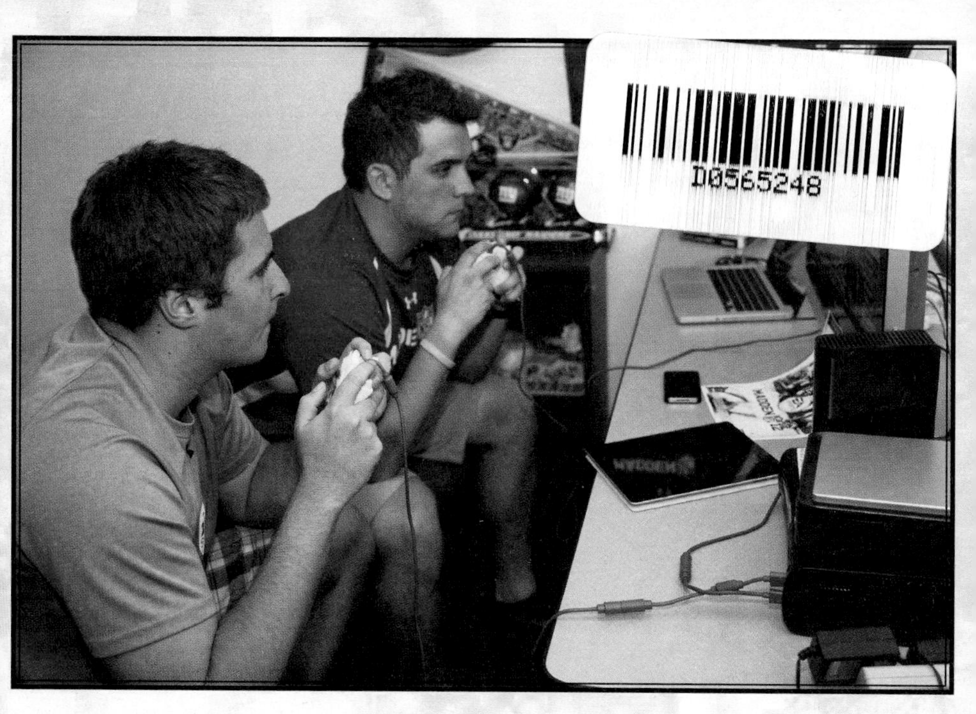

"Our goal for *Madden NFL 12* is to bring the most authentic football game ever. We changed the tackling system to give a more realistic feel to every collision in the game. We also made zone defense more aggressive than ever with dynamic reactions to patterns along with defenders eying and reacting to the QB's arm movement. This has added much more complexity to defensive play calling and the passing game. We added a pump fake mechanic so users can pump fake at specific receivers to give double move routes more value. And those are just a couple of the new features we have added to the greatest football simulation of all time.

We have worked closely with authors ZFarls and SGibs (pictured) in the creation of this strategy guide. They have been incredibly valuable in helping us ensure that we deliver the best product possible. These guys know this game inside and out. Take their tips and use them to improve your game, you'll be glad that you did."

Mike Scantlebury,
Designer I, *Madden NFL 12*

UPDATED ROSTERS AVAILABLE ONLINE!

Editor's note:
It has been quite an offseason for the NFL. And while the events of this summer hopefully ensure that we have football for years to come, they certainly made making the best player's guide possible very…challenging.

The team rosters in this guide were created using the final retail version of *Madden NFL 12*. Due to the NFL work stoppage and other circumstances beyond the control of Prima Games or Electronic Arts, some of the information contained in the guide may have changed after printing. Prima Games will provide roster and player updates for free on *www.PrimaMadden.com*

Now let's play football!
-Prima Games Team

Each year, *Madden NFL* adds new features to the game to keep the experience fresh. Sometimes, the changes are off-the-field additions that add more depth to the overall game experience. However, this year, almost all of the big changes focus on the *on-the-field* experience. *Madden NFL 12* is true to the game, and many of the changes give the game that authentic NFL feel. From how the game looks to how it feels and to how each player reacts, *Madden NFL 12* will be a great experience for football fans of any level!

DYNAMIC PLAYER PERFORMANCE

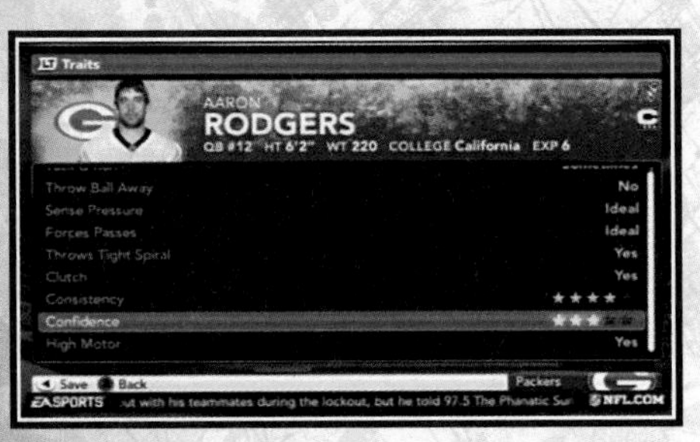

He will tuck and run

If you've ever wondered why certain receivers in NFL games drop open passes after hearing footsteps over the middle, but often hung on to them in *Madden NFL*, you will love dynamic player performance (DPP). Now the game has a way to distinguish between the rating of a player and his behavior on the field. If you can sack a scrambler like Michael Vick three times in the first half, he will look to take off at the first sign of pressure later in the game. If you can rip the ball loose from Adrian Peterson, he will make sure to cover up and take extra caution with the football. Each player has a confidence rating that shows how well he is playing; this can help a player's ratings without truly affecting his attributes, which will make the gameplay amazing. Now, a simple hot streak will result in a short-term boost without having to change too much around. If a player like Peyton Manning hits a cold streak, he won't sink as many points as a player who has proved less over the course of his career, like a Chad Henne.

Make sure to check out your players' tendencies by clicking the right thumbstick down at your roster screen. Also, when you pause the game, you will see what is going on with your players—pay attention and try to use these stats to your advantage!

FRANCHISE MODE

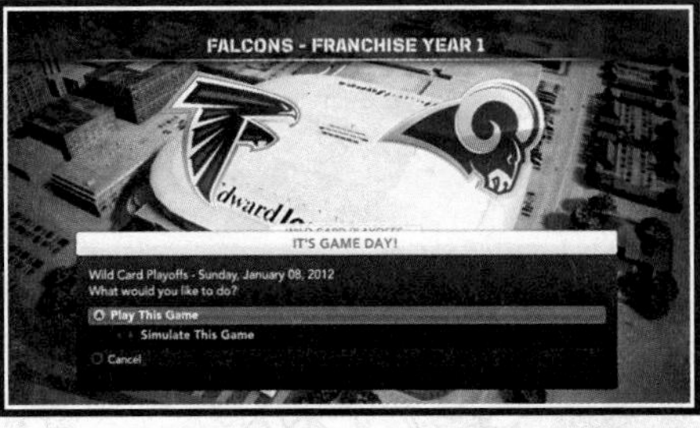

Our playoff run starts today!

Every season, Franchise is one of the most heavily played modes in *Madden NFL*. The team at EA SPORTS really added a whole new dimension to offline Franchise this season by listening to feedback and giving the users total control over their rosters. Now, you have to make so many hard decisions off the field that you may be thankful to get into the game! It has a new feel and menu system, so make sure to get into Franchise mode this season and attempt to take home the Lombardi Trophy!

Expanded Rosters and Cut Days

Come with me and bring your playbook...

Don't get fooled on a star like Julio Jones

EA SPORTS fully expanded the rosters this season to bring the training camp feeling of really putting together a roster. If you have a fourth QB who might be a gem someday, you can work him out to find out if he has what it takes to cling to the roster. The more action your backups get on the field, the more you can reveal about their stats. Each week you will be forced to cut down your roster to get it to the opening day size. You will likely lose a few players who could have helped your squad along the way, but that is what makes managing a team so tough! Can you pick out the few players who will be able to fill in if an injury occurs? The expanded roster feature adds great depth to Franchise mode this season.

Franchise-Specific DPP with Hot and Cold Streaks

When you're playing online, the rosters are updated very frequently and constantly shift the dynamic of the game. However, in Franchise mode the ratings never fluctuated in quite the same way—until now! Now, the ratings will shift every week in your franchise due to dynamic player performance. Depending on how your players perform, they will have consistency and confidence that can change their on-the-field performance. If your player is making all the plays, expect a boost with a hot streak that can carry into the next game. But if your player lets up on too many big plays, beware of the cold streak as well.

Free Agent Bidding

In the past, bidding on free agents didn't bring the high-pressure mentality that most teams experience every off season. That will all change this season as bidding on free agents is now a fast-paced interactive feature where you must take on 31 other teams in the experience. No longer will you get first crack at the top-rated players; you will be forced to outmaneuver and outbid your opponent. Do you risk offering that deal on the first day? Your stud may not be available very soon!

Player Roles

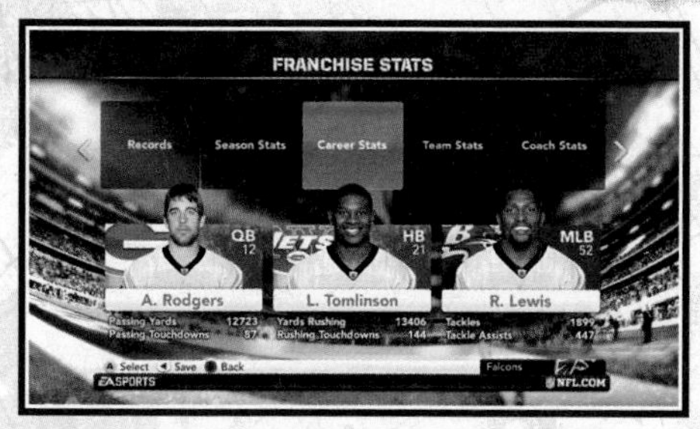

Are any of these veterans available?

When the Jets signed backup Mark Brunell last season, it wasn't because they wanted him to battle with QB Mark Sanchez for the starting role. It was because the savvy veteran Brunell had just won a Super Bowl and could bring tons of valuable experience to mentor Sanchez with. These roles bring a strategy element to your team and can help solidify your roster. Now rookies with potential will be given the chance to become "the QB of the future" rather than sitting behind an average QB who is rated only 1 point higher. These roles will affect the way players play on the field, and their impact could be the difference between winning and losing football games. This is just another way that EA SPORTS added depth to *Madden NFL* this season.

Community-Requested Features

This season, the community had as big a role in shaping the direction of Franchise mode as ever. The developers at EA SPORTS listened to your posts, blogs, and tweets and responded by adding multiple new features to the game. You can now trade future draft picks in order to keep stockpiling picks for the future (the New England Patriots' method). You now also can enter practice mode right from the Franchise menu. This will give your team the chance to work on specific plays and put some aces up your sleeve come Sunday! You also can put players on injured reserve. This can help free up roster space and allow you to hang on to players who will be fresh next season. This was a big year for Franchise mode and it was all because of the passion of the fans.

NEW COLLISION SYSTEM

This year's game offers so many new and unique tackles

The team at EA SPORTS took a lot of time to focus on the elimination of "suction" from the game this season. Now, the tackle doesn't start until the players make contact with each other. This means improved offensive line play, better player interaction, and tackles that look and feel incredible! Don't forget to press the new Tackle button to lunge and wrap up the ball carrier this season.

IMPROVED ZONE COVERAGE

Zones play to much better depth!

The team at Tiburon focused on making zone defenders not just play their zones, but work with the other zones in the area. Now, instead of playing just a spot on the field, defenders play the man inside their zone and pass him off to another defender when he leaves the area. This makes the ability to zone blitz more effective and the ability to switch between man and zone more deadly. If you gave up on zone in years past, now is the year to add it back into your scheme on defense!

CUSTOM PLAYBOOKS

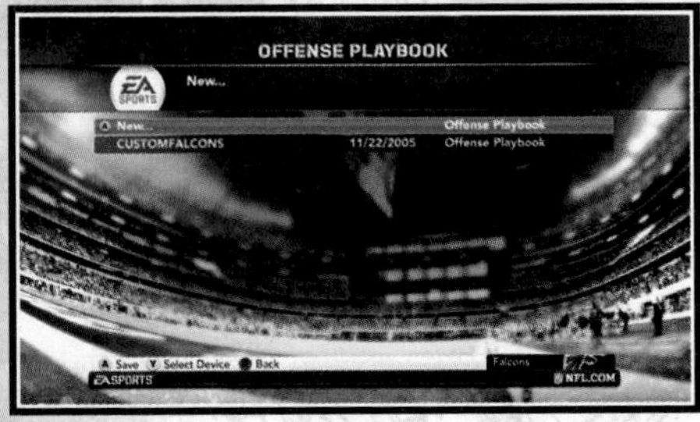

Give your book a unique name and load it at the team screen

The defense will not be ready for the Pistol next week

What if you were playing someone online and couldn't stop one of your opponent's formations? What if I told you that you now can add that formation to your playbook?! Custom Playbooks is one of the most talked about features in years; now you can run the Bronco Heavy formation with the Cowboys if you wish. This addition allows you to tweak all your plays and formations for offense and defense. If you want to take out a play that just is not working for your offense and add another play, go ahead. This will bring a new level of depth in-game and allow gamers to create totally unique offensive schemes. Players will be tinkering all season long with their playbooks! Each season the NFL has a breakout formation, like the Wildcat, and now gamers will be able to try it out with their team and the Custom Playbooks feature. Be ready!

NEW PRESENTATION

All-new camera angles

If there is one reason to try out every team in this year's game, it may be to see their new entrances! EA SPORTS actually went on a field trip to watch how a football game is directed and produced for live television! This year in *Madden NFL*, the stadium cameras are accurate for each stadium and really add to the overall game day experience. The team focused on new overlays for stats and in-game presentation as well. Now you will get to see Ray Lewis fire up the crowd and follow the Hawk out onto the field while listening to the deafening roar of the 12th man. *Madden NFL* is true to the game with its presentation this season.

DIVE CATCH

Put the team on his back

When throwing the deep ball, sometimes the pass is just out of reach and the WR must lay out for the football. Now, the ability is in your hands. This is one of the best additions to the game—it feels incredible when you take control of the WR and lay out for a game-breaking catch!

COMMUNITIES

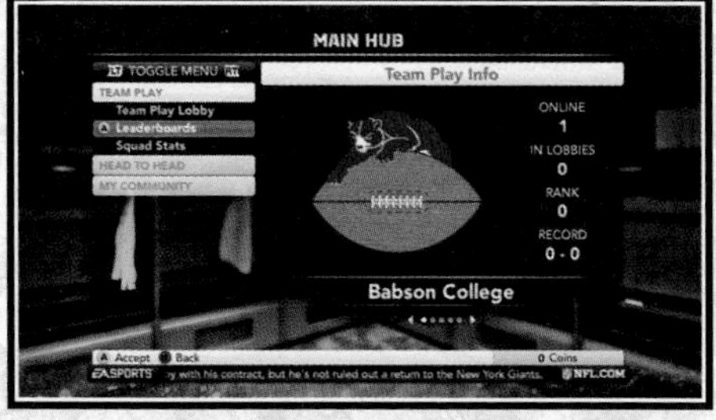

Your own protected Madden area

Find your friends and start a community

For online gamers who are trying to get better or simply want to play with a group of like-minded people, the Communities feature is the biggest addition to online play ever. You can now find a group of people online who play the same style and battle it out. The game will keep all your stats and matchups inside the community, and you can fight for bragging rights. This can help keep players who quit early out of your group. You can even password-protect your community. If you prefer longer quarters, you can set that up! If you want the default difficulty set to All-Madden, you can do that, too!

TRADES IN ULTIMATE TEAM

Madden Ultimate Team (MUT) has been one of the most popular game modes of the next generation. Now, players can trade their cards to other players! This adds a totally new dimension to the game and shows why MUT has been such a popular mode over the last few seasons! Now, if you are in control of a rare card, you can flip it for multiple players who can help you right now! If you have a solid team but need that one superstar, go make a big trade for your team!

SUPERSTAR MODE

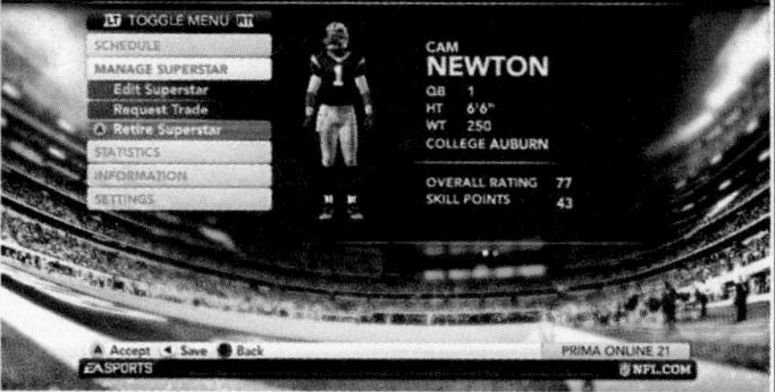

Your whole career is shown here

Keep getting better

Superstar mode has received big enhancements this season. As soon as you hit the main menu, you will see the changes. The entire system is easier to manage and clearly displays your progress. You still have the option to create your own fully customized player and put him at any position! You can also choose a rookie from the draft and guide him on his journey to becoming a top player in the league. If you want to be traded out of town, you have the option. Make sure to know where you would fit in on the depth chart before you swing the deal!

OFFENSIVE FUNDAMENTALS

Contents

RUNNING MOVES

Pounding the rock in *Madden NFL* has consistently been the style of the best players every year. When you develop a solid rushing attack and all the moves to go along with it, your offense is unstoppable. Pass-heavy players can be shut down at any moment, but a gamer who commits to the run and grinds out drives can keep the defense on their toes and win more games. Committing to the run is a challenge; everyone starts out running, but most people slowly abandon it during the game. If you harness the moves covered here, you will no doubt have a great running game in *Madden NFL 12*!

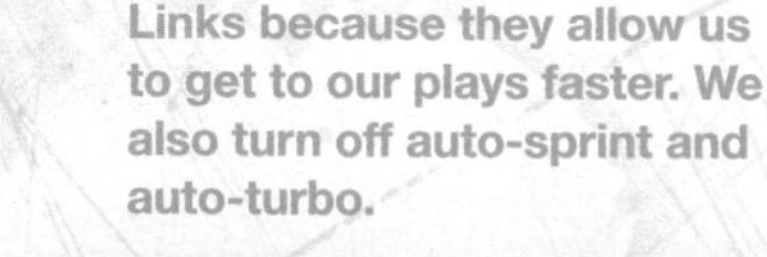

The game is set to use the Strategy Pad, but we use Quick Links because they allow us to get to our plays faster. We also turn off auto-sprint and auto-turbo.

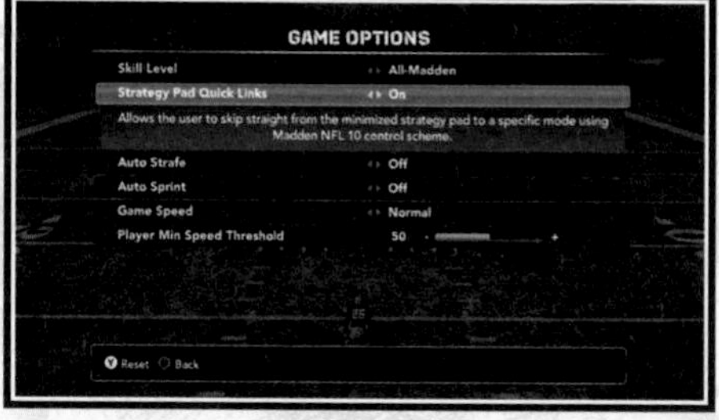

Make sure to check your options!

Juke

Xbox 360: Left or right on the right thumbstick

PlayStation 3: Left or right on the right thumbstick

The more elusive you are, the better!

The juke is one of the most heavily used moves in *Madden NFL*. It's best used in the open field to make one defender miss. If you get an overly aggressive defender, you can leave him in the dust. If you see two defenders closing in, you can also use back-to-back jukes. This is a more advanced move but one that will likely make your highlight reel!

Spin

Xbox 360: B

PlayStation 3: ●

Turn fast and continue upfield

A well-timed spin move is one of the best feelings in *Madden NFL*. One great place to use the move is when the defender has an angle on the sideline. The spin will keep your momentum going forward and allow you to gain yards. Work on the timing of this move—while it's not heavily used, it can be devastating. Beware of hard-hitting defenders; being on the wrong end of a hit stick while you're spinning can force the ball loose.

Stiff Arm

Xbox 360: A

PlayStation 3: ×

Great sideline move

When the ball carrier is approached from the side, a stiff arm can help him gain extra yards without having to cut. This is one of the most aggressive moves in football. Nothing fancy needed; just extend the arm straight out and leave the defender on his butt. This move is especially effective if you see a weaker player like a defensive back trying to tackle your player. Hold the button and keep journeying down the sideline to pay dirt.

Hurdle

Xbox 360: Y

PlayStation 3: ▲

Take to the air

The defender wins this battle

The hurdle is one of the more advanced moves in the game; while it's easy to perform most players don't realize they should have hurdled until after the play is over! If you are thinking quickly, you will know when to press the button to hop over downed blockers and stay out of trouble. This move must be used sparingly, however; if there are multiple defenders you can get punished for leaving your feet!

Lean and Shield

Xbox 360: Up on the right thumbstick

PlayStation 3: Up on the right thumbstick

The defender gets bested

When you use this move, the animation triggered depends on what type of player you're running with; if you have an elusive back he will shake the defender. If you have a power back he will lower his shoulder and truck the defender. EA SPORTS has done a great job making this move harder over the years—make sure to time it correctly, otherwise you will lose balance if you hold the stick for too long.

High Step

Xbox 360: Down on the right thumbstick

PlayStation 3: Down on the right thumbstick

Look to make one cut

The high step allows the RB to change what lane he is attacking in the run game. If you see that the initial read is clogged, hold back and make a sharp cut. By picking up his knees, the runner gains extra agility for a short time and can leave aggressive defense hanging their heads.

Dive

Xbox 360: ⓧ

PlayStation 3: ■

Lay out!

When you have crucial yards at stake, you need to bring out the dive. If you are within a few yards of the end zone, the runner will attempt to jump over the pile, and this can lead to clutch touchdowns. If you are within a few yards of a first down, look to lay out and get the tough yards. The ball carrier will likely be considered down, so only use it sparingly. You also leave yourself vulnerable to big hits and a potential fumble.

Protect Ball

Xbox 360: RB

PlayStation 3: R1

Heading into the danger zone

When you are powering up the field and come across a scrum of players, make sure to cover up the ball. Many online players use the strip move on defense, and it is especially important to cover up against these players. If you see a safety or LB with good hit power, make sure to cover up as well. These players can jar the ball loose. When you are running out the clock and sealing a win, controlling the ball is the most important goal, so cover up!

Hard Cut

Xbox 360: Left or right on the left thumbstick

PlayStation 3: Left or right on the left thumbstick

Throw on the brakes

Having "good sticks" means the ability to manually juke the defender. If you need to make a move, simply try cutting hard with the stick instead of pressing a button. This also lets you cut runs outside or choose a different gap at the last second. Mastering the left stick will give you more control of the ball carrier and comes with practice.

Switch Hands

Xbox 360: Ⓐ

PlayStation 3: ✕

The defender is eyeing the football

The back tucks the ball away safely

The running back always wants to carry the ball in his outside arm, away from trouble. If you are approaching a sideline, look to keep the ball in your outside hand. Any fumble will likely go out of bounds and your team will get the ball back. This is a subtle move but one that can really separate the men from the boys.

Dive Catch

Xbox 360: Hold ⓧ

PlayStation 3: Hold ■

Lay out for the ball

EA SPORTS added a dive catch to the game this season. If you are running downfield and the ball is just out of your reach, simply hold the button down to lay out for the ball. This is a tougher control to get down, but one that will absolutely come up big for you this season. Try it out in practice mode to get the timing; it's very addicting.

PASSING CONTROLS

The dream of being an NFL QB is something most teenagers have thought about constantly. While most never get a chance to play on Sundays, *Madden NFL 12* gives you the ability to run the offense and throw the ball however you like. Once you harness all the passing controls, you will be well on your way to all the glamour that comes with playing quarterback. While QB is often considered the most difficult position in all of sports, following the controls outlined here will make it much easier.

Bullet/Lob Pass

Xbox 360: A B X Y or LB

PlayStation 3: × ▲ ● ■ or L1

Throw it deep and let the WR create space

Squeeze it into the window

Every time you drop back to pass, you are looking for an open receiver to get the football to. On every pass play, the wide receivers will have specific icons over their heads. If you hold down the button matching the receiver's icon, you will bullet the pass into the receiver—this can be used when the defender has tight coverage or you need to get the ball out quickly. The other option is a lob pass, for which you just tap the button instead of holding it down. A lob pass is perfect when throwing the ball deep. This requires less touch and can help give the WR time to run under the football and make a catch. The difference between these two types of throws can mean big yards over the course of a game. Look to see what routes and coverages work best with both. Most often, a lob throw is for longer throws while you bullet in short throws. Having a QB with better accuracy ratings can really make throwing these passes easier.

Pass Lead

Xbox 360: Left, right, up, or down on the left thumbstick

PlayStation 3: Left, right, up, or down on the left thumbstick

The defender is shielded away from the football

Let him run onto the ball

Once you figure out how to throw the ball, learning where to place it can help your WRs get more yards. By using the left stick, we can lead the WR in any direction. If you can hit him in stride, he can pick up big yards after the catch. By using the left stick, you can protect your WR from big hits and also fit the ball into very tight spaces. Make sure to put the ball where only your receiver can get it!

Pump Fake

Xbox 360: RB or hold LT and press a WR icon

PlayStation 3: R1 or hold L2 and press a WR icon

Try to force the defender to bite

Madden NFL has always had a pump fake move; however, now gamers can actually target a specific WR. Now, you can use the controls to target a specific player rather than a side of the field. This should put some extra stress on the defenders. If you do get the defender to commit, look to go deep and make the defense pay for their mistake.

Sprint

Xbox 360: RT

PlayStation 3: R2

Break the pocket

When you hold turbo, your QB will tuck the ball and run. Most of the time, a faster QB will cause a headache for the defense. If you have a slower QB, you can still use this maneuver, but only if the defense drops too many defenders back. This is also good for plays where the pocket rolls because it cuts down half the field and makes for an easy throw.

Quarterback Slide

Xbox 360: Tap Ⓧ

PlayStation 3: Tap ■

Sliding can save your QB!

When you decide to sprint out of the pocket with your QB, you should look to run out of bounds or use the QB slide. Since the QB is one of your most valuable players on offense, you want to keep him safe. Sliding allows you to avoid taking a big hit and can also help avoid fumbles, which can devastate drives.

Throw Away

Xbox 360: RB

PlayStation 3: R1

Chuck it away and avoid the sack

Throwing the football away is often one of the smartest plays a gamer can make. Instead of taking a sack and losing yards, you simply lose one down. A player under pressure often just throws the ball up to a covered WR, and this frequently results in a loss of possession. Look to play another down and just throw the ball away! Make sure you get out of the pocket—otherwise it can be called intentional grounding.

OFFENSIVE PRE-SNAP CONTROLS

Before the play, the QB has the ability to make hundreds of adjustments at the line of scrimmage, depending on what he reads from the defense. Most football fans have seen Peyton Manning make multiple calls at the line of scrimmage. In *Madden NFL*, you can use the same tactics. Let's take a look at all of the controls we can use pre-snap to gain an advantage against the defense!

Motion

Xbox 360: Ⓑ to select player, then left or right on the left thumbstick

PlayStation 3: ● to select player, then left or right on the left thumbstick

We can easily read the coverage

Before the snap of the football, the QB has many weapons at his disposal. By motioning one of the receivers, we look to confuse the defense and force them to reveal their coverage. This is a tactic used by the top players online and a good habit to get into. We can also make our formations appear different by shifting where the receiver lines up before the snap. Try moving a receiver around in your favorite formation and see what you come up with!

Coach Cam

Xbox 360: RT

PlayStation 3: R2

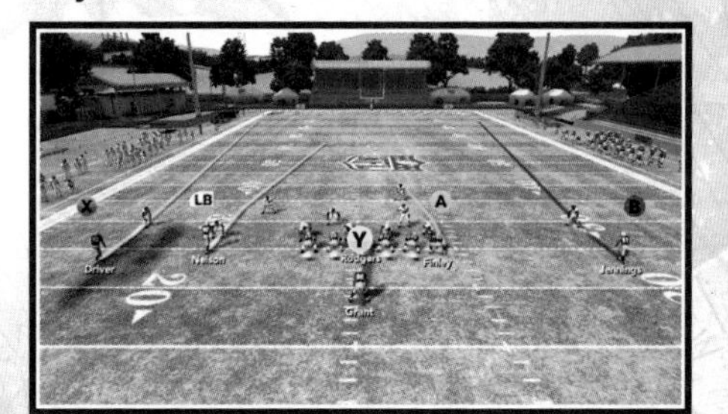

Coach cam shows the play, in case you forget what you called

By using the coach cam, you can quickly see what routes your players are going to run. This can help show weaknesses in the defensive coverage or guide you if you audibled to a different play. When playing online, only you can see the play art, so feel free to double-check on the play you called at any time.

Audibles

Xbox 360: Ⓧ to bring up the menu

PlayStation 3: ■ to bring up the menu

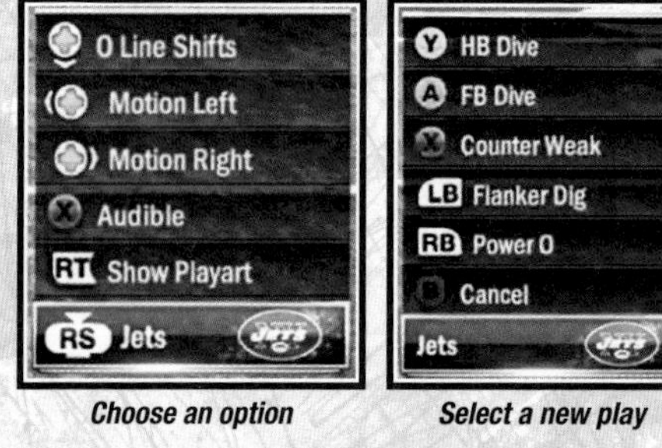

Choose an option *Select a new play*

If you don't like the play you chose at the menu screen, you can quickly make a change to a different play by using the Audible menu. Another great time to audible is if the defense is vulnerable to a certain formation or play. Because you have five audibles and four different quick audibles, you can get to a wide range of plays. You can also set them before the game so you can audible to your favorite at a critical time!

Quick Audibles

You always have access to four play types from whatever formation you are currently in. Quick audibles can be selected at any time by pressing the Audible menu button twice and then pressing the right thumbstick in a direction:

- Down activates a run—usually an up-the-middle quick run.
- Left activates a play action pass.
- Right activates a deep pass.
- Up activates a quick pass.

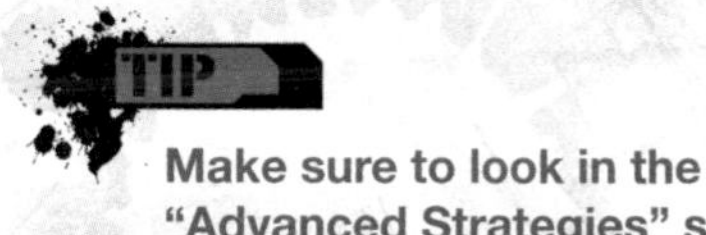

Make sure to look in the "Advanced Strategies" section to learn how to dominate your opponent with these plays.

Slide Protection

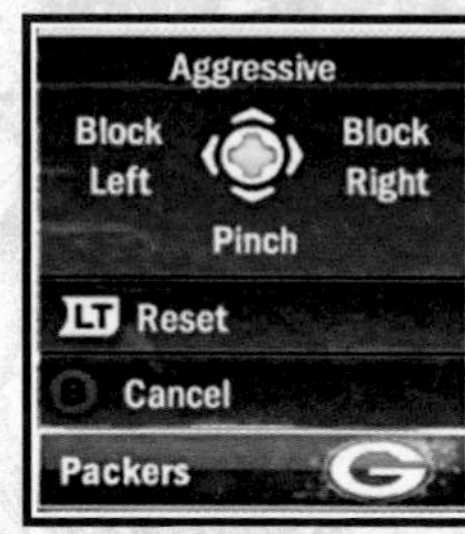

Give your offensive line a head start

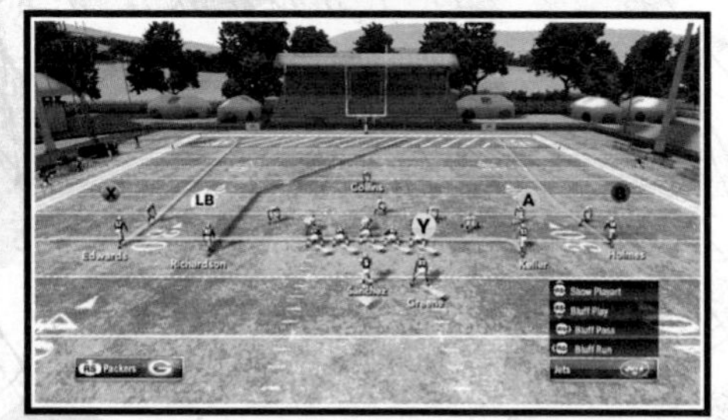

The LB is tipping us off to the blitz

If the QB senses pressure coming from a certain place on the field, he can call out to his linemen which direction and they will block that way. This is a great way to pick up blitzes that are targeting a certain area. Every QB does this on Sunday by letting the center know where to block, and now you have the power in *Madden NFL*. To call slide protection:

1. Bring up the Strategy Pad.
2. Select Slide Protection.
3. Choose a direction.

Hot Routes

Hot routes are a great way to quickly change a WR's route without changing the entire play. If we see that the defense is vulnerable to a certain type of route, we can quickly tell our WR to run that route. This can also be used to make our own plays by putting more than one player on a hot route. The top online players are constantly making hot routes and adjustments on every play. It is common to see three hot routes on any play, and more if the defense reacts to the initial changes. Once you get comfortable knowing how to change up the WR's routes, it will change the way you play *Madden NFL* forever. Let's take a look at how to perform these changes:

1. Use the Strategy Pad to select the Hot Routes option.
2. Choose the player you wish to send out on a hot route.
3. Select the type of route you would like him to run.

Receiver Hot Routes

Streak

Xbox 360: Up on the left thumbstick

PlayStation 3: Up on the left thumbstick

This is a very common route change

A streak is a great route if you catch the defense playing too close to the line of scrimmage. If you have a speedy WR who is matched up against a slower player like a linebacker, you can make a quick adjustment and allow the speed advantage to work for you. This route does take a long time to develop, so make sure you will have time to get the ball deep—otherwise it can result in a sack.

Out/In

Xbox 360: Left or right on the left thumbstick

PlayStation 3: Left or right on the left thumbstick

Bullet this throw outside so the defender can't cut it off

Look out for danger over the middle

Outs and ins are very good for beating man coverage in *Madden NFL 12*. If your WR has a good route-running rating, he should be able to get separation from the defender.

Once the receiver makes his cut, look to bullet a pass into him and lead him so he can pick up more yards after the catch. These are very short, high percentage throws that can help the offense move the chains.

Curl

Xbox 360: Down on the left thumbstick

PlayStation 3: Down on the left thumbstick

Outstanding route

Curls are a very effective way to beat both man and zone coverage. If the defender plays man coverage, look to use the WR's body to shield the ball as he makes his cut. If we throw a lead pass in a certain direction, this can help get extra separation. When the defense is in zone coverage, there may be a defender underneath, so you must be careful. However, if you put a few curls on multiple depths and areas of the field, the zone defenders will be forced to choose. Always look to throw as the WR is breaking. These are great routes to smart route (by clicking on the right thumbstick) as well because the WR will head to the first down marker before turning around!

Slant Out/Slant In

Xbox 360: Left or right on the right thumbstick

PlayStation 3: Left or right on the right thumbstick

Fight for inside position

Still effective, but no longer the best

In *Madden NFL 11*, the slant out was one of the most devastating routes in the game. However, it is now back to being simply a way to beat zone coverage. If you flood a zone, look to hit the slant out where the defense is weak. The slant in has always amazed me ever since watching Brett Favre throw the ball extremely fast to his cutting WR. The slant starts out like a streak but breaks very hard after only a few steps. If the WR can get inside position, the QB can lead him with a chance to pick up big yards after the catch. This forces the defense to respect the short throw.

Drag

Xbox 360: Down on the right thumbstick

PlayStation 3: Down on the right thumbstick

Hit him on the cut or wait to outrun the defender

Drags have been used heavily online due to their great ability to beat man coverage; however, they are not quite as powerful as in years past. If you can get a speed mismatch with a defender, you will still get separation. This is a great route if the defense is blitzing because it develops very quickly and is always a threat to go the distance pending one broken tackle.

Fade

Xbox 360: Up on the right thumbstick

PlayStation 3: Up on the right thumbstick

A go-to route in the red zone

The fade used to be a deep, developing route but now is good in short yardage and red zone situations. If you have a big WR who can out-jump his defender, look to call this play. The WR should be able to use his physical abilities to leap in the air and grab the ball at its highest point. This is one of our most reliable red zone routes and something even a newer player can pull off with ease.

Smart Route

Xbox 360: Click on the right thumbstick

PlayStation 3: Click on the right thumbstick

Smart routes allow almost any route to be adjusted to first down distance. If you need 12 yards on third down but the route is only running 8, simply call a smart route to extend the WR across the first down mark. This also works in shorter yardage situations. Try smart-routing some of your favorite or unique routes in the game to see what you come up with.

WR Block

Xbox 360: LT or RT

PlayStation 3: L2 or R2

Calling all blockers

If we need extra protection, we can quickly assign any WR to block. The player will slide into the line and help the offensive linemen out. This will leave an extra defender in coverage or allow the defense to blitz, so be prepared for either defensive reaction.

Running Back Hot Routes

RB Slants

Xbox 360: Left or right on the right thumbstick

PlayStation 3: Left or right on the right thumbstick

Send them out in either direction

A slant from the HB used to be the most devastating route out of the backfield in *Madden NFL*. Now, the route takes a little longer to develop but can still be effective when used under the right circumstances. Wait until the back makes his sharp cut and look to lead him outside.

RB Drags

Xbox 360: Down on the right thumbstick

PlayStation 3: Down on the right thumbstick

The player will head out to the open side of the field

Drags by the halfback give the QB a quick target and can allow unaccounted for players to run for days with just a short pass.

RB Fades

Xbox 360: Up on the right thumbstick

PlayStation 3: Up on the right thumbstick

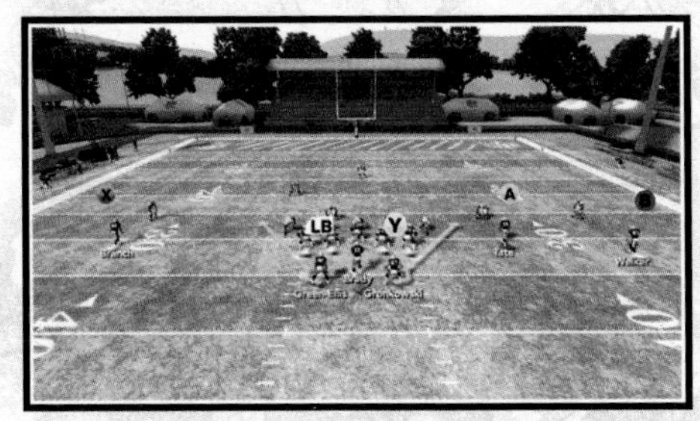

Try motioning these out for different effects

Fades by the halfback act differently depending on the formation you call them in. Here the RB will take a route just outside of the tackle, and this can really burn a defender who is playing too far outside of the hash marks.

RB Ins and Outs

Xbox 360: Left or right on the left thumbstick

PlayStation 3: Left or right on the left thumbstick

Deliver quickly or wait until the cut

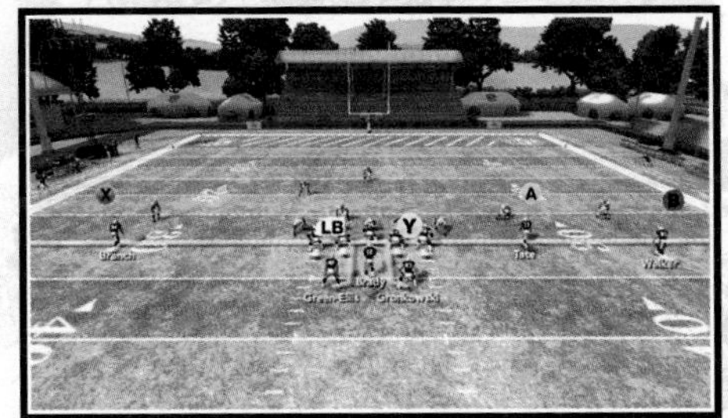

Here the backs will cross

An in or an out from the HB can give the QB two different windows to throw the ball. He can look to hit the back while he is making his initial cut upfield, or wait and deliver the ball once the back makes his cut. These take a little longer to develop than other routes, but having two spaces to throw the ball into is valuable.

RB Blocking

Xbox 360: LT or RT

PlayStation 3: L2 or R2

Learning how to pick up blitzers by blocking with the halfbacks is a quick way to become a great *Madden NFL* player. If you sense the blitz coming, look at all four directions where we can add extra protection.

HBs Block Left

Protect the QB's blind side

Here we can pick up anything the defense can throw at us from the left side. We block both backs to the left side of the formation.

HBs Block Right

They will both step over and pick up the heat

By sending both backs to block the right-hand side, we will be ready if the defense sends a blitz from the QB's right side.

HBs Block Middle

Plug the middle

If you block each halfback to the middle of the formation, they will both step up in the A gap and pick up pressure. Since this is the fastest way a defense can get pressure, it is a good place to block.

HBs Block Outside

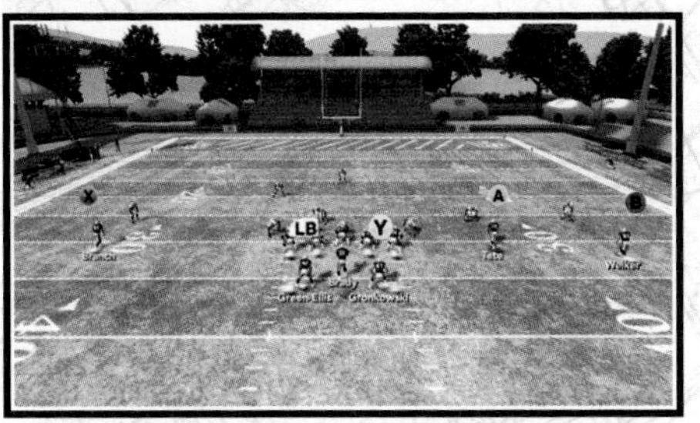

This will alleviate any pressure off the edge

If the defense is spreading out and rushing off the edges, hot route both backs outside and each will watch the outside. The blockers will step up and help out the offensive tackles.

You can also use the HB blocking with offensive line slide protection, which will allow you to pick up any blitz in the game!

Other Passing Tips

- Using delayed routes out of the backfield can often give you more time in the pocket. The back will block and then release to give you a late safety valve throw on the play.
- When you get up to the line of scrimmage, always try to figure out what type of coverage the defense is in. They will either be in man or zone, and using motion is a great way to know. If you motion a WR and a defender follows him, the defense is likely in man. If you motion the WR and the defenders don't run across, they are likely in zone defense.
- Look to see if the defense is sending a blitz—if you see that the safety who should be back 8–10 yards is creeping up near the line of scrimmage, that is one giveaway. Always look to throw to where the blitz came from since the defense should be weak there. If you have to adjust your play to give yourself a quick option, don't be afraid to make the change.
- Look at what types of players the defense has on the field. If they have four linebackers and you have four fast wide receivers, look to spread them out and use speed routes. If they have fast CBs on the field and you have big TEs, look to work shorter possession-style routes. Always look for mismatches and know each of your WR's strengths and weaknesses.
- Take what the defense gives you: If you see an open 5-yard pass, don't wait for something better. The longer you wait to deliver the pass the more risk the QB must take.
- Learn to maneuver around in the pocket. Most novice players do not trust their blockers and look to run around, away from the defense. However, the game sets up a nice pocket for you to stand in and this will make your throws more accurate.
- Set up the run game: While passing is glamorous, it is made a lot easier if the defense respects the run. The more worried they are about your HB, the easier it will be to make big throws down the field!

RUNNING STYLES

Now let's explore runs and what part of the defense they attack. There are two ideas behind running the ball—one is to go between the tackles (the inside run game), and the other is to take the ball outside the tackles (the outside running game). If you can master both types of runs and understand why they work, it will be impossible for the defense to defend all of your options.

Inside Run Game

The easiest way to run the ball is straight ahead. If you can dominate your opponent up front, simply hand off the football and keep moving the chains. Here are some of the up-the-middle runs that are effective on first down or short yardage situations. Simply look to hit the hole and pick up as much as possible.

HB Iso

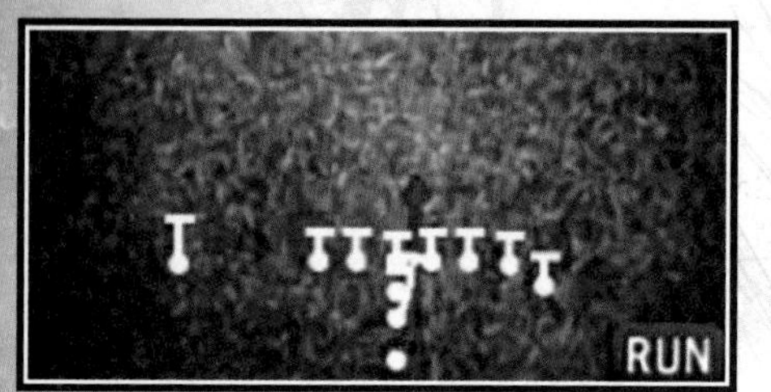

The HB Iso is the quickest straight-ahead run

The HB Iso is a straight-ahead run that utilizes a fullback to block straight ahead. This is a great run for short yardage and a great up-the-middle run in the three-headed rushing attack.

Follow the FB into the line

At the snap, the QB tries to hand the ball off quickly to the HB, who follows the FB through the A gap. Read the LBs to see if a cutback lane is available, but most of the time you will just follow the blocker and pick up as many yards as possible.

A hole opens up

As the FB seals off the lane to the right, our HB will now start to turbo and gash through the hole. In short yardage situations, simply get as many yards as possible instead of getting fancy.

Burst into space

As the defense approaches, make sure to cover up the ball and keep the legs moving forward. If you can get even 4 yards consistently with this play, it easily becomes one of the best runs in the game.

HB Dive

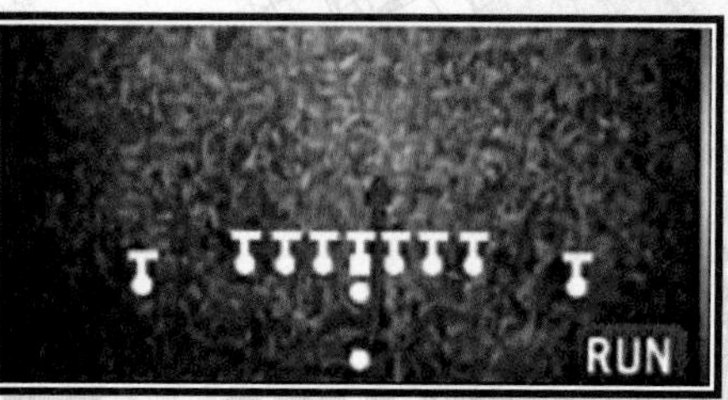

There's no fullback to follow

The dive is another straight-ahead run; however, we will not have the luxury of a fullback blocking for us. This is a great run when you see that the "box" has fewer defenders than you have blockers. This opens up lanes and can keep the defense honest. It's not a true power run, but it can gash defenses up the middle.

Read the defense pre-snap

The initial pre-snap read with the dive is extremely important since you have minimal lead blockers on the play. Here it looks like our six linemen can attack their six defenders in the box to open up holes.

Choose a hole after taking the handoff

The HB gets the football quickly and starts heading towards the hole. He sees that the linebacker may have a chance to attack the hole and decides to lay off the turbo and cut left.

Make one cut and go

Because the HB cut back to another gap, the linebacker is now out of position to make the tackle and the HB can pick up a good chunk of yards. The leading fullback on this play was replaced by making a sharp and well-timed cut to take the defender out of the play.

HB Draw

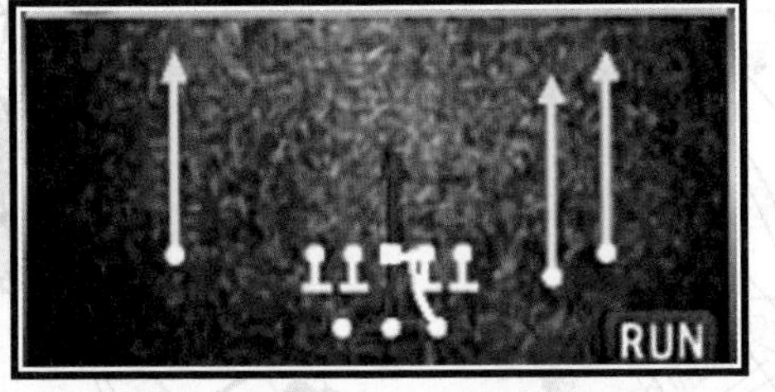

This is a great run for passing situations

The HB Draw is another up-the-middle run, but it should not be called in short yardage situations. The design of the play is to make the defense believe you are passing the ball so they back up and leave the middle vulnerable. When called during the right situations the draw can gain big yards, but it also can be blown up in the backfield more often than other runs.

The defense starts backing up

At the snap, the QB drops back as if he is going to pass the ball, and the receivers head upfield on passing routes. The HB then steps up and the QB hands him the football. Hopefully, the defensive ends have started their rush upfield and won't be able to recover. Ideally, there will be no penetration from the DTs at this point.

The back has tons of open space

If there is no penetration from the line, the draw is a great play to cut back into a different running lane. Here the left side is open and our HB quickly takes advantage of the hole.

Pick up as much yardage as possible

Draws have the ability to go the distance, and this most often happens right up the middle. A speedy RB can split the safeties and really do some damage. If the safeties close in, protect the ball and get as many yards as possible. This is often a shotgun run and can help keep defenses who are dropping linemen into coverage honest.

FB Dive

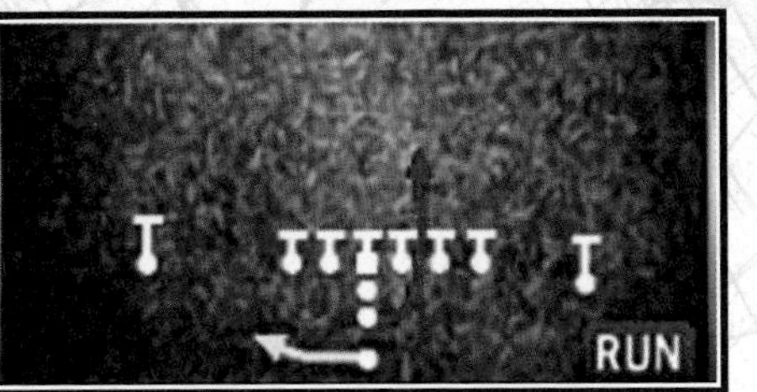

The FB Dive is great for short yardage

The FB Dive is a very quick run that can really hurt defenses who are weak up the middle. This was one of the best runs in prior years due to its very quick nature, but it has been toned down in recent years. This is a good short-yardage run as well since it quickly moves forward.

The QB quickly hands the ball off

The FB usually lead blocks for the HB, but if the defense is weak in the box, the QB simply gives the ball to the FB and he powers ahead. The FB is almost always a power runner who should look to put his head down and power forward for yards rather than trying to dodge defenders and cut back.

The defense is weak up the middle

The defense was weak; as the pre-snap look indicated, a giant hole opens up and our fullback gets to top speed as quickly as possible. The defense may have gone for the fake pitch to the HB and left the middle open.

Put your head down for extra yards on impact

As the defense approaches, the FB does what he knows best—lowers his head and tries to run the defender over. This can get you an extra 2–3 yards on any play and is the best way to break a tackle with bigger backs.

HB Blast

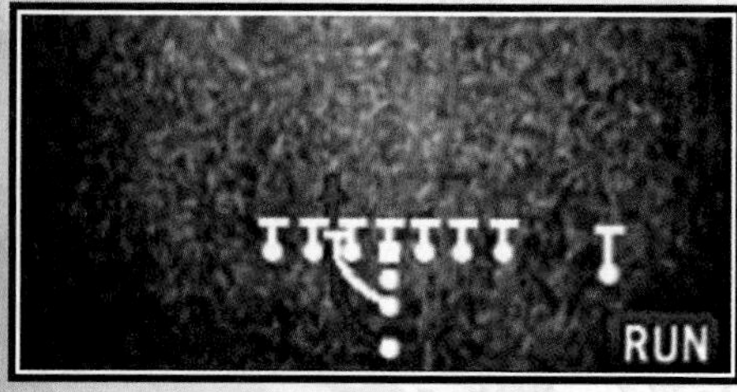

This is a great weak-side run

The HB Blast is a great weak-side run that can be utilized in our rushing attack. This run develops faster than a counter but attacks a similar area.

Key off the FB

The HB Blast attacks the B gap to the weak side. If the defense is stacking the strong side (the side with more blockers or an extra TE) then we can hit them to the other side.

Make a read depending on the block

The RB should look to get back to the line of scrimmage as quickly as possible before reading his blocks. Once he sees what is open, the back has a chance to cut it outside for big yards or stay inside and pick up as many yards as possible.

A great fake sucks the defense to the outside

The RB fakes to the outside to lure the safety to the right; this will set him up to be blocked by the FB when the back goes back inside. The blast is a misunderstood run, but when used properly it has many options to frustrate defenses.

HB Power O

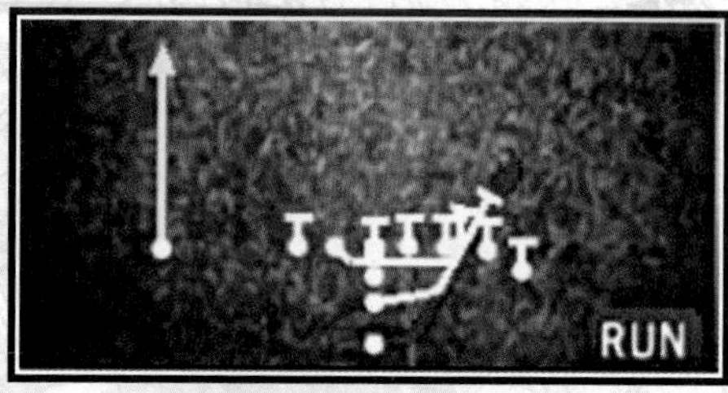

The guard pulls across the formation

The HB Power O is a very commonly run audible down. The key to the run is that the weak-side guard pulls to the strong side. One unique thing about the HB Power O is that it can be used to go up the middle or it can be broken outside. This makes it one of the most versatile options in the game and a great run for the three-headed rushing attack.

Don't turbo until the blocks set up

The QB hands off the ball to the RB, who sees the guard coming across to pick up a block. The RB should look to stay behind his blockers and attack the middle early in the run.

Still waiting to read the assignments

As the RB approaches the line, he must make a choice whether to keep it going up the middle or break the run outside. Here he appears to be heading to the inside as the safety is playing over the top.

Make a sharp cut

The RB busts through the first hole and sucks the safety inside, and he then uses his blockers to cut outside and shield himself from being tackled. This is the optimal way to run the Power O and why it is such a devastating run with so many options.

Outside Run Game

When a defense is getting pounded up the middle, it will be forced to commit extra defenders to the box and leave it vulnerable on the outside. This is when the offense should try to break containment and get the ball out wide. Another great time to use an outside run is on short yardage situations when you sense the defense is committing too many defenders inside to try and stop a predictable short run. Let's take a look at the different outside runs that can really burn an undisciplined defense.

HB Toss

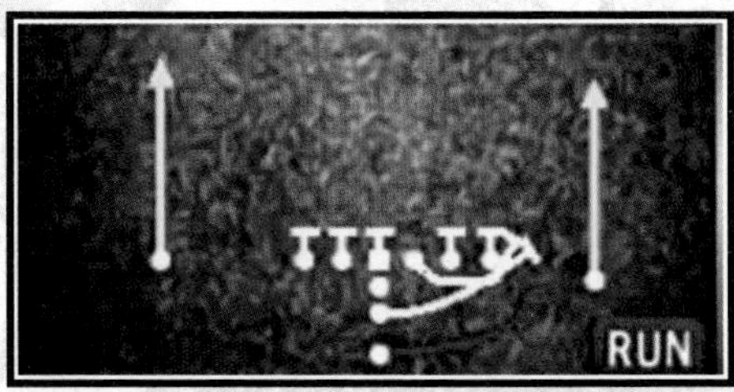

This play quickly gets the ball outside

The HB Toss is the fastest way to break containment against a defense to the outside. The toss is obvious because the QB actually pitches the ball rather than handing off. This play can be blown up in the backfield if the defense protects outside and can dodge your lead blocker.

The QB swings it out wide

At the snap, the RB and FB head quickly out to the right as the QB spins and pitches the ball. Hopefully there will be no penetration from the outside and the FB can get a head of steam to block.

Have great patience to wait for the FB

Not holding turbo right away and breaking outside is one of the keys to running a successful toss. Most players think they want to run towards the sideline right away, but it's best to keep the run inside until a lane outside becomes clear.

The cut inside is the best option here

Here the run outside is bottled up, but the back is able to stay inside for a great gain. Only take it outside right away if the defense overcommits and you have a wide open path to the end zone—otherwise find a lane and wait on getting to the corner.

HB Sweep

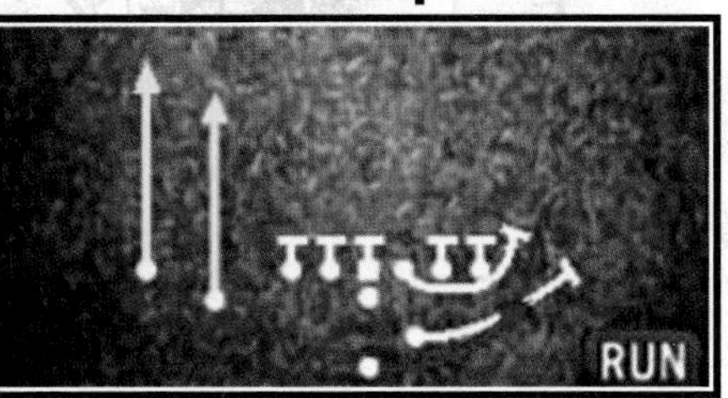

The lineman pulls on the sweep

The sweep is similar to the toss as the QB pitches the ball out wide, but the blocking is different. The offensive lineman pulls and adds extra weight towards where the ball carrier is running.

The QB pitches the ball outside

As the HB receives the pitch he waits for the guard to engage the blocker and hopes the FB can swing out wide to give him a convoy to the second level of the defense.

The FB gets out in front

Once the blocking is set up, the RB looks to turbo and get to the corner. Being patient with outside runs is one of the hardest things to do, but the most important. If you can master these runs, it will make the defense stay honest.

The HB is one-on-one against the safety

The HB finally turns the run outside and is left one-on-one with a defender. This will be a tough tackle for any defender, but having to take on a talented RB like Chris Johnson running at full speed can be deadly.

HB Stretch

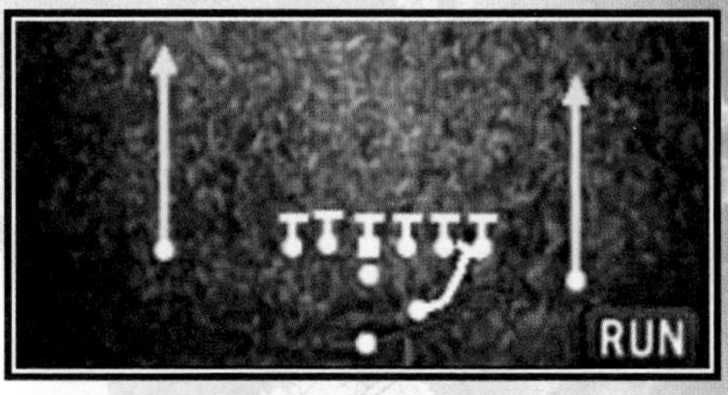

The run bangs off tackle

The stretch run has been made very popular by Peyton Manning and the Colts. It is a good outside run that is very clear due to the angle the QB takes to give the ball to the HB.

The patented handoff look of the stretch

The stretch run has been improving in *Madden NFL* over the last few seasons. If your team has a strong tackle who can hold up the point of attack this run can work for your offense.

Cut it hard off the edge

The RB follows the blockers to the edge as his team has done a good job of sealing off the edge. There is no need to cut hard on a stretch run as it has a distinct lane to follow.

Make sure to cover up

The defense is closing in, so the RB should cover up the ball and look to grab a few more yards. Using the stretch when the defense is expecting pass is a great way to make sure the defenders play their gaps.

Counter Weak

The best run in the game

The counter run is a staple of the three-headed rushing attack. It allows the offense a great way to run to the outside and can be effective to the outside or cut back against overly aggressive defenses. The key is the initial misdirection step that the HB takes to fool the defense.

The RB always takes a fake step to the strong side

While the HB is taking his false step, the FB and guard are busy pulling and getting ready to block the defenders.

The lineman pulls while the FB gets out in front

As the RB finally gets the football, he will have two blockers out in front. Now is the time to read the defenders and find out whether to cut the run outside or to make a move inside of the fullback.

The HB can cut it inside or outside depending on the defense

The counter is a great run because it can go for huge gains and rarely gets blown up in the backfield despite taking a little longer to develop.

Fake FB Dive HB Flip

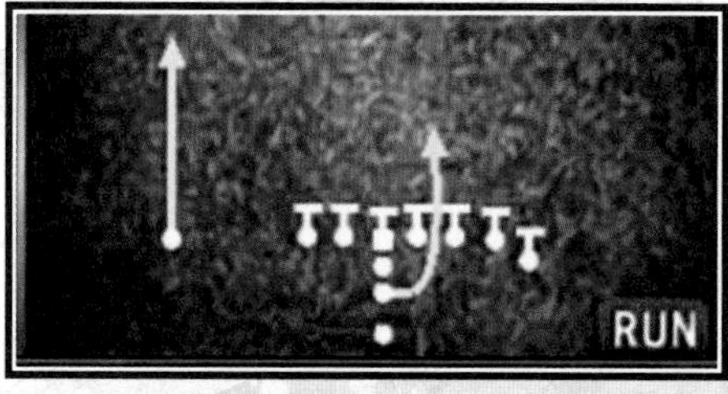

The HB will get the pitch here

This is another run that relies on misdirection to fool the defenders. The QB fakes the handoff to the FB in hopes that the defense will suck to the middle and lose containment on the edges. The QB then pitches the ball out wide to the HB.

A great fake by the QB

If we call the FB Dive a few times before running the pitch, the defense will have more respect for the fake. If we simply call this play without setting it up, our RB can be in trouble since he has no blockers.

The LB tries to cheat inside

The linebacker tries to storm through the B gap, but our halfback is already out wide and using his speed.

The RB gets outside one-on-one

The RB can hopefully get to the edge and make one move on the defender. This is a run that is used sparingly, but when called in the right situation, it can be the difference between a win and a loss.

PASSING STYLES

Short Passing Game

The short passing game was made famous during the 1980s with the invention of the West Coast Offense. Coaches quickly realized they could utilizing short passing to replace the run game and still keep the chains moving. Prior to this game plan, most coaches considered passing very risky and only used it in desperate situations. In *Madden NFL*, the most effective way to use a poorly rated QB is to throw short passes and let the receivers do the work. If you have an elite QB, you can throw pinpoint passes short to suck in the defense before stretching them deep. A great short passing game will unlock the ability to run the ball as well. Here are the types of routes that an effective short passing game employs.

Flat Route

The TE has outside position against the LB

A flat route is a great horizontal route that is most often run by a player coming out of the backfield. It develops very quickly and can easily beat defenses that back up too far from the line of scrimmage.

The speed mismatch allows the TE to get to the edge

At the snap of the ball, the receiver quickly heads to open space before turning to look for the ball. Once he gets into space he can secure the ball and look to get to the corner. Be careful not to throw late in the flats; if the route is open early, don't dump it off late assuming it is still going to be there.

Curl Route

The WR starts his cut and the QB should be releasing the ball

Curl routes have the ability to beat both zone and man coverage depending on the depth and style of coverage. The WR starts upfield and appears to be running a straight streak route, but he then sharply turns around and cuts back to the ball. When this pass is thrown well the play can be undefendable.

The WR gets his hands up and comes back to the ball

The curl relies on great timing from the QB and WR tandem. If the ball arrives too early, the receiver will not have turned around yet, but if it arrives too late, the defender will have a chance to make a play on the ball. If you need extra yards, try smart-routing the play so the player will run to the first down marker before turning around—this can come in handy on long third downs. Also lead the pass away from the defender; we had success throwing a low pass where only our player could go down and catch the ball.

Slant Route

A sharp cut results in inside position

Slants are a great way to take advantage of a soft defensive coverage. The WR appears to start upfield before cutting sharply across the middle of the field. If the WR earns inside position, the QB should be able to bullet a pass to him.

The QB does a good job and the WR can maintain top speed

The QB should try to lead the throw out in front of the receiver. If the player can catch the ball in stride, he can add extra yards onto the play. The slant also helps set up other routes, as the defender will be forced to play more aggressively if he is beaten early.

Out Route

The WR starts making his cut to the sideline

Out routes are a great way to beat zone coverage when combined with other route combinations. In *Madden NFL 12*, they also do a great job of beating man coverage. If your WR has good route running and your QB has a strong arm, use these to get separation from the defense.

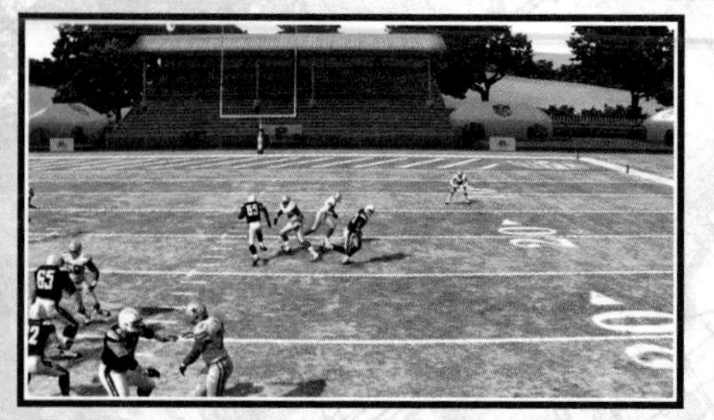

The defenders lose containment and the QB has a big window

As the WR makes his cut, the defender holds inside as there are two offensive players in position. The whole sideline is open and a QB with a strong arm can really make a good throw here. If you can keep the throw in-bounds, the receiver should be able to cut upfield for more yards. By running this play to the sideline with more space, you get more room to throw the ball.

Drag Route

The defender does a good job staying inside the drag

Drags are great because they allow the offense a chance to beat both man and zone coverage. If the offense has a speed player who has a skills advantage, he will be able to outrun man coverage and get open. If the offense reads zone coverage, the QB can be patient and wait until the receiver runs through a hole in the coverage. By using multiple drag routes on one play, the offense can create a mesh concept, which can mix up defenders, who have to run through congested areas.

The WR gets help from his teammate, who runs into the defender

An extra bonus to the drag is that it runs right in front of the QB—this makes for an easier throw and allows him to see any potential defenders that are sneaking into the play. Here, our second route runs into the main defender and forces him to lose a step on the WR; he is finally wide open, and staying patient will pay off for a huge gain.

Slant Out Route

The defender's hips are turned inside

Slant outs were a very popular route in *Madden NFL 11* due to their ability to get open against man coverage. Let's take a look at how they work this season. After the snap, the WR will start his cut around 2 yards; he looks to gain outside position and give his QB a window to throw to the sideline.

The player gets great separation

When the defense is in zone coverage, slant outs do a great job of finding a weak spot near the sideline. This gives the QB a safe throw to the sideline—an overthrow results in an out-of-bounds throw rather than an interception. Make sure to throw these passes with confidence, because if the defender jumps the pass, it could result in a pick 6.

Fade Route

The WR takes a step inside to set up the route

Fade routes have changed the last few years in *Madden NFL*, and this year this short route can be used inside the red zone. At the snap, the WR takes a quick step inside before heading out towards the sideline. The QB should look to throw a lob pass and trust the WR to get underneath the ball and make a play.

An athletic wideout will consistently win this battle

When utilizing a bigger target on the edge, the player should be able to go up and pick the ball right out of the air. Make sure to keep this pass within 20 yards of the end zone because the player won't go up for the pass unless he is past the goal line. This is one of our favorite routes and one that can cause the defense headaches if they don't use double coverage.

Angle Route

The RB starts his sharp cutback to the middle of the field

Angle routes are a great way to turn your players running out of the backfield into threats. This route gives the QB two options for when to throw the football. The QB can hit the back either when he is starting out on his route towards the sideline or after the player makes his cutback upfield. The cut should shake his defender loose as it is one of the sharpest in the game.

The defender can't keep up and the whole middle of the field is open

Make sure to bullet this pass into the back. The angle route is another route to feel confident using on third and short plays because of its consistency in getting the RB open. The more skilled players you can put into the position, the more separation you will get from the defender and the more yards you will gain. Learn the timing of the cut because throwing to a cutting player will result in an incompletion.

Post/Corner Route

The TE starts working his cut to get inside

Posts and corner routes are similar to slants except the initial streak route is longer. These give you the ability to stretch the defense a little more and can attack the middle or the edge of the field. When run from the inside slot or TE position, these can stress smaller LBs because they must defend a larger receiver.

The TE makes the catch in traffic

This play usually works best against zone coverage when mixed in with other routes. Here the safety has to respect the deep route and can't recover in time to break up the play. When you have a threat at TE, working him in tight areas can be one way to maximize his talents. When running the corner to the sideline, make sure to bullet the pass in and get the ball to the receiver quickly so he is protected.

Playmaker

The defender now must choose QB or RB

Using the Playmaker feature on offense is one of the best ways to make something out of nothing. Playmaker works best when the play is broken down and the QB breaks the pocket. Using Playmaker tells your nearest WR where to run!

The HB listens to his QB and looks for open space

On this play, the offense needs to pick up a critical third down. Although it's not looking good, the QB is able to keep the play alive with his feet. He lets his RB know to cut upfield and creates a two-on-one matchup! Now the HB is cutting upfield and the defender is paralyzed about what he should do. This should only be used under extreme circumstances, but it is a great thing to have in the back pocket.

WR Screens

Notice how the linemen will block outside

The blitzers think they have the QB!

The big offensive linemen are able to get out in front and crush the DBs.

A screen is a great way to catch a defense that is sitting too far back in coverage or is overly aggressive. If you can deliver the football quickly, you have a chance to make one move and rack up yards. There are multiple types of screens.

HB Screen

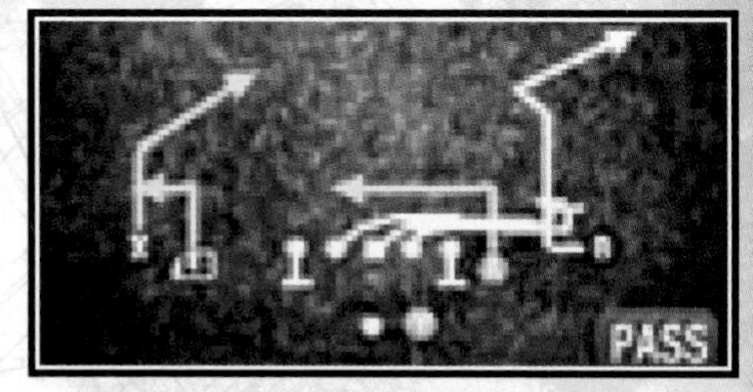

Clear out the area

The RB turns just in time

The back secures the ball and follows his blocks upfield

The HB Screen is another great way to catch the defense off guard. You can use a slip screen to sneak the HB out of the backfield and set up blocking downfield. You must be patient when running the screen; wait for the play to develop and it will pay dividends.

Deep Passing Game

Streak Route

Both receivers head on "go" routes

When looking to get a vertical passing attack going, a streak route is the simplest way to beat the defense over the top. The receiver simply looks to run a straight route and burn his defender deep. The streak can also be effective when trying to clear out an area against zone coverage.

If your WR can get a step on his defender, look to lob the pass deep and allow him time to run under the ball. In *Madden NFL 12*, you can have your player lay out for a catch just out of reach using the Dive Catch button.

The WR hauls in the deep pass

Streaks are best when thrown by a QB with good arm strength. If you can take the top off the defense, everything else will come easier.

Wheel Route

A short flat route can suck the defender in

The wheel route is a unique route; it starts with a short flat route but ends with a streak. The sharp cut at which the receiver cuts upfield often freezes the defender and earns the receiver space. Look to work the short route to get the defense to bite short and then throw a similar pass to the streak route.

A halfback with great speed is the ideal type of player to throw the ball to. If the defense allows the short option to be open, take it, because holding the ball for too long can be risky. This is a stock route that is commonly seen out of shotgun formations—try motioning the back out to put stress on the defense.

Air it out and allow your athlete to run under it

Deep Corner Route

The WR waits until he gets behind his defender

Deep corner routes allow your wideout to get into a zone-busting area on the field. Working these routes in combination with streaks will put stress on the defense. If running this route against man defense, release the football on the receiver's cut. The better QB you have the easier this throw is to make.

The sideline is a safe place to throw the ball

On this specific play the streak on the outside clears the defender over the top. Our slot WR waits until he gets behind his defender to start the cut to the sideline. This play is stock in many formations but can also be created by smart-routing certain routes.

Deep Post Route

The WR gets behind the midlevel zone

The deep post is a great way to get the ball deep without top-level QB accuracy. A streak must be thrown on one plane and can be hard to complete. The deep post allows the QB to really air the ball out and allow the defender to get under the ball. The margin for error is wider and the pass has a great chance of success.

Give your WR space to get under the ball

When calling the deep corner route, rolling the pocket is ideal. The WR will often get behind even deep zones and can run for miles after catching the ball. Make sure to step up in the pocket and really put air underneath the ball. A speedy wideout can toast a slower safety and allow the offense to rack up points fast.

DEFENSIVE FUNDAMENTALS

Contents

DEFENSIVE CONTROLS

With the addition of custom playbooks, offenses will have plenty of plays to throw at the defense in *Madden NFL 12*. If you can master the defensive controls, you can be ready for any scheme the offense comes up with this season. This chapter covers not only the individual controls that you need during the play, but all the adjustments you can make before the snap to take your game to the next level.

Audible

Xbox 360: ⓧ

PlayStation 3: ■

Y 2 Man Under
A Pinch
X Cover 2
LB Cover 4
RB Cover 3
B Cancel
Ravens

Make the quick adjustment

What if you choose your defensive play expecting the offense to run the ball, but when you get to the line of scrimmage, they have five wide receivers on the field? By calling an audible, you can switch to a new play before the offense snaps the ball and take away their advantage.

NOTE

Check out the "Advanced Gameplay Strategies" chapter to find out which five audibles will have you ready for any situation.

Coverage Audible

Xbox 360: ⓨ

PlayStation 3: ▲

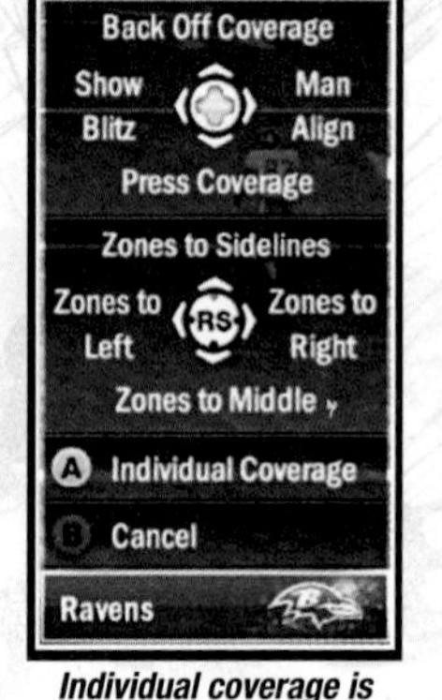

Individual coverage is new this year!

The Coverage Audible button quickly gives defenses the ability to move eight ways before the snap. If you need to protect deep, you can back up your coverage. If you want to jam the receivers you can move the secondary closer to the line of scrimmage. If the offense is beating you to a specific side of the field, this menu also gives you the option of shading your defenders to a specific side. By learning these quick controls, we can quickly make even more adjustments before the snap.

NOTE

Please see the "Coverage Audibles" section later in this chapter for details on each coverage audible.

Tackle

Xbox 360: ⓧ

PlayStation 3: ■

Press the new button to lunge for the tackle

To eliminate suction from the game, EA SPORTS added a brand-new collision system. This ensures that the tackle does not start until contact is made. Now, the optimal way to tackle is by pressing the Tackle button to lunge at the ball carrier and trigger the tackle animation. It may take a few games to learn how to wrap up, but this system adds in tremendous new tackles and lets you make some amazing plays.

Hit Stick

Xbox 360: Up or down on right thumbstick

PlayStation 3: Up or down on right thumbstick

The hit stick takes out the ball carrier

The hit stick is back in *Madden NFL 12*. When used in the proper situation, this can be an incredible way to unload on the ball carrier. Use a player with high hit power or make sure you have momentum. A well-timed hit stick can jar the ball loose or even cause an injury. Do not attempt this in the open field unless you have help.

Defensive Line Moves

Xbox 360: Move the right thumbstick in any direction

PlayStation 3: Move the right thumbstick in any direction

Control the lineman and get to the QB!

If you're a player who enjoys rushing the QB, be sure to use the moves in the game to free yourself up from the offensive lineman. If you have a finesse rusher, look to spin. If you're using a power rusher, simply attempt to bowl over the lineman on your way to the sack.

Strip

Xbox 360: LB

PlayStation 3: L1

The defender tries to rip the ball loose

The Strip button can be one of the best ways to bring down the ball carrier if you use it at the right time. Make sure that you have some teammates around to help because using this will lead to more broken tackles. If you need a turnover or are going against a player with a suspect carry rating, use the strip. Hold down the button while approaching the ball carrier and watch your player try to rip the ball out!

Make sure a teammate pounces on the ball

Defensive Playmaker

Xbox 360: Select a player, use the Strategy Pad, and then select an option

PlayStation 3: Select a player, use the Strategy Pad, and then select an option

Every tool the defense needs is here

Learning how to quickly and effectively use the defensive Playmaker is how good players become great. These assignments allow our defenders to stop offenses that are utilizing the same play against us. Go into practice mode and learn how to quickly adjust the defensive line; this is your first step to becoming great. Knowing how to quickly call a QB spy or a contain can help shut down fast QBs who can frustrate newer players. The best players are often making 3–5 adjustments on any play and know what each adjustment does and when to use it.

NOTE

Please see the "Defensive Playmaker—Individual Hot Routes" section later in this chapter for details on each option.

D-Line Swat Ball

Xbox 360: LB or RB

PlayStation 3: L1 or R1

If you can't get to the QB, get into his passing lane

When controlling the defensive line, you have the option to jump up and try to deflect the pass. This is a great option if you are just a few steps short of sacking the QB. Another good time to use the swat is when the QB is consistently dumping short routes over the middle or to the flats—try to swat the ball down and block his passing lane.

Swat Ball

Xbox 360: LB

PlayStation 3: L1

Knock it down

Knowing when to go for a swat and when to go for the interception is what separates great *Madden NFL* players. If you are one-on-one and trailing the WR, look to simply swat the ball away. However, if you have safety help and have time to get your defender set up, go for the interception. When in doubt, always go for the swat, as it is a more consistent option and can really frustrate the offense.

Catch

Xbox 360: Hold Y

PlayStation 3: Hold ▲

Go for the interception

Making a "user pick" is one of the best feelings in the game. However, it can also feel pretty bad if you let up a long touchdown while trying to go for the interception. Make sure that you have enough space and time to jump up and get the interception. Hold down the button and get to the spot where the throw is going for the best chance to make a big play!

Strafe

Xbox 360: Hold LT

PlayStation 3: Hold L2

Keep your hips square

When user-controlling the defender, strafing will keep your hips square to the line and keep your player shuffling. This is ideal to keep your body facing forward. It allows you to keep one eye on the QB and one on your receiver. One specific time to use strafe is when you are going for an interception. Hold down the Strafe and Catch buttons and get to the front of the circle; your player will sky up and grab the interception!

Defensive Assist

Xbox 360: Hold A

PlayStation 3: Hold ×

On every level but All-Madden, users can hold down the Defensive Assist button to allow the computer to control the defender they are playing. This is especially helpful when going in for a tackle, as it will lock you onto the ball carrier. Another good time to use defensive assist is when playing man coverage; it should keep you on target with your opponent's route. Simply stop holding the button at any time to take back control!

DEFENSIVE LINE SHIFTS

Learning how to successfully maneuver the defensive line to create optimal fronts is a great way to win the important trench battle in *Madden NFL*. By making sure your defenders are lining up in the proper gaps, you will be ahead of the offense when the ball is snapped; here are some of the changes we can make on any given snap.

By turning the Strategy Pad's Quick Links menu on, you can make shifts faster than using just the Strategy Pad.

Advanced players should turn on the Quick Links menu for maximum pre-play adjustments

3-4 vs. 4-3

The shifts covered in this section are shown with a 3-4 defense, since shifting is more drastic due to fewer defensive linemen. Let's take a look at the difference between the two main styles of base defense in the NFL.

NFL teams use a 4-3 or a 3-4 as a base defense. A 4-3 uses four linemen and three linebackers, while a 3-4 has three linemen with four linebackers.

3-4 Strengths

- This defense gives coordinators the creativity to blitz a linebacker on any play or have extra coverage quickly.
- Defensive ends are more focused on holding up the gap than rushing the QB. This defense doesn't require elite personnel at DE.

3-4 Weaknesses

- An elite nose tackle is required to play two gaps in the middle and anchor the line.
- You need smart linebackers who can pass rush or drop back and play coverage on any down.

4-3 Strengths

- If a team can get pressure with its front four rushers, it can play multiple coverages successfully.
- It's tougher to run inside the tackles due to the presence of two defensive tackles.

4-3 Weaknesses

- This defense requires talented linemen to win one-on-one battles and get penetration without blitzing.
- Outside LBs must be able to match up against elite tight ends and slot WRs depending on packaging.

Defensive Line Shift Right

Xbox 360: Strategy Pad then left on the D-pad

PlayStation 3: Strategy Pad then left on the D-pad

NOTE

The callout for the left defensive end is actually for the left-side-of-the-screen defensive end. Normally, the left end lines up against the right tackle, but in *Madden* when referring to the defense we refer to how you're looking at the TV, not the actual player's in-game position.

The left-of-screen LB is helping occupy the offensive line

Strengths

Plays the weak-side inside gaps with good balance.

Slows down the ability to call play action to the strong side.

Weaknesses

Allows the offense to run outside to the strong side.

Lets the TE run free on pass plays.

Defensive Line Shift Left

Xbox 360: Strategy Pad then right on the D-pad

PlayStation 3: Strategy Pad then right on the D-pad

The TE can't block him consistently

Strengths

Allows a DE to rush against a TE and slows him down if he runs a passing route.

Puts a linebacker against a tackle who can hopefully speed rush around him (think DeMarcus Ware).

Weaknesses

Leaves you vulnerable to weak-side counters.

Leaves the MLB to recover quickly against a fast back.

Defensive Line Pinch

Xbox 360: Strategy Pad then down on the D-pad

PlayStation 3: Strategy Pad then down on the D-pad

The middle is locked up

Strengths

Controls the inside rushing lanes, including the A gap.

Doesn't allow quick runs up the middle, especially on short yardage.

Allows linebackers to roam free behind the line and make tackles.

Weaknesses

The offense can toss the ball outside and run for days.

The defense is forced to use an extra linebacker to hold the edge.

The defense must commit a linebacker to spy the QB since the lineman will lose containment.

Defensive Line Spread

Xbox 360: Strategy Pad then up on the D-pad

PlayStation 3: Strategy Pad then up on the D-pad

Force the run inside

Strengths

In 4-3, allows the DEs to start their rush upfield quicker.

Can help occupy outside linemen, which lets LBs get a matchup against the HB.

Helps stop QBs from breaking the pocket on passing plays.

Weaknesses

Forces the linebackers to back up the middle of the field.

Disciplined offenses will continue to run the ball for solid gains up the middle.

Crash Left

Xbox 360: Strategy Pad then left on the right thumbstick

PlayStation 3: Strategy Pad then left on the right thumbstick

Attack the left side of the line

If you sense where the run is going or want to run a stunt, we can crash the line. Here we look to set the edge against a potential run to the left. Look to consistently attack whichever side of the line is weaker.

Crash Right

Xbox 360: Strategy Pad then right on the right thumbstick

PlayStation 3: Strategy Pad then right on the right thumbstick

Hopefully the end can loop around outside

Try using different shifts combined with crashing the line to make some unique fronts. This crash helps attack the right side of the line.

Crash Down

Xbox 360: Strategy Pad then down on the right thumbstick

PlayStation 3: Strategy Pad then down on the right thumbstick

Get penetration inside

This will put tremendous pressure on the interior linemen. If we suspect a straight-ahead run on third and short, look to push the line back by crashing inside.

Crash Out

Xbox 360: Strategy Pad then up on the right thumbstick

PlayStation 3: Strategy Pad then up on the right thumbstick

Your DEs will start upfield but be vulnerable to draws.

Crashing your defensive line out will help the ends play the edge. If you have a speedy line, they can often loop around and grab a QB who rolls out of the pocket.

LINEBACKER SHIFTS

LB Spread
LB Shift Left
LB Shift Right
LB Pinch
All LB Zones
ROLB Blitz
LOLB Blitz
All LB Blitz
Cancel
Ravens

Linebackers are the second level of the defense. If the offense breaks through into the second level, your LBs must be there to pick up the slack. With the 3-4, LBs are especially important since they should be protected by the linemen and have the ability to roam. Let's take a look at the shifts that can get them into position to make big plays.

Linebacker Shift Left

Xbox 360: Strategy Pad then left on the D-pad

PlayStation 3: Strategy Pad then left on the D-pad

The weak side is very strong

Strengths

The linebacker has a great angle to the QB.

Any plays to the weak side will be blown up.

Weaknesses

Allows the offense to run outside to the strong side.

The slot WR is uncovered.

Linebackers Shift Right

Xbox 360: Strategy Pad then right on the D-pad

PlayStation 3: Strategy Pad then right on the D-pad

Take away any thought of going to the strong side

Strengths

The right-of-screen LB can quickly match up in pass coverage vs. the TE or HB.

The defense will not be able to get past the free rushing LB.

Weaknesses

The LOLB can't hold the edge on the weak side.

The offense can simply slide protect or block an extra player to chip the LB.

Linebackers Pinch Align

Xbox 360: Strategy Pad then down on the D-pad

PlayStation 3: Strategy Pad then down on the D-pad

Attack the A gap

Strengths

Takes away the inside run.

Puts blitzers in the fastest gap to the QB.

Controls short throws to the middle of the field.

Weaknesses

Forces weaker safeties to hold the edge in the run game.

Can be burned by the QB rolling outside the pocket.

Linebackers Spread Align

Xbox 360: Strategy Pad then up on the D-pad

PlayStation 3: Strategy Pad then up on the D-pad

Get the LBs out wide

Strengths

Allows the user to send either LB off the edge.

Great balance, simply does not show a weakness.

Weaknesses

Can be hit up the middle by draws in the passing game.

Puts pressure on the MLB to slow down all runs to the inside.

All LB Blitz

Xbox 360: Strategy Pad then down on the right thumbstick

PlayStation 3: Strategy Pad then down on the right thumbstick

This sends everyone

Use this if you have a good feeling about the offense's play and need to quickly blitz all your linebackers. This is a dangerous maneuver, but it can pay off if you call it at the right time.

Left Outside LB Blitz

Xbox 360: Strategy Pad then left on the right thumbstick

PlayStation 3: Strategy Pad then left on the right thumbstick

Quickly call for the backer to blitz down

This is a great way to send the weak-side linebacker into the backfield, and you also can use it to reblitz the LB straight down. This should eat up any play action fakes.

Right Outside LB Blitz

Xbox 360: Strategy Pad then right on the right thumbstick

PlayStation 3: Strategy Pad then right on the right thumbstick

Get a good blitz angle from the strong side

This seals off the strong side of the formation against runs and challenges the weaker tackle in pass protection.

All LB Zone

Xbox 360: Strategy Pad then up on the right thumbstick

PlayStation 3: Strategy Pad then up on the right thumbstick

Quickly drop everyone into hook zones

This places all the linebackers into yellow zones, which is a good start against over-the-middle passes. If you have time, make sure to swap a few of the LBs into different types of zones, since four yellow zones over the middle is more than enough.

COVERAGE AUDIBLES

Coverage audibles allow our secondary to give the offense different looks pre-snap and then change where they play after the snap. Make sure you know what the rest of the defense is doing because your secondary is the final line of defense before the end zone.

Press

Xbox 360: Strategy Pad then down on the D-pad

PlayStation 3: Strategy Pad then down on the D-pad

The defender won't give him a free release

Strengths

Disrupts the timing of the passing game.

Forces the QB to wait and makes him vulnerable to the pass rush.

Weaknesses

Talented WRs can easily beat the coverage for large gains.

The offense should recognize the coverage and start to utilize unbumpable routes.

Back Off

Xbox 360: Strategy Pad then up on the D-pad

PlayStation 3: Strategy Pad then down on the D-pad

The DB can't get beaten here

Strengths

Keeps the threats in front of our defense and doesn't allow the big play.

Can switch up coverages and use less-talented players effectively.

Weaknesses

Allows the offense to use shorter routes to dink and dunk.

The corners can't support the run game.

Man Align

Xbox 360: Strategy Pad then right on the D-pad

PlayStation 3: Strategy Pad then right on the D-pad

When you have multiple DBs on the field, use this coverage audible to make sure they line up properly when in man coverage. This will help keep the formation balanced and not give your opponent an advantage.

Show Blitz

Xbox 360: Strategy Pad then left on the D-pad

PlayStation 3: Strategy Pad then left on the D-pad

By showing blitz, we can fool the offense into thinking we are bringing pressure. This will move all our defenders up close to the line and cut off short throws. Use this sparingly—it leaves the defense vulnerable to the deep pass and play action game. If you are expecting a run and don't have time to audible, use this to quickly bring the safeties up to the line.

Zones to Sidelines

Xbox 360: Strategy Pad then up on the right thumbstick

PlayStation 3: Strategy Pad then up on the right thumbstick

If expecting the QB to attack the sideline

If the offense is looking to get out of bounds or utilize the sideline, call this coverage audible. The safeties will spread out with this call and play closer to the sideline. This is solid if you are user-controlling the deep middle part of the field with a linebacker.

Zones to Middle

Xbox 360: Strategy Pad then down on the right thumbstick

PlayStation 3: Strategy Pad then down on the right thumbstick

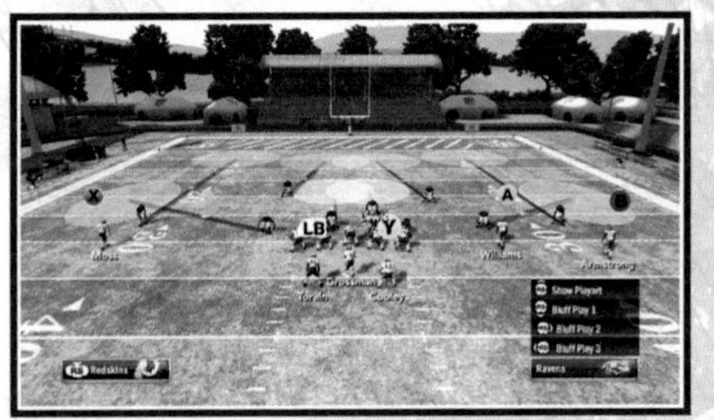

Protect the middle of the field

If the defense is trying to work us in the middle with the deep post, this can help shut them down.

Shade Safeties Left

Xbox 360: Strategy Pad then left on the right thumbstick

PlayStation 3: Strategy Pad then left on the right thumbstick

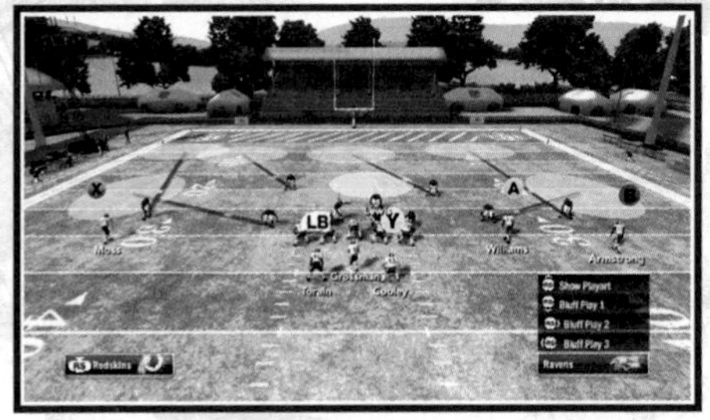

Watch the left side

If the offense is operating on the right hash mark, they might look to throw left since there is more room on that side of the field. Be ready!

Shade Safeties Right

Xbox 360: Strategy Pad then right on the right thumbstick

PlayStation 3: Strategy Pad then right on the right thumbstick

Extra shading to the right

Here the offense has an extra WR on the right side of the field, so we want to pay extra attention over there.

DEFENSIVE PLAYMAKER—INDIVIDUAL HOT ROUTES

In *Madden NFL 12*, the defense has seven seconds to make any adjustments that it needs to get ready for the upcoming snap. With the ability to change any defender's individual route to one of eight different assignments, the possibilities are nearly endless. To call a defensive hot route, first take control of the defender you intend to hot route.

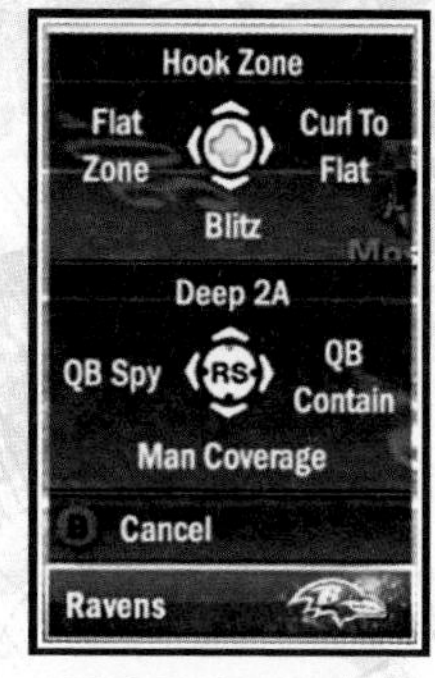

All eight of our options

If we are expecting a play to a specific player, we can quickly add another defender to cover him. If we think the QB might take off, we can call a QB Spy to watch him like a hawk. By mixing these routes up we can make average plays into great ones and lock up anything the offense is doing. Let's take a look at what each assignment does and how to make quick changes before the play.

QB Spy

Xbox 360: Press down on the D-Pad, then left on the right thumbstick

PlayStation 3: Press down on the D-Pad, then left on the right thumbstick

Orange zone

A QB Spy is great for a defensive lineman or LB if we think the QB might make a break for it. Another way that a QB Spy is good is when the offense is throwing a lot of short crossing throws. Since the defender steps back and waits for the QB, he is in good position underneath to intercept the ball. He is usually tough for the to see QB since he is usually rushing. If you place a DT on a spy, make sure he is fast enough to catch the QB, since he will not chase him until after he crosses the line of scrimmage.

Buzz Zone

Xbox 360: Press down on the D-pad, then right on the left thumbstick

PlayStation 3: Press down on the D-pad, then right on the left thumbstick

Purple zone or "curl to flat"

With the overhauled zone coverage in *Madden NFL 12*, curl to flat zones are a great way to defend the sideline and the flat at the same time. In years past, the buzz zone would often not defend the flat, but now it is a great way to slow down dink and dunk offenses. Since many playbooks lack a stock play with purple zones, these are a common hot route that you have to call. We usually find these popular with Cover 4 defenses. If you're an online-type player and have trouble defending corner routes, look to use the buzz zone to slow them down.

Hook Zone

Xbox 360: Press down on the D-pad, then up on the left thumbstick

PlayStation 3: Press down on the D-pad, then up on the left thumbstick

Yellow zone

Hook zones are a great way to defend 5- to 8-yard throws over the middle of the field. Even if the pass is completed in front of the zone, the defender will be there to quickly wrap up the ball carrier. These are most commonly used by LBs and slot defenders; if the offense is working an intermediate passing game, we can force the QB to make tough reads into crowded areas with these zones. When playing with a linebacker, this is a good route to user-control over the middle of the field. Try placing defensive ends on these routes and you might be able to steal an interception on passes to the TE!

Blitz

Xbox 360: Press down on the D-pad, then down on the left thumbstick

PlayStation 3: Press down on the D-pad, then down on the left thumbstick

Use this to change blitz angles

By sending additional defenders on blitzes, we can quickly add pressure on the offense to get rid of the ball quickly. Most of the time, we will not user-rush the player on the blitz, but quickly place him and change to another person. When we use the blitz Playmaker, it changes the angle of the blitz and can create some unique rushes. Try mixing the Playmaker blitz with other "stock" play calls to see what you can come up with!

Flat Zone

Xbox 360: Press down on the D-pad, then left on the left thumbstick

PlayStation 3: Press down on the D-pad, then left on the left thumbstick

Light blue zone

Flat zones have gotten a huge upgrade in this year's game. Before, they would often slide inside and not hold the outside. Now, they stay out wide and even guard the most difficult "slant out" route that is popular online. This allows the defense to utilize these routes now and can really make it tough for the QB to simply dump the ball off. These routes can result in interceptions if the QB gets lazy, and they often are returned for touchdowns! With Cover 2, these routes bump the WR before letting him go behind to pick up the flat route; this can disrupt the offense's timing.

QB Contain

Xbox 360: Press down on the D-pad, then right on the right thumbstick

PlayStation 3: Press down on the D-pad, then right on the right thumbstick

Keep everything in the pocket

Contains became very famous in *Madden NFL* due to their ability to bring pressure from unique angles and slow down popular online players like Michael Vick. In this year's game, contains do not mess with the offensive line anymore but still do a great job of keeping opposing threats inside the pocket. We can also use these on run plays that are suspected to go to the outside edge of the field. Make sure you know which way the contain is going, as it depends on which half of the field you call it on. If you bring pressure from the left side, contain the right side so when the QB rolls away from the blitz, your defender is there to meet him.

Man Up

Xbox 360: Press down on the D-pad, then down on the right thumbstick, and then the receiver's icon

PlayStation 3: Press down on the D-pad, then down on the right thumbstick, and then the receiver's icon

An extra man defender is placed on the TE

If we have a blitz that leaves someone uncovered or suspect that a pass is going to a certain player, we can give him extra attention by manning up a defender to guard him. Most of the time, we will simply user-control a player near him, but if we want the computer to take care of the job, we can assign a defender and focus our attention elsewhere.

Deep Zone

Xbox 360: Press down on the D-pad, then up on the right thumbstick

PlayStation 3: Press down on the D-pad, then up on the right thumbstick

Dark blue zone

Deep zones do a great job of keeping the WRs in front of them. Although you are vulnerable to shorter passes, it's a great way to add another layer of protection deep. If you have a Cover 2 that you suspect is vulnerable, simply add a deep zone to make it a Cover 3. This can force the QB into a bad read if he is not expecting this coverage. You can make this adjustment when using man or zone coverage, which makes it one of the most versatile in the game. While it might not make you huge plays, it is a very safe route and one we can call if we get lost or in trouble on defense.

RUN DEFENSE

Stopping the run is the most important thing on defense; if you can't control the line of scrimmage, the offense will simply work long drives and tire you out. If you can stop the run, you force the defense to pass and you can really start attacking the QB. Let's look at the two main types of run defense and how both work.

Inside Run Defense

By placing seven defenders (usually four linemen and three linebackers) inside the space between the offensive tackles, we can be ready for the most common types of inside run.

Two of our LBs hold their gaps at the snap

At the snap, our LBs are free to rush since our defensive linemen did a great job at picking up the initial linemen. We know have two free defenders while the offense only has one fullback in front of the RB. The run is designed to go up the middle, but the RB quickly realizes he has no chance to gain yards. He cuts outside and our LB wraps him up.

The HB is forced to cut outside

Outside Run Defense

By keeping five defenders (usually four linemen and one linebacker) inside the space between the offensive tackles, we have our two other LBs free to hold the edge and keep the run contained inside.

Our LB sets the edge at the snap

At the snap, the QB tosses the ball, which always signifies an outside run. Our LB rushes into the backfield; even if he is picked up by a blocker, this still helps contain the run and takes away a blocker.

Our second defender breaks up the play

Our first defender forces a hesitation and keeps the RB from breaking containment. This keeps the play inside and gives our LBs time to get over and make the play. If you are playing with the safety, make sure to stay out wide rather than trying to knife inside and make a play. The offense really wants to break the edge on the defense, and it is your job to hold it.

COVERAGE TYPES

Man Defense

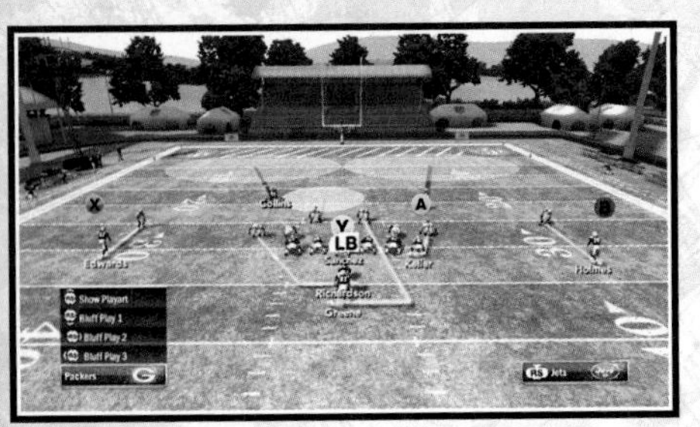

The defenders are assigned to man coverage

Man defense is very common for newer players because each player simply follows his assignment wherever he goes. The man defenders often have zone help over the top in case they get beaten deep, but for the most part it is their responsibility to cover just one WR.

The defender follows the WR on his crossing pattern

Here the man defender sees the person he is supposed to be covering break to the inside, and he runs right with him. This is an example of good coverage, because the defender is in good position to break up the pass or tackle the WR as soon as he catches the football. When calling man defense, make sure everyone is accounted for, and know where your help is over the top so you can play aggressively.

Zone Defense

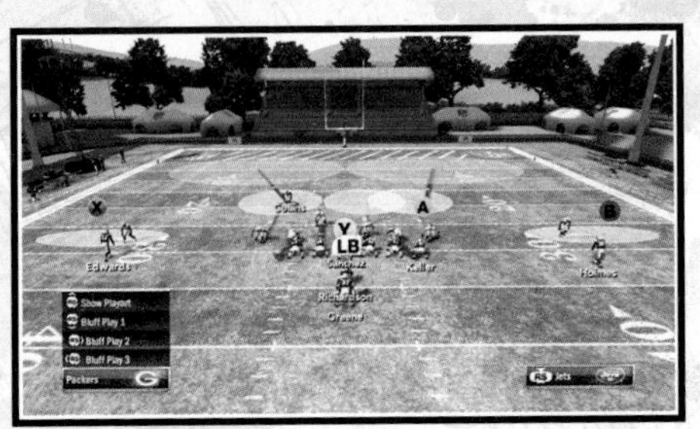

The defenders are assigned to zone coverage

Zone defense is a little bit more advanced because defenders only cover an area rather than a player. When a player runs through your zone, you play him man to man, but as soon as he leaves he is no longer your problem.

The defender lets the WR run out of his zone

Here the zone defender sees the person he is supposed to be covering break inside, but rather then following him, he passes him off to the zone next to him. This is an example of good defense because if the defender had followed him, the HB who is about to run through his zone would be open. The defender who is playing in the zone next to the first defender will pick the offensive player up and defend him while he is in his zone. Different types of zone are explored in the "Advanced Gameplay Strategies" chapter—make sure to know what types you will be using!

BLITZING 101

Blitzing is a great way to put pressure on the offense. Blitzing refers to sending five or more rushers at the QB and hoping to force a sack or an errant throw. When the defense blitzes they do have fewer defenders in coverage, which can leave them vulnerable to attack. The best blitzes look to confuse the offense and to get pressure while sending as few rushers as possible. Let's take a look at the most common types of blitzes and when to use them.

Man Blitz

We're setting this blitz up inside

With any man blitz, we have the option of bringing pressure inside the offensive line (usually with a linebacker) or rushing off the edge and making it an outside blitz (usually rushing a defensive back).

The line needs to pinch down

At the snap of the football, our LBs begin their rush. Our defenders are playing close to their WRs, so the QB can't quickly dump the ball off. We have one safety deep, but if we wanted to make a heavier blitz, we could also rush him.

The LB sneaks through

If the HB had stayed into block, he would likely have helped pick up the LB; however, we would have then been able to blitz his defender and still had the advantage! This makes it tough for offenses to choose who to keep in. The HB has made his cut and is starting to come open across the middle—thankfully our pressure is almost at the QB.

The QB can't get the ball off

Since we only had one-on-one coverage, the routes were getting open, but the blitz arrived in time and the QB is sacked. By blitzing in long yardage situations, we don't give the offense enough time to get the ball downfield, and that makes it a great time to send pressure. The line will adapt and pick up this pressure, but next time we will put the LB on the RB and send the player off the edge. If the line pinches down expecting the same blitz, our edge rusher will get in free. Working the inside/outside man blitz is a cat-and-mouse game with the offense.

Zone Blitz

A zone blitz still sends the same amount of pressure, but instead of man coverage, our players line up in zone behind the blitz. This tactic was made famous by Dick LeBeau and is now used by nearly every team in the NFL today.

The defense is in zone coverage

The defense lines up in the same blitz as the man defense and even has the extra LB looking like he is going to blitz off the edge. The offense has two backs next to the QB who may be helping block, but that also gives the QB fewer options to throw to.

The defenders rush at the snap

Our defenders attack the inside part of the field and force the linemen to slide and pick up the pressure. The left back is on a delayed route and will block before releasing. While the blitzing players get picked up, it allows one of the defensive linemen a good matchup, and he breaks into the backfield.

The QB is brought down for a loss

The zone coverage picks up the WRs and the blitz gets to the QB before anything opens up. Once again, we can switch which linebackers blitz next time and hope to fool the QB into making the wrong read. Playing zone coverage is good because you have less of a tendency to get beaten deep than with man if the blitz does not arrive. The more defenders we send, the riskier the blitz, but the better chance of success. Look at the "Advanced Gameplay Strategies" chapter to find out some of the best zone blitzes in the game!

Pro Tip: Many blitzes have man and zone versions that you can quickly change between.

EA SPORTS

MADDEN NFL 12

ADVANCED GAMEPLAY STRATEGIES

Contents

FIVE SETS FOR SUCCESS: OFFENSE

How many games have you played where you bounce around from play to play while the play clock runs down, resulting in a delay of game? We firmly believe that this is the result of not having an ironed-out game plan. After reading this section you will never have that problem again! "Five Sets for Success" is designed for both your offensive and defensive game plans. No matter the situation and no matter the opponent you will be prepared with a winning scheme. "Five Sets for Success" uses specific formations and play strategy to combat whatever your opponent is doing. To implement these formations we set them as our audibles so that we can call upon them at any time during the game. The goal is to read what our opponent is doing and to audible into the appropriate formation and the play that gives us the best advantage. In this section we break down the offensive formations used in the "Five Sets for Success." e. Make sure that you set your audibles to match up with this strategy.

Power Run (Three-Headed Rushing Attack)

Strong Close is found in many playbooks in* Madden NFL 12; *it is one of the best power run formations in the game

The main priority of our offensive attack is to run the ball effectively. Having a specific formation for running the ball is extremely important and sets the tone for our entire offensive scheme. We have all fallen victim to running just one overly effective run. A few runs that come to mind are the FB Dive in *Madden NFL 09*, HB Off Tackle in *Madden NFL 10*, and the HB Draw in *Madden NFL 11*. While those runs did a great job of picking up quality yardage, they didn't put complete pressure on the defense. That's because the defense always knew what to expect. Too many times in crucial situations we saw these runs not deliver because the defense was prepared to make a play. The remedy for this is to implement a run game where the defense has to respect all areas of the field. The "Three-Headed Rushing Attack" will do just that. We will use runs to the left, middle, and right, which will allow our offense to dictate to the defense how we want to play the game. While you can use any under-center formation for your power running set, we choose to use the Strong Close because we believe it is the best running formation in the game. Not only does it have the ability to pound the rock but it also has a balanced passing attack to complement the run game.

Run Middle

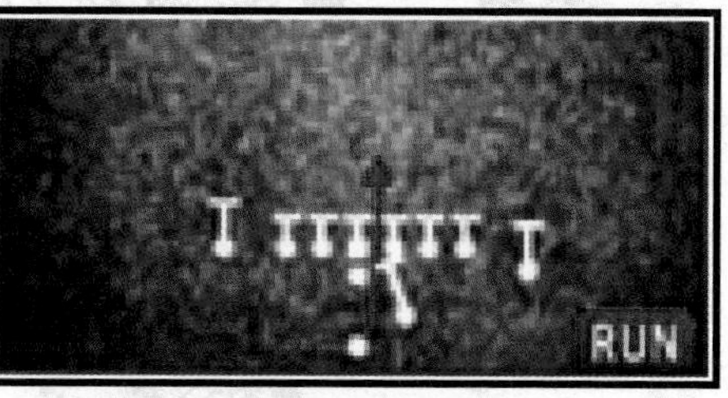

Strong Close—HB Dive

The Strong Close—HB Dive is the run to the middle in our three-headed rushing attack. Other middle run plays are isos, blasts, slams, and inside zones. The design of the play is to follow the fullback up through the offensive line. Be sure to stay consistent with this run and try to avoid the temptation to bounce outside.

The HB moves through the offensive line for the big gain

We followed our blocks and are rewarded with two open running lanes. The HB Dive is the staple of our rushing attack. Our goal is to force the defense to protect against the middle run. Once the defense adjusts to defend this we can anticipate our outside running lanes opening up.

Run Left

Strong Close—Counter Weak

We use the Counter Weak to run to the left in our attack. Other left runs are power O's, off tackles, tosses, and sweeps. The strong-side guard is set to pull left with the fullback at the snap of the ball. Be patient as the run develops and look to cut upfield once your blockers have engaged with a defender.

Our FB blocks the first defender while our pulling guard heads upfield

Notice that the FB's block has created two situations for the runner. He can cut either to the left or right of the fullback. Cutting right seems to be the better option because the defender out wide looks to have outside containment. Counters in *Madden NFL 12* are extremely effective, especially the Strong Close—Counter Weak.

Run Right

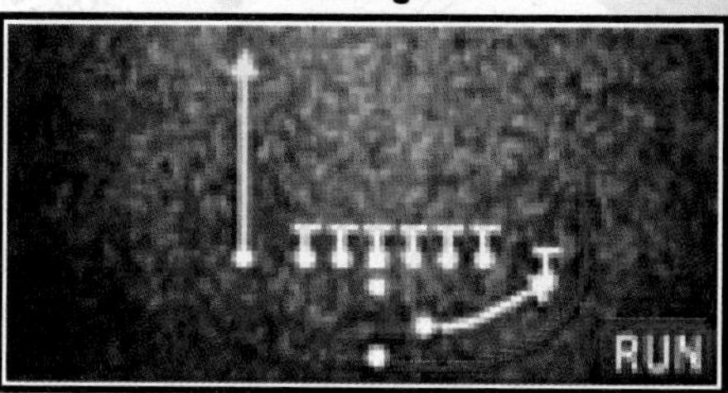

Strong Close—Quick Toss

The Strong Close—Quick Toss is the run right of our three-headed rushing attack. Other right runs are power O's, off tackles, tosses, and sweeps. Again, our strong-side guard and fullback will pull at the snap of the ball, only this time they will break out towards the right, helping to lead the way towards the sideline. Be just as patient with the toss as you were with the counter. Once the blocks are made move upfield.

Our TE makes a nice block while our FB and guard move towards the defense's second layer

Many times when running tosses you will be forced to cut the ball upfield prior to getting outside. This is because outside containment will be lost by our blockers, which forces the HB back up inside. Here our FB and guard have done a great job allowing us room to run outside.

Keys to the Power Run (Three-Headed Rushing Attack)

- Knowing your team's depth chart
- Substituting in your best run blockers over receiving threats
- Substituting in an extra offensive tackle for your TE for better run blocking
- Substituting TEs for your WRs for better run blocking.
- Running the ball until your opponents *prove* they can consistently stop the run
- Patience
- Commitment

Having success in the run game is about having a mind-set of playing smashmouth football. If you lose yards on one run don't be scared to run the ball again. Stick to your game plan and to the three-headed rushing attack and you will start winning more games than you could ever imagine. The defense can't account for all three options. They have to give up one of the three. Have patience, be committed, and pound the rock.

Quick Pass (Red Zone and Short Yardage)

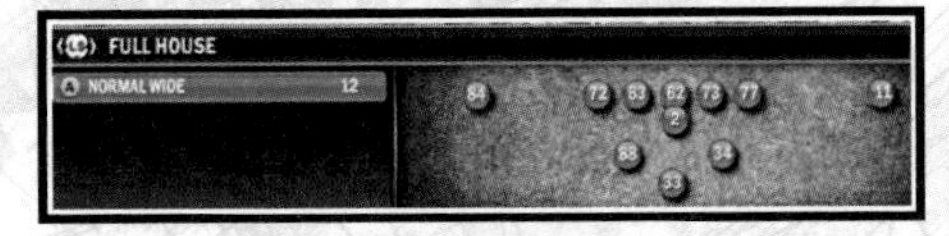

The Full House formation from the Atlanta playbook

The quick-pass formation can be under center or shotgun, but we prefer anything under center. We are looking for a formation that has a few options that allow us to consistently pick up gains in short yardage and red zone situations. Typically this type of pass is a "snap throw," meaning that it is all based on timing. Another important quality for a quick-pass formation is having two receivers split out wide near the sideline. This is imperative for red zone situations, where we throw a quick lob pass that is extremely difficult for the defense to defend. Quick-pass routes will most often come from the backfield. Routes to look for when searching for quick passes would be angles, up and outs, and red zone fades.

Without a doubt the Full House formation is the best quick-pass formation in the game. We have three offensive players in the backfield for quick-pass options as well as our two WRs split wide for the red zone quick lob pass. The quick-pass formation is also important for beating the blitz because high-pressure defenses are the status quo in the *Madden* community. Having the ability to score in the red zone, complete short yardage situations, and beat the blitz will do wonders for your confidence. In this section we look at one of our favorite passes from the Full House formation.

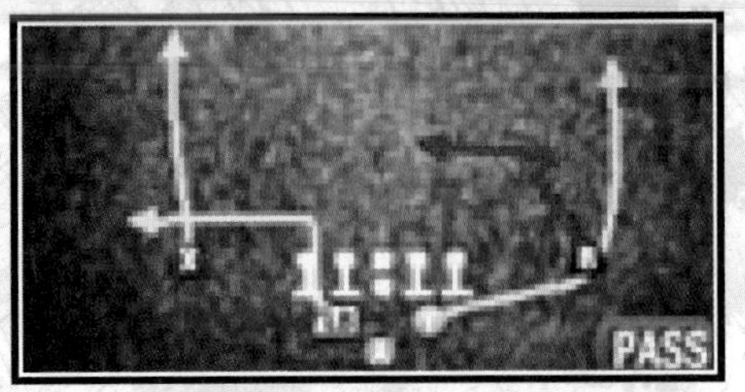

We focus on the TE out of the backfield on the up and out route

This play is all about timing, so be sure to head into practice mode and get a feel for the play yourself. This play is extremely difficult for defenses to stop. We throw the ball too quickly for pressure to get to the QB, man-to-man defenders won't be able to bump-n-run our TE, and zone defenders will drift from the short part of the field. The defense will have to user-defend the play, which helps to open up our other reads.

The defense is zone blitzing as our TE gets into position for the catch

At the snap of the ball we read the zone blitz and quickly look to get the ball to our TE. The zone defender is drifting away from the play and we don't see a user-controlled defender in the area.

Our TE hauls in the pass and goes in for the score

We complete the pass and our TE has enough momentum to carry into the end zone. The zone defense closed in on the TE too late and wasn't able to make a play on the ball. The blitz was a non-factor because we got rid of the ball lightning quick.

Keys to the Quick Pass (Red Zone and Short Yardage)

- Timing
- Repetition
- A formation with two receivers split wide near the sideline
- Substituting your larger WRs/TEs out wide for the red zone quick lob pass

Having confidence in your scheme in all situations is just as important as being able to deliver in crunch time. Knowing that you can score in the red zone, complete short yardage plays, and beat the blitz is a major advantage to have going into every game. Often these three situations are where many players break down. Once you perfect your quick-pass formation you will have the confidence to deliver time and time again.

Base Play

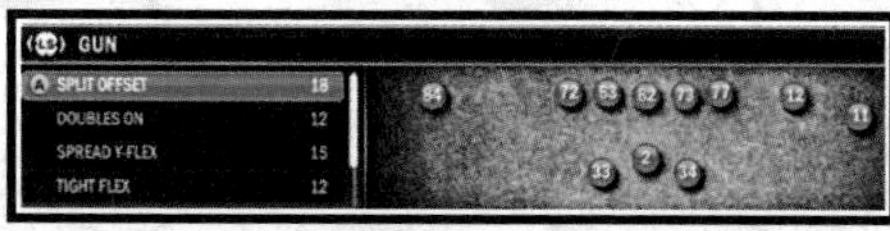

Gun Split Offset from the Atlanta playbook

We have all been flagged with a delay of game penalty because of a lack of game plan. If we look into this a bit more we can pinpoint the problem. The problem is a result of not having a game plan mixed with not having enough repetition of what we are doing. We are all creatures of habit, and we shouldn't treat *Madden NFL* any differently. We have a base play so that we will always come out in that one play. This helps to shape our identity and prevents us from wasting any time passing through the Play Call screen. We will now have more time to think about what the defense is doing rather than wondering "What play should I call?" During important parts of games the last thing to worry about is what play to choose. Your base play can be from any formation that's both in shotgun and under center. The base play helps to automate our scheme and allows us to stay focused on our opponent. You'll always be ahead of the curve and always know what play to call.

Your base play should contain a delayed blue route and have a flat route

We don't just pick a base play for the sake of having one. We have specific criteria for our base play. Our first order of business is to make sure it has a delayed blue route. Delayed blue routes are great for pass protection because the player first blocks any defensive pressure and then releases from the blocking duties to become a passing option. Next we like to have a passing option to the flat. This is so that we can always put pressure on defenses that play loose coverage and blitz heavily. Typically, the first area of the field the defense gives up when they bring pressure is the flat. Also, a popular style of defense is an all-out coverage defense, which is typically a Cover 4 zone coverage. In either of these situations we will be able to attack the flat with our base play. Another important factor of having a flat route in our base play is that it always gives us the option to beat zone coverage. With the addition of a few hot routes on the same side of the field as the flat route (a streak and a smart-routed slant out) we can flood zone coverage.

Our FB is heading to the flat

The defense is playing a Cover 1 man-to-man defense, which is our key to check the FB in the flat. The MLB is matched up against our FB as he breaks towards the flat. Next we look to the drag over the short middle. If the FB is open get the ball to him right away.

The throw is on time and the FB moves up the sideline

This play has two quick reads with the flat route and the short drag over the middle. Against zone the deep post will often get one-on-one matchups. If the defense sends pressure we have our blue route in the backfield to help in pass protection. Make sure to scan through your playbook to find an effective base play.

Keys to the Base Play

- Delayed blue routes
- Flat routes
- Always knowing what play to choose

Take a minute to think about how important the base play really is. It gives you the ability to have great pass protection, beat overzealous defenses, smash max coverage defenses, and hot route to beat any zone coverage. Having an effective base play sets the entire tone for your offensive attack. Don't limit yourself to having just one base play; in fact, having two or three for specific situations is recommended.

Man Beater (Compressed Formations)

Gun Tight Flex

Your man beater will come from compressed formations. This means that the alignment of the formation will be close to the offensive line. Against man-to-man defenses compressed formations allow for natural picks and rubs to occur as your receivers run their routes. This helps receivers spring free against their defenders. Typically, crossing patterns are the best way to do this. This would be a combination of drags, ins, slant ins, and angled slants.

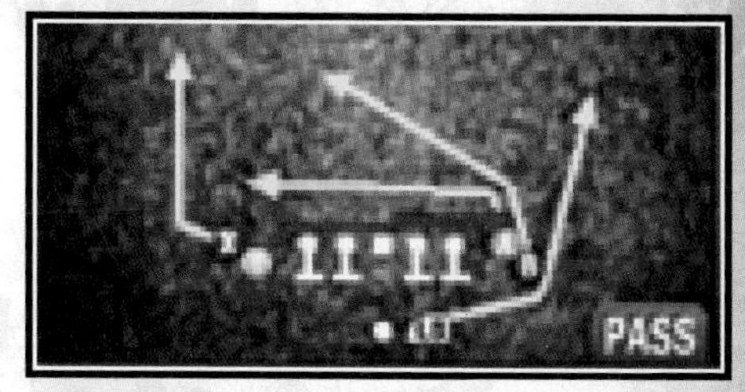

The Falcon Cross from Gun Tight Flex in the Atlantic playbook

Falcon Cross is one of the best plays in *Madden NFL 12,* and it's especially great at beating man-to-man defense. The crossing patterns torch man coverage while the outside wheel routes are great when the defense blitzes. The deep post is another great route against aggressive defenses.

The defense is playing 2 Man Under

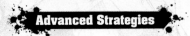

Here we can see the crossing patterns over the middle of the field beginning to open up. The underneath drag route receiver has inside position, so we could get him the ball now for the short gain. However, if we wait a bit longer for the other crossing route we should pick up more yards.

Our WR is matched up against the slower LB

The defense didn't send pressure so we waited in the pocket for our routes to develop. Look through your playbook for compressed formations and plays that have crossing patterns so that facing man-to-man coverage will be a walk in the park.

Keys to the Man Beater

- Compressed formations
- Crossing patterns
- Speedy receivers
- Route running

Man-to-man is typically the most-used style of defense in the game. For some it causes major problems because it always appears that your receivers are covered. Knowing that compressed sets and crossing patterns will open up your receivers should give you the confidence needed to attack any man-to-man defense you face. When in doubt look to hot route two of your receivers on drags to create your own crossing patterns!

Zone Beater (Bunch and Trips Formations)

Singleback Bunch

Beating zone defensive coverage is all about spacing on the field. Our goal when facing zone is to run specific route combinations to overload the zone coverage. Zone defenders play areas of the field rather than actual offensive players; this means that we can flood zones with a route combination of a streak, a corner, and a flat route. To do this effectively we need to make sure that we use a trips or bunched formation. Trips formations have three receivers split to one side of the field and typically have equal spacing. Bunched formations also have three receivers split to one side, but those receivers are stacked closely together. With both you will be able to attack zone coverage effectively.

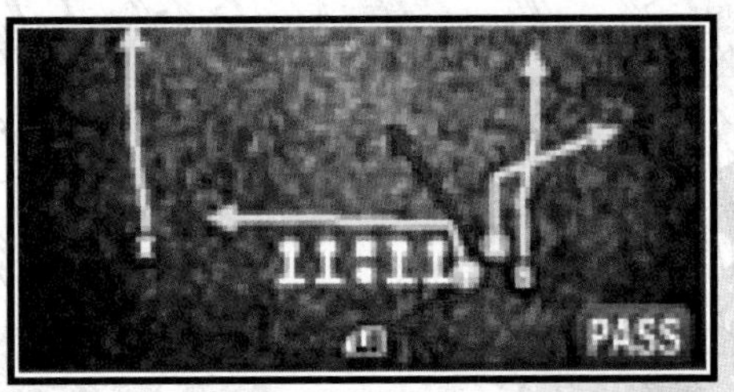

Singleback Bunch—Falcon Angle

Falcon Angle from Singleback Bunch is one of the best under-center plays in the game. This bunch formation calls for an isolated vertical route to the left of the field while the bunch side has a nice route combination with corner and vertical routes by the wide receivers. The HB out of the backfield is on an angle route that acts as a flat route with a quick pass and then cuts back over the middle of the field.

Notice that the flat defender has lost his depth on the sideline because of our HB's route

The defense is playing a Cover 3 zone and we are trying to sneak our corner route between the deep coverage and the underneath coverage. Our vertical route will pull coverage deep and our flat route will keep the flat defender from dropping back and defending our corner route.

Our receiver is wide open for the easy catch

Our route combination worked perfectly and our receiver was open in the corner. The corner receiver won't always be open—it all depends on the type of zone the defense is playing. Against Cover 2 look for the vertical route, against Cover 3 look for the corner, and against Cover 4 look to the flat.

Keys to the Zone Beater

- Trips formations
- Bunched formations
- Route combinations of vertical, corner, and flat routes

Most players will run a Cover 3 zone coverage, so be ready for it. Cover 3 is extremely weak against the corner route when we use the methods we've described. Zone coverage can be just as frustrating as man-to-man coverage for some. Be ready for it, audible to your trips or bunch formation, and dissect the defense!

Five Sets for Success Wrap-Up (Offense)

Utilizing the "Five Sets for Success" on offense allows you to be prepared for everything your opponent can throw at you. If your opponent gives you the run you will audible to your power run set. If the defense doesn't respect your inside running game you will audible to your run middle and play smashmouth football until they start respecting your rushing attack. Once in the red zone you will be ready to attack the defense with numerous quick passes for the easy score. If the defense looks to send pressure we will once again call upon our quick passes to force them out of the aggressive defense. By having a base play we will always be one step ahead of our opponent and be prepared for the most exotic defenses. If the defense plays man-to-man we will force them to play zone by using our man beaters, and once they are in zone we will force them out of zone with our zone beaters.

Our goal is to force our opponent to put the controller down by using the best strategy on the planet, and it doesn't get much better than the "Five Sets for Success!" Next we will break down the formations and play styles we use on the defensive side of the ball for the defensive "Five Sets for Success."

FIVE SETS FOR SUCCESS: DEFENSE

Run Defense (Inverted Cover 2)

46 Normal

Before we even step onto the virtual gridiron we need to make sure that we have a defense that can consistently stop the run. As much as the run game is about individual efforts by star athletes in the backfield, it is more about numbers. At every snap of the ball in running situations we want to try and outnumber the offense in the run game. Counting the five offensive linemen, the FB, and the TE, the offense has seven blockers in the middle of the field. The remaining players on the field for the offense are the two WRs, the QB, and the HB. Typically, the WRs will not be in position to help in the run game, and the QB hands the ball off to the HB, so neither the QB nor the HB will be blocking on any run plays. By doing the simple math here we can see that on average the offense will have seven players blocking and a maximum of nine. Our goal as a defense is to outnumber the offensive blockers. If we do this we put our defense in the best position to beat the offense on every single run.

We do this by playing an *inverted Cover 2*. An inverted Cover 2 is a zone defense where the outside cornerbacks split the deep halves of the field. Typically, safeties split the deep part of the field, which takes them out of position to play the run. By playing an inverted Cover 2 we allow our safeties to play in the box and help in run support. If we count the defenders in a normal Cover 2 we will have four defensive linemen and three linebackers playing in the box for run support. The outside cornerbacks will play the sideline and the safeties will drop deep. This gives our defense seven defenders in position to stop the run. An inverted Cover 2 has four defensive linemen, three linebackers, and two safeties who can all play in the box. This gives us nine defenders to play the run. Defensively we are still in the same coverage but we now are in better position to stop the run.

We know going in that most runs in the game will have seven blockers and at most nine. By playing the inverted Cover 2 we are setting our defense up to have one or more free defenders to take down the ball carrier. There are not many inverted Cover 2 defenses in the game, so we create our own by calling a Cover 3 zone. We then shade the safeties in and hot route the safety who is playing the deep middle of the field to a yellow zone. We user-control this player as well.

46 Normal—Cover 3

Here you can see that we shaded our secondary in, which has now created the inverted Cover 2. Count the defenders in the box—there are nine.

Nowhere to go up the middle!

The offense looked to run up the middle but there are no running lanes. The HB gains only 1 yard on this run.

The offense looks to go outside

Here the offense is trying their luck to the outside. We shoot the gap with our user-defender and are in great position to take the HB down for a big loss. Notice the free linebacker scraping towards the edge. He is our outside containment if we miss the tackle in the backfield.

The final attempt at running the ball is running the counter left

The offense tries running a counter left, but we once again have the numbers to take down the ball carrier. Our DT shot through untouched to take down the ball carrier.

Keys to Run Defense

- Numbers
- Balance
- Inverted Cover 2

Not only does the inverted Cover 2 do a great job of stopping the run, it is also a solid pass defense. At the snap of the ball, if the offense is actually passing look to drop deep with your user-controlled player. Also, note the balance on the field when you play the inverted Cover 2. We have the same coverage throughout the field, which helps to give this run defense an extremely well-balanced point of attack.

Red Zone Defense

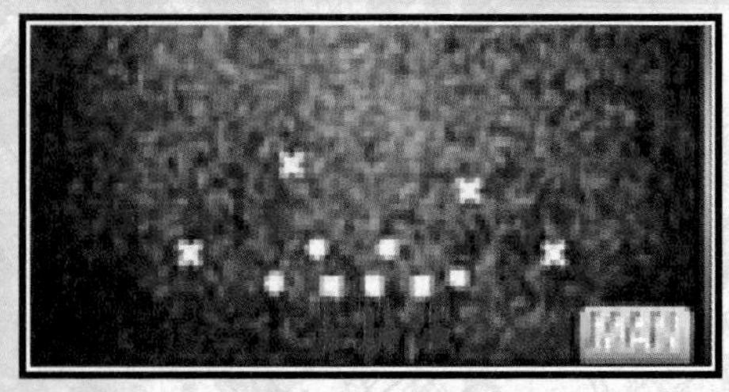

3-4 Under—Double Man

The red zone is the area of the field between your opponent's 20-yard line and in towards the end zone. In *Madden NFL* we refer to the red zone as the area of the field between your opponent's 10-yard line and in towards the end zone. Playing great red zone defense is all about shutting down your opponent's number one threat. We believe that in *Madden NFL 12* the number one option in the red zone will be the quick fade lob pass. Our main objective in the red zone is to stop this play. We call upon the 3-4 Under—Double Man because the outside WRs are double-covered with two man-to-man defenders. This helps to completely shut down the quick fade lob pass. We can also contain the run and stop quick passes. If you can't stop your opponent from scoring it doesn't matter how good your defense is outside the red zone.

The outside WRs are double-covered

The offense's outside threats have two defenders on them. They will be forced to go to their other options. We have a user-controlled defender with which we look to spy our opponent's other quick passes.

The outside WR is double-teamed!

As the play develops we can see we have all options covered. Our wide pass rush is keeping the QB in the pocket.

The QB forces the pass into double coverage

The QB knew that his number one option was double-covered but decided to force the ball in anyway. Our defense makes a play on the ball and swats it down for the incomplete pass.

Keys to Red Zone Defense

- Shutting down the offense's number one option

Stopping quick passes There are plenty of plays in the game that call for double coverage on outside WRs. Find the play that works best for you and stick with it. Remember that your goal in the red zone is to take away your opponents' *first* option. Anything after that will cause your opponents to feel uncomfortable with their reads. Once they are uncomfortable that is when mistakes happen.

Base Play

Cover 4 is our base defense

A base play on defense has the same principles as on offense. It helps to automate our play calling so that we are never stuck in deciding what play to choose. We will always know what play to call and we recommend using a Cover 4 zone coverage. Using a Cover 4 as your base play allows you to use your quick audibles to get to every basic defensive coverage in the game. No matter the situation you will be armed and ready to adjust to what your opponent is doing. The importance of the base play on defense is all about being able to make quick adjustments on the fly and to respond to what you are seeing.

The base play is also very effective early on in games. During the first drive you will typically not have a feel for what your opponent is doing. It is best to sit back and see how your opponent is going to attack you. With the base play we can call generic defenses according to the situation and see what type of player our opponent is. Every defensive play in the game has quick audibles from the same formation assigned to it: The quick audible up is a 2 Man Under, quick audible right is a Cover 3 zone, quick audible left is a Cover 2 zone, and the quick audible down is a blitz. Using the base play on the opening drive will make our opponents earn the first drive as we sit back and analyze their style of play.

The defense is in a Cover 4 and is giving up the flat

We come out in the Cover 4 to get a feel for what our opponent is doing. The flat is open and we are OK with giving that up for now.

The pass is completed to the TE in the flat

The defense caught us in the flat for the easy completion. We now have to play the chess game that is *Madden NFL 12*.

We quick-audible to a Cover 3 zone to take away the flat

Many times offenses will run a no-huddle offense to try to exploit a particular defense. However, with a quick audible to our Cover 3 we are in position to make a play in the flat.

The offense runs the same play and is looking to the TE in the flat

Our defender is in position in the flat if the offense throws to the TE. The quick audible to the Cover 3 looks like it was the right call.

Our defender swats the ball down!

Being able to call every basic defensive coverage allows our defense the flexibility to defend against whatever the offense throws at us.

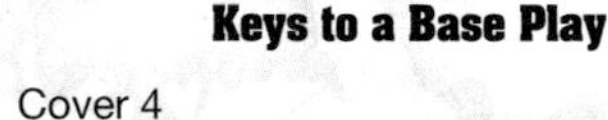

Keys to a Base Play

- Cover 4
- Great for opening drives
- Bend-but-don't-break defense
- Ability to call all basic defensive coverages

A base play should almost always be a Cover 4 variation. *Madden NFL 12* has seen the addition of the Cover 6 to its defensive arsenal and we can look to utilize the Cover 6 as our base play as well. Remember that the goal of the base play is to help put your defensive game in rhythm and to get a feel for what your opponent is doing.

Man/Zone Blitz

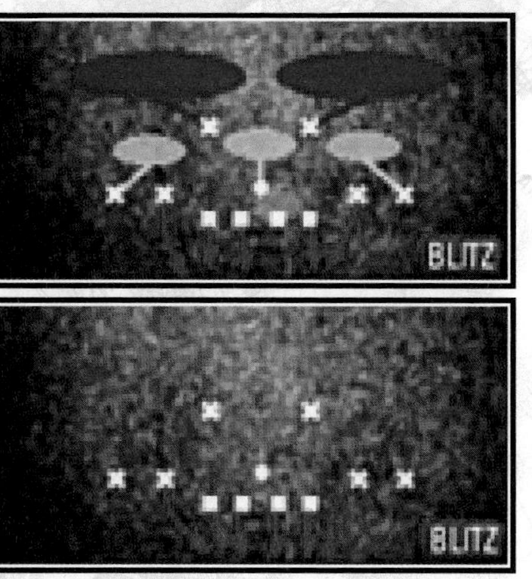

Strike 2 Deep and DB Blitz from the Dime formation

At some point during every game you will need to reach into your back pocket and dial up pressure. Not only do you need pressure but you need to have the same pressure from both man-to-man and zone coverage. The purpose of this is to confuse your opponent. They might call out where the pressure is coming from, but more times than not they won't know the type of coverage. Once we get the opposition thinking one thing, that is when we hit them with another. The plays we showcase here are from the Dime formation. Both plays call for pressure to come off the outside edge. You will find both these plays in most playbooks in *Madden NFL 12*.

Strike 2 Deep

We are set up in the Strike 2 Deep zone coverage on this play. We are user-controlling the MLB and are watching for any quick pass to the HB as well as any crossing patterns over the middle of the field.

The QB held onto the ball and paid the price

The pressure from the outside got to the QB before his routes over the middle of the field opened up. Our opponent couldn't handle the pressure on this play. We have the QB right where we want him; the next play we will bring the same pressure but change up to our man version. This should be an easy three and out!

DB Blitz

This time around our defense has called DB Blitz from the Dime formation. Notice how the play alignment looks exactly the same as if we were in Strike 2 Deep. This makes it extremely difficult for the offense to string together plays.

The QB looks to fit the pass over the deep middle

The offense calls the same play but makes a few minor adjustments to attack what they think is zone coverage. We have seen this happen more times than we can remember. The offense thinks we will keep our defense the same but we are smarter than that! We switch it up to our man-to-man version!

Our safety is in position for the swat!

Our deep safety is matched up on the TE in man-to-man coverage. The QB expected the TE to be open, but instead he is blanketed by our safety.

Keys to the Man/Zone Blitz

- Different coverage; same pressure
- Deception
- Turnovers and sacks

The man/zone blitz is one of the most important aspects of the defensive "Five Sets for Success." Getting crucial stops in games comes down to being able to bring effective pressure. There is no better way to blitz in the game than using a combination of coverages. Get creative with your man/zone blitzes and dive into your playbook to find the best ones for your defensive scheme.

X-Factor

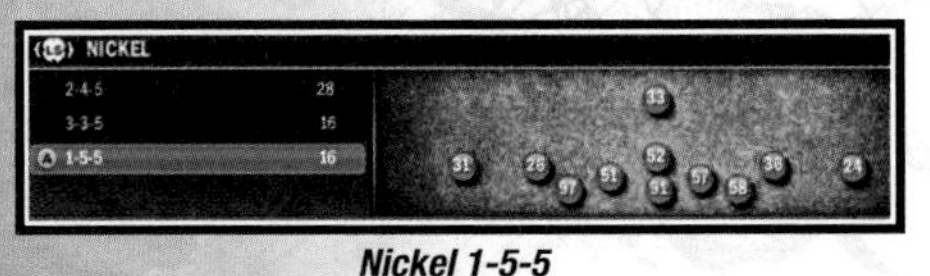

Nickel 1-5-5

The X-Factor defense is what we call upon in specific late-game situations. This is your third down and 10 defense. It is a play that dials up pressure but also has the flexibility to mix in max coverage defenses. Our X-Factor defense of choice is the Nickel 1-5-5. The 1-5-5 is unique because of its five linebackers on the field. Using the global LB command we can instantly blitz all five LBs or drop all five back into coverage. This means we can create blitzes extremely quickly as well as play complete coverage. We like to save our X-Factor play for those late-game situations where our opponent hasn't yet seen our ace in the hole.

We globally blitz all our LBs

The pressure is coming fast and the QB has to make a quick decision. Be ready for the quick throw and try to make a user play on the ball!

The pass was thrown to the short flat, where our defender drives the receiver out of bounds

The QB was forced to get rid of the ball quickly to the flat. Our defender was in position to push the receiver out of bounds for the short gain.

We globally drop back all our LBs

This time around we decide to globally drop back all our LBs to play yellow zones. Then we hot route our OLBs to purple zones. We hope to catch the offense off guard with this max coverage defense.

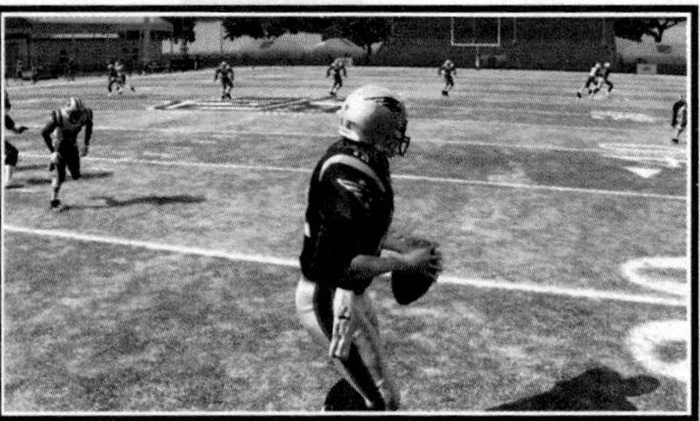

The QB sees only defenders!

The field is covered with defenders and the offense has nowhere to go with the ball.

Our one-man rush finally closes in

We only sent one defender to pass rush the QB, but he was able to work his way to apply pressure. The QB is forced to throw the ball into coverage.

Keys to the X-Factor

- Save it for crucial situations
- Look for all-out pressure or max coverage

Five Sets for Success Wrap-Up (Defense)

Defense is all about adjusting to what the offense is doing. Early in games you will use your base play to get a feel for the game tempo. Make your opponent earn that first drive as you tinker with your coverages until you feel confident about what type of offensive player you are facing. If your opponents look to run the ball you will call upon your run defense to slow them down. When looking to bring pressure make sure to use your man/zone blitz to confuse your opponents. If your opponents get inside the red zone don't panic. Take away their number one option and force them elsewhere. In late-game situations save your X-Factor defense to catch your opponents off guard.

ADVANCED PASSING CONCEPTS

A passing concept is a plan of attack against defenses. Offensive coordinators look to attack defenses either horizontally or vertically. By putting together specific route combinations and specific formations offenses can effectively take advantage of defenses by using passing concepts. In this section of the guide we will showcase many different passing concepts that you will find in *Madden NFL 12*.

Horizontal Concepts

Spacing is an example of a horizontal passing concept

Horizontal passing concepts spread defenses from sideline to sideline. Horizontal passing is used to attack laid-back defenses. If you run into an opponent who plays a lot of Cover 4 you will want to call upon a horizontal passing concept, such as Spacing. The approach of the concept is to overload the underneath coverage with more offensive players than defensive players. Avoid using this concept when facing Cover 2 zone but look to use it against Cover 3 and Cover 4 zones. Horizontal concepts work best when your opponent expects a vertical attack.

Vertical Concepts

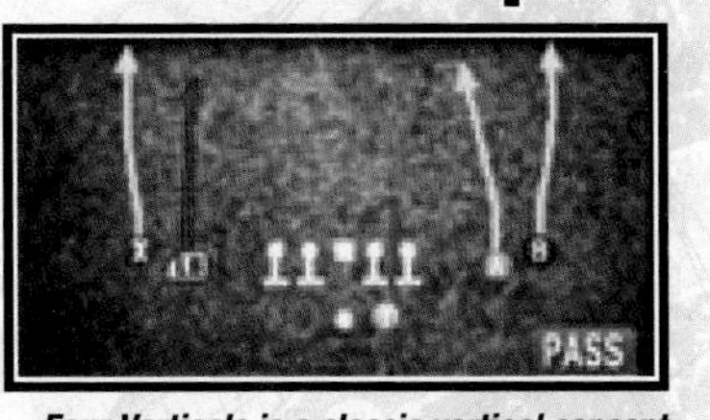

Four Verticals is a classic vertical concept

Vertical passing concepts are used to spread defenses from end zone to end zone. Aggressive defenses can be burned by a vertical passing concept. When facing a aggressive zone blitzer look to call upon a vertical concept, such as Four Verticals. If your opponent expects you to attack underneath and plays a Cover 2 or Cover 3 zone the vertical concept will work perfectly. Defenses need to play a Cover 4 or man-to-man coverage to defend this concept. Vertical concepts work best when your opponent expects a horizontal attack.

Individual Passing Concepts

Bench

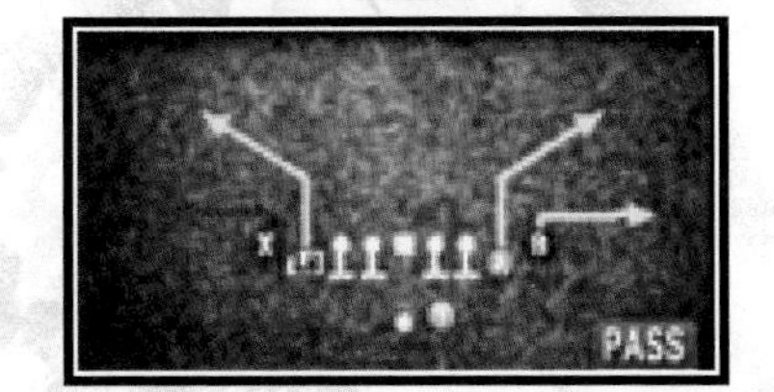

The Bench concept is a great base play. It can be used to attack all types of coverages in *Madden NFL 12*. Against man-to-man look for the quick out routes. Against Cover 2 and Cover 3 zone look to the deep corner routes. When facing Cover 4 you will want to hit the out routes. The Bench concept is a high-low read. Look underneath to the outs and then to the corner route up top.

Curl Flat

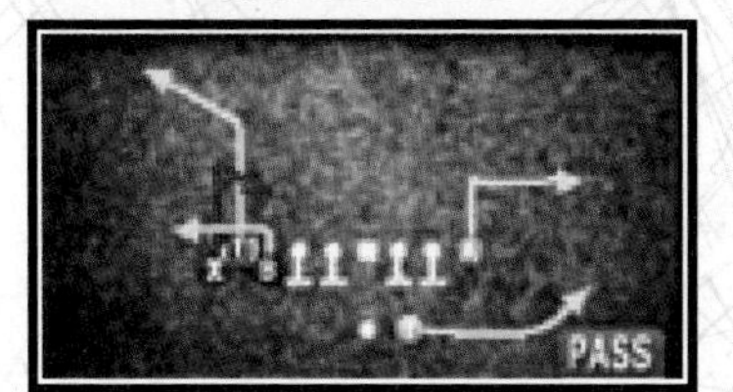

The Curl Flat passing concept is one of the most effective and most used concepts in the game. The read is extremely easy and effective. This concept will work against both man-to-man and zone coverage. First look to the flat receiver, and if he is open deliver him the ball. If the flat is covered the curl should be open against zone coverage. Against man look to the curl route.

Curl Flat Corner

Using a Curl Flat Corner concept is great when attacking zone coverages. The idea behind this play is to have three receivers run different routes at different depths to overload the zone coverage. This play is one of our favorites when facing Cover 3 zone. The play-side defensive back will be forced deep with the corner route while the underneath flat defender will be forced to defend either the flat receiver or the curled receiver. Watch the defender and deliver the ball to the uncovered receiver.

Curls Attack

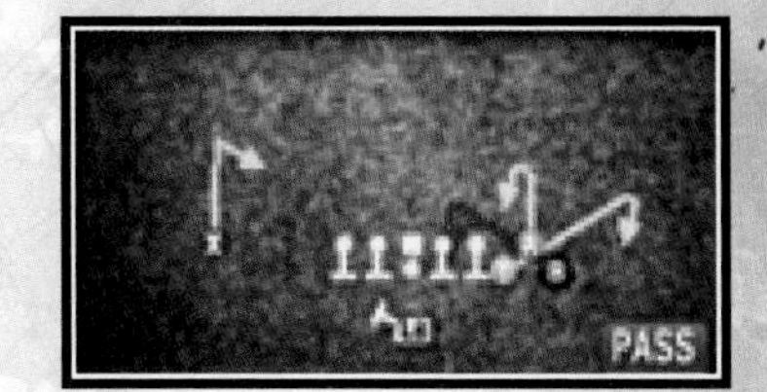

Curls Attack is a horizontal passing concept that looks to flood underneath zone defenses. All our receivers are running short curls while our HB out of the backfield is on a flat route. Look for the isolated receiver towards the far left of the field as well as the far right receiver running his curl over the short middle. These two routes open up the most consistently when using this play.

Double Slant

This concept is a nice option when attacking man-to-man coverage as well as zone blitzing. Against man-to-man coverage read the inside slant receiver as he breaks towards the middle of the field look to see if he has inside position on the defender. If he is covered move to the outside slant and look for the same read and deliver the ball. Against the zone blitz you will need to read the zone defender in the area. Look to see where his positioning is. If he plays in front of the slot slant look for the back-side slant. If he plays between the two slants look to hit the slot slant.

Drive

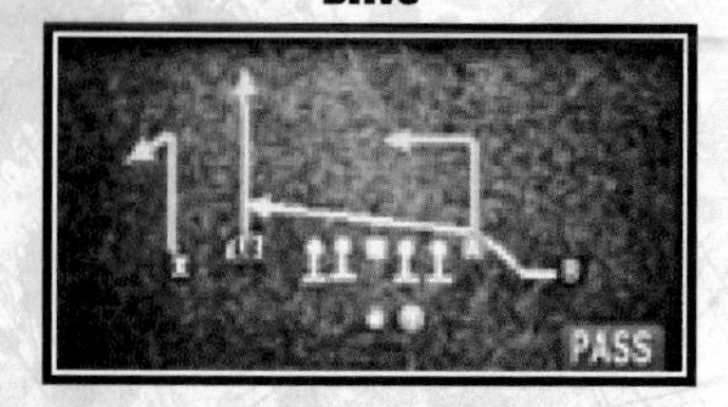

The Drive concept is designed to attack zone coverage and key on zone defenders in the middle of the field. The goal with the drive is to create a high-low read against the zone and force the defender to choose a receiver to cover. We have an inside in route that is our high read and an outside drag route that is our low read.

Flood

The Flood passing concept is similar to the Curl Flat Corner. It is great for attacking zone coverage and it works by forcing an isolated zone defender to choose a specific offensive player, leaving the other open. The streak route will pull coverage deep, allowing the deep in and flat routes to work a high-low option against the zone defender in the flat. The majority of the time the defender will cover the flat and leave the deep in open.

Follow

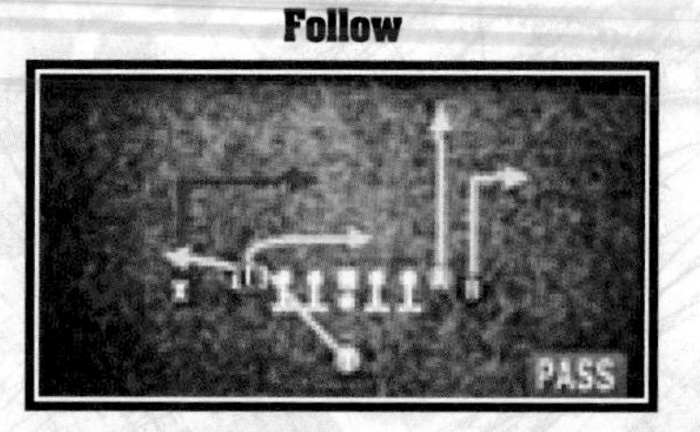

Similar to the Drive passing concept is the Follow concept. This is another high-low read for the quarterback. The inside receiver runs a short drag over the middle of the field while the outside receiver runs a deep in. If the zone defender covers the high read look to your low option and vice versa. Against man-to-man look for the flat route by the HB or the comeback route on the sideline.

Hitch Seam

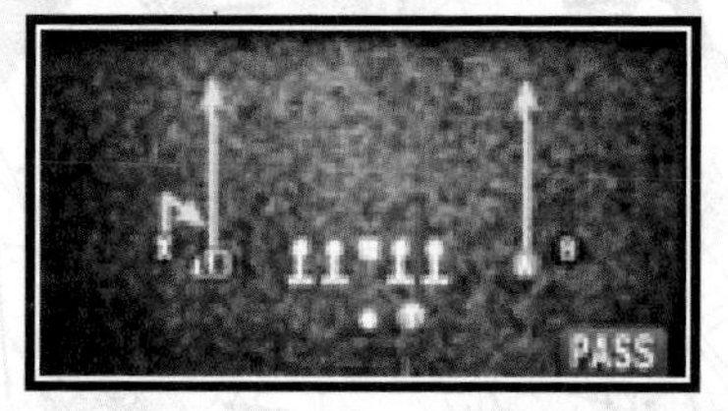

The Hitch Seam concept is a go-to option when facing Cover 2 or Cover 4 zone. The play is designed to attack both by having your outside receivers run short curl routes and the seam receivers run streaks. Against Cover 4 zone look to the short curls on the outside, and against Cover 2 zone look for the one-on-one matchups in the seam. The HB on the delay route will be your last option and should be used against Cover 3 zone.

Inside Cross

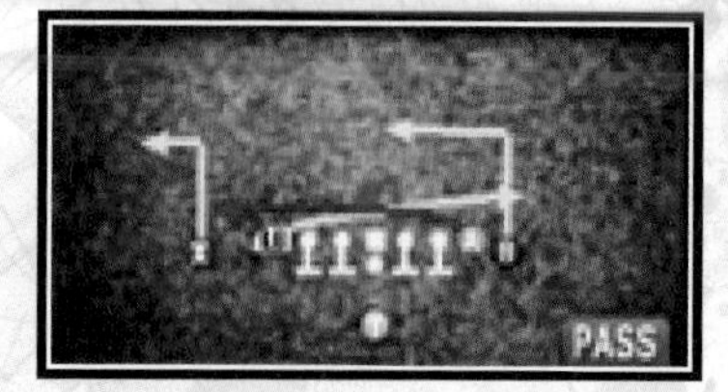

The Inside Cross is an excellent passing concept when facing man-to-man coverage. It calls for double crossing patterns over the middle of the field. The offensive players will cross through each other, which should rub free one of our receivers. Hot route this passing concept with some of your favorite zone beaters. There are many different combinations of the Inside Cross that have different receivers crossing patterns with each other. Scan your book and make sure you implement this concept into your offensive game plan.

Levels

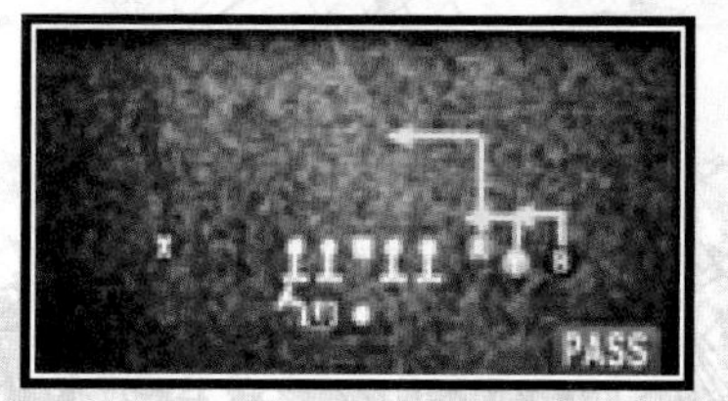

Levels is another nice passing concept that works extremely well against zone coverage. It works by attacking individual zone defenders with multiple offensive targets. Levels has identical patterns running at different depths. The QB makes the read depending on where the zone defender is positioned. If he is playing the high receiver look to dump the ball off to the underneath receiver. If the defender chooses the underneath receiver deliver the ball to the high receiver. Typically, zone defenses in *Madden NFL 12* will have defenders play underneath routes, so be prepared for this.

Mesh

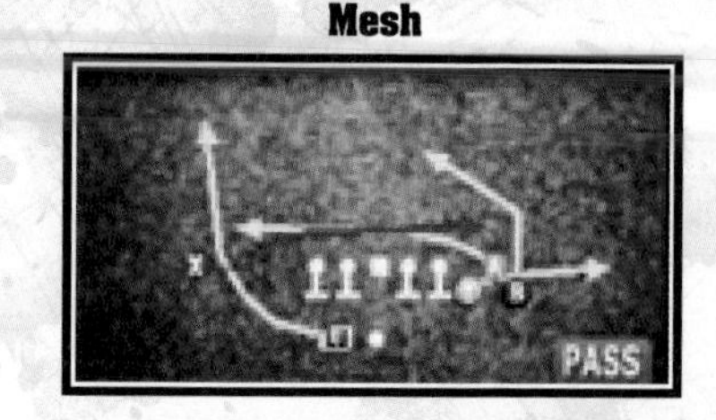

Mesh is one of the most effective passing concepts in the game. It is used to beat both man-to-man and zone coverage. The crossing patterns over the middle of the field will get great separation against man-to-man, while the wheel route by the HB will often be open against zone. Against the zone blitz the flat route will typically run free. The post over the middle will also put pressure on defenses that are overly aggressive.

Shallow Cross

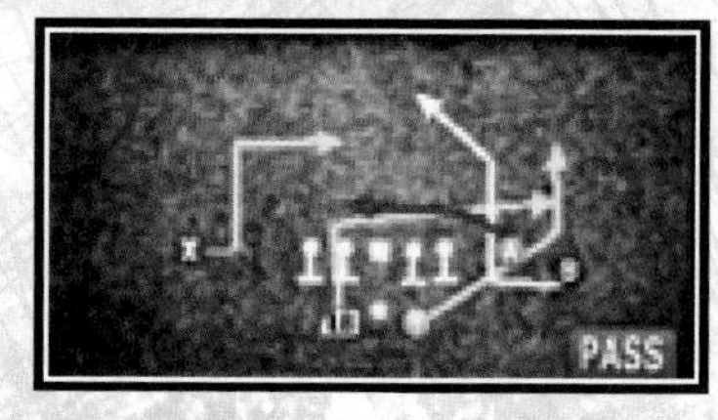

The Shallow Cross concept works off a high-low read where one receiver runs a shallow drag route and a receiver on the opposite side runs an in route. We are keying on the zone defender once again and forcing him to choose someone to defend. As the QB we want to find the open receiver and deliver the ball to him in open space. Against man-to-man coverage look for the HB out of the backfield, who is moving towards the flat.

Slant Flats

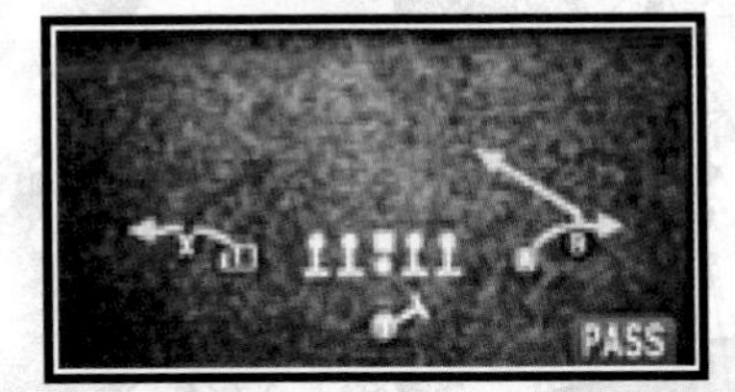

The Slant Flats concept is very similar to the Curl Flats concept. Your first read should be to the flat receivers. If they are open deliver the ball to them right away. If they are covered, whether it be man-to-man or zone coverage, the inside slants should open up as they break over the middle. Look to deliver the ball before they cross the face of the QB. This is one of the most fun ways to read a defense. It can be extremely easy making this read, but it is very effective in *Madden NFL 12*.

Smash

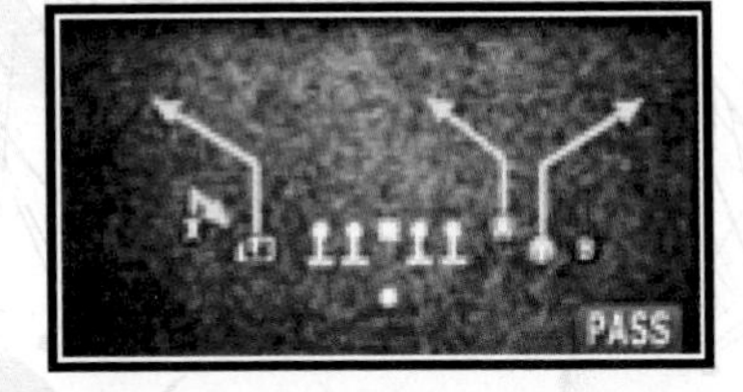

The Smash concept is extremely effective when facing Cover 2 and Cover 4 zone coverage. You want to key in on the short curl receiver; if a defender drops back to defend him the corner should open up top. This read is another high-low passing concept. If the high read is covered then the low read should be open. Cover 4 will have a defender in a buzz zone that can play the underneath curl. Typically the buzz zone will allow for a catch to be made, but yards after the catch are hard to come by. The Smash concept is one of our favorite in the game for attacking zone coverage.

Spot

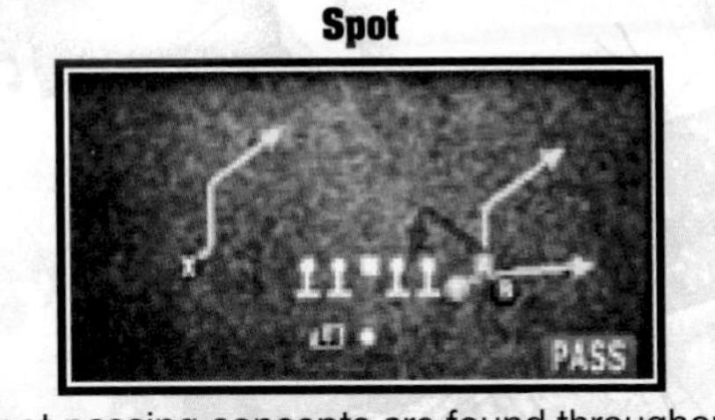

Spot passing concepts are found throughout *Madden NFL 12* in many trips and bunch formations. They can attack man-to-man coverage as well as zone. Your first read is to the flat; if that receiver is covered check down to your corner route. Against zone this will be a high-low read depending on where the defender is positioned. If the low read is covered look to the high read and vice versa. The spot route receiver will be a bit delayed as he waits for the other receivers in the bunch to clear out. Against man-to-man throw the ball just as he begins making his break towards the middle of the field. Against zone wait for him to turn back towards the QB and deliver a high lead pass.

Stick

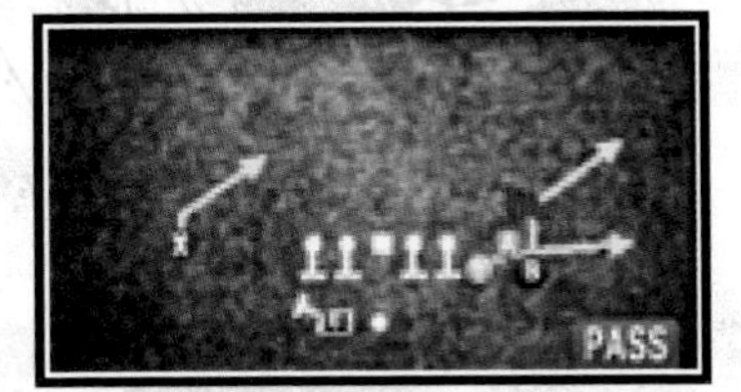

The Stick passing concept has been the most used and most effective passing concept over the past few seasons in the *Madden* community. It has a quick flat read at the snap of the ball that can be used to beat man-to-man or zone coverage. If the flat is covered check down to the short curl, which should open up against zone coverage. The deep corner route creates a high-low concept with the flat route. If all else fails look to the back-side slant breaking over the middle of the field.

Texas

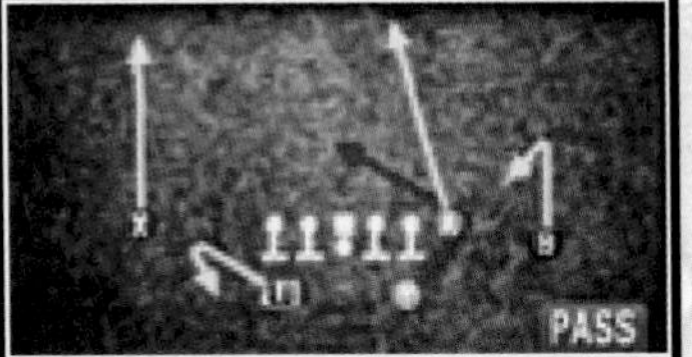

The Texas passing concept is the single best way to get the ball out to your HB against zone coverage. Texas relies on the TE's ability to pull zone coverage deep to allow the HB's angle route to run clear into space. Zone defenses will be forced to guard the TE as he breaks over the deep middle of the field, and this opens up the short middle of the field for the HB as he breaks over the middle. Against zone coverage this is one of the best passing concepts in *Madden NFL 12*.

Wheel Out

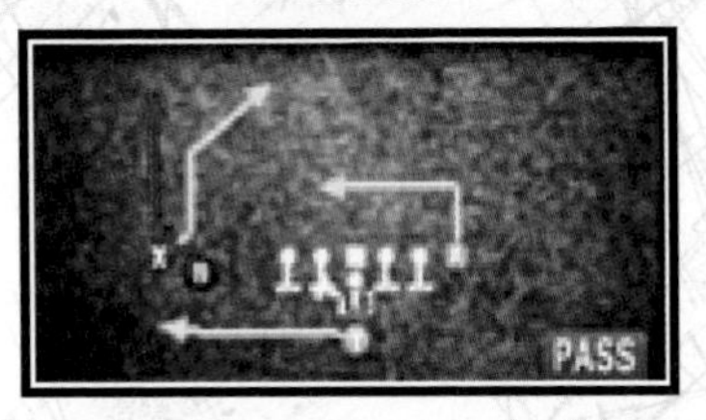

The Wheel Out works extremely well against all defensive coverages in the game. Against any type of blitz look to the slot receiver as he breaks to the sideline. The zone blitz should leave this area uncovered, and against man-to-man you will rely on your receiver to break one tackle and then be off to the races. Against a Cover 2 zone look to the outside receiver running the post. Against Cover 3 zone look to the wheel route as the receiver breaks up the sideline; the post should clear out enough room for the wheel route to open up down the sideline. Against Cover 4 hit the wheel route in the flat. The Wheel Out concept makes for a great base play.

In this section we have covered the most popular passing concepts in *Madden NFL 12*. Look to mix and match them. Many plays in the game will overcommit to attacking one type of defense. Learn to create plays (by using hot routes) that will attack both man-to-man and zone. See the "Advanced Hot Routing" section later in this chapter to see how we like using hot routes to beat defenses all over the field!

READING AND UNDERSTANDING DEFENSIVE COVERAGES

One of the first factors in running a successful offense in *Madden NFL 12* is learning how to read and understand the strengths and weaknesses of defensive coverages. In this section of the guide we break down every coverage you will see, how to read those coverages, and also their strengths and weaknesses.

The first place to read the defense's coverage starts with the safeties. In most scenarios reading what the safeties do will tell you what the overall defense is doing. There are three basic types of safety coverage that you will come across as you read the deep coverage. Those coverages are zero safeties, one safety, and two safeties. Each coverage type will give you a base understanding of what the defense is in.

Reading Defensive Coverages

Reading Zero Safeties

If you read zero safeties dropping into coverage you can be almost positive that the defense is blitzing. From this read we also know that the defense is in man-to-man as there are no safeties dropping deep into coverage. There are a few plays in *Madden NFL 12* that have the safeties doubled up on receivers, so watch out for this scenario. If you see double coverage on the outside or slot this is also Cover 0, only there will be no blitz.

What to Expect Against Zero Safeties Deep

- A blitz (expect six or more pass rushers)
- Man-to-man defense
- A small chance of double coverage on your outside or slot WRs

NOTE

A few zone defenses in the game have CBs dropping deep into coverage while the deep safeties either blitz or play the middle of the field. This is inverted coverage and is the only type of zone coverage that will have zero safeties deep.

Reading One Safety

If you see only one safety dropping into deep coverage you can assume that the blitz is coming, just as you did with zero safeties. The defense can be either man-to-man or a Cover 3 zone, so be ready for both. If the defense is in man-to-man watch out for a zone defender over the middle of the field. If the defense isn't blitzing, often they will drop a defender over the short middle of the field.

What to Expect Against One Safety Deep

- Man-to-man blitz (expect five or more pass rushers in this situation)
- Man-to-man with one defender in a zone, spy, or double coverage
- Cover 3 zone
- Cover 3 zone blitz

Reading Two Safeties

When reading two safeties playing deep it is safe to assume the defense is not sending pressure. You should expect man-to-man, Cover 2 zone, or Cover 4 zone. Be ready to attack the coverage defense; the field will be blanketed with coverage.

What to Expect Against Two Safeties Deep

- 2 Man Under with no blitz
- Cover 4 zone with no blitz

Understanding Defensive Coverages

Cover 0

Once you read zero safeties dropping deep we know that the defense is in a Cover 0. Expect the blitz and be prepared to attack the defense accordingly. The pressure will be quick and your reads will need to be quicker. Typically the defense will send six defenders after the QB.

Strengths

- Sends six pass rushers
- Forces offenses to block extra defenders
- Applies quick pressure
- Strong against play action
- Strong against scrambling quarterbacks
- Strong against vertical passing schemes

Weaknesses

- No deep coverage
- Results in big plays for the offense if pressure is picked up
- Needs excellent man coverage defenders
- Needs elite defensive speed to be run consistently
- Weak against crossing patterns
- Weak against quick passes

Examples of Cover 0 Defenses

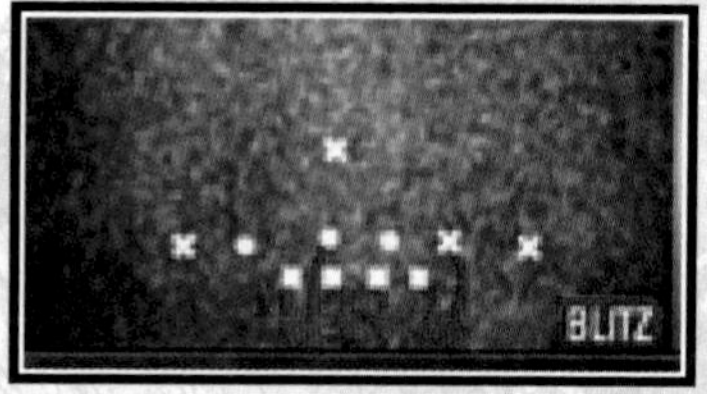

46 Normal—SS Blitz

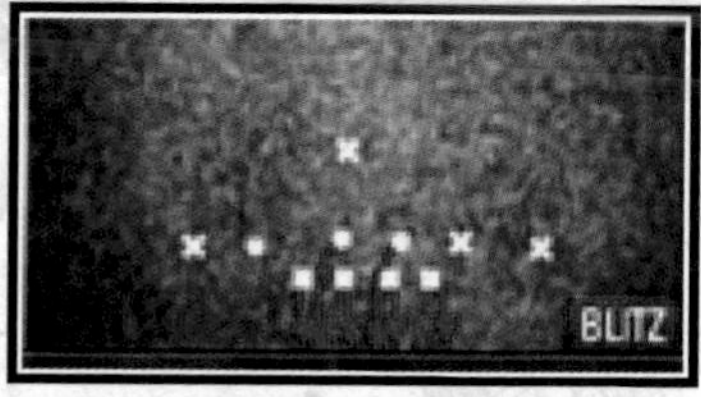

46 Normal—Inside Blitz

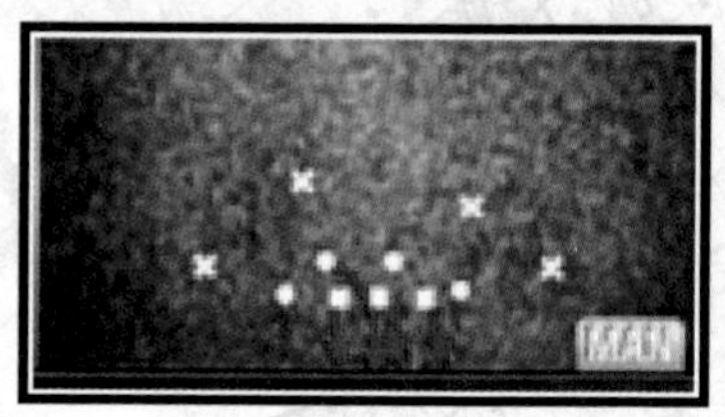

3-4 Under—Double Man

Cover 1

The defense will have one safety dropping to defend deep. Facing a Cover 1 defense is very similar to facing Cover 0. The defense often is blitzing but will only be sending five pass rushers after the QB instead of six. There are other instances where Cover 1 can be called and the defense will drop a defender into a short zone, spy, or even double coverage rather than blitz him.

Strengths

- Sends five pass rushers
- Has one deep defender
- Strong against scrambling QBs
- Strong against play action
- Strong against vertical passing schemes
- Can disguise which safety is dropping into coverage

Weaknesses

- Weaker pass rush than Cover 0
- Weak against crossing patterns
- Weak against curls
- Weak against quick passes

Examples of Cover 1 Defenses

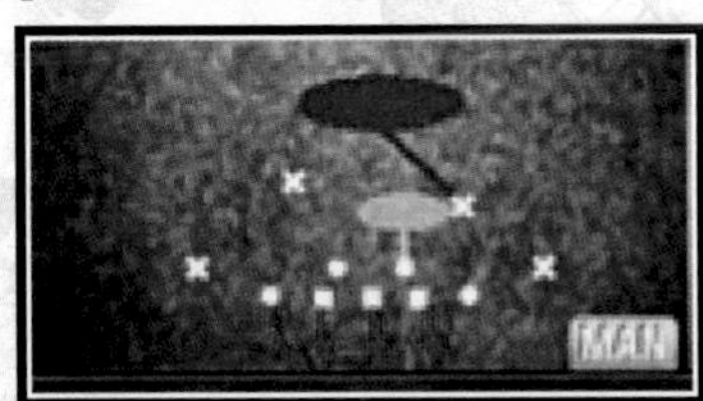

3-4 Under—Cover 1

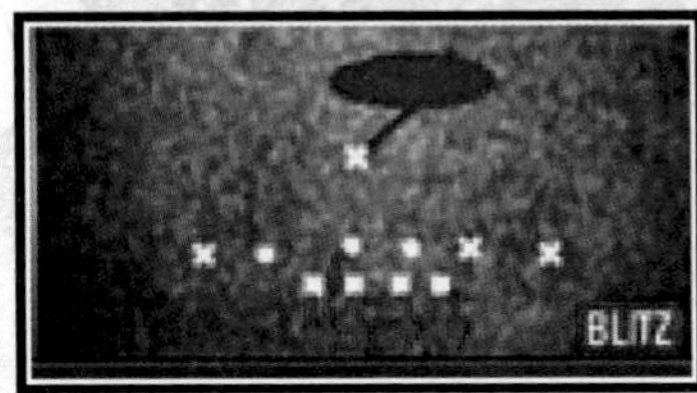

46 Normal—Cover 1

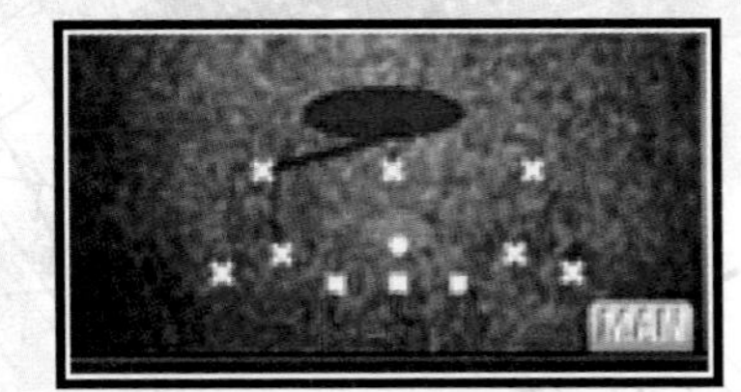

Quarter Combo—Double Z LB Spy

Cover 2

Unlike Cover 1 and Cover 0, Cover 2 can be either man-to-man or zone coverage. In both instances the deep safeties will split the deep half of the field. Man-to-man will have the underneath defenders play individual receivers, while zone will have them play areas of the field. Cover 2 Man Under is one of the most popular defenses in the game, so expect to see a lot of it in *Madden NFL 12*. Cover 2 zone is a great defense for short situations but needs a solid four-man pass rush to be truly effective.

Strengths (Cover 2 Man Under)

- Strong against vertical passing schemes
- Can be disguised to look like a blitz or zone coverage
- Strong against flooding

Weaknesses (Cover 2 Man Under)

- Weak against play action
- Relies on the defensive line pass rush for pressure
- Weak against crossing patterns
- Weak against curls
- Weak against quick passes

Strengths (Cover 2 Zone)

- Strong against crossing patterns
- Strong against curls
- Strong against quick passes
- Strong against flats
- Strong against horizontal passing schemes
- Strong run defense

Weaknesses (Cover 2 Zone)

- Weak against vertical passing concepts
- Weak against trips/bunch formation flooding
- Relies on the defensive line pass rush for pressure

Examples of Cover 2 Defenses

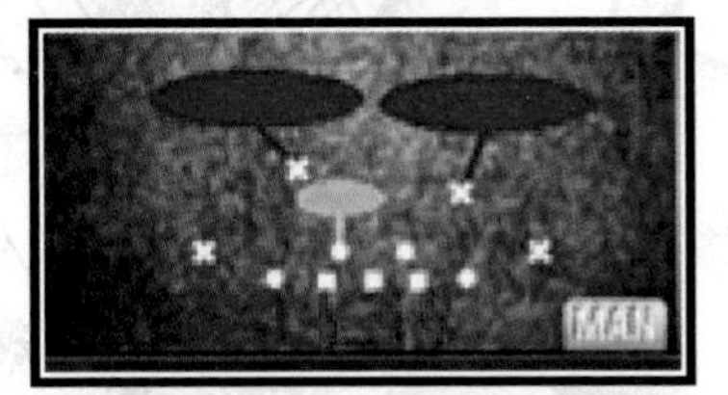

3-4 Under—2 Man Under

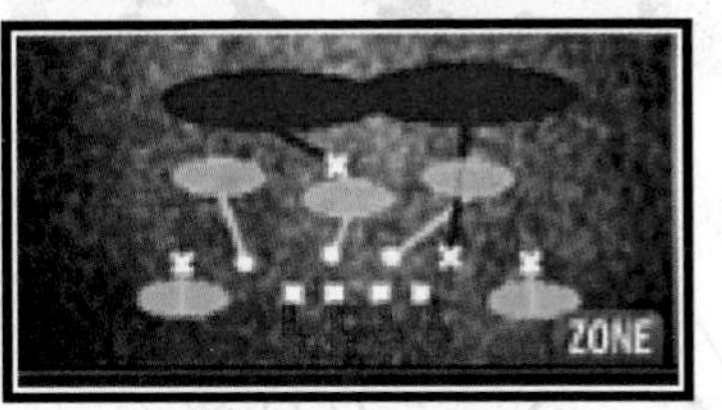

46 Normal—Cover 2

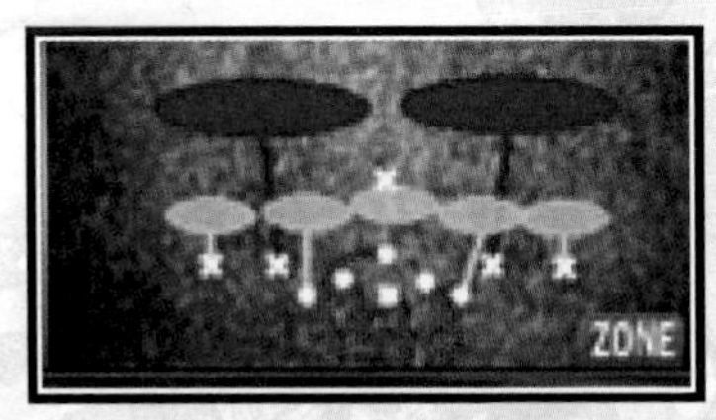

Nickel 1-5-5—Cover 2 Sink

Cover 3

One of the most used plays in the game is the Cover 3 zone. It is great for deep coverage as well as short coverage. It can be extremely difficult to beat Cover 3 because it is the most balanced defense in the game. Expect to see a lot of Cover 3 zone during the *Madden NFL 12* season. Most zone blitzes are run using a Cover 3 shell, so be ready for both coverages as well as the blitz. Cover 3 zone calls for three deep defenders with four underneath defenders. If it is a Cover 3 zone blitz expect there to be only two or three underneath defenders with three over the top.

There are a few plays in *Madden NFL 12* where the defense is in man-to-man with three deep defenders.

Strengths

- Disguised blitzing and coverage
- Strong against horizontal passing concepts
- Strong against flats
- Strong against crossing patterns
- Strong against quick passes
- Strong against curls
- Good run defense
- Protects against deep routes
- Defends the TE

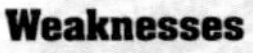

Weaknesses

- Weak against vertical passing concepts
- Weak against trips/bunch formation flooding
- Leaves huge holes if the blitz is recognized

Examples of Cover 3 Defenses

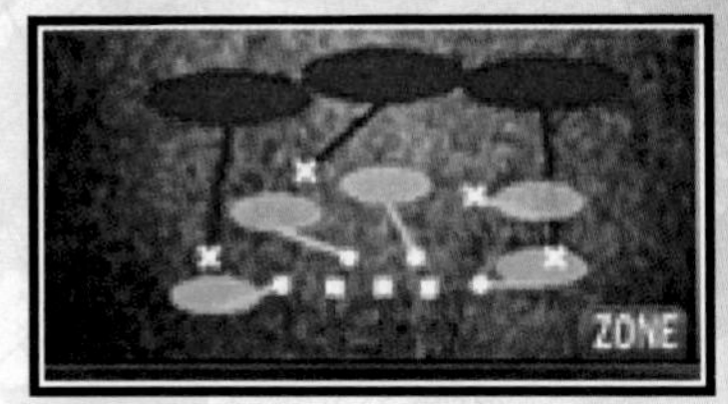

3-4 Under—Cover 3

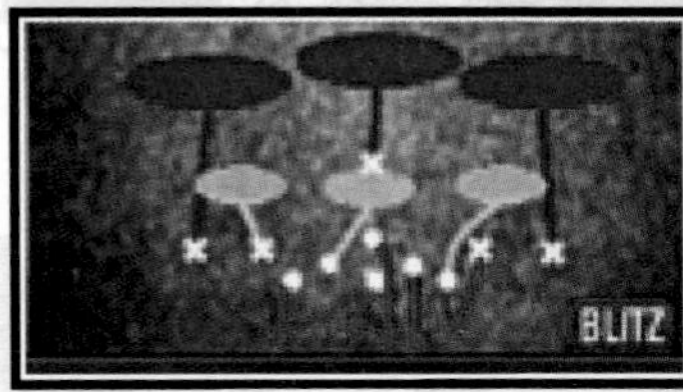

Nickel 1-5-5—SS Zone Blitz

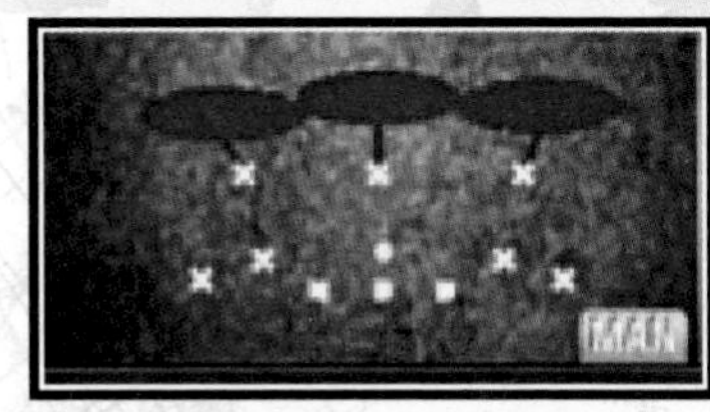

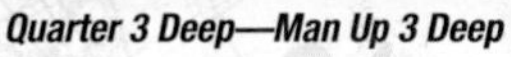

Quarter 3 Deep—Man Up 3 Deep

Cover 4

The Cover 4 can be one of the most frustrating defenses in the game. At first glance it appears that the field is completely covered both short and deep. That is because most players like to attack downfield early and often. With both CBs and the safeties dropping deep to split the deep part of the field into quarters, your first option should be to the short flat. The underneath defenders will protect the sidelines as well as middle of the field, leaving the flat uncovered. Beating the Cover 4 is all about learning to take what the defense gives you. Don't expect the blitz when facing Cover 4, as it's a sure sign that the defense is playing a bend-but-don't-break defense.

In *Madden NFL 12* there are a few plays where the deep coverage is Cover 4 zone but the underneath coverage is man-to-man.

Strengths

- Strong against vertical passing concepts
- Strong against crossing patterns
- Strong against curls
- Strong against quick passes

Weaknesses

- Weak against flats
- Weak against horizontal passing concepts
- Weak against trips/bunch formation flooding
- Relies on the defensive line pass rush for pressure

Examples of Cover 4 Defenses

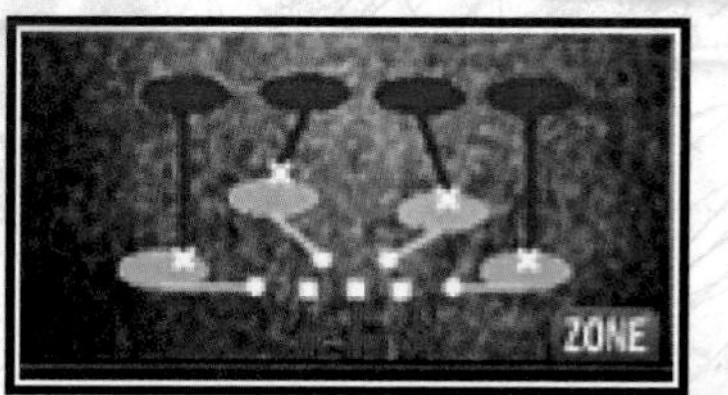

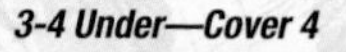
3-4 Under—Cover 4

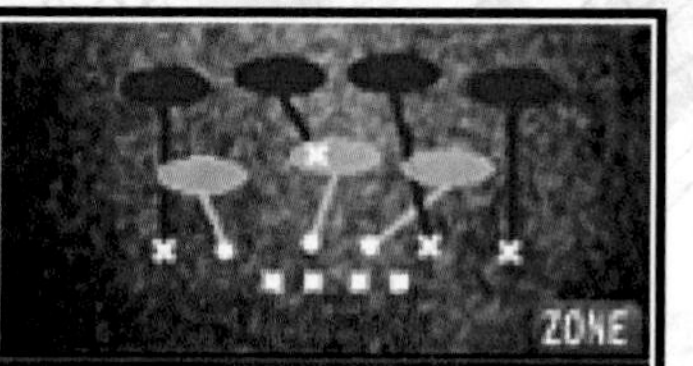

46 Normal—Cover 4

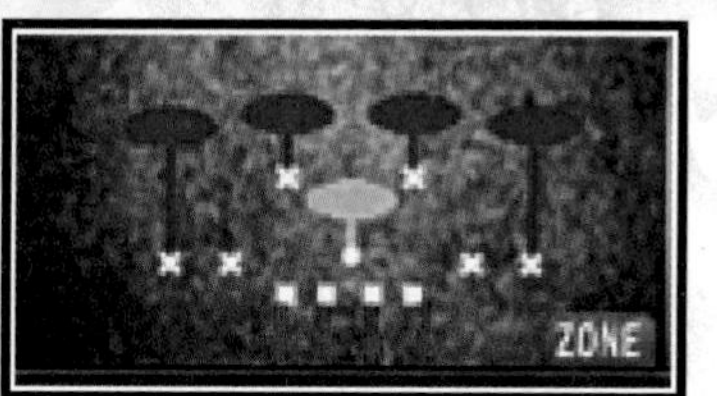

Dime Normal—Quarters Man

New Coverages in *Madden NFL 12*

Madden NFL 12 has seen two new types of coverage with the addition of the Cover 6 and roll coverage. It will be interesting to see how these plays will be implemented into defensive schemes around the country. We are extremely excited about both, especially the roll coverage.

Roll Coverage

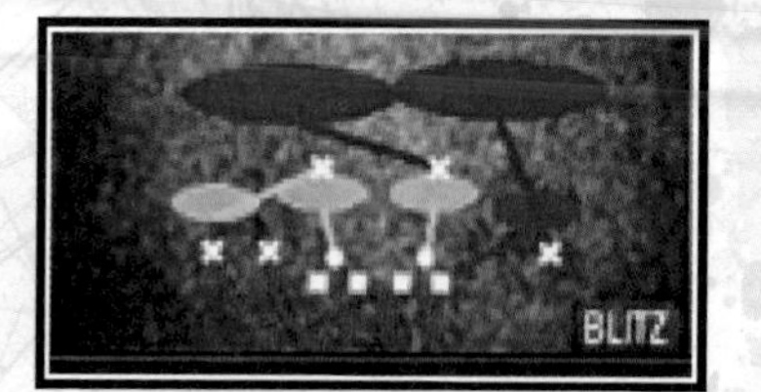

Nickel Normal—Corner Fire 2 Roll

Roll coverage is designed to confuse QBs into reading a Cover 2 shell and expecting typical Cover 2 coverage. However, with the roll coverage we will have one CB drop to play one deep half of the field and the safety above him drop to split the other half. This allows our defense to sneak our blitz off the back edge of the play. This type of defense can be very confusing, especially with what the pre-snap read looks like. In most instances QBs will read either Cover 3 or Cover 1 as they see only one safety dropping back into coverage. This can lead to late throws to the flat, resulting in turnovers!

Cover 6

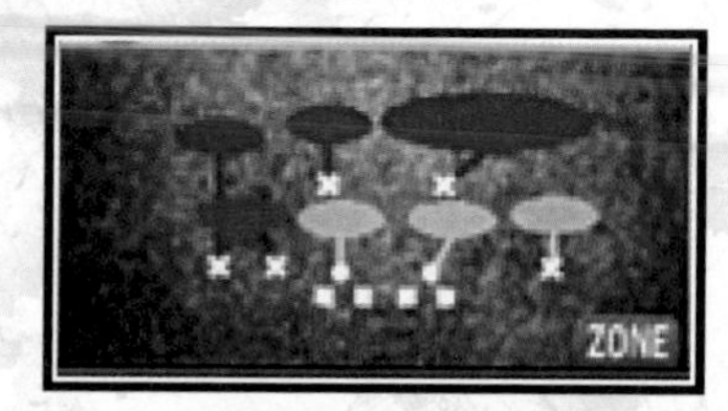

Nickel Normal—Cover 6

The Cover 6 defense is used to yet again confuse QBs by giving them false pre-snap reads. Pre-snap, the defense looks like it is in a Cover 2 shell. However, at the snap of the ball one CB will drop back to play a deep zone and the safety above him will also drop back to the same side deep. Meanwhile, the opposite side safety drops back into a Cover 2 deep assignment. This means that one-half of the deep field is in Cover 4 while the other half is in Cover 2. The underneath coverage will mimic the up-top coverage. This type of defense is great against elite downfield WRs, especially if defenses have star safeties that are able to play in coverage. QBs will read Cover 4 to one side of the field and Cover 2 to the other. If they read Cover 4 and look to attack the flat we will have a defender waiting to make a play. The same goes for a Cover 2 read; if they look to attack deep there's a good chance they will throw into double coverage!

ATTACKING DEFENSIVE COVERAGES

Now that you know how to read and understand all the coverages in *Madden NFL 12*, let's focus on how you will attack them. This section of the guide shows you the plays you need to run to beat whatever defenses send your way. We will also break down key labbing techniques to enhance each play!

Cover 0

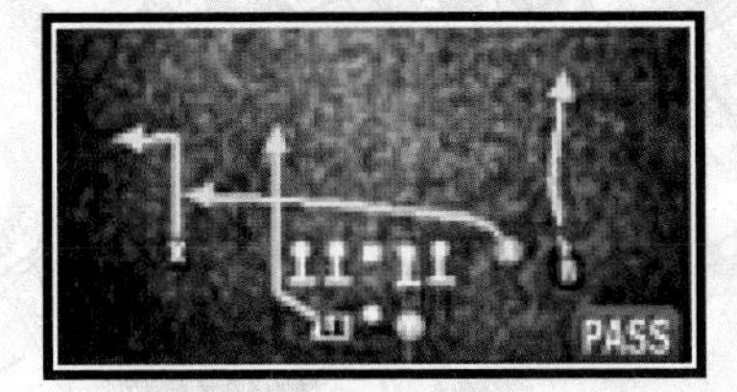

Gun Split Cowboy—Cowboy Y-Out

When facing a Cover 0 defense you know that pressure will be coming quickly. That means you need to get the ball out even quicker. You want to look for a play that gives you at least one quick-pass option. With the Cowboy Y-Out we have three quick-pass options. Both players out of the backfield run routes where we can deliver the ball as they break upfield. The slot receiver over the middle is also a nice option.

Pressure is coming in from the left edge

Our slot receiver has inside position, but his defender is right on top of him. Notice the deep safety assigned to the FB out of the backfield; he isn't in position to defend the quick pass.

Our FB makes the catch and looks to move upfield!

Focus on getting the right animation when you deliver the ball to any of the options. To the receivers out of the backfield make sure to throw a high lead pass. The high lead pass will give you a little speed burst animation upfield, which helps to increase your yards after catch.

What is great about this play for beating the blitz is that we can attack pressure from whatever angle it is coming from. A general rule of thumb for beating aggressive defenses is to attack them from where they are sending pressure. This play gives us the ability to hit the defense to the short left, short middle, and short right. No matter where they blitz we can beat the defense. The Cowboy Y-Out is a must for any playbook or scheme. It can be found in the Dallas Cowboys playbook.

Lab Tips

- Use slide protection to create better passing angles to your routes out of the backfield. The offensive tackles can slow down your receivers. If you want to throw to the left HB, slide protect right; if you want to throw to the right FB, slide protect left.
- Sub in a TE for the FB. TEs are typically taller and have better catch in traffic ratings.
- Sub in taller WRs/TEs on the outside with good catch in traffic ratings.
- Your two outside WRs can be hot routed to any route combination. We recommend one streak route and one curl route. Look for the curl route in one-on-one coverage and throw a low ball as the receiver turns around. Go up top to the streak WR as he has one-on-one coverage down the sideline.

Cover 1

Gun Split Cowboy—Cowboy Go's

Against Cover 1 we like to create multiple one-on-one matchups and take our chances with one of those matchups. To do this we send a decoy WR towards the one deep safety and then have a few iso routes to complement the decoy. With the Cowboy Go's we have our slot WR on a post over the middle of the field. His route should keep the attention of the one deep safety. On both sidelines we are running angled streak routes that will carry both WRs towards the deep sideline. Underneath we have our HB on an out route as our checkdown. For extra protection we keep our FB in to block to keep a safe pocket.

The deep safety is waiting on the slot post

At the snap of the ball we immediately look to the safety to see where his drop-back is. He drops back directly over the middle of the field. We know right away that both sideline routes will have the one-on-one coverage we are looking for. Our checkdown route should be available as well.

Touchdown!

We had the matchup we were looking for up top and took the chance deep. Our receiver hauled in the pass and held on for the touchdown.

Remember; when facing Cover 1 try to create one-on-one matchups. Make sure to have a checkdown option if your up top reads are taken away. With this play we created three different one-on-one matchups and took advantage of the poor downfield coverage.

Lab Tips

- Cover 1 typically sends five pass rushers, so you don't have to keep the FB in to block. We like to keep him in for the added protection, especially if we are looking downfield. Use your hot routes to find what option you like the best to complement your other routes.
- Keep your checkdown receiver in mind. He will be matched up against slower linebackers on most plays. The throw will be short but there is big potential for yards after catch.
- If the safety drops to either sideline the slot post receiver will have inside position on his defender. Deliver the lead pass into open space across the middle of the field.

Cover 2 (Man-to-Man and Zone)

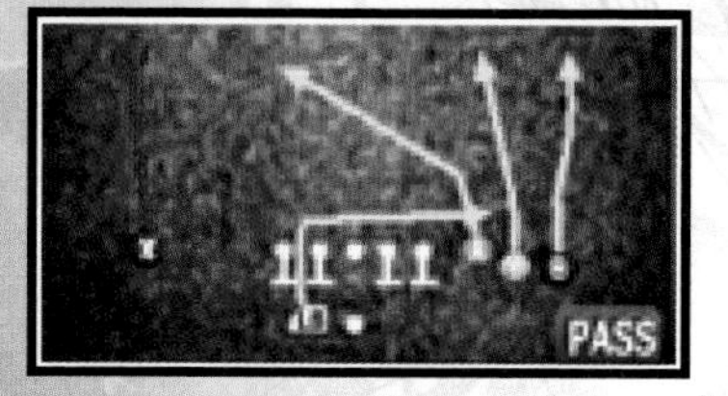

Gun Y-Trips—Four Verticals

Cover 2 can be either man-to-man or zone coverage; we need to keep in mind our route combinations so that we are prepared to beat either. We call upon the Gun Y-Trips—Four Verticals and make one adjustment to attack either Cover 2 defense. If we see zone we make sure we have at least three vertical routes, and if it's man-to-man we make sure we have at least one curl route underneath. For this play we recommend leaving both slot receivers on their designed routes and then hot routing one of the outside receivers on a curl route. This will create a scenario where we will flood a Cover 2 zone defense deep and have an underneath curl against man-to-man.

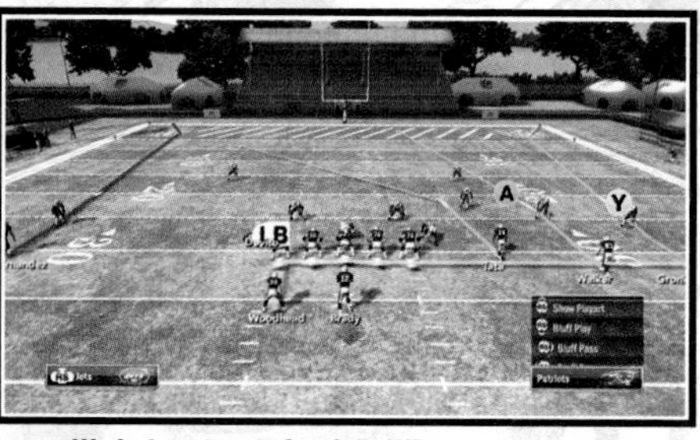

We hot route our far right WR on a curl route

If it's man-to-man we will look to the curl, and if it's zone we will look to the angled short post over the middle of the field. The two deep verticals will pull the Cover 2 zone safeties deep, leaving the post open over the middle of the field.

It was man-to-man and we delivered the low ball to the curl

Another nice option would have been the HB on the underneath out route. However, we had the matchup we were looking for with our big receiver on the outside. We throw a low lead pass and our receiver hauls it in.

This time the defense is in zone

We hot route our far left WR on a curl and leave our far right WR on the deep streak. Notice how the flooding takes place against the deep zone coverage.

Our receiver down the sideline is wide open for the score

Cover 2 zone can't defend three receivers deep. Our flood worked perfectly against the zone coverage.

Going into the play we didn't know what type of Cover 2 the defense was going to call, but with a few adjustments and knowing how to properly attack both types we were prepared for either. Four Verticals is one of the better plays in the game, and it can help you beat many defenses in *Madden NFL 12*. It can be found in a variety of formations and playbooks.

Lab Tips

- Another option for beating man-to-man would be to place the curl receiver on a drag route to mesh with the HB out of the backfield. The routes will work well off each other and will be a nice change of pace.
- Try using double curl routes on the outside. This will increase your chances for beating man-to-man coverage and still give you good odds against zone. You will have one-on-one matchups deep against Cover 2 zone.

Cover 3

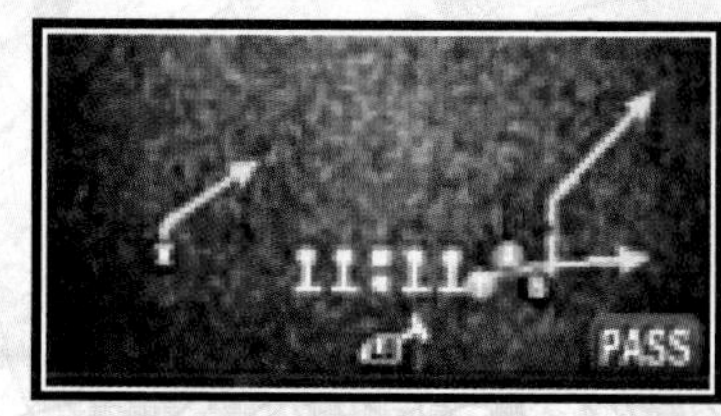

Singleback Bunch—Stick

Expect to see a lot of Cover 3 zone, because it will be one of the most used defenses in *Madden NFL 12*. Beating Cover 3, however, is simple. The formula for attacking Cover 3 involves any trips/bunch formation and a flat route. From that you can hot route a streak and a slant out that will flood the zone. Typically the slant out will be open near the sideline, but sometimes the zone will defend the play differently, so be ready with your reads in case that happens. Singleback Bunch—Stick requires one hot route to be successful against Cover 3. We hot route the short curl to a streak to help pull coverage deep to open up the corner route.

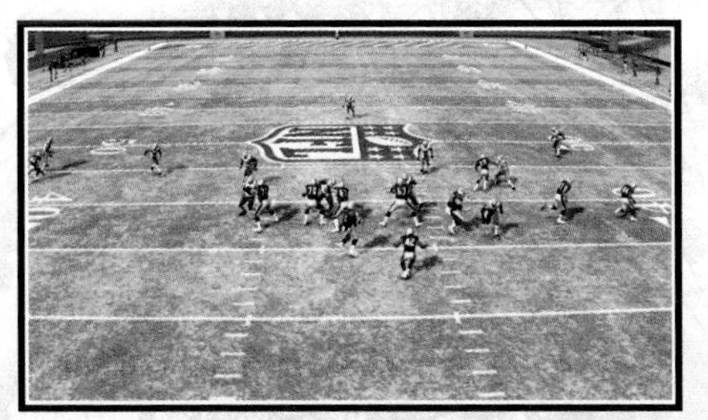

The flat defender is caught bumping our streaked WR

The defender who's supposed to be in the flat bumps our WR on the streak. This leaves both our flat WR and our corner receiver open. This is why we mentioned not sitting on just one route. Be prepared for whatever opens up and take what the defense gives you.

Our QB delivers the ball on time for the completion

We could have waited for the corner route to get open, but that would allow more time for the defense to recover or pressure the QB. The defense gave us the flat so we took it and picked up a big gain down the sideline.

Any time you see zone you should be audibling to your zone beater, which should come from a trips/bunch formation. This game can be simple; don't complicate things!

Lab Tips

- Hot route the far left isolated WR on a curl. If you make a bad read and the defense is in man-to-man he will be your checkdown.
- Place the HB on a fade and get a feel for a quick pass to him.

Cover 4

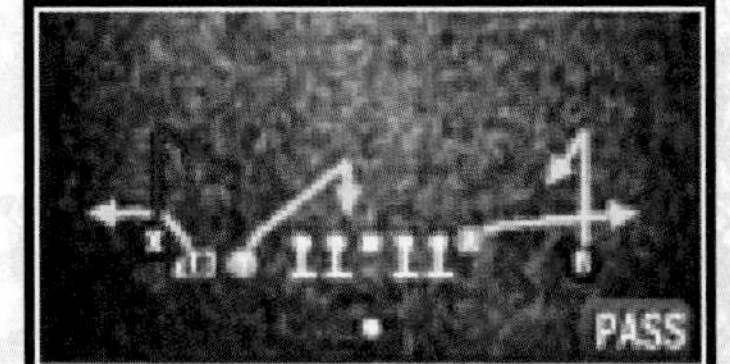

Gun Empty—Curl Flats

Cover 4 should scream flats to you. There is no other place to attack Cover 4 than the flats. The defense is literally giving them to you to take. Look directly to the flat and be ready to get rid of the ball as soon as you see an opening. In case of a bad read look to hot route in a couple of man-to-man beaters, such as curls and drags, as checkdowns if the defense is playing man-to-man.

The flat is opening up to the right

At the snap of the ball the field looks completely covered. If you are late to the flat against Cover 4 it often seems to have everything covered. Deliver the ball to the open receiver early.

The pass is completed in the flat

Our receiver was open and we delivered the ball on time. Cover 4 looks to lull you into making bad decisions. While Cover 4 doesn't apply pressure on the QB you still need to make quick reads and get the ball out just as quickly because of the great coverage on the field.

When you think Cover 4 think flats. All day, every day. What are you going to do against Cover 4? That's right—pass to the flats!

Lab Tips

- Be prepared for bad reads and make sure to hot route a few man-to-man beaters.
- Run this play against Cover 4 but don't deliver the ball right away. Go back into instant replay and watch how the defense works against the flats. Keep that image in your head so you are prepared for it when you see it in game.

Cover 6

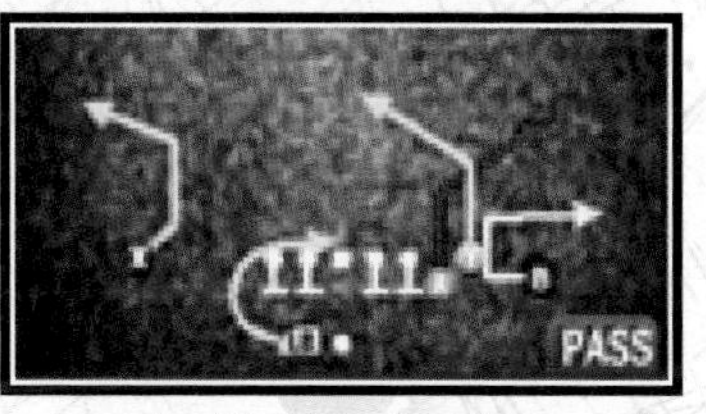

Gun Flip Trips—Deep Fork

Cover 6 is a difficult defense to gauge because it plays Cover 4 on one side of the field and Cover 2 on the other. Our goal when attacking Cover 6 is to focus on finding the Cover 2 side of the field and exploiting the one deep safety. Deep Fork is a unique play that vertically attacks the defense at many different points. We hot route the far right WR on a deep streak. To the trips side we now have three deep routes with one of those routes being a post. If the defense is in a Cover 2 on the trips side our deep corner will be open. If the defense is in a Cover 2 to the left the post would be open over the middle of the field. Key in on the CBs; whichever side has the CB playing the flat is your Cover 2 side. Make your read and deliver the ball to the open receiver.

Cover 2 is to the right!

Notice a few things with this coverage read. The right CB is playing extremely shallow, so we know that that is the Cover 2 side. Also notice the read you get in the deep secondary. To the left there are two deep defenders and to the right there is only one defender. This read takes place later in your route progression, but you can still rely on it.

Our receiver makes the catch on the sideline

Our corner receiver is wide open as our hot routed streak receiver pulls the single high safety deep. It's a beautiful thing when you make the right reads and deliver the ball for a completion.

Cover 6 could take the community by storm, so be prepared with knowing how to beat it. Deep Fork can be found in the Arizona Cardinals and Dallas Cowboys playbooks. It's hands down the best play in the game for attacking Cover 6.

Lab Tips

- Your HB is your only checkdown, so be ready to hit him if need be. Practice the quick pass to him because the C route out of the backfield is extremely difficult to defend. This makes the play that much harder to defend.
- For added protection against the blitz, block the HB. You will lose your checkdown but you will pick up extra pressure.

Max Coverage Defense

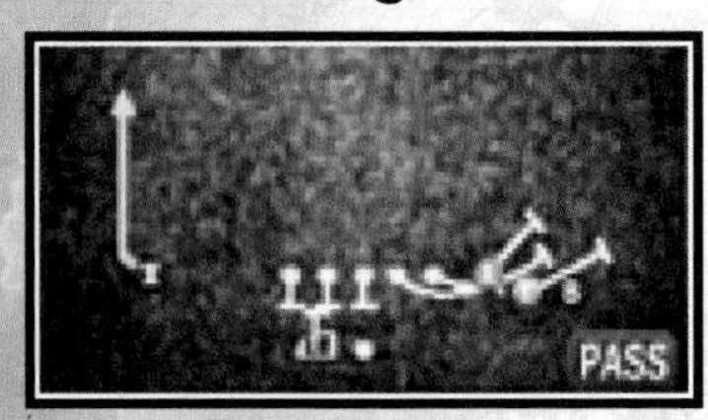

Gun Y-Trips—WR Screen

While "Max Coverage Defense" isn't a specific coverage you will find in the game, it is a strategy that is used by many. Max coverage defense is when defenses drop nine or more defenders into coverage. They are playing the ultimate bend-but-don't-break defense. It can be very frustrating playing against this style of defense, but we will show you two ways to absolutely crush opponents who play it.

The WR Screen is the first way we like to attack max coverage. If the defense isn't going to send any pass rushers after our QB we are going to use our offensive linemen as blockers for our WRs.

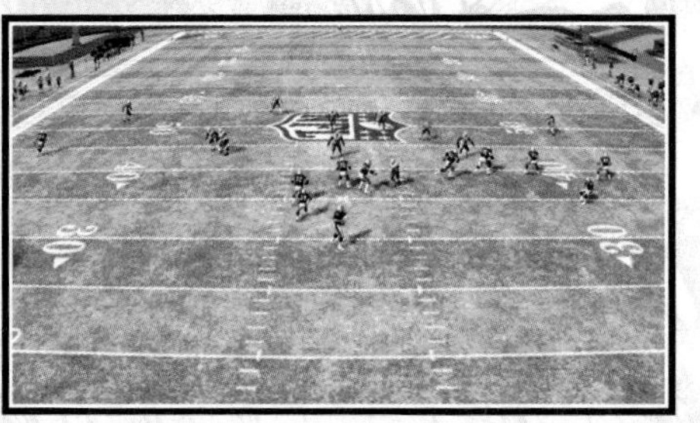

The defense rushes only one defender

Here the defense is in a zone Cover 4 and dropped three defensive linemen into coverage. Our linemen, however, are getting in position to block for our WR Screen.

Our blockers are in position and there is green grass ahead!

We get the ball out to our play-making WR and have blockers upfield. WR Screens will destroy max coverage defense, so be sure to call upon them if you face it.

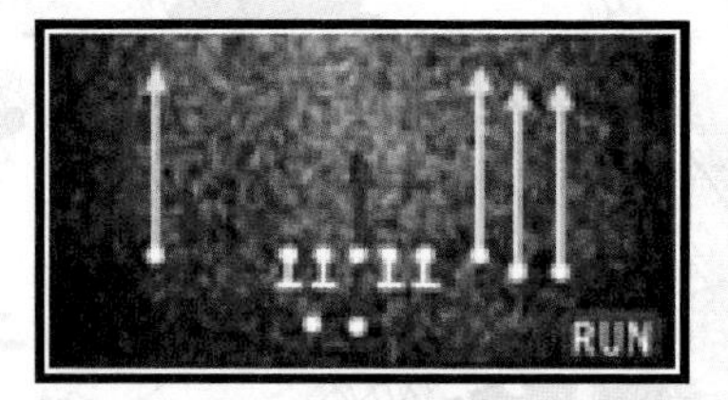

Gun Y-Trips—HB Draw

Another great way to attack max coverage defense is by running HB Draws. We again are involving our offensive linemen in the play. The draw allows our linemen to get upfield and block defenders up the middle of the field.

Our linemen begin to move upfield as our HB gets the delayed handoff

Be patient with draws and let the linemen get in position for their blocks. Once they have made their initial blocks move upfield quickly.

Our HB cuts up between the blockers

We picked up big yardage on the HB Draw as the defenders sat back on their heels. Patience was the key to the yards gained. Don't try and outrun your blocks; let them develop first.

Don't panic against max coverage defense; it's a natural reaction to get frustrated with your opponent if you think "Who plays that way?" Take what they give you, which is the WR Screen and HB Draw!

Lab Tips

- Substitute in your fastest and most agile player as your screen WR.
- Substitute in your fastest and most agile HB.
- Consider substituting in TEs for the slot WRs to get better blocking on the field for the WR Screen and HB Draw.

ADVANCED USER-CATCHING

Many games in *Madden NFL 12* come down to the ability to "out-user-control" your opponent. User-control is manually controlling a specific player during any play. In this section of the guide we break down user-catching and our three favorite ways to do it. User-catching is extremely important because often the computer will be out of position to make a play on the ball when a pass is in the air. Rather than let an incompletion happen—or worse, an interception—we will click onto our offensive player and manually put our receiver in better position for the completion.

We like using tight formations to execute user catches on the sideline

Using tight formations allows us to get the best angle for the user catch on the sideline. From any tight formation hot route your outermost receivers to slant outs.

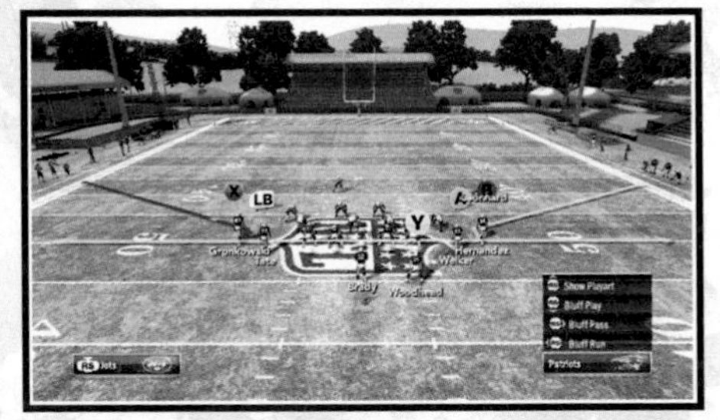

We hot routed both outside receivers on slant outs. We hot routed the slot receivers to drags.

The play is set up and we first must be prepared for pressure and to check down to our receivers on drags. This play requires time in the pocket, so make sure to get the ball out to your checkdowns if needed.

Our outside receivers begin to approach the sideline

Our pass protection is good and we feel no pressure in the pocket. We sit and wait for the receivers to get a few yards away from the sideline. Once they are in position we throw a down and away lead pass, click onto the receiver, drag the receiver back towards the QB, and go for the catch by holding down the Catch button.

Our receiver goes up for the ball and makes the catch!

We spin our receiver around and make the catch. Height is extremely important for good user-catching. Make sure to substitute in your tallest receivers when you plan on doing this in-game.

We can user-catch to the other sideline as well

Our receiver is getting into position, and we hang in the pocket as he approaches the sideline.

Click on and spin the receiver around towards the QB

As the receiver turns toward the QB make sure to hold down the Catch button. Once the ball gets in range you will launch up for the ball.

Nice catch!

We once again have the height advantage and our receiver makes the catch!

Our second option for user-catching is using out routes to our receivers near the sideline. We like using any formation where we have two receivers that are split out wide close to the sideline.

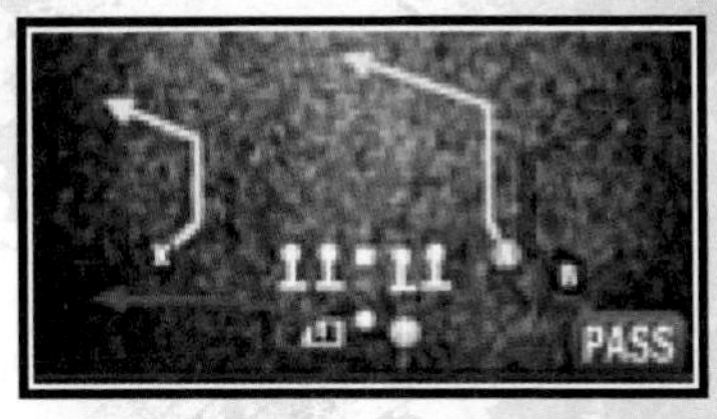

Gun Split Cowboys—Cowboy Corners

We choose to come out in Gun Split Cowboys—Cowboy Corners because it has double blue routes, which help with our pass protection. We hot route both our outside receivers on out routes towards the sideline. As the receiver approaches the sideline throw a high lead pass, click onto the receiver, and drag him back towards the QB while holding the Catch button.

Our far left receiver approaches the sideline

Our out route is open and we sit in the pocket waiting for the receiver to get close enough to the sideline for the user catch.

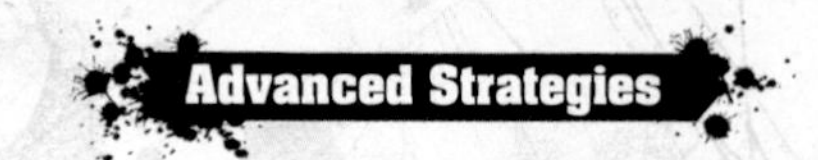

Another nice user catch!

The defense will have a difficult time defending the user catch unless they click onto the defender and make a user play themselves.

Our final option for user-catching is with hot routed streaks. This user catch is the easiest of the three and is just as effective as the others. Height is once again important for the success of this play, so make sure to substitute your biggest players on the field. It can be done from any play and any formation, so work it in with your scheme however you like.

Our receiver moves upfield on his hot-routed streak

Notice that at the snap of the ball we have inside position on the defender. However, as the play develops more we will lose that inside position. This user catch is all about making sure that our offensive player has inside position on the defender. We wait for our receiver to get 10–15 yards downfield, where we then throw an inside lead pass. Click onto the receiver and move him inside towards the ball. Hold the Catch button as you approach the circle indicator.

Click on and move the receiver inside

Notice that we clicked onto the receiver and moved him inside towards the ball. This gives us a better angle to make a play on the ball.

We make the catch in front of the defender!

We get a great animation and snatch the ball away from the defender. Work on your pass lead throws because different QBs call for different timings for this throw.

This time we look for the user-catch streak on the other side of the field

We move to the right side of the field and look to user-catch to our other big target. Throw an inside pass lead left and click on for the catch!

Our receiver goes up and makes the catch!

The user catch works best with accurate QBs and tall receivers with good catch in traffic ratings. Look for receivers who are 6'4" or taller and have 88-plus catch in traffic ratings. QBs should have 85 or better deep throw accuracy. User-catching takes lots of practice, so be sure you put in time in practice mode to perfect it.

PASS PROTECTION

Pass protection sometimes gets put in the back of the closet in terms of its importance to winning. If you can identify where pressure is coming from and make adjustments to pick up that pressure you will not only frustrate your opponent but you will find passing extremely easy in *Madden NFL 12*. There are four ways we like to increase our pass protection: delayed routes, a swing receiver, double delayed routes, and power blocking.

Delayed Routes

Delayed routes are any play in the game where an offensive player, at the Play Call screen, is on a route that is colored blue. This player will first look to block any pressure coming towards the QB, and he will then release on his route. Delayed routes are ideal because they help to add pass protection without ever thinking of where pressure is coming from. What is also great about them is that at the snap of the ball our offense will have a six-man protection scheme. This means the defense is forced to send seven defenders to outnumber our blockers. If the defense doesn't send pressure our delayed route will still release out as a passing option. Oftentimes around the *Madden* community we hear "Why not just hot route someone to block?" The reason we don't just block a receiver is because if we guess wrong we lose a passing option. Delayed blue routes are single-handedly the easiest way to instantly better your pass protection.

Gun Snugs Flip—Cowboy In

Here we have our HB on a delayed route. The defense has the box loaded with defenders, so the blue route should step up and pick up outside pressure. The offensive line in *Madden NFL 12* looks to protect the middle of the field first and everything outside second.

Our HB steps up and makes the block

Don't hang in the pocket thinking you will be safe forever! Often the HB will only chip the defensive player, giving you just enough time to deliver the ball for the completion. Here our HB makes an amazing block and stands up the pass rusher.

Our receiver makes the catch and tiptoes on the sideline

The extra time in the pocket is exactly what we needed to make the completion. We would have had to rush the throw without the delayed route and could have thrown into coverage.

Swing Receiver

The swing receiver is any player on the field whom we add to our pass protection scheme who is not on a delayed route. This receiver should balance out the formation's overall protection. You should also not block effective individual routes for protection. For example, if you are using a play that has only one flat route, you should never block that player for extra protection. The flat route is often vital to the overall success of a play. Often we mix delayed routes with swing receivers. This helps to increase the number of blockers we have in pass protection, but it doesn't limit our offense by losing too many receivers to blocking.

Gun Snugs Flip—Cowboy In

We use the same play as for the delayed routes example and first look to see who our swing receiver can be. As you get more comfortable with your offensive scheme, start identifying who your swing receivers are. For this play we use our left slot receiver. The defense has four down linemen and has positioned two linebackers to the left of the formation. With this play we now have one extra blocker to the right of the field (our delayed route) and then one extra blocker to the left of the field (our swing receiver). The balance we have with our protection scheme will make it extremely difficult for defenses to get pressure against us.

Our swing receiver steps up and makes the block!

Notice that our HB on the delayed route is also looking to help with protection. However, there is no one for him to block, and he will release on his route shortly.

Great protection and a great pass

We sit in the pocket and deliver a strike to our receiver. The swing receiver plays a vital role in the success of your team's protection scheme. Make sure to devote extra time to identifying who he is in all your offensive formations.

Double Delayed Routes

There are only a handful of plays in *Madden NFL 12* that have two delayed routes, and they can drastically change the landscape of some games. Double blue routes with the addition of a swing receiver give our offense an eight-man protection scheme. That means that defenses would need to send nine defenders to have a plus-one advantage! Last I checked defenses only have 11 defenders—if they blitzed nine that would mean there would only be two players left in coverage. When you utilize double delayed routes in combination with your swing receiver expect to have time to take a nap in the pocket!

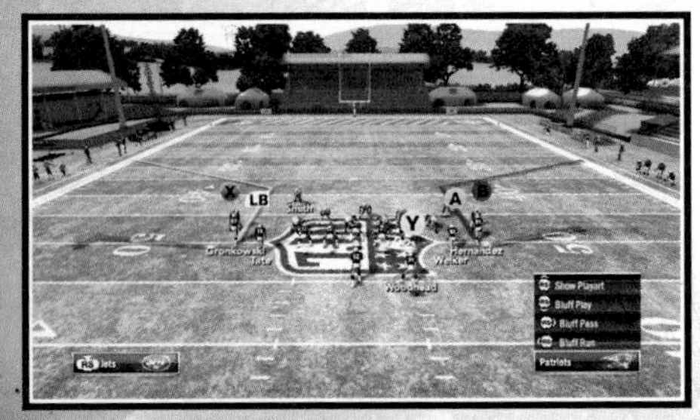

Gun Snugs Flip—PA WR Stops

We choose our HB as our swing receiver and block him. Remember; one of the keys to the swing receiver is to balance the field. If we blocked either of the outside receivers we wouldn't have offensive threats on that side of the field. Our HB is the perfect option to block, and he helps to create our mega pocket!

The pressure is stuffed

The defense sent seven defenders and dropped four in zone coverage. After our delayed route receivers deliver their blocks they will release to the flat, giving us safety checkdowns.

Our receiver makes the grab

Defenses that send seven defenders are really looking to pressure the QB. However, we are confident that we can pick up *any* pressure in the game. Use delayed routes, find your swing receiver, and hang in the pocket.

Power Blocking

Our last pass protection tip is power blocking. We use power blocking specifically from Gun Split Close sets. Power blocking is when we force our blockers to block specific gaps. In *Madden NFL 12* we can block the middle A gap and the outside C gap.

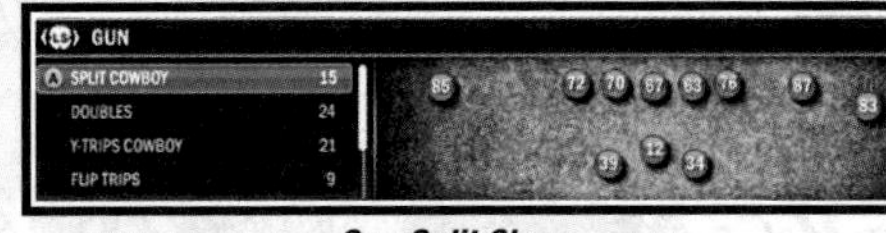

Gun Split Close

The A gap is the area between the center and guards, and the C gap is the area outside the offensive tackles. We power-block by blocking our player in the backfield towards the direction we want him to block. For example, if we want our HB to block the A gap we simply block him by hot routing him to block right. If we want the TE on the opposite side to block the A gap we would hot route him to block left. To block the HB towards the C gap we would hot route him to block left. To block the TE towards the C gap we would hot route him to block right. Power blocking is extremely effective in blocking called out pressure.

We power-block both players towards the A gap

Here we expect the defense to blitz the A gap. We decide to power-block both our players in the backfield to prevent any pressure from coming through the A gap.

Pressure is coming from the left!

Notice that both our players step up into the A gap to protect the QB. Pressure is coming from the left, but the rusher will have to get past both our A gap blockers.

Touchdown!

We go up top and get the touchdown. The pressure was quick but we were able to assign our players to block the A gap.

We power-block both players towards the C gap

The defense appears to set up a blitz that will come off the C gap. We prepare for the pressure by power-blocking the C gap.

Notice the difference between power-blocking the A and C gaps

Pressure did come from the outside, but power-blocking the C gap worked perfectly.

The ball is delivered to the TE over the middle of the field

We make the easy completion with the extra time in the pocket. The pressure would have been quick but we didn't feel a thing!

Put the time in and analyze your team's playbook and plays to find the best way to maximize your pass protection scheme. Many never even consider having a protection scheme, but to truly elevate your game this is something you will need to focus on.

NOTE

All the plays discussed here can be found in the Dallas Cowboys offensive playbook.

ADVANCED HOT ROUTING

Offensive hot routing can help to balance any offensive play in the game. The purpose of the hot route is to make adjustments to your offensive play to better fit your overall scheme. Many plays in *Madden NFL 12* will have effective routes that we want to take advantage of but then have routes that get wasted as they don't follow along with the route progression of the play. Also, many plays are great for beating man-to-man but don't have checkdowns in case it is zone and vice versa. By hot routing in adjustments we make sure that we can attack one coverage and then have a safety checkdown in case our read is wrong.

One of the first things we do when we analyze a play is to call the play without any adjustments and determine what our route progression would be. Route progression is when we move from receiver to receiver looking for one to be open. There are three windows that routes can fall into. For example, drag routes and flat routes are the quickest developing routes in the game—these would be our first window. Routes such as curls, slants, deep ins, and deep outs fall into our second window of route progressions. Our third window would be routes such as posts, deep corners, and streaks. Our reads should always start with the first window, then move to the second and end with the third.

Hot routes should also be used to create checkdowns. A checkdown is a route that we use in case our read of the defense is wrong. For example, if we read zone and look to audible to our trips or bunch formation we want to make sure that we set our play up to beat zone coverage, but we also like to audible in a route that will beat man-to-man. That way if the defense is actually playing man-to-man we will check down to that option and vice versa. In this section we break down a few plays and show you the hot routes we like to add.

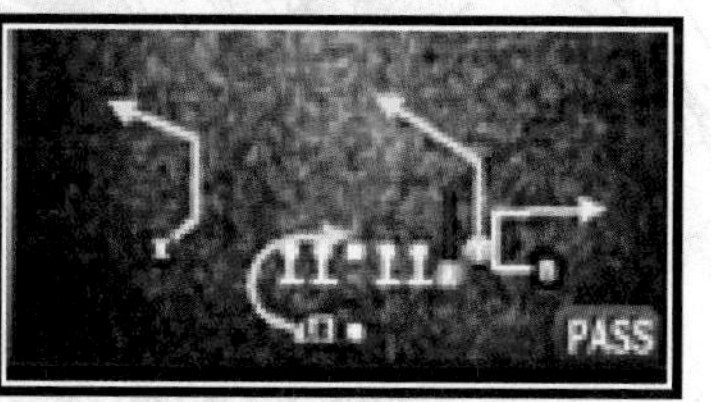

Gun Flip Trips—Deep Fork

This play has a nice quick pass out of the backfield as well as a nice auto-motion route by our far right WR. The inside slot WRs are running deep posts and corner routes while our far left WR is on a corner route.

Our auto-motion route is open right after the snap

We see that our receiver on the auto-motion out route opens up right after the snap of the ball. We look to deliver the ball to him as soon as he breaks out wide.

He makes the catch with room to run up the sideline

Our receiver brings the pass in and completes a nice 6-yard gain. Let's take a look at our other routes at the time of the throw.

Our HB begins his cut inside

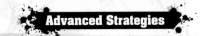

Our HB is open, and he is a great option for a quick pass. However, the Deep Fork is a great play for attacking the defense vertically. We choose the HB as our swing receiver, and in case the defense blitzes we like to block him to help with our protection scheme.

Our post and corner routes haven't got downfield yet!

Here we see our third-window receivers beginning to get into position. We choose to leave them on their assigned routes. Notice how the route progression works here. These receivers have yet to open up on their routes, compared to our auto-motioned WR and our HB out of the backfield.

Our far left receiver hasn't made his move towards the corner

Here we have our far left receiver moving towards the corner. The defender is draped all over him and the pressure is just about to get to the QB. This renders the corner route useless.

Let's break down what's happening here. We have three routes that fall into our third window of progressions and two first-window reads. However, to help with protection we are going to block our HB. This leaves us with only one short read and three deep reads. If the defense covers our first and only short read we could be in trouble. We choose to hot route our far left receiver to a curl. This now gives us one first-window, one second-window, and two third-window progressions. Our protection should be good, and if our first-window read is covered we can check down to our curl route. If we have time in the pocket we can deliver the ball downfield to our third-window reads.

This shows the Deep Fork with our hot routes

We hot routed the HB to block and the far left receiver to a curl. Our play is now better set up to pick up pressure and protect ourselves in case we made a bad read on the defense.

Our first-window read is covered

The defender is in better position on our first read. We might still be able to squeeze the pass towards the sideline, but if our opponent clicks on and tries to make a play on the ball it could result in a pick 6!

The pressure is picked up and we sit comfortably in the pocket

Look at our route progressions working here! Our first-window read has come and gone and now we quickly scan over to our second window to the far left. That receiver is just beginning to turn around on his curl route; meanwhile, our deep reads are still not in position.

We throw a low lead pass for the easy completion

If we hadn't made the adjustments to this play we most likely would have been looking at a sack or even a poor pass to a receiver who was either covered or not in position to make a play on the ball.

We also want to show you what would happen if the defense were playing in zone coverage and how this play would still be effective against zone.

Both our first- and second-window reads are covered

We kept our HB in to block because we expected pressure. However, the defense is playing coverage defense and is also in zone. Our first- and second-window reads are covered, but we still have our third-window options to rely on. We have tons of time in the pocket to wait for them to get open.

Our corner route is wide open!

Our read of the defense was wrong and our first two options were covered. Many players would panic in this situation, but when you know what your route progression is and mix that with effective hot routing you can feel confident even when things go wrong.

The next play we look at focuses on creating balance on the field with our hot routes. We will also be creating a checkdown in case our initial read is incorrect.

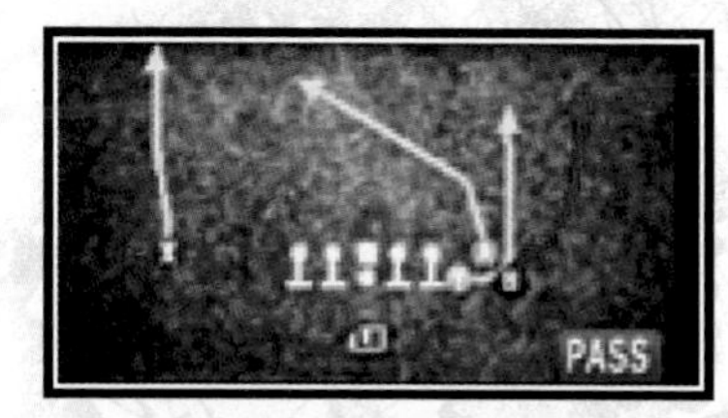

Singleback Bunch—Verticals

By default this play has one first-window read and three third-window reads. Your first read is the wheel route; next you would move to the three vertical routes. We like this play for the wheel route to the right flat, the HB on the delay route, and the deep post over the middle. Let's take a look at the route progression of this play.

The wheel route is open in the flat

Our wheel route receiver is open in the flat so we look to get him the ball. Notice how the inside receiver on the sharp wheel route is congesting the area with his route.

The pass is completed for the big gain

We get upfield and pick up the first down. Let's look at the other routes on the play to see what adjustments we want to make.

This area of the field is congested with receivers and defenders

The sharp wheel route isn't an option at this point and has also brought another defender into the area to help defend our first-window read.

Our far left receiver is still early in his deep route

The HB is on a delayed route out of the backfield. We like this option and will leave him on the delayed route. The far left receiver, however, is nowhere near being open. The post over the middle is also not in position to get open.

If the defense sends pressure we will be OK with our HB on the delayed route. However, if our first-window read is covered we won't have a second option to check down to. We also don't have a good way to beat man-to-man coverage. The wheel route to the flat is great for beating zone, but we can't rely on it for beating man-to-man. We decide to create a mesh over the middle of the field by hot routing our far left receiver on a drag route and our inside receiver on the right of the field on a slant in. This gives us a great option for attacking man-to-man coverage.

Our play is now set up with our hot routes

The field is more balanced with these hot routes, and we also have great route progression; we will look to the wheel route in the flat and then to the crossing patterns over the middle of the field. We will then look to the deep post and then back to the wheel route down the sideline. Our last option is the delayed route out of the backfield.

Our wheel route is covered in the flat

We move to the crossing patterns now that our wheel route is covered in the flat. The defense is in man-to-man, so one of the crossing patterns should be open.

Our slant is beginning to get open

Our drag receiver has inside position but has a defender on his back. We look to the slant route receiver because he has a few steps on his defender.

The pass is completed for the easy gain

Hot routing is all about having a method to your madness. Use it to create balance in your offensive attack. Give yourself checkdowns in case you make a bad read on the defense. Utilize them to your advantage and give yourself as many options as possible.

ADVANCED PLAYER POSITIONING

In the first part of this chapter we broke down the "Five Sets for Success" and how important it is to have a scheme. With this section we take our offensive scheme to the next level by teaching you how to position your players in such a way that you can utilize their skill sets for each of your formations. The base play is where you start and make your adjustments, because when you audible to your other formations you will notice that your players will move to different points on the field depending on the formation. Make sure that when you do go to these formations you can still run your scheme effectively.

We figure out our scheme's positioning by audibling to each of our audibles and looking at where specific players line up. If we feel things are out of whack we need to adjust our base play.

Gun Snugs Flip—Cowboy In

We have made no adjustments to this play and we have not moved any of the players around to fit our scheme. With our specific scheme we focus on height towards the outside of the formation. We want to make sure that our tallest receivers are positioned here. The inside receivers need to be fast enough to get to the flat as well as downfield, and we also need to make sure that we have a receiver with a good catch in traffic rating, because we can expect the receivers to take big hits as they cross over the middle of the field.

We make a few hot routes and are ready to go

Our far left receiver looks to stretch the field, while our left slot receiver looks to get to the flat and make the defense respect the short part of the field. Our right slot receiver will be crossing over the middle of the field, so he should have a good catch in traffic rating. The far right receiver we are looking to utilize as a user-catch option on the sideline. Make sure he has good height for it to be effective.

Our sideline user-catch receiver isn't tall enough!

We can't get our receiver high enough to make a play on the ball. The taller defensive back makes a play on the ball instead of our receiver. We need to get more height at this position.

Our receiver over the middle gets crushed by the MLB

The receiver hangs onto the ball here, but we want to make sure one of our best catch in traffic receivers runs this route.

The flat route receiver doesn't have the speed to get separation

The flat route is useless because our receiver can't separate from the defender. We need more speed here!

Our deep streak receiver can't match up downfield with the bigger defenders

Our receiver is nowhere near making a play on this ball. He is stuck between two bigger defenders and doesn't even give us a fighting chance to make a play on the ball. We need a lot more height here.

This is only one setup, but you should be breaking down each of your plays in this manner and make sure that you have the best players for each specific route. The positioning we have with the initial breakdown is the default setup of receivers. Although the game says this is our best lineup it is not. Know this and make adjustments accordingly.

We made key adjustments to our player positioning

We subbed in our 6'6" TE for the far left streak route. The left slot WR was subbed out for our WR with a 94 speed rating, and the right slot WR was subbed out for our receiver with a 97 catch in traffic rating. The far right user-catch receiver is now a 6'1" TE with good jump and catch in traffic ratings.

User-catch for the win!

The extra height allows us to go up and make the user catch!

Our right slot receiver has a 97 catch in traffic rating

We have complete confidence going over the middle because our receiver has a catch in traffic rating of 97.

Our left slot flat route now gets open with the extra speed on the field

A speed rating of 94 is enough for us to get to the edge with our flat route. This play is now effective because of the speed difference.

The 6'6" TE downfield now gives us the advantage against the defense!

We now have the advantage over the defense. Expect double-teams to stop a player who is 6'6" and streaking downfield.

Now let's look at each of our audibles and see if the player positioning will work for our overall scheme.

Power run

When we audible to our power run formation we have our two big TEs lined up on the outside. This is perfect for user-catching on the sideline as well as attacking the defense downfield with their height. In the backfield we have our 94 speed receiver to hit in the flat once again, and lined up at TE we have our receiver with 97 catch in traffic. For passing purposes this is everything we would want. We will lose blocking ability by having WRs lined up at FB and TE, but we are OK with that. If we really want to pound the rock we will come out in our power run set and substitute in our heavy package.

Quick pass

Here we audible to our quick pass and once again have perfect player positioning. Both our speed players are in the backfield for quick passes. Our 97 catch in traffic receiver is in the slot and going over the middle of the field. Once again our big targets are on the outside for user-catching.

Man beater

Our man beater formation will also be our base play, but we also like to use the Gun Flip Trips—Deep Fork. Here we have our best route runner on an auto-motioned out route, which is ideal for this play. We have one of our speed receivers running a deep corner and one of our tall receivers running a deep post. To the far left we have our 6'6" TE matched up for curls and user catches.

Zone beater

Our zone beater once again gives us our tallest targets lined up on the outside. We have our catch in traffic receiver over the middle of the field and our speed threat going deep over the middle of the field.

Player positioning can elevate your game so much when done properly. Scan your roster and plan out your offense to find where specific players need to be according to your scheme. If we didn't make adjustments to our scheme with this breakdown the overall scheme wouldn't be as effective as it could be with the appropriate players. Know your roster, know your scheme, and start winning ball games!

ATTACKING THE ONLINE PLAYER: OFFENSE

This section of the guide is going to break down what we believe will be the most used defensive blitz packages online in *Madden NFL 12*. Our goal is to show you how to attack these defenses when you come across them in online games. We are going to highlight 46 Normal—Inside Blitz, Dime Normal—Strike 2 Deep, and the 3-4 Over—Sting Pinch Zone. Both the Dime Normal—Strike 2 Deep and 3-4 Over—Sting Pinch Zone are zone coverage defenses that also have man-to-man versions of the blitz, which we will also cover. These blitzes are quick, easy to set up, and well known around the community as being the most effective ways to get pressure on the QB.

46 Normal—Inside Blitz (Speed Package)

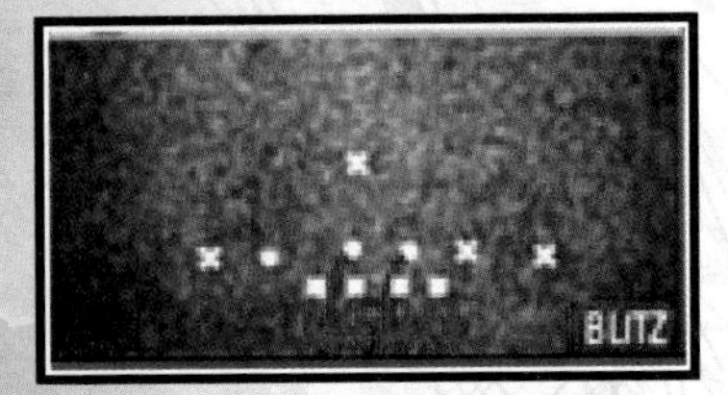

46 Normal—Inside Blitz

The 46 Normal—Inside Blitz is one of the most effective and most used blitzes in the game. The nature of this defense is a very up-in-your-face, beat-me-if-you-dare style of play. The box is loaded with eight defenders, so the defense is taunting you to throw deep. However, if you use the speed package, the 46 Normal gets six defensive backs on the field. That allows this formation to be one of the most flexible in the game. The Inside Blitz will bring pressure through the A gap and can also be used to manually set up pressure from the inside and outside.

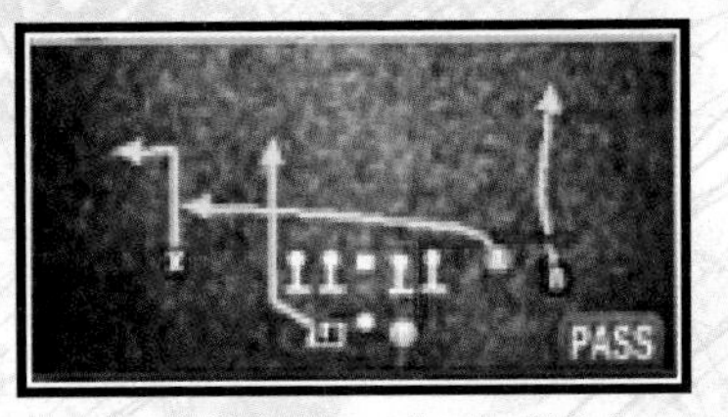

Gun Split Cowboy—Cowboy Y-Out

The Inside Blitz is high-powered, but it is weak in defending quick passes and downfield plays. We can either focus on pass protection and look to get the ball downfield or quick-pass the defense into submission. First we will show the quick-pass option and then show how we attack downfield against this play.

We hit our HB out of the backfield

Our first option is either HB out of the backfield. Both break out wide of the line of scrimmage and set up nicely for a quick pass. The defense can't defend both these options at the same time. The pressure can be overwhelming, but don't panic. Trust your play and trust your homework. You know that this play and, generally speaking, all blitzing defenses are weak against quick passes. Hang in the pocket and deliver the strike.

We are looking to attack downfield

Here we are looking to hit the defense deep because they have no safety help over the top. We power-block our backfield so that we have time in the pocket. We placed our best deep threat on a streak in the slot and have our underneath receivers running a drag over the middle of the field and a user-catch option with the out on the sideline. Bring it on, defense!

The pressure is picked up!

Our power blocking worked perfectly. We have a nice pocket and have time to wait for our streak to burn past the slower defender.

Touchdown!

We took advantage of the aggressive defense and made them pay deep. Yes, the Inside Blitz is effective, and yes, you will see it many times this year, but having a plan of attack is the best way to combat whatever the defense is doing to you. Put this in your back pocket and be ready to make a big play when needed!

Dime Normal—Strike 2 Deep (Zone) and DB Blitz (Man)

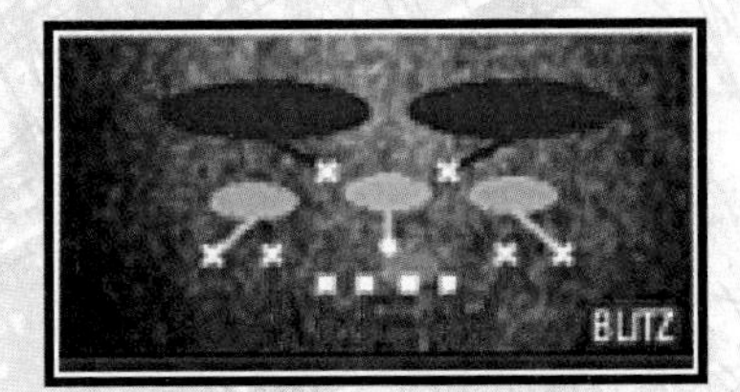

Dime Normal—Strike 2 Deep

This defense falls into the category of "oldie but goodie." It has been a popular play in *Madden NFL* for as long as we can remember and for good reason. It is one of the simplest ways to bring effective pressure. The coverage is good, there is a lot of speed on the field, and defenses can switch the coverage on the play but still bring the same pressure by calling DB Blitz. Mix in a few max coverage defenses and you have yourself a sound defensive attack.

We are focusing on attacking the defense at three points with this setup

Focus not on a specific play but rather on a specific set of route combinations. As an offense we can't be 100 percent sure if the defense is playing man-to-man or zone coverage. So we prepare for both by picking a play that has specific routes to attack both coverages. We scan our playbook to find an angle out of the backfield and a flat route. We want to attack the defense vertically if it is zone coverage because we know the defense only has two defenders deep. We also know that if it is man-to-man coverage we will have our HB matched up one-on-one on a slower linebacker over the middle of the field. Another read we have is the flat route—against zone coverage look to the flat as your first read and see if the zone defender is pulled back from the deep receiver's route. If there is space fire the ball in for a first down. If not, hang in the pocket and look to your vertical flood to the right of the field.

The flat was covered so we look to go deep

Notice that downfield the safety is stuck between a rock and a hard place. We have two receivers deep and there is only one defender. The safety can't guard both receivers—we deliver the ball to the inside receiver.

We celebrate in the end zone

Our QB had the matchup he was looking for and delivered a perfect ball, which resulted in a score. Be careful with this play because we have no pass protection, so you need to be precise with when you get the ball out to the receivers.

Dime Normal—DB Blitz

The defense switched up its coverage this time and is now playing man-to-man. We use the same setup as before and stick to the same reads. If the flat is covered and it's man-to-man, check down to the HB over the middle of the field.

Our HB begins making his cut over the middle of the field

The slower linebacker is no match for our HB. We get the ball just as he breaks away from the linebacker and look to head upfield.

First down!

We complete the pass over the middle of the field and have rendered this defense useless. The defense had better find another way to get pressure!

3-4 Over—Sting Pinch Zone

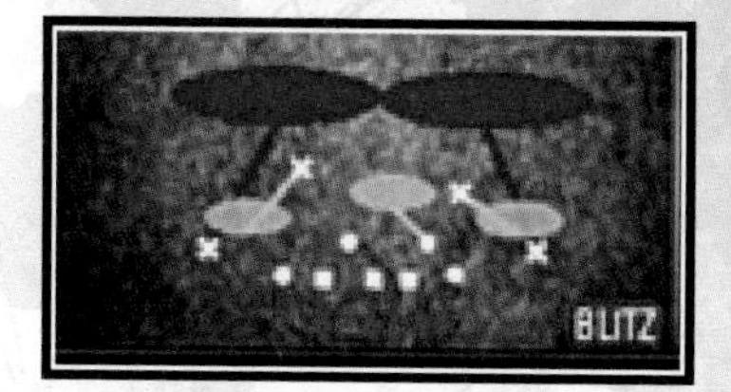

3-4 Over—Sting Pinch Zone

The 3-4 Over—Sting Pinch Zone came onto the *Madden* community scene strong during the *Madden NFL 10* season. It took the community by storm because of its fast setup and inverted Cover 2 look. The underneath hook zones also are some of the best in the game. They play the flat extremely well and also get enough depth to defend balls over the deep middle. All around, this defense is arguably one of the most reliable in the game. Pressure will come from the outside but can also come through the A gap. This defense can often seem like the entire field is covered.

Four Verticals

Attacking the 3-4 Over—Sting Pinch Zone is all about looking to hit the defense deep. Any vertical concept will work here, but we specifically like using Four Verticals as our play of choice. You will find Four Verticals in many different formations and playbooks in *Madden NFL 12*. The underneath hook zones do such a great job defending underneath we like taking our chances deep. We keep the HB in to block for extra pass protection and wait for our routes to open up downfield.

The pressure is picked up

The hook zones do an amazing job of dropping back and defending the vertical routes but we need to wait a bit longer for them to clear space. Once this happens we will have four receivers against two defenders deep. Find the open receiver and deliver the pass!

We coast into the end zone for the easy score

Our receiver was wide open in the end zone and we completed the pass for the touchdown. If possible, stay away from attacking the underneath zones of the Sting Pinch Zone. Call out your pass protection and sit in the pocket for your deep routes to develop!

Over the course of the *Madden NFL 12* season you will run into many different variations of these defenses, and you will also run into completely different defenses overall. However, let this section build the foundation for the mind-set you need to have to combat what the more popular trends will be this year.

IMPORTANT RATINGS—FINDING OFFENSIVE MADDEN GEMS

One of the most asked questions is, "How do we find 'Madden Gems'?" Oftentimes the only rating that people look at is the overall rating. It can't be assumed that just because someone has a high overall rating that he is one of the best, just as it can't be assumed that a low overall rating means he is one of the worst. Each position in the game has specific ratings that make those players either stand out in the crowd or get blown away with the wind. Following this formula will help you to unlock the true power of your team's roster and allow you to find the next Madden Gem that everyone will be talking about! Here we showcase the four most important position-specific ratings to look for in *Madden NFL 12*.

Quarterbacks

- Short Throw Accuracy: 88+
- Deep Throw Accuracy: 80+
- Speed: 70+
- Medium Throw Accuracy: 88+

Every QB in the game needs to be able to throw a 5-yard out with precision. Short throw accuracy is the most important rating that a QB can have in *Madden NFL 12*. If your QB can't make this throw, good luck. The next most important rating is our QB's ability to attack downfield with deep throw accuracy. After short throws most passes we will be throwing are deep downfield.

We ranked speed as being the third most important rating for a QB because having extra speed adds an element to your game plan that defenses typically don't plan for. The last rating is our QB's medium throw accuracy, because most of the routes in the game will fall into either the short throw category or deep throw category.

Halfbacks

- Speed: 94+
- Acceleration: 95+
- Agility: 95+
- Trucking/Elusiveness: 92+

The single most important aspect to a halfback's game is his speed rating. Without speed HBs can't get to the edge and stretch the defense. Speed determines if your HB can make the big play or settle for a short gain. After speed comes acceleration and agility. These two ratings help HBs get to top speed and then cut on a dime as they pass through running lanes. Trucking or elusiveness helps HBs finish out plays by either running defenders over or slipping past them.

Wide Receivers

- Speed: 92+
- Height: 6'3"+
- Catch in Traffic: 88+
- Route Running: 90+

The perfect combination for a receiver in *Madden NFL 12* is to be 6'4" with 95+ speed. Unfortunately, not many fall into this category. Speed helps stretch defenses out while height helps to slow games down and play a possession-style game. To hold onto catches WRs need to have a high catch in traffic rating so that when they take the big hit they come down with the ball. Route running is great for routes that have sharp cuts such as ins and outs. WRs with good route running run crisp routes, which help them get more separation. Auto-motion plays typically work well for good route runners.

Tight Ends

- Height: 6'4"+
- Speed: 80+
- Catch in Traffic: 88+
- Impact Block: 60+

TEs play an interesting role in game plans. Some players use them as pure run blockers while others use them as receiving threats. Shorter teams in the NFL usually have a few TEs that have good height, which helps to create mismatches downfield in the passing game. Height is the single most important stat for a TE. Speed is a luxury for TEs—if you have a TE with some speed consider that a gift and find a way to get him on the field. TEs typically run their routes over the middle of the field, so they need to hold onto the ball, and thus their catch in traffic rating needs to be high. The last rating we look at is impact block. We care about the bone-crushing block that we get every now and then from our TE. A TE will never be as good as an offensive lineman, but if we have one with a good impact block rating he can seal off a few edges during the game, and that can make a huge difference in the outcome.

Search for these ratings for each position and be sure to look at not only your team's roster but your opponent's roster. Know who the *Madden* playmakers are. Find your own Madden Gem and get him in the lineup however you can. Knowing the most important ratings is all about maximizing your team to its fullest potential. You will never overlook that WR with a 62 overall rating again—because he's 6'6", has a 97 jump rating, and has an 85 catch in traffic score. Put me in, coach—I'm ready to play!

Top 10 Players by Position: Offense

Now that you know the important ratings in *Madden NFL 12* and what to look for, let's look at the top 10 players for each position and then show you *our* top 10 for each position. For the most part the lists are the same, but you will see a few Madden Gems in each category climb to the top!

Madden NFL 12 Top 10 QBs

- Tom Brady
- Aaron Rodgers
- Peyton Manning
- Philip Rivers
- Drew Brees
- Ben Roethlisberger
- Michael Vick
- Matt Ryan
- Joe Flacco
- Matt Schaub

Our Top 10 QBs

- Michael Vick
- Aaron Rodgers
- Tom Brady
- Philip Rivers
- Peyton Manning
- Drew Brees
- Cam Newton
- Ben Roethlisberger
- Josh Freeman
- Tony Romo

Madden NFL 12 Top 10 HBs

- Adrian Peterson
- Chris Johnson
- Jamaal Charles
- Maurice Jones-Drew
- Steven Jackson
- Michael Turner
- Ray Rice
- Arian Foster
- Peyton Hillis
- Frank Gore

Our Top 10 HBs

- Jamaal Charles
- Chris Johnson
- Adrian Peterson
- Darren McFadden
- Peyton Hillis
- Michael Turner
- Reggie Bush
- Maurice Jones-Drew
- Jahvid Best
- Danny Woodhead

Madden NFL 12 Top 10 WRs

- Andrew Johnson
- Roddy White
- Larry Fitzgerald
- Reggie Wayne
- Calvin Johnson Jr.
- Greg Jennings
- Brandon Marshall
- DeSean Jackson
- Dwayne Bowe
- Wes Welker

Our Top 10 WRs

- Andre Johnson
- Calvin Johnson Jr.
- DeSean Jackson
- Brandon Marshall
- Larry Fitzgerald
- Roddy White
- Marques Colston
- Devin Hester
- Mike Wallace
- Ramses Barden

Madden NFL 12 Top 10 TEs

- Antonio Gates
- Dallas Clark
- Jason Witten
- Tony Gonzalez
- Vernon Davis
- Jermichael Finley
- Marcedes Lewis
- Zach Miller
- Kellen Winslow
- Chris Cooley

Our Top 10 TEs

- Antonio Gates
- Jason Witten
- Zach Miller
- Marcedes Lewis
- Dallas Clark
- Vernon Davis
- Jermichael Finley
- Tony Gonzalez
- Greg Olsen
- Jimmy Graham

What are your thoughts on our top 10? What's your top 10? What do you value the most? These should be some questions to ask yourself as you create your own top 10 list for *Madden NFL 12*.

DEFENSIVE FORMATIONS

Defense wins championships, and without it don't expect to win many games in *Madden NFL 12*. In this section of the guide we showcase the defensive formations in the game. Learning how to play defense starts with understanding what each formation does and what its strengths and weaknesses are.

3-4 Defense

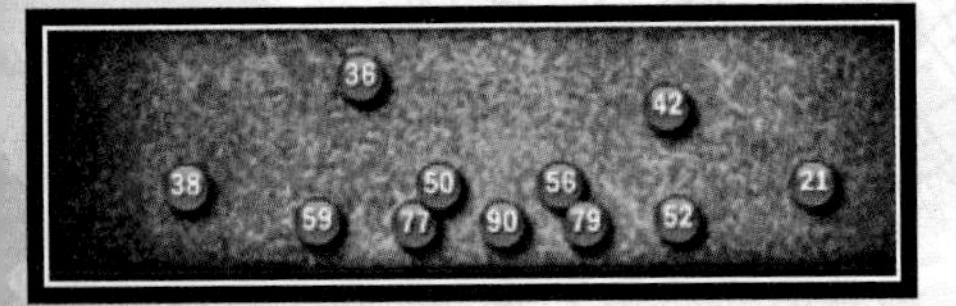

The 3-4 formation calls for three down defensive linemen and four linebackers with the remaining four defenders as defensive backs. The 3-4 has caught the NFL by storm in recent years thanks to the success of teams like the Pittsburgh Steelers and the New England Patriots. The idea is to remove a slower defensive lineman and replace him with a faster linebacker to aid in pass coverage. The 3-4 looks to get pressure off the edge with blitzing linebackers and also have those same linebackers drop back into coverage for passing situations. The 3-4 is a great all-around defense for either passing or running situations.

4-3 Defense

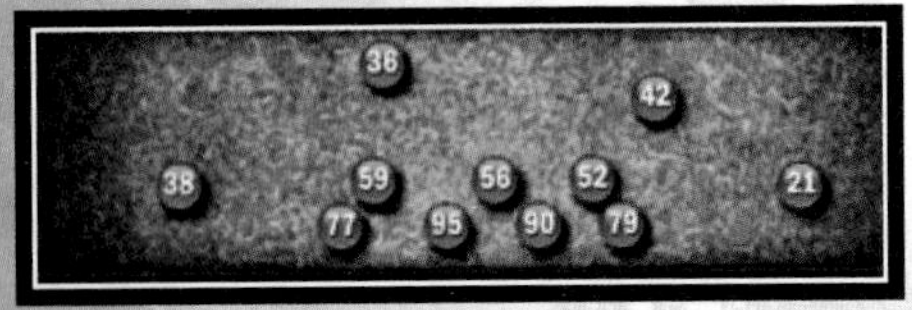

The 4-3 formation calls for four defensive linemen and three linebackers with the remaining four defenders as defensive backs. The 4-3 is one of the most used formations in the NFL as it has seven big bodies to help stop the run. The 4-3 can struggle in passing situations because there is not a lot of speed on the field for coverage. The 4-3 should be used as your run-stopping formation in many instances, so look to package all your big players in for the 4-3.

46 Defense

The 46 formation calls for four defensive linemen and three linebackers with the remaining four defenders as defensive backs. The 46 is identical to the 4-3 formation but calls for the deep strong safety to play up in the box, creating an eight-man defensive front. This not only adds run support but also helps to disguise pressure. This defense was made famous by the Chicago Bears in the mid-'80s. Look to use the speed package from this formation; it substitutes two defensive backs for two linebackers. This helps to add more speed on the field for blitzing and coverage purposes. This is hands down one of the most effective formations to use in *Madden NFL 12*.

5-2 Defense

The 5-2 formation calls for five defensive linemen and two linebackers with the remaining four defenders as defensive backs. The 5-2 is very similar to the 3-4 formation but calls for two extra defensive linemen to replace the outside linebackers of the 3-4. The 5-2 formation can generate great pressure because each defender is in a one-on-one battle with the offensive lineman in front of him. Beat your man and you are getting to the quarterback. This formation in man-to-man coverage will typically rush all five defensive linemen, leaving only one defender in deep coverage. If you need to stop the run in late-game situations call upon the 5-2.

Nickel Defense

The Nickel formation calls for four defensive linemen and two linebackers with the remaining five defenders as defensive backs. The Nickel defense is the most versatile formation in the game. It can be used to stop the run and pass and has enough speed to blitz or play effective coverage. The Nickel is our favorite; it is the ultimate formation in *Madden NFL 12*.

Dime Defense

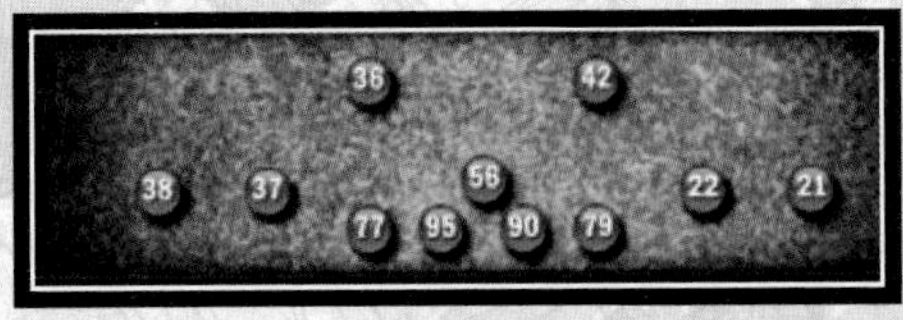

The Dime formation calls for four defensive linemen and one linebacker with the remaining six defenders as defensive backs. You should call upon the Dime when your opponent is in passing situations. The extra speed on the field helps to slow down pass-heavy offenses. The Dime defense is also great at bringing pressure off the edge; many blitzes from this formation come off the outside edges.

Quarter Defense

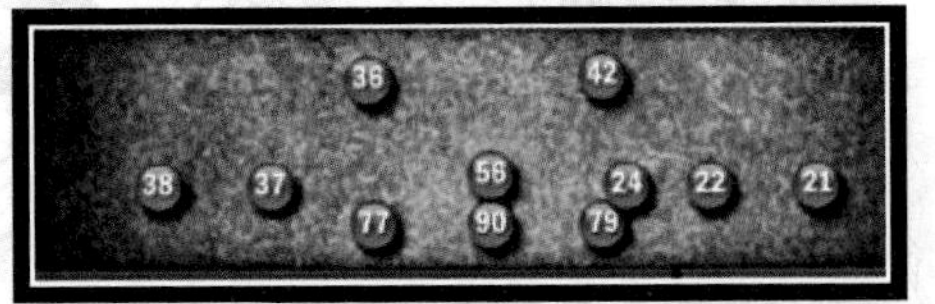

The Quarter formation calls for three defensive linemen and one linebacker with the remaining seven defenders as defensive backs. The Quarter formation is absolute lockdown defense for passing situations. This is how you get the most speed possible on the field to shut down all-out passing offensives. One issue with the Quarter formation is that most teams don't have seven good defensive backs. Make sure your team has the talent and depth to use this formation. Quarters has emerged as a *Madden* community favorite over the years.

RUN DEFENSE GAP ASSIGNMENTS

Madden NFL 12 has three different gap assignments based on formation: The 3-4, 4-3, and 5-2 each force different responsibilities on defenders. It is essential to learn your base front's gap assignments to play run defense in *Madden NFL 12*. Learning your defender's gap assignments will help your user control in the run game because you will always know where to go on the field. Many times gamers will grab hold of a defensive player and run him around the field, taking him out of position and hurting the team's overall defense. In this section we show what the responsibilities are and how they change for each formation.

Three-Man Front

The 3-4 formation is a three-man front

With the 3-4 formation the defensive tackle is responsible for the A gaps while the defensive ends are responsible for the offensive tackles. The outside linebackers cover the outside C gaps while the inside linebackers are in control of the B gaps.

All our players are filling in the correct gaps

Notice that the center has control of the A gap and our defensive ends are in control of the offensive tackles. Our inside linebackers are in position to close in on the B gaps.

When controlling any of these defenders be sure you stick to these gaps when in a three-man front. This will help your defense get more stops over the course of the year.

Four-Man Front

The 4-3 formation is a four-man front

The defensive ends in a four-man front are responsible for the outside C gaps. The weak-side defensive tackle is in charge of the weak-side A gap. The strong-side defensive tackle will take control of the inside B gap. The outside linebackers need to attack the outside B gaps, and the middle linebacker will go after the strong-side A gap.

Once again our defense is in perfect position

Our defenders have stuck to their gap responsibilities up and down the line of scrimmage. It's not always about being a hero and making a big play—sometimes it's all about knowing your role and executing.

Five-Man Front

The 5-2 formation is a five-man front

The 5-2 formation calls for the defensive ends to control the outside C gaps. The interior defensive tackles are responsible for the B gaps (the strong-side DT should control the outside B gap). The defensive tackle over the center is responsible for the strong-side A gap. The weak-side linebacker will cover the weak-side A gap and the strong-side linebacker will hold the inside B gap.

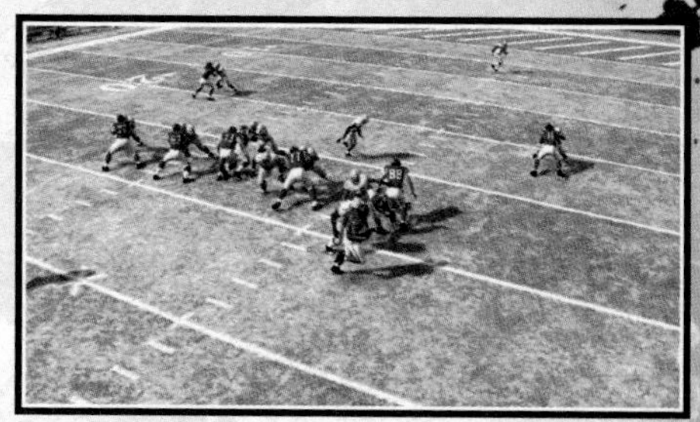

The HB is taken down for a loss

The HB tried to break the run outside, but because our defenders stuck with their responsibilities they were in position to make a play. The strong-side DT broke free from his outside B gap and made a play on the ball carrier.

Defensive fronts can change depending on how you manually position defenders and shift your defensive line. This section is all about an understanding of what you should be looking for when facing the run. Learn your gap assignments and stick to them to crush your opponent's rushing attack!

DEFENDING THE SHORT PASS

Top-level players online look to find as many short passing options as possible. The longer a QB holds onto the ball the greater the chance for mishaps and bad decisions. That is why short passes are vital to the success of most *Madden* offenses. Some of the most popular routes you will come across are quick passes out of the backfield, screens, drags, slants, and crossing patterns. With this section we slow the game down for you and show you how we like to adjust on the fly to stop the most effective passing routes in the game.

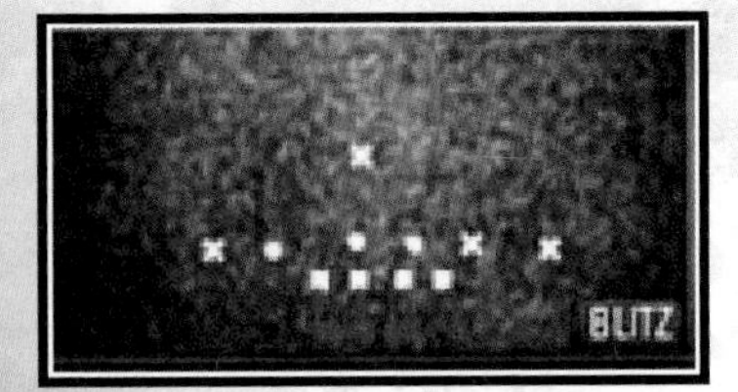

46 Normal—Inside Blitz (Speed Package)

The defensive play we use for every breakdown in this section is the 46 Normal—Inside Blitz. We used the speed package to get more speed on the field. Using just one play we will show you that with the right adjustments you can stop anything in *Madden NFL 12*!

Defending the Quick Pass

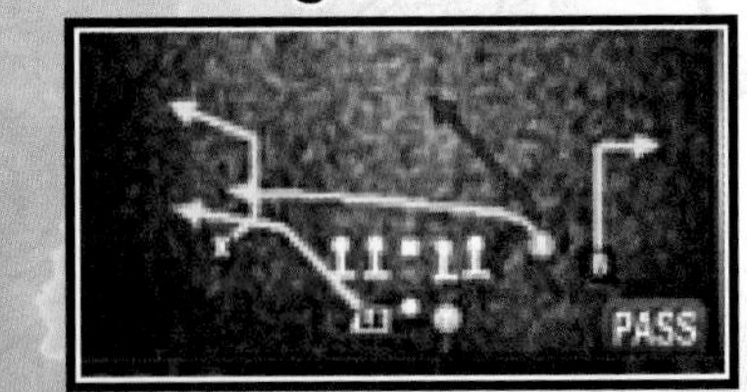

This play is designed to attack defenses at three different points near the line of scrimmage

Offenses love quick passes because they are highly efficient and are timing based. With enough practice players can be extremely confident in their quick passes no matter the situation.

The pass is completed for a first down and then some

Our defense is playing man-to-man and we tried bringing pressure, but the offense got the ball out to the HB before we could make a play on it.

We drop the right-of-screen DE into a hook zone

With a few adjustments we should be able to shut down the quick-pass options. We hot route our right-of-screen DE to a hook zone so that he will play the area where the FB will break out of the backfield. Then we hot route the left-of-screen DT to a QB spy. The QB spy does an excellent job of defending drag routes. Hook zones drop back too deep and don't play the same depth as drags, but the QB spy sits right at the drag route's depth. The last adjustment is to take the right-of-screen blitzing defender and user-control him in a deep zone. At the snap of the ball we break on the short pass and look to make a user play. If the QB doesn't throw to the quick pass we immediately drop into deep coverage.

There's no way the FB is catching this ball!

With the adjustments we made we had three defenders in the area of the quick pass. With this many defenders around the ball don't expect many completions.

Defending Screens

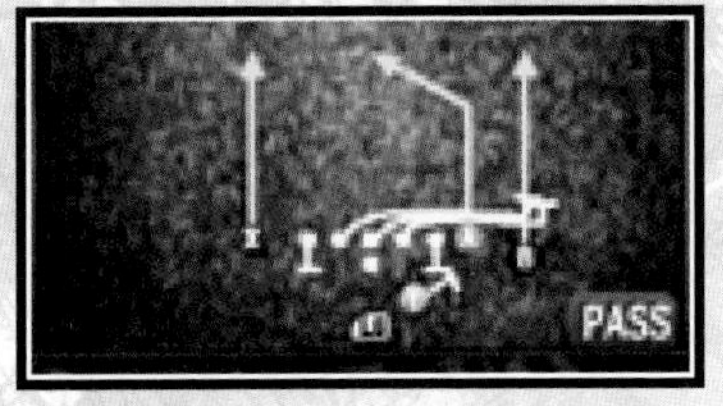

Strong Close—HB Slip Screen

Nothing screams instant offense more than screens. Screens do a great job of countering aggressive defenses. Called at the right time they can give fits to defenses. Most if not all players have a few screens mixed in with their offensive scheme.

The HB gets a few blocks and moves down the sideline

The HB breaks containment and gets down the sideline for a big gain. With a few adjustments we can get another defender in the area to congest the screen's blocking.

Hot route the screen-side DE into a flat zone

The adjustments we make are to drop the screen-side DE into a flat and then user-control the blitzing defender to the right of the field. If the offense calls a screen we sprint over to the screen, fighting through blockers and looking to make a play on the ball.

The HB is taken down for a loss

Notice our big defensive linemen just waiting to lay a hit stick on the HB. Our user-controlled player takes down the HB.

Defending Drags

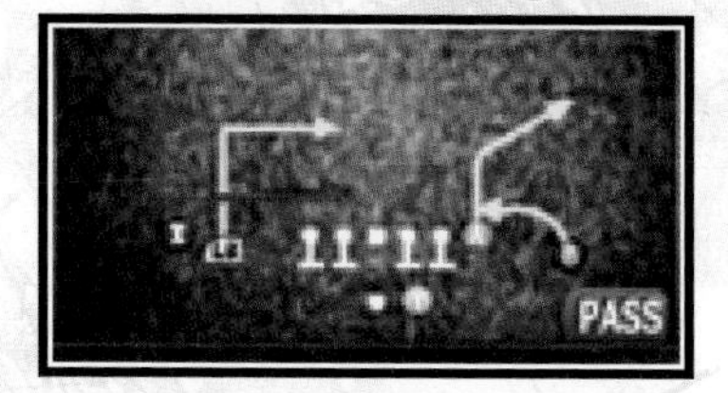

What's the best route in football? The drag route! It gets open against any defense and has the potential to spring off huge gains. Against man-to-man, speed helps create separation as the drag receiver runs across the field. In zone you need to find the holes and deliver the ball as the drag crosses through open space. The staple of a lot of offenses is the drag route. Let's look at how we stop it cold in its tracks!

The WR gets inside position and cuts upfield after the catch

Here the WR turns the drag upfield and gets tons of yards after the catch. The biggest threat of the drag is the individual WR's ability to turn nothing into something.

Pressure will come off the right edge

Here we hot route our left-of-screen DT to a QB contain to prevent the QB from rolling away from pressure. We set up the play by taking our blitzing defender on the right of the screen and stacking him in the right B gap. This will bring pressure off the right edge. The last adjustment is dropping the left-of-screen DE into a QB spy. The goal with this play is to make the QB roll away from his throwing side and throw into coverage.

Interception!

Just as we wrote it up! The QB was forced away from his throwing side and threw into coverage. This resulted in our spy defender making the interception. It is important to know that a QB spy only slows down drag routes; once the drag clears past the spy the QB can deliver the ball.

Defending Slants

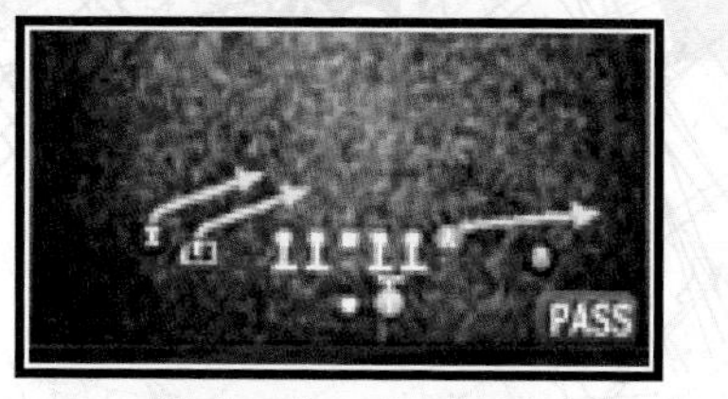

Shotgun Normal—Slants

The slant is very similar to a drag route. They both run shallow underneath routes, but the slant route gets deeper downfield as the route develops. This creates different throwing lanes for QBs and also stretches defenses a bit farther downfield. Bigger WRs are great for slants as they tend to break off bump-n-run coverage and also are bigger targets for QBs once they get inside position on the defender.

The WR hauls in the pass for the easy gain

For the slant route we drop a defensive lineman into a hook zone to defend against it. Hook zones will sit right in the path of the oncoming slant. Slant routes are also easier to user-defend because we can get into better position to make a play on the ball because of the angle the route takes.

Pressure once again comes off the right edge

We use the same setup as we did defending the drag route but this time drop the left-of-screen DE into a hook zone rather than a QB spy. The QB spy wouldn't drop deep enough to defend the slant but the hook zone will.

Another interception!

The extra defender in the area messed up the timing of the WR and QB. It resulted in an interception and a headache for your opponent!

Defending Crossing Patterns

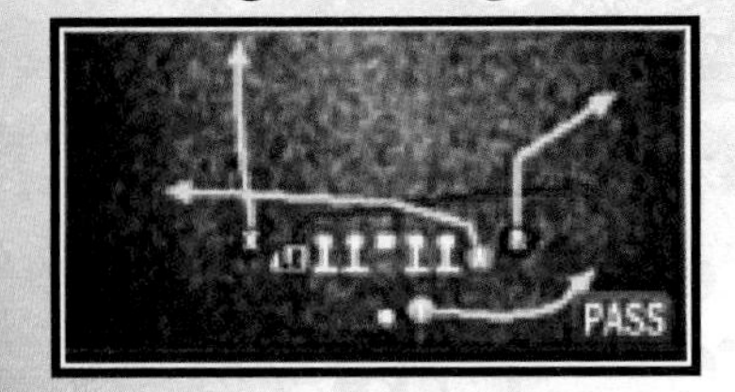

Gun Snugs Flipped—Mesh

Mesh is one of the most popular plays in the game. It is set up to beat both man-to-man and zone coverage. It is also very effective against any blitz. The crossing patterns over the middle of the field make this play tick by destroying man-to-man coverage. The deep streak attacks zone coverage and Cover 0. The corner route and flat route create a nice high-low passing concept to attack zone coverage.

The QB reads which crossing pattern receiver has a step on his defender

The open receiver with the crossing patterns will be different nearly every play. It is very difficult to user-defend because you have to guess which WR will get the pass.

The speed of the WR results in a touchdown

The danger of the crossing pattern is if a speed WR turns upfield and gets into open field. Here the WR turned his step on the defender into a touchdown.

Our defense is set up to shut down the crossing patterns!

Rather than send pressure we decided to play a more max coverage approach. We drop our left-of-screen DE into a QB spy. Then we hot route the left-of-screen DT into a buzz zone and also drop our blitzing defender to the right of the field on a buzz zone. The left blitzing defender we user-control in a deep zone.

The QB has to wait for the crossing patterns to clear the QB spy

The QB has an earlier read on the crossing patterns but needed to wait for the routes to cross past the QB spy. The WR running to the left of the field looks to be open, but our buzz zone is in position to make a play on the ball.

The WR is taken down for no gain!

This time the WR couldn't turn the ball upfield. Our extra defender in the area slowed down his progress and we stopped him for no gain.

Mix and match the different combinations to stop short passing schemes. We used one formation and one play to show you that with a few minor adjustments you can defend just about everything offenses can do to you. Try your own formation and implement these adjustments to other formations to leave your opponents scratching their heads!

DEFENDING THE LONG PASS

There is no better way to score a lot of points in a hurry than to attack defenses vertically. You don't always run into offensive schemes that are focused around the deep ball, but when you do they can often be devastating. Mixing in deep vertical routes with quick and short passes underneath can spell disaster for defenses. Deep routes that you can expect to see are streaks, posts, and deep corners. In this section we show you that sending pressure is your best friend when facing a vertical threat and how to best position your defense to defend whatever deep ball you are going against.

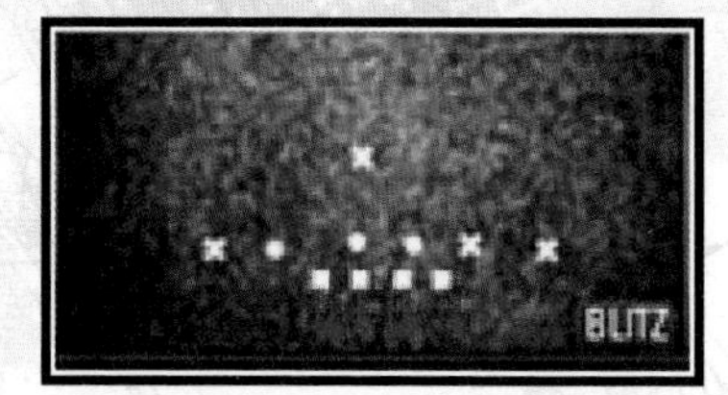

46 Normal—Inside Blitz (Speed Package)

We again use the 46 Normal—Inside Blitz (speed package) as our only play for this section.

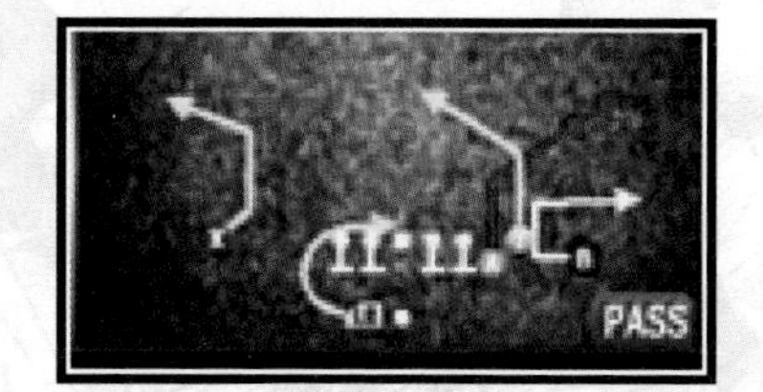

Gun Flip Trips—Deep Fork

Offensively, the Gun Flip Trips has every deep vertical route that you can expect to face in *Madden NFL 12*: A deep streak (a hot route to the far left WR), a deep post, and a deep corner. For this section we use only this offensive play.

Defending the Deep Streak

The offense hot routes the far left WR on a deep streak

The offense is looking to attack us with their isolated WR to the left of the field. This creates a few problems for deep safeties. The right side of the field is flooded with receivers, so as a defense we are more aware of this side of the field. We need to make sure we don't lose sight of the isolated WR.

Pressure is coming!

Our pressure from the Inside Blitz is closing in on the QB. However, notice that the isolated WR is matched up one-on-one down the sideline.

The receiver makes the catch

The bigger receiver won the one-on-one matchup, and it's a huge gain for the offense. We need to adjust to what the offense is doing and make sure we defend the sideline streak.

Our adjustment is to drop a deep zone towards the sideline

We drop our weak-side blitzing defender into a deep zone and shade safety coverage to the left of the field. Now our deep zone will drop back to the sideline at the snap of the ball. Pressure will come flying off the right edge, forcing the QB to make an early throw into coverage.

Interception!

Our adjustment pays off as we get the turnover with the interception. The simplest adjustment can make all the difference in the world. If your opponents key in on the sideline deep ball, make this type of adjustment and shut them down!

Defending the Deep Corner

The offense focuses on the deep corner route

This time around the offense is keying in on the deep corner route. Once again our pressure is good but our coverage in the secondary is weak.

The WR snags the ball out of the air for the big gain

The separation the WR got was minimal but was just enough for one-on-one coverage. To stop this play we again hot route one of our defenders deep. Having the extra defender typically forces QBs to wait an extra second before throwing the ball, which can allow our pressure to get to him.

We drop our strong-side DE into a deep zone

To defend the deep corner we drop our DE into a deep zone and shade coverage towards the right sideline. Dropping defensive linemen deep into coverage can seem foolish, but because their speed is usually slow they will trail plays and be in position underneath while our main coverage will be step-for-step with the receiver. The underneath coverage is good for knocking balls loose with big hits and for batting down balls that are thrown too low.

Incomplete pass!

There is no way the WR is coming down with this ball. Two defenders right in his face plus an under-thrown ball equals incomplete pass for the offense.

Defending the Deep Post

Pressure is coming!

Our pressure for the third time is closing in on the QB. However, he gets the ball off just before the defender takes him down.

The QB drops the pass in for a big gain

Our defensive secondary is good but not good enough to defend WRs this far downfield. The pressure was good but we need to adjust and drop a defender deep to defend against the post.

We drop the weak-side blitzer deep over the middle of the field

This time we drop the weak-side blitzer over the deep middle but we don't shade coverage. We leave the deep coverage over the middle so that the defender will help with the deep post.

I-N-T-E-R-C-E-P-T-I-O-N

That spells interception! The adjustment we made was simple but effective. The pressure was still good and we added the extra touch to our deep coverage to lock down the offense.

It's important to send pressure against the offense when they are looking to attack you vertically. We sent at least five defenders after the QB on all the plays; that is a good chunk of our defense to go after the QB. We adjusted to how the offense was attacking us and responded with huge plays in the secondary. Pressure the QB and you won't have to worry about the deep ball!

ADVANCED BLITZING

Blitzing, blitzing, and more blitzing. This is the section I'm sure a lot of you turned to right away. Without a doubt the biggest question every year is "How can I generate pressure on the QB?" In this section we showcase our favorite blitzes using the 46 Normal—Inside Blitz (speed package). At this point I'm sure you are noticing a recurring theme: We use the 46 Normal—Inside Blitz a lot! That is indeed fact, not opinion, but we are constantly evolving the way we run it so that it never truly is the same play twice. We show you six different blitzes from this one play, and the blitzes you see here will work with Cover 3 zone, Cover 2 zone, and Cover 4 zone from this formation. If you do the math that equals 24 blitzes at your fingertips. This is only from one formation—the same ideas and concepts will carry from formation to formation.

The goal with any blitz is to "plus-one" the offensive line. That means always having a one-man advantage at a given area of the offensive line so that we can squeeze one pass rusher through untouched towards the QB. For example, if we run the 46 Normal—Inside Blitz against a shotgun five-wide set we know a few things right away. The offensive line has five players and we are sending six after the QB. This is a plus-one scenario because we are sending one more defender than the offense can block. To take this a step farther we like to break the offensive line into segments: Anything to the left of the center is considered the one gap, and anything to the right of the center is considered the two gap. Our goal as a defense is to try to occupy the center and then attack either the one gap or the two gap with a plus-one blitz. If we do this we force the weak side of the offensive line to sprint back and recover to help in pass protection. This is asking a lot from 300-pound men.

46 Normal—Inside Blitz (Speed Package)

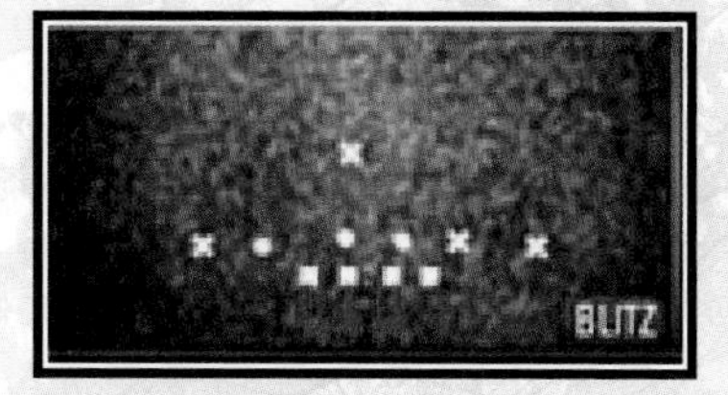

46 Normal—Inside Blitz (Speed Package)

This play calls for six players rushing the QB with five defenders in man-to-man coverage. The pressure with this play is quick and it's intense. However, without adjustments and deception it can be beaten.

Setup #1

Our first setup

- Reblitz the right-of-screen DE.
- Reblitz the right-of-screen LB and stack him in the B gap.
- QB contain the left-of-screen DT.
- QB spy the left-of-screen DE.
- Hot route the MLB into a deep zone.
- User-control the deep safety who is covering the HB.

The pressure is coming through the right B gap

The offensive line to the left is paying attention to the contain while the pressure sneaks in off the right edge. We have a three-vs.-two scenario here as we send three rushers against one guard and one tackle. Someone is coming in untouched!

Incomplete pass

The pass falls incomplete as the QB has to hurry the throw. The ball actually bounced off the HB's helmet because he hadn't even turned around on his route yet. The pressure was so intense the QB had nowhere to go with the ball.

Setup #2

Our second setup

- Reblitz the right-of-screen LB and stack him in the left-of-screen B gap.
- Reblitz the MLB and stack him in the left-of-screen B gap.
- Reblitz the left-of-screen DE.
- Hot route the right-of-screen DT to a QB spy.
- User-control the deep safety covering the HB.

Pressure is coming in off the left edge

The pressure is quick and the offensive line can't pick it up here! Notice the plus-one scenario once again as we send four pass rushers to the offensive line's three blockers.

Sack!

Not much the QB can do here. His hot read was taken away over the middle of the field because the QB spy stepped in nicely to force the QB to hold the ball a bit longer than he wanted. The beauty of this play is that if the offense slide protects, our weak-side DE will sneak in off the back edge untouched!

The offensive line slide protects left

The offense picks up the pressure but forgot about our weak-side pass rusher. He has a clear path to the QB.

Almost another sack

The QB got rid of the ball just in time and the half-attempted pass falls incomplete. This play setup is awesome because the offense can't slide protect to pick up the pressure. They will need to use delayed routes or a swing receiver to pick up the pressure.

Setup #3

Our third setup

- Spread the defensive line out.
- Reblitz the entire defensive line.
- Reblitz the MLB and stack him in the left-of-screen B gap.
- Place the right-of-screen LB in the right-of-screen B gap and hot route him on a deep zone.
- User-control the deep safety covering the HB.

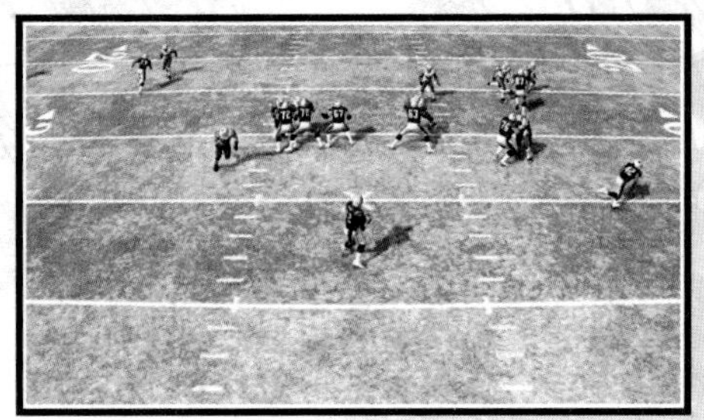

Pressure off the left edge!

Pressure looked like it could have come from either C gap. The offense will have a difficult time figuring out where pressure is coming from as long as you keep a balanced look on defense.

A big hit on the QB

The pressure gets to the QB, and once again the plus-one blitzing method works to perfection. The offense doesn't know where to call out pass protection, so it's making it difficult to pick up any pressure.

Setup #4

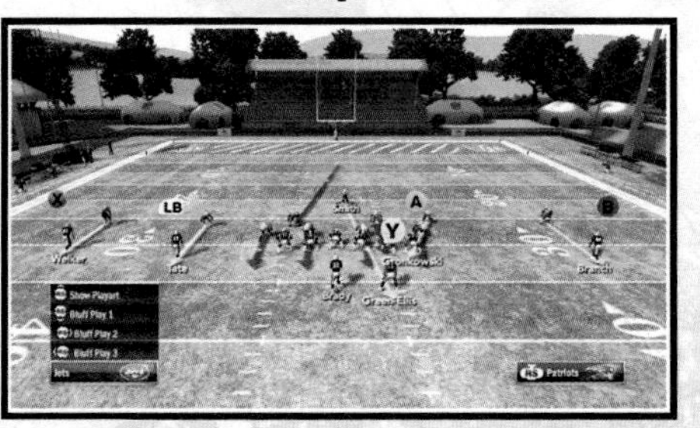

Our fourth setup

- Spread the defensive line out.
- Reblitz the entire defensive line.
- Reblitz the right-of-screen LB and stack him in the right-of-screen B gap.
- Place the MLB in the left-of-screen B gap and hot route him to a deep zone.
- User-control the deep safety covering the HB.

Pressure right!

This time we attempt to trick the offense by making the setup look like #3 but bringing pressure from the right of the field. Remember; we are focusing on deception with our blitzing.

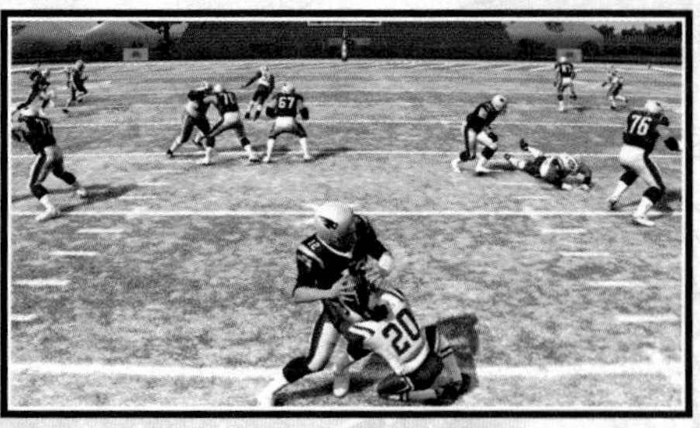

The QB goes down

The QB was no match for the speed of the blitz. It got to him in a hurry and he was forced to live to fight another day.

Setup #5

Our fifth setup

- Spread the defensive line out.
- Reblitz the entire defensive line.
- Reblitz the right-of-screen LB and stack him in the right-of-screen B gap.
- Reblitz the MLB and stack him in the left-of-screen B gap.
- User-control the deep safety covering the HB.

The center doesn't know what to do

Notice that the center is confused by this pressure. We have two guys running free off both edges. The QB is about to get swallowed by the defense.

The QB has no chance

The QB was a sitting duck. He had no one to throw to and nowhere to run. All he could do was sit there and let the sack happen!

Setup #6

Our sixth setup

- Spread the defensive line out.
- Reblitz every defensive lineman.
- Place the MLB in a deep zone and stack him in the left-of-screen B gap.
- User-blitz the right-of-screen LB in the right-of-screen B gap.

Our user blitz is about to smash the QB

You will need to time the user blitz, so make sure you work on this in practice mode. At the snap of the ball fire through the B gap and get after the QB. The offensive line doesn't pay as much attention to you as you pass through the open lane.

We sack the QB for the big loss

Make sure you mix in zone coverage with these blitzes, and remember that every setup will work with the Cover 3, Cover 2, and Cover 4 zones from the 46 Normal formation. The blitzes here will help to smash the competition into submission and help you get more wins throughout the season!

ADVANCED MAX COVERAGE DEFENSE

Max coverage defense is any time a defense drops back nine or more defenders into coverage. The goal with max coverage defense is to play bend-but-don't-break defense. However, we feel that if you mix in coverage defense with blitzing packages correctly then your defense will be a force to reckon with in *Madden NFL 12*. In most cases max coverage defenses come from a Cover 4 zone.

3-4 Over—Drop Zone

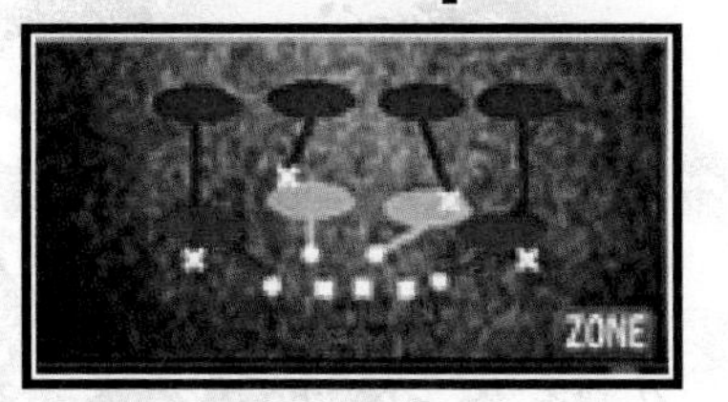

3-4 Over—Drop Zone

Here we have a standard Cover 4 zone with three pass rushers and eight defenders in coverage. We make a few minor tweaks to make this defense the ultimate coverage defense. Cover 4 zone without adjustments can be difficult to beat; add in the adjustments we make and it's lights-out coverage defense!

Setup

We create a Cover 5 zone

- Hot route the right MLB to a deep zone.
- Shade the safeties out.
- Pinch the defensive line.
- Place both DEs on QB spy.
- User-control the left MLB in coverage.

We only rush one player after the QB

The field is covered with defenders at the snap of the ball. This look can startle a lot of players because the field is literally covered everywhere. The goal with this defense is to force your opponent to either scramble with the QB, call HB Draws, or force throws into coverage. QBs scrambling is a good thing because we can either injure them or make them fumble—most QBs aren't accustomed to running with the football. HB Draws leave the HB wide open for crushing hit sticks, and throwing into coverage means interception time for our secondary!

The ball is batted down in the end zone

We have four defenders in the area that have a chance to make a play on the ball. That is ridiculous coverage! Good luck finding passing lanes!

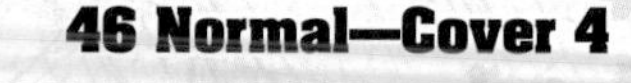

46 Normal—Cover 4

46 Normal—Cover 4

Here we have the 46 Normal—Cover 4 from the same formation as the Inside Blitz. This is a nice mix-up to use since your opponent will see a number of different blitzes from this formation. We make sure to set up the positioning of our max coverage defense to be identical to our blitzing packages. That makes it hard for offenses to read what we are doing pre-snap.

Setup

The field is covered

- Hot route both DEs to flat zones.
- Hot route the left-of-screen DT to a QB spy.
- Hot route both outside LBs to buzz zones.
- User-control the MLB.

Both these setups will cause fits for offenses when called at the right time. Look to use them in late-game situations when you have a lead. It really helps to slow the game down, and when time important this defense helps put stress on the offense. Use any variation of the Cover 4, create your own hot routes, and find out what your favorite max coverage defense is.

ADVANCED RUN DEFENSE

Dime Normal—All Out Blitz

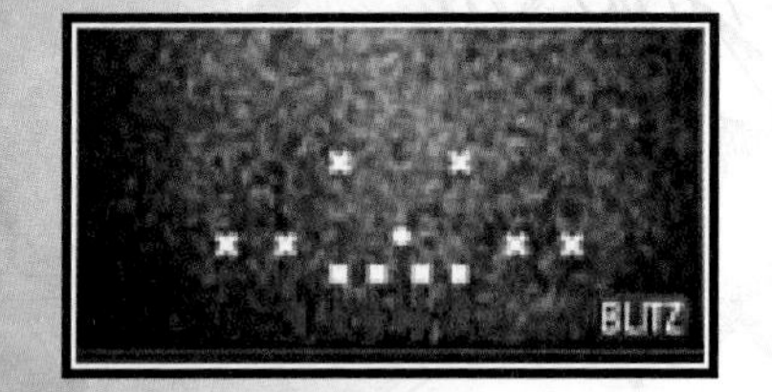

We all need a back-pocket run defense to bust out in late-game situations—a defense that we can use when we know we need a stop. The Dime Normal—All Out Blitz is that defense. Let's take a quick look at what the gap assignments are with this play.

Setup

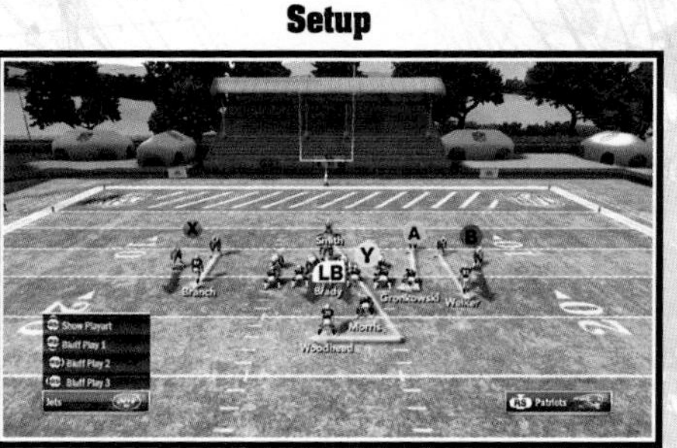

We make a few minor adjustments

- Pinch the defensive line.
- Stack the MLB between the two DTs.
- User-control the defender covering the HB.

If we take a look at this play we can see that the DEs are responsible for the outside B gaps (they need to control the tackles but look to drive inside to out) while the inside DTs need to control the inside B and outside A gaps. Our MLB is responsible for the inside A gaps. The wild cards with this defense are our two blitzing defensive backs. They are in control of the outside C gaps. The blitzing defensive backs make this play work; they control any run that has lateral movement while our user defender in the secondary is in charge of anything up and through the offensive line. This run defense is extremely aggressive but also extremely effective. It relies heavily on the ability of the cornerbacks and your user-controlled defender to make big-time plays in the open field. If you feel you are up for the challenge then give this defense a test spin and see how you like it.

The blitzing DBs are waiting outside

Our user defender is controlling the middle of the field while our defensive backs are waiting for the HB to cut outside.

Nowhere to go!

Our big DT makes the tackle. The HB had no running lanes open and had to cover up and lose a few yards on the play.

Can't go outside

The HB looks for running room outside but the door is closed!

Denied!

The HB tries his luck to the left and is once again stopped dead in his tracks.

This defense will get you big stops in the run game. However, you should be aware that every once in a while this defense gives up a big gain. The aggressive nature of this defense is begging for the big run. However, that's the name of the game—high risk equals high reward!

ADVANCED USER SKILLS

What are user skills? User skill is when a gamer manually controls an on-field player. Most *Madden NFL* gamers control defensive linemen, perhaps for one of these reasons: They never thought to control anyone else, they think the computer can do a better job of controlling their defensive secondary, or they are afraid of messing up the coverage by making mistakes. Well, now you know that you should control someone other than a defensive lineman, you know you can make better decisions and bigger plays than the computer can, and you know you have to fail hundreds of times before you succeed just once. Making the leap from controlling a defensive lineman to controlling a linebacker or safety is the single most important factor in elevating your game. In this section of the guide we will help you learn how to start user-defending with the best of the best!

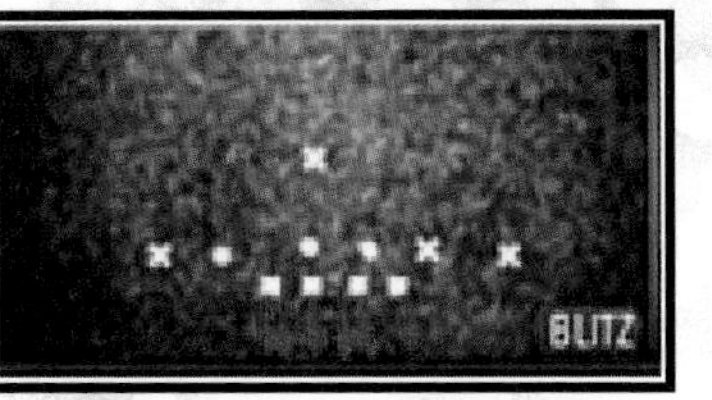

46 Normal—Inside Blitz

As with most of our breakdowns we will stick with our base play, the 46 Normal—Inside Blitz. We can make quick adjustments to play max coverage defense or bring major heat. This defense is extremely flexible, so for this section of the guide know that all the setups are being done from this play. We will also show a few zone breakdowns that are quick audibles from the 46 Normal formation.

Gaining a Extra Defender (Man-to-Man)

The HB delivers the block

Without making any adjustments we can increase the coverage of the 46 Normal—Inside Blitz. We do this by manually covering whomever the free safety is defending. Typically this is the HB. Going into this play we know a couple of things—we know that we are sending six pass rushers and we know that the offense only has five blockers. To stop the pressure the offense needs to block the HB in the backfield. We want to take advantage of this knowledge, so at the snap you need to quickly read if the HB is going out for a pass or if the HB is staying in to block. If the HB goes out for a pass then we will manually defend him on his route; if the HB stays in to block then we will drop back into coverage.

With this play we can see that the HB has been hot routed to stay in and block. We immediately key in on this and drop back into pass coverage.

Incomplete pass

The QB went for the out route towards the sideline. However, we read the play and got in position to make a play on the ball. We went for the swat and knocked the pass down for the incomplete pass. This strategy mimics gaining an extra defender on the field.

Gaining a Extra Defender (Zone)

Our deep safety is playing up in the box

To gain an extra defender while playing zone we look to use Cover 3 zone and stack the deep safety up into the box. The safety up in the box will mimic an extra short defender as he breaks towards the deep secondary. This is a very useful trick to help make our zone coverage have more defenders than there really are.

Our safety makes the tackle

The offense threw a short slant over the middle of the field and our safety was in position to take down the WR. If we had had him in the deep secondary this WR could have sprung the run upfield for more yards.

User Picks vs. User Swats

User Picks

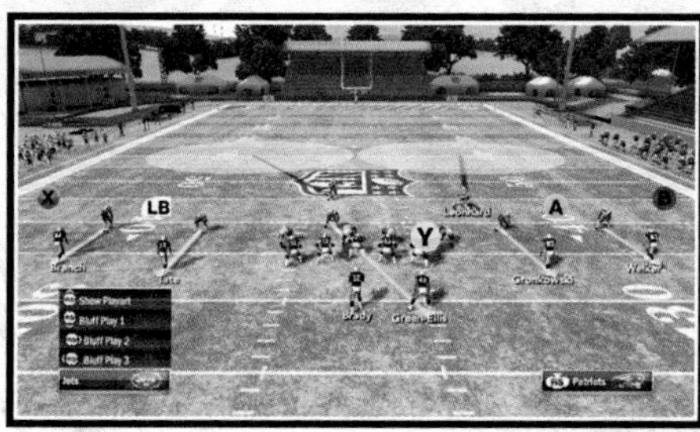

There is a very fine line between going for a user pick and going for a user swat. Gamers all around the country claim to have the best user skill. Often, user picks and user swats help define a player's game. Making a big user pick in a game can change the entire momentum. We will show you when to go for the user pick and when to go for the user swat.

We quick-audible to a 2 Man Under

At the snap of the ball we drop deep into coverage with the deep strong safety. We see the far right WR streaking down the sideline. The QB doesn't throw a quick pass, so we immediately begin to get into position over the top of the streaking WR.

We are in position for a user pick here

Notice that we are well ahead of the WR and that we have great depth to turn around and strafe for the user pick. As the ball is in the air, make sure to get to the back of the circle that appears on-screen. Once you are in position you need to press and hold the Strafe button while holding the Catch button down at the same time. As the ball approaches your defender will leap into the air for the user pick.

At the back of the circle and starting to strafe

Here we are moving towards the back of the circle and beginning our strafe.

Interception!

We come down with the ball and look to make a play in the return game. Only go for the user pick when you can get in position. This means that if you can't get to the back edge of the catch circle and strafe in time then you should go for the user swat instead.

User Swat

The user swat is less glamorous than the user pick. No one writes home to Mom about user swats. However, a saying we like to use is "User pick for show and user swat for dough." User picks are flashy and get all the attention, but many games are won because of good decision-making and user swats. If you go for a user pick and you aren't in position you can cost your team points and big plays. The user swat is almost guaranteed as long as you are somewhat near the WR.

At the snap of the ball we know right away that we are out of position to make a user pick. We don't have the depth that we need to get into position. As we break down the sideline we will be stride for stride with the WR.

We are only one step ahead of the WR

We can't get to the back edge of the circle so we look to user swat instead.

We knock down the pass

It was a good decision to go for the user swat. If we had missed on the user pick the offense would have likely scored a touchdown. The user pick is high-risk high-reward, while the user swat is low-risk but results in the defense living to fight another day.

Advanced Cover Skills

We have talked about moving the safety in a Cover 3 zone up in the box to mimic having an extra defender in the box. We can take this a step farther by user-controlling this defender in the box and then recovering deep to our designed coverage. This strategy is used by the best online competitors and for good reason. The computer will do a nice job dropping into coverage and will congest the middle of the field, but oftentimes it won't make the big play. By user-controlling the deep safety in the box and recovering deep we can prevent all sorts of options for the offense.

We will be able to help in run support, stop quick passes, jump hot routes, and also recover deep to defend the deep pass.

We are controlling the deep safety in the box

Our initial goal is to defend our opponents' favorite quick pass at the snap of the ball and then drop deep into coverage. We know they like to throw to the FB out of the backfield, so we creep into the box and show our opponents we are ready to make a play. At this point we are daring them to make this throw, and if they do we will be ready to make a big play.

We sit on the quick pass

We sit right where the quick pass will go and show our opponents we aren't afraid to make a big play! Either your opponents will test your user skills or they will shy away and look for another WR.

Now we have to recover deep

The QB made a great decision and decided not to try our user-pick skills. However, now we have to sprint back to defend the deep middle of the field.

User pick!

We get into position and make the user pick. On this play we defended the quick-pass option and then recovered deep and made the user pick. This alone is why user skill on defense is very important to your overall success in *Madden NFL 12*. With strong user skill we defended two passing options, which led to the turnover.

Don't be afraid to click on and make big plays!

ATTACKING THE ONLINE PLAYER: DEFENSE

Here we break down what we believe will be the most-used plays and styles of offenses you will come across in *Madden NFL 12*. The resurgence of Michael Vick took not only the NFL by storm but also the *Madden* community. Many offenses revolve around Vick being able to create plays with his legs as well as his rocket arm. We will break down how to stop the Gun Tight Flex—Falcon Cross, Michael Vick's scrambling, and the Full House WR Dbl Shake.

Defending the Vick Scramble

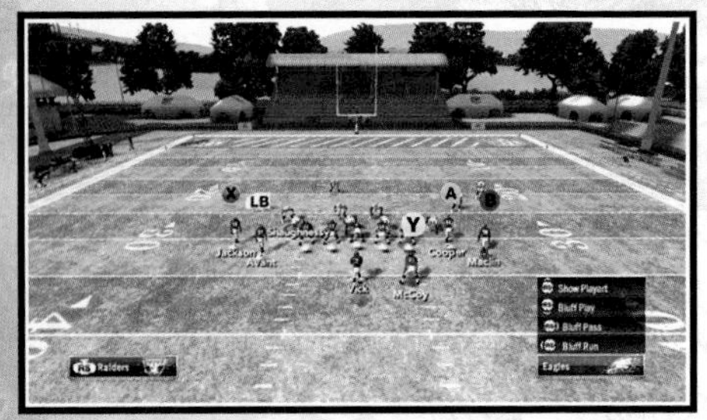

Gun Tight Flex

In this play the offense has blocked every single passing option other than the HB. They will try to scramble outside the pocket with Vick, and if they lose the edge to the defense they will look to dump the ball off to the HB on the delay route. Yes, this play is unconventional, but it will be effective without proper adjustments.

Vick gets to the edge

Even against the Oakland Raiders defense Vick gets to the edge and gains 15 yards on the play. The Raiders have the fastest defense in the game, and they couldn't contain Vick without proper adjustments.

Our defense kept containment, but Vick playmakered the HB deep

The other half of the equation is that with savvy user skills gamers can playmaker the HB deep if they can't get to the edge. That is exactly what happens here and we are in trouble deep!

Touchdown for the offense

The HB got deep in the secondary, and with Vick's throwing power he gets the ball downfield for the easy score.

We have our Vick defense set up

To contain Vick we hot route both our DEs to QB contains and we hot route one of our free linebackers on a QB spy. We also have a deep safety to protect against the deep ball.

Sack!

Vick looks to scramble wide, but our QB contain defender gets wide enough to take him down for the huge loss.

This time Vick looks to throw deep

Vick rolls out again but can't get to the outside edge. He playmakers the HB deep and takes a chance downfield.

Our QB spy makes the interception

The containment to the outside prevented Vick from letting the deep route develop. He had to either take another sack or hope for the HB to make a play on the ball. Instead, our QB spy steps in and makes the interception!

"Contain Vick" is a mind-set that you need to have *all game long*. We have seen it happen so many times where someone will contain Vick for three quarters and then get comfortable and the defensive coverage will get sloppy in the fourth quarter. Then Vick makes a few big plays and next thing you know we have to listen to their story about why they lost. Stay focused and pay attention to him for all four quarters and you will be able to control him.

Defending Falcon Cross

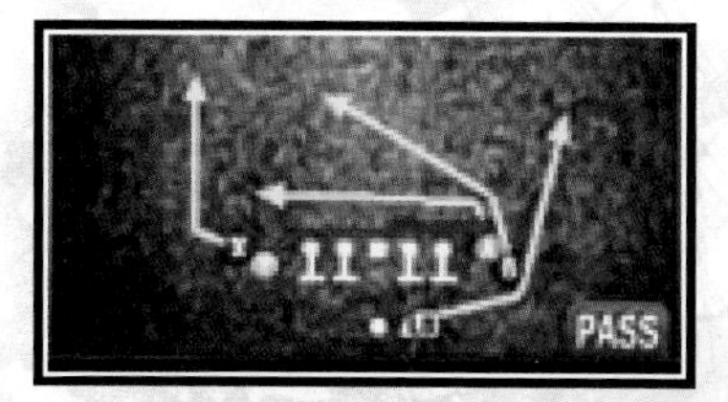

Gun Tight Flex—Falcon Cross

Without a doubt the best play in the game, with no adjustments, is the Gun Tight Flex—Falcon Cross. This play is the staple of many *Madden NFL* gamers. It has two quick flat reads that turn into vertical threats, it has two great crossing patterns to beat man-to-man coverage, and it has a nice deep post that crushes one-on-one coverage. This play is essentially the perfect play. Let's take a look at how we like to slow down the toughest play in *Madden NFL 12*.

We bring pressure in hopes of slowing it down

One of the first things to try to slow down any play is to pressure the QB. Not all players can handle pressure and you will be surprised at how you can rattle your opponent by doing this.

Bad decision—the offense completes the deep pass to the post

The deep post is a deadly route against one-on-one coverage. It is a tough throw for a lot of QBs to make because of the sharp angle the route takes. However, it can crush the backbone of many defenses.

We call Cover 3 with a few adjustments to defend Falcon Cross

To stop Falcon Cross we call a Cover 3 zone and make a few minor adjustments. We hot route the right-of-screen DT to a QB spy and the left-of-screen DT to a QB contain. We then user-control either the deep safety or one of the LBs in a hook zone. We use the Cover 3 to stop this play because the flat zones of the Cover 3 will stop the quick flat reads. The QB spy and the two hook zones will prevent the quick pass to the crossing patterns, and the three-deep coverage will defend the three vertical routes of the play as well.

Every option is covered

Here you can see that every passing option is covered. The QB can either scramble or throw into coverage.

The QB throws the ball downfield to the deep post

Bad decision by the QB. He decided to try and squeeze the deep post in between three deep defenders. It resulted in an interception for the offense and a big play for the defense!

When defending Falcon Cross your first goal is to stop the flat routes and then contain the crossing patterns. The play you are willing to give up is the deep post. It is a difficult throw for QBs to make. Stick to this formula and you will shut this play down all season long!

Defending WR Dbl Shake

Yes, the Full House—WR Dbl Shake is our favorite play in the game, and it has been for the past two seasons. It will without a doubt be the most effective under-center play in the game once again for *Madden NFL 12*. The quick-pass options from this play are great, and in the red zone you can see a lot of headaches coming from this play. Let's take a look at how we will stop it.

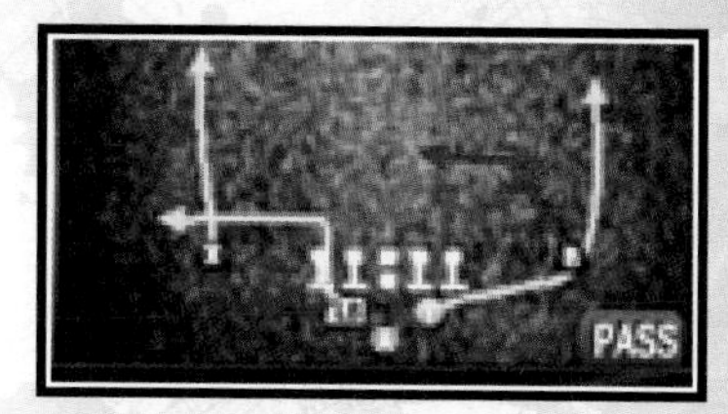

Full House—WR Dbl Shake

In the red zone most players will hot route the outside WRs on fade routes and lob the ball up to them in the end zone. With taller receivers this produces a crazy animation that is extremely difficult to defend. The quick pass to the left and the right are great inside the red zone for easy scores. The delay route out of the backfield is also extremely difficult to stop when used properly.

The quick pass to the TE is completed for a touchdown

This quick pass is the best in the game. It is extremely quick and very tough to defend.

Yet another touchdown scored by using the delayed blue route

The offense blocked both the TE and FB to help free the delay route. It will release extremely quickly to the short flat. The offense delivered the pass for the easy score.

The fade lob in the end zone

Here is the fade lob in the back of the end zone for a score. It is extremely difficult to defend in *Madden NFL 12*.

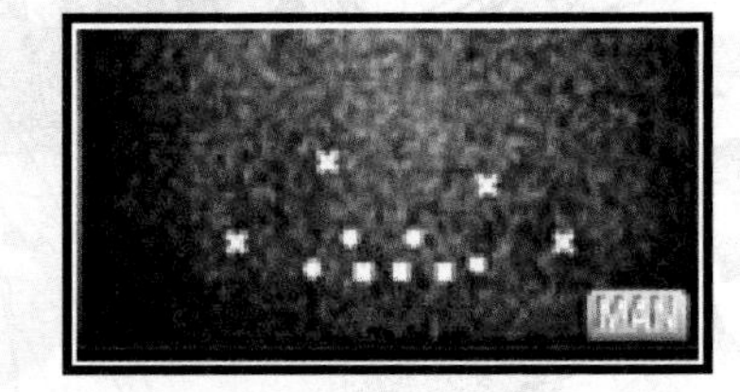

3-4 Under—Double Man

We use the 3-4 Under—Double Man because it double-covers both outside receivers. Our first goal in stopping this play is to slow down the fade lob. By putting two defenders on both options we increase our chances of getting a stop.

Incomplete pass!

We get the incompletion thanks to our two defenders in the area. The extra defender delivered the big hit on the WR as he exposed himself going up for the ball.

We intercept the delay route

Not having to worry about the fade lobs we can user-control the blitzing linebacker on the QB's hot reads. Defend the left quick pass first and then drop off to the other options.

The run is stuffed as well

We have seven big defenders in the box to help stop the run. If the defense tries to be tricky and run the ball when we expect the quick pass we will still be in good position to make the stop.

The WR Dbl Shake is a play that you should see being used many times during the *Madden NFL 12* season. Double the outside WRs and then user-control the left quick pass and you should start seeing more stops than scores!

Throughout the *Madden NFL 12* season you will come across many other offensive plays that give you headaches. If you have any questions feel free to let us know by heading over to primafootball.com.

IMPORTANT RATINGS—FINDING DEFENSIVE MADDEN GEMS

We are often asked how to find "Madden Gems." Sometimes gamers only look at the overall rating. Just because someone has a high overall rating, that doesn't mean he is one of the best, and a low overall rating doesn't mean he is one of the worst. Each position in the game has specific ratings that make those players either stand out in the crowd or get blown away with the wind.

Cornerbacks

- Speed: 94+
- Agility: 95+
- Acceleration: 95+
- Man Coverage: 90+

Man-to-man defense tends to be more reliable, so speed is extremely important for the success of a CB. Playing a lot of man coverage also means that CBs need to be able cut on a dime, so a high agility rating is a must. Just as WRs need to get off the line quickly, so do CBs. They need to be able to keep up with WRs in the passing game, so that makes acceleration number three on our list. Man coverage is our last rating because we believe that a high percentage of our defensive play calls will rely on our secondary playing man-to-man.

Safety

- Speed: 88+
- Acceleration: 90+
- Hit Power: 85+
- Catch: 70+

Safety is a unique position because safeties need to be able to play coverage as well as have ball skills. They also need to be able to play up in the box for run support. Speed and great acceleration allow our safeties to play coverage against WRs and TEs. Hit power allows them to play up in the box and deliver crushing blows on ball carriers. The last rating is catch; with good catch our safeties can be ball hawks in the deep secondary and make QBs pay for making a bad throw!

Linebackers

- Speed: 80+
- Tackle: 90+
- Hit Power: 90+
- Agility: 85+

Once again speed is most important, in this case to the success of our linebacking core. Anything over 80 speed should be considered starter worthy. Speed allows linebackers to roam around the field tracking down HBs as well as TEs and WRs. We also need to make sure our LBs are tackle machines that can lay a devastating hit on any ball carrier. Tackle and hit power come in at numbers two and three. LBs' lateral movement from gap to gap needs to be great so that they can take down shifty HBs. Without good agility LBs would need HBs to run right into them in order to make a tackle.

Defensive Linemen

- Speed: 80+
- Strength: 92+
- Block Shed: 90+
- Acceleration: 90+

Defensive linemen need to be either fast and quick or big and strong. We have a mix with our ratings because depending on how you play, you might value bigger defensive linemen over slower ones. For our fast pass rushers we care about speed and their acceleration to the QB. For our slower hogs to stop the run we care about strength and their block shedding ability.

Top 10 Players by Position: Defense

Now that you know the important ratings in *Madden NFL 12* and what to look for let's take a look at the top 10 players for each position and then show you *our* top 10 for each position. For the most part the lists are the same, but a few Madden Gems in each category climb to the top!

Madden NFL 12 Top 10 CBs

- Darrelle Revis
- Nnamdi Asomugha
- Champ Bailey
- Asante Samuel
- Charles Woodson
- Tramon Williams
- Brandon Flowers
- Leon Hall
- Cortland Finnegan
- Corey Webster

Our Top 10 CBs

- Dominique Rodgers-Cromartie
- Champ Bailey
- Patrick Peterson
- Antonio Cromartie
- Nnamdi Asomugha
- Darrelle Revis
- DeAngelo Hall
- Chris Johnson
- Terence Newman
- Tramon Williams

Madden NFL 12 Top 10 Safeties

- Troy Polamalu
- Ed Reed
- Nick Collins
- Antoine Bethea
- Adrian Wilson
- Michael Griffin
- LaRon Landry
- O.J. Atogwe
- Eric Berry
- Kerry Rhodes

Our Top 10 Safeties

- Troy Polamalu
- Ed Reed
- Taylor Mays
- LaRon Landry
- Nick Collins
- Eric Berry
- Adrian Wilson
- Tyvon Branch
- Michael Huff
- Earl Thomas

Madden NFL 12 Top 10 LBs

- Patrick Willis
- DeMarcus Ware
- James Harrison
- Jon Beason
- Ray Lewis
- Clay Matthews
- Terrell Suggs
- Brian Urlacher
- LaMarr Woodley
- Lance Briggs

Our Top 10 LBs

- Patrick Willis
- DeMarcus Ware
- Jon Beason
- James Harrison
- Clay Matthews
- Ray Lewis
- Brian Urlacher
- Ernie Sims
- Keith Rivers
- Manny Lawson

Madden NFL 12 Top 10 Defensive Linemen

- Kevin Williams
- Haloti Ngata
- Vince Wilfork
- Julius Peppers
- Justin Tuck
- Jared Allen
- Dwight Freeney
- Robert Mathis
- Kyle Williams
- Richard Seymour

Our Top 10 Defensive Linemen

- Dwight Freeney
- Robert Mathis
- Julius Peppers
- Casey Hampton
- Terrence Cody
- Haloti Ngata
- Elvis Dumervil
- Justin Tuck
- Vince Wilfork
- Jason Pierre-Paul

What do you think about our top 10? What do your lists look like? What do you value the most?

TEAM STRATEGY

Contents

SAN FRANCISCO 49ERS

OFFENSIVE SCOUTING REPORT

The San Francisco 49ers cater to a traditional offensive player. Allow RB Frank Gore to lead the charge on an offense that will let players grind out drives. Develop a scheme with SF that focuses on TE Vernon Davis. He has the athletic ability to stretch defenses in the seam like a WR but has the frame of a TE. On the outside, Michael Crabtree will hang on to whatever ball is thrown his way. Get Crabtree across the field, which will leave a shorter throw for the QB. The 49ers have some speed in the slot with return man Ted Ginn. Look for routes that run him at an angle into the deep secondary. The quarterback position will be a question mark in *Madden NFL 12*, but the talent surrounding this position should help any player succeed.

DEFENSIVE SCOUTING REPORT

The 49ers' defense is one of the most solid in *Madden NFL 12* due to the strength of their LB core. They possess the best MLB in the game with Patrick Willis holding down the middle. At safety, a young talent like Taylor Mays is waiting to show off his athleticism. If you can utilize a strong possession offense, your defense should be able to keep it a low-scoring battle. The great strength at DT really lets the talented LBs roam free and cause havoc.

TEAM RATING

Overall	77
Offense	83
Defense	83

DYNAMIC PLAYER PERFORMANCE TRAITS

Frank Gore
RB #21

Fights for Yards	Yes
Consistency	★★★★★
Cover Ball	★★★★★
Confidence	★★★★★
Clutch	No

RATINGS BY POSITION

Quarterbacks	75	Defensive Tackles	88
Halfbacks	91	Outside Linebackers	78
Fullbacks	77	Middle Linebackers	98
Wide Receivers	77	Cornerbacks	83
Tight Ends	91	Free Safeties	79
Tackles	83	Strong Safeties	78
Guards	84	Kickers	85
Centers	84	Punters	90
Defensive Ends	84		

DEPTH CHART

POS	OVR	FIRST NAME	LAST NAME
3DRB	71	Kendall	Hunter
C	84	Eric	Heitmann
C	56	Daniel	Kilgore
CB	84	Nate	Clements
CB	81	Shawntae	Spencer
CB	72	Tarell	Brown
CB	70	Tramaine	Brock
CB	66	Chris	Culliver
DT	88	Aubrayo	Franklin
DT	67	Ricky	Jean Francois
FB	77	Moran	Norris
FB	51	Bruce	Miller
FS	79	Dashon	Goldson
FS	58	Curtis	Taylor
FS	66	C.J.	Spillman
HB	91	Frank	Gore
HB	68	Anthony	Dixon
HB	71	Kendall	Hunter
HB	59	Xavier	Omon
K	85	Joe	Nedney
KOS	85	Joe	Nedney
KR	72	Ted	Ginn
KR	52	Kyle	Williams
LE	76	Isaac	Sopoaga
LE	72	Ray	McDonald
LG	88	Mike	Iupati
LG	67	Mike	Person
LG	67	Chris	Patrick
LOLB	80	Manny	Lawson
LOLB	76	Ahmad	Brooks
LOLB	64	Thaddeus	Gibson
LS	61	Brian	Jennings
LT	88	Joe	Staley
LT	74	Barry	Sims
MLB	98	Patrick	Willis
MLB	87	Takeo	Spikes
MLB	73	NaVorro	Bowman
MLB	68	Scott	McKillop
P	90	Andy	Lee
PR	72	Ted	Ginn
QB	75	Alex	Smith
QB	70	Colin	Kaepernick
QB	65	David	Carr
RE	92	Justin	Smith
RE	64	Demetric	Evans
RE	63	Will	Tukuafu
RG	79	Chilo	Rachal
RG	79	Adam	Snyder
ROLB	76	Aldon	Smith
ROLB	78	Parys	Haralson
ROLB	71	Travis	LaBoy
RT	77	Anthony	Davis
RT	60	Alex	Boone
SS	78	Reggie	Smith
SS	71	Taylor	Mays
SS	62	Chris	Maragos
TE	91	Vernon	Davis
TE	70	Delanie	Walker
TE	58	Nate	Byham
WR	81	Michael	Crabtree
WR	78	Josh	Morgan
WR	72	Ted	Ginn
WR	60	Dominique	Zeigler
WR	59	Ronald	Johnson
WR	53	Kevin	Jurovich

OFFENSIVE STRENGTH CHART

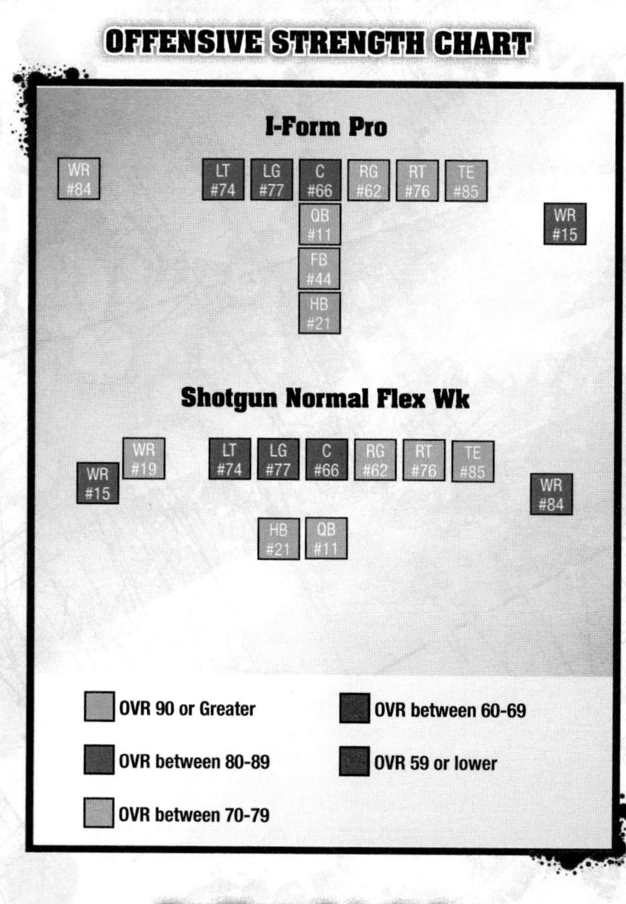

Key Player Substitution

Player: Ted Ginn

Position: #2 WR

Key Stat: 97 Speed

What He Brings: Ginn is a force on special teams; however, smart coordinators will look to get him the ball more than a few times a game. Ginn can catch screens in space, but he's also a threat to beat the defense deep.

#85 Vernon Davis
Tight End

Overall	91
Speed	90
Catch	82
Jump	94
Catch in Traffic	75

#21 Frank Gore
Running Back

Overall	91
Speed	91
Agility	92
Trucking	89
Catch	77

#7 Colin Kaepernick
Quarterback

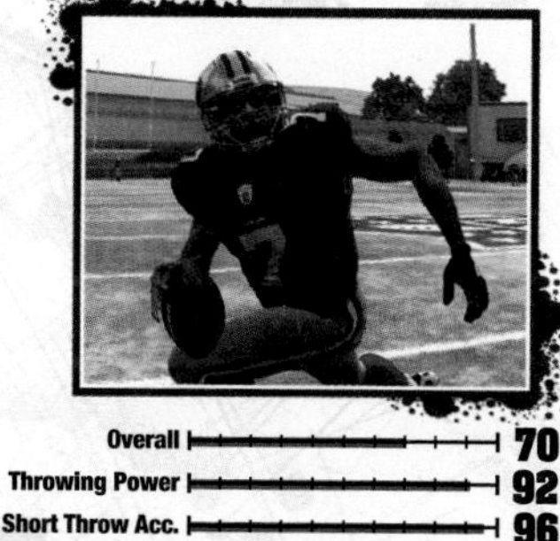

Overall	70
Throwing Power	92
Short Throw Acc.	96
Med. Throw Acc.	84
Deep Throw Acc.	74

#52 Patrick Willis
Middle Linebacker

Overall	98
Speed	90
Awareness	90
Tackle	98
Hit Power	94

#99 Manny Lawson
Outside Linebacker

Overall	80
Speed	89
Awareness	73
Tackle	75
Hit Power	72

#23 Taylor Mays
Strong Safety

Overall	71
Speed	95
Tackle	66
Hit Power	91
Play Recognition	48

DEFENSIVE STRENGTH CHART

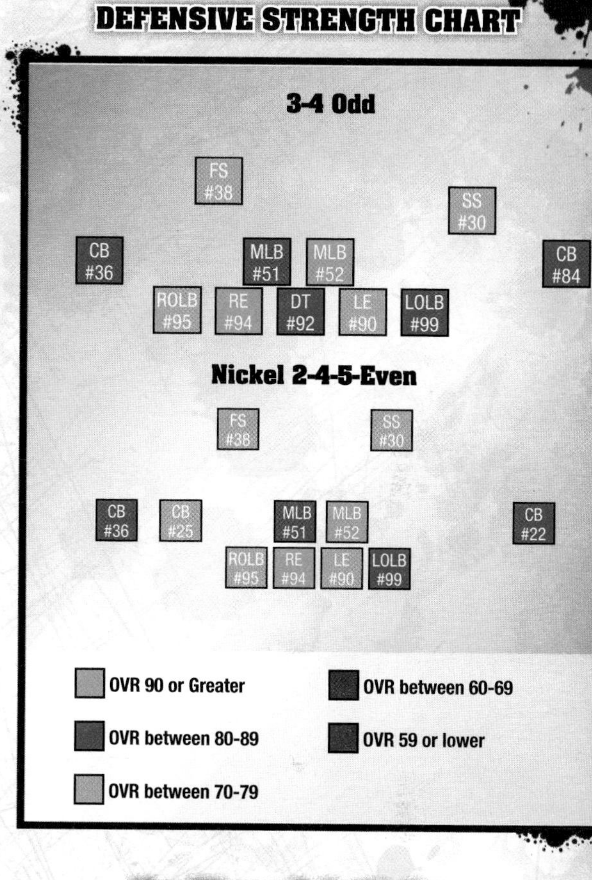

Key Player Substitution

Player: Taylor Mays

Position: #1 FS

Key Stat: 95 Speed

What He Brings: Taylor Mays has elite athletic talent and should be on the field for every snap. By user-controlling Mays, we also unlock his 95 agility.

Playbook Tips

Offensive Style: Run Balanced

Offense

- Rookie QB Colin Kaepernick has a unique skill set after running the pistol offense at Nevada. Look to work a few plays into your offense for him.
- Frank Gore is good enough to carry the load full-time.
- Use multiple-TE sets to help out your offensive line in the run game.

Defense

- Stay in your base defense as much as possible; your LBs are that good.
- Use a 4-3 Under scheme to maximize rookie Aldon Smith.
- On passing downs, utilize the LB Rush package on the Play Call screen.

OFFENSIVE FORMATIONS

FORMATION	# OF PLAYS
Gun Bunch HB STR	9
Gun Empty Trey Flex	9
Gun Normal Flex WK	15
Gun Split Y-Flex	15
Gun Trey Open	12
Gun Y-Trips HB WK	18
I-Form Pro	24
I-Form Tight	15
I-Form Slot Flex	12
I-Form Tackle Over	9
I-Form Twins Flex	18
Singleback Ace	18
Singleback Ace Pair	18
Singleback Bunch	12
Singleback F Pair Twins	15
Singleback Flex	18
Singleback Trey Open	12
Singleback Y-Trips	18
Strong H Pro	15
Weak Pro	15

OFFENSIVE PLAYCOUNTS

PLAY TYPE	# OF PLAYS
Quick Pass	22
Standard Pass	64
Shotgun Pass	48
Play Action Pass	59
Inside Handoff	45
Outside Handoff	15
Pitch	11
Counter	11
Draw	13

Three-Headed Rushing Attack

I-Form Tackle Over—HB Iso

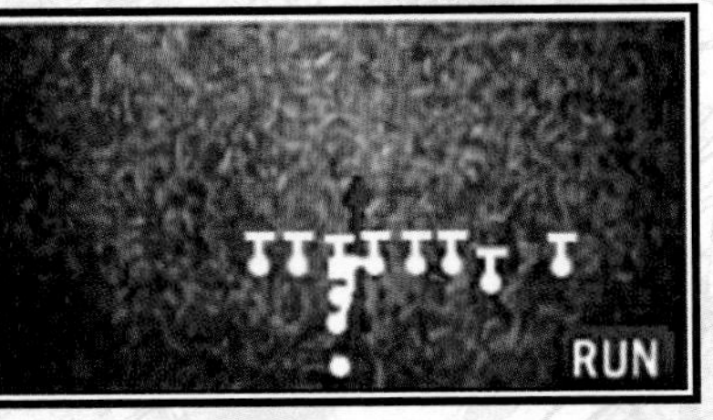

The Tackle Over formation will overload the right side of the line with an extra tackle. Our run left will actually hit the middle gap since running to the left would give the back no protection.

Our extra tackle should be able to manhandle his end and help us get a push at the snap. This leaves the guard unblocked and heading into the second level to block a backer.

The FB is also moving straight ahead on the iso and our RB should follow him. Between the guard and FB, our running back should be well over the line of scrimmage before having to make any kind of cut. The Tackle Over is a dominating power run formation.

PRO TIP Beware of a defense that stacks the weak side; they might try an edge rush to quickly grab the QB behind the line.

I-Form Tackle Over—HB Toss

With the right side of the line overloaded by the offense, our QB should be able to pitch the ball outside. Tosses are usually quick hitters that catch the defense losing containment. However, in a Tackle Over formation there are no surprises; we are simply looking to overpower the D.

The guard pulls at the snap, all the way around two tackles! He lead blocks once he gets to the corner. Smaller CBs that try to keep containment will not be able to get around him.

The WR on the short side of the field does a good job of keeping the play inside, but our RB has a nice lane to cut back inside. It is important to realize that not all tosses must go outside and to the house; they can be cut back in for a good chunk of yards.

PRO TIP Top online players will quickly learn about the lack of runs to the left from this formation and look to stack the strong side.

Tackle Over - HB Power O

The San Francisco 49ers' ground attack is vital to the team's success. The Tackle Over formation creates an unbalanced line that overloads the right side of the field with an extra tackle on the line of scrimmage. We have a major advantage in the run game while using this formation.

The HB Power O can run between the tackles and can bounce outside. We can see here that the approaching linebacker has shut down the outside running lane. Look to cut the ball up into the opening running lanes.

Always look to follow your blockers. Be patient with the running game. It is tempting to bounce the ball outside and go for the big gain. However, in this situation, we chose to run between the tackles and pick up five yards.

PRO TIP Sub in an extra offensive lineman for your second TE to get even better blocking.

Quick Pass

Tackle Over - PA Power O

Once you have the opponent thinking about the run, this is when we want to work in our play action. The Tackle Over PA Power O looks exactly the same as our running play, but we want to catch the defense off guard and hit them with the pass!

Our first option off the play action is to the FB in the flat. With the play fake, we are trying to get the man defender to be a step slow in coverage. We can see here that the FB is heading to the flat with no one following him. Look to get the ball to him as quickly as possible.

We were able to get the pass off after the play fake and have an extra step on the defender. As soon as you make the catch, look to head upfield and pick up extra yardage.

PRO TIP Sub in a faster TE at FB to have a better receiving threat out of the backfield.

Man Beater

Bunch HBSTR - Durham

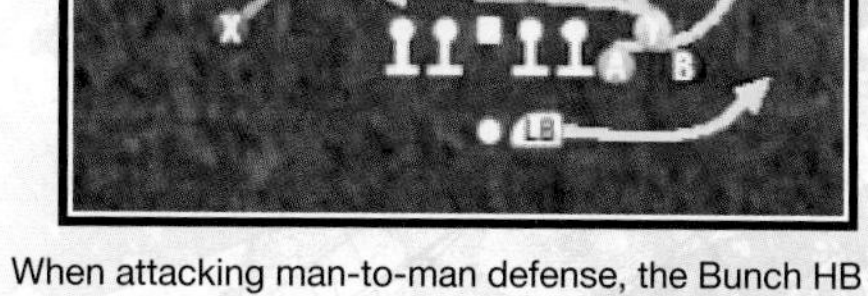

When attacking man-to-man defense, the Bunch HB STR Durham does a great job of overloading the right side of the field with routes. The alignment of the formation makes it difficult to guard all our offensive threats when in a man-to-man defense.

Our HB releases to the flat after the snap of the ball. We see the man-to-man defense with two safeties dropping deep into coverage. The linebacker in the middle of the field is responsible for covering our HB. He is way behind in coverage as our HB runs to the flat.

We complete the pass and the linebacker is still trailing the HB. We break upfield, looking to take advantage of our HB's speed as we fight for extra yardage. The Bunch HB STR formation causes major matchup problems for any man-to-man defense and should be called upon in many situations.

PRO TIP When on the sideline, look to avoid a big hit and possible fumble by heading out of bounds.

Zone Beater

I - Tight - Angle

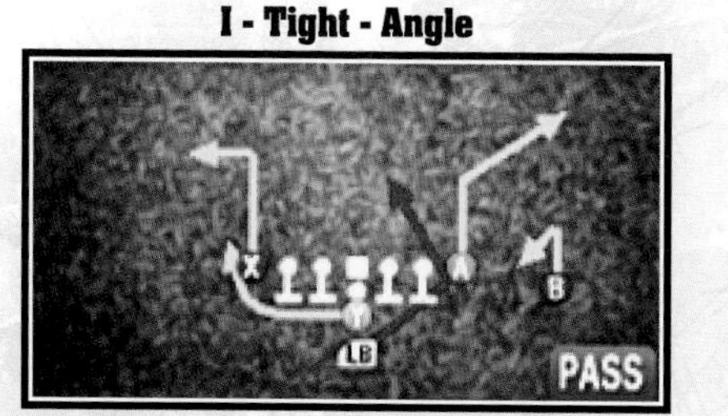

The I-Tight formation is typically a power-run formation. Expect the defense to load up the box with extra defenders. We have a couple quick pass options on this play, but against a blitzing defense, we look to take advantage downfield with our big TE.

At the snap of the ball, we see our TE heading upfield in a one-on-one matchup with a smaller safety. There are no other defenders in the area. This means that the defense is in a man-to-man blitz. We can dump the ball off to our HB on the angle route or our FB to the left flat, or we can hang in the pocket and attack them downfield with our TE running the corner route.

We decide to hang in the pocket and deliver the pass downfield to our TE. He makes the catch and has no one around him. The trailing defender can't match up to the size and speed of our TE.

PRO TIP Look to hit your checkdown routes to your HB and FB against the zone blitz!

Base Play

Gun Empty Trey - WR Screen

When facing any type of blitz, such as zone or man, the Gun Empty Trey WR Screen is a solid option to use to take advantage of the aggressive defense. What is great about this screen is that we are in an empty set. It will be easier to see where pressure is coming from presnap as the defense is forced to spread out to cover our formation.

At the snap of the ball, we see that the middle of the field is wide open because of the zone blitz. The safety drops deep over the middle of the field so we expect the zone to be a Cover 3. The WR Screen is the perfect play call in this situation.

We deliver the pass on time and look to follow the blockers. Be patient when following your blockers. Let them get upfield and clear out space for your WR. We do exactly this and see only green grass in front of us!

PRO TIP Sub in your fastest and most agile WR for this play.

CHICAGO BEARS

OFFENSIVE SCOUTING REPORT

The Chicago Bears rode a hot defense and dynamic QB play from Jay Cutler into the NFC Championship game. For success with the Bears, look to get the ball quickly out of Jay Cutler's hands. The Bears have two speedy WRs who can burn almost any CB in the game one-on-one. The Bears were at their best last season when getting the ball to Matt Forte. Not only did he take the pressure off the offensive line with the run game, but he also excelled at catching passes. Avoid taking big hits with Jay Cutler; otherwise the offense can change in a blink of an eye.

DEFENSIVE SCOUTING REPORT

The consistency of the Bears' defense has been incredible over the last few seasons. When healthy, star LB Brian Urlacher is the emotional leader and heart and soul of the defense. Urlacher has plenty of help, though; DE Julius Peppers is a force off the edge and must be double-teamed on a consistent basis. This allows other players like LB Lance Briggs to shine through. The Bears' ability to force turnovers and leave a short field for the offense is one of the biggest assets in *Madden NFL 12*. The Bears should continue to be a popular team for fans of hard-hitting old-school football action.

RATINGS BY POSITION

Quarterbacks	85
Halfbacks	89
Fullbacks	68
Wide Receivers	78
Tight Ends	86
Tackles	75
Guards	80
Centers	82
Defensive Ends	89
Defensive Tackles	81
Outside Linebackers	86
Middle Linebackers	94
Cornerbacks	83
Free Safeties	88
Strong Safeties	74
Kickers	93
Punters	84

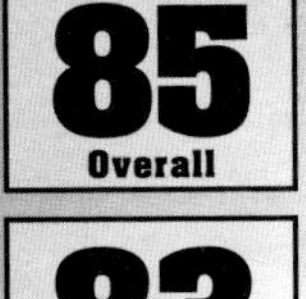

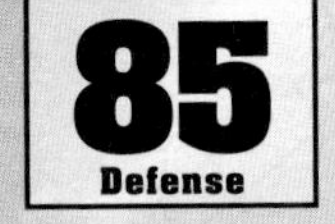

Matt Forte
RB #22

Cover Ball	★★★★★
Consistency	★★★★★
Confidence	★★★★★
Fights for Yards	Yes
Clutch	No

DEPTH CHART

POS	OVR	FIRST NAME	LAST NAME
3DRB	77	Chester	Taylor
C	82	Olin	Kreutz
CB	86	Charles	Tillman
CB	80	Tim	Jennings
CB	74	Zackary	Bowman
CB	66	Corey	Graham
DT	81	Anthony	Adams
DT	77	Matt	Toeaina
DT	67	Henry	Melton
DT	65	Marcus	Harrison
FB	68	Brandon	Manumaleuna
FB	58	Harvey	Unga
FS	88	Chris	Harris
FS	68	Major	Wright
HB	89	Matt	Forte
HB	77	Chester	Taylor
HB	63	Kahlil	Bell
HB	65	Garrett	Wolfe
K	93	Robbie	Gould
KOS	93	Robbie	Gould
KR	79	Johnny	Knox
KR	74	Danieal	Manning
LE	82	Israel	Idonije
LE	76	Corey	Wootton
LG	84	Chris	Williams
LG	59	Edwin	Williams
LG	62	Herman	Johnson
LOLB	78	Pisa	Tinoisamoa
LOLB	70	Nick	Roach
LOLB	55	J.T.	Thomas
LS	68	Patrick	Mannelly
LT	74	Gabe	Carimi
LT	75	Frank	Omiyale
MLB	94	Brian	Urlacher
MLB	62	Rod	Wilson
P	84	Brad	Maynard
PR	79	Devin	Hester
QB	85	Jay	Cutler
QB	72	Caleb	Hanie
QB	64	Nathan	Enderle
RE	95	Julius	Peppers
RE	57	Nick	Reed
RG	75	Roberto	Garza
RG	72	Lance	Louis
RG	69	Johan	Asiata
ROLB	93	Lance	Briggs
ROLB	65	Brian	Iwuh
ROLB	54	Chris	Johnson
RT	75	J'Marcus	Webb
RT	62	Levi	Horn
SS	74	Danieal	Manning
SS	74	Josh	Bullocks
SS	72	Craig	Steltz
TE	86	Greg	Olsen
TE	66	Kellen	Davis
TE	74	Desmond	Clark
WR	79	Johnny	Knox
WR	79	Devin	Hester
WR	76	Earl	Bennett
WR	72	Devin	Aromashodu
WR	66	Rashied	Davis

OFFENSIVE STRENGTH CHART

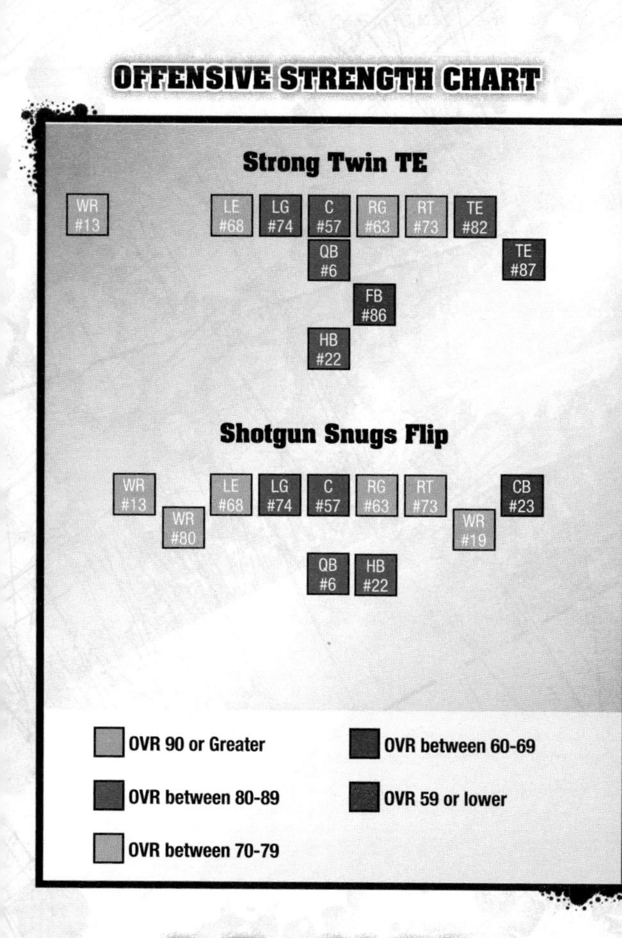

Key Player Substitution

Player: Garrett Wolfe

Position: #1 FB

Key Stat: 93 Agility

What He Brings: Wolfe is a speedy back who will be a great addition in the passing game. Make sure to sneak him into your attack to run plays like FB Angle. If the defense forgets about him for even a second, he will make them pay.

#6 Jay Cutler
Quarterback

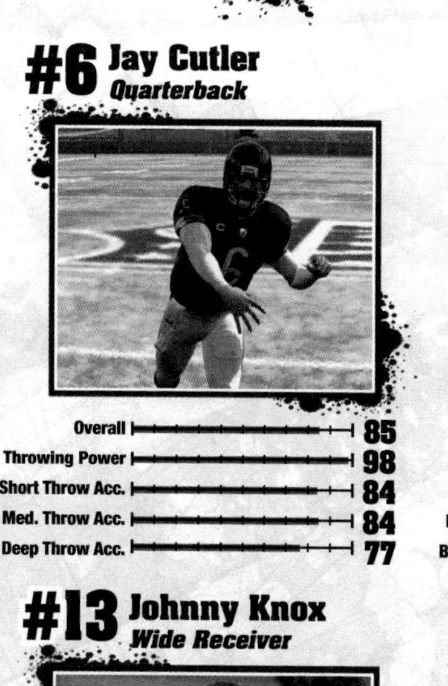

Overall	85
Throwing Power	98
Short Throw Acc.	84
Med. Throw Acc.	84
Deep Throw Acc.	77

#13 Johnny Knox
Wide Receiver

Overall	79
Speed	97
Catch	86
Route Running	79
Acceleration	97

#23 Devin Hester
Wide Receiver

Overall	79
Speed	98
Catch	76
Route Running	77
Acceleration	98

#90 Julius Peppers
Defensive End

Overall	95
Speed	85
Strength	85
Finesse Moves	96
Block Shedding	65

#54 Brian Urlacher
Linebacker

Overall	94
Speed	84
Awareness	95
Tackling	96
Hit Power	91

#26 Tim Jennings
Cornerback

Overall	80
Speed	49
Man Coverage	84
Zone Coverage	82
Awareness	82

DEFENSIVE STRENGTH CHART

4-3 Stack

FS #46
SS #38
CB #26
LOLB #55
DT #54
LOLB #59
CB #33
RE #90
DT #75
DT #95
LE #71

Dime Normal

FS #46
SS #38
CB #26
CB #35
DT #54
CB #21
CB #33
RE #90
DT #75
DT #95
LE #82

OVR 90 or Greater
OVR between 60-69
OVR between 80-89
OVR 59 or lower
OVR between 70-79

Key Player Substitution

Player: Tim Jennings

Position: #3 CB Slot

Key Stat: 94 Speed

What He Brings: Tim Jennings is a great weapon to match up with a speedy slot WR. Charles Tillman is sure-handed against slower WRs. Look to match up Jennings against the team's speedy deep-threat WR.

Playbook Tips

Offensive Style: Balanced

Offense

- The offensive line can be hit or miss; don't hold the ball for too long early in the game.
- Mike Martz loves to take shots down the field to keep the defense honest.
- Work a run game from the Strong Pro formation to get the D on its heels.

Defense

- Keep Briggs and Urlacher on the field even in passing situations.
- Bring one safety down into the box on run downs to help support Julius Peppers.
- Blitz from the opposite side of Peppers to allow him one-on-one matchups with the tackle.

OFFENSIVE FORMATIONS

FORMATION	# OF PLAYS
Gun Doubles WK	15
Gun Empty Trey	12
Gun Snugs Flip	12
Gun Split Offset	15
Gun Spread Y-Flex	12
Gun Y-Trips WK	15
I-Form Pro	18
I-Form Tight	18
Singleback Ace	21
Singleback Ace Twins	18
Singleback Bunch	15
Singleback Doubles	21
Singleback Spread Flex	12
Singleback Trey Open	15
Singleback Y-Trips Bear	21
Strong Pro	18
Strong Twin TE	15
Weak Slot	12
Weak Twins Flex	12

OFFENSIVE PLAYCOUNTS

PLAY TYPE	# OF PLAYS
Quick Pass	21
Standard Pass	73
Shotgun Pass	55
Play Action Pass	52
Inside Handoff	41
Outside Handoff	12
Pitch	10
Counter	8
Draw	16

Singleback Ace Pair Twins—WR Screen

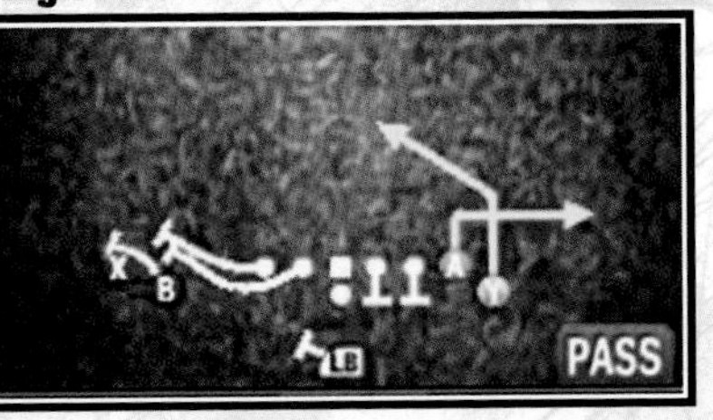

The Bears have power run formations, but this Singleback is one of the most distinctive in the game. Rather than looking to run straight ahead, we can use the short passing game and the WR Screen as an extension of the run game when the defense is sitting back. Here are two screen passes we can sub into our scheme!

Since the Bears have dynamic playmakers on the edge, it is best to get them the ball in space. By swinging it out to the left to a dangerous player like Devin Hester, the D won't be able to pack the box.

Hester quickly receives the throw and looks to get upfield. His blocker does a great job on pinning the defender and Hester is able to make one sharp cut and get upfield. Look to get outside if the block doesn't make it out in time.

PRO TIP Devin Hester can also be used as a decoy on this play—look to hit your other stud, Johnny Knox, instead.

Three-Headed Rushing Attack

Singleback Ace Pair Twins—HB Slip Screen

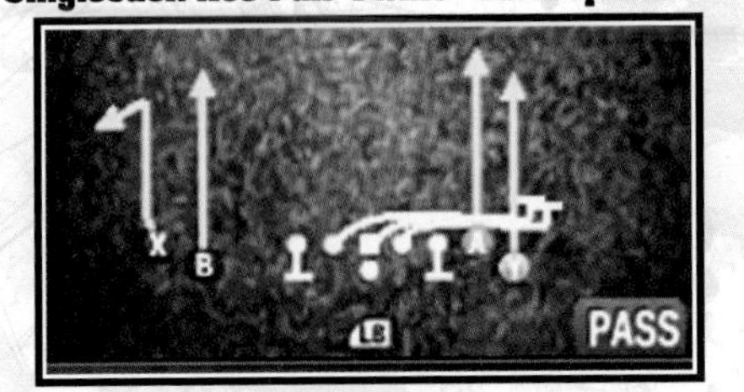

Now that the defense must worry about the WR Screen, we are going to send the HB out to the right for a very high-percentage passing play. This will work as an extension of the run game, which can pay big dividends.

The idea of a slip screen is to get the running back out into space with some blockers in front of him. At the snap, the linemen will head out towards the sideline to set up their blocks; this will leave their defenders rushing towards the QB.

The QB has rolled back far enough to avoid pressure, and the linemen realize the screen is coming but are too far committed to make a play on the running back. The HB is going to make a wide-open catch on the right side with three huge linemen out in front! This play will go for huge yards if you let the blockers clear the way downfield.

PRO TIP Calling this early in the game will keep the defense worrying about the possible screen every time you call this formation.

Singleback Ace Pair Twins - HB Draw

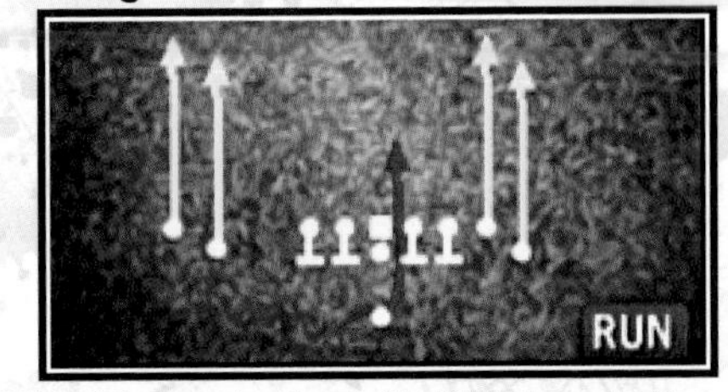

With all the passing threats the Bears have working, HB Draw can open up the run game. Matt Forte is a great mix between size and speed. At the snap of the ball, the defense's initial read will be pass play. Look to take advantage of this as we move upfield.

Be patient when running HB Draw. Running lanes will develop, and when they do, try to explode through the line of scrimmage. Cover the ball as you move through the offensive line to protect against fumbling.

As you get into the open area, stop covering the ball and fight for extra yardage. The HB gets past the offensive line and is deep into the secondary for the big gain.

PRO TIP If you are looking for more blocking on the play, motion one of your TEs behind the line of scrimmage and snap the ball when he slides past the center.

Quick Pass

Singleback Ace Pair Twins - WR Screen

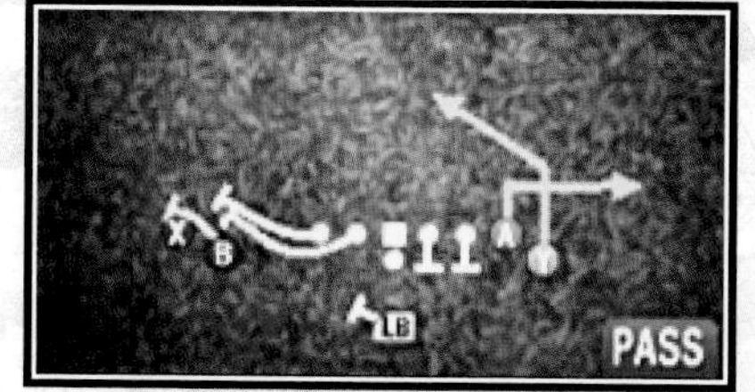

Against the blitz, a WR Screen is a great option. The defense is being aggressive, and that is exactly what we want. With the speed the Bears have on offense, we can break the game wide open with the Singleback Ace Pair Twins WR Screen.

The pressure is coming up the middle. The offensive linemen look to get into position for the screen. The pressure will come quick, so be sure to get the ball off as soon as the WR is set.

We beat the blitz and have our speedy WR moving upfield. Do a quick juke and make the defender miss. The WR Screen has big play potential when called upon in the right situations.

PRO TIP Save this play for late in the game. You will catch your blitz-happy opponent off guard!

Man Beater

SinglebackY-TripsBear-EmptyChiUnder

An effective way to find out what the defense is doing is to enter into an Empty Set play. The Singleback Y-Trips Bear Empty Chi Under forces the defense to show its hand. The defense is in man-to-man coverage with two safeties deep. Hang in the pocket and find the open WR.

One of the better ways to attack man coverage is to use drag routes and slants. We have two drags crossing paths with each other and a slant route running on top of the drags. Both drags have tight coverage, but we can see that our WR on the slant has created separation from the defender.

We deliver the pass as soon as we see the separation. Our WR hauls it in for a big gain. It is important to trust that one of these three options will open up against man coverage. Hang in the pocket and find the open WR.

PRO TIP Watch out for a robber defender in man defense. This is a zone defender in man coverage looking to take away this read.

Zone Beater

Empty Trey - Levels

A great way to beat zone defense in *Madden NFL 12* is to use Empty Trey Levels. This play overloads the zone defense with the same route but attacks the defense at different depths. The zone defender cannot be in more than one place at once. Sit back and find the open man!

As the play develops, we see two of the WRs initially covered. Be patient and let them pass the defenders. Read the zone defenders and look to see who they defend. Will it be the above WR or the underneath WR?

The underneath WR cleared through the defense, and the ball was delivered on time. We have open space to run into. The key to beating zone defense is to trust your play call. Be patient and wait for your routes to open up!

PRO TIP Roll out with your QB to the natural flow of the play. This will give you better passing angles!

Base Play

Gun Snugs - PA Wheels

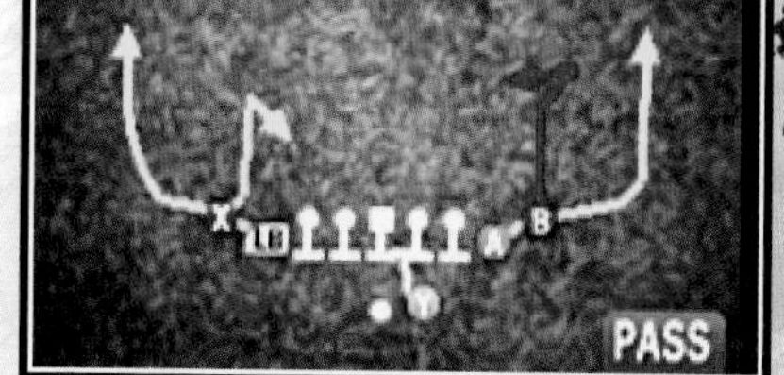

When facing zone coverage, we love the dual threat of the Gun Snugs PA Wheels. Wheel routes first break to the flat and cut upfield into a vertical threat. This is critical to beating zone coverage. If the initial flat read is covered, wait for the wheel route to extend into the vertical route and sneak the pass behind the coverage.

The zone defender in the flat covers the WR. If we hit our WR early, there is a good chance the defensive player will make a play on the ball. Because the WR is running a wheel route, he will get behind the defensive player and into the open field.

When the WR breaks into the open field, we deliver the pass. It gets there just in time to prevent the deep safety from recovering and making a play on the ball. It is important to get this pass off early so the deep defender cannot recover.

PRO TIP Sub in one of your taller WRs for this play. Height is more important than speed for this play!

CINCINNATI BENGALS

OFFENSIVE SCOUTING REPORT

The Cincinnati Bengals roster underwent big shake-ups this off-season, but they will still be a force in *Madden NFL 12*. By drafting WR A.J. Green in the first round, the Bengals took away much of the pain of losing their former superstar wideouts. New offensive coordinator Jay Gruden will bring a new West Coast style to Cincinnati. This offense will help any QB by making short throws and committing to the run game. Cedric Benson is a strong RB who is capable of fighting for yards. Also look to Bernard Scott if you're trying to beat a Contain on a defense. TE Jermaine Gresham will excel on short slants in this offense and will keep defenders on his back with his size. WR Jordan Shipley will also fit into this new offense by being fearless over the middle of the field. WR Quan Cosby has great agility and acceleration. If Shipley needs rest, put Cosby in and look for him to beat defenders with sharp cuts.

DEFENSIVE SCOUTING REPORT

The Bengals ended up having a solid defense last season. Cornerback Johnathan Joseph allows the defense to use many different styles since he can really lock down the other team's main option. LB Rey Maualuga has continued his ascension towards becoming a top-tier LB. Look to unleash him on passing downs to attempt to create turnovers. On the line of scrimmage, RE Antwan Odom has a solid blend of speed and strength. For gamers who don't mind making a few adjustments and bringing blitzes the Bengals are a very capable defense. This is good news for Bengals fans since the offense will likely struggle early because of their youth.

TEAM RATING

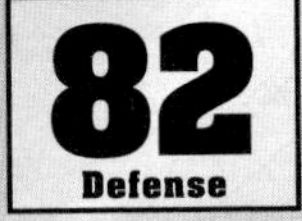

DYNAMIC PLAYER PERFORMANCE TRAITS

Cedric Benson
HB #32

Cover Ball	★★★★★
Consistency	★★★★★
Confidence	★★★★★
Fights for Yards	Yes
Clutch	No

RATINGS BY POSITION

Quarterbacks	83
Halfbacks	81
Fullbacks	68
Wide Receivers	80
Tight Ends	80
Tackles	81
Guards	83
Centers	78
Defensive Ends	80
Defensive Tackles	84
Outside Linebackers	77
Middle Linebackers	83
Cornerbacks	90
Free Safeties	81
Strong Safeties	75
Kickers	73
Punters	74

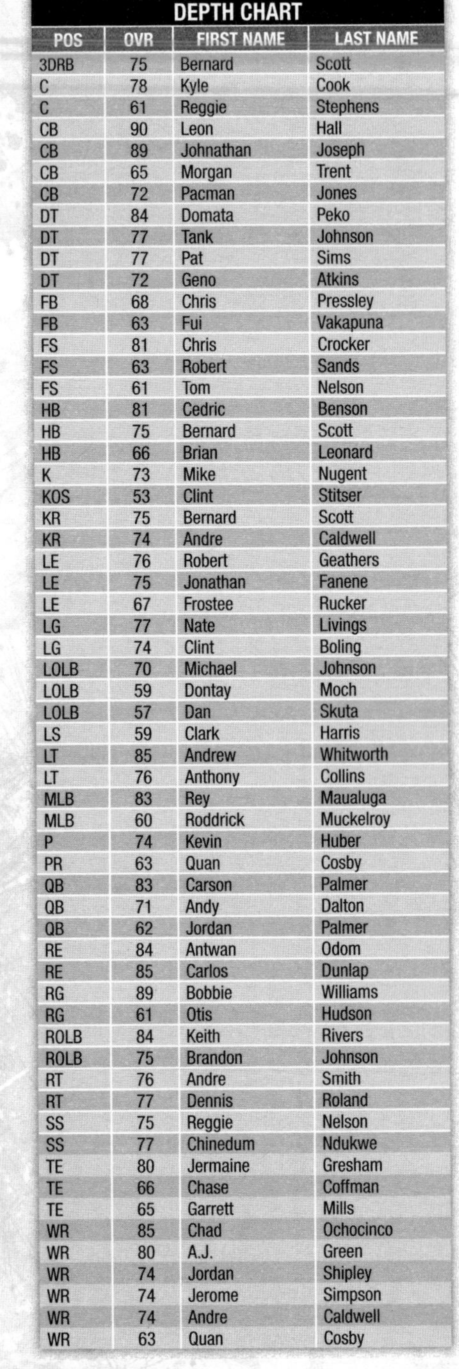

DEPTH CHART

POS	OVR	FIRST NAME	LAST NAME
3DRB	75	Bernard	Scott
C	78	Kyle	Cook
C	61	Reggie	Stephens
CB	90	Leon	Hall
CB	89	Johnathan	Joseph
CB	65	Morgan	Trent
CB	72	Pacman	Jones
DT	84	Domata	Peko
DT	77	Tank	Johnson
DT	77	Pat	Sims
DT	72	Geno	Atkins
FB	68	Chris	Pressley
FB	63	Fui	Vakapuna
FS	81	Chris	Crocker
FS	63	Robert	Sands
FS	61	Tom	Nelson
HB	81	Cedric	Benson
HB	75	Bernard	Scott
HB	66	Brian	Leonard
K	73	Mike	Nugent
KOS	53	Clint	Stitser
KR	75	Bernard	Scott
KR	74	Andre	Caldwell
LE	76	Robert	Geathers
LE	75	Jonathan	Fanene
LE	67	Frostee	Rucker
LG	77	Nate	Livings
LG	74	Clint	Boling
LOLB	70	Michael	Johnson
LOLB	59	Dontay	Moch
LOLB	57	Dan	Skuta
LS	59	Clark	Harris
LT	85	Andrew	Whitworth
LT	76	Anthony	Collins
MLB	83	Rey	Maualuga
MLB	60	Roddrick	Muckelroy
P	74	Kevin	Huber
PR	63	Quan	Cosby
QB	83	Carson	Palmer
QB	71	Andy	Dalton
QB	62	Jordan	Palmer
RE	84	Antwan	Odom
RE	85	Carlos	Dunlap
RG	89	Bobbie	Williams
RG	61	Otis	Hudson
ROLB	84	Keith	Rivers
ROLB	75	Brandon	Johnson
RT	76	Andre	Smith
RT	77	Dennis	Roland
SS	75	Reggie	Nelson
SS	77	Chinedum	Ndukwe
TE	80	Jermaine	Gresham
TE	66	Chase	Coffman
TE	65	Garrett	Mills
WR	85	Chad	Ochocinco
WR	80	A.J.	Green
WR	74	Jordan	Shipley
WR	74	Jerome	Simpson
WR	74	Andre	Caldwell
WR	63	Quan	Cosby

OFFENSIVE STRENGTH CHART

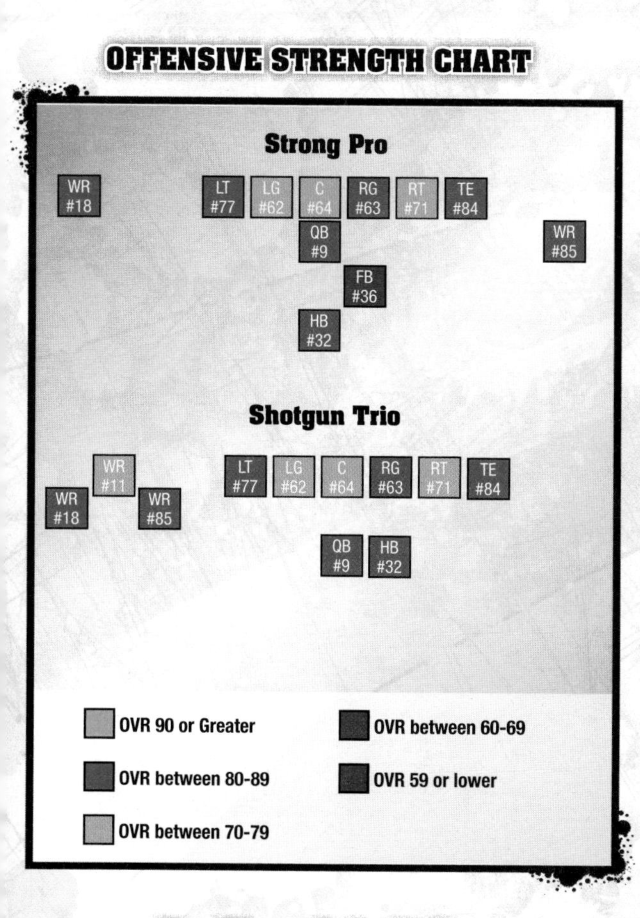

Key Player Substitution

Player: Chase Coffman

Position: #2 WR in Red Zone

Key Stat: 90 Catch in Traffic

What He Brings: Coffman isn't as consistent as Jermaine Gresham, but these two players can tag team in the red zone. The Bengals already have a solid playmaker on the edge in rookie WR A.J. Green. Swing Coffman outside in the red zone and let him take on defenders in traffic.

#32 Cedric Benson
Halfback

Overall	81
Speed	87
Agility	82
Trucking	92
Catch	48

#22 Johnathan Joseph
Cornerback

Overall	89
Speed	95
Man Coverage	90
Zone Coverage	85
Awareness	86

#18 A.J. Green
Wide Receiver

Overall	80
Speed	89
Catch	89
Route Running	75
Acceleration	90

#55 Keith Rivers
Linebacker

Overall	84
Speed	87
Awareness	76
Tackling	87
Hit Power	88

#80 Chase Coffman
Tight End

Overall	66
Speed	71
Catch	86
Jump	76
Catch in Traffic	90

#20 Reggie Nelson
Strong Safety

Overall	75
Speed	93
Tackling	55
Hit Power	73
Play Recognition	80

DEFENSIVE STRENGTH CHART

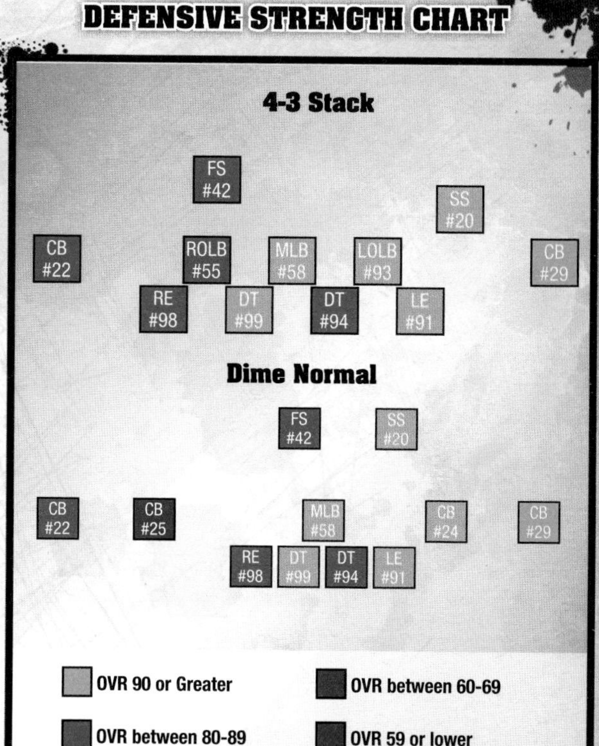

Key Player Substitution

Player: Dontay Moch

Position: #2 DE Slot

Key Stat: 91 Speed

What He Brings: In passing situations, Moch has the ability to get off the edge in a hurry. He is still a very raw talent, but using him in this one situation can make him an effective player.

Playbook Tips

Offensive Style: Pass Balanced

Offense

- The Bengals are thought of as a pass-first team, but the best option is the run game.
- Make sure to work dual TEs into the game to help out at the line of scrimmage.
- The Bengals playbook has lots of play action passes, set these up early.

Defense

- Don't be afraid to let the corners play man coverage; they can handle the load.
- Coordinator Don Zimmer likes to stop the run by keeping stronger defensive linemen in the game.
- Manually control safety Reggie Nelson to get the most bang for your buck.

OFFENSIVE FORMATIONS

FORMATION	# OF PLAYS
Full House Normal Wide	12
Gun Bunch Weak	12
Gun Doubles Wing	15
Gun Empty Trey	15
Gun Split Slot	18
Gun Spread	12
Gun Tight	12
Gun Trio	15
Gun Y-Trips WK	21
I-Form Pro	15
I-Form Pro Twins	12
I-Form Tight Pair	18
Singleback Ace	15
Singleback Ace Pair	18
Singleback Doubles	21
Singleback Y-Trips	15
Singleback Bunch	15
Singleback Snugs Flip	12
Strong Pro	21
Weak Pro Twins	12
Wildcat Bengal	3

OFFENSIVE PLAYCOUNTS

PLAY TYPE	# OF PLAYS
Quick Pass	19
Standard Pass	56
Shotgun Pass	87
Play Action Pass	54
Inside Handoff	40
Outside Handoff	10
Pitch	11
Counter	9
Draw	15

Three-Headed Rushing Attack

Weak Pro Twins—Toss Weak

Establishing the ground attack is crucial for the Bengals this season because they don't have the dynamic playmakers they once had on the outside. Cedric Benson is a very capable back and can break enough tackles to get the job done.

The toss to the weak side is a unique run that can really catch the defense off guard. The twin WRs block rather than head upfield, which can really help seal the edge. On this play, our player gets the ball out in space and the LB gets sucked inside.

Our HB has blockers who managed to seal the edge for him. This is a run that will consistently try to break containment rather than being cut back inside. If we have Bernard Scott, our speedy backup RB, in the game, this can be even more deadly.

PRO TIP Look to flip the toss to the strong side if the defense is not lined up for it.

Weak Pro Twins—HB Inside

The HB Inside is a run that attacks the weak side up the middle. This is the perfect run to keep the defense honest. This run sends the HB through the gap first and gives our runner a lane to follow.

At the snap, the HB takes the ball and sees two holes have opened up; one has an extra blocker and he should take that option. Many players choose the wrong side because they are used to hitting the middle with iso runs.

Once the back gets to the line of scrimmage, he should make one move before getting upfield. Here the LB is filling in from the right-hand side, so our back looks to make a sharp cut to the left to spring free. Flip this run in short yardage situations to minimize the amount of penetration the defense can get at the snap.

PRO TIP The quick-pass audible can help us counteract an overly aggressive defense on third and short.

Pro Twins - Offtackle

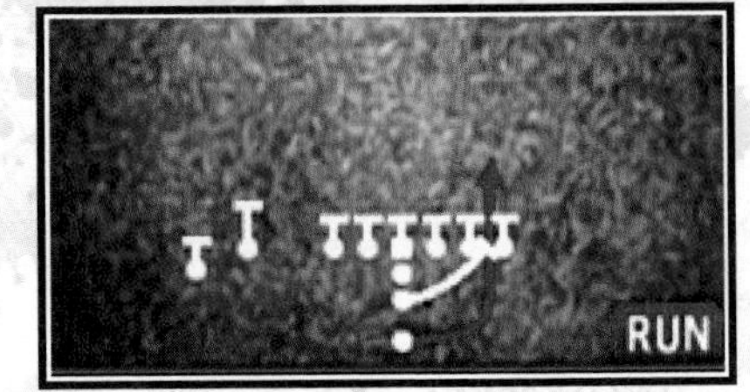

The Pro Twins Off Tackle is a dual-run threat. You can bounce it to the outside and cut it up inside. You decide. Find the open lane and get upfield!

At the snap of the ball, try to take the run up the middle of the field. However, the middle linebacker has other plans. We can either try to take him head-on or bounce the run outside.

We decide to go outside and avoid the middle linebacker. The HB can pick up extra yardage with this decision. Instead of facing the bigger linebacker, we are taken down by a smaller safety as we pick up five yards.

PRO TIP Look to cover the ball against bigger defenders. Against smaller defenders, look to use the Highlight stick!

Quick Pass

Strong Pro - FB Angle

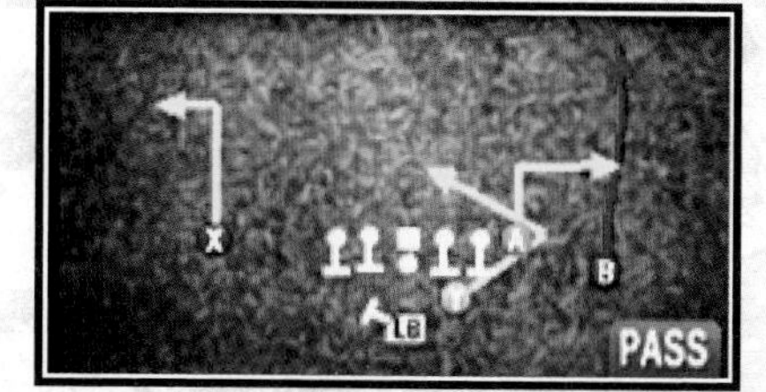

When facing the blitzing defense, you must be able to get rid of the ball quickly. The Strong Pro FB Angle has a great route to this. The FB will break outside the offensive tackle and cut toward the middle of the field.

The opponent is playing man-to-man coverage and is sending the blitz. The middle linebacker is again looking to cause havoc. He's coming straight at us. That's okay, because we have the FB running into space behind the blitz.

The pass is delivered before the pressure can get to us. Facing an aggressive defense can often force bad decisions that result in turnovers. When you are prepared to face the blitz, it can result in big gains!

PRO TIP Always attack a blitzing defense from where they are sending pressure.

Man Beater

Gun Tight - Circle

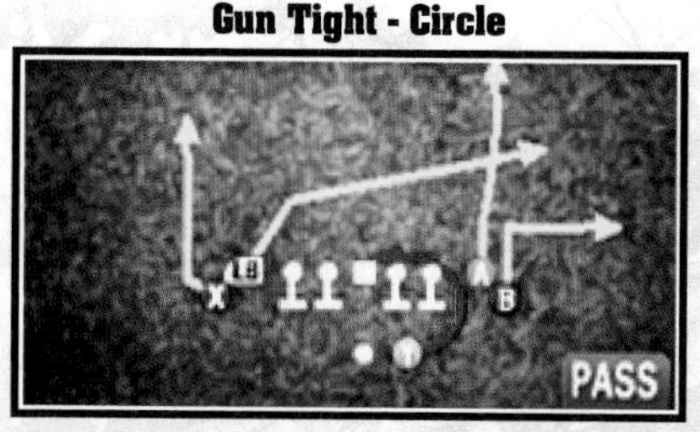

Facing a press-style defense can throw off the offense's rhythm. Gun Tight Circle is a nice play to utilize the sideline. The Gun Tight formation creates more space toward the sideline for our WRs to run routes.

We are targeting the WR running the out route. At the snap of the ball, he is getting jammed by the defender. Hang in the pocket as the WR breaks toward the sideline.

As the WR breaks to the sideline, we throw a lead pass in that direction. The defender is out of position after the press coverage, and we are able to use the extra space as we approach the sideline.

PRO TIP Substitute the WR with a higher Route Running rating to get more separation from the defender.

Zone Beater

Gun Trio - Curl Flat

When attacking a zone defense, you are looking to force the zone defender to choose where they will defend. In this example, we have a curl-flat concept. We have one WR running a flat route and then another WR running a curl route on top of it. This forces the zone defender in that area to choose who he will cover.

Once the ball is snapped, key in first on the WR in the flat. If he springs free, quickly throw the pass to him. If the zone defends against him, the WR running the curl route will open up. The zone defender chose to defend against our WR in the flat.

When you see the zone defender drop off to the flat WR, immediately target the WR on the curl route. Deliver the pass before the zone defender can recover. Attacking zone defense is about making good decisions and not forcing the ball into players who are covered.

PRO TIP Substitute a taller WR in for the curl route. This will make it harder for the defense to defend against.

Base Play

Split Slot - Flat Combo

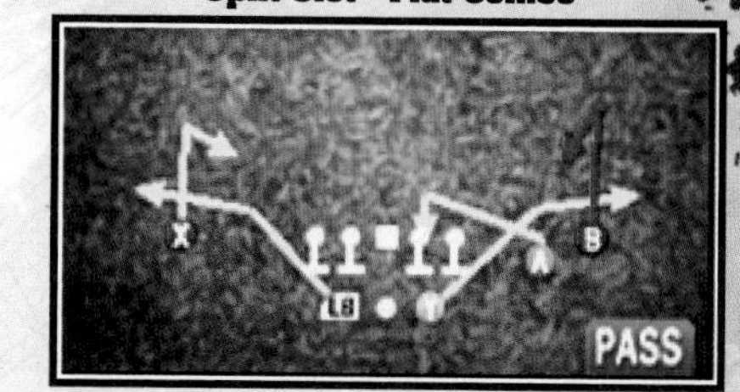

We are going to again attack the zone defense with a curl-flat combo but with the Split Slot formation. This formation gives us the ability to run the curl-flat concept on both sides of the field. Read the zone defender and deliver the pass to the open receiver!

The zone defender is signaling that he has the flat receiver. He is passing off the WR running upfield. We now know that our WR running the curl route will have a small window in which we can fit the ball for the completion.

The pass is on time, and we complete the pass between the zone defenders. The curl-flat concept is one of the best ways to attack zone defenses in *Madden NFL 12*. Be sure to scan the rest of your playbook to find similar plays!

PRO TIP To free up the curl route, hot-route your slot WR on a streak. He will pull the deep defender with him upfield.

BUFFALO BILLS

OFFENSIVE SCOUTING REPORT

While the Bills' record didn't meet expectations in 2010, fans were happy with the emergence of WR Stevie Johnson and QB Ryan Fitzpatrick. The Bills hung tough during the season and showed grit despite missing the playoffs. In *Madden NFL 12*, do not take Buffalo lightly. Gamers should look to start RB C.J. Spiller, who showed flashes of athletic brilliance during his first season. Wide receiver Lee Evans has speed that can stretch the defense vertically. Look to use Ryan Fitzpatrick from the Shotgun to give him extra time with the Bills' offensive line. For tough yards, RB Fred Jackson should be taking the handoffs. With the right scheme, Buffalo can be a force!

DEFENSIVE SCOUTING REPORT

The Buffalo Bills did a tremendous job improving their defense through the draft by selecting Marcell Dareus. Not many teams are able to get instant help at a position by this method. After switching to the 3-4 defense last season, Buffalo should be more comfortable. While they don't have the fastest linebacking core in the league, they are all pretty solid, and that leads to great depth. The secondary has a few athletic players who can turn on the jets if needed. Buffalo should be a much improved team this season.

TEAM RATING

73	Overall
78	Offense
83	Defense

DYNAMIC PLAYER PERFORMANCE TRAITS

Stevie Johnson
WR #13

Consistency	
Confidence	
Cover Ball	
Feet in Bounds	Yes
Drops Open Passes	Yes

RATINGS BY POSITION

Quarterbacks	81
Halfbacks	80
Fullbacks	71
Wide Receivers	79
Tight Ends	69
Tackles	71
Guards	82
Centers	77
Defensive Ends	83
Defensive Tackles	93
Outside Linebackers	76
Middle Linebackers	87
Cornerbacks	80
Free Safeties	84
Strong Safeties	85
Kickers	83
Punters	89

DEPTH CHART

POS	OVR	FIRST NAME	LAST NAME
3DRB	75	C.J.	Spiller
C	77	Geoff	Hangartner
CB	83	Terrence	McGee
CB	77	Drayton	Florence
CB	80	Leodis	McKelvin
CB	71	Aaron	Williams
CB	68	Reggie	Corner
DT	93	Kyle	Williams
DT	66	Torell	Troup
DT	60	Kellen	Heard
FB	71	Corey	McIntyre
FS	84	Jairus	Byrd
FS	64	Jon	Corto
HB	80	Fred	Jackson
HB	75	C.J.	Spiller
HB	66	Johnny	White
HB	65	Quinton	Ganther
K	83	Rian	Lindell
KOS	83	Rian	Lindell
KR	75	C.J.	Spiller
KR	80	Leodis	McKelvin
LE	82	Marcell	Dareus
LE	68	Alex	Carrington
LE	64	John	McCargo
LG	82	Andy	Levitre
LG	62	Cordaro	Howard
LG	74	Chad	Rinehart
LOLB	71	Chris	Kelsay
LOLB	69	Reggie	Torbor
LOLB	57	Danny	Batten
LS	58	Garrison	Sanborn
LT	73	Demetrius	Bell
LT	60	Ed	Wang
MLB	87	Paul	Posluszny
MLB	76	Andra	Davis
MLB	71	Keith	Ellison
MLB	67	Kelvin	Sheppard
P	89	Brian	Moorman
PR	75	C.J.	Spiller
QB	81	Ryan	Fitzpatrick
QB	65	Brian	Brohm
QB	63	Levi	Brown
RE	83	Dwan	Edwards
RE	69	Spencer	Johnson
RG	82	Eric	Wood
RG	64	Kraig	Urbik
ROLB	80	Shawne	Merriman
ROLB	70	Arthur	Moats
ROLB	58	Aaron	Maybin
RT	68	Mansfield	Wrotto
RT	70	Chris	Hairston
RT	70	Erik	Pears
SS	85	Donte	Whitner
SS	75	George	Wilson
SS	79	Bryan	Scott
TE	69	David	Martin
TE	67	Jonathan	Stupar
TE	73	Shawn	Nelson
WR	81	Lee	Evans
WR	86	Steve	Johnson
WR	71	Roscoe	Parrish
WR	69	David	Nelson
WR	59	Donald	Jones
WR	56	Naaman	Roosevelt

OFFENSIVE STRENGTH CHART

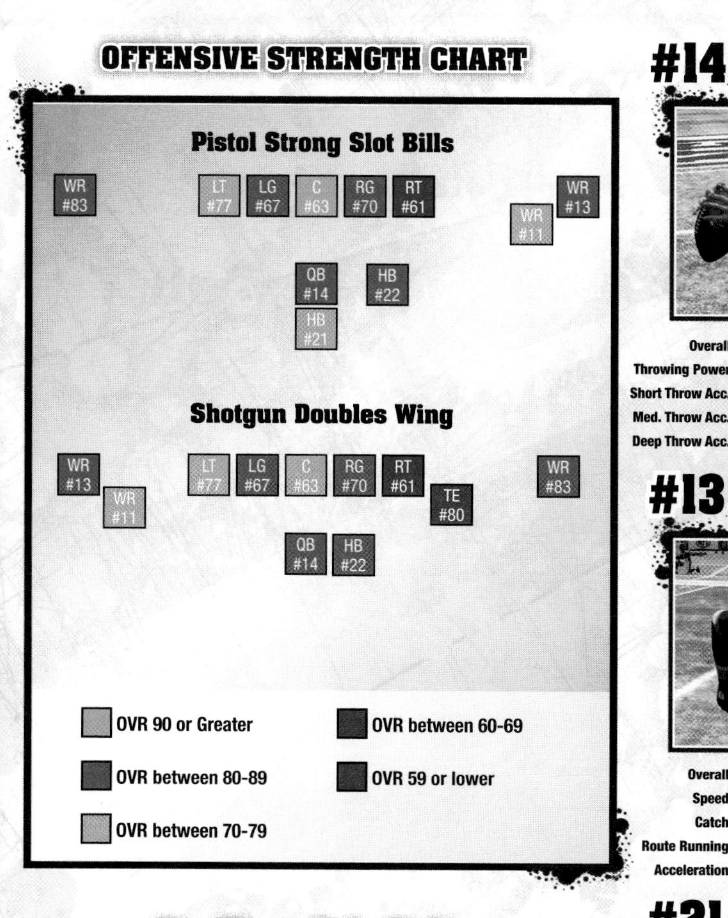

Key Player Substitution

Player: C.J. Spiller

Position: #1 HB

Key Stat: 95 Speed

What He Brings: C.J. Spiller brings the threat to go the distance every time he steps on the field. This agile back looks to prove that he can carry the load full-time this season. This will also free up stronger HB Fred Jackson to move to FB.

#14 Ryan Fitzpatrick
Quarterback

Overall	81
Throwing Power	80
Short Throw Acc.	84
Med. Throw Acc.	83
Deep Throw Acc.	64

#13 Stevie Johnson
Wide Receiver

Overall	86
Speed	88
Catch	84
Route Running	88
Acceleration	92

#21 C.J. Spiller
Halfback

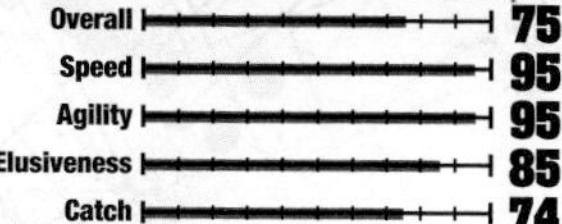

Overall	75
Speed	95
Agility	95
Elusiveness	85
Catch	74

#99 Marcell Dareus
Defensive End

Overall:	82
Speed	73
Strength	92
Power Moves	88
Block Shedding	94

#24 Terrence McGee
Cornerback

Overall	83
Speed	92
Man Coverage	87
Zone Coverage	81
Awareness	82

#58 Aaron Maybin
Linebacker

Overall	58
Speed	84
Awareness	43
Tackling	65
Hit Power	74

DEFENSIVE STRENGTH CHART

3-4 Odd

FS #31, SS #20, CB #29, MLB #54, MLB #51, CB #24, ROLB #55, RE #98, DT #95, LE #99, LOLB #90

Sub 2-3-6 Even

FS #31, SS #20, CB #29, CB #28, MLB #51, SS #37, CB #24, ROLB #55, RE #98, LE #99, LOLB #90

OVR 90 or Greater
OVR between 60-69
OVR between 80-89
OVR 59 or lower
OVR between 70-79

Key Player Substitution

Player: Aaron Maybin

Position: #1 LOLB

Key Stat: 84 Speed

What He Brings: There is no denying his athleticism. Look to user-control him off the edge to counter his low awareness. This player can bring down the QB on any play!

Playbook Tips

Offensive Style: Quick Passing

Offense

- Utilize the Pistol formation because it is one of the most distinctive in the game.
- Look to keep the TEs in to block, giving you more time to pass downfield.
- The Bills work out of the shotgun more than most teams.

Defense

- Unleash rookie Marcell Dareus on the field in pass-rushing situations because he is very quick inside.
- Leave LB Paul Posluszny inside in the new 3-4 scheme for Buffalo.
- New defensive coordinator George Edwards comes from a rich LB tradition in Miami, which means the team should improve.

OFFENSIVE FORMATIONS

FORMATION	# OF PLAYS
Gun Bunch WK	12
Gun Doubles Wing	15
Gun Split Slot	18
Gun Spread	15
Gun Trio Open	15
Gun Trips Open	21
Gun Y-Trips WK	12
I-Form Pro	18
I-Form Tight	15
I-Form Tight Pair	15
Pistol Strong Slot Bills	15
Singleback Ace	15
Singleback Ace Pair Twins	15
Singleback Bunch	12
Singleback Doubles	18
Singleback Tight Doubles	9
Singleback Wing Trips	18
Strong Normal	15
Weak H Slot	12
Wildcat Normal	3

OFFENSIVE PLAYCOUNTS

PLAY TYPE	# OF PLAYS
Quick Pass	15
Standard Pass	40
Shotgun Pass	83
Play Action Pass	54
Inside Handoff	34
Outside Handoff	19
Pitch	8
Counter	10
Draw	12

Three-Headed Rushing Attack

Singleback Ace—Bills Zone Wk

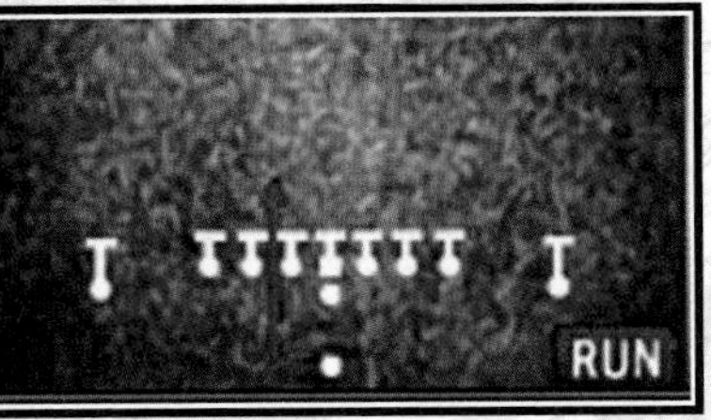

The Bills Zone Wk is a solid run that allows the HB to either run between the tackles or break the run outside to the left. While we don't have a FB, we do have an extra TE on the line who can really seal any player rushing off the edge.

The back takes the handoff and does a tremendous job reading the defender. He can clearly see the LB approaching through the B gap and looks to be cutting the run outside.

When he gets to the line of scrimmage, the back's vision pays off. He can see the LB starting to get to the edge of the defense and cuts back to his original assignment for what could be big yards. When you don't have a lead blocker, choosing a hole at the last possible second allows you time to fool the defense and get them out of position.

PRO TIP The Singleback Ace is a perfectly balanced formation, which makes it easy for the QB to read the defense's alignment.

Singleback Ace—HB Dive

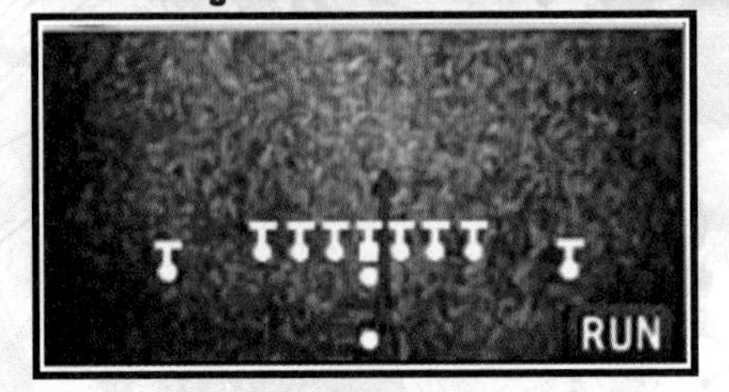

The HB Dive is a straight-ahead run that will make sure the defense does not sneak outside to stop the toss. We can call this with either our speed back or a bruiser who can put his head down and take on a defender.

A hole opens up quickly and the linebackers are unable to shoot through. The only time we would avoid this gap is when the defense gets penetration. This is a smashmouth run meant to pick up 4–5 yards up the middle.

Our linemen do a great job of holding the blocks until the back can make his way into daylight. Now, the running back's job is to set the safety up for a move and not get caught from behind. This is a solid run that will force the defense to keep its linebackers in the box.

PRO TIP Use a stronger HB in this role because running through the tackles can be tough against strong defenses.

Singleback Ace HB Toss

C.J. Spiller has amazing speed. Take full advantage of this and get to the outside into space. The Singleback Ace HB Toss is the perfect play for this.

Spiller receives the toss, and there is an outside running lane. We look to cut upfield right away, as the outside WR is still holding his block. The deep safety is the only man to beat!

The defense closes in as we make our move upfield. Spiller's speed allows us to get a huge chunk of positive yards. We gain six yards on the play!

PRO TIP Just prior to contact, be sure to cover up the ball to avoid fumbling it!

Quick Pass

Tight Doubles Bills Fade

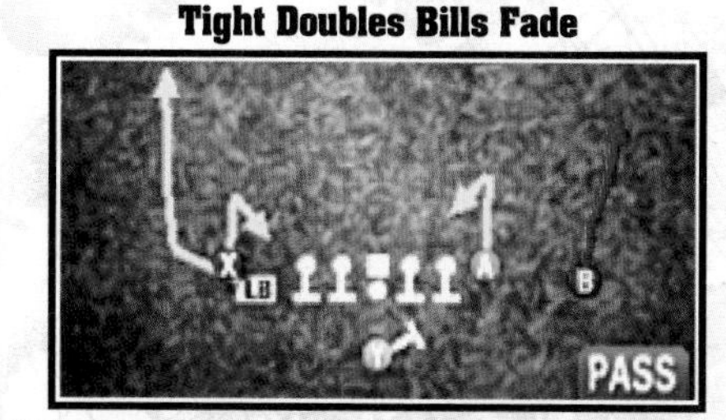

When your opponent looks to bring heavy pressure with the blitz, you will need a play that will quickly result in positive yards. The Tight Doubles Bills Fade allows for a quick pass to our slot WR just after the snap. Read the blitz and get the ball out of the QB's hands!

The man-to-man blitz is coming off the edge. We see the deep safety is going to cover our slot WR. With a quick pass, we can get the ball to our open WR for positive yards!

The pressure was intense, but the safety was late in coverage. We beat the blitz and pick up big yardage in the process.

PRO TIP Sub in one of your higher-rated speed players in the slot position.

Man Beater

Pistol - Mesh

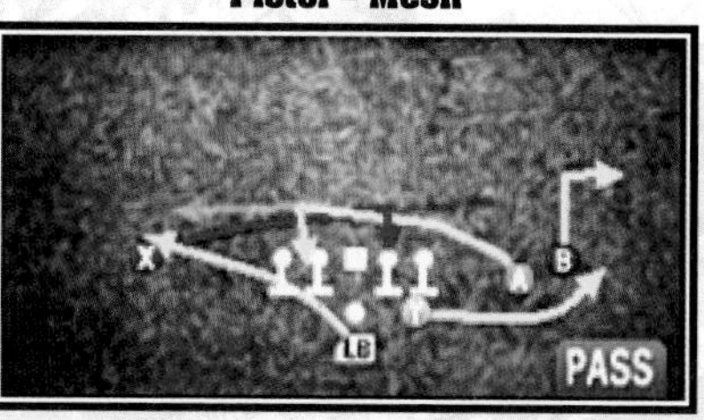

The Pistol is a unique set that allows for extra time in the pocket to read the defense. We are not under center, and we are not in a traditional Shotgun set either. With the extra time in the pocket, we can decipher man coverage or zone coverage much quicker!

We see that the defense is in man-to-man coverage with two safeties deep. Look to your short reads and hit the open man. Our HB is matched up against a slower linebacker as he heads to the flat.

Our faster HB gets upfield as he takes the big hit from the linebacker. The Pistol formation will cause headaches for opponents all season long in *Madden NFL 12*.

PRO TIP If you can't find anything open down the field, check down to your HB. Look to the crossing routes over the middle of the field for a bigger gain.

Zone Beater

Singleback Bunch Z Spot

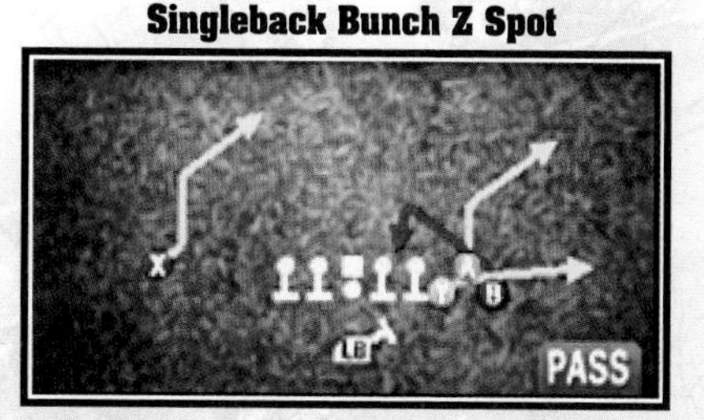

After consistently beating your opponent's man-to-man defensive sets, they will look to play zone coverage. The key to the Singleback Bunch Z Spot is to look at the flat defender. If he chooses to cover our flat WR, then we want to hit our WR on the inside.

The zone defender is covering the flat, and our inside WR has now gained inside position on the zone. Wait for him to turn and face the QB. Throw a high pass to the WR and look to cut upfield.

The pass is delivered on the money with no defenders around him. Make a move upfield to gain extra yards after the catch.

PRO TIP Sub in a taller WR, as this will provide a larger target for your QB.

Base Play

Bills Deep Attack

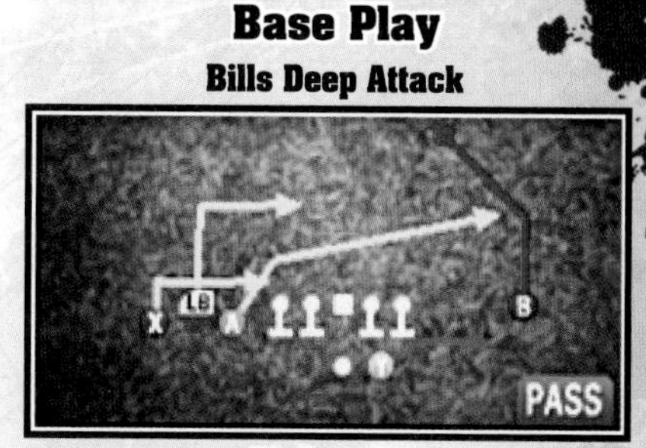

We are looking to take advantage of our downfield threats with this play. We have great route progression that will help free up our main target. In this play, the deep safety must either cover the short crossing pattern or drop back and defend against the deep pass.

Here we have one of our faster WRs going downfield. You can see that in this zone defense, the defender is giving free release to the WR and is telling the deep safety that he is now responsible for covering him.

Our underneath crossing pattern forces the deep safety to step up to guard him. However, our deep route now makes the deep safety drop back into coverage. Here the defender is late in getting back as we make the catch for the big gain. Facing zone defense is about patience and letting routes develop. Hang in the pocket and wait for good things to happen!

PRO TIP The underneath crossing pattern will be completed on a more consistent basis.

DENVER BRONCOS

OFFENSIVE SCOUTING REPORT

The Denver Broncos are a very unique team in *Madden NFL 12*. They have an interesting QB situation where fan favorite QB Tim Tebow can make the defense very anxious with his running ability. Pairing him in the backfield with the very agile RB Knowshon Moreno gives this team a solid ground game. For fans of the full aerial attack, play QB Kyle Orton and look for athletic WR Demaryius Thomas and the reenergized WR Brandon Lloyd. The Bronco's have plenty of great Shotgun formations for your offense to try out.

DEFENSIVE SCOUTING REPORT

The Broncos have plenty of speed on defense to rush the QB off the edge. Set Von Miller and Elvis Dumervil as the OLBs and let them wreak havoc. On the outside, don't worry about leaving CB Champ Bailey on an island. He has the experience to lock up the other team's best threat despite his age. New coach John Fox expects a lot out of this defensive group and will look to maximize their potential by switching to a 4-3 look. Make sure to get star LB D.J. Williams on the field for all downs. He has the speed and hit power to hold things down in the middle. The Broncos should be solid in *Madden NFL 12*!

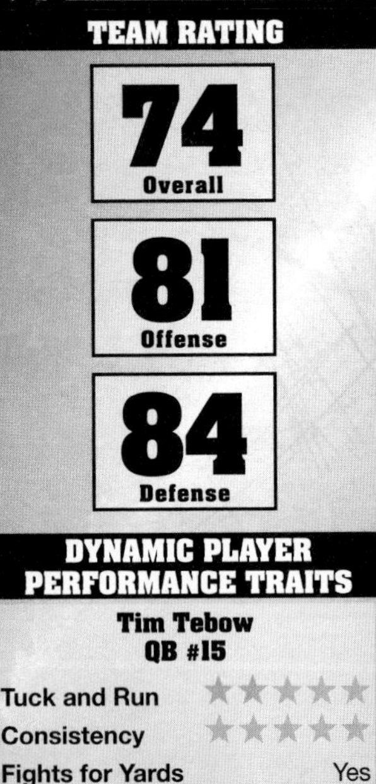

TEAM RATING

74 Overall

81 Offense

84 Defense

DYNAMIC PLAYER PERFORMANCE TRAITS

Tim Tebow
QB #15

Tuck and Run	★★★★★
Consistency	★★★★★
Fights for Yards	Yes
Throws Tight Spiral	No
High Motor	Yes

RATINGS BY POSITION

Quarterbacks	77	Defensive Tackles	77
Halfbacks	85	Outside Linebackers	84
Fullbacks	64	Middle Linebackers	76
Wide Receivers	79	Cornerbacks	92
Tight Ends	67	Free Safeties	87
Tackles	89	Strong Safeties	80
Guards	81	Kickers	80
Centers	71	Punters	72
Defensive Ends	82		

DEPTH CHART

POS	OVR	FIRST NAME	LAST NAME
3DRB	85	Knowshon	Moreno
C	71	J.D.	Walton
C	75	Russ	Hochstein
CB	97	Champ	Bailey
CB	86	Andre'	Goodman
CB	66	Perrish	Cox
CB	67	Nathan	Jones
CB	68	Syd'Quan	Thompson
DT	77	Ronald	Fields
DT	74	Marcus	Thomas
DT	72	Kevin	Vickerson
DT	75	Ryan	McBean
FB	64	Spencer	Larsen
FB	63	Kyle	Eckel
FS	87	Brian	Dawkins
FS	75	Darcel	McBath
FS	73	Rahim	Moore
HB	85	Knowshon	Moreno
HB	76	Correll	Buckhalter
HB	71	Laurence	Maroney
HB	66	Lance	Ball
K	80	Matt	Prater
KOS	80	Matt	Prater
KR	76	Eddie	Royal
KR	73	Demaryius	Thomas
LE	73	Robert	Ayers
LE	77	Jason	Hunter
LG	78	Zane	Beadles
LG	64	Eric	Olsen
LOLB	89	D.J.	Williams
LOLB	55	Lee	Robinson
LS	67	Lonie	Paxton
LT	92	Ryan	Clady
LT	55	Chris	Clark
MLB	76	Joe	Mays
MLB	78	Mario	Haggan
MLB	65	Nate	Irving
MLB	53	Mike	Mohamed
P	72	Britton	Colquitt
PR	76	Eddie	Royal
QB	77	Tim	Tebow
QB	82	Kyle	Orton
QB	72	Brady	Quinn
RE	91	Elvis	Dumervil
RE	73	David	Veikune
RE	64	Jeremy	Beal
RG	84	Chris	Kuper
RG	68	Stanley	Daniels
ROLB	79	Von	Miller
ROLB	66	Wesley	Woodyard
ROLB	61	Braxton	Kelley
RT	85	Ryan	Harris
RT	67	Orlando	Franklin
RT	71	Herb	Taylor
SS	80	Renaldo	Hill
SS	66	David	Bruton
SS	64	Kyle	McCarthy
TE	67	Richard	Quinn
TE	64	Julius	Thomas
TE	63	Virgil	Green
WR	88	Brandon	Lloyd
WR	76	Eddie	Royal
WR	73	Jabar	Gaffney
WR	73	Demaryius	Thomas
WR	69	Eric	Decker
WR	64	Matthew	Willis

OFFENSIVE STRENGTH CHART

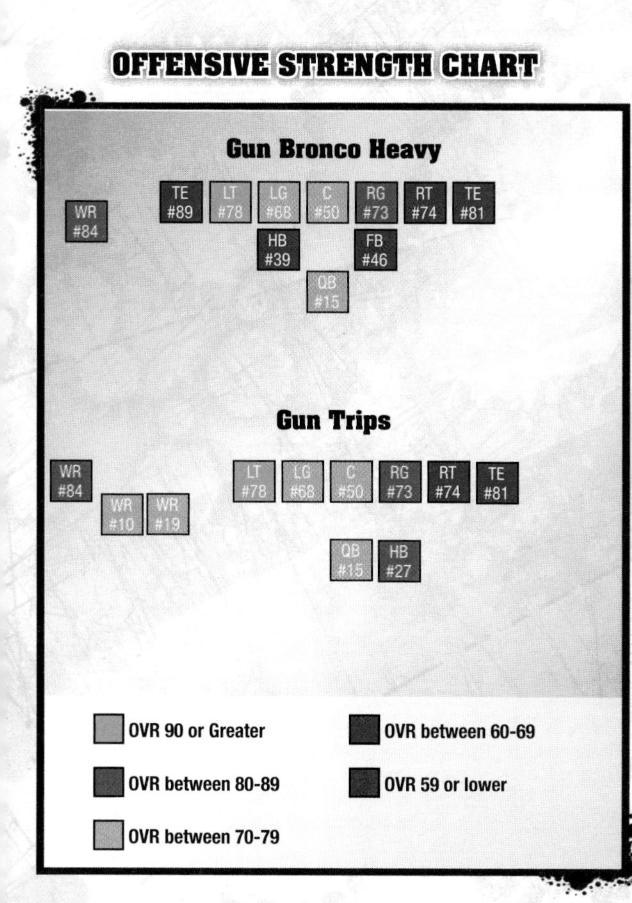

#15 Tim Tebow
Quarterback

Overall	77
Throwing Power	88
Short Throw Acc.	76
Med. Throw Acc.	75
Deep Throw Acc.	77

#24 Champ Bailey
Cornerback

Overall	97
Speed	95
Man Coverage	97
Zone Coverage	90
Awareness	98

#27 Knowshon Moreno
Halfback

Overall	85
Speed	88
Agility	97
Elusiveness	90
Catch	80

#55 D.J. Williams
Linebacker

Overall	89
Speed	83
Awareness	88
Tackling	92
Hit Power	95

#88 Demaryius Thomas
Wide Receiver

Overall	73
Speed	96
Catch	81
Route Running	59
Acceleration	92

#59 Wesley Woodward
Right Outside Linebacker

Overall	66
Speed	85
Awareness	68
Tackling	76
Hit Power	82

DEFENSIVE STRENGTH CHART

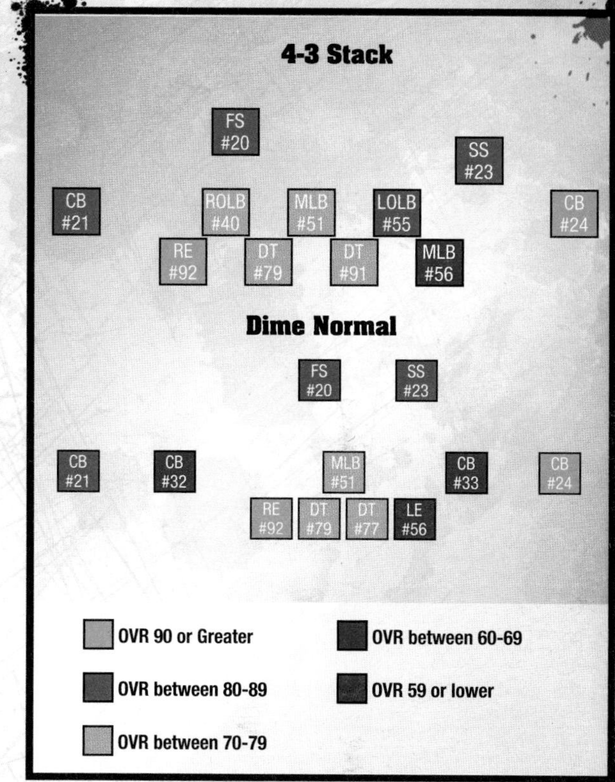

Key Player Substitution

Player: Tim Tebow

Position: #1 QB (Red Zone)

Key Stat: 84 Trucking

What He Brings: Tim Tebow is not only a fan favorite, he is a dual threat in the red zone. Look for him to steamroll defenders on his way in for 6. If the defense crowds the line, get ready to unleash one of his famous passes over the line!

Key Player Substitution

Player: Von Miller

Position: #2 LB (Nickel)

Key Stat: 94 Acceleration

What He Brings: Von Miller is a great rookie addition for the Broncos. John Fox has been able make use of similar talent in the past. Look to send Miller off the edge opposite from Dumervil because no pair of tackles can match up with the burst of these two rushers.

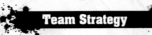

Playbook Tips

Offensive Style: Pass Balanced

Offense

- The Gun Bronco Heavy formation allows users to substitute in Tim Tebow while leaving Kyle Orton as the starter. Use this formation to catch the defense off guard.
- Depending on your game plan, use Orton for short accurate passes that let the WRs get in space.
- Denver has compiled a solid WR core to go along with more than 80 shotgun passing plays.

Defense

- The Broncos are switching back to a 4-3 defense this season under coach John Fox.
- A healthy Elvis Dumervil is essential to the Broncos getting pressure without sending extra blitzers.
- Move Brian Dawkins to strong safety to play the run.

OFFENSIVE FORMATIONS

FORMATION	# OF PLAYS
Gun Bronco Heavy	9
Gun Bunch WK	15
Gun Doubles Flex	15
Gun Empty Spread	9
Gun Normal Y-Slot	12
Gun Snugs Flip	9
Gun Split Bronco	15
Gun Trips	15
Gun Wing Trips WK	21
I-Form TE Flip	15
I-Form Tight	15
I-Form Tight Pair	12
Singleback Ace	15
Singleback Ace Twins	12
Singleback Doubles	15
Singleback Flip Trips	12
Singleback Jumbo Z	9
Singleback Trips Open	9
Singleback Y-Trips	18
Strong Pro	15
Weak Tight Pair	12
Wildcat Wild Horse	3

OFFENSIVE PLAYCOUNTS

PLAY TYPE	# OF PLAYS
Quick Pass	15
Standard Pass	46
Shotgun Pass	83
Play Action Pass	47
Inside Handoff	31
Outside Handoff	15
Pitch	12
Counter	5
Draw	12

Three-Headed Rushing Attack

Singleback Jumbo Z—PA Middle

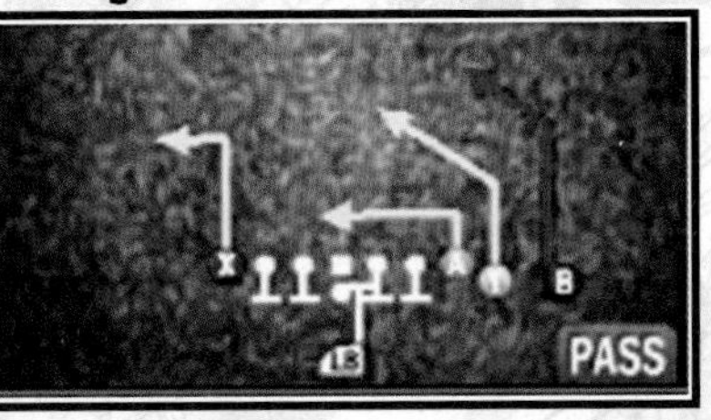

The Singleback Jumbo Z does a great job of bringing extra beef into the game to help with run blocking. However, a run to the weak side is not beneficial since our power is on the strong side. Instead, our run left will utilize a play action fake and then hit the player crossing back over the middle.

The defense should have its power run personnel in the game because of our package. If we have success pounding the rock early, we can set them up for the fake. Here the QB uses the same drop-back as the run middle.

The play fake works, holding the defenders for just a minute. The defense fails to get any motion into the backfield and our QB has plenty of time to make a good throw back across the middle. This is a great run substitute and will force the defense to respect another aspect of our game.

PRO TIP If the defense loses contain, scramble with QB Tim Tebow, who can punish smaller defenders with his trucking.

Singleback Jumbo Z—H Zone Str

The H Zone Str has a nice auto-motion that puts an extra blocker in a great area to help in the run game. As soon as the RB gets the handoff, feel your way from the inside out. This is the most effective way to run this play.

The defense is doing a good job of closing up the primary hope of getting outside, but the shifty running back will be able to cut inside and avoid trouble on the edge.

[illegible] the [illegible] the [illegible] the middle, he can keep the

chains moving and make sure the defense is more disciplined next time they see this run. When mixed in with the HB Dive from the same formation this combo can be deadly. Having the extra TEs on the strong side can really help the back hit the outside.

PRO TIP The Jumbo Z formation is essential for the Broncos, who have the right personnel to utilize it.

Singleback Jumbo Z HB Dive

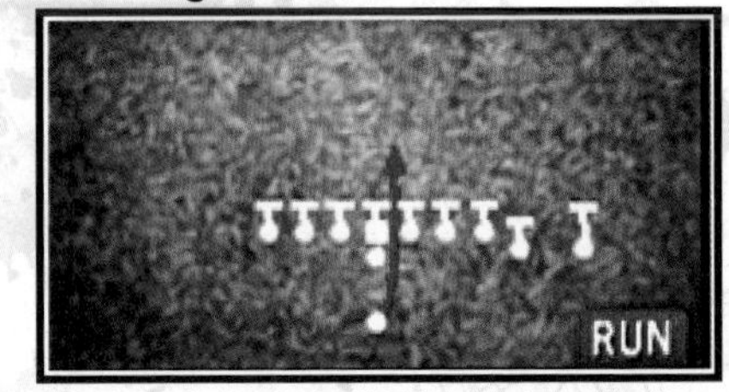

The Singleback Jumbo Z HB Dive loads up the line of scrimmage with extra TEs to aid in run blocking. The HB Dive is a north-south run; you will want to keep this run inside. As soon as you receive the handoff, look to get the ball upfield as you read your running lanes.

The HB gets the handoff, and you immediately see two running lanes open up. You can cut to the left hole or go straight ahead. If you go left, you will have to shake the linebacker who is free. By choosing straight ahead, you will be able to pick up easy yards until the defense closes in.

We choose to go straight ahead and avoid the initial contact with the linebacker. As we make our move upfield, the deep safety clamps down on the run. We can pick up six yards on the HB Dive.

PRO TIP Avoid using spin moves and jukes on HB Dives. Find the open hole and hit it hard!

Quick Pass

Bronco Heavy - Bronco Corner

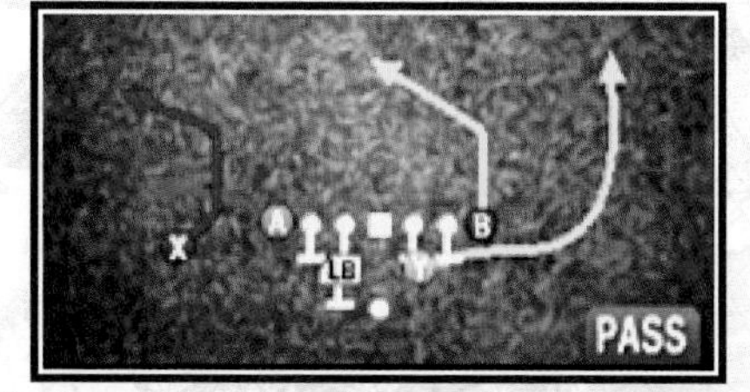

The Bronco Heavy formation was designed for QB Tim Tebow. This is a solid formation for mobile QBs to use their athletic ability to attack the defense. What makes QBs such as Tebow dangerous is their ability to run and pass. The Bronco Corner has nice protection to sit in the pocket and find the open man.

One of the best ways to have solid pass protection is to utilize blue routes. These are designed to block any initial pressure and then release out for a pass. The TE looks to block the DE off the left edge. As soon as he releases, we will look to get him the ball.

The TE released into the flat and picked up extra yards after the catch. We were able to trick the defense, as they initially thought the TE was going to stay in to block. After the release, the defender was a step behind our TE. Blue routes are highly effective tools for all offensive schemes!

Man Beater

Gun Snugs Stick

Against man-to-man coverage, Gun Snugs Stick is one of the best plays in the game. It is fast-developing and has dual flat routes. This play can cause major problems for all defenses.

Here we can see the quick nature of this play. Our WR is heading straight to the flat. Meanwhile, his man-to-man defender is already a step behind in coverage. Get the ball out quick to the WR and look to get upfield.

The pass is delivered, away from the defender. We still have a few steps on the defender and will look to break upfield as quick as possible. Be sure to check the opposite side of the field, as we have the same route concept being run there.

PRO TIP Substitute your highest-rated speed player for this play.

Zone Beater

Gun Wing Trips WK TE Deep Out

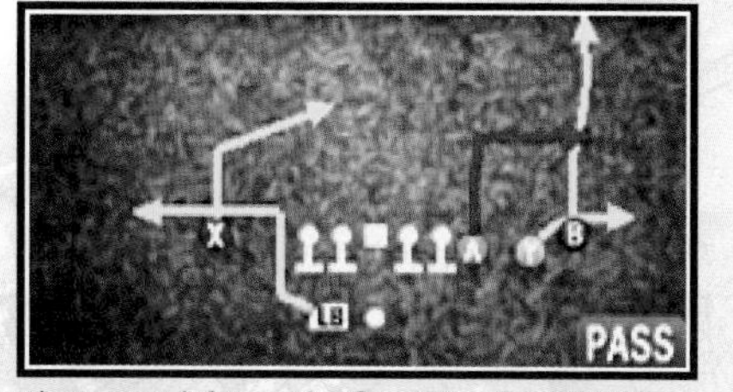

Against zone defense, the Gun Wing Trips WK TE Deep Out does a nice job at attacking the deep part of the field. At the snap of the ball, the short flat route will draw the attention of the defense. The TE running the deep out route will help keep the safety honest as he drives upfield. Meanwhile, our deep streak route looks to create a one-on-one matchup downfield.

There are two things happening here: The underneath defender is choosing to go after our flat WR, and the safety's attention is drawn to our TE over the middle of the field. This gives us the matchup we are looking for with the deep ball.

The deep ball is thrown perfectly, and we are able to jump up and make the catch. Zone defense can be difficult to beat. If attacked properly, it can be one of the easier things to do.

Base Play

Singleback Flip Trips Bronco Fork

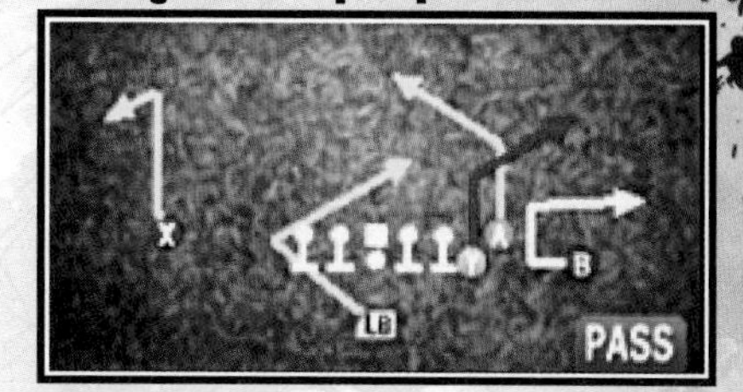

The Singleback Flip Trips Bronco Fork has one of the best HB routes in the game. Sharp angle routes are great for beating man-to-man blitz packages. They are quick to develop, which helps attack the blitz.

At the snap of the ball, the HB will release to the short flat and then cut back toward the middle of the field. Against the blitz, you will want to throw just prior to the HB's cut upfield. The blitzing linebacker is steps away from our QB. Deliver the pass before the HB makes his initial cut toward the middle of the field.

We haul in the pass before the pressure is able to get to us. The HB makes the catch well before the defender can make a play on the ball. We beat the blitz and gain seven yards on the play!

PRO TIP In third-down situations, make sure to substitute a HB with a High Catch rating in the game.

CLEVELAND BROWNS

OFFENSIVE SCOUTING REPORT

The Cleveland Browns are best used as a ball-control offense. The Browns made off-season news when fans voted HB Peyton Hillis as the *Madden NFL 12* cover athlete. The HB exploded onto the scene and easily eclipsed 1,000 yards and 10-plus TDs in 2010. The Browns also look to switch their offense under new head coach Pat Shurmur. Colt McCoy had a promising rookie season and will blossom with a West Coast–style attack. McCoy can deliver the ball on short throws (88 Short Throw Acc) and keep this offense marching downfield. If we can deliver the ball to dynamic players like Joshua Cribbs in space (98 Agility, 96 Acceleration), the Browns are a threat!

DEFENSIVE SCOUTING REPORT

Joe Haden reenergized the city of Cleveland last season with his dynamic play and commitment to the franchise. With T.J. Ward also playing strong, the Browns' pass D is looking solid. Where the team could use some help is with the pass rush. The team simply did not generate enough pressure on opposing QBs. However, new defensive coordinator Dick Jauron and his new 4-3 regime look to be very aggressive. With a solid ground attack on offense, the Browns defense only needs a few big stops a game; if you can force turnovers with them, you can bring them to prominence.

TEAM RATING

74	Overall
82	Offense
81	Defense

DYNAMIC PLAYER PERFORMANCE TRAITS

Peyton Hillis
RB #40

Cover Ball	★★★★★
Consistency	★★★★★
Fights for Yards	Yes
Clutch	Yes
High Motor	Yes

RATINGS BY POSITION

Quarterbacks	77	Defensive Tackles	81
Halfbacks	91	Outside Linebackers	84
Fullbacks	90	Middle Linebackers	83
Wide Receivers	75	Cornerbacks	85
Tight Ends	83	Free Safeties	80
Tackles	86	Strong Safeties	85
Guards	79	Kickers	87
Centers	88	Punters	62
Defensive Ends	69		

DEPTH CHART

POS	OVR	FIRST NAME	LAST NAME
3DRB	91	Peyton	Hillis
C	88	Alex	Mack
C	71	Steve	Vallos
CB	86	Joe	Haden
CB	84	Sheldon	Brown
CB	81	Eric	Wright
CB	73	Mike	Adams
CB	62	Coye	Francies
DT	81	Ahtyba	Rubin
DT	74	Phil	Taylor
DT	71	Brian	Schaefering
DT	72	Derreck	Robinson
DT	56	Travis	Ivey
FB	90	Lawrence	Vickers
FB	67	Owen	Marecic
FS	80	Abram	Elam
FS	63	Ray	Ventrone
HB	91	Peyton	Hillis
HB	71	Mike	Bell
HB	71	Montario	Hardesty
K	87	Phil	Dawson
KOS	87	Phil	Dawson
KR	79	Josh	Cribbs
KR	86	Joe	Haden
LE	66	Jayme	Mitchell
LE	55	Brian	Sanford
LG	86	Eric	Steinbach
LG	64	Pat	Murray
LOLB	86	Matt	Roth
LOLB	79	Chris	Gocong
LOLB	73	Jason	Trusnik
LS	64	Ryan	Pontbriand
LT	95	Joe	Thomas
LT	56	Phil	Trautwein
MLB	83	D'Qwell	Jackson
MLB	69	Kaluka	Maiava
P	62	Reggie	Hodges
PR	79	Josh	Cribbs
QB	77	Colt	McCoy
QB	73	Seneca	Wallace
QB	73	Jake	Delhomme
RE	72	Jabaal	Sheard
RE	75	Marcus	Benard
RG	72	Shawn	Lauvao
RG	63	Jason	Pinkston
ROLB	82	Scott	Fujita
ROLB	64	Titus	Brown
ROLB	62	Steve	Octavien
RT	77	Tony	Pashos
RT	62	Brandon	Braxton
SS	85	T.J.	Ward
SS	73	Sabby	Piscitelli
SS	57	Eric	Hagg
TE	83	Benjamin	Watson
TE	75	Evan	Moore
TE	72	Alex	Smith
WR	76	Mohamed	Massaquoi
WR	70	Greg	Little
WR	79	Josh	Cribbs
WR	70	Brian	Robiskie
WR	68	Chansi	Stuckey
WR	65	Demetrius	Williams

OFFENSIVE STRENGTH CHART

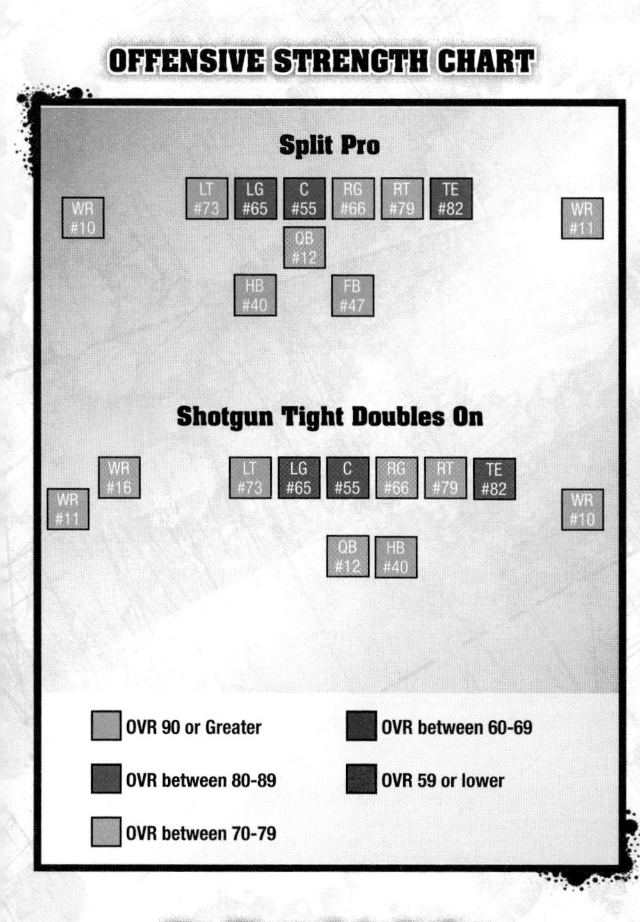

Key Player Substitution

Player: Seneca Wallace

Position: #2 QB Slot

Key Stat: 84 Speed

What He Brings: Seneca Wallace is a great option to bring into the game if you're looking to catch the defense off guard. He has solid speed and can really gash the defense with his legs. Play him sparingly and try using the hurry-up to keep the defense off balance.

#40 Peyton Hillis
Halfback

Overall	91
Speed	87
Agility	86
Trucking	99
Catch	79

#16 Joshua Cribbs
Wide Receiver

Overall	79
Speed	92
Catch	69
Route Running	70
Acceleration	96

#6 Seneca Wallace
Quarterback

Overall	73
Throwing Power	78
Short Throw Acc.	74
Med. Throw Acc.	70
Deep Throw Acc.	71

#53 Matt Roth
Linebacker

Overall	86
Speed	75
Awareness	86
Tackling	90
Hit Power	79

#23 Joe Haden
Cornerback

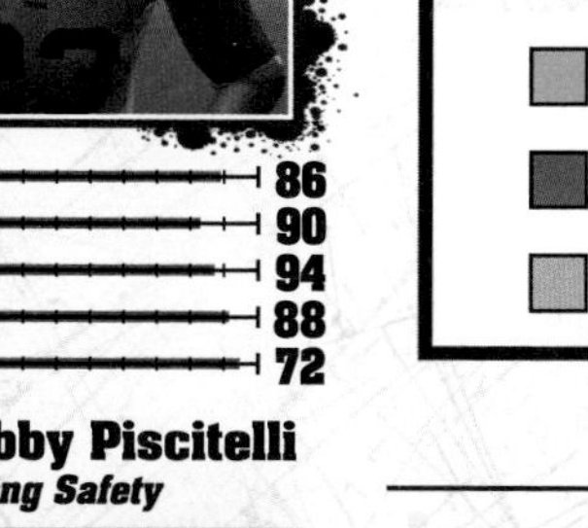

Overall	86
Speed	90
Man Coverage	94
Zone Coverage	88
Awareness	72

#28 Sabby Piscitelli
Strong Safety

Overall	73
Speed	87
Tackling	74
Hit Power	86
Play Recognition	56

DEFENSIVE STRENGTH CHART

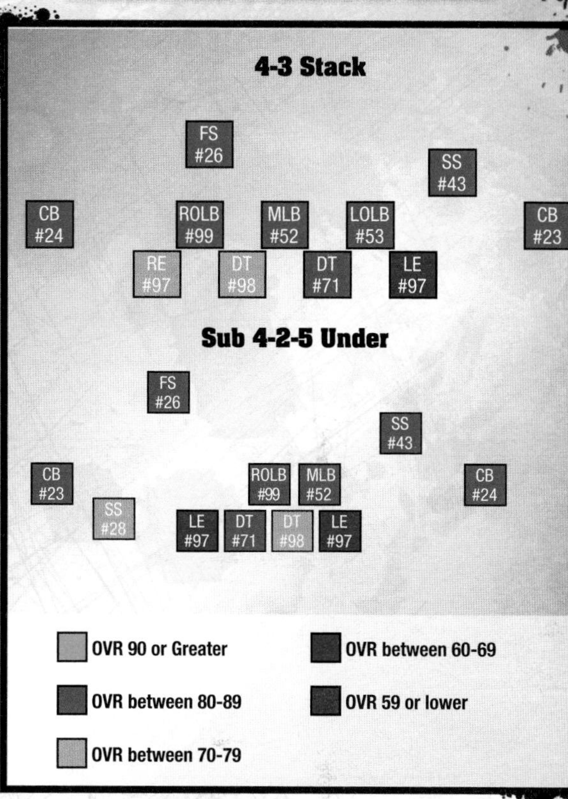

Key Player Substitution

Player: Sabby Piscitelli

Position: #1 FS

Key Stat: 87 Speed

What He Brings: Sabby is a *Madden NFL* favorite due to his solid speed and great hit power. If you properly user-control him, he will play way above his rating and bring good size to your secondary.

Playbook Tips

Offensive Style: Run Heavy

Offense

- Peyton Hillis is one of the best power backs in the game; get him running downhill.
- Use Colt McCoy's legs to roll out and stress the defense.
- Cleveland can excel by throwing short passes to Joshua Cribbs underneath the defense.

Defense

- Help out the defensive line by bringing some extra blitzers on long yardage downs.
- Allow CB Joe Haden to work alone against a team's top threat until he gets beaten consistently.
- Shaun Rogers can eat up space and allow your MLBs to make plays behind him all game.

OFFENSIVE FORMATIONS

FORMATION	# OF PLAYS
Far Pro	12
Flash Split	3
Flash Trio	3
Gun Doubles On	15
Gun Empty Trey	12
Gun Split Offset	21
Gun Snugs Flip	12
Gun Tight Doubles On	12
Gun Trey Open	15
I-Form Pro	18
I-Form Tight	12
I-Form Twin TE	15
Singleback Ace	12
Singleback Ace Pair Twins	12
Singleback Bunch	18
Singleback Doubles	21
Singleback Jumbo	12
Singleback Y-Trips	15
Split Pro	9
Strong Pro	18
Strong Twins Flex	12
Weak Tight Pair	12

OFFENSIVE PLAYCOUNTS

PLAY TYPE	# OF PLAYS
Quick Pass	21
Standard Pass	56
Shotgun Pass	62
Play Action Pass	53
Inside Handoff	39
Outside Handoff	17
Pitch	12
Counter	6
Draw	9

Three-Headed Rushing Attack

I-Form Tight—HB Lead Toss

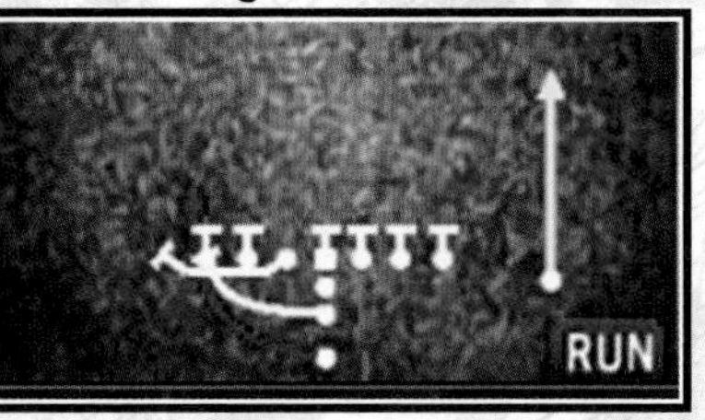

The HB Lead Toss is a great way to get outside to the weak side of your formation. The play is set to run left; however, at the snap our QB reads that the defense is weak to the right. Our QB playmakers for the run to go right and quickly snaps the ball while the defense is off guard.

Peyton Hillis swings out wide and picks up the toss. With most big backs, you want to get them running north and south quickly, but the HB Lead Toss has enough blocking that the back can get to top speed before meeting any defenders.

With a hole opened up around to the right, our HB is cutting outside instead of taking the sure yardage up the middle. This is actually a good cut because he is using the wall of blockers between him and the safety as a wall. He holds the inside until the last second and looks to get the safety stuck inside and unable to recover on the play.

PRO TIP Use the play action quick audible early to stop the defense from creeping the safeties up into the box.

I-Form Tight—Zone Stretch

The stretch run is used when we want to run outside of the tackle but prefer to hand the ball off. Make sure to follow the FB, as he is our only lead blocker on the play.

This run is set up to attack the strong side of the formation, and at the snap our FB gets out in front of the halfback. The QB quickly gets the ball to the halfback. The WR on the right looks to block his safety and hold the edge of the field down, but his assignment beats him and starts heading down the line of scrimmage.

This is where the FB comes in handy; he picks up the CB and easily blows him out of the water. However, this leaves nobody to block the safety downfield. This is where Peyton Hillis and his great trucking ability come in handy. Look to maintain your speed and put your head down to bowl over the safety. No need to make a cut—just try to demolish him.

PRO TIP Make sure to cover up the football with HB Peyton Hillis; many defenders go for the ball since it takes so long to bring him down.

I-Tight Browns Zone WK

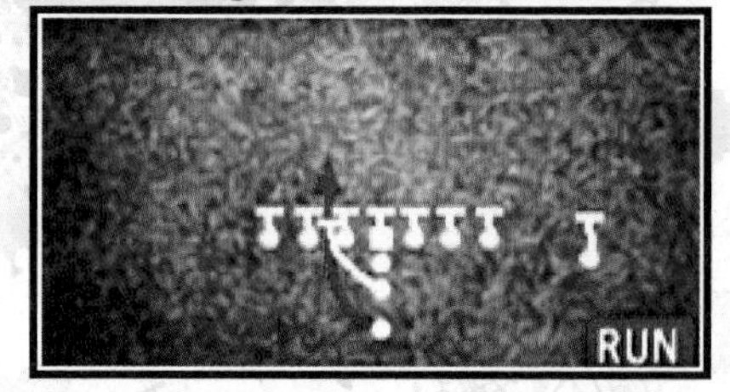

The I-Tight Browns Zone WK is ideal for a HB like Peyton Hillis. The formation allows us to run the ball to the left and right while maintaining balance on both sides of the field. The Browns Zone WK gives us the ability to go both inside and outside with the ball.

As soon as the ball is snapped, we see the balance of the I-Tight formation paying off. We have three running lanes that have opened up. We can hit the hole to the right and take on the safety, follow our FB up the middle, or bounce the ball outside.

We choose the outside lane and take the contact head-on. Peyton Hillis is a big guy who does not shy away from contact. We are able to plow through the defender and pick up a tough four yards!

PRO TIP When using a big back like Peyton Hillis, look to create contact, as he will often fall forward for extra yards.

Quick Pass

Singleback Jumbo - PA Drag Wheel

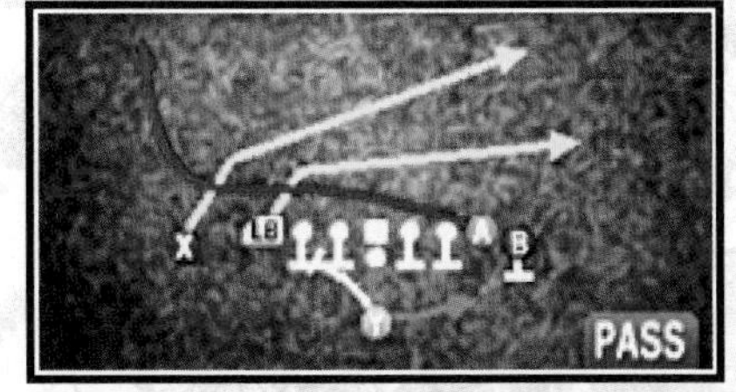

Once we get our opponent thinking about the run, we will want to capitalize on the play action. With the PA Drag Wheel, we are looking to get the ball to our playmaking TE. Look for the defense to freeze on the play action and deliver the ball to the TE.

Here we see the play action to the HB. Key in on the linebackers in the middle of the field. Look for them to bite on the play action and be out of position for the pass.

We deliver the pass to the TE who can utilize his speed to gain extra yards after the catch. Play action looks to make a return in *Madden NFL 12*. When matched together, using play action in the run game can be very difficult to stop!

Man Beater

Y-Trips WR Screen

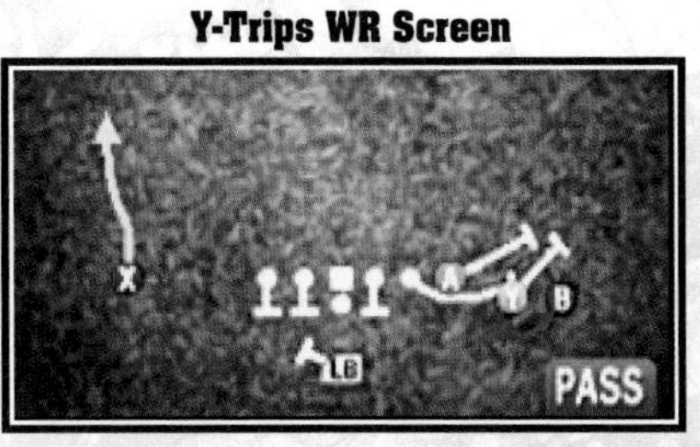

When teams look to bring the blitz, the Y-Trips WR Screen is a great play to get playmaker Joshua Cribbs into the action. Cribbs's explosive speed and agility make him a threat every time he touches the ball.

At the snap of the ball, we see the WR Screen develop. The blitzing defender is looking to close in on the QB. However, we are looking to counter the blitz with the screen to Cribbs.

Cribbs makes the catch and gets upfield in a hurry. We have only one man to beat down the sideline. It is all about getting the ball to your playmakers.

PRO TIP Substitute a TE for the slot WR. The TE will provide better blocking for the WR Screen.

Zone Beater

Split Pro Texas

An effective way to attack a blitzing defense is to utilize the mobility of your QB. Colt McCoy can move around in the pocket. With the Split Pro Texas, we are looking to roll out to the right to create a better passing angle for a FB out of the backfield.

The blitz is on and is again closing in on our QB. We look to roll out to the right with McCoy. As our HB makes his break toward the middle of the field, we will deliver the pass.

We elude the blitz with our mobile QB and deliver the pass. Our FB makes the catch and has room to run afterward. Make sure to cover the ball up as the defense closes in.

PRO TIP Substitute a TE for the FB to give your QB a better receiving threat out of the backfield.

Base Play

Gun Tight Doubles On WR Cross

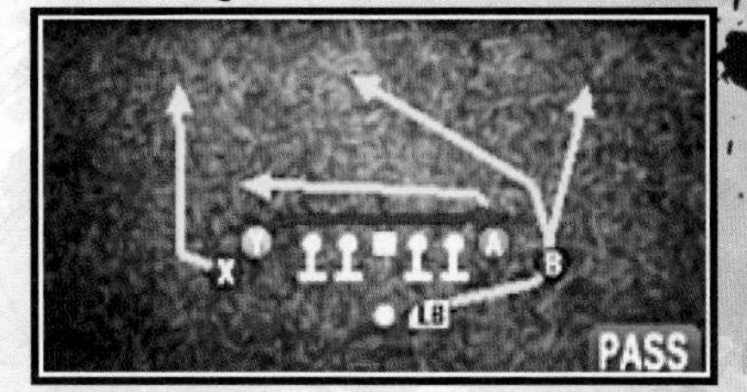

The Gun Tight Doubles On WR Cross is one of the best plays in the game. The route combinations make this play ideal for both man and zone. Be careful, as this play lacks pass protection, and be quick with your offensive reads.

At the snap of the ball, we see that the defense is in man-to-man with two safeties over the top. Both our crossing routes over the middle of the field have opened up. We also see the deep middle of the field is open.

We decide to pass to our TE, who is matched up against the slower linebacker. This is a favorable matchup for yards after the catch, so look to cut upfield as soon as the catch is made!

PRO TIP The deep post over the middle of the field is good for the big play. For a high-risk, high-reward target, throw to this WR.

TAMPA BAY BUCCANEERS

OFFENSIVE SCOUTING REPORT

The Tampa Bay Buccaneers are a huge sleeper team in *Madden NFL 12*. Josh Freeman is a talented young QB with a knack for making the big play. Freeman has a unique blend of strength, speed, and throwing power that will only improve this season. QB Josh Johnson is a secret weapon off the bench. Work some short throws into your game plan and look to use Johnson's legs if the defense doesn't respect his speed. At the WR position, Mike Williams proved he was a consistent big-play threat with a nose for the end zone. The Buc's playbook will set up better this season for RB LeGarrette Blount, who proved to be a punishing runner. If you want to get a RB involved in the passing game, look for Cadillac Williams, who has solid hands out of the backfield. TE Kellen Winslow established himself as a threat by blocking in the run game and leading the team in receptions. Winslow has a big 6'4" frame and is the Buc's best and most athletic target on offense.

DEFENSIVE SCOUTING REPORT

The Buccaneers have seemingly been rebuilding their defense ever since Jon Gruden left the scene. The team has been shifting around its style under Raheem Morris and finally looks to be ready to go. After a solid 10-6 season last year, the defense will have to ramp it up just one more level to put the Bucs into the playoffs. Ronde Barber is a solid player in zone coverage. The Bucs will also have to quickly find a replacement for departed CB Aqib Talib. Thankfully, the defensive line showed great improvement last season and should be one season stronger. If they can get anything from talented rookie Da'Quan Bowers, it will be a big bonus. This may be the first time the offense looks to help out the defense in Tampa Bay.

RATINGS BY POSITION

Quarterbacks	87
Halfbacks	81
Fullbacks	78
Wide Receivers	76
Tight Ends	89
Tackles	81
Guards	81
Centers	85
Defensive Ends	76
Defensive Tackles	81
Outside Linebackers	80
Middle Linebackers	86
Cornerbacks	86
Free Safeties	70
Strong Safeties	81
Kickers	71
Punters	58

TEAM RATING

84 Overall

85 Offense

80 Defense

DYNAMIC PLAYER PERFORMANCE TRAITS

Josh Freeman
QB #5

Senses Pressure	★★★★★
Consistency	★★★★★
Confidence	★★★★★
Throws Tight Spiral	Yes
Clutch	Yes

DEPTH CHART

POS	OVR	FIRST NAME	LAST NAME
3DRB	76	Carnell	Williams
C	85	Jeff	Faine
C	73	Jeremy	Zuttah
CB	86	Aqib	Talib
CB	85	Ronde	Barber
CB	69	E.J.	Biggers
CB	66	Myron	Lewis
CB	65	Elbert	Mack
DT	81	Gerald	McCoy
DT	71	Roy	Miller
DT	71	Brian	Price
DT	63	Al	Woods
FB	78	Earnest	Graham
FB	60	Erik	Lorig
FS	70	Cody	Grimm
FS	67	Corey	Lynch
FS	58	Dominique	Harris
HB	81	LeGarrette	Blount
HB	76	Carnell	Williams
HB	60	Kareem	Huggins
HB	62	Kregg	Lumpkin
K	71	Connor	Barth
KOS	71	Connor	Barth
KR	67	Micheal	Spurlock
KR	55	Preston	Parker
LE	78	Adrian	Clayborn
LE	70	Kyle	Moore
LE	66	Tim	Crowder
LG	73	Ted	Larsen
LG	59	Brandon	Carter
LOLB	77	Quincy	Black
LOLB	61	Dekoda	Watson
LS	61	Andrew	Economos
LT	87	Donald	Penn
LT	51	Will	Barker
MLB	86	Barrett	Ruud
MLB	62	Tyrone	McKenzie
MLB	65	Mason	Foster
P	58	Robert	Malone
PR	67	Micheal	Spurlock
QB	87	Josh	Freeman
QB	67	Josh	Johnson
QB	59	Rudy	Carpenter
RE	74	Da'Quan	Bowers
RE	71	Stylez	White
RE	72	Michael	Bennett
RG	88	Davin	Joseph
RG	64	Derek	Hardman
ROLB	82	Geno	Hayes
ROLB	66	Adam	Hayward
RT	75	James	Lee
RT	71	Jeremy	Trueblood
RT	61	Demar	Dotson
SS	81	Sean	Jones
SS	64	Larry	Asante
SS	69	Ahmad	Black
TE	89	Kellen	Winslow
TE	71	Luke	Stocker
TE	59	Daniel	Hardy
WR	84	Mike	Williams
WR	76	Arrelious	Benn
WR	69	Sammie	Stroughter
WR	67	Micheal	Spurlock
WR	68	Maurice	Stovall
WR	55	Preston	Parker

OFFENSIVE STRENGTH CHART

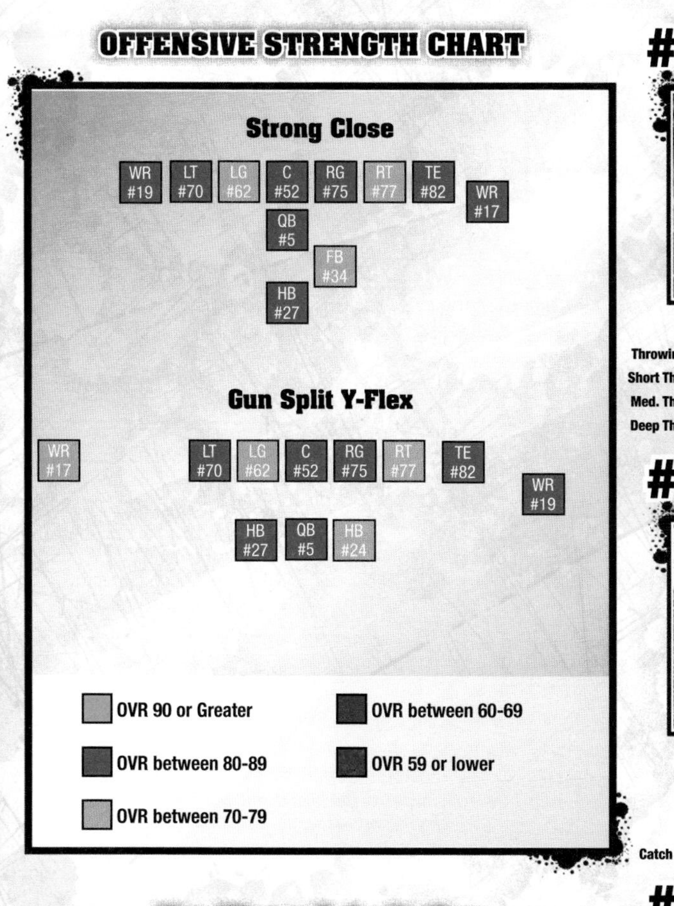

Key Player Substitution

Player: Josh Johnson

Position: #2 QB

Key Stat: 95 Jump

What He Brings: Josh Johnson has been a tremendous threat in the game over the last few seasons. Look to use him sparingly on bootlegs and for play action to catch the defense off guard. He can really hurt a defense that loses contain or forgets to place a spy on him. Try to find a way to get him five snaps a game.

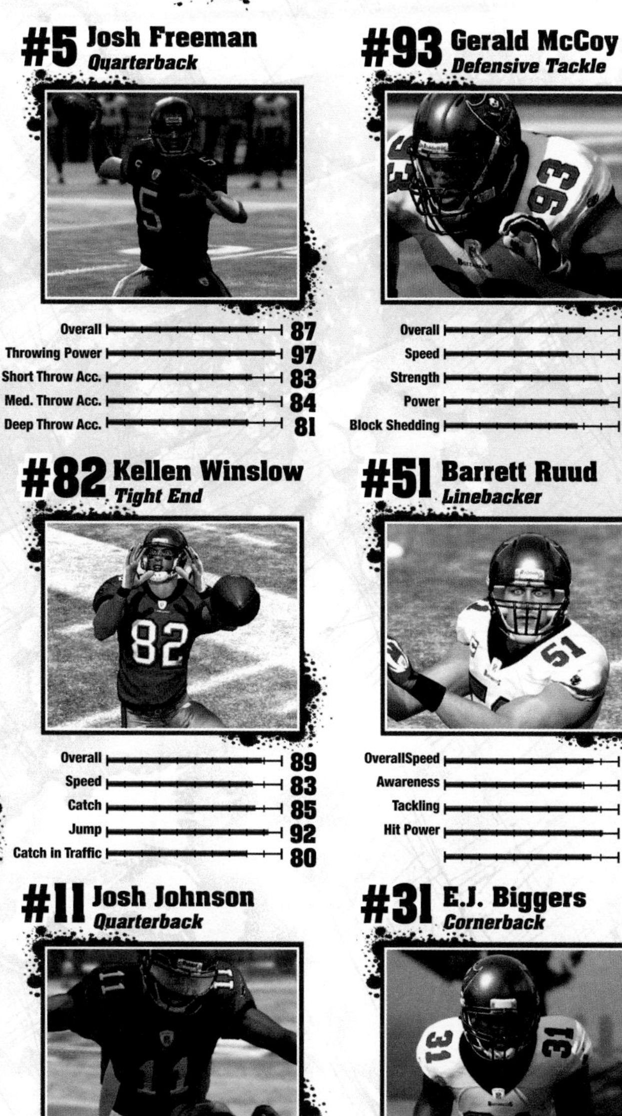

DEFENSIVE STRENGTH CHART

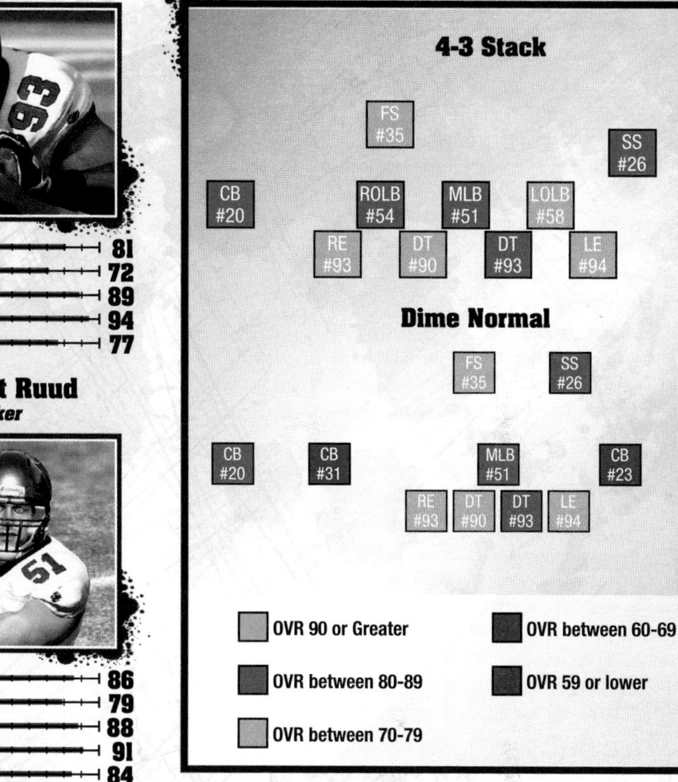

Key Player Substitution

Player: E.J. Biggers

Position: #2 CB

Key Stat: 94 Speed

What He Brings: Ronde Barber is still a tremendously smart player and will play solid with the new zone defensive system in *Madden NFL 12*. However, look to get Biggers in the game when matching up in man coverage. He simply has better ability to match up with younger, speedier wideouts.

Playbook Tips

Offensive Style: Run Balanced

Offense

- Josh Freeman has an elite arm but is best used after you've established a run game.
- The Bucs have a solid array of I-Form sets; test them all out to find their strengths.
- Despite being a run-first team, Tampa has 60-plus shotgun plays to pass from.

Defense

- Tampa Bay has focused on rebuilding its defensive line to hold up against the run.
- Look to utilize zone coverage to bring out the best in CB Ronde Barber.
- Tampa has always been solid in the middle of the field, and the tradition continues with MLB Barrett Ruud.

OFFENSIVE FORMATIONS

FORMATION	# OF PLAYS
Gun Bunch	9
Gun Doubles	15
Gun Empty Trey	12
Gun Snugs Flip	9
Gun Split Y-Flex	12
Gun Spread	12
Gun Y-Trips HB WK	18
I-Form Pro	18
I-Form Tight	12
I-Form Tight Pair	12
Singleback Ace	15
Singleback Ace Pair	12
Singleback Ace Pair Twins	12
Singleback Doubles	15
Singleback Wing Trips	9
Strong Close	9
Strong Pro	15
Weak Pro Twins	12

OFFENSIVE PLAYCOUNTS

PLAY TYPE	# OF PLAYS
Quick Pass	12
Standard Pass	30
Shotgun Pass	62
Play Action Pass	46
Inside Handoff	34
Outside Handoff	14
Pitch	10
Counter	4
Draw	10

Three-Headed Rushing Attack

Strong Close—Counter Weak

The Counter Weak is our favorite run to counter an aggressive defense. If we can get the defenders to take one false step, we will really have the advantage on this run. The WRs do a great job clearing out in this formation.

The back gives the guard time to get set up to the left before taking the handoff. After that, it's his job to read whether to cut the run inside or break it outside. The best way to go is between the guard and FB before heading outside.

It appears the defender is waiting for us on the edge of the defense; however, he will quickly be sealed by the FB or guard. This will allow the HB to hammer down on the turbo and get outside the defense for big yards. If our blockers weren't able to seal the edge, we would simply have kept the run in tight for a smaller but effective gain.

PRO TIP Blount is known for hurdling defenders, so if players try to go low with a hit stick, hit the Hurdle button.

Strong Close—Quick Toss

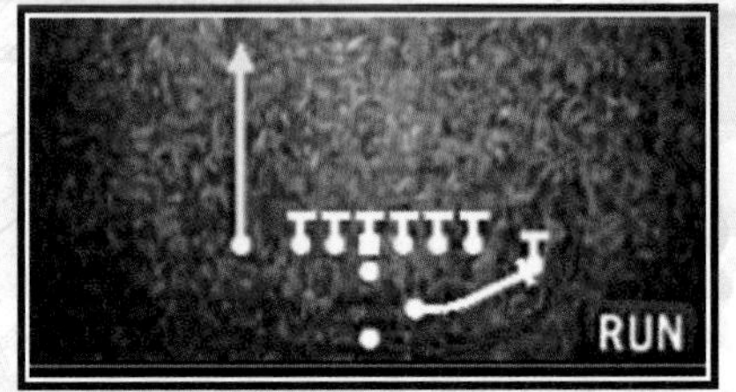

The Quick Toss is a great way to beat a pesky man defense that brings a safety down into the box. By motioning the WR on the right towards the middle of the formation, you will bring the man defender with him and clear out space for the toss.

Here, the QB reads that the defense is in zone coverage, so he allows the WR to stay out on the right and add an extra body to the formation. He will turn quickly at the snap and look to pitch the ball out to the HB, who is already starting towards the corner.

The blockers do a good job of getting to the corner and setting up a lead for the back. He has a few players approaching from his left that he must outrun. Effectively mixing in the toss with the Bucs will keep the middle of the field open for the dive, where their personnel is most effective.

PRO TIP If you place QB Josh Johnson in, even just to hand off, the defense will be forced to consider the consequences of not containing him pre-snap.

Strong Close - HB Dive

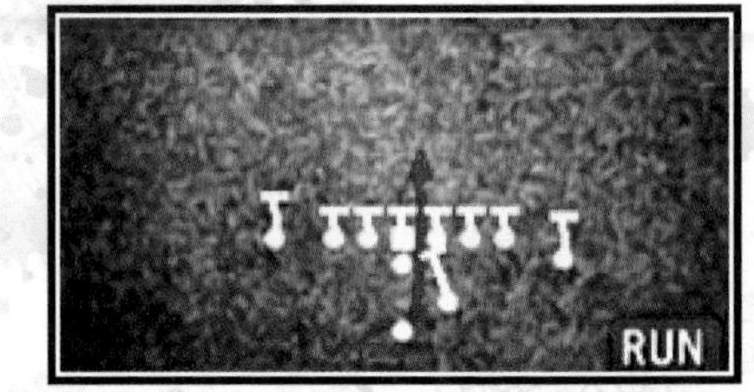

The Strong Close formation was one of the best running formations in *Madden NFL 11*. It looks to be just as effective in *Madden NFL 12*. The HB Dive is a great run for our HB, who looks to pick up yards between the tackles.

We receive the handoff and have a few options to make. We see that a hole has opened up to the left, middle, and right of the offensive line. If we go left, we will run into two linebackers. Following our FB up the middle, we might get stuck in traffic. To the right, we will have only one linebacker to beat.

We choose the hole on the right of the field. With a big HB, we can take on the hit from the linebacker. We take the contact and fall forward for the extra yards.

PRO TIP Make sure your highest-rated FB is in the game so he can deliver the bone-crushing block!

Quick Pass

Strong Close - Inside Post

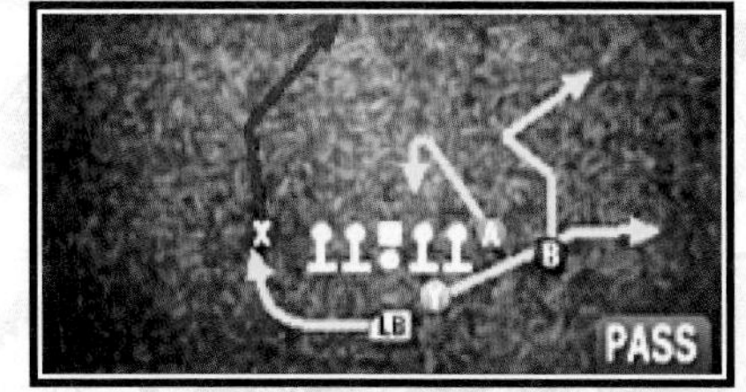

The threat of the inside run will make your opponent send in extra defenders to stop the run. The Strong Close Inside Post attacks the middle part of the field with our TE. Attack the defense from where it sends pressure.

We can see the two blitzing linebackers coming off the edge to stop the run. The remaining linebacker is calling out the coverage on the TE. We want to take advantage of the blitzing linebackers by hitting our TE as soon as he breaks over the middle of the field.

The blitzing linebackers gave us a favorable matchup over the middle of the field. We deliver the pass on time and before the blitz can get to the QB. Make sure to cover up the ball to avoid a dropped catch or fumble.

Man Beater

Gun Split Y Flex - Mesh

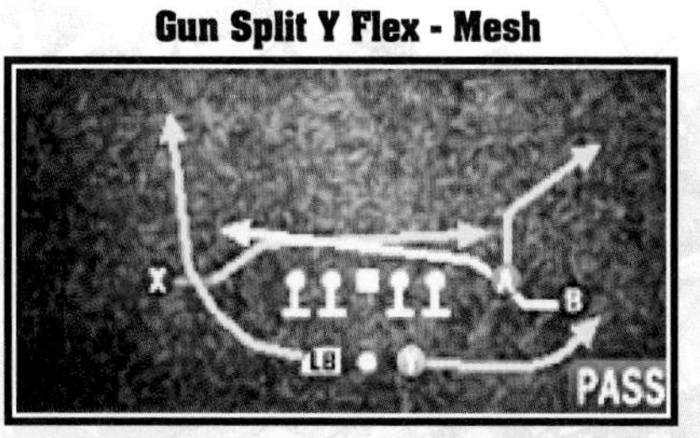

Auto-motion in *Madden NFL 12* is great for beating press coverage, and it is effective as a decoy. Whenever a WR is put into motion, the defense's attention is brought to that WR. The Gun Split Y-Flex does a good job against man coverage, as we have dual drag routes over the middle of the field.

The WR is set in motion. The defense will now be paying extra attention to this WR. That is exactly what we want. Your first read should be to the flat to see if the HB is open; if not, look back to the drags over the middle of the field.

Our drag opposite the auto-motioned WR is able to get open over the middle of the field. We deliver the pass, and the WR makes a spectacular one-handed catch. With no defenders in the area, we can look to get upfield for extra yards.

PRO TIP Make sure that your highest-rated WR is set into motion. This will cause the defense to pay even more attention to the auto-motion.

Zone Beater

Gun Bunch - Bucs Sail

The Gun Bunch Bucs Sail is a good play to call when facing zone coverage. The TE will break to the flat and draw the zone defender with him. Meanwhile, our WR running the streak route will pull coverage deep. This route combination will help create space for our WR running the C route.

We can see the flat defender guarding the TE. The deep safety is taking the bait with our streak route. The vacated space behind the flat defender and in front of the deep safety is starting to develop.

Space between the defenders clears out, and we are able to deliver the pass to an open WR. Look to get upfield to gain yards after the catch. Beating zone defense is about route combinations, and the Bucs Sail destroys zone coverage.

PRO TIP Against a Cover 2 defense, look for the streak route; against a Cover 4 defense, look for the flat route.

Base Play

Singleback Doubles - Curls HB Angle

The Singleback Doubles Curls HB Angle is a multi-faceted play that is capable of beating zone coverage, man coverage, and a blitz from your opponent. On the outside, the play has a curl-flat concept that beats zone coverage. If we read man coverage or suspect a blitz, the HB angle route will open to allow a quick throw for yards up the middle.

We roll out as we notice the pressure is coming. Our offensive tackle has lost containment on the outside pass rush. We wanted to hit our curl route, but the pressure is coming in too quick. However, our HB has inside position on his defender.

The ball is delivered to the HB, on time and before the pressure can get to the QB. We have the matchup we want in the open field. Our HB looks to make the defense pay for bringing the pressure as he gets upfield!

PRO TIP Substitute an HB with higher-rated hands and speed to maximize this play.

ARIZONA CARDINALS

OFFENSIVE SCOUTING REPORT

The Arizona Cardinals are looking to return to prominence. They still have one of the best big-play WRs in Larry Fitzgerald. Fitzgerald will attract tons of attention from the defense and give your QB a big target. Whichever QB you choose, make sure it's one who fits your style. QB Derek Anderson has a strong arm but has limited mobility around the pocket. Both backup QBs can deliver accurate short passes. Take to the ground and start RB Beanie Wells over Tim Hightower. Look for talented WR Steve Breaston in the slot on crucial third downs, and sneak the speedy RB LaRod Stephens-Howling into the game on passing downs.

DEFENSIVE SCOUTING REPORT

After selecting Patrick Peterson in the first round of the NFL Draft, the Cardinals have one of the top three secondaries in *Madden NFL 12*. Peterson immediately becomes a top 10 CB with elite speed. On the other side is Dominique Rodgers-Cromartie, who has a huge frame and the speed to match Peterson. Having two of these players is a luxury, so make sure to really work the press coverage on the outside. Adrian Wilson is a game changer who will be able to play in the box as an extra linebacker. The defensive line is one of the strongest in the league but needs some help to rush the QB from the LB core. The Cardinals' defense is their strength since they lack a great option at QB.

TEAM RATING

70 Overall

76 Offense

83 Defense

DYNAMIC PLAYER PERFORMANCE TRAITS

Larry Fitzgerald
WR #11

Confidence	★★★★★
Consistency	★★★★★
Feet in Bounds	Yes
Drops Open Passes	No
Clutch	Yes

RATINGS BY POSITION

Quarterbacks	70
Halfbacks	75
Fullbacks	69
Wide Receivers	83
Tight Ends	70
Tackles	74
Guards	77
Centers	71
Defensive Ends	85
Defensive Tackles	74
Outside Linebackers	80
Middle Linebackers	81
Cornerbacks	84
Free Safeties	88
Strong Safeties	92
Kickers	89
Punters	74

DEPTH CHART

POS	OVR	FIRST NAME	LAST NAME
3DRB	72	LaRod	Stephens-Howling
C	71	Lyle	Sendlein
C	65	Ben	Claxton
CB	85	Dominique	Rodgers-Cromartie
CB	82	Patrick	Peterson
CB	75	Gregory	Toler
CB	71	Trumaine	McBride
CB	65	Michael	Adams
DT	74	Bryan	Robinson
DT	74	Dan	Williams
DT	69	Gabe	Watson
FB	69	Anthony	Sherman
FB	69	Reagan	Mauia
FS	88	Kerry	Rhodes
FS	66	Rashad	Johnson
HB	75	Tim	Hightower
HB	73	Beanie	Wells
HB	73	Ryan	Williams
HB	72	LaRod	Stephens-Howling
K	89	Jay	Feely
KOS	89	Jay	Feely
KR	72	LaRod	Stephens-Howling
KR	66	Andre	Roberts
LE	80	Calais	Campbell
LE	66	Kenny	Iwebema
LE	60	Jeremy	Navarre
LG	72	Rex	Hadnot
LG	64	Tom	Pestock
LOLB	78	Clark	Haggans
LOLB	61	Will	Davis
LOLB	59	Cyril	Obiozor
LS	68	Mike	Leach
LT	70	Levi	Brown
LT	60	D'Anthony	Batiste
MLB	81	Gerald	Hayes
MLB	74	Daryl	Washington
MLB	78	Paris	Lenon
MLB	60	Reggie	Walker
P	74	Ben	Graham
PR	66	Andre	Roberts
QB	70	Derek	Anderson
QB	68	Max	Hall
QB	69	John	Skelton
RE	89	Darnell	Dockett
RE	71	Alan	Branch
RE	58	David	Carter
RG	82	Deuce	Lutui
ROLB	81	Joey	Porter
ROLB	70	O'Brien	Schofield
ROLB	64	Sam	Acho
RT	77	Brandon	Keith
RT	74	Jeremy	Bridges
SS	92	Adrian	Wilson
SS	73	Matt	Ware
SS	69	Hamza	Abdullah
TE	70	Stephen	Spach
TE	71	Ben	Patrick
TE	66	Rob	Housler
WR	96	Larry	Fitzgerald
WR	78	Steve	Breaston
WR	74	Early	Doucet
WR	61	Stephen	Williams
WR	66	Andre	Roberts
WR	63	Max	Komar

OFFENSIVE STRENGTH CHART

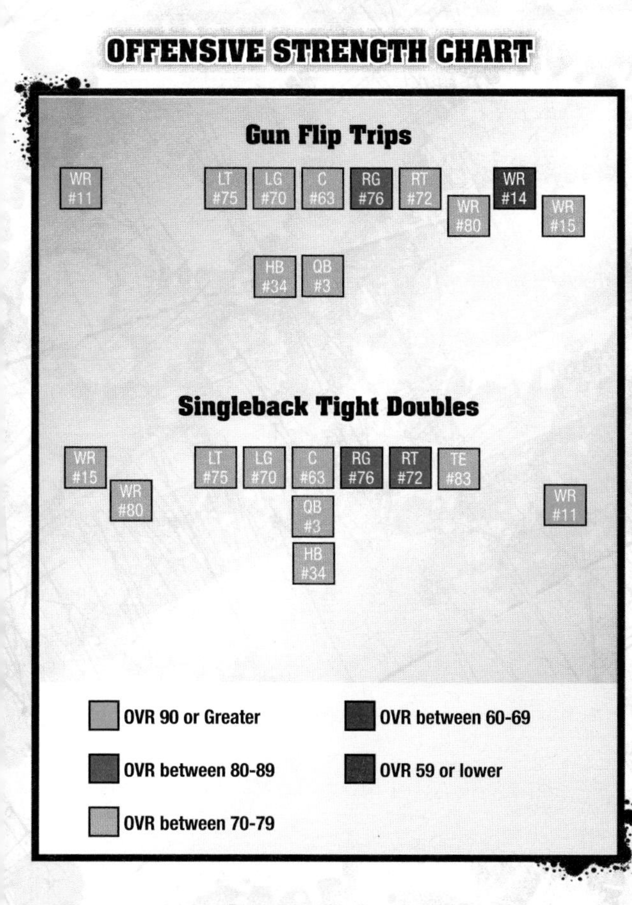

Key Player Substitution

Player: Rob Housler

Position: #1 TE Slot

Key Stat: 85 Speed

What He Brings: If you need to get the ball downfield bring in Housler to help stretch the defense in the seams with his speed. When running, bring in a stronger TE who can offer support in the run game.

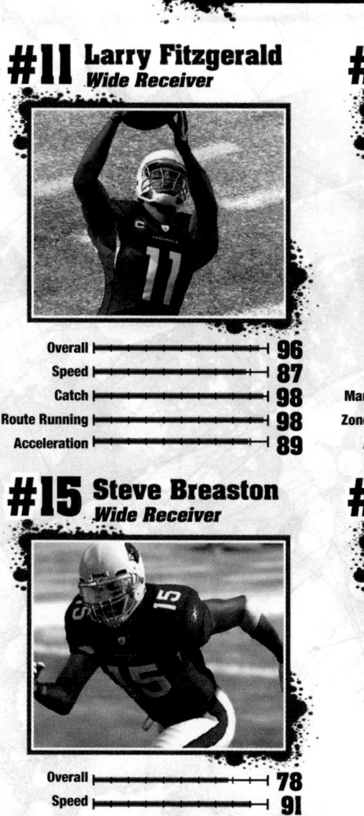

#11 Larry Fitzgerald
Wide Receiver

Overall	96
Speed	87
Catch	98
Route Running	98
Acceleration	89

#15 Steve Breaston
Wide Receiver

Overall	78
Speed	91
Catch	81
Route Running	76
Acceleration	94

#84 Rob Housler
Tight End

Overall	66
Speed	85
Catch	78
Jump	82
Catch in Traffic	81

#29 Dominique Rodgers-Cromartie
Cornerback

Overall	85
Speed	98
Man Coverage	95
Zone Coverage	84
Awareness	71

#27 Patrick Peterson
Cornerback

Overall	82
Speed	97
Man Coverage	89
Zone Coverage	88
Awareness	60

#58 Daryl Washington
Linebacker

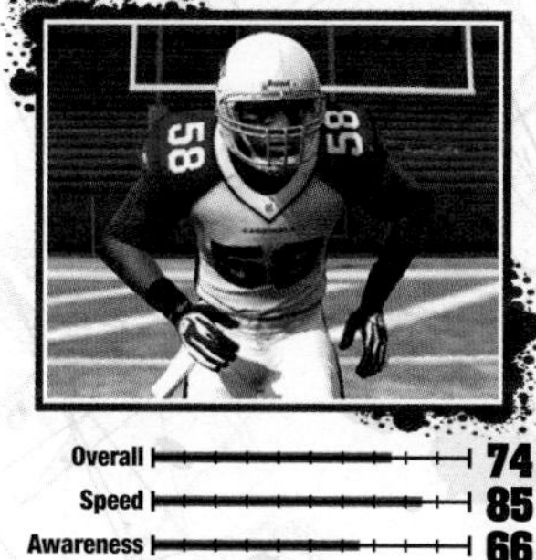

Overall	74
Speed	85
Awareness	66
Tackling	86
Hit Power	79

DEFENSIVE STRENGTH CHART

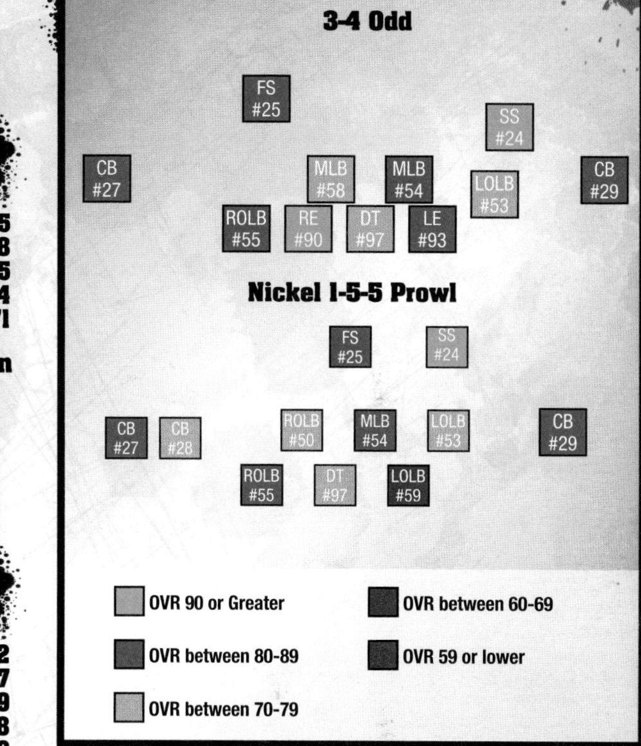

Key Player Substitution

Player: Daryl Washington

Position: Nickel LB

Key Stat: 85 Speed

What He Brings: The Cardinals' strength at secondary is incredible, but if you need run support, bring in Daryl Washington. He has a bigger frame than your defensive backs but still has solid speed to match up if needed in pass coverage.

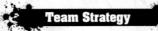

Playbook Tips

Offensive Style: Pass Heavy

Offense

- The Singleback Tight Doubles formation is one of the best under-center passing formations in the game.
- The defense will be eyeing your playmaker, Larry Fitzgerald, but force the ball to him anyway.
- Try all of the Cards' QBs out to see who gives you the best chance to win.

Defense

- Play plenty of coverage defense with Arizona as they have an amazing secondary.
- The Cardinals have a strong defensive line that can hold the point of attack.
- Use Joey Porter in the middle on passing downs because his hit power can jar the ball loose.

OFFENSIVE FORMATIONS	
FORMATION	# OF PLAYS
Gun Bunch WK	12
Gun Doubles WK	12
Gun Empty Trips	15
Gun Flip Trips	9
Gun Split Offset	15
Gun Spread	12
Gun Tight	12
Gun Trips HB WK	18
Gun Y-Trips Open	12
I-Form Pro	18
I-Form Tight	12
Singleback Ace	15
Singleback Ace Pair	15
Singleback Ace Pair Twins	15
Singleback Bunch Base	12
Singleback Doubles	18
Singleback Tight Doubles	12
Singleback Y-Trips	18
Strong Pro	15
Weak Slot	15
Weak Twin TE	12

OFFENSIVE PLAYCOUNTS	
PLAY TYPE	# OF PLAYS
Quick Pass	20
Standard Pass	52
Shotgun Pass	92
Play Action Pass	46
Inside Handoff	34
Outside Handoff	16
Pitch	10
Counter	4
Draw	12

Three-Headed Rushing Attack

Strong Pro—Z Close Ctr Wk

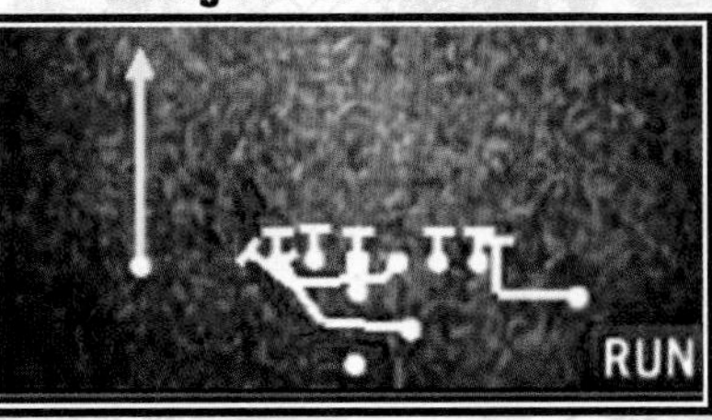

The Z Close Ctr Wk has an auto-motion to the right side of the formation that can let the defense know the play call. The Z WR to the right will line up a little tighter to the line, but this run was so successful in our practice tests we simply had to include it.

The counter is effective if the defense is looking to overplay the strong side of the formation. With a force like Larry Fitzgerald out there, the defense should leaving the weak side open plenty. The weak-side WR does a great job clearing out on this play and leaving a lane open behind him. The FB fills it in and the play starts to develop.

Our HB sees the inside defender slip off his block so he takes his cut out wide. This is a good way to run the counter, but the longer you can keep the run inside, the more defenders you can suck to the middle before making a cut. We like to have our faster RB in the game to maximize yards—we shouldn't be forced to break too many tackles here.

PRO TIP Use other passing plays with similar auto-motion to keep the D honest.

Strong Pro—HB Blast

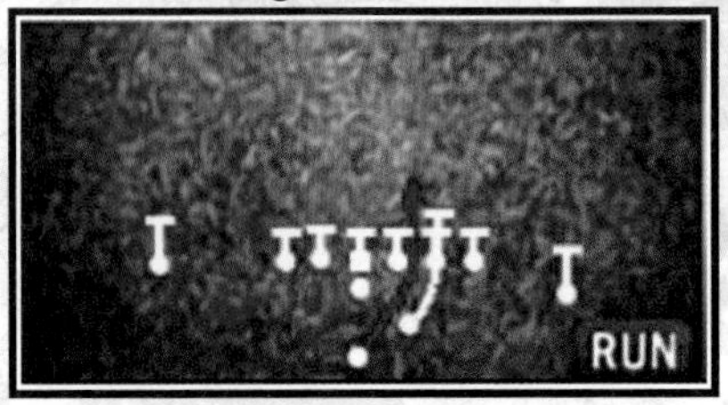

HB Blast is a great way to pick up solid yards on first down. If the defense spreads out for any reason, we can really deliver a powerful attack up the middle. Unlike a dive, the HB Blast sends the FB to the B gap and our HB to the middle of the field. This makes for a run different from the iso, which many players are used to, but it can often lead to big holes.

The FB heads out and gets to the line of scrimmage without any penetration. This lets him get into the second level and give our back a great lead blocker to follow. Get through the gap quickly as you don't want it to close up on you.

The HB busts through the line of scrimmage and can now make a cut to turn a 7-yard run into a 15-yard run. With the safety approaching from the left, he has to quickly veer to the right while letting the FB stay engaged on his block. He also must be aware of all the traffic behind him and not slow down.

PRO TIP Use formation subs to get an extra TE at WR to help with blocking.

Strong Pro - Power O

The HB Power O is the staple of many *Madden NFL 12* offenses. The pulling offensive lineman adds a boost to the run blocking on this play. You will want to follow the pulling offensive linemen, but be sure to read which running lanes are open.

The running lane to the left is blocked by a defender who has broken off his block. We can try and run through this defender or look to the right running lane for positive yards. Our FB could not get the push upfield that we wanted, and we are forced to react quickly.

We hit the left running lane hard and are able to break the initial tackle. Head upfield and follow your blocker. Be patient and let your blocks get to the next level.

PRO TIP Be patient with the HB Power O. Let the pulling guard get into position before you break into the running lane.

Quick Pass

I - Form Normal - FL Smoke

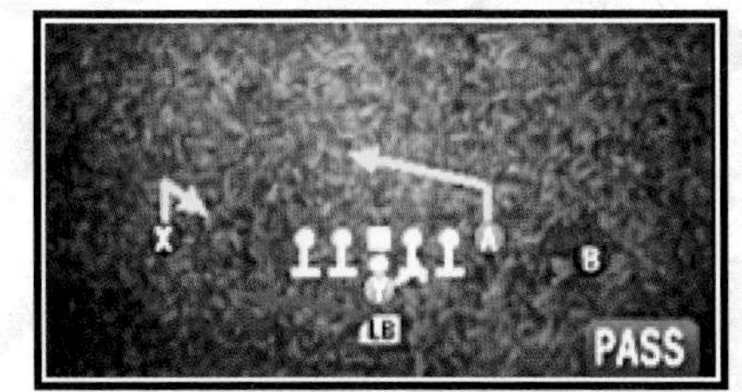

I-Form Normal FL Smoke is one of the best plays in the game for beating press defensive coverage. Add in Larry Fitzgerald and it makes this play very difficult to stop. FL Smoke develops quickly and will keep the defense on its toes.

Larry Fitzgerald looks to get past the press coverage and into his route. Wait for the jam to take place. Once Fitzgerald gets past the DB, deliver the ball.

Fitzgerald is able to beat the press coverage and get behind his defender. We deliver the ball as soon as the coverage is beat. Fitzgerald makes the grab and is off to the races!

PRO TIP Make sure to use a tall WR for the FL Smoke, as height is vital for the success of the play!

Man Beater

Flip Trips - Deep Fork

Another way to attack zone defense is to flood the field deep. Earlier we went over the Four Verticals passing concept. With the Deep Fork, we still attack the defense downfield, but we have viable short passing options. The route progression of the deep post and deep corner will put pressure on the defense.

As our WRs head downfield, we can see that both begin to make cuts into their routes. The deep safety must decide if he will break to defend the post or the corner route.

The deep safety chose to defend the deep corner, which allowed our deep post to be left open over the middle of the field. We delivered the pass for the easy score. The defense was in a Cover 2, which allowed for the deep middle to be open. Look for the deep corner to be open against a Cover 3.

PRO TIP A WR with both speed and height is ideal for the deep post and deep corner.

Zone Beater

Y - Trips - Four Verticals

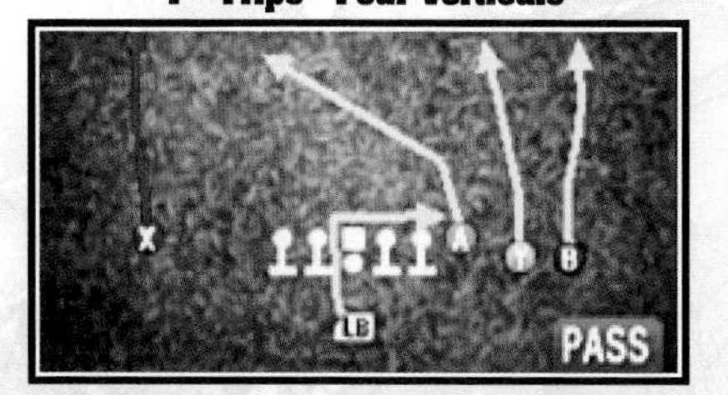

Any time a defense is in zone coverage, the Y-Trips Four Verticals is an effective play to run. The offense is sending four WRs deep in hopes that the defense is in a Cover 2 or Cover 3 defensive coverage. If the defense is in Cover 2 or Cover 3, we will outnumber the defense downfield.

You can see the zone defender passing off Larry Fitzgerald to the deep defender. Because we are running a Four Vertical passing concept, the deep safety is forced to leave Larry Fitzgerald open.

Larry Fitzgerald gets behind the defense for the easy score. The deep safety is not able to recover to defend Fitzgerald. The Four Vertical passing concept is one of the best ways to attack zone defensive coverage in the game.

PRO TIP The Four Vertical passing concept is found in many offensive formations in *Madden NFL 12*. Be sure to check your playbook to find them all!

Base Play

Tight Doubles - Close Under

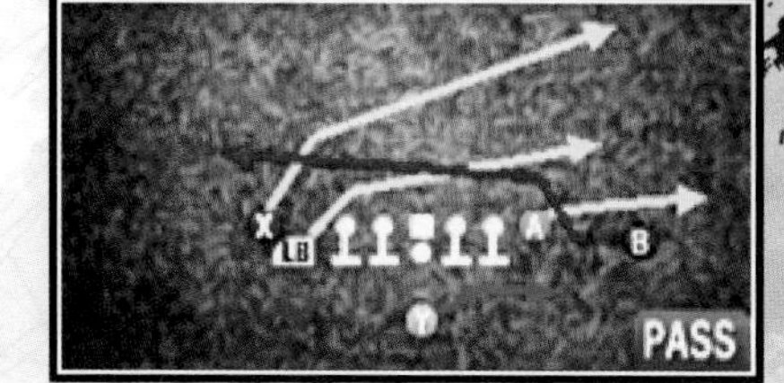

The Tight Doubles Close Under has a combination of crossing patterns and quick-developing routes. It also has an element of surprise with the HB on a delayed blue route. The HB will first look to block any pressure and will then release to the flat.

At the snap of the ball, we can see the HB look for a defender to block. His defender is frozen in the middle of the field. Notice that the TE to the short flat is open.

We decide to wait on the HB to release to the flat. The favorable matchup is the linebacker on the HB. The QB rolls to the right and hits the HB in stride for the easy completion.

PRO TIP Be prepared for the blue route to not release. If your opponent sends pressure, the blue route will stay in to block and will not release to the flat.

SAN DIEGO CHARGERS

OFFENSIVE SCOUTING REPORT

The San Diego Chargers have possessed elite *Madden NFL* talent for years. Good news for Bolts fans—they will once again have plenty of firepower in *Madden NFL 12*. Philip Rivers has quietly put up some incredible numbers, and his passing accuracy will reflect that in this year's game. With SD, a proper game plan includes attacking the middle of the field and using Rivers' big receivers to create matchup problems. The Chargers are not for the rookie user; they cater to the player who has patience and knows how to attack a zone defense. WR Vincent Jackson will hang on to almost anything thrown his way, while TE Antonio Gates is a huge safety valve on third downs. Ryan Mathews showed flashes of talent, and the offense is set up to use his speed in the run game. Mike Tolbert should be out in front blocking at FB, and he has solid hands out of the backfield. Make sure to cover up the football after securing the catch. Throwing to the middle of the field can be dangerous against a safety with good hit power. The Chargers' playbook is set up to block and allow routes to get downfield. Do not settle for short throws—step up and avoid the rush, and deliver a strike downfield.

DEFENSIVE SCOUTING REPORT

The Chargers have had a very solid defense the last few years in *Madden NFL*. By utilizing a strong front line with players like Luis Castillo, SD is able to send LBs off the edge. They seem to have plenty of LBs to fit into their 3-4 scheme, including Shaun Phillips and Larry English. In the secondary, Quentin Jammer plays better than his rating while safety Eric Weddle can clean up any play downfield. SD's defense might let through a few points in shootouts because of their own high-powered offense, but they'll make a timely play to seal the win.

RATINGS BY POSITION

Quarterbacks	96	Defensive Tackles	81
Halfbacks	77	Outside Linebackers	84
Fullbacks	73	Middle Linebackers	83
Wide Receivers	80	Cornerbacks	86
Tight Ends	99	Free Safeties	87
Tackles	83	Strong Safeties	77
Guards	87	Kickers	93
Centers	86	Punters	83
Defensive Ends	80		

TEAM RATING

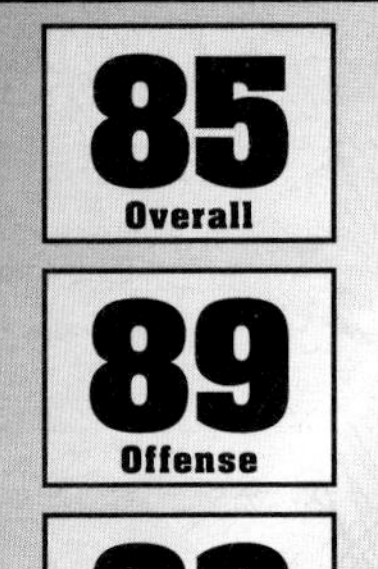

85 Overall

89 Offense

83 Defense

DYNAMIC PLAYER PERFORMANCE TRAITS

Philip Rivers
QB #17

Senses Pressure	★★★★★
Consistency	★★★★★
Throws Tight Spiral	No
Throws Ball Away	No
Clutch	Yes

DEPTH CHART

POS	OVR	FIRST NAME	LAST NAME
3DRB	62	Jordan	Todman
C	86	Nick	Hardwick
C	73	Scott	Mruczkowski
CB	89	Quentin	Jammer
CB	83	Antoine	Cason
CB	68	Donald	Strickland
CB	69	Marcus	Gilchrist
CB	63	Dante	Hughes
DT	81	Antonio	Garay
DT	60	Cam	Thomas
FB	73	Jacob	Hester
FB	64	Billy	Latsko
FS	87	Eric	Weddle
FS	74	Darrell	Stuckey
HB	77	Ryan	Mathews
HB	77	Mike	Tolbert
HB	79	Darren	Sproles
HB	62	Jordan	Todman
K	93	Nate	Kaeding
KOS	93	Nate	Kaeding
KR	79	Darren	Sproles
KR	74	Patrick	Crayton
LE	75	Corey	Liuget
LE	65	Ogemdi	Nwagbuo
LG	94	Kris	Dielman
LG	67	Steve	Schilling
LOLB	91	Shaun	Phillips
LOLB	71	Antwan	Barnes
LOLB	61	Jonas	Mouton
LS	69	David	Binn
LT	89	Marcus	McNeill
LT	66	Brandyn	Dombrowski
MLB	83	Stephen	Cooper
MLB	77	Brandon	Siler
MLB	76	Kevin	Burnett
MLB	65	Kion	Wilson
P	83	Mike	Scifres
PR	79	Darren	Sproles
QB	96	Philip	Rivers
QB	69	Billy	Volek
RE	84	Luis	Castillo
RE	53	Vaughn	Martin
RG	80	Louis	Vasquez
RG	66	Tyronne	Green
ROLB	77	Antwan	Applewhite
ROLB	75	Larry	English
ROLB	72	Jyles	Tucker
RT	76	Jeromey	Clary
RT	69	Eric	Young
SS	77	Steve	Gregory
SS	68	Paul	Oliver
SS	66	Quinton	Teal
TE	99	Antonio	Gates
TE	77	Randy	McMichael
TE	72	Kris	Wilson
WR	87	Vincent	Jackson
WR	80	Malcom	Floyd
WR	73	Legedu	Naanee
WR	74	Patrick	Crayton
WR	71	Buster	Davis
WR	68	Vincent	Brown

OFFENSIVE STRENGTH CHART

Strong Pro

WR #80 | LT #73 | LG #68 | C #61 | RG #65 | RT #66 | TE #85 | WR #83

QB #17 | FB #22 | HB #24

Gun Normal Y-Flex Tight

WR #83 | WR #11 | LT #73 | LG #68 | C #61 | RG #65 | RT #66 | TE #85 | WR #80

QB #17 | HB #24

OVR 90 or Greater | OVR between 60-69 | OVR between 80-89 | OVR 59 or lower | OVR between 70-79

Key Player Substitution

Player: Jordan Todman

Position: #1 FB Passing Downs

Key Stat: 94 Speed

What He Brings: Jordan Todman has solid speed to go along with RB Ryan Mathews. Look to get these two players on the field together as they can both burn LBs in the game.

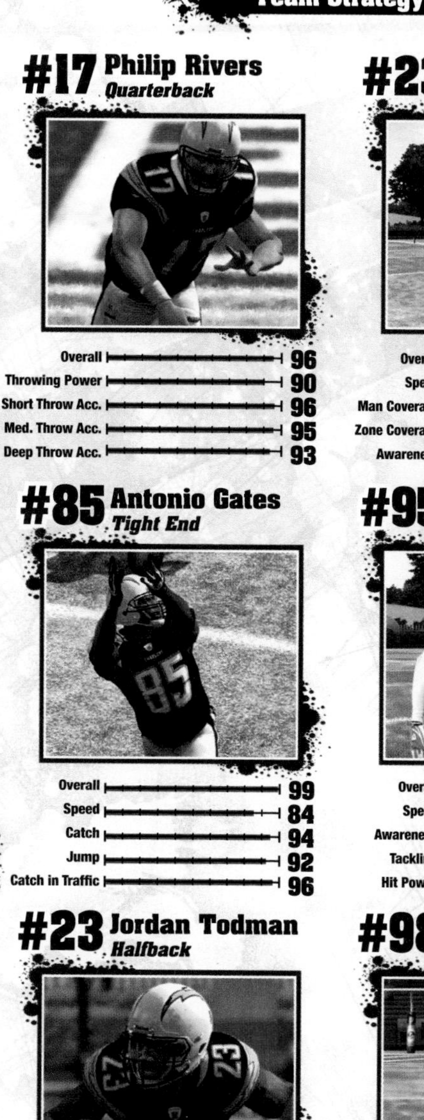

#17 Philip Rivers
Quarterback

Overall	96
Throwing Power	90
Short Throw Acc.	96
Med. Throw Acc.	95
Deep Throw Acc.	93

#85 Antonio Gates
Tight End

Overall	99
Speed	84
Catch	94
Jump	92
Catch in Traffic	96

#23 Jordan Todman
Halfback

Overall	62
Speed	94
Agility	90
Elusiveness	73
Catch	69

#23 Quentin Jammer
Cornerback

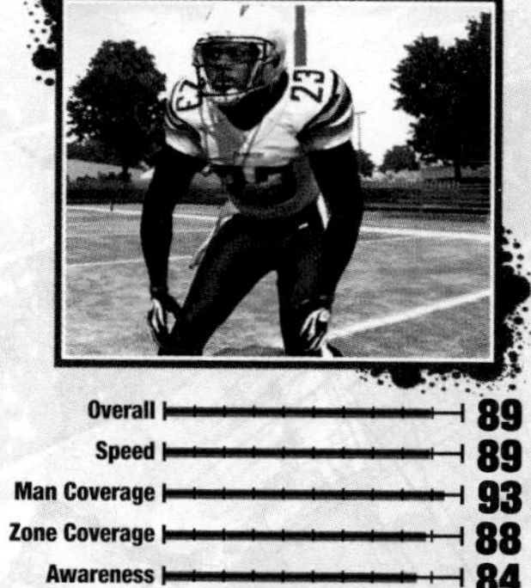

Overall	89
Speed	89
Man Coverage	93
Zone Coverage	88
Awareness	84

#95 Shaun Phillips
Linebacker

Overall	91
Speed	84
Awareness	88
Tackling	87
Hit Power	88

#98 Antwan Barnes
Linebacker

Overall	71
Speed	86
Awareness	65
Tackling	74
Hit Power	84

DEFENSIVE STRENGTH CHART

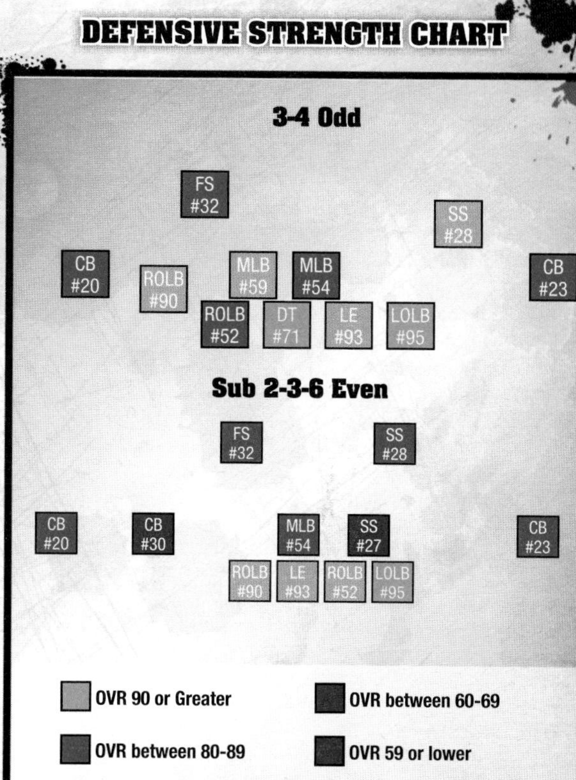

Key Player Substitution

Player: Antwan Barnes

Position: #2 MLB

Key Stat: 86 Speed

What He Brings: Barnes has been an athletic specimen in San Diego. You can really cause trouble for the offense by controlling him. Look to lay some hit stick over the middle with his solid hit power.

Playbook Tips

Offensive Style: Pass Heavy

Offense

- Rely on Philip Rivers's deep accuracy—it is tops in the game.
- San Diego has two of the bigger targets in the league with WR Vincent Jackson and TE Antonio Gates.
- Chargers love the Gun Y formations, so make sure to test them all out in practice mode.

Defense

- San Diego has eliminated some star names from its defense, but they still are capable of getting the job done .
- Utilize a 3-4 attack only on first and second downs because the linebackers lack great pass coverage skills.
- Leave LB Shaun Phillips in on passing downs and send him after the QB.

OFFENSIVE FORMATIONS

FORMATION	# OF PLAYS
Gun Doubles	15
Gun Normal Y-Flex Tight	15
Gun Normal Y-Slot	15
Gun Split Y-Flex	18
Gun Tight Doubles On	9
Gun Trips TE	12
Gun Y-Trips Open	15
I-Form Pro	21
I-Form Tight Pair	12
I-Form Twins	15
Singleback Ace	21
Singleback Ace Pair Twins	15
Singleback Bunch	15
Singleback Doubles	18
Singleback Jumbo	12
Singleback Wing Trio	12
Strong Pro	24
Weak Pro	15
Weak Pro Twins	15

OFFENSIVE PLAYCOUNTS

PLAY TYPE	# OF PLAYS
Quick Pass	13
Standard Pass	53
Shotgun Pass	66
Play Action Pass	65
Inside Handoff	46
Outside Handoff	14
Pitch	7
Counter	6
Draw	14

Three-Headed Rushing Attack

I-Form Pro—FB Fake HB Flip

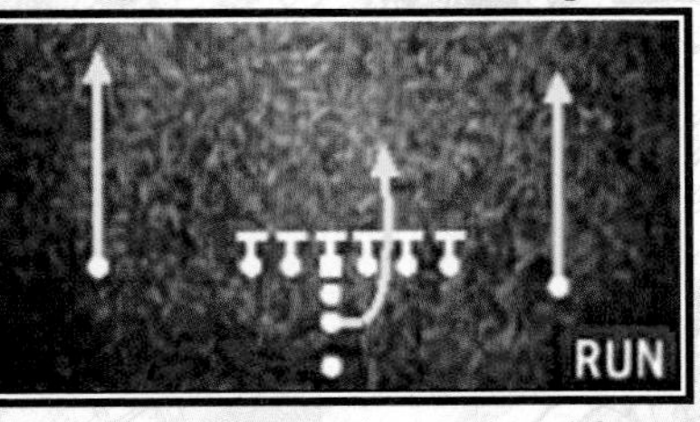

The RB has the ability to catch an anxious defense off guard here and go the distance. Make sure to call the FB Dive a few times to get the defense set up for it. When this play is used at the right time, it can win you the game!

The QB threatens to hand off the ball to the FB, who puts his head down and sells the fake. If this can pull a defender inside, the HB should get a free release to the edge. Rivers gets the ball out wide to the HB.

Since our FB got the handoff fake, he is unable to block for us on the outside. This play is all up to the RB. If you called it at the right time and the defense packed the middle, you will be off to the races. Here, the defenders appear to be recovering, so look to get back to the line and make one move and fight for yards.

PRO TIP Your FB must threaten the defense; use a second HB to really strike fear into the defense.

I-Form Pro - Inside Zone

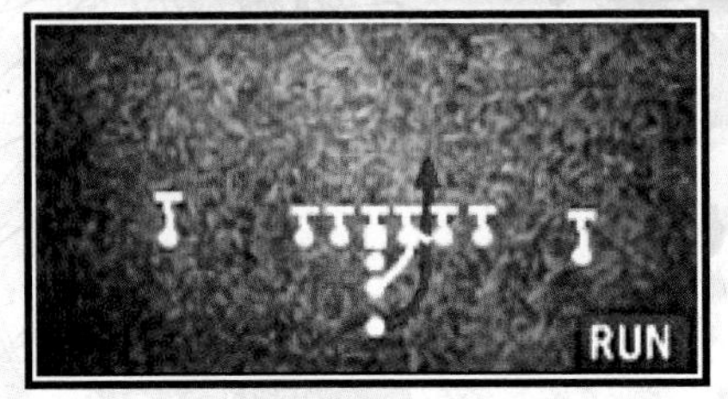

It is important when running the I-Form Pro Inside Zone to keep the ball inside and only look to go outside if the hole develops. Running lanes with the Inside Zone will develop toward the inside and will occasionally open up outside. Ryan Mathews is versatile enough that he can run between and outside the tackles.

We bust the ball outside as we see a running lane develop. We see our blocks downfield and look to cut the run back toward the middle of the field. Mathews has the speed to get the ball to the edge, but he also has the strength to fight through tackles of larger defenders.

Mathews takes the big hit from the linebacker but not before we pick up big yardage on the ground. The Inside Zone is a staple run for any offense.

PRO TIP The Inside Zone can be found in many formations in *Madden NFL 12*. We feel that it is the best overall run play in the game.

I-Form Pro - HB Counter WK

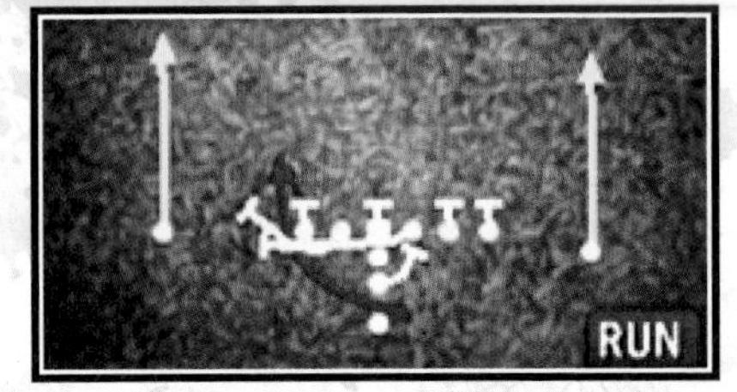

For the I-Form Pro HB Counter WK, we substitute our faster, more agile back in the game. With this play, we are looking to get the defense to bite on the run fake right while the play is designed to run left. Make sure to not outrun your blockers, as you are running this play to the weak side of the offensive line.

Our HB gets the handoff, and we can see that the linebacker in the middle of the field is already out of position. Our pulling guard is in position to get upfield and help lead the way for our speedy HB.

We break outside for positive yards and prepare for the hit. With smaller backs, it is important that we do not take many big hits from the defense. Look to avoid the pressure by taking the run outside toward the sideline, or be sure to cover up when running into defenders.

PRO TIP Substitute a FB or a TE with a high Impact Blocking rating. We are looking for the big play with the HB Counter WK.

Quick Pass

I-Form Pro—HB Lead Draw

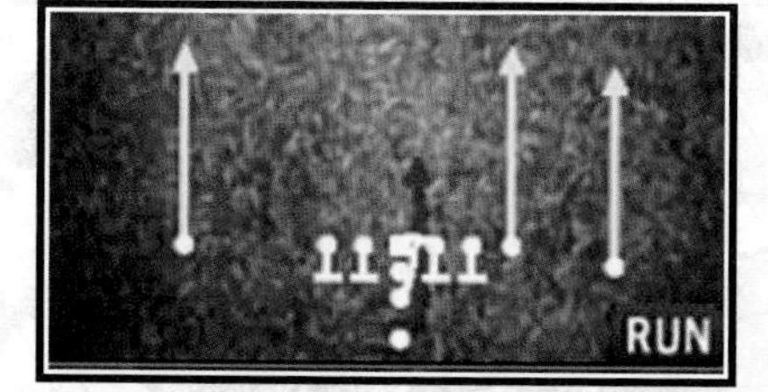

Quick passes are primarily used for beating the blitz and keeping the defense honest. Here we have a play that will do just that, but it's a run! By staying in our run formation the defense will likely bring some defenders down into the box. Calling the HB Lead Draw here is a perfect sub for a quick pass because our WRs even start to head upfield on routes.

The key to this play is QB Philip Rivers selling the look like he is going to pass. This will get the defensive ends running upfield and past the HB, who will then take the handoff. This should allow the HB to choose his lane at the line of scrimmage, depending on how far back the LBs drop due to the pass fake.

The RB follows the lead blocker through the hole and looks to make one move. He sees some defensive linemen approaching but knows he can simply outrun them without making a move. The safety is about to enter the play, but our back will have time to set him up for one move. Using the draw in place of a quick pass is excellent on first and second downs. But on short yardage downs where the quick pass is solid, check out the PA Pass later in the scheme.

Man Beater

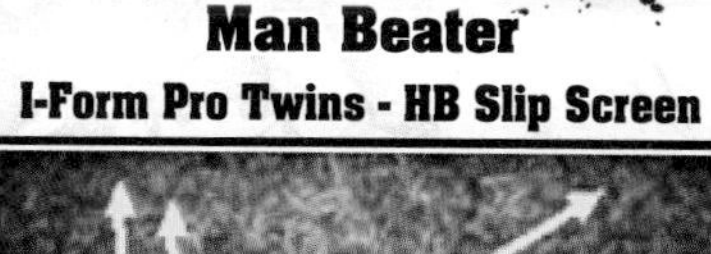

I-Form Pro Twins - HB Slip Screen

One way to speed-start your offense is with the I-Form Pro Twins HB Slip Screen. The explosiveness of this play can get your offense back in the groove if it has stalled. At the snap of the ball, look to roll back away from the pass rush. Wait for the HB to get set up behind his blockers and deliver the throw.

Our HB is getting in position. The pulling offensive linemen are setting their blocks to help move the ball downfield. All we need to do now is deliver an accurate throw.

The pass is perfect, and we are able to get into position to get upfield. There is a trailing defender, so we need to move quickly. Follow your lead block and look to gain extra yardage.

PRO TIP Against zone coverage, consider hot-routing one of your WRs to a drag route for extra blocking on the screen.

Zone Beater

Trips TE - Flex SD HB Wheel

Another good formation to use against defensive zone coverage is Trips TE. The Flex SD Wheel gives us plenty of nice passing options to flood zone coverage and shred man-to-man defensive coverage. The HB is your first read out of the backfield. Then look toward the middle of the field where the crossing routes are occurring.

The HB is open toward the flat. We decide to wait on this pattern and look to see if we can hit a route farther downfield. This can be risky, as we are passing up a short gain in the hopes that one of our WRs will be open for more yards.

Antonio Gates opens up over the short middle of the field. We deliver the pass between the zone defenders for the big gain. Patience in the passing game can often pay dividends!

PRO TIP The deep sideline route is typically isolated downfield because of the route combination of this play. Look to take a few shots down the sideline.

Base Play

I-Form Pro - PA Charger Wheel

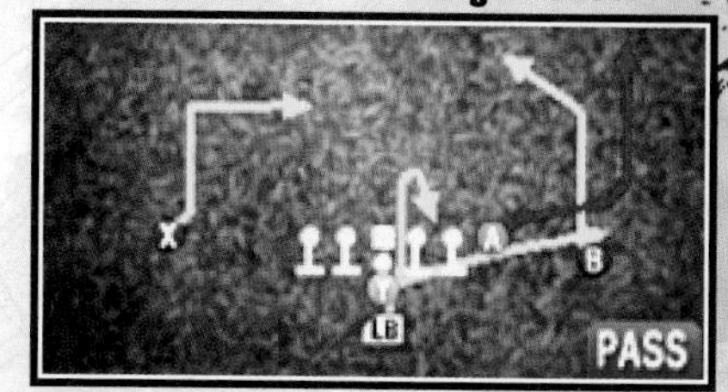

With all the running that we are doing from the I-Form Pro formation, we will look to attack the defense with play action. The Chargers have the perfect threat in TE Antonio Gates. A perfectly timed play-action pass can destroy a defense that anticipates a run.

The play action has occurred, and we can already see how open TE Antonio Gates is toward the sideline. We wait a bit longer for him to begin his cut upfield; as soon as he makes his move, we deliver the pass.

Gates's height and jumping ability make him nearly impossible to stop. The pass was delivered just out of reach of the defender and in bounds where Gates can make a play on the ball. Gates is able to haul in the catch for the huge gain.

PRO TIP Hot-route your FB to a drag as a safety valve if Gates is covered downfield.

KANSAS CITY CHIEFS

OFFENSIVE SCOUTING REPORT

The Kansas City Chiefs are a sleeper team in *Madden NFL 12*. Their offensive setup allows them to switch between many different types of runs. Jamaal Charles is an absolute game breaker and should be the focal point of your offense. Don't waste Charles' speed on power runs; instead, focus on getting him to the edge of the defense. Thomas Jones can handle the interior runs and will protect the football better late in the game. On the outside, Dwayne Bowe has the skill set to exploit man defense. Use Matt Cassel to extend plays in the red zone, and target Dwayne Bowe, who has a nose for the end zone. Once a game, test the defense deep with some play action with hybrid Dexter McCluster in the slot. Use a bruising TE like Leonard Pope in the running game, and use his giant size advantage against smaller defenders in the passing game.

DEFENSIVE SCOUTING REPORT

Kansas City made a run to the playoffs last season behind a solid defense who continually closed out games. Tamba Hali was a force off the edge but will draw a lot of attention from the offense due to his high profile. While not the faster players in the game, the Chiefs CBs are very balanced and can play physical defense. Eric Berry should also take a leap and become a full-fledged star this season. Hopefully, Derrick Johnson and Glenn Dorsey will finally be able to make the jump from good to great. With a balanced offensive attack, the Chiefs' defense can remain the same and make the playoffs again, but they have the potential for more.

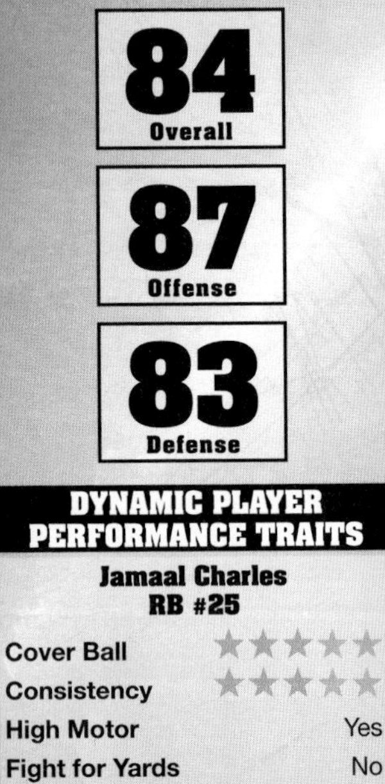

TEAM RATING

Overall	84
Offense	87
Defense	83

DYNAMIC PLAYER PERFORMANCE TRAITS

Jamaal Charles
RB #25

Cover Ball	★★★★★
Consistency	★★★★★
High Motor	Yes
Fight for Yards	No
Clutch	No

RATINGS BY POSITION

Quarterbacks	86	Defensive Tackles	81
Halfbacks	95	Outside Linebackers	84
Fullbacks	73	Middle Linebackers	86
Wide Receivers	79	Cornerbacks	86
Tight Ends	75	Free Safeties	74
Tackles	82	Strong Safeties	88
Guards	89	Kickers	77
Centers	83	Punters	88
Defensive Ends	79		

DEPTH CHART

POS	OVR	FIRST NAME	LAST NAME
3DRB	95	Jamaal	Charles
C	83	Casey	Wiegmann
C	73	Rudy	Niswanger
CB	91	Brandon	Flowers
CB	81	Brandon	Carr
CB	73	Javier	Arenas
CB	69	Maurice	Leggett
CB	59	Jackie	Bates
DT	81	Ron	Edwards
DT	68	Anthony	Toribio
DT	60	Jerrell	Powe
FB	73	Tim	Castille
FB	66	Mike	Cox
FS	74	Jon	McGraw
FS	73	Kendrick	Lewis
FS	63	Ricky	Price
HB	95	Jamaal	Charles
HB	84	Thomas	Jones
HB	66	Jackie	Battle
K	77	Ryan	Succop
KOS	77	Ryan	Succop
KR	73	Javier	Arenas
KR	74	Dexter	McCluster
LE	76	Tyson	Jackson
LE	75	Shaun	Smith
LE	52	Dion	Gales
LG	91	Brian	Waters
LG	75	Jon	Asamoah
LOLB	77	Mike	Vrabel
LOLB	75	Andy	Studebaker
LOLB	64	Justin	Houston
LS	65	Thomas	Gafford
LT	86	Branden	Albert
MLB	86	Derrick	Johnson
MLB	76	Jovan	Belcher
MLB	76	Demorrio	Williams
MLB	71	Corey	Mays
P	88	Dustin	Colquitt
PR	73	Javier	Arenas
QB	86	Matt	Cassel
QB	67	Brodie	Croyle
QB	68	Ricky	Stanzi
RE	81	Glenn	Dorsey
RE	64	Wallace	Gilberry
RE	62	Allen	Bailey
RG	86	Ryan	Lilja
RG	64	Darryl	Harris
ROLB	91	Tamba	Hali
ROLB	65	Cameron	Sheffield
ROLB	59	Gabe	Miller
RT	78	Barry	Richardson
RT	74	Ryan	O'Callaghan
SS	88	Eric	Berry
SS	68	Donald	Washington
SS	67	Reshard	Langford
TE	75	Leonard	Pope
TE	76	Tony	Moeaki
TE	57	Jake	O'Connell
WR	91	Dwayne	Bowe
WR	71	Jonathan	Baldwin
WR	74	Dexter	McCluster
WR	74	Chris	Chambers
WR	61	Verran	Tucker
WR	57	Quinten	Lawrence

OFFENSIVE STRENGTH CHART

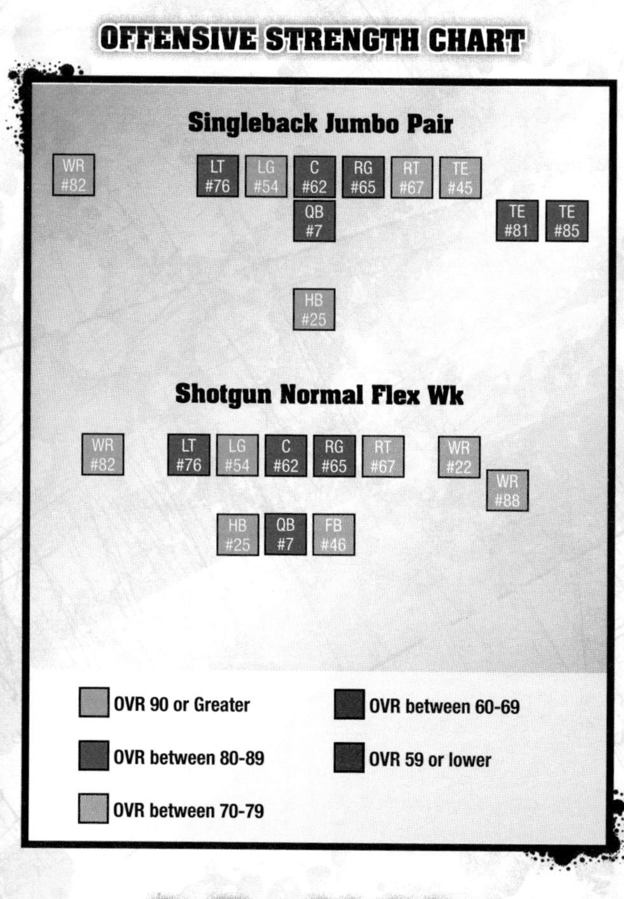

Key Player Substitution

Player: Dexter McCluster

Position: #2 WR

Key Stat: 96 Acceleration

What He Brings: Dexter McCluster is a playmaker who can fit into a role at either HB or WR. With Jamaal Charles carrying the load at HB, look to split McCluster out wide and make the most of his elite athletic talent. He is the perfect complement to a big physical WR like Dwayne Bowe.

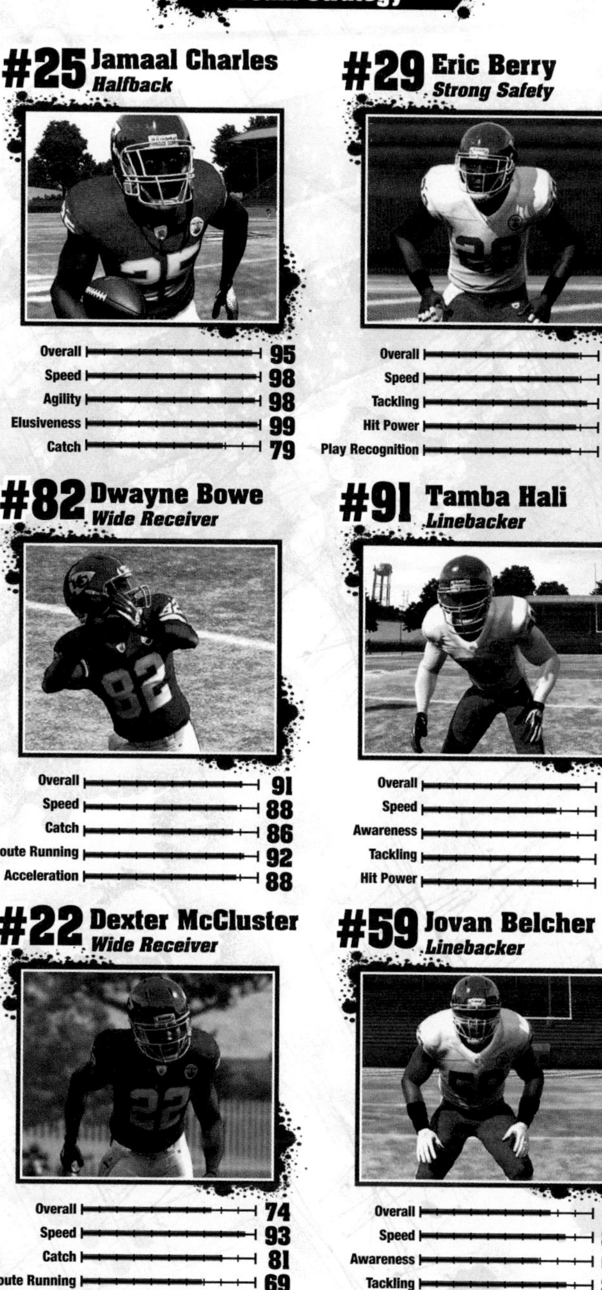

#25 Jamaal Charles *Halfback*

Overall	95
Speed	98
Agility	98
Elusiveness	99
Catch	79

#29 Eric Berry *Strong Safety*

Overall	88
Speed	92
Tackling	82
Hit Power	91
Play Recognition	80

#82 Dwayne Bowe *Wide Receiver*

Overall	91
Speed	88
Catch	86
Route Running	92
Acceleration	88

#91 Tamba Hali *Linebacker*

Overall	91
Speed	78
Awareness	86
Tackling	92
Hit Power	87

#22 Dexter McCluster *Wide Receiver*

Overall	74
Speed	93
Catch	81
Route Running	69
Acceleration	96

#59 Jovan Belcher *Linebacker*

Overall	76
Speed	83
Awareness	69
Tackling	86
Hit Power	88

DEFENSIVE STRENGTH CHART

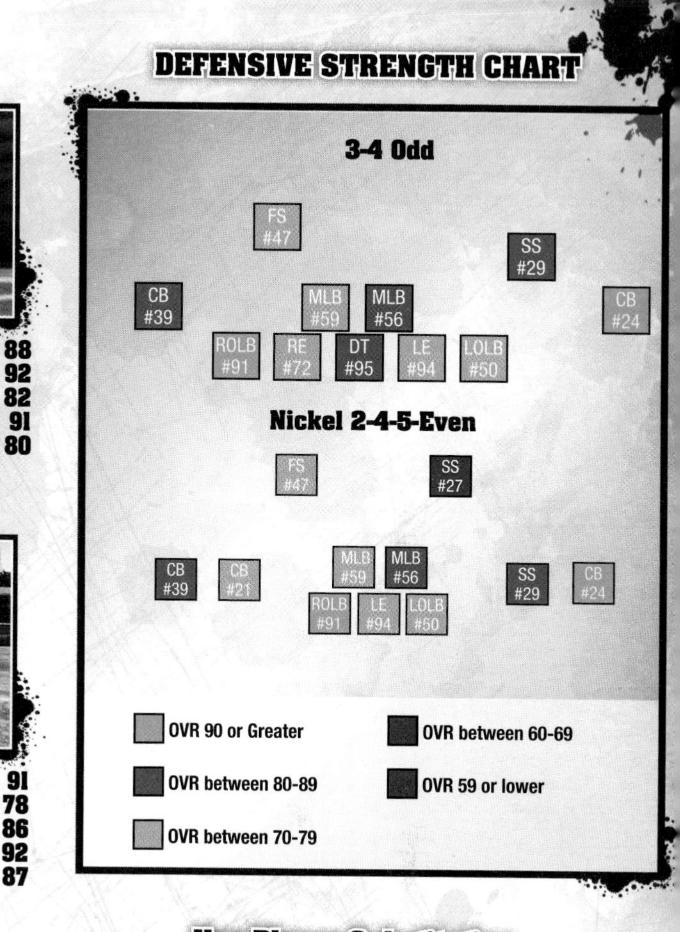

Key Player Substitution

Player: Jovan Belcher

Position: #4 LB

Key Stat: 88 Hit Power

What He Brings: The Chiefs have all the makings for a solid 3-4 system. Use Jovan Belcher in the middle of the field to back up Tamba Hali, who should be left free to rush off the edge.

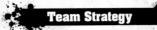

Playbook Tips

Offensive Style: Run Balanced

Offense

- Feature HB Jamaal Charles heavily; there's no need to split carries.
- Utilize the high number of pitches and outside runs in the playbook for max success.
- The Chiefs have strong WRs who set up great for the possession passing game.

Defense

- Defensive coordinator Romeo Crennel looks to improve upon his 3-4 scheme, which led NE to three Super Bowls.
- Utilize OLB Tamba Hali as an edge rusher in the 3-4 system.
- User-control safety Eric Berry and bring him up in the box to blow up the run.

OFFENSIVE FORMATIONS

FORMATION	# OF PLAYS
Full House Normal Wide	9
Gun Bunch	12
Gun Doubles	21
Gun Empty Base	9
Gun Empty Y-Flex	9
Gun Normal Y-Slot	18
Gun Snugs	12
Gun Split Close	12
Gun Trips HB WK	9
Gun Wing Trips WK	21
I-Form Pro	15
I-Form Tight	12
Singleback Ace	15
Singleback Ace Pair	18
Singleback Ace Pair Chief	15
Singleback Doubles	27
Singleback Jumbo Pair	9
Singleback Y-Trips	18
Strong Twins	12
Weak Pro	15
Wildcat Chief	3

OFFENSIVE PLAYCOUNTS

PLAY TYPE	# OF PLAYS
Quick Pass	16
Standard Pass	49
Shotgun Pass	88
Play Action Pass	47
Inside Handoff	36
Outside Handoff	18
Pitch	10
Counter	6
Draw	10

Three-Headed Rushing Attack

Strong Twins—HB Dive

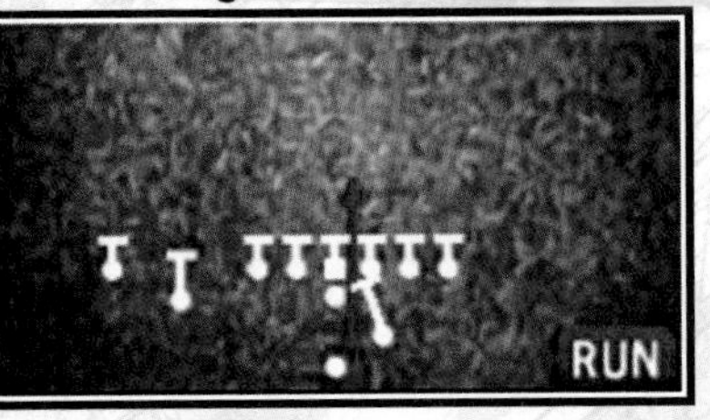

The dive will help give your offense a starting point and set up your other plays. Make sure to call this play until the defense proves they can consistently stop it. Once the offense crams the middle, utilize your other running plays.

The QB will hand the rock off to the HB while the FB powers forward and terminates defenders. The dive is great because we can quickly shift to another gap if the defense plugs the primary read. Here, the RB has to quickly avoid a defender in the backfield but is free the rest of the way. His FB gets out in front and should help him avoid the linebacking core.

The center is also out in front and can really crush smaller defenders. You can either run past him and get as many yards as possible now, or be patient and allow him to get in front. This can be risky but can really pay off for advanced runners. The dive is a no-nonsense run and is super effective with a star like Charles who can go the distance on any play.

PRO TIP Near the goal line use the Dive button to jump over the pile and into the end zone.

Strong Twins—Bubble Screen

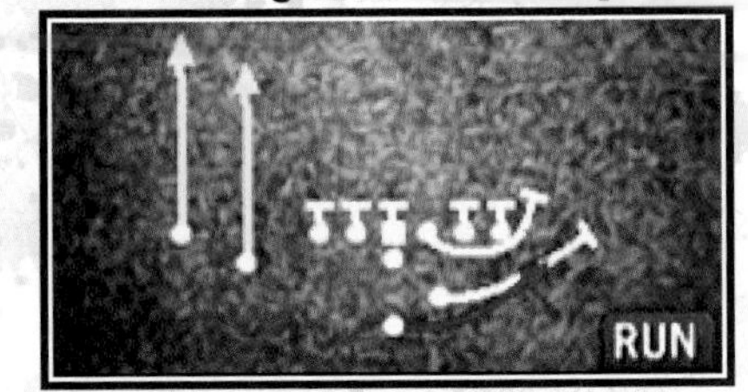

By using a pass in our running attack, the offense can quickly get the ball out in space to our playmakers. This will be a great read and something that makes the Strong Twins formation excellent to use in a three-headed attack.

Most outside runs look to quickly get the ball to the edge. Since there is no faster way than throwing it, this is a great tactic to use. This pass is very high percentage and is a great extension of the run game.

Once the WR hauls in the pass, he is turned into a running back. Make sure to read your blocks and determine if the inside or outside is open. Make sure to wait for the WR to get into position before throwing the pass; this will let your blockers set up and make the play even more effective.

PRO TIP Place a TE at WR to really ramp up the blocking on this play.

Strong Twins - HB Sweep

The explosive run game plays a vital role in the success for the Chiefs. This is due to HB Jamaal Charles being a huge threat when he touches the ball. The Strong Twins HB Sweep is a perfect play to take advantage of Charles's blazing speed.

When running the HB Sweep, it is important that the run blocking gets an outside push on the defense. We can see here that our blockers have sealed off the outside edge. Our FB is also getting into position to get upfield to the next level. Have patience when following your block and bust it upfield as soon as the FB has made his block.

The FB has chipped the outside defender, and we now have room to cut back upfield. There is only one man to beat—the trailing linebacker. Charles has the advantage in this situation with his lightning speed and super agility.

PRO TIP Pound the inside run to force the defense to protect the middle of the field. This will open up the HB Sweep.

Quick Pass

Strong Twins - WR Streak

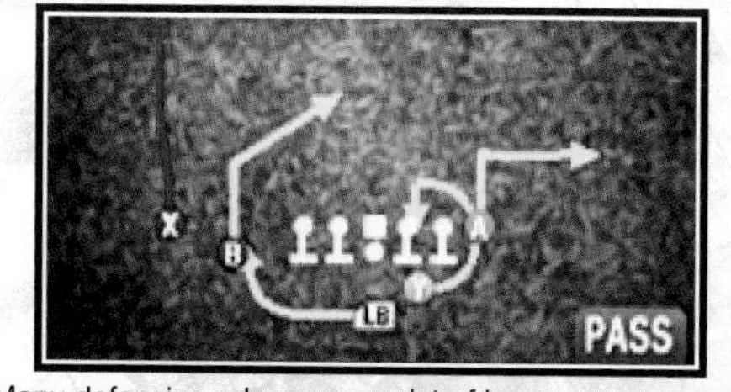

Many defensive schemes consist of heavy man-to-man defensive blitz packages. We need to be prepared for this style of play if we want to consistently move the ball down the field. The Strong Twins WR Streak has a quick pass option out of the backfield to our FB.

The man-to-man defensive blitz is on, and our TE is covered downfield. The pressure is coming, and we need to get the ball off quickly. Look to the FB out of the backfield. As soon as he makes his break upfield, make the pass.

We complete the pass before the defender can make a play on the ball. Timing is crucial to the success of this play. Throw too soon and the FB won't pick up positive yards; throw too late and the defender will be in a position to make a play on the ball. Be prepared to attack the blitz with one of the better quick passes in the game!

PRO TIP Keep your HB in to block for extra protection and extra time in the pocket to deliver the pass.

Man Beater

Split Close - KC Cross

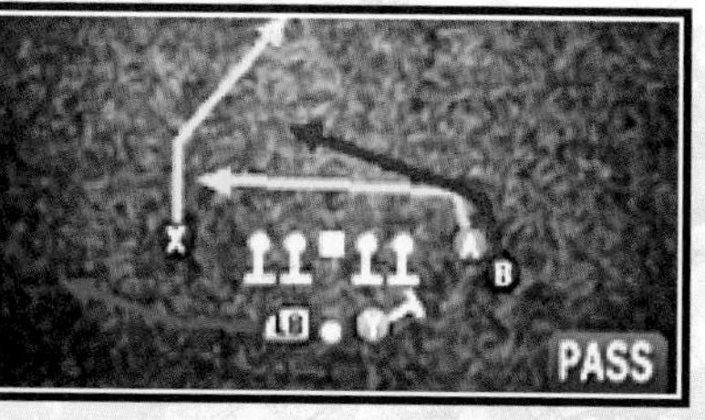

Another way to attack zone defense is by pinpointing a specific part of the field and target it with precise timing and different depths of routes. The Split Close KC Cross has an amazing combination of crossing patterns in the middle of the field. These route combinations make it extremely difficult for a zone defense to defend.

The QB drops back in the pocket and scans the field. He sees that two zone defenders are defending the middle of the field. Our offense is targeting the middle of the field with three crossing patterns all at different depths. Wait in the pocket and find the open WR.

Our big WR is targeted deep downfield for the big gain. We have the matchup we want with the smaller safety defending one of our taller WRs. Remember that zone defense is meant to confuse you as a player. The goal is to force throws into coverage where the defense can make a play on the ball. You must trust your route combinations and defensive reads!

Zone Beater

Ace Pair Chief - KC Smash

Frequently you will face a defense who plays maximum coverage. This will result in the defense rushing only two or three defenders at the QB while the remaining defenders will drop into coverage. One way to attack this style of defense is with delayed blue routes out of the backfield.

After the snap of the ball, the defense is rushing only three defenders. The HB looks to block any would-be pressure. Since the defense is playing a coverage style of defense, we know that our HB will release to the flat.

The pass is completed in stride to the HB out of the backfield. Blue routes are very important in this game. They aid in pass protection, and they are threats in the receiving game. Scan your playbook and find ways to utilize plays that have them!

PRO TIP After the snap of the ball, block an extra offensive player to ensure the blue route releases.

Base Play

Gun Bunch - KC Bunch Trail

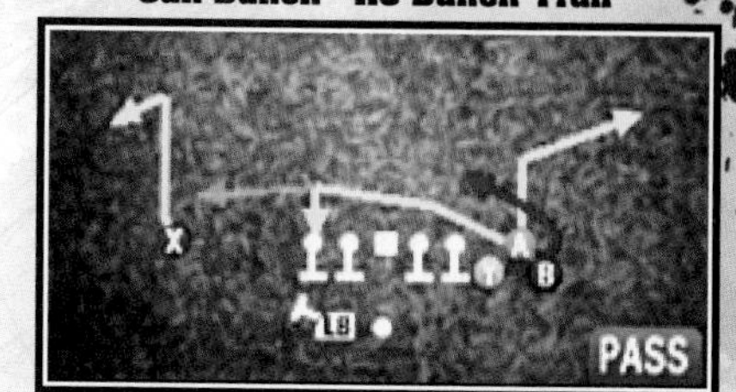

The Gun Bunch KC Bunch Trail is one of our favorite plays because of the route combinations on the Bunch side. We have a corner, drag, and trail route. We know that no matter the zone defensive coverage, our route combination will provide an open receiver.

We read that the deep safety has dropped into a Cover 2 zone. We immediately know that the deep safety will cover our corner route, and we know that our trail route should be open behind the drag route. Let the play develop and watch the corner route push the zone defense deep and the drag pull the zone defense away from the trail route.

We hang in the pocket and deliver a strike to our TE. The routes worked off each other to open up the trail to our TE. Defensive zone coverage can cause a lot of problems to an impatient QB. Stay calm and trust your route combinations.

PRO TIP Make sure your TE is a threat for the defense to guard by substituting your receiving TE for this play.

INDIANAPOLIS COLTS

OFFENSIVE SCOUTING REPORT

The Indianapolis Colts fought their way to the play-offs during the 2010 season. Along the way, Indy discovered many new talents to be used in *Madden NFL 12*. Look to use two TE sets with Jacob Tamme and dynamic playmaker Dallas Clark. This will keep franchise QB Peyton Manning's eyes upfield while his new offensive line learns the ropes. Reggie Wayne has consistently produced and has outstanding route running. Austin Collie and Blair White emerged as go-to receivers for Peyton Manning on third down. Pierre Garçon is effective, and he can stretch defenses that focus too much on Wayne and Clark. Pound the ball with Joseph Addai if the defense stops respecting the run. The Colts have one of the most unique playbook styles in *Madden NFL*, and players who harness its powers will reap big rewards.

DEFENSIVE SCOUTING REPORT

Any conversation about the Colts defense begins and ends with Dwight Freeney and Robert Mathis. These two defense ends have elite speed and can cause loads of trouble all by themselves. When the Colts' offense gets the lead, these two players tee off on the QB and really slow the offense down. The rest of the defense is solid as well—MLB Gary Brackett has consistently held down the middle of the field and helped lead the defense. Elsewhere, the Colts' secondary is solid, since they never have to cover too long with Freeney and Mathis up front!

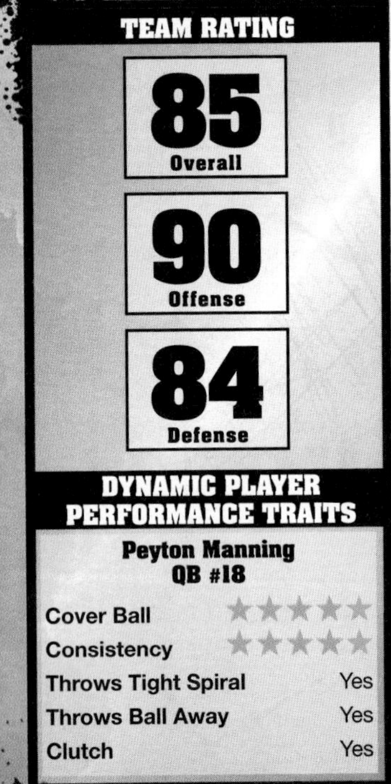

TEAM RATING

85 Overall

90 Offense

84 Defense

DYNAMIC PLAYER PERFORMANCE TRAITS

Peyton Manning
QB #18

Cover Ball	★★★★★
Consistency	★★★★★
Throws Tight Spiral	Yes
Throws Ball Away	Yes
Clutch	Yes

RATINGS BY POSITION

Quarterbacks	98
Halfbacks	82
Fullbacks	61
Wide Receivers	85
Tight Ends	96
Tackles	82
Guards	76
Centers	95
Defensive Ends	93
Defensive Tackles	75
Outside Linebackers	78
Middle Linebackers	87
Cornerbacks	83
Free Safeties	93
Strong Safeties	79
Kickers	93
Punters	73

DEPTH CHART

POS	OVR	FIRST NAME	LAST NAME
3DRB	82	Joseph	Addai
C	95	Jeff	Saturday
CB	85	Kelvin	Hayden
CB	81	Jerraud	Powers
CB	70	Jacob	Lacey
CB	75	Justin	Tryon
CB	58	Cornelius	Brown
DT	75	Daniel	Muir
DT	77	Fili	Moala
DT	72	Antonio	Johnson
DT	66	Ricardo	Mathews
FB	61	Gijon	Robinson
FS	93	Antoine	Bethea
FS	72	Al	Afalava
HB	82	Joseph	Addai
HB	72	Donald	Brown
HB	68	Delone	Carter
HB	63	Javarris	James
K	90	Adam	Vinatieri
KOS	73	Pat	McAfee
KR	75	Justin	Tryon
KR	58	Devin	Moore
LE	93	Robert	Mathis
LE	71	Eric	Foster
LE	68	Jerry	Hughes
LG	76	Kyle	DeVan
LG	70	Jamey	Richard
LOLB	75	Pat	Angerer
LOLB	70	Philip	Wheeler
LOLB	59	Nate	Triplett
LS	55	Justin	Snow
LT	80	Charlie	Johnson
LT	76	Anthony	Castonzo
LT	56	Michael	Toudouze
MLB	86	Gary	Brackett
MLB	54	Cody	Glenn
P	73	Pat	McAfee
PR	67	Blair	White
QB	98	Peyton	Manning
QB	61	Curtis	Painter
RE	93	Dwight	Freeney
RE	67	Keyunta	Dawson
RE	55	John	Chick
RG	76	Mike	Pollak
RG	65	Jacques	McClendon
ROLB	81	Clint	Session
ROLB	69	Tyjuan	Hagler
ROLB	65	Kavell	Conner
RT	83	Ryan	Diem
RT	65	Jeff	Linkenbach
RT	60	Joe	Reitz
SS	79	Melvin	Bullitt
SS	76	Aaron	Francisco
SS	65	Mike	Newton
TE	96	Dallas	Clark
TE	83	Jacob	Tamme
TE	61	Brody	Eldridge
WR	95	Reggie	Wayne
WR	82	Pierre	Garcon
WR	79	Austin	Collie
WR	70	Anthony	Gonzalez
WR	67	Blair	White
WR	60	Taj	Smith

OFFENSIVE STRENGTH CHART

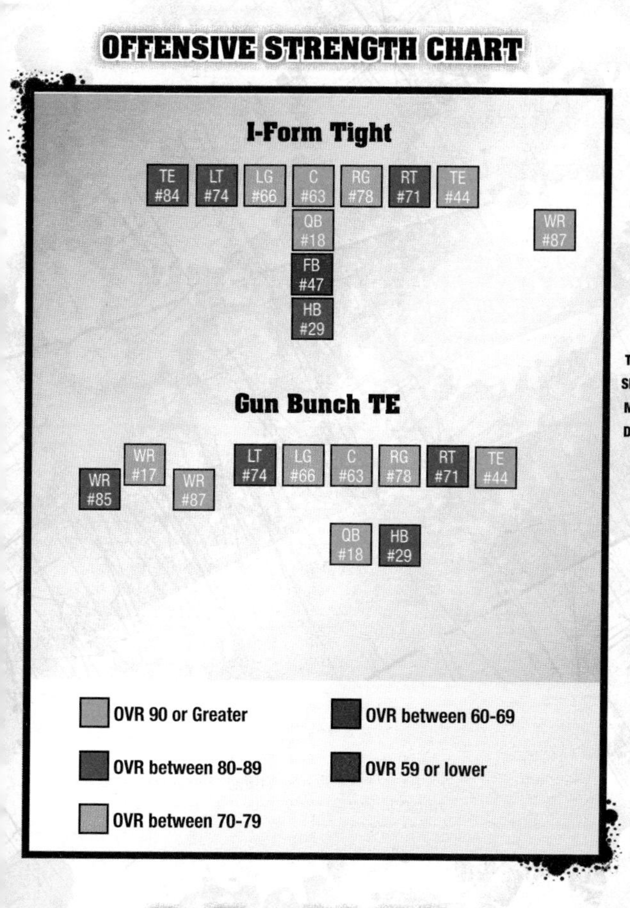

Key Player Substitution

Player: Austin Collie

Position: #2 WR

Key Stat: 93 Agility

What He Brings: While fan favorite WR Anthony Gonzalez will be back from injury, give Austin Collie the start behind Reggie Wayne. He is more agile and can hang onto the ball in tight places.

#18 Peyton Manning *Quarterback*

Overall	98
Throwing Power	94
Short Throw Acc.	96
Med. Throw Acc.	92
Deep Throw Acc.	86

#87 Reggie Wayne *Wide Receiver*

Overall	95
Speed	87
Catch	98
Route Running	99
Acceleration	93

#17 Austin Collie *Wide Receiver*

Overall	79
Speed	87
Catch	92
Route Running	90
Acceleration	89

#93 Dwight Freeney *Right End*

Overall	93
Speed	87
Strength	80
Finesse Moves	97
Block Shedding	67

#98 Robert Mathis *Left End*

Overall	93
Speed	86
Strength	76
Finesse Moves	96
Block Shedding	67

#92 Jerry Hughes *Left End*

Overall	68
Speed	85
Strength	64
Finesse Moves	78
Block Shedding	57

DEFENSIVE STRENGTH CHART

4-3 Stack

FS #41
SS #33
CB #25
LOLB #55
DT #58
LOLB #51
CB #26
RE #93
DT #95
DT #90
LE #98

Dime Flat

FS #41
SS #33
CB #25
CB #26
CB #27
MLB #58
CB #20
RE #93
DT #95
DT #90
LE #98

OVR 90 or Greater
OVR between 60-69
OVR between 80-89
OVR 59 or lower
OVR between 70-79

Key Player Substitution

Player: Jerry Hughes

Position: #2 DT

Key Stat: 93 Acceleration

What He Brings: While the Colts already have two monsters rushing from the edge, try to get Jerry Hughes in the game on passing downs. Shift Mathis into the DT spot and line him up against weaker guards. Hughes can rush inside or out.

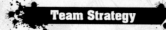

Playbook Tips

Offensive Style: Pass Heavy

Offense

- Indy only has one I-Form formation, which means lead blockers are rare.
- Indy operates nearly all its plays from Gun or Singleback.
- The Colts allow QB Peyton Manning to change between plays at the line of scrimmage depending on his read.

Defense

- The Colts 4-3 defense should be used with stunts from the defensive line.
- Indy used to run a Cover 2 scheme under Tony Dungy similar to the "Tampa 2."
- Look to utilize heavy zone coverage with this base defense.

OFFENSIVE FORMATIONS

FORMATION	# OF PLAYS
Gun Bunch	12
Gun Bunch TE	12
Gun Deuce Trips	12
Gun Dice Slot	24
Gun Dice Slot WK	21
Gun Dicey-Flex	15
Gun Empty Trey	14
Gun Split Flex	15
Gun Y-Trips WK	21
I-Form Tight	12
Singleback Bunch	12
Singleback Deuce	21
Singleback Deuce Slot	18
Singleback Deuce Twins	15
Singleback Dice Slot	27
Singleback Trips Colt	21

OFFENSIVE PLAYCOUNTS

PLAY TYPE	# OF PLAYS
Quick Pass	11
Standard Pass	42
Shotgun Pass	105
Play Action Pass	46
Inside Handoff	25
Outside Handoff	14
Pitch	7
Counter	3
Draw	10

Three-Headed Rushing Attack

Singleback Deuce—Weak Zone

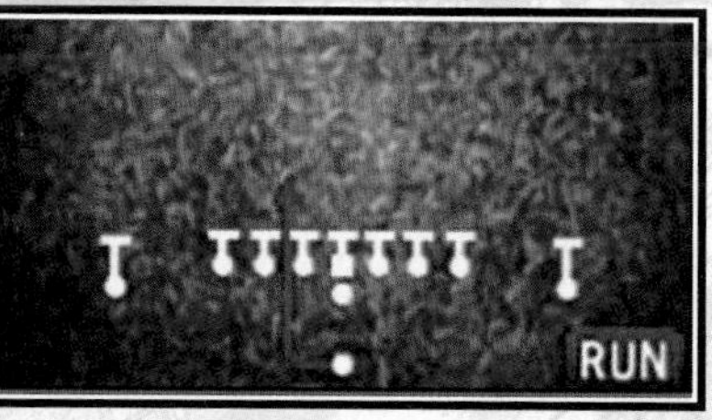

The Colts only run when they have the advantage in the box. Peyton Manning is constantly reading the defense and looking to play the numbers game. Since the Colts rarely employ a lead blocker, they must make sure they can block everyone in front.

This particular run can beat strong-side blitzes and alleviate pressure. The HB takes the ball and looks to see what opens up. He can bust it to the B gap or continue outside if the defense gets sucked in.

As the back approaches the line of scrimmage, he notices that the edge is not being held by the defense. The Colts have a very balanced group of HBs, and any one of them is capable of taking the ball outside. The back should pick up a good chunk of yards and force the defense to be more cautious next time.

PRO TIP Never come out in this play call—simply audible to it when the defense is vulnerable.

Singleback Deuce—HB Dive

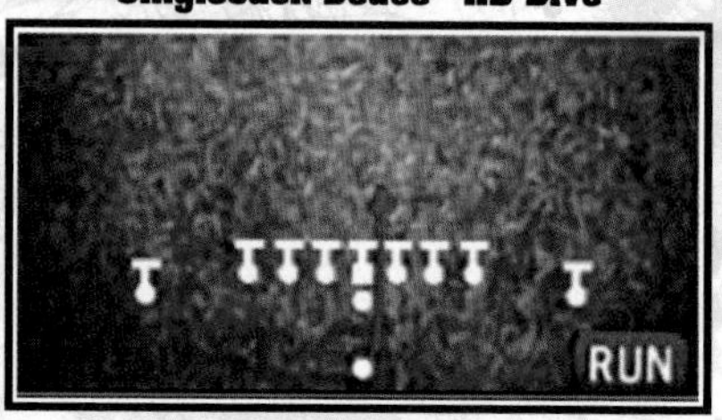

While the true staple of Indy is the stretch run, a straight-ahead run like a dive employs a similar concept of taking whatever the defense is offering. This is the fastest way to attack the defense and a great way to pick up short yardage and scores in the red zone.

Before the play, Manning sees the linebackers fan out to cover the TE threats. He quickly makes one adjustment and changes the play to the run. The back is ready to hit the hole hard and knows that dancing behind the line is out of the question.

The halfback sees that the expected hole is in fact cleared out. He breaks through to the second level of the defense. He should put his head down and ram forward for as many yards as possible. While the dive is not a game-breaking run, it does have the ability to frustrate defenses who get too worried about coverage.

PRO TIP If the LBs pack the middle, use the quick-pass audible to get the TEs into open space.

Singleback Duece - HB Stretch

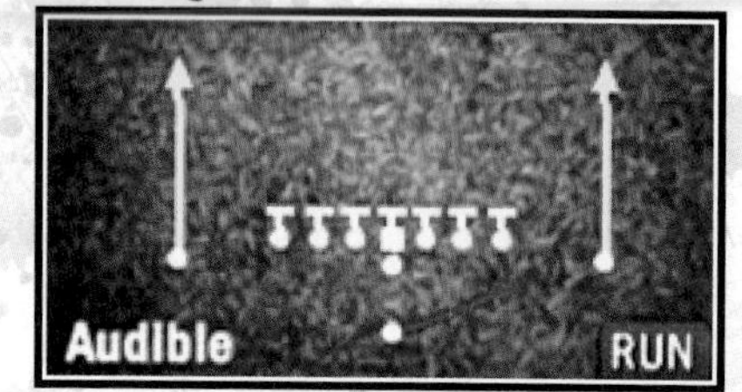

The staple of the Colts› running attack over the past few seasons has been the HB Stretch. The effectiveness of the run depends on the success of the HB to read the appropriate running lane to attack. Use the HB Stretch to get outside the defense.

QB Peyton Manning hands off to the HB. The design of the play is for the run to go outside. A few running lanes in the middle of the field have opened up. Only with a more agile HB will cutting back toward the open running lanes be ideal.

Our nimble HB was able to make the cut back toward the open running lanes. We get up inside the offensive line and follow the blocks upfield. Running between the tackles is not our first option with the HB Stretch, but being able to adjust midplay is vital for success in *Madden NFL 12*.

PRO TIP With a bigger HB, look to avoid the cutback. Stay on course and plow your way off tackle!

Quick Pass

Singleback Dice Slot - PATE Screen

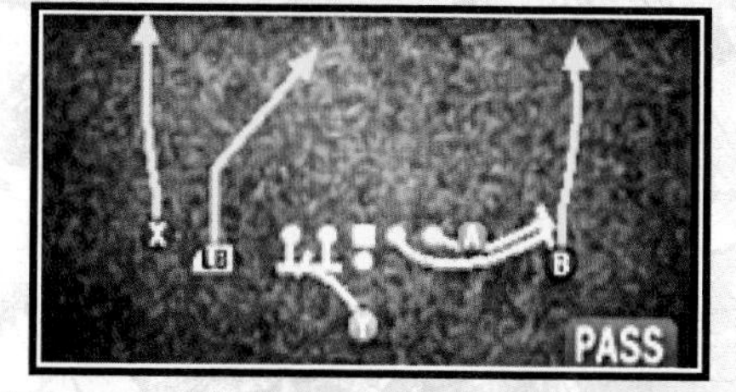

Having a star TE in Dallas Clark will make the defense anticipate that he will stretch the middle of the field. The Colts› offense looks to get the ball to its playmakers in unique ways. The PA TE Screen shows play action to suck the defense in and then get the ball out quick to Clark.

The defense is in man-to-man coverage, which will work to our advantage. The play action freezes the defense and allows Dallas Clark to get open behind his blocker. After the play action, deliver the pass.

The defense is out of position as we deliver the ball to Clark. Our pulling offensive lineman lays the block in the open field. We break upfield to gain as many yards as possible.

PRO TIP The more you run the ball, the better the play action will work.

Man Beater

Split Flex - Colts HB Wheel

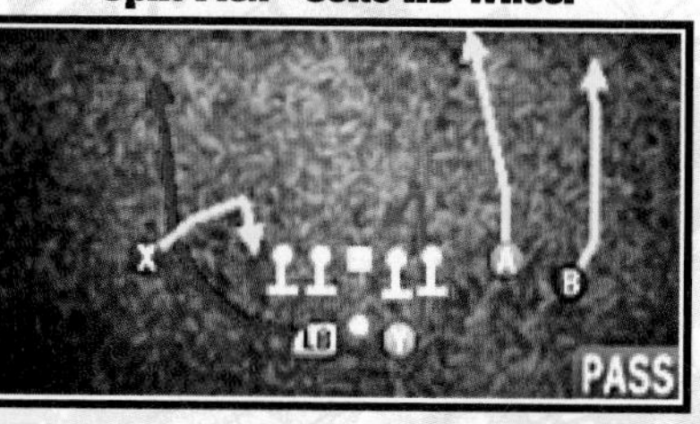

The Split Flex Colts HB Wheel is designed to attack a defense deep downfield, but it also has a few quick hot reads in case the defense sends the blitz. After the blitz, determine to checkdown or look for the big play with one of the vertical routes.

Short, quick routes are the best way to beat a man-to-man blitzing defense. We see the blitz coming off the edge in this play. We also see our inside WR breaking free over the middle of the field. His defender is virtually out of the play.

The defender is completely out of position as we make the grab. We will gain major yards after the catch. If you can consistently beat your opponent when they blitz, you will dictate the pace of the game.

PRO TIP The HB wheel route out of the backfield is killer against the zone blitz.

Zone Beater

Singleback Bunch - Stick

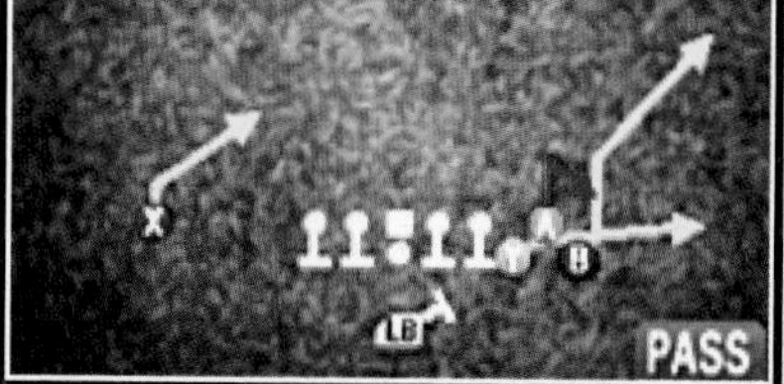

A popular way to beat zone coverage is by utilizing the stick concept. From the Bunch formation, one of the receivers will break to the flat, forcing the zone defense his way. One of the WR will run a short curl route behind the flat route. What is so unique about the Bunch Stick play is the added corner route.

The corner route puts immense pressure on the zone defense. Not only do they have to worry about the short curl, but the deeper corner route can sit behind the flat defender for a bigger gain. The defense is forced to pick its poison with this play.

The pass is delivered before the safety can make a play on the ball. The zone defense stands no chance in defending against the stick concept. This same style of play is found in many formations throughout the Colts› playbook.

PRO TIP Be sure to substitute a WR with a good Catch in Traffic rating.

Base Play

Gun Bunch - TE Corner

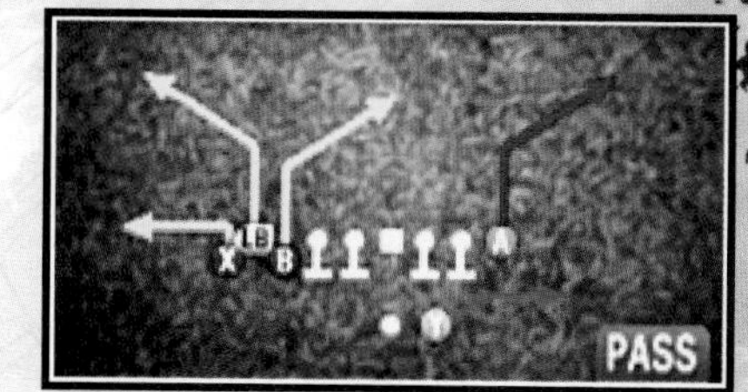

The Gun Bunch TE Corner is one of our favorite zone defensive coverage beaters. The route combination on this play calls for two deep corners and one deep post. Against the Cover 3 zone, this gives us three one-on-one matchups. Against the Cover 2 zone, the post will be open.

We target Dallas Clark running the deep corner. Notice the deep safety over the middle of the field. This is our clue that the defense is in a Cover 3 zone. We now know that we have the matchup we want with Clark in the corner.

Clark hauls in the pass and tiptoes on the sideline. Anytime we have a one-on-one matchup with Clark, the advantage belongs to the offense. Attacking zone defense is all about route combinations!

PRO TIP Substitute in your best blocking HB or FB to get added blocking protection.

DALLAS COWBOYS

OFFENSIVE SCOUTING REPORT

The Dallas Cowboys have possessed elite *Madden NFL* talent since *Madden NFL 09*. They have had speed and power out of the backfield and a unique combo of size and speed at wideout every season. With a healthy Tony Romo in *Madden NFL 12*, the Cowboys are poised to be a top-five team. Dallas has playmakers to run any type of game plan. Dez Bryant and Miles Austin are deceptively strong on the outside, while Jason Witten owns the middle of the field. Start Felix Jones at RB due to his speed and catch ratings. Romo has solid short accuracy and the ability to keep plays alive with his legs. Use a reserve player on special team returns to keep your starters fresh. Dallas has no shortage of speed. For the online players, get used to seeing Dallas as a top-tier team.

DEFENSIVE SCOUTING REPORT

Superstar DeMarcus Ware is arguably the best linebacker in the game. His rare combination of speed and size allows you to utilize him in coverage as well as pass-rushing situations. The secondary of the Cowboys has plenty of studs for man-to-man coverage. Terence Newman, Orlando Scandrick, and Mike Jenkins can all play in one-on-one situations, so don't be afraid to dial up the pressure with the Cowboys. Defensive tackle Jay Ratliff is not only big and powerful but he has pass-rushing abilities to complement his strength. Having a defensive tackle that can get after the quarterback is a luxury in *Madden NFL 12*

TEAM RATING

Overall	82
Offense	86
Defense	82

DYNAMIC PLAYER PERFORMANCE TRAITS

Demarcus Ware
LB #94

Swim Move	Yes
Bull Move	Yes
Spin Move	Yes
Clutch	Yes

RATINGS BY POSITION

Position	Rating	Position	Rating
Quarterbacks	88	Defensive Tackles	92
Halfbacks	81	Outside Linebackers	90
Fullbacks	69	Middle Linebackers	83
Wide Receivers	84	Cornerbacks	81
Tight Ends	96	Free Safeties	76
Tackles	81	Strong Safeties	77
Guards	83	Kickers	67
Centers	87	Punters	90
Defensive Ends	75		

DEPTH CHART

POS	OVR	FIRST NAME	LAST NAME
3DRB	74	Tashard	Choice
C	87	Andre	Gurode
C	62	Travis	Bright
CB	85	Terence	Newman
CB	77	Mike	Jenkins
CB	70	Orlando	Scandrick
CB	63	Bryan	McCann
CB	64	Josh	Thomas
DT	92	Jay	Ratliff
DT	59	Clifton	Geathers
FB	69	Chris	Gronkowski
FB	66	Shaun	Chapas
FS	76	Alan	Ball
FS	64	Akwasi	Owusu-Ansah
FS	63	Danny	McCray
HB	81	Felix	Jones
HB	75	Marion	Barber
HB	74	Tashard	Choice
HB	57	Lonyae	Miller
K	67	David	Buehler
KOS	67	David	Buehler
KR	63	Bryan	McCann
KR	63	Kevin	Ogletree
LE	72	Stephen	Bowen
LE	65	Jason	Hatcher
LE	54	Alex	Daniels
LG	82	Kyle	Kosier
LG	69	Montrae	Holland
LG	68	David	Arkin
LOLB	82	Anthony	Spencer
LOLB	67	Bruce	Carter
LOLB	69	Victor	Butler
LS	54	L.P.	Ladouceur
LT	84	Doug	Free
LT	60	Jermey	Parnell
LT	59	Robert	Brewster
MLB	83	Bradie	James
MLB	82	Keith	Brooking
MLB	73	Sean	Lee
MLB	72	Leon	Williams
P	90	Mat	McBriar
PR	63	Bryan	McCann
QB	88	Tony	Romo
QB	76	Jon	Kitna
QB	67	Stephen	McGee
RE	78	Igor	Olshansky
RE	63	Sean	Lissemore
RG	84	Leonard	Davis
RG	70	Phil	Costa
ROLB	98	DeMarcus	Ware
ROLB	57	Brandon	Williams
RT	77	Tyron	Smith
RT	78	Marc	Colombo
RT	67	Sam	Young
SS	77	Gerald	Sensabaugh
SS	70	Barry	Church
TE	96	Jason	Witten
TE	73	Martellus	Bennett
TE	69	John	Phillips
WR	89	Miles	Austin
WR	83	Dez	Bryant
WR	79	Roy	Williams
WR	65	Sam	Hurd
WR	63	Kevin	Ogletree
WR	61	Manuel	Johnson

OFFENSIVE STRENGTH CHART

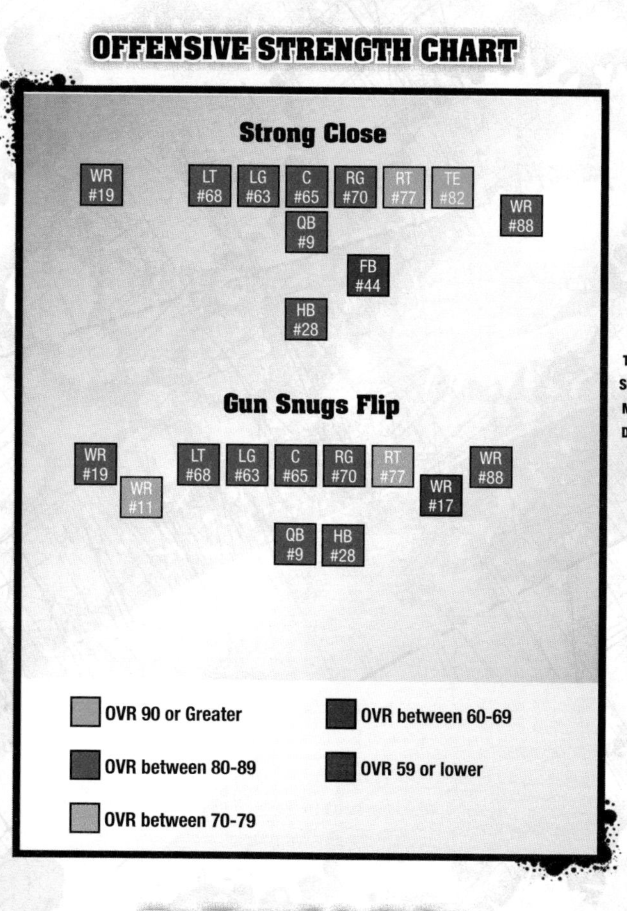

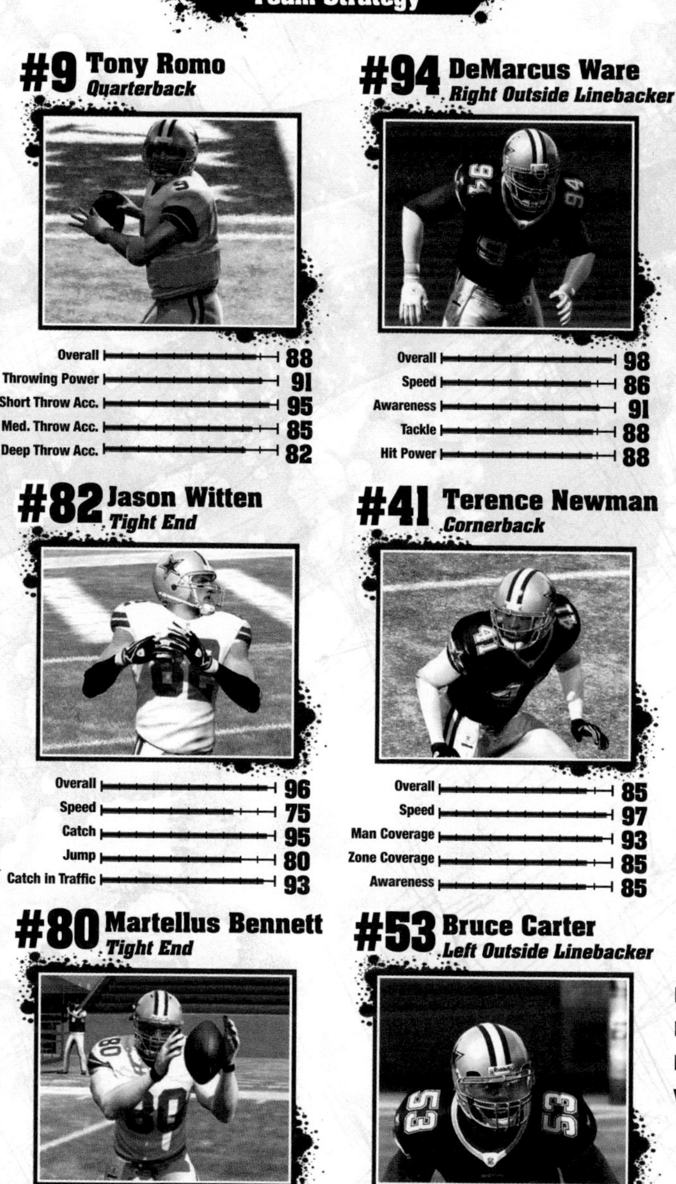

DEFENSIVE STRENGTH CHART

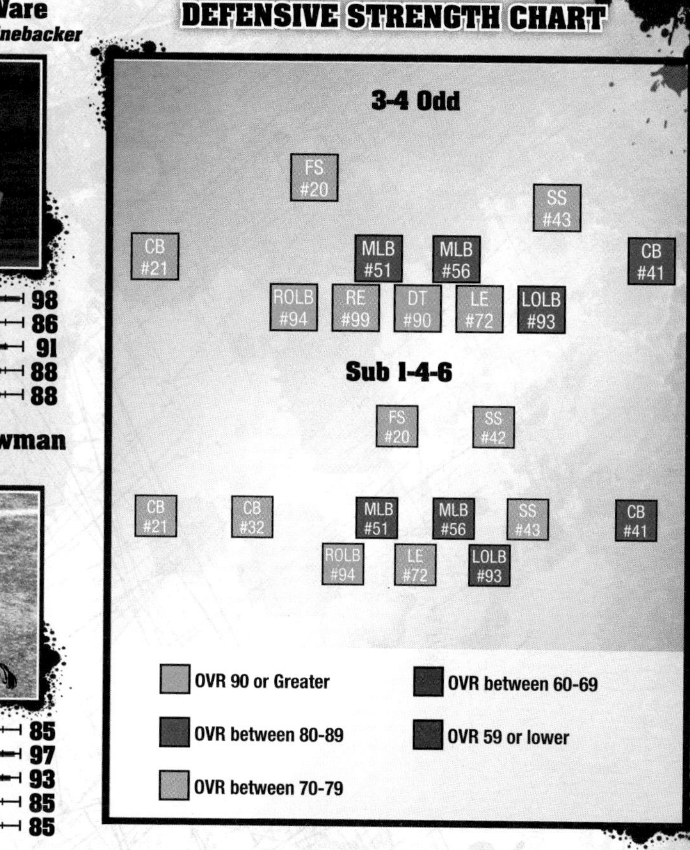

Key Player Substitution

Player: Kevin Ogletree

Position: #3 WR Slot

Key Stat: 96 Speed

What He Brings: Kevin Ogletree is able to keep up in the speed department. Get him in the game to bring an element of quickness to your scheme.

Player: Bryan McCann

Position: #4 CB Slot

Key Stat: 98 Acceleration

What He Brings: The Cowboys have tremendous depth in the secondary and are able to throw out many different lineups. They can match up physically against teams, but McCann is valuable against a fast team like Philadelphia, which the Cowboys see twice a year.

Playbook Tips

Offensive Style: Balanced

Offense

- Use speedy RB Felix Jones when trying to break big runs outside.
- The Dallas offense has many different styles of draws; find out which works best for your scheme.
- Dallas's core WRs have tremendous depth and have elite size for their position.

Defense

- Allow LB DeMarcus Ware to rush on every third down passing situation.
- Don't be afraid to leave the Cowboys' CBs on an island; they can handle their own.
- Get FS Akwasi Owusu-Ansah into the game in passing situations—he has solid athletic talent.

OFFENSIVE FORMATIONS	
FORMATION	# OF PLAYS
Gun Doubles	24
Gun Empty Trips TE	12
Gun Flip Trips	9
Gun Snugs Flip	9
Gun Split Cowboy	15
Gun Spread Y-Slot	12
Gun Trey Open	12
Gun Y-Trips Cowboy	21
I-Form Pro	18
I-Form Slot Flex	15
I-Form Tight Pair	15
Razorback Cowboys	3
Singleback Ace	18
Singleback Ace Pair	12
Singleback Ace Pair Flex	15
Singleback Bunch	18
Singleback Doubles	21
Singleback Jumbo	12
Strong Close	15
Strong Pro	12

OFFENSIVE PLAYCOUNTS	
PLAY TYPE	# OF PLAYS
Quick Pass	15
Standard Pass	57
Shotgun Pass	82
Play Action Pass	44
Inside Handoff	39
Outside Handoff	14
Pitch	11
Counter	4
Draw	11

Three-Headed Rushing Attack

Strong Close—Counter Weak

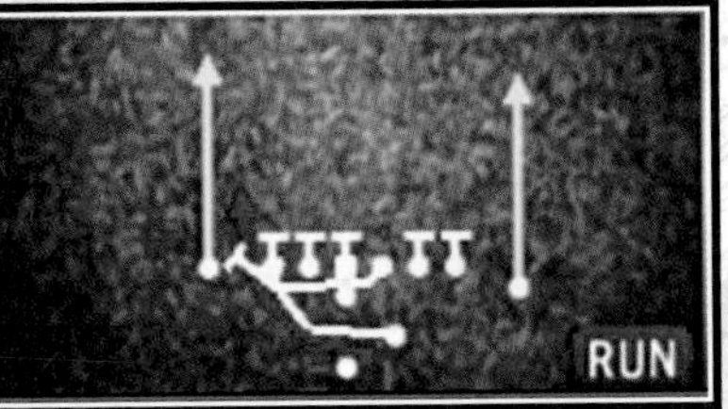

The counter is thought of as a slow-developing run, but out of the Strong Close formation it rarely ever gets blown up in the backfield. The reward of calling this run at the right time is worth the risk and can really deliver huge yards.

At the snap, the offense seems to be outnumbered, but when the WR clears out of the area he takes two defenders with him. The HB does a good job of waiting for the FB to get upfield and block the defense.

As a defender slips in, the HB makes a move to get around him. Now, he decides to cut inside and get as many yards as possible. If he had taken it outside, he would have run the risk of being taken down. At least he picked up a nice chunk of yardage and set the offense up for an easy second down.

PRO TIP Against zone coverage, motion your right WR to the weak side to help prevent penetration in the backfield.

Strong Close—HB Dive

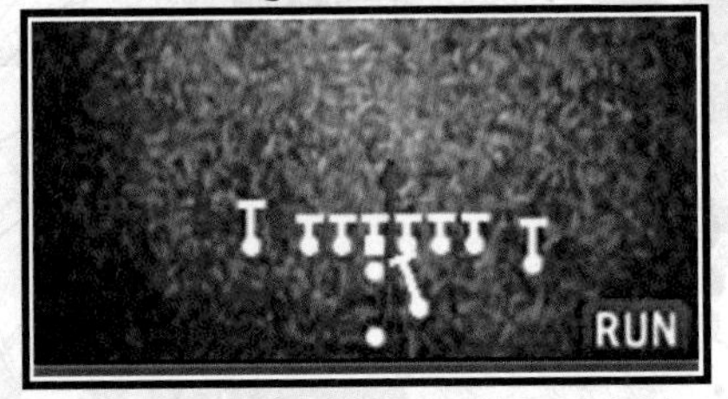

HB Dive is the best way to attack a defense that is not respecting the middle of the field. It takes discipline to run the ball constantly for 5 yards a carry, but it will open up all other aspects of your game.

Dallas has powerful tackles who can really demolish weaker ends in the run game. Here the middle of the field is opened as the defense gets knocked off the ball. Look to get the running back quickly up the hole and moving into the secondary.

Once into the secondary, the safeties will approach the ball carrier. You can line one up for a move, but if two approach simply cover up the ball and get down. After a few dives, the defense will sneak the safeties down and the passing game will open up.

PRO TIP Use play call subs to add a tackle to the TE position. Then place Jason Witten at WR, which will help add bulk to this run-heavy package

Strong Close - HB Toss

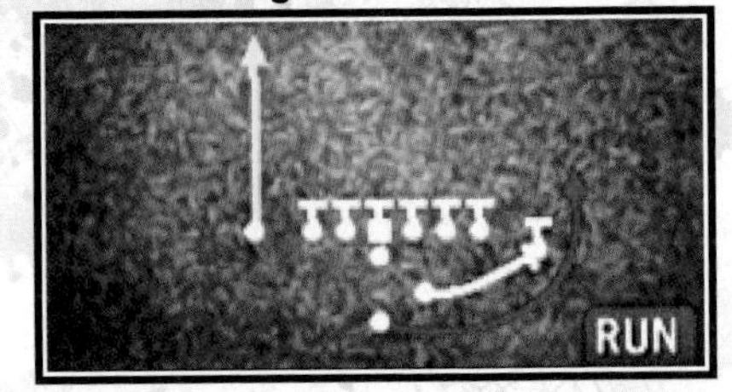

The offensive speed of Felix Jones in the backfield creates major matchup problems for the defense. The Strong Close HB Toss forces the defense to protect the middle part of the field. The design of this play is to get Jones out toward the sideline where he can use his game-changing speed.

Jones gets the pitch, and we can see the offensive line sealing off the edge. Our outside running lane has opened, and we look to get upfield quickly. Jones's speed allows us to take full advantage of the HB Toss.

Brace for impact, as Jones is a smaller back. Cover up the ball to avoid fumbling it. Follow your blocks and the design of the run, and the HB Toss can be a staple of your running game.

Quick Pass

Split Cowboy - Cowboy Y - Out

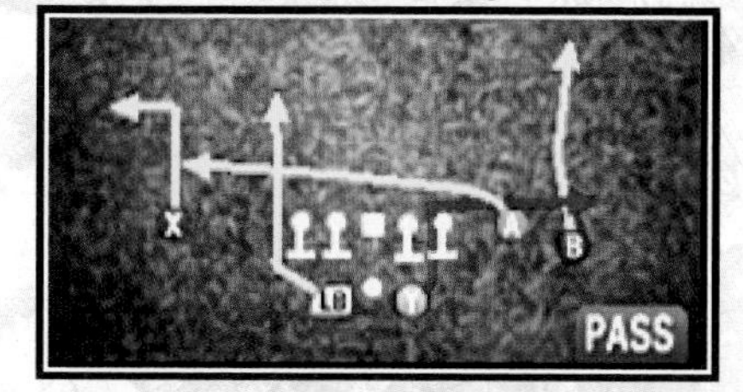

Over the past few seasons, the Cowboy Y-Out has been one of our favorite quick passing options against blitz pressure. The quick threats out of the backfield make blitz packages pay for being overly aggressive. The secret to this play is that it is designed to attack the defense from every angle it can send the blitz.

Our HB runs a vertical route, our TE runs an out and up route, and our slot WR runs a drag over the middle of the field. No matter where pressure comes from, we can expect to beat the blitz. Here we see the pressure coming off the TE side. We wait for the TE to break upfield before delivering the ball.

The pass is thrown high to where only the TE can make the catch. We threw to where the pressure was coming from. This is the golden rule when attacking the blitz and a must-have against blitz-heavy opponents!

Man Beater

Gun Snugs - Cowboy In

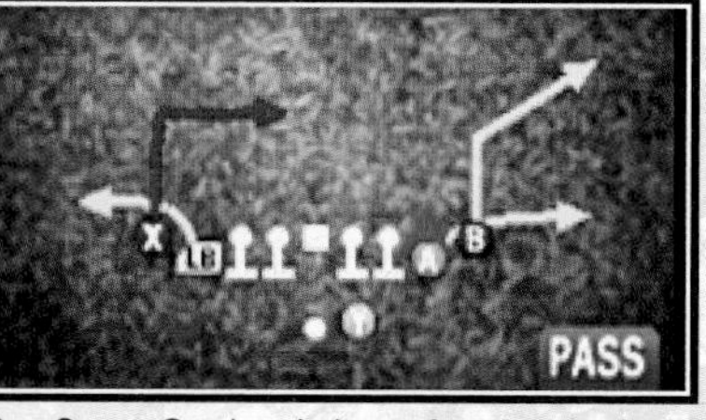

The Gun Snugs Cowboy In is our favorite play in the Cowboys' playbook. The dual flat routes force our opponent to protect against the flat. The blue route by the HB protects against the blitz, and we have a corner route to attack a Cover 3 zone defense.

We see the defense is in man-to-man coverage. The WR is open in the flat. Hit the WR in the flat to force the defense out of man coverage.

Our number-one rule is to never be late when passing to the flats! This only allows for the defense to make a play on the ball. When passing to the flat, be quick and precise. We are able to get upfield with our speedy WR!

PRO TIP Against a coverage-style defense, look for the HB out of the backfield. This route is very difficult to defend!

Zone Beater

Singleback Bunch - Y Trail

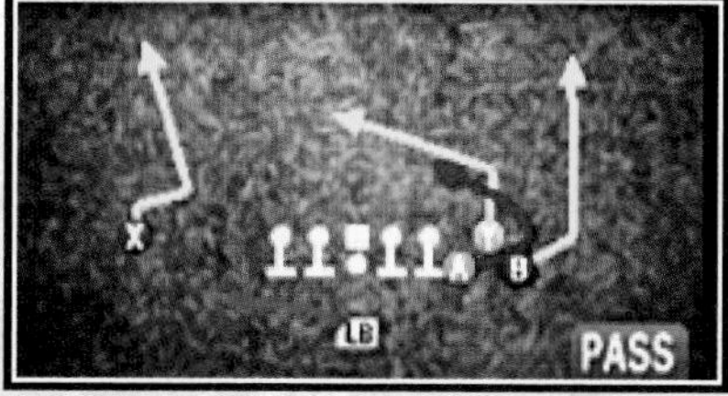

Using a Bunch formation is one of the better ways to beat zone defensive coverage. With the Y Trail, we can attack the defense short and deep with the route combinations on the field. We want to key in on the vertical route, as we are looking to sneak the pass in behind the zone defense.

We know that the defense is in a Cover 2 zone, as we see the flat defender point off to the deep safety to cover the streaking WR. With proper timing, we can squeeze the ball between coverages to complete the pass!

The timing of the throw is perfect as we utilize one of our best WRs in the open field. Expect a big hit from the deep safety. You can either break for the sideline or look to cover the ball while anticipating contact. Bunch formations put pressure on zone defensive coverage because of their ability to overload the zone defense.

Base Play

Flip Trips - Slot Trail

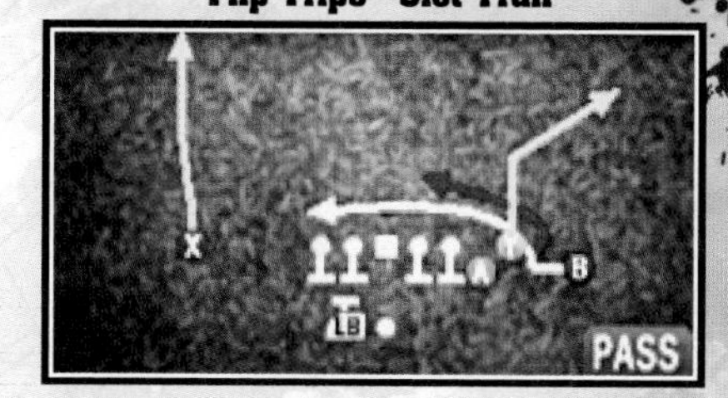

One of the most popular plays in*Madden NFL 11*—Slot Trail, out of the Flip Trips formation—will make its comeback in *Madden NFL 12*. We love this play because of its threat to beat zone defensive coverage and man defensive coverage. It can also beat press coverage with the designed auto-motion!

The defense is in man-to-man press coverage looking to slow down our explosive offense. Our WR goes into motion, and we anticipate his free release. The auto-motion will not allow the defender to press our WR, which is a major advantage for our offense.

Our WR springs free past the pressing defender. Against zone defense, the auto-motion route is still a great option, but look for the trail route opening up behind the auto-motion. Against the Cover 3 zone, the deep corner will be in a one-on-one matchup.

PRO TIP Speed kills with auto-motion. Substitute in your WR with the highest Speed rating.

MIAMI DOLPHINS

OFFENSIVE SCOUTING REPORT

The Miami Dolphins' true strength will finally translate into a successful team. With an up-and-coming offensive line that can push people back, the Dolphins will be able to grind out wins. The Miami playbook is finally set up to run plays that will work with bruising RBs like Ronnie Brown. Brown is often overlooked as a top RB; however *Madden NFL 12* allows players to grind out drives, and Brown will finally get respect. Chad Henne is the best option at QB, and Brandon Marshall is a big threat who will hang on to the ball in the toughest areas of the field. Look for TE Anthony Fasano on delayed (blue) routes where he can block and then release as a safety valve for Henne. Use Brian Hartline as the second WR; he is a better blocker and a huge threat when you add him to the slot against an inferior defender on passing downs. Avoid relying on the Wildcat formation, as the defense is not slowed down by the handoff options on the virtual gridiron.

DEFENSIVE SCOUTING REPORT

Vontae Davis has emerged as one of the league's lockdown cornerbacks. His ball-playing skills have helped to form the Dolphins' overall defense. Cameron Wake is a quarterback's nightmare with his pass-rushing ability off the edge. Wake has explosive speed to get after the quarterback, and offenses will be required to double-team him to slow him down. Cornerback Sean Smith is a *Madden NFL* superstar. At 6'3" Smith can cause major matchup problems a lot of times on the outside. The Dolphins' defense has the ability to blitz every down.

RATINGS BY POSITION

Quarterbacks	77	Defensive Tackles	86
Halfbacks	84	Outside Linebackers	83
Fullbacks	90	Middle Linebackers	90
Wide Receivers	81	Cornerbacks	82
Tight Ends	75	Free Safeties	76
Tackles	94	Strong Safeties	87
Guards	78	Kickers	79
Centers	79	Punters	83
Defensive Ends	87		

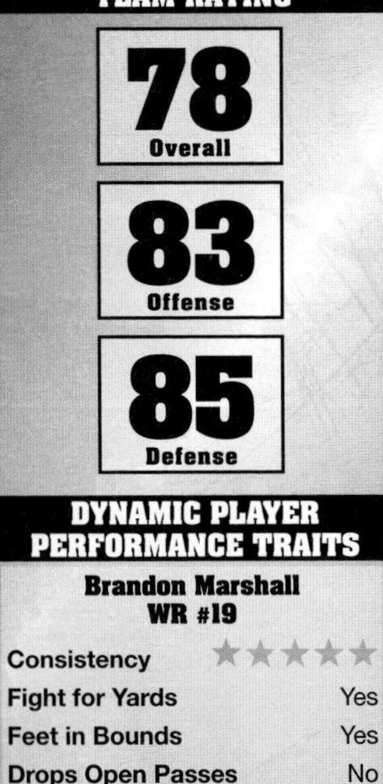

TEAM RATING

78 Overall

83 Offense

85 Defense

DYNAMIC PLAYER PERFORMANCE TRAITS

Brandon Marshall WR #19

Consistency	★★★★★
Fight for Yards	Yes
Feet in Bounds	Yes
Drops Open Passes	No
High Motor	No

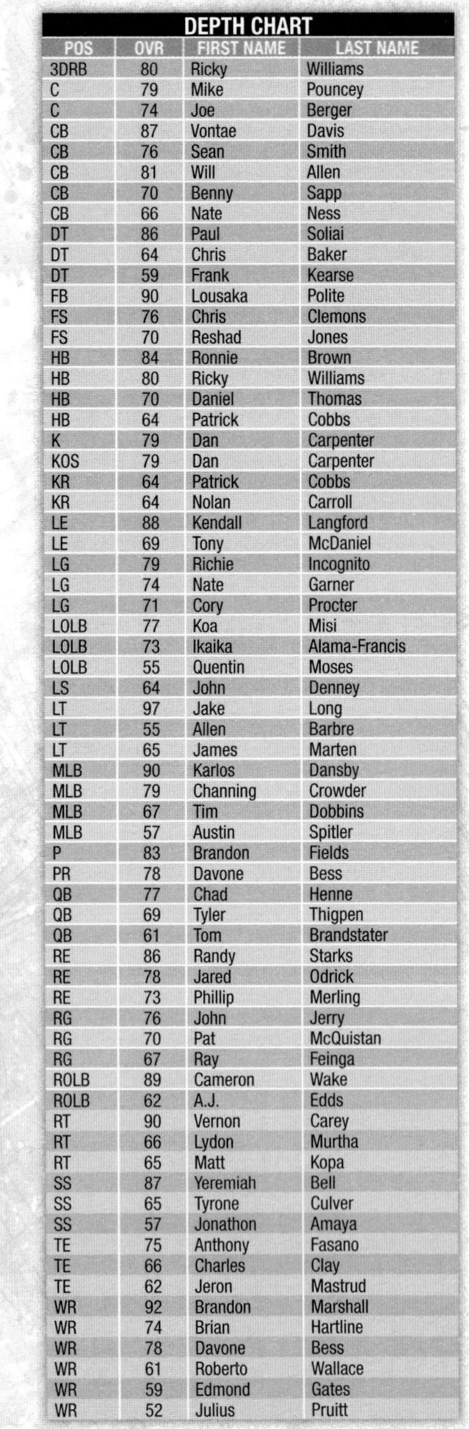

DEPTH CHART

POS	OVR	FIRST NAME	LAST NAME
3DRB	80	Ricky	Williams
C	79	Mike	Pouncey
C	74	Joe	Berger
CB	87	Vontae	Davis
CB	76	Sean	Smith
CB	81	Will	Allen
CB	70	Benny	Sapp
CB	66	Nate	Ness
DT	86	Paul	Soliai
DT	64	Chris	Baker
DT	59	Frank	Kearse
FB	90	Lousaka	Polite
FS	76	Chris	Clemons
FS	70	Reshad	Jones
HB	84	Ronnie	Brown
HB	80	Ricky	Williams
HB	70	Daniel	Thomas
HB	64	Patrick	Cobbs
K	79	Dan	Carpenter
KOS	79	Dan	Carpenter
KR	64	Patrick	Cobbs
KR	64	Nolan	Carroll
LE	88	Kendall	Langford
LE	69	Tony	McDaniel
LG	79	Richie	Incognito
LG	74	Nate	Garner
LG	71	Cory	Procter
LOLB	77	Koa	Misi
LOLB	73	Ikaika	Alama-Francis
LOLB	55	Quentin	Moses
LS	64	John	Denney
LT	97	Jake	Long
LT	55	Allen	Barbre
LT	65	James	Marten
MLB	90	Karlos	Dansby
MLB	79	Channing	Crowder
MLB	67	Tim	Dobbins
MLB	57	Austin	Spitler
P	83	Brandon	Fields
PR	78	Davone	Bess
QB	77	Chad	Henne
QB	69	Tyler	Thigpen
QB	61	Tom	Brandstater
RE	86	Randy	Starks
RE	78	Jared	Odrick
RE	73	Phillip	Merling
RG	76	John	Jerry
RG	70	Pat	McQuistan
RG	67	Ray	Feinga
ROLB	89	Cameron	Wake
ROLB	62	A.J.	Edds
RT	90	Vernon	Carey
RT	66	Lydon	Murtha
RT	65	Matt	Kopa
SS	87	Yeremiah	Bell
SS	65	Tyrone	Culver
SS	57	Jonathon	Amaya
TE	75	Anthony	Fasano
TE	66	Charles	Clay
TE	62	Jeron	Mastrud
WR	92	Brandon	Marshall
WR	74	Brian	Hartline
WR	78	Davone	Bess
WR	61	Roberto	Wallace
WR	59	Edmond	Gates
WR	52	Julius	Pruitt

OFFENSIVE STRENGTH CHART

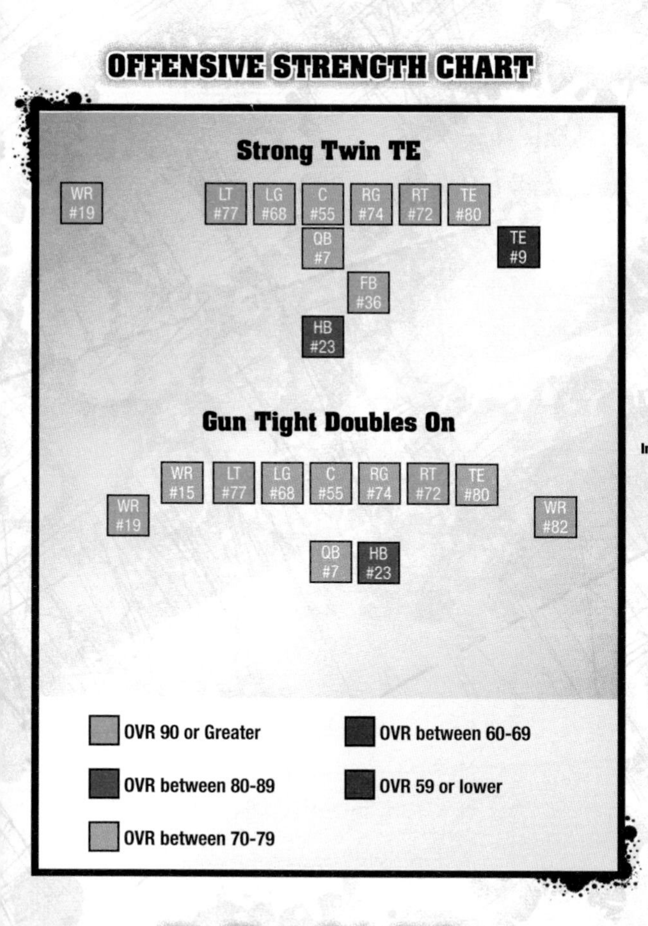

Key Player Substitution

Player: Edmond Gates

Position: #4 WR

Key Stat: 94 Speed

What He Brings: While Davone Bess has great acceleration, he lacks the top end speed of Gates. Look to work Bess over the middle while Gates stretches the defense in the seams with his jets.

#77 Jake Long
Left Tackle

Overall	97
Strength	97
Run Block Str.	98
Pass Block Str.	97
Impact Blocking	93

#19 Brandon Marshall
Wide Receiver

Overall	92
Speed	88
Catch	96
Route Running	90
Acceleration	87

#15 Davone Bess
Wide Receiver

Overall	78
Speed	85
Catch	95
Route Running	97
Acceleration	96

#58 Karlos Dansby
Middle Linebacker

Overall	90
Speed	79
Awareness	91
Tackle	92
Hit Power	88

#91 Cameron Wake
Right Outside Linebacker

Overall	89
Speed	84
Awareness	79
Tackle	85
Hit Power	88

#28 Nolan Carroll
Cornerback

Overall	71
Speed	93
Man Coverage	74
Zone Coverage	66
Awareness	44

DEFENSIVE STRENGTH CHART

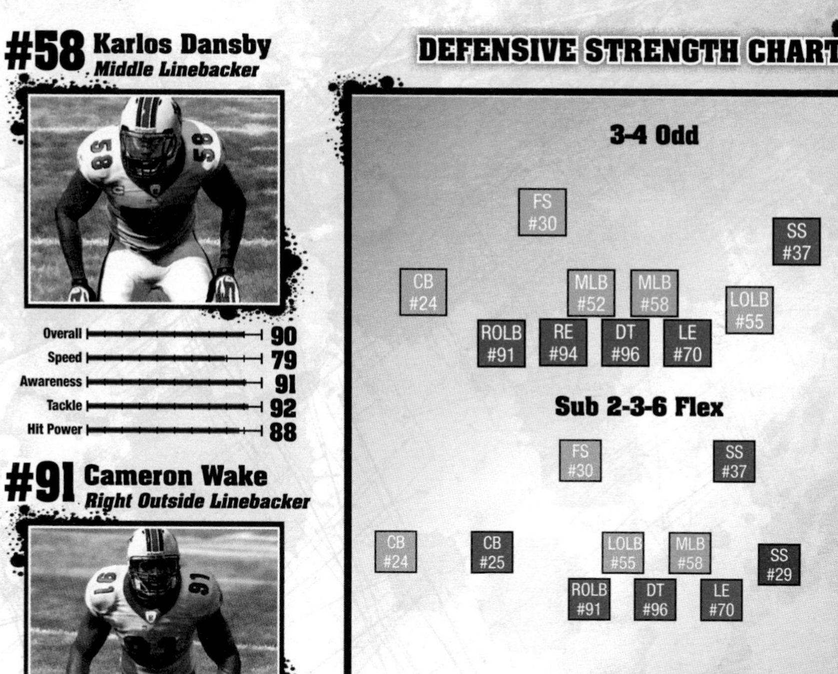

Key Player Substitution

Player: Koa Misi

Position: #1 MLB on Passing Downs

Key Stat: 88 Speed

What He Brings: When the offense drops back to pass, make sure to have Misi on the field. He is a strong defender against the pass because of his speed, and this will allow Cameron Wake to rush the passer.

Playbook Tips

Offensive Style: Run Balanced

Offense

- The Dolphins have 12 Wildcat plays from two different formations to explore and frustrate the defense with.
- Work your run game behind franchise cornerstone LT Jake Long.
- Use the Gun Split Dolphin to allow extra time in the pocket for your QB.

Defense

- Cameron Wake can really pressure the offense from the edge; allow his primary job to be rushing the passer.
- Allow the Dolphins physical corners to get up on the line of scrimmage and bump their WRs.
- Keep LB Karlos Dansby on the field even in passing situations because he is the anchor in the middle.

OFFENSIVE FORMATIONS

FORMATION	# OF PLAYS
Gun Doubles WK	15
Gun Doubles Wing TE	12
Gun Empty Trey	9
Gun Snugs Flip	9
Gun Split Dolphin	15
Gun Tight Doubles On	12
Gun Trey Open	12
Gun Trips TE	12
I-Form Pro	21
I-Form Pro Twins	15
I-Form Slot Flex	15
Singleback Ace	18
Singleback Ace Pair	15
Singleback Bunch	15
Singleback Doubles	21
Singleback Jumbo	12
Singleback Y-Trips	18
Strong Pro	18
Strong Twin TE	15
Weak Pro Twins	12
Wildcat Normal	6
Wildcat Trips Over	6

OFFENSIVE PLAYCOUNTS

PLAY TYPE	# OF PLAYS
Quick Pass	15
Standard Pass	59
Shotgun Pass	60
Play Action Pass	61
Inside Handoff	44
Outside Handoff	14
Pitch	13
Counter	8
Draw	12

Three-Headed Rushing Attack

Strong Twin TE—Counter Weak

The Strong Twin TE formation is an announcement to the defense that you are taking no prisoners. When you use this as your power running set, the defense will be forced to bring extra linemen on the field to contend with it.

At the snap, the LT blocks to the right and leaves the player on the edge free. Our FB will work over and pick him up, but now we are down one blocker. When we get to the edge, our RB cuts back inside to try and get more yards.

The defense does a good job of holding the edge to prevent the huge run but is still getting burned up the middle for a decent gain by the HB. When we cut back inside, the guard is heading over to pick up our left side to spring us for a few extra yards.

PRO TIP Place a stronger WR into the game who will hold his block against his defender.

Strong Twin TE—HB Dive

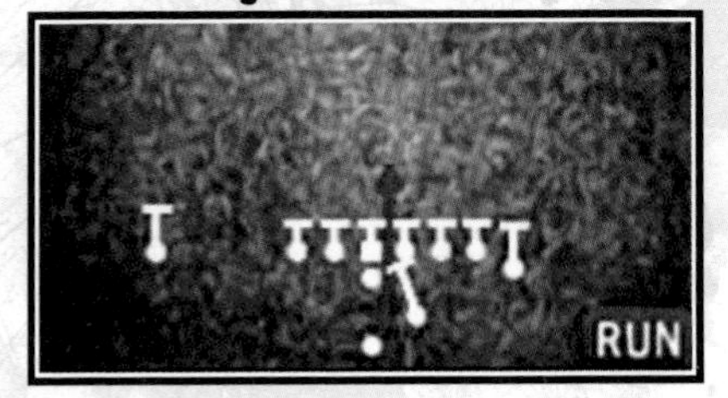

When an offense has the best success with a running attack, it is because they are simply running it right at the defense and still are picking up yardage. The dive is the type of run that can make for a long afternoon if the defense struggles to defend it.

The QB quickly gets the ball into the hands of the HB. He is waiting to see where the FB picks up his block and attempts to follow him through the line of scrimmage.

The RB gets into the secondary before getting touched and still has a lineman leading the way. This is a bad sign for the defense. Now the safety will have to come up and make the tackle, and then move closer to the line the next time this formation is seen.

PRO TIP If the defense cheats, you can cut this run outside to the left even after the snap by using the High Step button.

Strong Twin TE - HB Power O

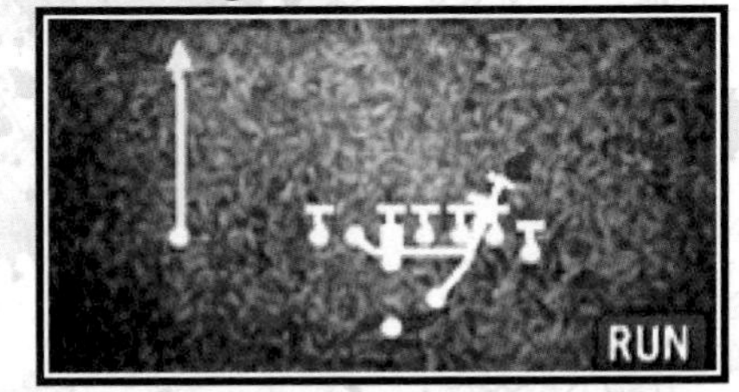

The Strong Twin TE formation is known to many around the *Madden NFL* community as an "old-school formation." This is because of its run-first mentality. The package calls for two TEs, a FB, and our split-end WR. We are not concerned with the defense keying in on the run, as we are confident with the play call.

We can see that our running lane to the outside has been shut down, and we are forced to cut the ball back up the middle and follow our blockers. If you decide to bounce the run outside, make sure the blockers seal off the outside edge.

It is important to follow your pulling offensive linemen on the HB Power O. They will lead the way for you upfield. Let them get into position before looking to break outside or back up inside. Patience is the key when running HB Power O.

PRO TIP Substitute an extra offensive lineman for your second TE to get extra blocking on the field.

Quick Pass

Tight Doubles On - PA Deep Curls

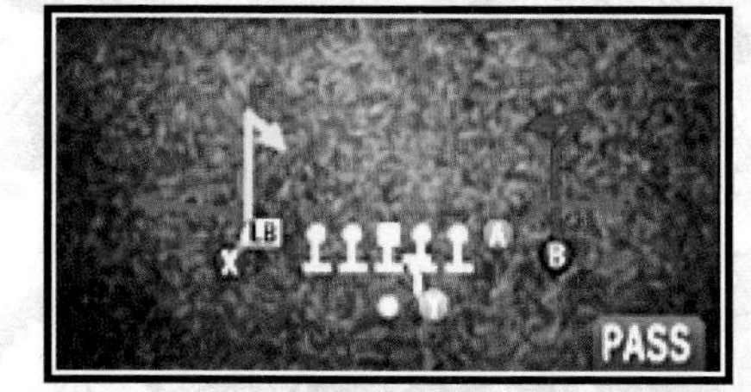

The Tight Doubles On PA Deep Curls is one of the most unique plays in the game. It has two blue routes assigned to the play. This means that we will have nice pass protection after the snap of the ball. We call upon this play when we are facing an opponent who has an aggressive blitz package.

We are going to target Brandon Marshall once again. Marshall's size creates major matchup problems for any defense in the game. To go along with the deep blues, we have two of our WRs running curl routes. The curl routes are effective against the blitz because we can get one-on-one matchups with the defender.

The blitz is on and Marshall is able to snag the ball between two defenders. If you make an incorrect read and the defense is dropping into coverage, the blue routes will release into the flat. Both of these WRs should have a step on their defenders.

PRO TIP Block your HB to gain another blocker to aid in protection.

Man Beater

I-Form Pro - Mesh

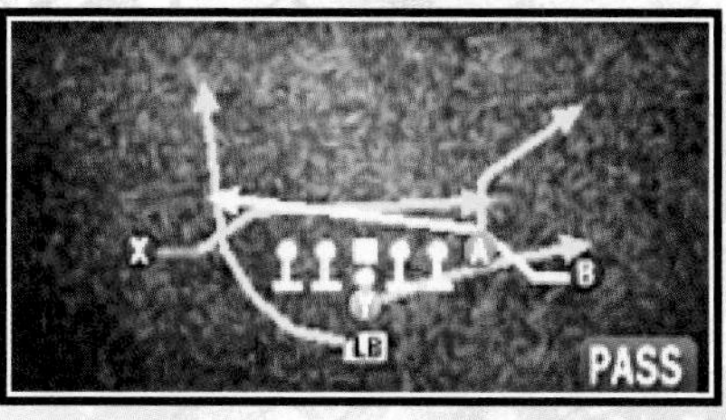

The I-Form Mesh is an excellent play call when facing man-to-man coverage or a Cover 2 zone. The dual drag routes will open up from the natural picks, and the corner route is a Cover 2 zone killer. Our quick pass option is to our HB out of the backfield on the wheel route. This same route is great for hitting the seam against the Cover 3 zone.

We look to get the ball to Ronnie Brown in the passing game. He breaks out of the backfield and has the matchup we want against the slower linebacker. Wait for Brown to begin his move upfield and then deliver the pass.

Brown's playmaking ability in the open field allows us to pick up a big chunk of yardage after the broken tackle. The linebacker is no match for his mix of speed and power. The I-Form Mesh is a great play to attack both man and zone defensive coverages. It will give you confidence for every play because of its ability to beat any type of defense!

Zone Beater

Trips TE - Xspot

Another way to attack zone coverage is by utilizing the Trips TE formation. We love the route combinations with the X Spot, as we are able to take advantage of Brandon Marshall's height and awesome Catch in Traffic rating. Against a Cover 4 Zone defense, the flat route will be open. Against the Cover 3 and Cover 2 zone defense, look for Brandon Marshall posting up the defense on the curl route.

We drop back and scan the field and recognize the Cover 3 zone defense. Our WR in the flat is open, but it would only be for a short gain. We wait for the defender to choose who he will guard. Will it be the flat WR or Brandon Marshall on the curl route?

We deliver the pass to Marshall for the sure catch. The defender is in position to take him down right after the catch. We are confident he will hang on to the ball after the big hit!

Base Play

Split Dolphin - Slot Cross

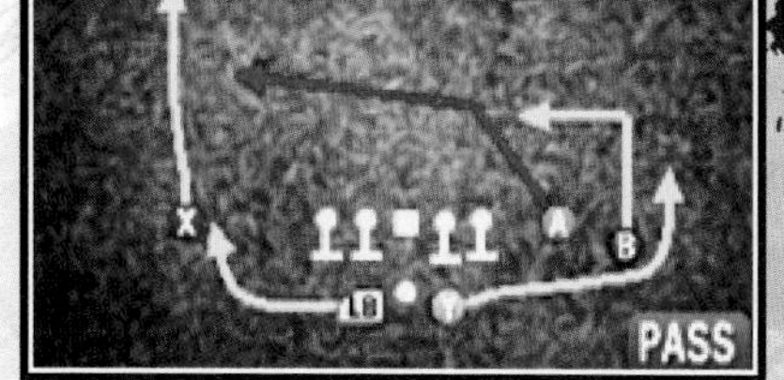

The Split Dolphin Cross puts pressure on the defensive zone blitz. The defense will typically have three defenders deep and three defenders short. The deep coverage will still be solid, but the underneath coverage will be weak. We are looking to attack the defense in both flats and in the middle of the field.

Our TE heads to the flat where there is no zone defense. We also see the outside defensive backs dropping back deep in coverage. This tells us that our opponent is in Cover 3 zone defense. The pressure is coming but the coverage is weak.

The catch is made with no zone defenders around our TE. We are able to get upfield and gain extra yards before the defense is able to take us down. The zone blitz uses the same tactic of confusion to try and force you into a bad decision. By mastering the Slot Cross, you will be able the zone blitz no matter where they send the pressure from. Your opponent may try and roll the coverage to confuse you. Stick with the basic understanding of the Slot Cross and you will have no problem beating the zone blitz!

PHILADELPHIA EAGLES

OFFENSIVE SCOUTING REPORT

The Eagles signing of Michael Vick paid huge dividends in 2010. This dynamic QB threw for over 3,000 yards and averaged 6.8 yards per carry. The Eagles returned to the postseason by capitalizing on their elite speed at skill positions. In *Madden NFL 12*, Philadelphia is best utilized by getting its playmakers in the open field. Gamers should look to focus on hitting RB LeSean McCoy out of the backfield and throwing strikes to WRs like DeSean Jackson. The Eagles' playbook contains unique spread formations that will force the defense to try and hang with their speed. The best players force the defense to hot-route defenders into a QB Spy. This will limit the amount of defenders giving help, which will lead to one-on-one matchups.

DEFENSIVE SCOUTING REPORT

There is no telling what scheme the Eagles will go with under new defensive coordinator Juan Castillo this season. However, the Philadelphia Eagles' defense has been known over the years to be very aggressive in nature. With cornerback Asante Samuel the Eagles have the confidence to play lockdown defense in the secondary. Linebacker Ernie Sims is a *Madden NFL* superstar. Sims has a great combination of pure speed and power. He can be the ultimate playmaker by forcing fumbles and covering the field with his speed. We recommend using nickel packages with the Eagles and leaving Trent Cole one-on-one to rush off the edge. If the Eagles can add one more special piece via free agency, they could be a go-to team in *Madden NFL 12*!

TEAM RATING

Overall	86
Offense	88
Defense	83

DYNAMIC PLAYER PERFORMANCE TRAITS

Michael Vick
QB #7

Tuck and Run	★★★★★
Forces Passes	★★★★★
Throws Tight Spiral	Yes
Clutch	No
High Motor	No

RATINGS BY POSITION

Quarterbacks	93	Defensive Tackles	86
Halfbacks	88	Outside Linebackers	79
Fullbacks	87	Middle Linebackers	69
Wide Receivers	85	Cornerbacks	87
Tight Ends	83	Free Safeties	77
Tackles	84	Strong Safeties	88
Guards	83	Kickers	90
Centers	78	Punters	69
Defensive Ends	86		

DEPTH CHART

POS	OVR	FIRST NAME	LAST NAME
3DRB	88	LeSean	McCoy
C	78	Jamaal	Jackson
C	65	Mike	McGlynn
CB	94	Asante	Samuel
CB	79	Dimitri	Patterson
CB	74	Joselio	Hanson
CB	64	Trevard	Lindley
DT	86	Mike	Patterson
DT	79	Brodrick	Bunkley
DT	75	Antonio	Dixon
DT	67	Trevor	Laws
FB	87	Leonard	Weaver
FB	76	Owen	Schmitt
FS	77	Nate	Allen
FS	75	Marlin	Jackson
FS	63	Jamar	Adams
HB	88	LeSean	McCoy
HB	77	Jerome	Harrison
HB	67	Dion	Lewis
HB	63	Eldra	Buckley
K	90	David	Akers
KOS	66	Alex	Henery
KR	58	Jorrick	Calvin
KR	63	Eldra	Buckley
LE	78	Juqua	Parker
LE	76	Brandon	Graham
LE	73	Victor	Abiamiri
LG	90	Todd	Herremans
LG	66	Julian	Vandervelde
LG	64	Dallas	Reynolds
LOLB	76	Moise	Fokou
LOLB	71	Casey	Matthews
LOLB	74	Rashad	Jeanty
LS	49	Jon	Dorenbos
LT	89	Jason	Peters
LT	58	Austin	Howard
MLB	69	Jamar	Chaney
MLB	62	Greg	Lloyd
MLB	63	Omar	Gaither
P	69	Sav	Rocca
PR	91	DeSean	Jackson
QB	93	Michael	Vick
QB	84	Kevin	Kolb
QB	67	Mike	Kafka
RE	93	Trent	Cole
RE	72	Darryl	Tapp
RE	59	Ricky	Sapp
RG	76	Danny	Watkins
RG	72	Max	Jean-Gilles
ROLB	81	Stewart	Bradley
ROLB	74	Akeem	Jordan
ROLB	78	Ernie	Sims
RT	78	Winston	Justice
RT	69	King	Dunlap
RT	61	Fenuki	Tupou
SS	88	Quintin	Mikell
SS	68	Kurt	Coleman
SS	71	Jaiquawn	Jarrett
TE	83	Brent	Celek
TE	66	Clay	Harbor
TE	64	Cornelius	Ingram
WR	91	DeSean	Jackson
WR	86	Jeremy	Maclin
WR	77	Jason	Avant
WR	64	Riley	Cooper
WR	61	Chad	Hall
WR	61	Sinorice	Moss

OFFENSIVE STRENGTH CHART

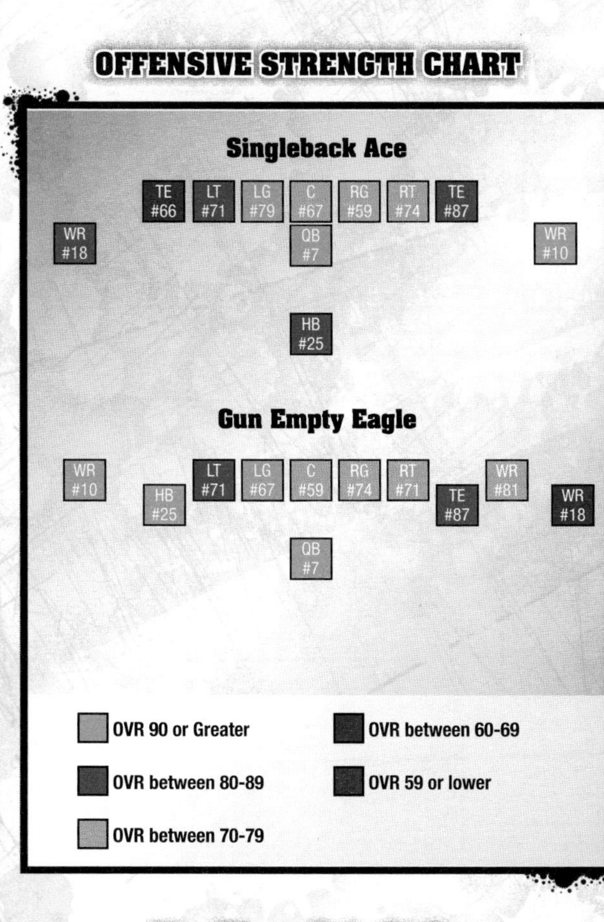

Key Player Substitution

Player: Riley Cooper

Position: #3 WR

Key Stat: 87 Jump

What He Brings: The Eagles' offense has the best team speed in the game, but they don't have an intimidating lineup with their size. By placing Riley Cooper on the outside, Philly gets a little bigger and tougher to defend.

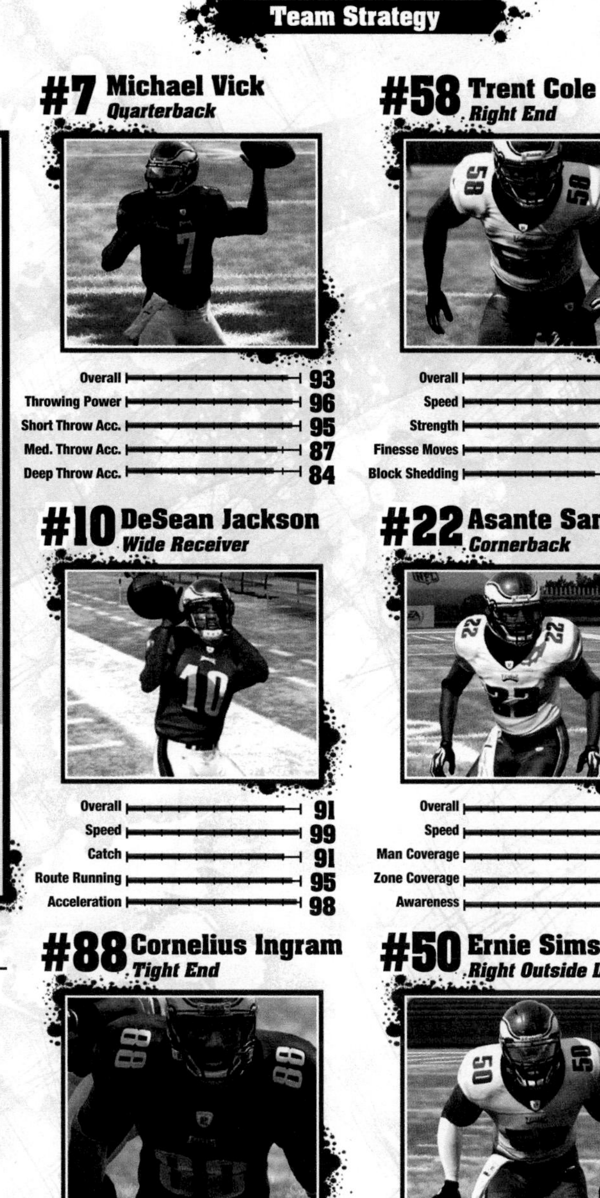

#7 Michael Vick
Quarterback

Overall	93
Throwing Power	96
Short Throw Acc.	95
Med. Throw Acc.	87
Deep Throw Acc.	84

#10 DeSean Jackson
Wide Receiver

Overall	91
Speed	99
Catch	91
Route Running	95
Acceleration	98

#88 Cornelius Ingram
Tight End

Overall	64
Speed	84
Catch	78
Jump	87
Catch in Traffic	76

#58 Trent Cole
Right End

Overall	93
Speed	84
Strength	78
Finesse Moves	97
Block Shedding	76

#22 Asante Samuel
Cornerback

Overall	94
Speed	90
Man Coverage	94
Zone Coverage	98
Awareness	95

#50 Ernie Sims
Right Outside Linebacker

Overall	78
Speed	88
Awareness	66
Tackle	85
Hit Power	91

DEFENSIVE STRENGTH CHART

4-3 Stack

FS #29 · SS #27 · CB #23 · LOLB #55 · MLB #51 · LOLB #53 · CB #22 · RE #58 · DT #97 · DT #98 · LE #75

Nickel Normal

FS #29 · SS #27 · CB #22 · CB #23 · CB #21 · LOLB #55 · MLB #51 · RE #58 · DT #97 · DT #98 · LE #75

OVR 90 or Greater · OVR between 60-69 · OVR between 80-89 · OVR 59 or lower · OVR between 70-79

Key Player Substitution

Player: Ernie Sims

Position: #1 LOLB Full-Time

Key Stat: 88 Speed

What He Brings: Ernie Sims is an athletic specimen who needs to be on the field for every snap. When you're user-controlling Sims, he will play high above his rating and force the offense to be cautious over the middle.

Playbook Tips

Offensive Style: West Coast

Offense

- Always take a shot deep in the first quarter to DeSean Jackson—even when it's unsuccessful it will still scare the defense.
- Make sure to utilize Vick's legs, but slide to keep him safe because he is very valuable to your offense.
- LeSean McCoy has great hands out of the backfield; make sure to use him on screen passes.

Defense

- Trent Cole will command a double team on most passing downs, and this will help slow down TEs and HBs who have to chip him at the line.
- Asante Samuel is a lockdown corner who is capable of making game-changing plays at any moment.
- The Eagles' strength is depth in the secondary, so make sure to take LBs off the field in passing situations.

OFFENSIVE FORMATIONS

FORMATION	# OF PLAYS
Gun Bunch WK	12
Gun Doubles	18
Gun Doubles WK	12
Gun Empty Eagle	9
Gun Empty Trey	9
Gun Snugs Flip	12
Gun Split	12
Gun Split Offset	18
Gun Spread Flex	12
Gun Trey Open	18
Gun Y-Trips WK	21
I-Form Pro	21
I-Form Slot Flex	15
I-Form Tight Pair	12
Singleback Ace	12
Singleback Ace Pair Twins	18
Singleback Bunch	15
Singleback Double Flex	9
Singleback Eagle Doubles	24
Weak Pro	15
Wildcat Philly	3

OFFENSIVE PLAYCOUNTS

PLAY TYPE	# OF PLAYS
Quick Pass	14
Standard Pass	44
Shotgun Pass	100
Play Action Pass	52
Inside Handoff	31
Outside Handoff	11
Pitch	7
Counter	2
Draw	14

Three-Headed Rushing Attack

I-Form Pro—Iso

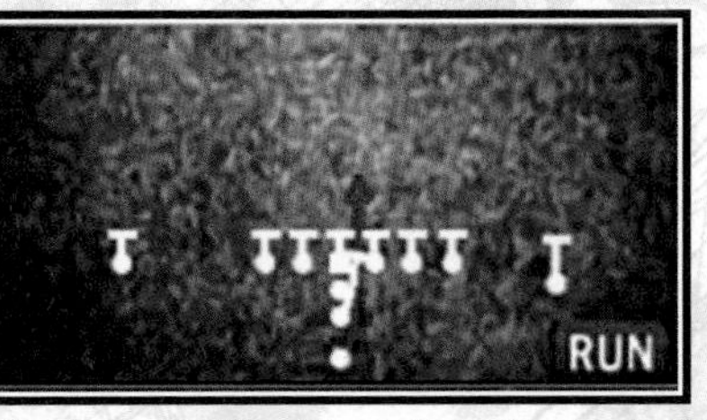

The Iso play is only meant to run through one gap. By following the FB this run can be used in short yardage situations or to test a defense trying to contain Michael Vick in the middle.

Our FB gets a full head of steam on his way to the line of scrimmage to clear space for the HB. The defender on the right of the screen is doing a great job playing his assignment and holding the edge, but this run won't be affected by him.

This is an ideal run for second and 4 because it is not likely to be an overwhelming running down. As the back breaks into the second level, he knows he only has a few men to beat. He places his hand behind him to gauge the traffic behind him while making one more cut to try and get in the end zone.

PRO TIP Place a back with good trucking in the game only in short yardage situations.

I-Form Pro—Toss

The Toss is a great way to get speedy RB LeSean McCoy out into space. The receivers will clear out and leave the right guard to pull around the strong side. This will let McCoy make those cuts he is famous for.

At the snap Vick quickly turns and pitches the ball out. The defense tries to sneak through the hole created by the pulling guard but can't keep up with the play. This will keep them locked inside and behind the play without containment.

As the RB approaches the edge, his guard has sealed the corner and he still has the FB out in front. The WR loses his man but has taken him far enough out of the play it won't be an issue. Now is the time to really hold down the turbo and get as many yards as possible. If you can outrun the defense behind you, this run can go all the way.

PRO TIP The toss is a great way to beat overly aggressive defenses like the Nickel 1-5-5, which are very popular online.

I-Form Pro—Inside Zone

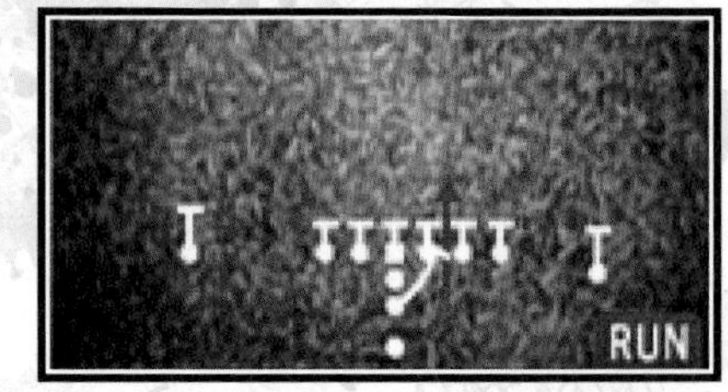

Having a go-to run play is crucial for short yardage situations. The I-Form Pro—Inside Zone leads the fullback through the hole into the second level.

Follow him through the line and look to make a cut when he blocks the linebacker.

McCoy has breakaway speed and you should look to get him to the second level of the defense. His speed will force the defense to respect his home run ability every time he touches the ball.

PRO TIP Use stronger WRs and motion them behind the offensive line to add an extra blocker to the play.

Quick Pass

I-Form Pro—HB Inside Zone

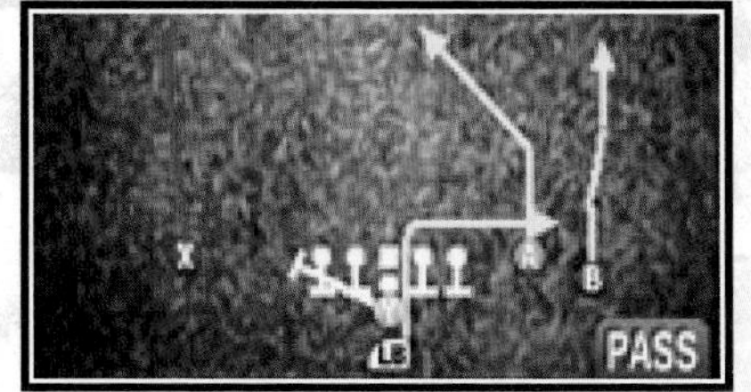

Use the I-Form Pro—HB Inside Zone in the red zone. This under-center quick pass is a great way to fit the ball in tight spaces. Wait until the RB cuts sharp upfield and throw him a bullet pass.

If the defense does not press the receivers, look to hit them quickly and make a move to the red zone. Here we throw a quick pass that is great on third down situations. We utilize our WR's big body to sheild off the defenders.

Hold the Icon button to bullet the ball to the WR to deliver it faster. Use the left stick to direct the pass and shield it away from the defender.

PRO TIP Use a lob throw when in the redzone to a bigger target like Cooper or Maclin.

Man Beater

Eagles Switch

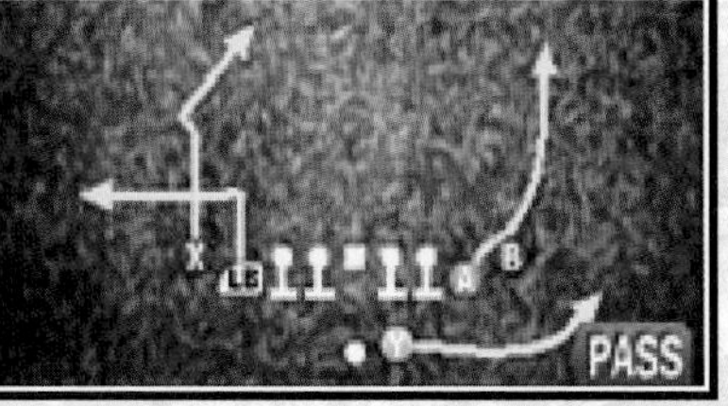

The Eagles Switch utilizes a Compressed set to allow defenders one-on-one matchups. Here the defender must switch off his assignment due to the alignment.

The CB swaps to cover the RB, leaving the linebacker on a WR. We can utilize the size and speed of the WR against the linebacker to get a possession catch.

If the defense is unable to switch, we can reap huge rewards.

PRO TIP If you can get enough time in the pocket, the route on the far left can really do damage down the field.

Zone Beater

Singleback Bunch—Eagles Drive

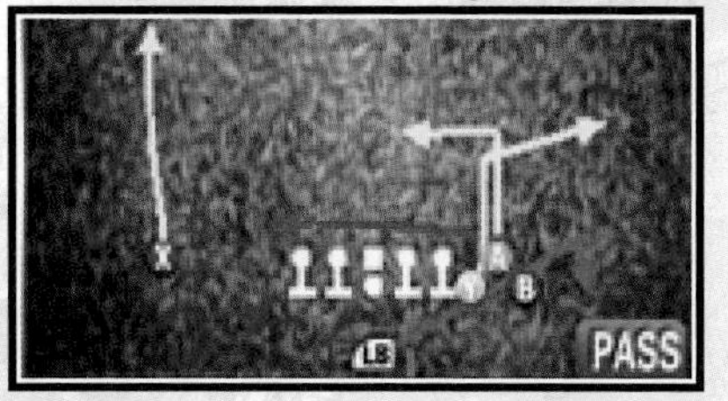

When taking on a zone defense, a Singleback Bunch—Eagles Drive set creates a flood and forces a defender to commit to one receiver.

On this play, we have our offense clear out the linebacker, which leaves room for the WR to sneak in his drag route.

The defender has to respect the deep receiver through his zone, and this creates a gaping hole in the middle of the offense for big yards.

PRO TIP Use this play to beat zone coverage and Smart Route the TE to get a shorter depth and easier throw to undercut the zone defender.

Base Play

Shotgun Eagle Empty—Eagle Deep In

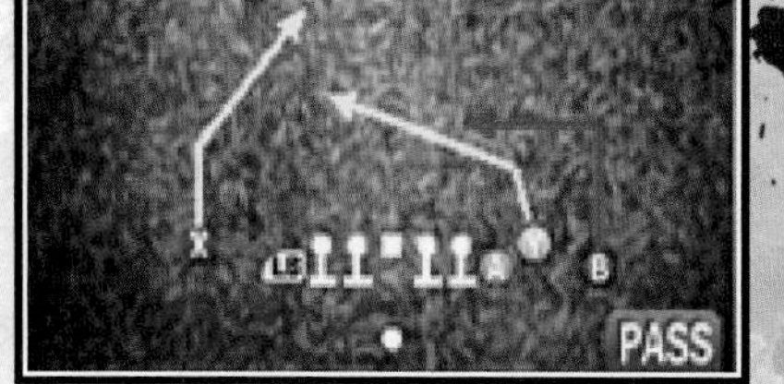

Emptying the backfield can be dangerous in *Madden NFL*; however, with Shotgun Eagle Empty—Eagle Deep In, the blue routes give you seven blockers on the line of scrimmage. These routes will block and delay their routes until the pocket is safe.

They will then release giving the QB a late release valve. DeSean Jackson will stress the secondary with a deep route, while the underneath routes give you a medium throw window.

Here we look to get the ball to McCoy in space. His speed allows us to pick up extra yards after the catch.

PRO TIP Try streaking to the outside right WR with Jeremy Maclin to give you a dual depth crossing threat. Slide protect the pocket left and roll out. The crossing routes will follow you, and the linebacker's release will force the defense to respect Vick as a running threat.

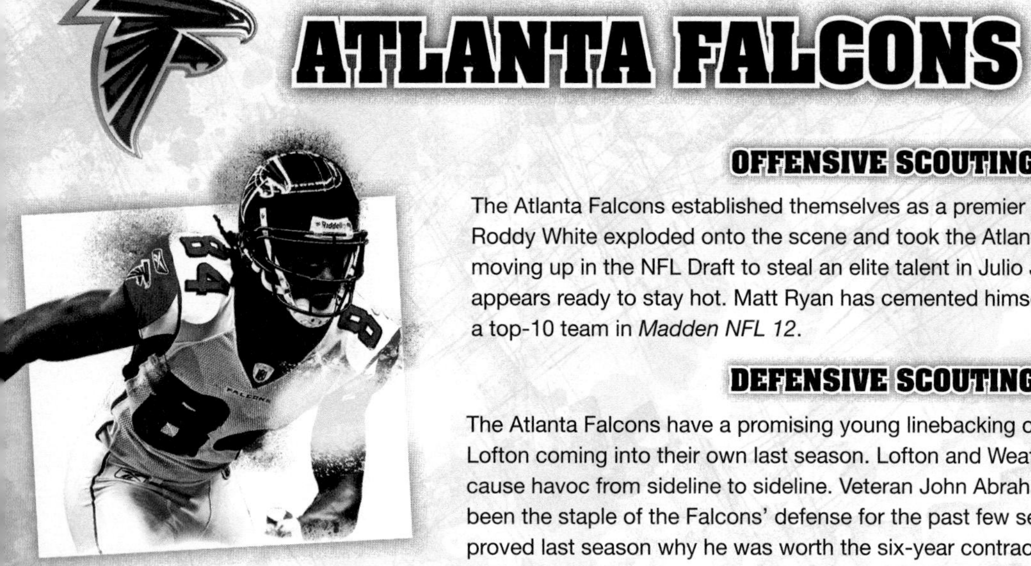

ATLANTA FALCONS

OFFENSIVE SCOUTING REPORT

The Atlanta Falcons established themselves as a premier team during the 2010 NFL season. WR Roddy White exploded onto the scene and took the Atlanta passing game to a new level. After moving up in the NFL Draft to steal an elite talent in Julio Jones, the Falcons' passing game appears ready to stay hot. Matt Ryan has cemented himself as a top-tier QB, and Atlanta will be a top-10 team in *Madden NFL 12*.

DEFENSIVE SCOUTING REPORT

The Atlanta Falcons have a promising young linebacking core with Sean Weatherspoon and Curtis Lofton coming into their own last season. Lofton and Weatherspoon are fast and athletic and will cause havoc from sideline to sideline. Veteran John Abraham controls the defensive line and has been the staple of the Falcons' defense for the past few seasons. Cornerback Dunta Robinson proved last season why he was worth the six-year contract and then some. His speed and ball skills help the Falcons get creative with their defensive scheme.

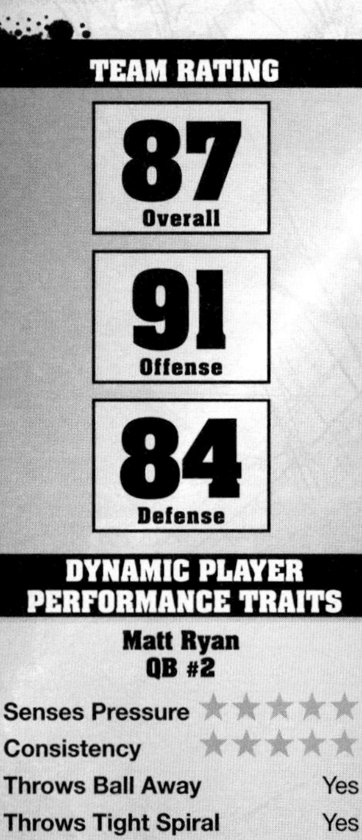

TEAM RATING

87	Overall
91	Offense
84	Defense

DYNAMIC PLAYER PERFORMANCE TRAITS

Matt Ryan
QB #2

Senses Pressure	★★★★★
Consistency	★★★★★
Throws Ball Away	Yes
Throws Tight Spiral	Yes
Clutch	No

RATINGS BY POSITION

Quarterbacks	90
Halfbacks	93
Fullbacks	94
Wide Receivers	83
Tight Ends	92
Tackles	90
Guards	85
Centers	90
Defensive Ends	85
Defensive Tackles	87
Outside Linebackers	76
Middle Linebackers	90
Cornerbacks	88
Free Safeties	80
Strong Safeties	82
Kickers	84
Punters	79

DEPTH CHART

POS	OVR	FIRST NAME	LAST NAME
3DRB	69	Jacquizz	Rodgers
C	90	Todd	McClure
C	68	Joe	Hawley
CB	89	Dunta	Robinson
CB	86	Brent	Grimes
CB	76	Brian	Williams
CB	70	Chris	Owens
CB	63	Dominique	Franks
DT	87	Jonathan	Babineaux
DT	77	Corey	Peters
DT	74	Peria	Jerry
DT	67	Vance	Walker
FB	94	Ovie	Mughelli
FS	80	Thomas	DeCoud
FS	60	Rafael	Bush
HB	93	Michael	Turner
HB	74	Jason	Snelling
HB	69	Jacquizz	Rodgers
HB	61	Jerious	Norwood
K	84	Matt	Bryant
KOS	56	Matt	Bosher
KR	70	Eric	Weems
KR	63	Dominique	Franks
LE	77	Kroy	Biermann
LE	75	Jamaal	Anderson
LE	69	Chauncey	Davis
LG	83	Justin	Blalock
LG	67	Mike	Johnson
LOLB	76	Stephen	Nicholas
LOLB	67	Coy	Wire
LS	60	Joe	Zelenka
LT	87	Sam	Baker
LT	62	Will	Svitek
MLB	90	Curtis	Lofton
MLB	66	Akeem	Dent
MLB	58	Bear	Woods
P	79	Michael	Koenen
PR	70	Eric	Weems
QB	90	Matt	Ryan
QB	72	Chris	Redman
QB	62	John Parker	Wilson
RE	93	John	Abraham
RE	63	Cliff	Matthews
RE	59	Lawrence	Sidbury
RG	87	Harvey	Dahl
RG	68	Andrew	Jackson
ROLB	75	Sean	Weatherspoon
ROLB	67	Spencer	Adkins
ROLB	66	Robert	James
RT	93	Tyson	Clabo
RT	67	Jose	Valdez
RT	67	Garrett	Reynolds
SS	82	William	Moore
SS	67	Shann	Schillinger
TE	92	Tony	Gonzalez
TE	66	Justin	Peelle
TE	57	Michael	Palmer
WR	96	Roddy	White
WR	78	Julio	Jones
WR	76	Michael	Jenkins
WR	71	Harry	Douglas
WR	70	Eric	Weems
WR	60	Kerry	Meier

OFFENSIVE STRENGTH CHART

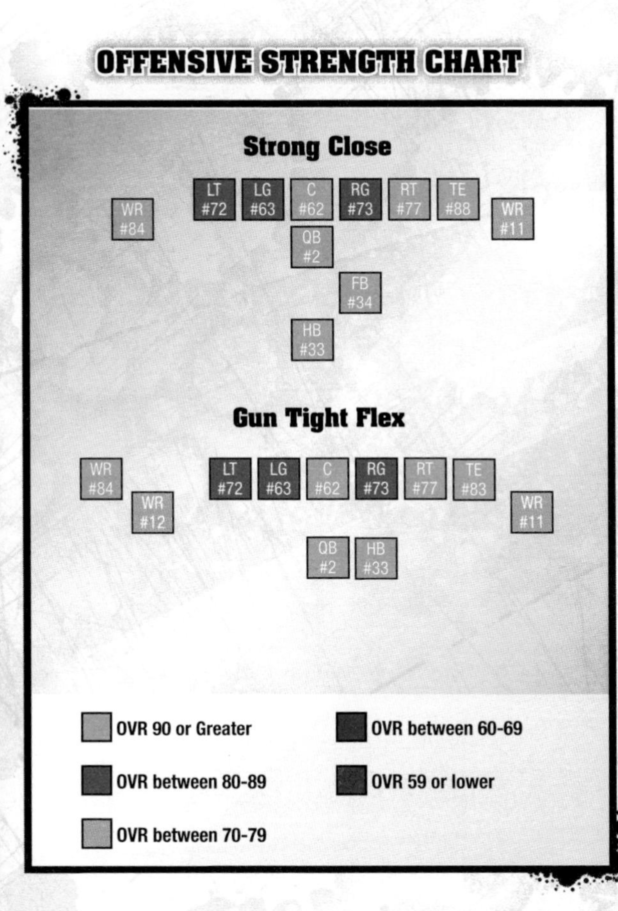

#84 Roddy White
Wide Receiver

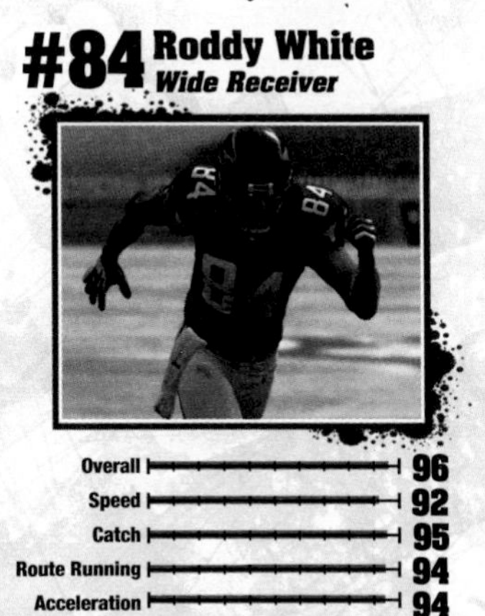

Overall	96
Speed	92
Catch	95
Route Running	94
Acceleration	94

#2 Matt Ryan
Quarterback

Overall	90
Throwing Power	89
Short Throw Acc.	92
Med. Throw Acc.	89
Deep Throw Acc.	85

#32 Jerious Norwood
Halfback

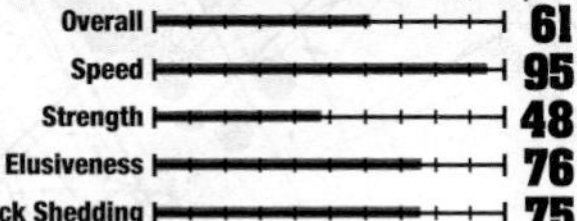

Overall	61
Speed	95
Strength	48
Elusiveness	76
Block Shedding	75

#55 John Abraham
Right End

Overall	93
Speed	81
Strength	85
Power Moves	94
Block Shedding	77

#50 Curtis Lofton
Middle Linebacker

Overall	90
Speed	79
Awareness	86
Tackle	96
Hit Power	89

#52 Coy Wire
Left Outside Linebacker

Overall	67
Speed	84
Awareness	66
Tackle	74
Hit Power	69

DEFENSIVE STRENGTH CHART

4-3 Stack

FS #28 · SS #25 · CB #20 · ROLB #56 · MLB #50 · LOLB #54 · CB #23 · RE #55 · DT #91 · DT #95 · LE #71

Dime Normal

FS #28 · SS #25 · CB #20 · CB #29 · MLB #50 · CB #21 · CB #23 · RE #55 · DT #91 · DT #95 · LE #71

OVR 90 or Greater · OVR between 80-89 · OVR between 70-79 · OVR between 60-69 · OVR 59 or lower

Key Player Substitution

Player: Jerious Norwood

Position: #2 RB

Key Stat: 95 Speed

What He Brings: Michael Turner can handle the bulk of the carries, but having a speedster like Norwood in the backfield to spell him is important. Defenses will have a tough time keeping up with him on the edge.

Key Player Substitution

Player: Coy Wire

Position: #1 LOLB

Key Stat: 84 Speed

What He Brings: Coy Wire has made the transition from safety to LB. This gives him solid speed at the linebacking core and really helps solidify the final spot in Atlanta's 3-4 scheme.

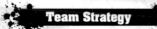

Playbook Tips

Offensive Style: Run Balanced

Offense

- The Falcons' playbook is easily the best stock playbook in the game.
- Use the Full House formation to maximize the Falcons' depth at running back.
- Very few teams will be able to match up with the talent at WR with Roddy White and Julio Jones.

Defense

- If John Abraham can win one-one-one battles the defense will have a great day.
- Atlanta's secondary proved it could make big plays last season; look to seal wins with turnovers.
- Curtis Lofton gives Atlanta the consistency in the middle it hasn't had since Keith Brooking left town.

OFFENSIVE FORMATIONS

FORMATION	# OF PLAYS
Full House Normal Wide	12
Gun Doubles On	12
Gun Empty Falcon	9
Gun Split Offset	18
Gun Spread Y-Flex	15
Gun Tight Flex	12
Gun Trey Open	18
I-Form Pro	18
I-Form Pro Twins	12
I-Form Tight Pair	18
Singleback Ace	15
Singleback Bunch	15
Singleback Doubles	18
Singleback Jumbo	12
Singleback Twin TE	15
Singleback Y-Trips	18
Strong Close	12
Strong Pro	12
Weak Tight Twins	12

OFFENSIVE PLAYCOUNTS

PLAY TYPE	# OF PLAYS
Quick Pass	22
Standard Pass	51
Shotgun Pass	60
Play Action Pass	50
Inside Handoff	40
Outside Handoff	11
Pitch	12
Counter	8
Draw	12

Three-Headed Rushing Attack

Strong Close—Counter Weak

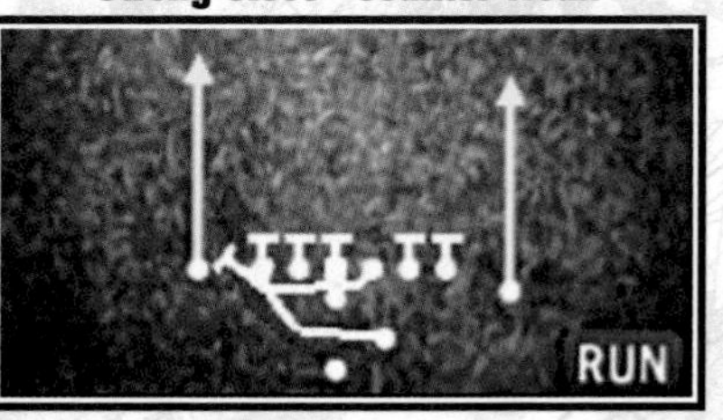

The counter is one of the best runs when trying to beat an aggressive defense. By using an element of misdirection, we can make the defense head the wrong way for a second. This also gives our blockers time to set up.

Another good thing about the misdirection is it allows the FB to get back across the formation and find someone to block. When the back gets the football he must see where the guard is and read how he wants to make the run.

This is the ideal situation for this run. A hole is open to the inside and we elect to hit it. However, after heading through we will then break outside. Why not just head that way at first? Because this allows us to get the safety inside and holds our blocks longer.

PRO TIP Try to playmaker the counter to the strong side if the defense suspects it's coming.

Strong Close—Quick Toss

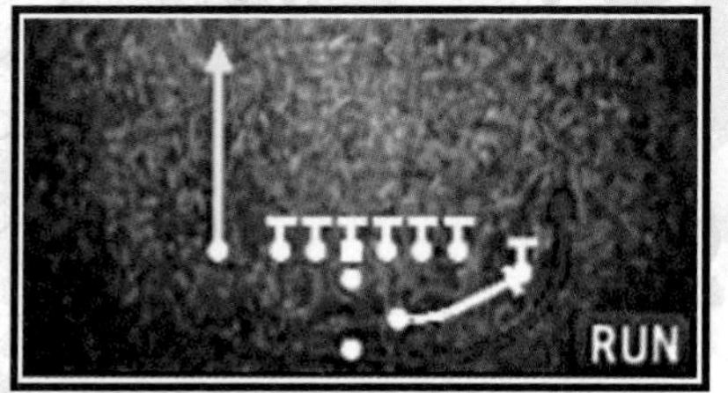

The Quick Toss is a great way to get past man defenses who try to pack guys onto the line of scrimmage. When we read that the defense is vulnerable to the outside, we look to quickly snap the ball before they can line up.

On this run, the QB realizes the man coverage and motions the WR who is where we are going to be running to get out of the way! This clears up a lane to the outside. The guard pulls on the play, so we allow him to lead since he is better than a wideout.

With the blockers holding the edge, we hardly need to hold turbo but will to get to the edge faster. No need for any fancy cuts, just put the jets on and head toward the sideline. This will force the defense to respect the run, and it's a great way to pick up big chunks of yards.

PRO TIP Matt Ryan is the colonel on offense; trust his reads to know when is the right time to hit the defense with the toss.

Strong Close HB Dive

The Falcons have a strong runner in the backfield. With the Strong Close HB Dive, we utilize his power in the red zone to pick a lane and find the end zone.

We make the initial burst toward the gap and see the defender attack the hole. The back is skilled enough to make a sharp cut and leave him in the dust.

Running the ball with Atlanta is essential to keeping the defense on their heels. This specific dive is a very powerful run and will force the defense to keep its stronger but slower players in the game.

PRO TIP Add a counter or toss to your audibles in Strong Close. This will allow you to quickly change the running lane if the defense overcrowds the gap. Do not use Turbo until you hit the hole and see daylight; this allows you to cut sharp.

Quick Pass

Full House Normal Wide WR Double Shake

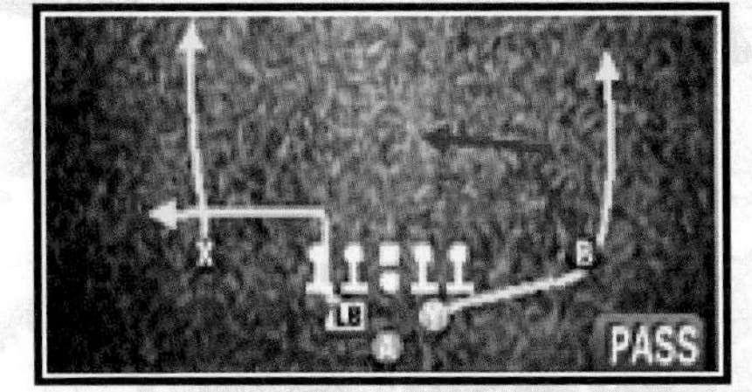

The Full House Normal Wide WR Double Shake is our red zone go-to play. The Falcons utilize a Full House formation and put star TE Tony Gonzalez in the backfield. We snap the ball and quickly throw a bullet pass. The TE shields himself from the defender and hangs on for a tough catch.

If the defender covers the TE, we can wait until the RB releases on his blue route and sneak him a pass. The defense will often forget about the blocker, and we can capitalize for six!

Get comfortable with all the options on this play, when the game is on the line, you will be confident knowing you can call this play to pick up crucial yardage!

PRO TIP Hit the RB before he curls on his route. This will keep him running toward the end zone.

Man Beater

Shotgun Empty Falcon ATL Hitch Seams

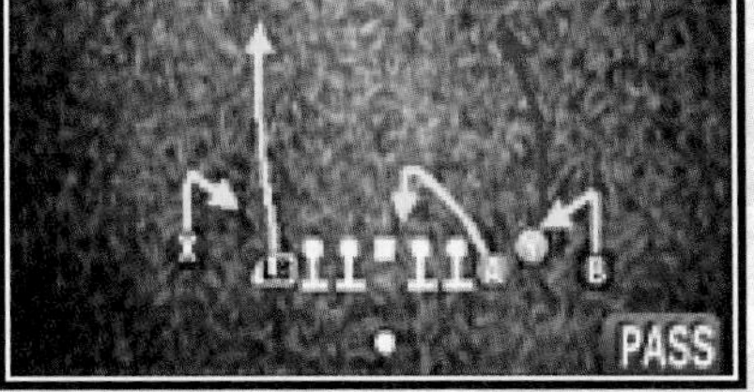

The spread set Shotgun Empty Falcon ATL Hitch Seams stresses the defense in the seams. Few teams have the speed to match up with Atlanta; this will force the defense into zone coverage. We look to see in which direction the linebacker sets his feet, and we deliver a bullet pass in the seam to his weak side.

We are able to shield the ball from the defenders outside the route.

Our speedy WR is able to shield the ball from the defenders outside the route. Look to make one more quick cut up the middle to pick up some yards after the catch. This is a safe throw for your QB and one you should make with confidence.

PRO TIP Drag the inside left WR to give your scheme some horizontal stretch, and use a bigger player like Tony Gonzalez in the seam to maximize possession catches.

Zone Beater

Singleback Bunch Falcon HB Angle

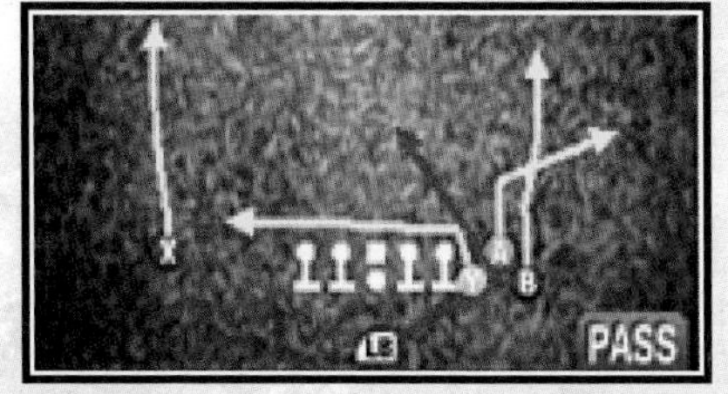

Zones are very strong in *Madden NFL 12*. With the Singleback Bunch Falcon HB Angle, we look to beat a Cover 3 with a Bunch concept. The Falcon HB Angle forces one safety to cover two WRs.

The safety must respect the deep route, leaving the underneath route wide open at the corner of the field.

As soon as the defender commits to a WR, look to bullet a pass to the other WR. Watch the defensive back's movements as he will often point and pass off the WR to another defender, this is your cue to deliver the ball.

PRO TIP Smart-route the corner route to have the WR start his cut to the sideline earlier. This can make the throw angle easier and make the play develop quicker.

Base Play

Shotgun Tight Flex Falcon Cross

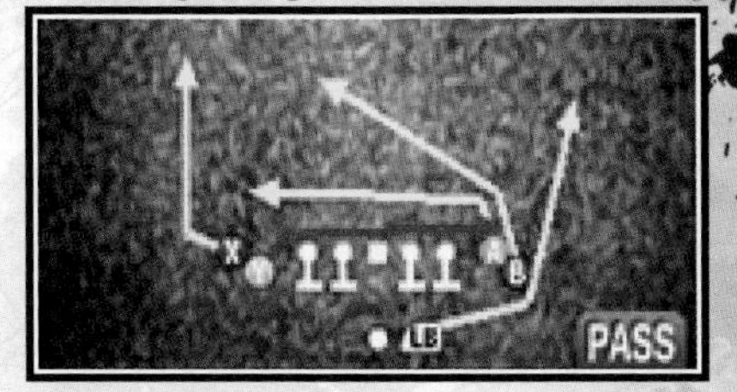

The Shotgun Tight Flex Falcon Cross is a dynamic play capable of beating man and zone coverage. Look at the middle linebacker and hold the pass until the WR clears him. We have two different depths running the route and can sneak a WR behind him for big yards.

Against man coverage, the drag routes across the middle allow fast WRs to burn their man. The defenders will have to respect every route, and this play is very tough to defend. Look to see who smokes their man and deliver a nice bullet throw with an upfield lead.

Keep running this play until the defense proves they can stop it, they will be forced to manually defend the crossing routes which can often lead to bigger holes downfield.

PRO TIP Motion the left slot receiver and snap after five steps; this will give him a free release and force man defenders to switch off.

NEW YORK GIANTS

OFFENSIVE SCOUTING REPORT

The NY Giants ranked in the top 10 in all major offensive and defensive statistics during the 2010 season. A successful game plan starts with speedy RB Ahmad Bradshaw taking the starting role. Bruising RB Brandon Jacobs will play the closer role. Be sure to utilize both of the Giants' HBs in the run game. Jacobs is your north-south runner, and Bradshaw should be used to stretch the field horizontally. Capitalize on their tremendous depth at the WR core with playmaker Hakeem Nicks. The Giants have tremendous height at wideout with TE Kevin Boss and WR Ramses Barden exposing smaller defenders for big gains. Eli Manning has plenty of weapons in the slot with Steve Smith and Mario Manningham using their route running and agility to dodge linebackers. New York has added speed and now boasts one of the most balanced rosters for any type of game plan in *Madden NFL 12*.

DEFENSIVE SCOUTING REPORT

The New York Giants have one of the best defensive lines in the game. There incredible depth on defense allows the user to mix and match lineups depending on game situations. If the offense is looking to pass the ball late in the game, bring in stud athlete Jason Pierre-Paul to rush off the edge and also move strong Justin Tuck inside. While LB Michael Boley is better in coverage, keep Jonathan Goff behind the line against the run because he has tremendous hit power. The secondary is vastly improved with the addition of first round pick Prince Amukamara this off season. He should start at your first CB slot because he has better athleticism than Corey Webster. The secondary proved its value last season and Kenny Phillips and Antrel Rolle should be ready to have huge seasons this year in *Madden NFL 12*!

TEAM RATING

83	Overall
86	Offense
84	Defense

DYNAMIC PLAYER PERFORMANCE TRAITS

Eli Manning
QB #10

Forces Pass	★★★★★
Senses Pressure	★★★★★
Consistency	★★★★★
Cover Ball	★★★★★
Clutch	Yes

RATINGS BY POSITION

Quarterbacks	87
Halfbacks	85
Fullbacks	83
Wide Receivers	84
Tight Ends	77
Tackles	84
Guards	89
Centers	92
Defensive Ends	92
Defensive Tackles	86
Outside Linebackers	76
Middle Linebackers	79
Cornerbacks	88
Free Safeties	85
Strong Safeties	81
Kickers	74
Punters	62

DEPTH CHART

POS	OVR	FIRST NAME	LAST NAME
3DRB	85	Ahmad	Bradshaw
C	92	Shaun	O'Hara
C	67	Adam	Koets
CB	90	Corey	Webster
CB	85	Terrell	Thomas
CB	79	Aaron	Ross
CB	81	Prince	Amukamara
CB	75	Bruce	Johnson
DT	84	Barry	Cofield
DT	81	Chris	Canty
DT	69	Marvin	Austin
DT	69	Linval	Joseph
DT	73	Rocky	Bernard
FB	83	Madison	Hedgecock
FB	72	Bear	Pascoe
FS	85	Antrel	Rolle
FS	62	Brian	Jackson
FS	67	Cary	Harris
HB	85	Ahmad	Bradshaw
HB	80	Brandon	Jacobs
HB	63	D.J.	Ware
HB	58	Da'Rel	Scott
K	74	Lawrence	Tynes
KOS	74	Lawrence	Tynes
KR	61	Darius	Reynaud
KR	56	Duke	Calhoun
LE	94	Justin	Tuck
LE	78	Jason	Pierre-Paul
LE	55	Dave	Tollefson
LG	81	Rich	Seubert
LG	68	Kevin	Boothe
LG	73	Ikechuku	Ndukwe
LOLB	80	Michael	Boley
LOLB	65	Gerris	Wilkinson
LOLB	51	Kenny	Ingram
LS	71	Zak	DeOssie
LT	77	David	Diehl
LT	73	Shawn	Andrews
LT	73	William	Beatty
MLB	79	Jonathan	Goff
MLB	64	Phillip	Dillard
MLB	65	Greg	Jones
P	62	Matt	Dodge
PR	61	Darius	Reynaud
QB	87	Eli	Manning
QB	70	Sage	Rosenfels
RE	89	Osi	Umenyiora
RE	79	Mathias	Kiwanuka
RE	65	Alex	Hall
RG	96	Chris	Snee
RG	65	Mitch	Petrus
ROLB	71	Clint	Sintim
ROLB	64	Adrian	Tracy
RT	91	Kareem	McKenzie
RT	69	James	Brewer
RT	66	Jamon	Meredith
SS	81	Kenny	Phillips
SS	75	Michael	Johnson
SS	59	Tyler	Sash
TE	77	Kevin	Boss
TE	71	Travis	Beckum
TE	56	Jake	Ballard
WR	89	Hakeem	Nicks
WR	84	Steve	Smith
WR	80	Mario	Manningham
WR	64	Derek	Hagan
WR	62	Ramses	Barden
WR	68	Devin	Thomas

OFFENSIVE STRENGTH CHART

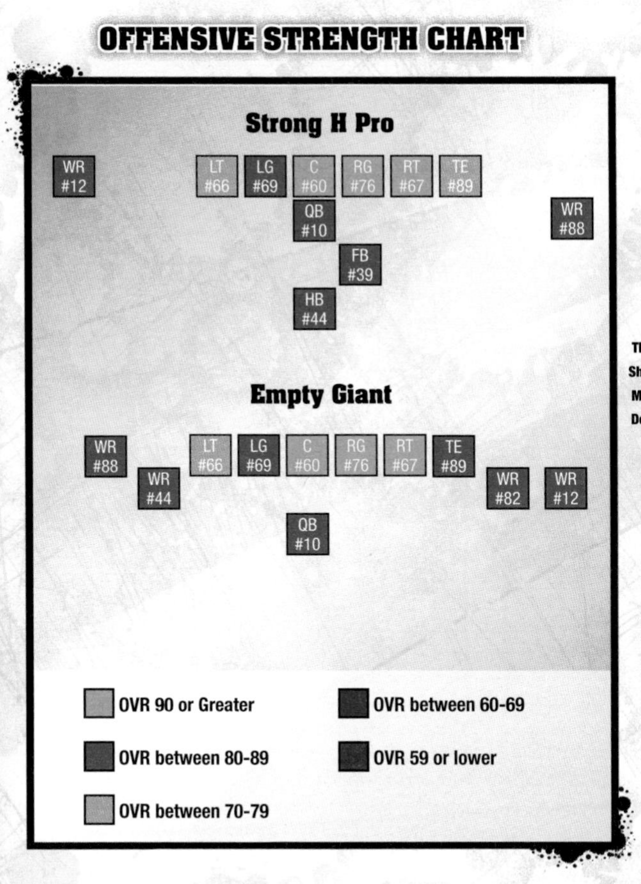

Key Player Substitution

Player: Ramses Barden

Position: #2 WR Slot

Key Stat: 95 Jump

What He Brings: Ramses Barden is one of the tallest receiving threats in *Madden NFL 12*. His size and jumping ability make him very difficult to defend, especially near the sideline and in the red zone.

#10 Eli Manning *Quarterback*

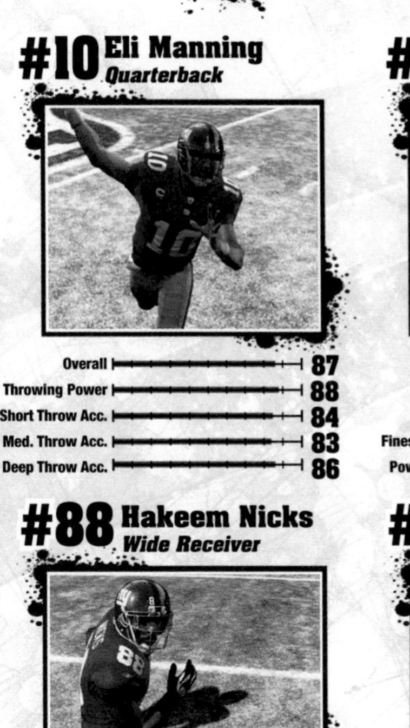

Overall	87
Throwing Power	88
Short Throw Acc.	84
Med. Throw Acc.	83
Deep Throw Acc.	86

#88 Hakeem Nicks *Wide Receiver*

Overall	87
Speed	90
Catch	90
Acceleration	93
Route Running	87

#13 Ramses Barden *Wide Receiver*

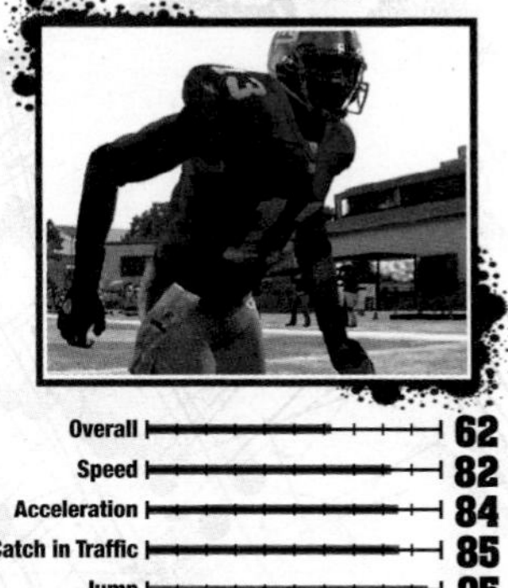

Overall	62
Speed	82
Acceleration	84
Catch in Traffic	85
Jump	95

#91 Justin Tuck *Defensive End*

Overall	94
Speed	84
Strength	87
Finesse Moves	93
Power Moves	83

#21 Kenny Phillips *Strong Safety*

Overall	81
Speed	90
Acceleration	93
Hit Power	85
Tackling	74

#90 Jason Pierre-Paul *Defensive End*

Overall	78
Speed	84
Acceleration	97
Finesse Moves	93
Power Moves	85

DEFENSIVE STRENGTH CHART

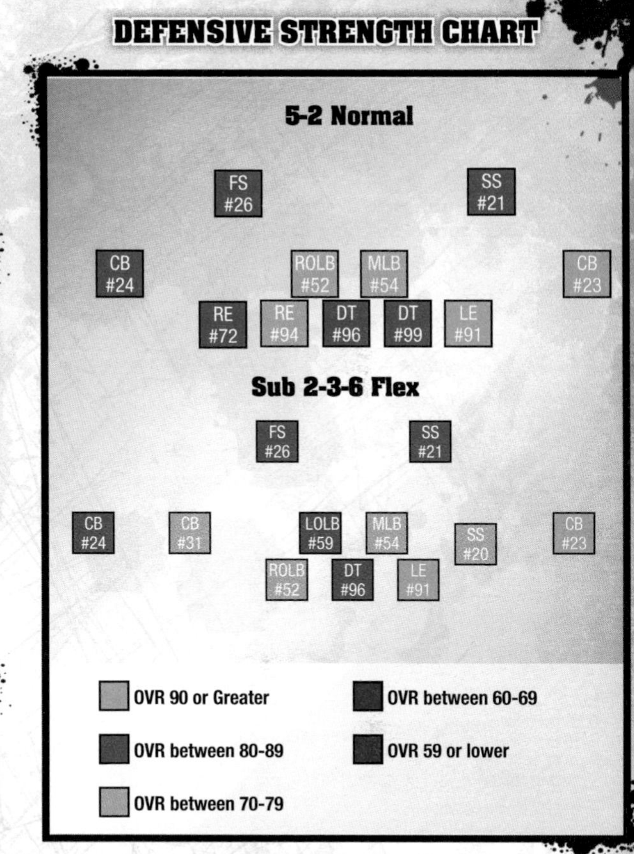

Key Player Substitution

Player: Bruce Johnson

Position: #3 CB

Key Stat: 93 Strength

What He Brings: Bruce Johnson has solid athletic skills that catapult him into the Giants' slot CB position. This will leave Terrell Thomas in the fourth slot, which allows him to become a linebacker in the 46 speed package and utilizes his sure tackling.

Playbook Tips

Offensive Style: Balanced

Offense

- Use Brandon Jacobs in the red zone and on short-yardage runs.
- Eli is a very solid QB; he can make any throw the offense needs.
- The team has great depth and range at WR, so look to utilize each player's specific talents.

Defense

- Allow the defensive line to get pressure without adding extra blitzers.
- Use faster defensive ends at LB to counter the Giants' weak depth at LB.
- The team has a slew of slower but zone ready CBs to drop into coverage.

OFFENSIVE FORMATIONS

FORMATION	# OF PLAYS
Gun Doubles WK	18
Gun Empty Giant	9
Gun Empty Spread	12
Gun Snugs	9
Gun Split Giant	15
Gun Spread	18
Gun Wing Trips WK NY	15
Gun Y-Trips WK	18
I-Form Pro	18
I-Form Pro Twins	12
I-Form Tight	15
I-Form Tight Pair	12
Singleback Ace	18
Singleback Ace Pair Twins	15
Singleback Bunch	15
Singleback Doubles Giants	21
Singleback Jumbo	12
Singleback Y-Trips	18
Strong H Pro	15
Weak H Pro	15

OFFENSIVE PLAYCOUNTS

PLAY TYPE	# OF PLAYS
Quick Pass	18
Standard Pass	53
Shotgun Pass	83
Play Action Pass	57
Inside Handoff	40
Outside Handoff	9
Pitch	10
Counter	8
Draw	13

Three-Headed Rushing Attack

Singleback Ace—Counter Wk

The pulling guard on this play will act as our leading blocker because there's no fullback. The ability of the HB to choose a good lane will be a big factor in making this run a success.

With dual TEs on the line of scrimmage, this play can be tough for a non-base defense to handle. The guard will need a second to get out in front, so our RB takes a fake step to the right to give him time.

As our players come around the edge of the line, the RB is very patient and waits for his blocks to set up. The WR ran his defenders out of the area but couldn't hold his block. The HB is doing a good job setting up the safety outside and his best move is to cut back sharp inside and take whatever he can pick up.

PRO TIP Try Rookie Da'Rel Scott on this play, he has tremendous speed once he puts it in high gear.

Singleback Ace - HB Dive

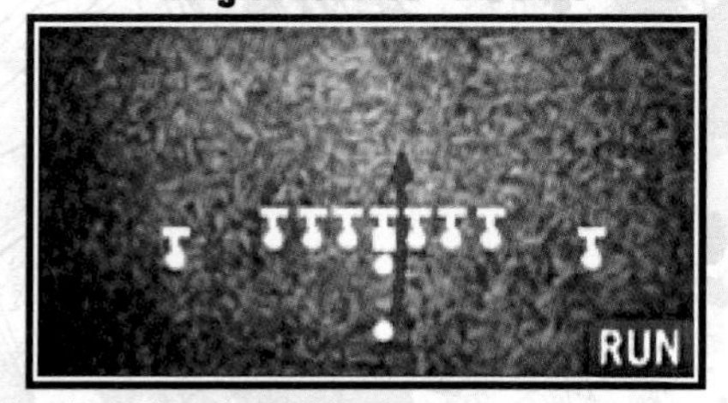

New York Giant football involves a steady dose of Brandon Jacobs. Jacobs is one of the biggest HBs in *Madden NFL 12*. He is extremely difficult to take down, and we want to force the defense to try and stop him. One of the best ways to get Jacobs involved in the game is with the Singleback Ace HB Dive.

Jacobs receives the handoff, and we quickly look for running lanes. Do not be fancy with the HB Dive. Look to get upfield at the snap of the ball. Be sure to use the Truck stick when approaching oncoming defenders.

We get up into the hole and smash through the defense. It takes two defenders to take down Jacobs. Over the course of the game, the defense will again be forced to protect the HB Dive. This will help to open up other plays!

PRO TIP When the defense loads up to stop the HB Dive, look to package in HB Ahmad Bradshaw to attack the defense on the outside.

Singleback Ace - HB Stretch

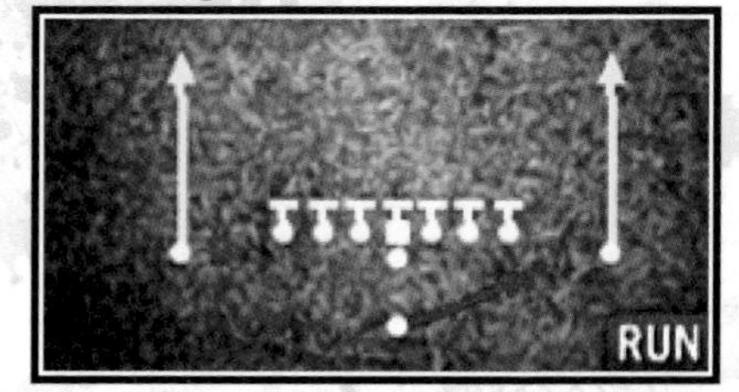

A dominating run game can sap the willpower of the defense. We call upon the HB Stretch to build upon the foundation that we set with Brandon Jacobs. With the HB Stretch, we are going to substitute Ahmad Bradshaw into the game and look to utilize his speed to get to the outside edge.

This package has two extra TEs on the line of scrimmage, which help out to balance the offensive line. At the beginning of the play, look to the outside TE and see if he has the blocking angle on the defender. If the defender has the inside advantage on our blocker, we will want to cut the run back up inside. We can see that the TE has the leverage we need to get outside.

Bradshaw gets into open field, and the defense is forced to chase him down. We can stay in the Singleback Ace formation and continually pound the ball all game. Not only will this demoralize the defense but it will also set up the play action.

Quick Pass

Singleback Ace—Giants Middle

By staying in the Singleback Ace formation, you can use a quick pass if the defense starts to look for the run. If the defense crams the middle or doesn't align properly, you can hit the TE quickly up the seam.

At the snap, the defense sends pressure, but the two blue routes pick it up. After making a good block, the TE releases off the line and the QB starts to feel the heat.

The QB delivers a throw to the flat, and the defense will think twice about blitzing next time. Utilizing plays with blue routes is one of the best ways to defeat pressure in *Madden NFL*. This play is great because it is out of our run formation and contains double delayed routes.

PRO TIP TE Travis Beckum is a better overall target in the passing game.

Man Beater

Gun Spread - Slant Bubble

Being creative in the passing game can help stalled drives turn into scoring drives. The Gun Spread Slant Bubble might not be a trick play, but it certainly is a drastic change of pace. Look to the slants when facing zone coverage, as the zone defender will cover the bubble routes. The ideal situation for the bubble routes is when the defense is playing loose man coverage.

We see our WR on the slant is being guarded by his man defender. Our slot WR breaks into the flat. The bubble route is unique in that it attacks the flat, but it is not a traditional flat route. Our WR will drift away from the line of scrimmage until we deliver the ball.

We make the grab and catch the defense off guard. Our opponent was not prepared to defend the bubble route and was left out of position. We pick up five yards on the play as the defense closes in.

PRO TIP Substitute your fastest WRs into both slots for the Slant Bubble.

Zone Beater

Gun Empty - Spacing

The Gun Empty formation is a favorite because of its ability to tip the defense's hand. We can spread the defense out and see where pressure is coming from, and we can better determine the base coverage of the defense. Many times, online players will use the Gun Empty to attack the defense downfield. We will be looking to do the exact opposite!

Spacing is an amazing way to attack a zone defense horizontally. Even if the defense is in a Cover 2 zone, we will be able to overload the zone across the field. Our responsibility as QB is to sit back in the pocket and find the open WR. We can see that our HB Ahmad Bradshaw is open in the left slot.

Bradshaw is not our ideal target, but he was the open receiver. We deliver the ball just as he takes the hit from the defense. The open receiver will change, depending on the play and the defense. Make sure to scan the field and do not key in on any specific WR.

Base Play

GunWingTripsWKNY

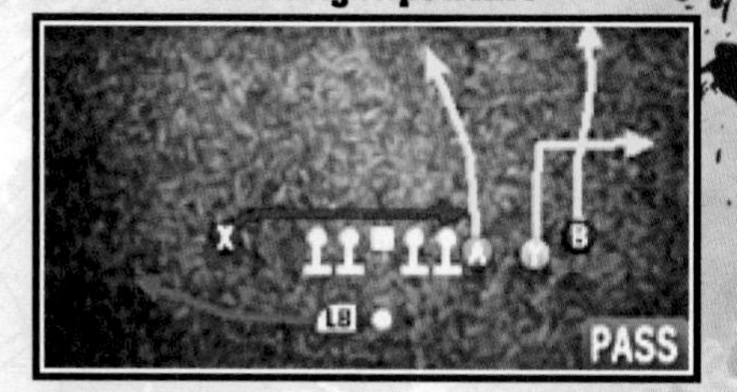

The Giants Iso Drag is a zone-crushing defense. We have a few ways that we can beat many different zone coverages. Our drag route is also killer against man defensive coverage. If the defense zone blitzes, look to the TE running the vertical route up the middle of the field. This is also an effective route against Cover 2.

The defense is in a zone blitz and has left the middle of the field open. Our big TE gets into space and has only one defender in front of him. Get the ball to the TE quickly; the longer we wait, the easier it will be for the deep safety to make a play on the ball.

We get the ball out to the TE and gain ten yards on the play. If you make a bad read and the defense is in man-to-man coverage, look for the drag underneath. This route is good for attacking man defensive coverage.

PRO TIP If the defense is in a standard Cover 3 zone coverage, the TE over the middle of the field will be a risky throw. Wait for the drag underneath or for the out route on the sideline.

JACKSONVILLE JAGUARS

OFFENSIVE SCOUTING REPORT

The Jacksonville Jaguars will be a tough team to defend in *Madden NFL 12*. Their offense relies heavily on RB Maurice Jones-Drew, whose athleticism makes him very tough to tackle at only 5'7". FB Greg Jones has a high truck rating and can be used in short yardage situations if Maurice Jones-Drew is tired. Mike Thomas has solid Agility and Acceleration ratings. TE Marcedes Lewis was a nice option in the red zone for QB David Garrard, who allowed Lewis and his 6'6" frame to snag 10 TDs. Rookie QB Blaine Gabbert will excite Jaguars fans, but Garrard still gives the team the best chance to win in *Madden NFL 12*.

DEFENSIVE SCOUTING REPORT

One of the best cornerbacks in *Madden NFL 12* is Rashean Mathis. Mathis's experience has yet to slow him down, and he is still able to cover any receiver in the game. Trust in his one-one-one coverage ability and leave him on an island while you bring pressure towards the QB. Linebacker Kirk Morrison is a wrap-up tackler who is starting to fit in with the Jaguars' defensive scheme. On the defensive line Aaron Kampman can be a one-man wrecking crew—he is a workhouse when getting after QBs. Play a mixture of man-to-man and zone blitzing with the Jaguars for the best chance of success. The Jaguars should continue to improve under Jack Del Rio's lead this season on defense and will be ready to go when the season kicks off.

TEAM RATING

75	Overall
85	Offense
81	Defense

DYNAMIC PLAYER PERFORMANCE TRAITS

Maurice Jones-Drew
HB #32

Consistency	★★★★★
Covers Ball	★★★★★
Fights for Yards	Yes
High Motor	Yes
Clutch	Yes

RATINGS BY POSITION

Quarterbacks	83
Halfbacks	95
Fullbacks	84
Wide Receivers	70
Tight Ends	90
Tackles	83
Guards	83
Centers	85
Defensive Ends	81
Defensive Tackles	87
Outside Linebackers	77
Middle Linebackers	90
Cornerbacks	82
Free Safeties	71
Strong Safeties	77
Kickers	81
Punters	63

DEPTH CHART

POS	OVR	FIRST NAME	LAST NAME
3DRB	95	Maurice	Jones-Drew
C	85	Brad	Meester
C	62	John	Estes
CB	89	Rashean	Mathis
CB	75	Derek	Cox
CB	67	David	Jones
CB	58	Scotty	McGee
CB	67	William	Middleton
DT	87	Terrance	Knighton
DT	84	Tyson	Alualu
DT	71	C.J.	Mosley
DT	60	Leger	Douzable
FB	84	Greg	Jones
FB	84	Montell	Owens
FS	71	Don	Carey
FS	64	Tyron	Brackenridge
FS	66	Chris	Prosinski
HB	95	Maurice	Jones-Drew
HB	74	Rashad	Jennings
HB	66	Deji	Karim
K	81	Josh	Scobee
KOS	81	Josh	Scobee
KR	66	Deji	Karim
KR	62	Tiquan	Underwood
LE	76	Jeremy	Mincey
LE	64	Austen	Lane
LE	58	Derrick	Harvey
LG	82	Vince	Manuwai
LG	62	Kevin	Haslam
LOLB	70	Russell	Allen
LOLB	59	Alvin	Bowen
LS	53	Jeremy	Cain
LT	81	Eugene	Monroe
LT	65	Guy	Whimper
MLB	90	Daryl	Smith
MLB	79	Kirk	Morrison
P	63	Adam	Podlesh
PR	79	Mike	Thomas
QB	83	David	Garrard
QB	72	Luke	McCown
QB	75	Blaine	Gabbert
RE	86	Aaron	Kampman
RE	60	Larry	Hart
RE	54	Aaron	Morgan
RG	84	Uche	Nwaneri
RG	83	Justin	Smiley
ROLB	83	Justin	Durant
ROLB	57	Jacob	Cutrera
ROLB	56	Slade	Norris
RT	85	Eben	Britton
RT	57	Daniel	Baldridge
SS	77	Courtney	Greene
SS	72	Sean	Considine
SS	71	Michael	Hamlin
TE	90	Marcedes	Lewis
TE	73	Zach	Miller
TE	56	Zach	Potter
WR	79	Mike	Thomas
WR	71	Jason	Hill
WR	61	Jarett	Dillard
WR	63	Kassim	Osgood
WR	62	Tiquan	Underwood
WR	60	Cecil	Shorts

OFFENSIVE STRENGTH CHART

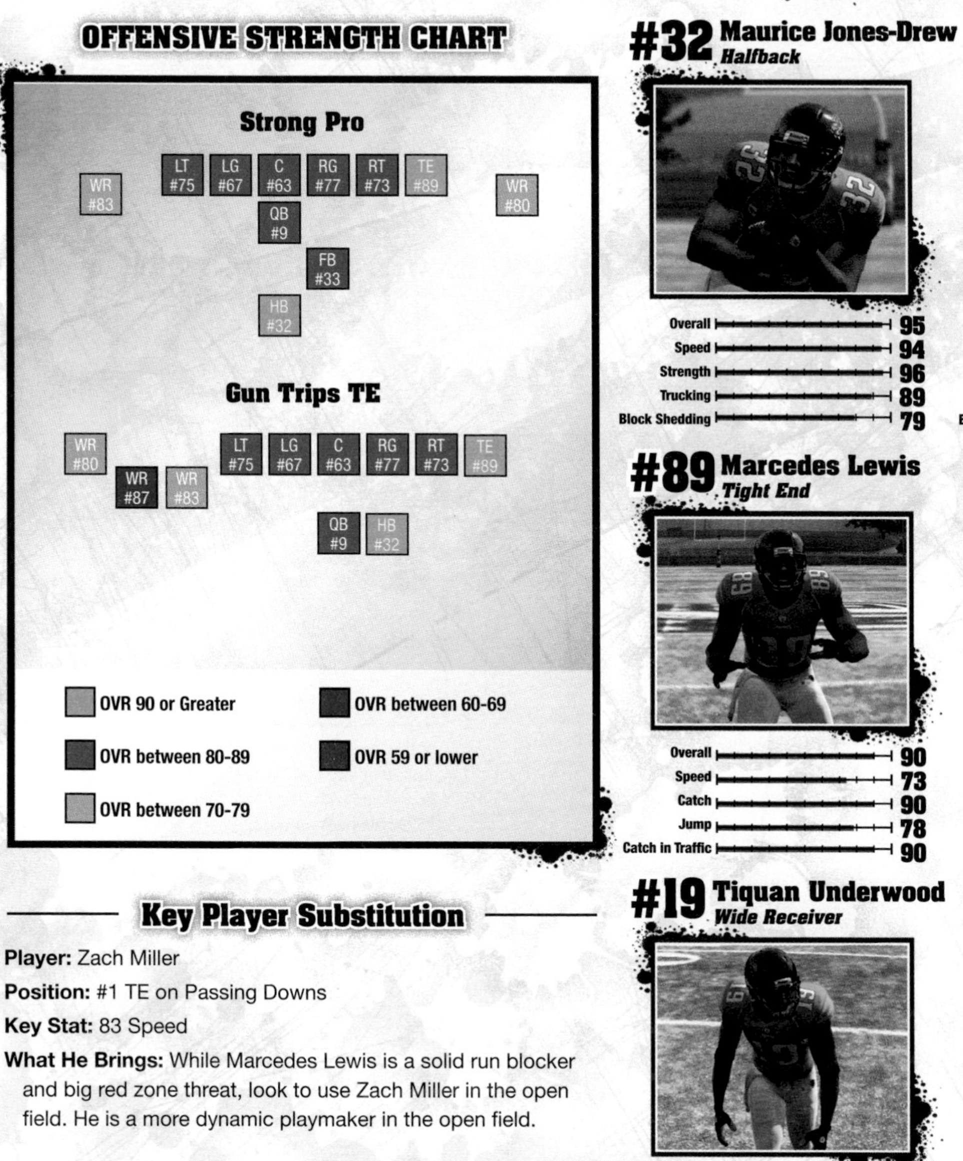

Key Player Substitution

Player: Zach Miller

Position: #1 TE on Passing Downs

Key Stat: 83 Speed

What He Brings: While Marcedes Lewis is a solid run blocker and big red zone threat, look to use Zach Miller in the open field. He is a more dynamic playmaker in the open field.

#32 Maurice Jones-Drew
Halfback

Overall	95
Speed	94
Strength	96
Trucking	89
Block Shedding	79

#74 Aaron Kampman
Right End

Overall	86
Speed	75
Strength	85
Power Moves	91
Block Shedding	78

#89 Marcedes Lewis
Tight End

Overall	90
Speed	73
Catch	90
Jump	78
Catch in Traffic	90

#27 Rashean Mathis
Cornerback

Overall	89
Speed	91
Man Coverage	88
Zone Coverage	94
Awareness	87

#19 Tiquan Underwood
Wide Receiver

Overall	62
Speed	95
Catch	67
Route Running	62
Acceleration	92

#42 Chris Prosinski
Free Safety

Overall	66
Speed	93
Tackle	74
Hit Power	68
Play Recognition	47

DEFENSIVE STRENGTH CHART

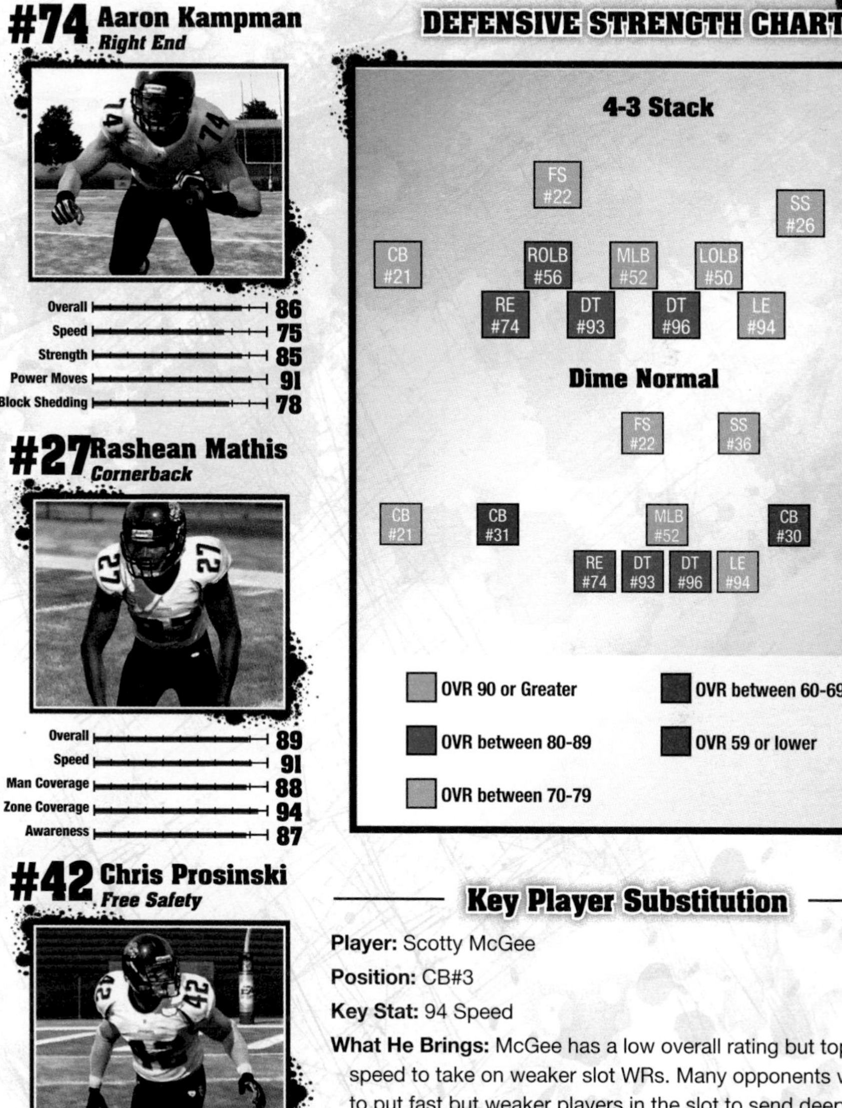

Key Player Substitution

Player: Scotty McGee

Position: CB#3

Key Stat: 94 Speed

What He Brings: McGee has a low overall rating but top-end speed to take on weaker slot WRs. Many opponents will try to put fast but weaker players in the slot to send deep, and McGee can take the threat away.

Playbook Tips

Offensive Style: Run Heavy

Offense

- TE Marcedes Lewis is a big target who can act as a safety valve inside the red zone.
- Make sure to test rookie QB Blaine Gabbert, as he brings a unique skill set to the table.
- Maurice Jones-Drew is the straw that stirs the drink for the offense—don't limit his carries.

Defense

- Don't worry about leaving CB Rashean Mathis alone; he can cover a majority of the top threats in the league.
- Aaron Kampman is a great power player who can really hold his spot down on the line of scrimmage.
- Look for second-year defender Tyson Alualu to continue to develop into an anchor for the line.

OFFENSIVE FORMATIONS	
FORMATION	# OF PLAYS
Gun Normal Wing TE	12
Gun Split Jaguar	12
Gun Spread Y-Flex	18
Gun Trey Open	15
Gun Trips TE	15
Gun Y-Trips WK	15
I-Form Pro	24
I-Form Pro Twins	15
I-Form Tight	15
I-Form Tight Pair	15
Singleback Ace	18
Singleback Ace Twins	15
Singleback Bunch	18
Singleback Doubles	21
Singleback Twin TE Slot	15
Singleback Y-Trips	15
Strong Pro	18
Weak Pro	15

OFFENSIVE PLAYCOUNTS	
PLAY TYPE	# OF PLAYS
Quick Pass	16
Standard Pass	63
Shotgun Pass	53
Play Action Pass	61
Inside Handoff	39
Outside Handoff	15
Pitch	11
Counter	10
Draw	12

Three-Headed Rushing Attack

I-Form Pro—PA Comeback Slide

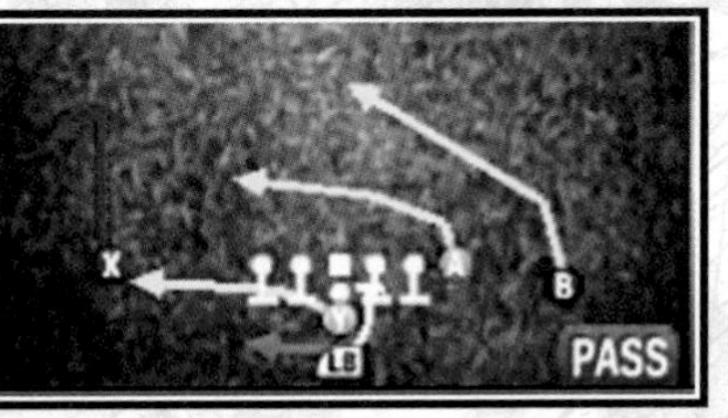

Using play action is an excellent way to make the I-Form Pro a deadly part of our three-headed rushing attack. This will get our QB rolling out and will get our WRs all rolling one way. The play is designed to roll the QB to the left along with our targets.

This play will only work with the proper setup; make sure to run similar handoffs so the defense can't cue in on the run or pass fake. We flip the play here to roll the pocket out to our QB's strong side. This will help make the throw easier because we only have to focus on half the field.

The QB really sells the fake and it causes the defense to hold for just one second. This allows our player to wrangle free over the middle of the field and catch the ball in stride. When play action works, it leads to high-percentage throws that supplement the run game and keep the defense on their heels.

PRO TIP If you sense the blitz, cancel the play action and look to run the play without the fake.

I-Form Pro—Stretch

The Stretch run is a great way to hand the ball off for an outside run. Maurice Jones-Drew is excellent at pounding the ball off tackle, and the Stretch is a great way to utilize that strength. We flip the run at the line of scrimmage since the defense decides to bracket our TE on the strong side.

Jones-Drew starts heading out wide and receives the handoff. He has a blocker out in front to pick up the seal to the corner. A player is approaching from the right, but we know our TE will drop off the double-team and pick him up at the second level. This allows us to cut inside instead of taking the ball immediately to the edge of the defense.

Our HB heads inside the blockers before making a hard cut to get outside. The reason to make this cut is to set up the safety, who is still 10 yards away. That is the type of advanced thinking that will turn average gains into game-breaking runs. Always try to think about your next move!

I-Form Pro - HB Draw

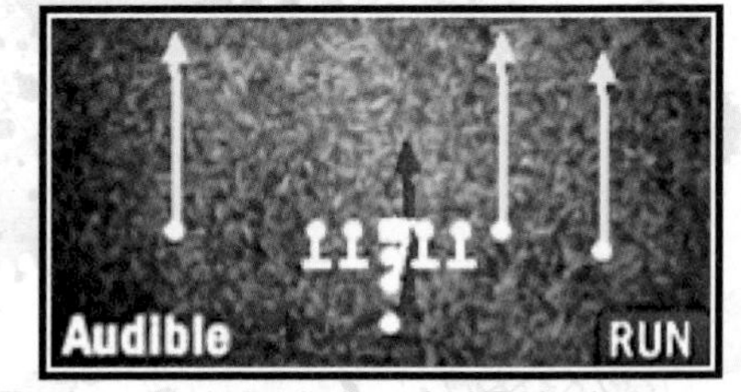

The Jaguars' playbook allows for HB Maurice Jones-Drew to be involved in both the run game and pass game. The I-Form Pro HB Draw is a nice change of pace to try and catch our opponent off guard. We want to get the ball to Jones-Drew as often as possible, and working in draws is a great way to get him extra carries.

Another reason we love the HB Draw is because we have complete control of finding open running lanes. Many times with traditional running plays, the defense will force its will on our offensive line. The HB Draw fakes the pass first, which makes the defense drop back into coverage. As soon as we get the ball, we are able to slash our way through the defense.

Jones-Drew slips past the defense and gets into the secondary. He is a rare combination of speed and strength for a HB his size. One of the most frustrating things for a defense is the inability to stop the run. The HB Draw was a *Madden NFL* community favorite last season and looks to make its return this year.

Quick Pass

Singleback Ace - Y Shallow Cross

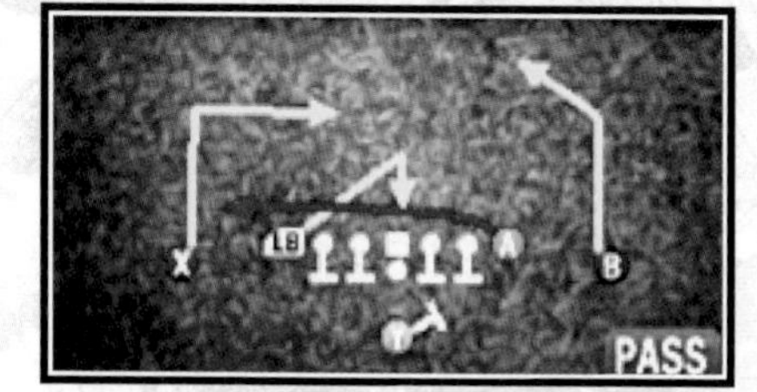

A man-to-man blitz defensive scheme can be very difficult to beat. All of the receivers are covered by defenders, and the pressure will get to the QB quickly. A general rule to follow is to attack the blitz from where it came from. The Y Shallow Cross has two quick routes to our inside TEs that can expose a man-to-man blitz.

Notice that both of our TEs release toward the short middle of the field. We can see the blitzing linebacker vacating that same area. Our TE has not turned around yet, but we deliver the pass prior to him turning around.

We deliver the pass just as the pressure gets to the QB. Our TE is led upfield because of the timing of our throw. Remember we threw the ball prior to the TE turning back toward the QB; because of this, we are able to pick up a few extra yards after the catch!

PRO TIP If the defense keys in on this TE's route, look to the other TE running the drag underneath.

Man Beater

Singleback Y - Trips - Smash

The Singleback Y-Trips Smash has been a staple of our offense for a long time. The reason is the route combinations run to the trip's side of the formation. The routes we want to focus on are the corner and the curl.

At the snap of the ball, we notice that the defense is in a Cover 2 zone. This is because the deep safeties drop back and split the field in half. We also see the flat defender is guarding our curl route.

Our read of the defense was right. We deliver the pass to our WR running the corner route. We fall forward just shy of the end zone. The Smash is a universal concept that you will be able to find in many different formations through the Jaguars' playbook.

PRO TIP Substitute height for the WR running the corner route. It will make the catch easier in coverage.

Zone Beater

Trips TE - Flex Jags Po Co

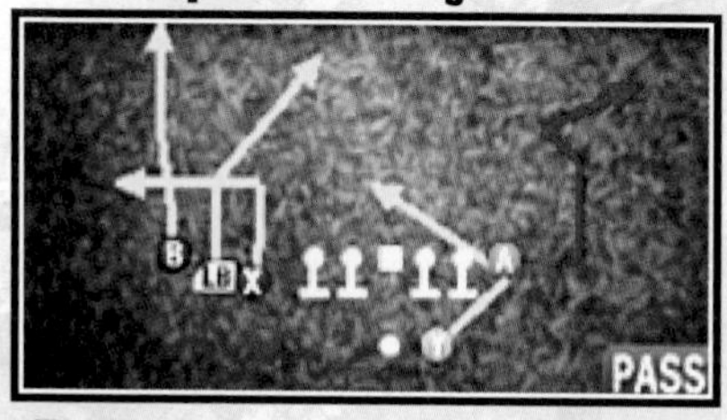

The Flex Jags PoCo is a play that we will use to attack zone defensive coverage. We want to attack the coverage downfield and use our underneath routes to fool the defense.

We can see the defense is in a Cover 3 zone. We run one vertical route down the left sideline and then have an underneath route run to the sideline. This will create an open passing window to hit our WR running the post.

The safety delivers a huge hit, but our WR hangs on to the ball! The route combination worked perfectly, as our underneath route was able to clear space below for us to connect with our deeper route downfield. Against the Cover 2 zone, our WR running the streak down the sideline will be a great option.

PRO TIP Make sure your highest rated Catch in Traffic WR is running the post on this play.

Base Play

Split Jaguar - Jags Deep In

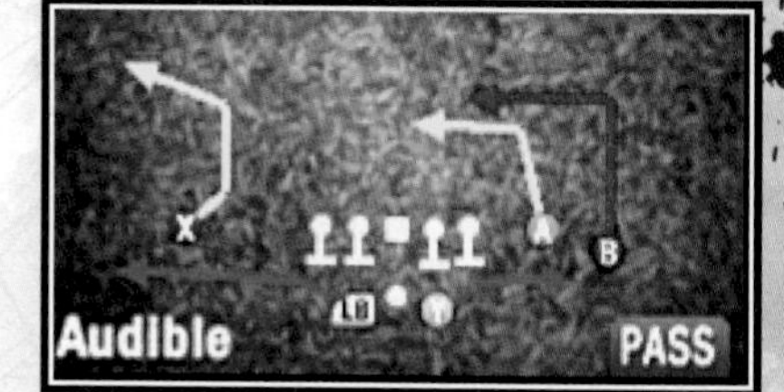

When facing an opponent who likes to send multiple blitz packages, we like to call upon the Split Jaguar Jags Deep In. This play has two blue routes in the backfield that will help in pass protection. Once pressure has been avoided, the blue routes will release into the flat.

We can see our blue routes step into the pocket to pick up the blitz. They do a great job at preventing the pressure from getting to the QB. We have the extra time to hang in the pocket and find the open WR.

We find our open WR down the sideline and deliver the pass. The defense brought the blitz, and we were able to get the one-on-one matchup on the outside. If the defense does not send the blitz, look to the blue routes releasing to the flats for the easy gain.

PRO TIP Substitute your tallest WRs on the outside to make the easy catch on the sideline.

NEW YORK JETS

OFFENSIVE SCOUTING REPORT

The New York Jets made its second consecutive run in the play-offs behind a strong ground game and great defensive game planning from head coach Rex Ryan. While the Jets' defense will be dominating in *Madden NFL 12*, their success relies heavily on QB Mark Sanchez. We must focus on getting the ball into good third-down situations where he can hit his favorite target, TE Dustin Keller. If the defense begins to overly focus on HB Shonn Greene, we need Sanchez to come up big and connect on a deep pass. This ability to keep the defense honest is what will drive the Jets from good to great in *Madden NFL 12*.

DEFENSIVE SCOUTING REPORT

If only every defensive coordinator had the luxury of lockdown coverage in the defensive secondary. The Jets can literally not worry about one-half of the field in the deep secondary. Cornerback Darrelle Revis will shut down whatever receiver he is covering. To complement Revis, cornerback Kyle Wilson is becoming a great player on the outside. This allows players to get crazy with their blitz packages as the Jets have great pass rushers to get after the QB. Linebacker Bart Scott is the vocal leader of the Jets defense, and he will anchor the team's run defense. There is no doubt the Jets will be a popular team online after another run deep into the playoffs last season. Make sure to try out many of the unique plays in the Jets' defensive book to unleash the fury on the opposing quarterback.

TEAM RATING

87 Overall

85 Offense

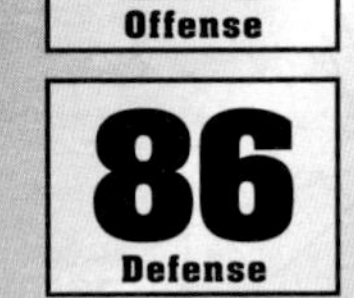

86 Defense

DYNAMIC PLAYER PERFORMANCE TRAITS

Mark Sanchez
QB #6

Consistency	★★★★★
Senses Pressure	★★★★★
Throws Ball Away	No
Throws Tight Spiral	No
Clutch	No

RATINGS BY POSITION

Quarterbacks	83
Halfbacks	80
Fullbacks	88
Wide Receivers	84
Tight Ends	85
Tackles	83
Guards	83
Centers	97
Defensive Ends	86
Defensive Tackles	81
Outside Linebackers	82
Middle Linebackers	92
Cornerbacks	93
Free Safeties	78
Strong Safeties	85
Kickers	71
Punters	66

DEPTH CHART

POS	OVR	FIRST NAME	LAST NAME
3DRB	84	LaDainian	Tomlinson
C	97	Nick	Mangold
C	58	Robert	Turner
CB	99	Darrelle	Revis
CB	86	Antonio	Cromartie
CB	71	Dwight	Lowery
CB	74	Kyle	Wilson
CB	71	Drew	Coleman
DT	81	Sione	Pouha
DT	63	Kenrick	Ellis
DT	62	Marcus	Dixon
DT	55	Carlton	Powell
FB	88	Tony	Richardson
FB	78	John	Conner
FS	78	Eric	Smith
FS	76	Brodney	Pool
FS	64	Emanuel	Cook
HB	80	Shonn	Greene
HB	84	LaDainian	Tomlinson
HB	62	Joe	McKnight
HB	65	Bilal	Powell
K	71	Nick	Folk
KOS	71	Nick	Folk
KR	76	Brad	Smith
KR	74	Kyle	Wilson
LE	90	Shaun	Ellis
LE	70	Muhammad	Wilkerson
LE	71	Ropati	Pitoitua
LG	75	Matthew	Slauson
LG	63	Dennis	Landolt
LOLB	80	Bryan	Thomas
LOLB	62	Jamaal	Westerman
LS	51	Tanner	Purdum
LT	94	D'Brickashaw	Ferguson
MLB	92	David	Harris
MLB	90	Bart	Scott
MLB	66	Josh	Mauga
MLB	60	Lance	Laury
P	66	Steve	Weatherford
PR	79	Jerricho	Cotchery
QB	83	Mark	Sanchez
QB	73	Mark	Brunell
QB	70	Kellen	Clemens
RE	81	Mike	Devito
RE	83	Trevor	Pryce
RG	90	Brandon	Moore
RG	55	Marlon	Davis
ROLB	84	Calvin	Pace
ROLB	63	Cody	Brown
RT	71	Vladimir	Ducasse
RT	72	Wayne	Hunter
SS	85	Jim	Leonhard
SS	58	James	Ihedigbo
TE	85	Dustin	Keller
TE	57	Matthew	Mulligan
TE	57	Jeff	Cumberland
WR	87	Santonio	Holmes
WR	85	Braylon	Edwards
WR	79	Jerricho	Cotchery
WR	76	Brad	Smith
WR	63	Patrick	Turner
WR	63	Logan	Payne

OFFENSIVE STRENGTH CHART

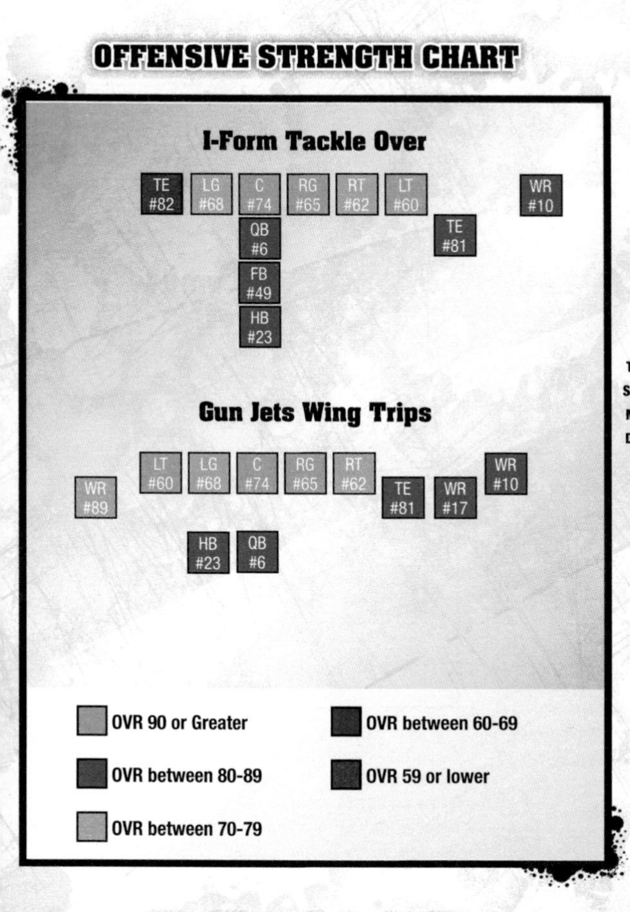

Key Player Substitution

Player: Joe McKnight

Position: #1 Third Down Back

Key Stat: 94 Acceleration

What He Brings: Having an up-and-coming talent like Joe McKnight to use in passing situations is a luxury. Shonn Greene is not a threat to go the distance in pass situations. Look to continue McKnight's relationship with Mark Sanchez, who can dump the ball off to him with screen passes.

#6 Mark Sanchez
Quarterback

Overall	83
Throwing Power	88
Short Throw Acc.	94
Med. Throw Acc.	84
Deep Throw Acc.	78

#81 Dustin Keller
Tight End

Overall	85
Speed	86
Catch	83
Jump	88
Catch in Traffic	85

#16 Brad Smith
Wide Receiver

Overall	76
Speed	92
Catch	76
Route Running	87
Acceleration	70

#24 Darrelle Revis
Cornerback

Overall	99
Speed	93
Man Coverage	99
Zone Coverage	96
Awareness	92

#52 David Harris
Middle Linebacker

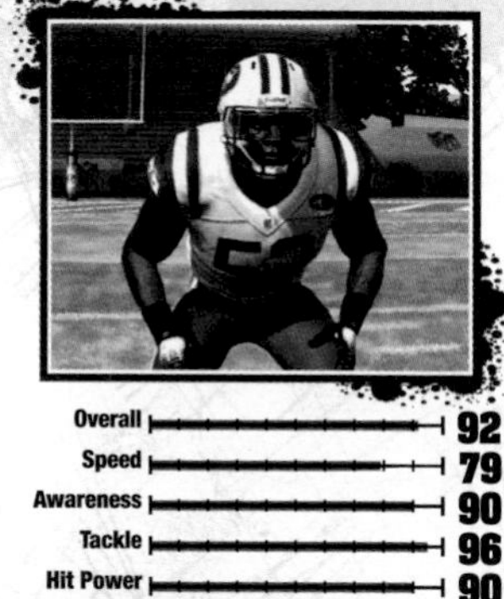

Overall	92
Speed	79
Awareness	90
Tackle	96
Hit Power	90

#22 Brodney Pool
Free Safety

Overall	76
Speed	87
Tackle	63
Hit Power	74
Play Recognition	72

DEFENSIVE STRENGTH CHART

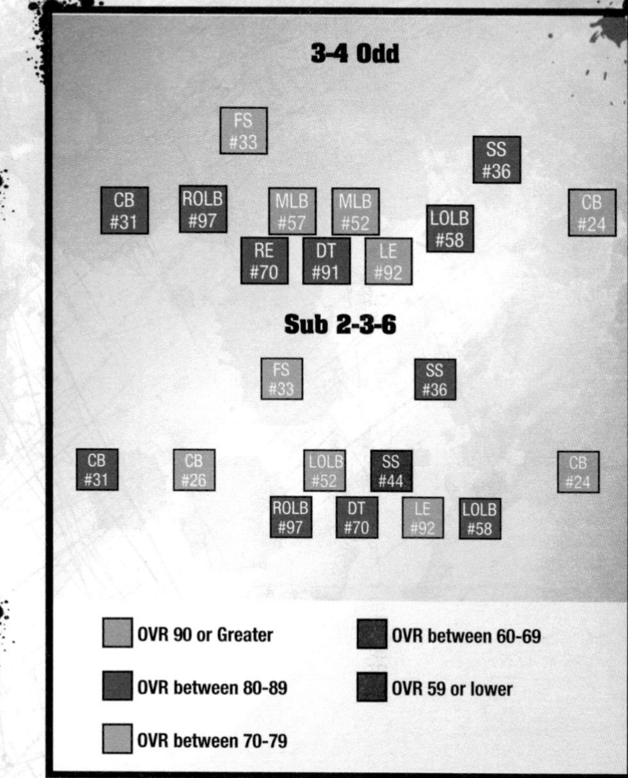

Key Player Substitution

Player: Ropati Pitoitua

Position: DT #3

Key Stat: 89 Strength

What He Brings: The Jets' defensive line has an incredible amount of depth, especially with the strength rating. Look to use goal line or the 5-2 to create a wall of strong defenders to stop the run. Use Pitoitua to help lead the charge in the middle.

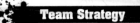

Playbook Tips

Offensive Style: Run Heavy

Offense

- Get QB Mark Sanchez started with easy passes to the TE before working the ball deep.
- The Jets have a solid backfield that allows for a split carry system, keeping both players fresh.
- Brad Smith is a great weapon for the New York Jets—he can line up at nearly any spot on offense!

Defense

- The Jets are a heavy blitzing team that relies on confusing the opponent with zone blitzing schemes.
- The Jets can bring heat because half of the field is locked down by elite CB Darrelle Revis.
- Creating a front to stop the run is easy with New York, which has many hogs to put on the interior line.

OFFENSIVE FORMATIONS

FORMATION	# OF PLAYS
Gun Bunch WK	15
Gun Jets Wing Trips	15
Gun Snugs	9
Gun Split Jet	15
Gun Spread Y-Slot	18
Gun Trey Open	18
I-Form Pro	15
I-Form Tackle Over	9
I-Form Twin TE	12
Singleback Ace	12\5
Singleback Ace Pair	12
Singleback Bunch Base	12
Singleback Doubles	18
Singleback Y-Trips	18
Strong Close	15
Strong Pro	15
Strong Y-Flex	12
Weak Pro	15
Weak Pro Twins	12
Wildcat Jet	3

OFFENSIVE PLAYCOUNTS

PLAY TYPE	# OF PLAYS
Quick Pass	17
Standard Pass	46
Shotgun Pass	63
Play Action Pass	53
Inside Handoff	46
Outside Handoff	12
Pitch	13
Counter	7
Draw	10

Three-Headed Rushing Attack

I-Form Tackle Over—HB Iso

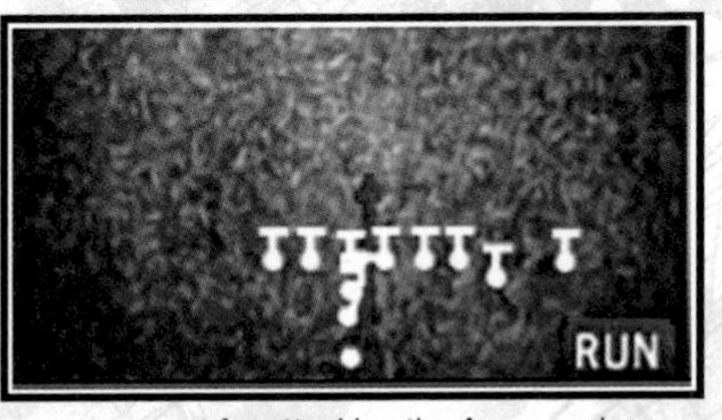

Iso runs are great for attacking the A gap under normal circumstances. However, with the Tackle Over formation employed by the Jets, this will actually be considered our run left. Since we are very weak to the left, we do not want to try anything out wide, so we will consider the middle run our left side.

Our dual tackles on the right side of the formation cause plenty of attention, and the defense will likely overplay this side. Make sure to stay up the middle as the run can get penetrated from the left side of the line. Follow the FB through the line of scrimmage for a huge gain.

When getting into the secondary, look to put your head down and cover up the ball. Most defenses have at least one safety who can pop the ball loose with a big hit. We don't want to let it slip out in traffic and cancel out our big gain.

PRO TIP Elite players online will know most of the runs out of the Tackle Over formation, so make sure to switch up your plays and make every play look the same.

I-Form Tackle Over—HB Toss

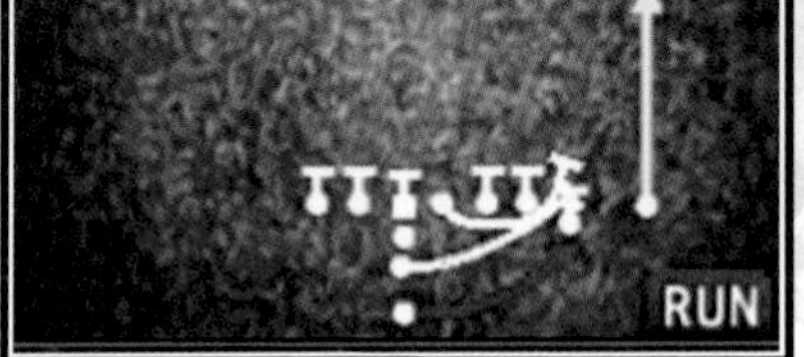

Tosses are not called as often because they have a certain risk-reward factor. Every time we break a run for a touchdown, we also have the possibility of getting dropped in the backfield for a loss. However, with the Tackle Over formation, we should have a wall that will not allow for penetration before we get back to the line.

Our guard pulls outside the formation to become a lead blocker. Since he has to run extra wide on the play, lay off the turbo to let him get set up. Our WR does a good job of clearing out his man, and the corner is sealed.

As we approach the corner, we can continue outside or cut in to hold our blocks a little longer. Here Greene appears to be heading outside, but if he can squeeze through the gap, he will reengage the blockers for another second and pick up big yards.

PRO TIP Only using speed backs on runs outside and power backs on runs inside will tip the defense off to what is coming.

I-Form - Tackle Over - HB Slam

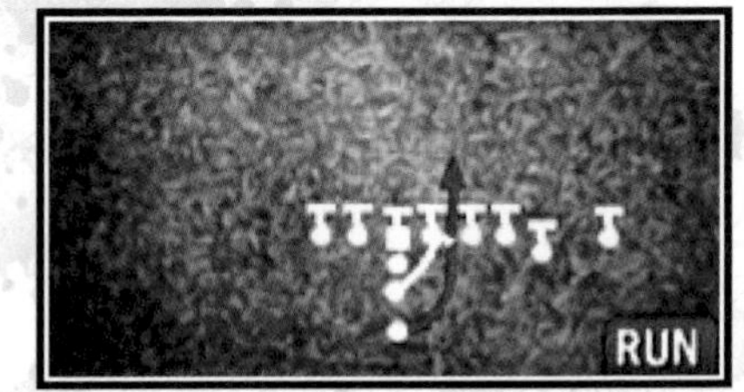

There is nothing more demoralizing for a defense than the inability to stop the run. A staple of the Jets' run game is the Tackle Over formation. The left tackle and TE switch positions on the field. This allows for us to overpower the defense and play smashmouth football with the run game.

The Jets' bruising back Shonn Greene is the perfect player for the run scheme we plan on using. Green is difficult to stop inside the offensive line. The HB Blast helps us attack the defense as we follow the lead block of our extra offensive tackle. Our offensive line gets an amazing push upfield for Greene.

As we move upfield, we take the run outside and look to get Greene into the open field. We use his amazing Trucking rating to punish the defense as they look for the tackle. Look to initiate contact with Greene, as he will fall forward for extra yards after the hit.

PRO TIP Substitute in a backup offensive tackle for your TE for extra run blocking.

Quick Pass

I-Form Tackle Over - Slants

Once we get the focus of the defense on the run, we will look for the pass. We substitute our HB with a good Catch rating, as we plan to target him in the flat. The steady dose of the run will make your opponent anticipate the run and be a step behind the pass.

At the snap of the ball, we look to the slant over the middle of the field. We want to see if the defense is blitzing. The slant will be a great route to attack blitzing defenses over the middle of the field. The defense is not blitzing, and we see that our HB in the flat has a step on the defender.

The HB makes the catch and gets upfield for the big gain. A key ingredient for success is making plays from the same formation all look the same presnap. We do that here and reap the benefits of the play call.

Man Beater

Gun Snugs - Jets Slot Posts

The Jets Slot Posts has a few amazing routes that we want to take advantage of. The HB's blue route will help with pass protection, and the two wheel routes on this play are great in beating the Cover 2 zone. Over the middle of the field, we have a hi-lo crossing pattern concept, which can help beat man-to-man and zone coverage.

Our WR running the deep post gets pressed as he breaks off the line of scrimmage. In the secondary, we can see the strong safety drop back into a Cover 2 zone. We now know that our pressed post will be a nice option as he goes downfield.

Our WR is able to find the opening in the middle of the field against the Cover 2 zone. The free safety is not quick enough to make a play on the ball, and we haul in the catch for a big gain.

PRO TIP Watch out for underneath zones running press coverage in *Madden NFL 12*. This can give the illusion of man coverage.

Zone Beater

Bunch Base - Jets Drive

We are looking to call upon the same play as the last breakdown. This time we want the defense to shade the Bunch side flat and take away our quick option to the HB. If the defense protects against the Bunch side flat, we will go up top to our split-end WR.

At the snap of the ball, we see that the defense is in the same coverage. Only this time the deep safety is over toward the sideline protecting against the HB downfield. This is where we want to take a chance downfield.

Our WR comes down with the ball just inside the end zone. The defense paid the price in defending against the HB down the opposite sideline. We recognized the weakness in the defense and capitalized for the big score!

PRO TIP Substitute in your fastest and tallest WR at the split end to stretch the field deep.

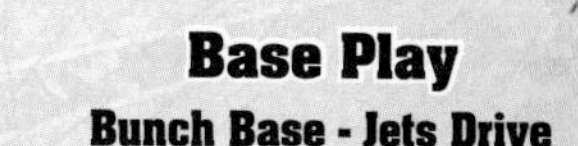

Base Play

Bunch Base - Jets Drive

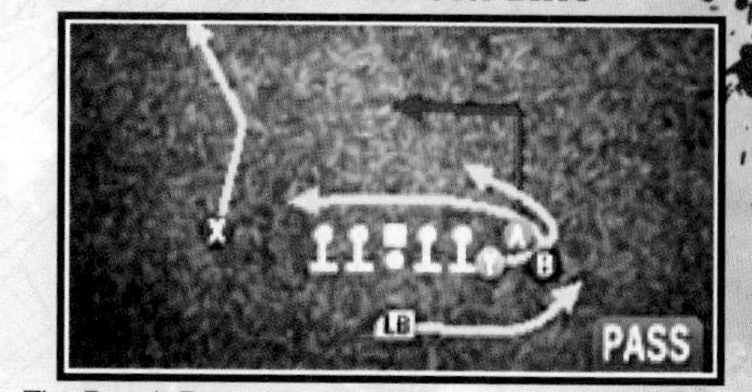

The Bunch Base Jets Drive has great route combinations for beating both man defensive coverage and zone defensive coverage. Our drag and trail route will be great for attacking underneath zone coverage. The flat will be solid against man coverage, and we even have a nice route for one-on-one situations.

We can see how open the HB gets against man-to-man coverage. The alignment of the offensive formation makes it difficult for man coverage to defend against this route. All we have to do now is deliver an accurate pass!

The pass is put on target so the HB can get upfield against the man coverage. The alignment of the bunch allows us to attack the bunch side with our HB on the flat route. This type of route combination matched with the formation itself can cause major issues for defenses in the game.

PRO TIP Look to run a flat route to any trips or bunch sides to create this type of separation against man defensive coverage.

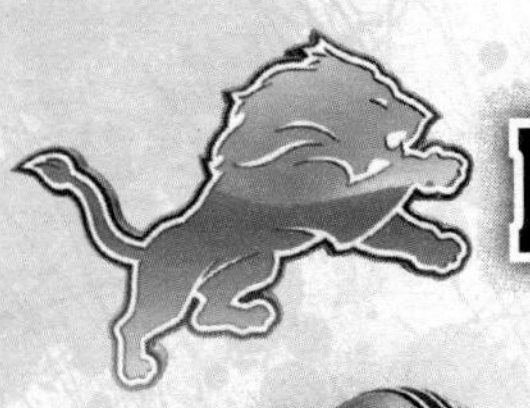

DETROIT LIONS

OFFENSIVE SCOUTING REPORT

Matthew Stafford showed promise despite being injured early during the 2010 season. The key to success for Detroit is keeping him upright in the pocket. The Lions are fortunate to have the best receiving threat in the game with Calvin Johnson. "Megatron" is an absolute beast in all aspects of the game. Look for his 6'5" frame to make plays over smaller DBs. Use Big formations to capitalize on the Lions' depth at the tight end. In the backfield, the Lions now have a two-headed attack. Start Jahvid Best, who has breakaway speed and can sneak out on-screen passes. Rookies Mikel Leshoure and Titus Young add tremendous depth to the skill positions. Both players will help spread the field and turn the Lions' attack into a big deal in *Madden NFL 12*.

DEFENSIVE SCOUTING REPORT

Safety Louis Delmas controls the defensive secondary for the Detroit Lions. Delmas is an emerging ball hawk who has all the skills to become an elite player in *Madden NFL 12*. The defensive line for the Lions is stacked with the recent draft picks of Nick Fairley and Ndamukong Suh. Expect both Fairley and Suh to pressure QBs into making bad decisions all season long. The combination of Suh and Fairley will be extremely difficult for teams to defend against. Sit back in coverage and look to rush only three or four and let your big DTs do work. Make sure to test the new 5-2 formation out as well. This will help protect your LBs, where the team is weakest.

TEAM RATING

76	Overall
82	Offense
78	Defense

DYNAMIC PLAYER PERFORMANCE TRAITS

Calvin Johnson
WR #81

Consistency	★★★★★
Covers Ball	★★★★★
Fights for Yards	Yes
Feet in Bounds	Yes
Drops Open Passes	No

RATINGS BY POSITION

Quarterbacks	80
Halfbacks	80
Fullbacks	76
Wide Receivers	79
Tight Ends	81
Tackles	82
Guards	80
Centers	80
Defensive Ends	83
Defensive Tackles	89
Outside Linebackers	72
Middle Linebackers	77
Cornerbacks	77
Free Safeties	84
Strong Safeties	73
Kickers	88
Punters	73

DEPTH CHART

POS	OVR	FIRST NAME	LAST NAME
3DRB	77	Maurice	Morris
C	80	Dominic	Raiola
C	64	Dylan	Gandy
CB	75	Alphonso	Smith
CB	78	Chris	Houston
CB	68	Nathan	Vasher
CB	69	Brandon	McDonald
CB	71	Tye	Hill
DT	89	Ndamukong	Suh
DT	86	Corey	Williams
DT	77	Nick	Fairley
DT	74	Sammie	Hill
DT	58	Andre	Fluellen
FB	76	Jerome	Felton
FB	51	Jake	Nordin
FS	84	Louis	Delmas
FS	66	John	Wendling
HB	80	Jahvid	Best
HB	72	Mikel	Leshoure
HB	74	Kevin	Smith
HB	77	Maurice	Morris
K	88	Jason	Hanson
KOS	88	Jason	Hanson
KR	63	Stefan	Logan
KR	63	Derrick	Williams
LE	85	Cliff	Avril
LE	77	Lawrence	Jackson
LE	69	Jared	DeVries
LG	84	Rob	Sims
LOLB	73	Bobby	Carpenter
LOLB	68	Ashlee	Palmer
LOLB	59	Doug	Hogue
LS	52	Don	Muhlbach
LT	83	Jeff	Backus
LT	69	Tony	Ugoh
MLB	77	DeAndre	Levy
MLB	67	Isaiah	Ekejiuba
MLB	61	Jordon	Dizon
P	73	Nick	Harris
PR	63	Stefan	Logan
QB	80	Matthew	Stafford
QB	76	Shaun	Hill
QB	68	Drew	Stanton
RE	80	Kyle	Vanden Bosch
RE	66	Turk	McBride
RE	62	Willie	Young
RG	75	Stephen	Peterman
RG	74	Donald	Thomas
ROLB	71	Zack	Follett
ROLB	70	Landon	Johnson
RT	80	Gosder	Cherilus
RT	71	Corey	Hilliard
RT	68	Jason	Fox
SS	73	Amari	Spievey
SS	80	Erik	Coleman
TE	81	Brandon	Pettigrew
TE	75	Tony	Scheffler
TE	63	Will	Heller
WR	93	Calvin	Johnson Jr.
WR	78	Nate	Burleson
WR	67	Titus	Young
WR	63	Derrick	Williams
WR	68	Bryant	Johnson
WR	63	Stefan	Logan

OFFENSIVE STRENGTH CHART

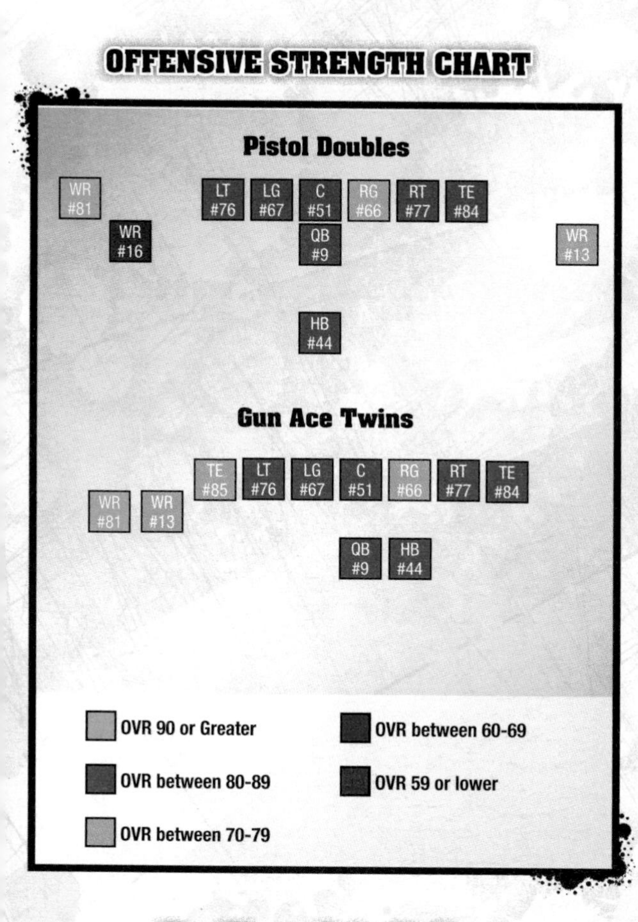

Key Player Substitution

Player: Aaron Brown

Position: #2 RB

Key Stat: 95 Speed

What He Brings: Picking up Mikel Leshoure in the draft is nice for Lions' fans who prefer the power run, but to spell the speedy HB Jahvid Best, use Aaron Brown. He has the speed to give Best a breather on outside runs and screen passes.

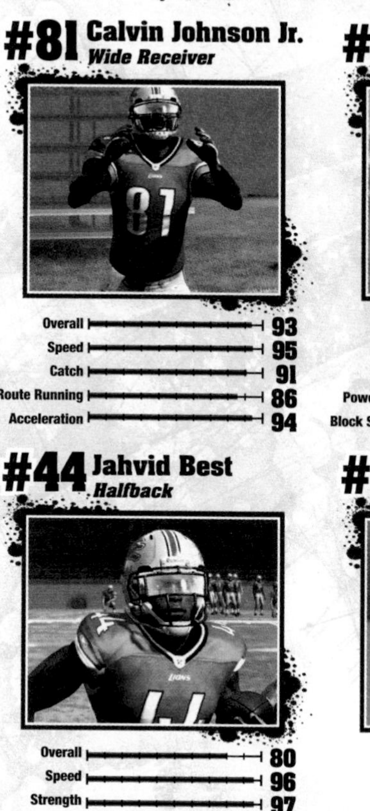

#81 Calvin Johnson Jr.
Wide Receiver

Overall	93
Speed	95
Catch	91
Route Running	86
Acceleration	94

#44 Jahvid Best
Halfback

Overall	80
Speed	96
Strength	97
Elusiveness	85
Block Shedding	72

#21 Aaron Brown
Halfback

Overall	85
Speed	95
Strength	89
Elusiveness	97
Block Shedding	77

#90 Ndamukong Suh
Defensive Tackle

Overall	89
Speed	72
Strength	95
Power Moves	90
Block Shedding	94

#26 Louis Delmas
Free Safety

Overall	84
Speed	87
Tackle	71
Hit Power	85
Play Recognition	81

#24 Tye Hill
Cornerback

Overall	71
Speed	97
Man Coverage	76
Zone Coverage	67
Awareness	66

DEFENSIVE STRENGTH CHART

5-2 Normal

FS #26
SS #42
CB #23
ROLB #49
MLB #54
CB #27
RE #93
DT #98
DT #90
DT #99
LE #92

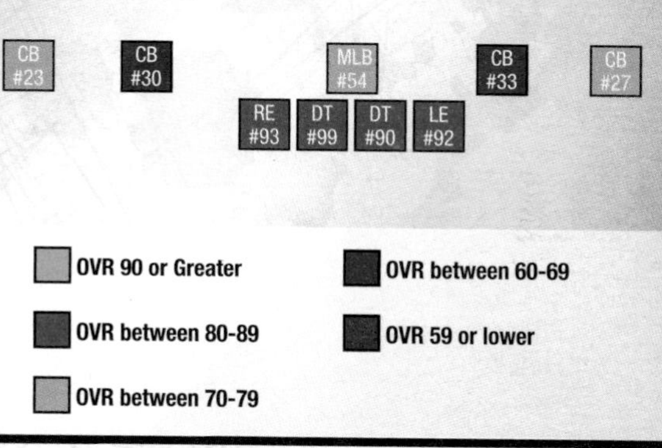

Key Player Substitution

Player: Turk McBride

Position: #1 LE in Run Situations

Key Stat: 85 Strength

What He Brings: The Lions have a powerful defensive line, but their starter at LE is more of a pass rusher. To anchor down on runs, insert Turk McBride into the game since he is a backup to the elite Kyle Vanden Bosch at RE.

Playbook Tips

Offensive Style: Balanced

Offense

- Calvin Johnson is an elite talent who can be relied upon even when tightly covered by a defender.
- The Lions have great balance at TE, so work routes to either player depending on defensive coverages.
- Jahvid Best is a slippery threat out of the backfield who can go the distance when he gets the ball in his hands via screen passes.

Defense

- The Lions solidified their defensive line through the draft by choosing Nick Fairley of Auburn.
- Utilize the new 5-2 formation on defense with Detroit as Ndamukong Suh will be explosive in the middle.
- Louis Delmas can put fear into opposing WRs who have to cross the middle of the field.

OFFENSIVE FORMATIONS

FORMATION	# OF PLAYS
Gun Ace Twins	15
Gun Doubles	18
Gun Snugs Flip	12
Gun Split Lion	15
Gun Spread Flex WK	15
Gun Trey Open	15
Gun Trips Open	15
Gun Y-Trips WK	18
I-Form Pro	15
I-Form Pro Twins	15
I-Form Tight Pair	12
Pistols Doubles	9
Singleback Ace	18
Singleback Ace Pair Flex	15
Singleback Bunch	15
Singleback Doubles	18
Singleback Tight Slots	9
Singleback Y-Trips Lion	18
Strong Close	12
Strong Twins	12
Weak Pro	15

OFFENSIVE PLAYCOUNTS

PLAY TYPE	# OF PLAYS
Quick Pass	19
Standard Pass	59
Shotgun Pass	91
Play Action Pass	51
Inside Handoff	36
Outside Handoff	11
Pitch	10
Counter	7
Draw	13

Three-Headed Rushing Attack

Strong Close—HB Off Tackle

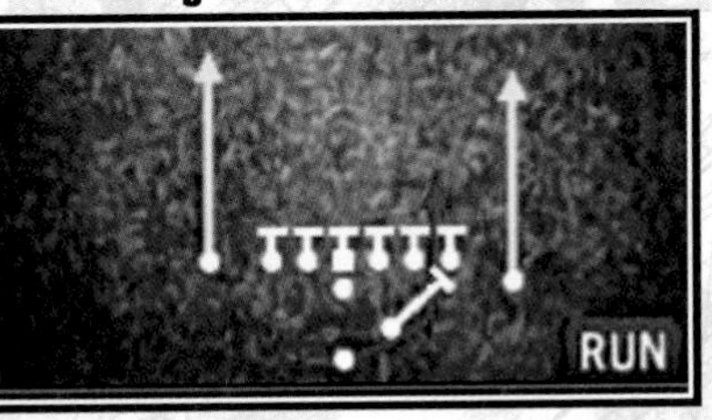

The Off Tackle run can be considered a run up the middle or a run up the right depending on what hole opens up. The optimal way is a run just inside the tackle that can punish the defense.

This was easily one of the best runs in *Madden NFL 11,* and you can see why it will be successful again this year. Our WRs clear out on both sides in case the run needs to go outside. At the snap, the back has the option of hitting the B gap or taking the run off tackle. It appears he is going to cut inside.

At the last second, the HB cuts back to the outside and takes the run off tackle. This is a true power run and allows him to set up his defenders. While Best is not a true power back, he has the speed to get to the edge after making the hard cut.

PRO TIP Place a TE at WR to really have the edge on lockdown.

Strong Close—Quick Toss

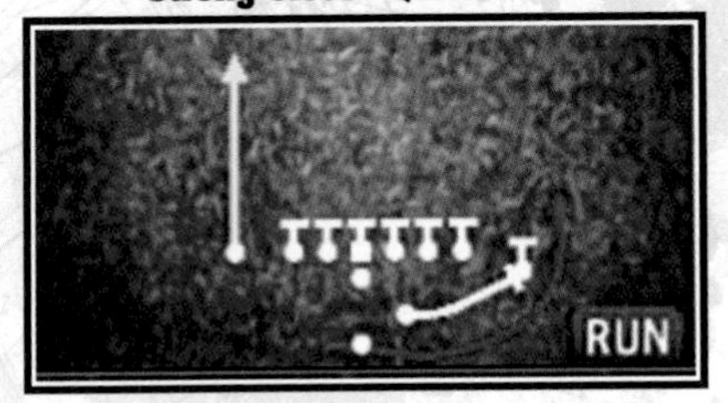

The Quick Toss is a great way to beat a man defense that is overcrowding the middle of the field. Look to quickly audible to the Quick Toss, which has the FB already offset to the strong side. This lets him get out in front.

Our QB turns and quickly pitches the ball to the dynamic HB Best. As he catches the toss, he sees the linemen crashing down towards the middle and knows he can go the distance with the right cuts.

The blockers hit the corner and seal the edge. All the defenders try to recover straight at the back rather than playing the angle towards the sideline. This proves to be fatal, as Best has elite speed and is almost never caught from the side. As soon as he finishes his cut upfield, he is gone.

PRO TIP If the defense places the linemen on contains, try using a quick juke to avoid the slower defender

Strong Close - Counter Weak

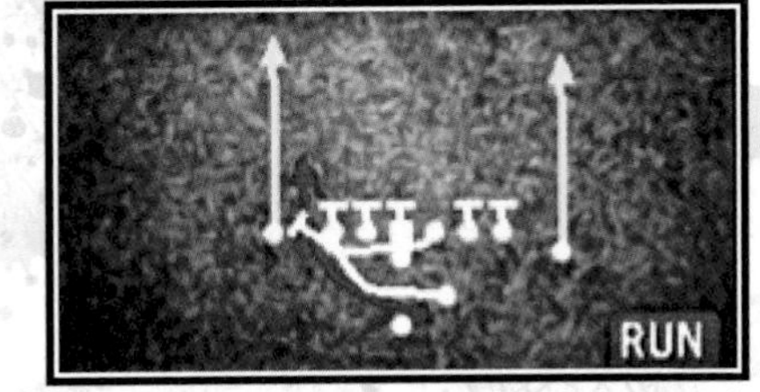

The Strong Close formation is one of the best running formations in the game. The balance of run plays in this formation is what makes it so versatile. We are looking to use the Counter Weak to get our speedy HB into the open field.

Best receives the handoff and sees room to run outside. If the outside lane is clogged, cut the run back inside. It is important to not outrun your pulling guard, as you can put yourself out of position for a positive run.

We use Best's speed to get around the edge of the defense. One good juke move and we are off to pay dirt! The Counter Weak has home run potential, especially with an HB like Jahvid Best.

PRO TIP Follow the pulling offensive linemen. Breaking away too early can result in a big play for the defense.

Quick Pass

Strong Close - TE Option

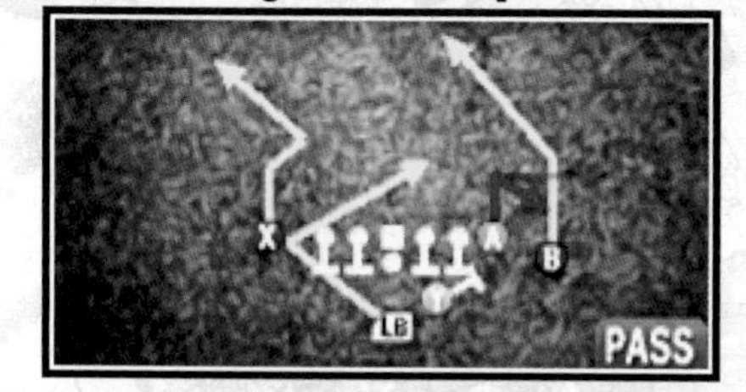

The Strong Close formation possesses a unique balance of passing threats and running threats. We will use one of our most dangerous weapons, HB Jahvid Best. His angle route out of the backfield is perfect for beating man coverage and the blitz.

Our QB sees that pressure is closing in. One of the offensive linemen has blown his block, and the defender is coming straight for us. We wait for Best to make his cut toward the middle of the field.

We deliver a strike, and Best is off to the races. Best's speed can break open any game on any play. So much attention is needed in defending Best that he will often free up our other offensive threats!

PRO TIP Throw the ball too early and Best will not have the angle to run upfield. Throw the ball too late and Best will not have any cutback angles.

Man Beater

Pistol - PA Boot

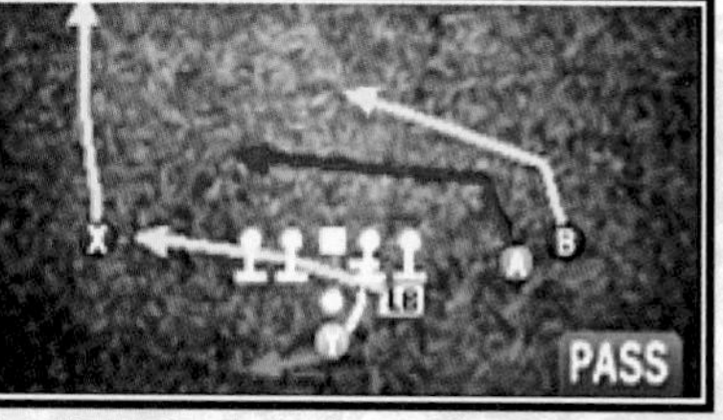

The Pistol formation makes its return in *Madden NFL 12*. The PA Boot is designed to get QBs with mobility outside the pocket. The flow of the play is to the field's right, and we look to take advantage of the unique throwing angles as we move away from the pocket.

Matthew Stafford has a big arm and excellent mobility for a QB. One way to avoid pressure is to roll away. This causes a few problems for the defense. Typically, defenses are only responsible for covering five offensive threats. Now with a mobile QB, they have to account for the added dimension the speed creates.

We love blue routes! The TE on the PA Boot looks to block first and then releases to the short flat. Stafford avoids the pressure of the blitz and gets outside where he can look to scramble or pass to the releasing TE. Our TE releases in time, and we get him the ball as he moves downfield.

PRO TIP Avoid rollouts with QBs with a Speed rating lower than 70.

Zone Beater

Trips Open - Deep Attack

The Detroit Lions have one of the best deep threats in the game. Calvin Johnson is not only one of the biggest players on the field, but he is also one of the fastest. We are trying to free him up downfield with Deep Attack. Against blitzing defenses, we will need to checkdown to one of our shorter options over the middle of the field. If we have time in the pocket, we can look to hit Johnson deep over the middle of the field.

The defense comes out in a Cover 3 zone. We know this because we see both defensive backs and one deep safety drop into coverage. The defense is not blitzing, so we should have time in the pocket to deliver the pass. Even with time, we have to wait for Johnson's route to develop. Here we can see the pressure coming just as we begin our throw.

The extra time in the pocket allowed us to deliver the perfect pass to Johnson. As much as we love the deep option of this play, it's important to understand the defensive coverage. If the blitz is on, get the ball to your crossing patterns or get the HB out of the backfield.

Base Play

Ace Twins - Smash

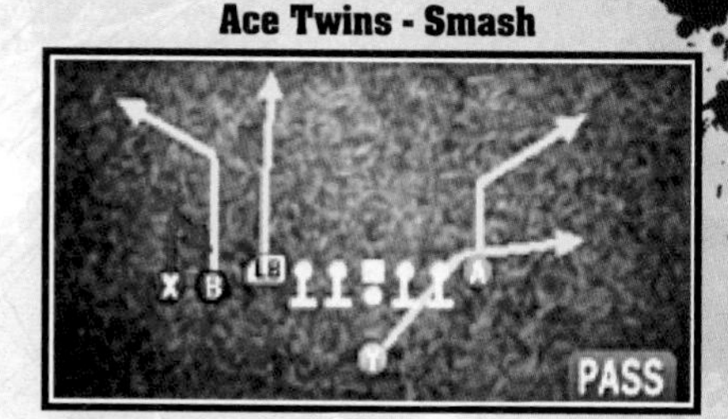

Get creative with how you use your star players. With the Ace Twins Smash, we use WR Calvin Johnson as a decoy. He is a big threat on offense, and the defense must account for him. The Smash concept is good for beating Cover 2 and Cover 4 zones. It is even a solid option against man-to-man coverage.

The defense drops back into a Cover 2 zone. The defense keys in on Johnson but leaves our WR running the corner route wide open. A perfect pass will be a huge gain for our offense.

Johnson did not make the catch on this play, but he did get our corner route open. We could also have Johnson post up his defender by throwing a high-lead pass.

PRO TIP The Smash concept is in many other formations in the game. Look to find it elsewhere in your playbook.

GREEN BAY PACKERS

OFFENSIVE SCOUTING REPORT

The Super Bowl champion Green Bay Packers will ascend into the top-three overall *Madden NFL* ratings this season. Aaron Rodgers has become a top passer and has sneaky good speed. Green Bay has every type of WR, with strong James Jones, quick Jordy Nelson, and veteran Donald Driver. Greg Jennings is a dynamic WR in every aspect of the game and is capable of putting the team on his back. Look to spread the defense out with a heavy aerial attack. Work TE Jermichael Finley into the game at every opportunity. His speed stresses out linebackers, and he is too big for most safeties. Nobody could keep up with the Packers' offense last season, and it appears to be the case in *Madden NFL 12*.

DEFENSIVE SCOUTING REPORT

The Green Bay Packers have tremendous depth at the secondary position. Sam Shields and Tramon Williams emerged as breakout players last season to go along with seasoned veteran Charles Woodson. Nick Collins is a playmaker and has elite speed for his position. At the LB position, Clay Matthews can control the middle of the defense. This is simple when you have stars like B.J. Raji holding down the middle and winning the battle at the line of scrimmage. The Green Bay defense is very fast and should play superbly in *Madden NFL 12*.

TEAM RATING

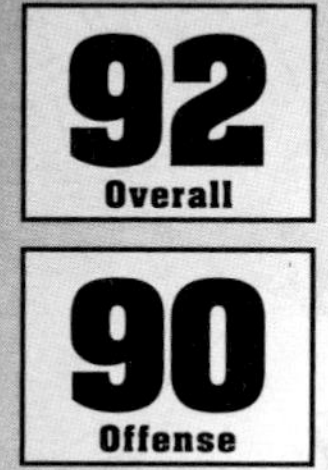

92 Overall

90 Offense

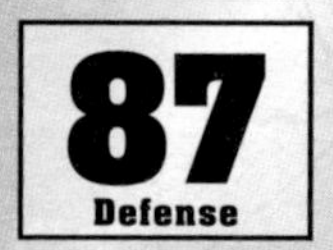

87 Defense

DYNAMIC PLAYER PERFORMANCE TRAITS

Aaron Rodgers
QB #12

Senses Pressure	★★★★★
Consistency	★★★★★
Throws Tight Spiral	Yes
High Motor	Yes
Clutch	Yes

RATINGS BY POSITION

Quarterbacks	98
Halfbacks	82
Fullbacks	79
Wide Receivers	85
Tight Ends	90
Tackles	85
Guards	87
Centers	84
Defensive Ends	86
Defensive Tackles	88
Outside Linebackers	85
Middle Linebackers	88
Cornerbacks	93
Free Safeties	95
Strong Safeties	77
Kickers	72
Punters	76

DEPTH CHART

POS	OVR	FIRST NAME	LAST NAME
3DRB	72	Brandon	Jackson
C	84	Scott	Wells
C	77	Jason	Spitz
CB	93	Charles	Woodson
CB	92	Tramon	Williams
CB	75	Sam	Shields
CB	68	Pat	Lee
CB	63	Brandon	Underwood
DT	88	B.J.	Raji
DT	70	Howard	Green
FB	79	John	Kuhn
FB	73	Korey	Hall
FS	95	Nick	Collins
FS	67	Jarrett	Bush
HB	82	Ryan	Grant
HB	77	James	Starks
HB	72	Brandon	Jackson
HB	64	Alex	Green
K	72	Mason	Crosby
KOS	72	Mason	Crosby
KR	75	Sam	Shields
KR	79	Jordy	Nelson
LE	83	Ryan	Pickett
LE	64	C.J.	Wilson
LE	59	Lawrence	Guy
LG	82	Daryn	Colledge
LG	65	Caleb	Schlauderaff
LG	61	Nick	McDonald
LOLB	95	Clay	Matthews
LOLB	70	Brady	Poppinga
LS	59	Brett	Goode
LT	88	Chad	Clifton
LT	73	Derek	Sherrod
LT	67	T.J.	Lang
MLB	88	Nick	Barnett
MLB	85	A.J.	Hawk
MLB	82	Desmond	Bishop
MLB	68	Brandon	Chillar
P	76	Tim	Masthay
PR	92	Tramon	Williams
QB	98	Aaron	Rodgers
QB	75	Matt	Flynn
QB	66	Graham	Harrell
RE	89	Cullen	Jenkins
RE	62	Jarius	Wynn
RE	70	Mike	Neal
RG	92	Josh	Sitton
RG	61	Marshall	Newhouse
ROLB	74	Brad	Jones
ROLB	71	Erik	Walden
ROLB	70	Frank	Zombo
RT	82	Bryan	Bulaga
RT	86	Mark	Tauscher
SS	77	Morgan	Burnett
SS	76	Atari	Bigby
SS	77	Charlie	Peprah
TE	90	Jermichael	Finley
TE	68	Andrew	Quarless
TE	68	D.J.	Williams
WR	93	Greg	Jennings
WR	82	Donald	Driver
WR	79	Jordy	Nelson
WR	76	James	Jones
WR	70	Randall	Cobb
WR	64	Brett	Swain

OFFENSIVE STRENGTH CHART

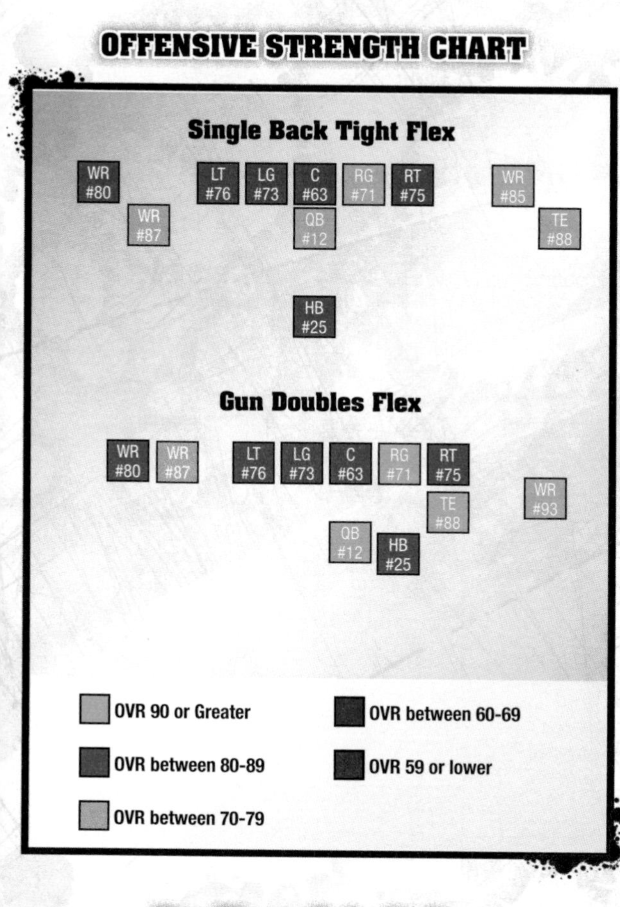

Key Player Substitution

Player: James Starks

Position: #1 HB

Key Stat: 91 Speed

What He Brings: James Starks showed up big for the Packers last season during their title run. Starks is very athletic.

#12 Aaron Rodgers
Quarterback

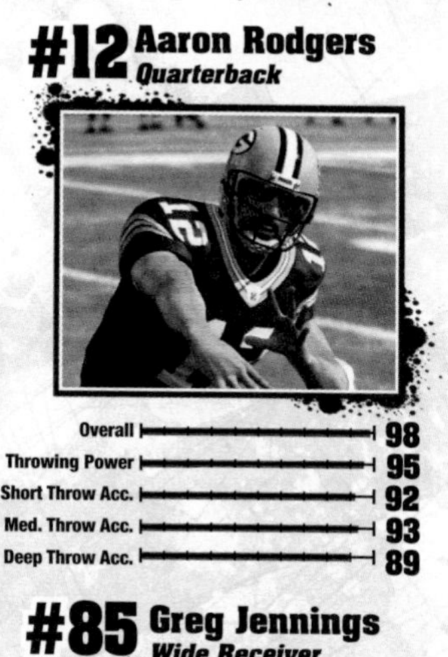

Overall	98
Throwing Power	95
Short Throw Acc.	92
Med. Throw Acc.	93
Deep Throw Acc.	89

#85 Greg Jennings
Wide Receiver

Overall	93
Speed	94
Catch	94
Route Running	93
Acceleration	95

#87 Jordy Nelson
Wide Receiver

Overall	79
Speed	88
Catch	85
Route Running	87
Acceleration	90

#52 Clay Matthews
Left Outside Linebacker

Overall	95
Speed	86
Awareness	85
Tackle	94
Hit Power	88

#38 Tramon Williams
Cornerback

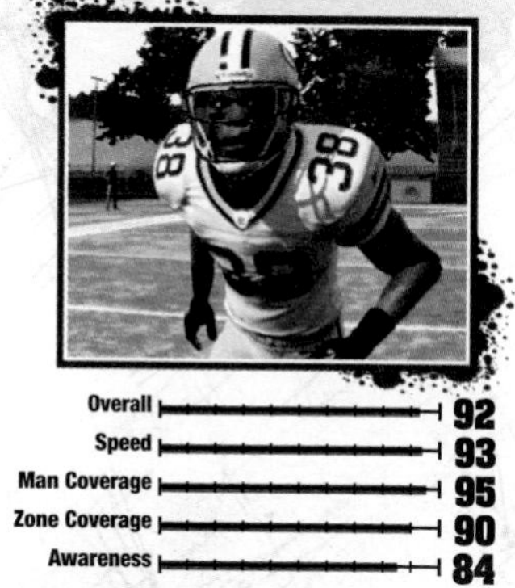

Overall	92
Speed	93
Man Coverage	95
Zone Coverage	90
Awareness	84

#37 Sam Shields
Cornerback

Overall	75
Speed	97
Man Coverage	79
Zone Coverage	78
Awareness	67

DEFENSIVE STRENGTH CHART

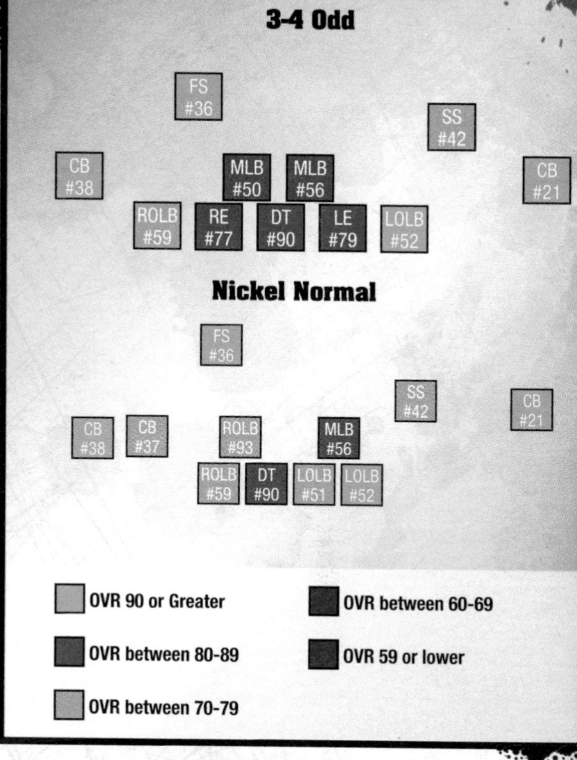

Key Player Substitution

Player: Atari Bigby

Position: #4 CB Slot (46 Speed Package)

Key Stat: 88 Hit Power

What He Brings: Use the speed package in the 46 defense to allow Atari Bigby to play the LB position. This will get all of your fast CBs on the field and let Bigby and his solid hit stick control the box with Clay Matthews.

Playbook Tips

Offensive Style: Pass Heavy

Offense

- Gun Doubles Flex Wing is a unique formation that helped the Packers throughout their playoff run.
- Jermichael Finley is a unique talent who can run routes from inside the hash marks as well as out wide against CBs.
- Don't be afraid to run with Aaron Rodgers, but make sure to slide as he is your most valuable asset in this offense.

Defense

- Cornerback Charles Woodson is not only a great cover man, but he can also rush the QB off the edge with great consistency.
- Look to keep Clay Matthews on the field in passing situations; he can shed blocks on the rush or drop back into coverage.
- The Packers have an elite secondary that lets their zone blitz schemes get very creative; check out the Nickel Psycho formation.

OFFENSIVE FORMATIONS

FORMATION	# OF PLAYS
Full House Wide	12
Gun Bunch WK	15
Gun Double Flex	12
Gun Doubles Flex Wing	12
Gun Doubles On	18
Gun Flex Trey	12
Gun Normal Y-Flex Tight	9
Gun Pack Trips	18
Gun Y-Trips WK	18
I-Form Pro	21
I-Form Slot Flex	15
I-Form Tight	12
I-Form Tight Pair	15
Singleback Ace	18
Singleback Ace Pair	18
Singleback Ace Twins	12
Singleback Bunch	15
Singleback Flex	18
Singleback Tight Flex	9
Strong Close	12
Weak Pro	15

OFFENSIVE PLAYCOUNTS

PLAY TYPE	# OF PLAYS
Quick Pass	14
Standard Pass	51
Shotgun Pass	77
Play Action Pass	65
Inside Handoff	43
Outside Handoff	21
Pitch	10
Counter	2
Draw	11

Three-Headed Rushing Attack

Singleback Tight Flex—HB Dive

Offenses love to run out of passing formations. This allows them to keep their weapons on the field but forces the defense to be ready for multiple looks. The Singleback Tight Flex is a great formation that will have the defense ready for anything.

The dive here is actually to the left side of the line and looks to pick up as many yards as possible. Ryan Grant is a solid overall back who can take the ball outside the tackle if the game calls for it.

Grant does a good job starting inside, which leads the deception. The D looks to pack the middle but Grant then simply cuts outside. While the dive won't often follow this path, it can reap huge rewards and it happens more often out of the Singleback Tight Flex.

PRO TIP Get Jermichael Finley into this formation inside; he is a great receiver but can still block in the run game.

Singleback Tight Flex—HB Screen

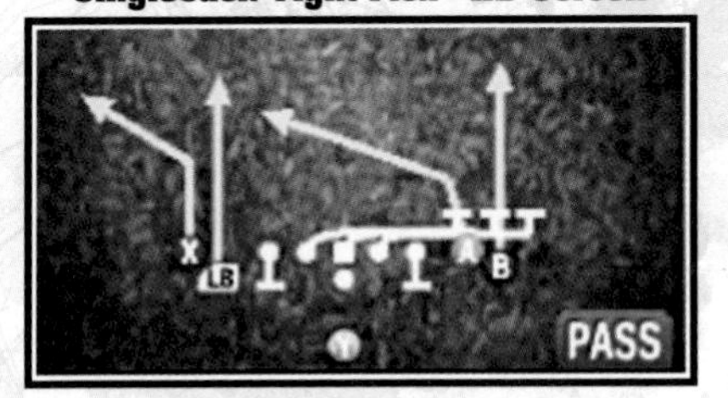

Adding in screen passes as an extension of the run game is a great way to fool the defense in *Madden NFL 12*. This is a great way to get the running back out in space while still getting the high percentage chance for yards of the run game.

The defense quickly busts through the line at the snap and thinks they have a shot at the QB. However, the speedy Aaron Rodgers rolls away from the pressure and knows he will have a great spot to dump off the ball.

The defenders realize something is not right when they see the ball dumped over their heads. The back will catch the ball in space with plenty of blocking in front. Be patient and don't outrun your blockers downfield.

PRO TIP Make sure to add a player with great hands into your third down RB spot. This is a pass that can't be dropped

Singleback Tight Flex - HB Slam

The Packers' HB Ryan Grant is perfect for the HB Slam. After the snap of the ball, find the open running lane, which should be the A or B gap. The HB Slam is not designed to go outside, so be sure to stick with the flow of the play.

Grant has a few running lanes to choose from. Both of the gaps we thought would be open are ready for Grant to bulldoze through. Be prepared for contact from the middle linebacker.

Grant gets into the open field, and the linebacker takes him down. Use Grant as the workhorse for your running attack. Over the course of the game, he will help to wear down the defense.

PRO TIP Work the play action after consistently giving the ball to Grant. Use Grant's great running ability to open up the pass.

Quick Pass

Fullhouse - Angle Swing

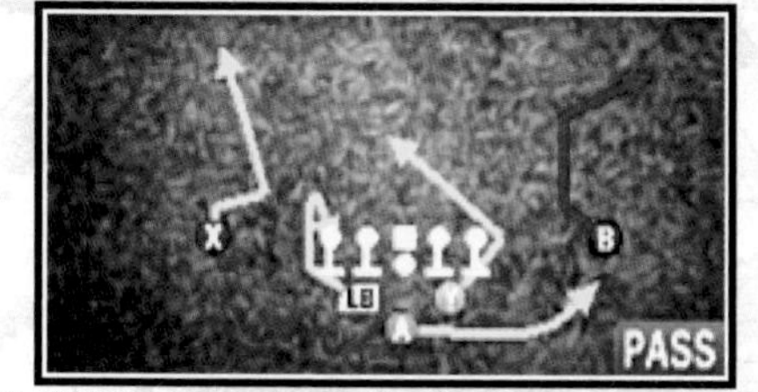

The Full House package in the Packers' playbook creates an interesting backfield. We have our TE, HB, and FB all behind the line of scrimmage. The defense will have difficultly defending against the quick passing options out of the backfield and stopping the run from this formation.

We see the defense is completely guessing at what we are going to do. The Full House package has forced the defense to overload the blitz and leave our TE wide open off the left edge. The deep safety is the only defender left to take Finley down in the open field.

The pressure was quick, but the defense made a bad decision in sending too many defenders to stop the run. The Full House appears to be a run-first formation, but appearances can be deceiving. We deliver the ball on time for the big gain!

PRO TIP To get more speed on the field, substitute your backup HB for your FB. This will help in the passing game.

Man Beater

Singleback Ace Twins - Smash

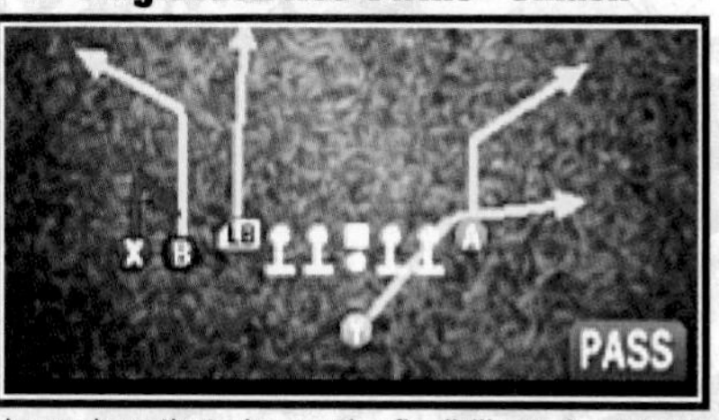

We love plays that give us the flexibility to beat both man and zone coverage. The last setup showcased how the Ace Twins Smash beats zone coverage. Now let's look at how we use this play to beat man coverage.

Jermichael Finley begins his route upfield. We see the smaller linebacker is matched up in man coverage against our TE. This matchup is what we are looking for, as the linebacker cannot defend Finley's speed and size. The deep safety is fading away from the corner route, so we feel confident in Finley getting open.

Finley gets open, and both the safety and the linebacker are out of position. We are able to isolate Finley into the one-on-one matchup that we were looking for. The Smash concept is very effective, especially when you have a playmaker at the TE position.

PRO TIP Read the deep safeties to determine man or zone coverage. If pressure is coming, check down to the HB in the flat.

Zone Beater

Singleback Ace Twins - Smash

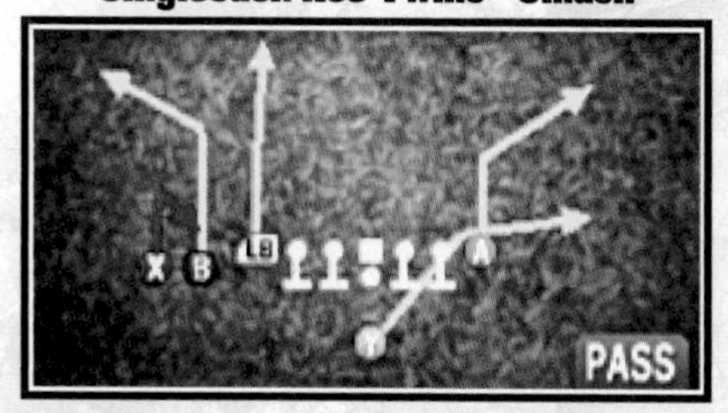

The Smash concept from Singleback Ace Twins can attack zone defensive coverage to the left and can attack man defensive coverage to the right. Against a Cover 2 zone, our slot WR on the corner route is a fantastic option to get behind the defense. Against man coverage, we like to isolate TE Jermichael Finley to the right of the field. The HB in the flat is a nice safety valve against the blitz.

The defense is in a zone blitz. The pressure is coming off the edge, and we see our routes starting to develop downfield. Our corner route is not open yet, so we will need to hang in the pocket a bit longer.

Our patience paid off, and the corner route is open. When pressure is coming, we want to get rid of the ball as quickly as possible. However, our route has not had enough time to get open. Be patient and trust that your route combinations will open up the WR.

PRO TIP Consider using one of your TEs or HB to block to gain extra pass protection for this play.

Base Play

Gun Doubles Flex Wing - Packers Comebacks

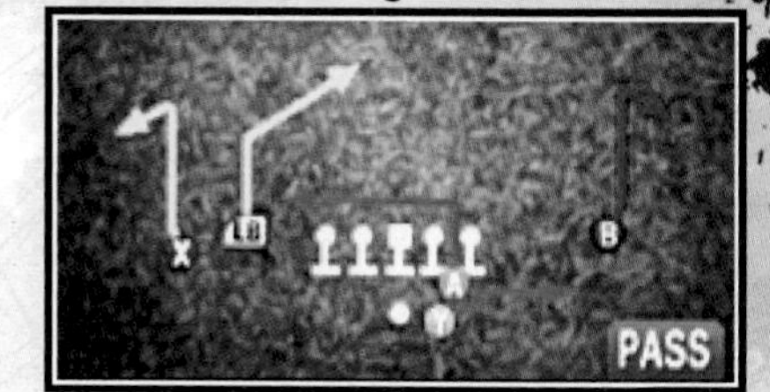

Blue routes are one of the most effective ways to defend against the blitz. On this play, we have two blue routes in the backfield. Both our TE and HB will block first and then release for a passing option.

The blitz is on, and we can see our TE and HB looking to aid in pass protection. We can hang in the pocket and wait for them to release on their routes, or we can look to the outside where our WRs are in one-on-one matchups.

Our outside WR is open, so we are not going to wait on the blue routes. The comeback route gets our WR the extra step he needs to get open. We deliver the pass toward the sideline and get the big gain.

PRO TIP Make sure to not use blue routes as your first option. If they get caught in their block, they will not release on their route.

CAROLINA PANTHERS

OFFENSIVE SCOUTING REPORT

Despite a disappointing season, the Carolina Panthers remained a popular *Madden NFL* team last season. Carolina will be heavily used once again due to their selection of Cam Newton, the number-one overall pick in the draft. Newton is a dual-threat QB who has the speed and strength to play above his rating. In the backfield, Carolina has always had a two-headed monster. RB Mike Goodson will fill any holes and can pound the rock to take the pressure off Newton. WR David Gettis looks poised to continue raising his play, and his size should give Newton a big window to throw the ball. WR Steve Smith has been a staple of the Panthers' offense for years; hopefully they hang on to him and his elite speed. Former QB/WR Armanti Edwards remains a hidden weapon on the Carolina bench; work to use his high acceleration and agility ratings.

DEFENSIVE SCOUTING REPORT

The Carolina Panthers' defense starts and ends with linebackers Jon Beason and Thomas Davis. These two linebackers control games with their speed and knowledge of the game. Look to use Beason as your main run support player. Use Davis for coverage purposes and also look to use him off the edge to rush the QB. This will allow you to play your base formation a good portion of the game. The defensive line has great overall strength and should let the players behind them run free. Chris Gamble holds down the defensive secondary and can defend just about every WR in the NFL.

TEAM RATING

72 Overall

84 Offense

84 Defense

DYNAMIC PLAYER PERFORMANCE TRAITS

Jon Beason
LB #52

Consistency	★★★★★
Confidence	★★★★★
Big Hitter	Yes
High Motor	Yes
Clutch	No

RATINGS BY POSITION

Quarterbacks	77
Halfbacks	89
Fullbacks	63
Wide Receivers	78
Tight Ends	81
Tackles	89
Guards	81
Centers	86
Defensive Ends	82
Defensive Tackles	76
Outside Linebackers	85
Middle Linebackers	97
Cornerbacks	84
Free Safeties	76
Strong Safeties	84
Kickers	89
Punters	79

DEPTH CHART

POS	OVR	FIRST NAME	LAST NAME
3DRB	74	Mike	Goodson
C	86	Ryan	Kalil
C	60	Zack	Williams
CB	86	Chris	Gamble
CB	81	Richard	Marshall
CB	73	Captain	Munnerlyn
CB	67	Brandon	Hogan
CB	57	Robert	McClain
DT	76	Ed	Johnson
DT	69	Terrell	McClain
DT	65	Sione	Fua
DT	66	Andre	Neblett
DT	71	Derek	Landri
FB	63	Tony	Fiammetta
FB	58	Rashawn	Jackson
FS	76	Sherrod	Martin
FS	68	Jordan	Pugh
FS	74	Gerald	Alexander
HB	89	DeAngelo	Williams
HB	81	Jonathan	Stewart
HB	74	Mike	Goodson
HB	60	Tyrell	Sutton
K	89	John	Kasay
KOS	66	Rhys	Lloyd
KR	74	Mike	Goodson
KR	60	Tyrell	Sutton
LE	88	Charles	Johnson
LE	74	Greg	Hardy
LG	85	Travelle	Wharton
LG	74	Mackenzy	Bernadeau
LOLB	83	Thomas	Davis
LOLB	66	Lawrence	Wilson
LOLB	68	Jamar	Williams
LS	56	J.J.	Jansen
LT	92	Jordan	Gross
LT	75	Garry	Williams
LT	59	Jacob	Bender
MLB	97	Jon	Beason
MLB	80	Dan	Connor
MLB	67	Abdul	Hodge
P	79	Jason	Baker
PR	73	Captain	Munnerlyn
QB	77	Cam	Newton
QB	70	Jimmy	Clausen
QB	73	Matt	Moore
RE	75	Tyler	Brayton
RE	70	Everette	Brown
RE	68	Eric	Norwood
RG	76	Geoff	Schwartz
RG	65	Duke	Robinson
ROLB	87	James	Anderson
ROLB	67	Jordan	Senn
ROLB	69	Nic	Harris
RT	85	Jeff	Otah
RT	65	Lee	Ziemba
SS	84	Charles	Godfrey
SS	68	Marcus	Hudson
TE	81	Jeremy	Shockey
TE	69	Jeff	King
TE	68	Gary	Barnidge
WR	89	Steve	Smith
WR	74	David	Gettis
WR	71	Brandon	LaFell
WR	64	David	Clowney
WR	63	Armanti	Edwards
WR	59	Kealoha	Pilares

OFFENSIVE STRENGTH CHART

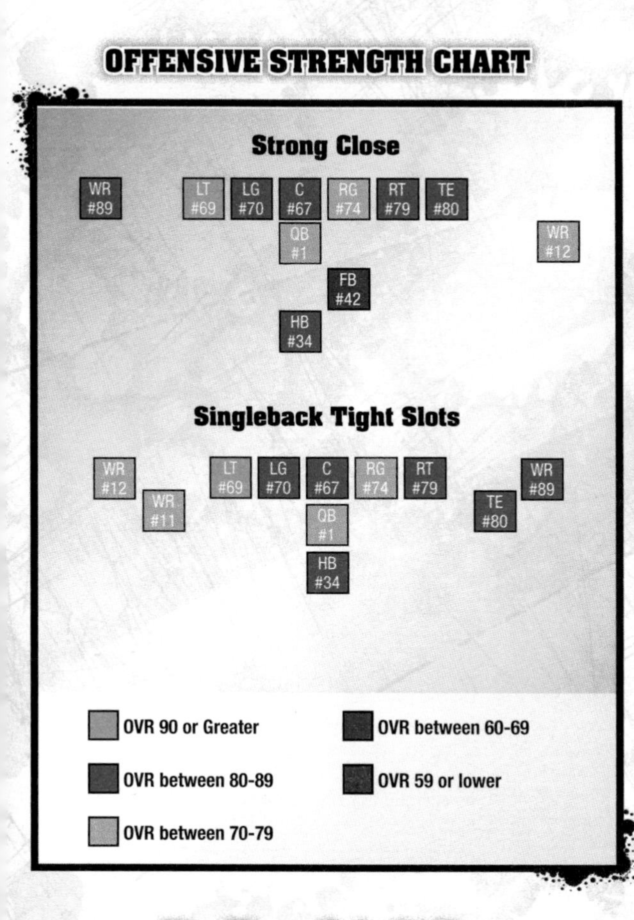

Key Player Substitution

Player: Gary Barnidge

Position: #2 TE Slot on Passing Downs

Key Stat: 82 Speed

What He Brings: Get Barnidge into the game to add another threat onto the field in the passing game. He can act as a safety valve for young QB Cam Newton.

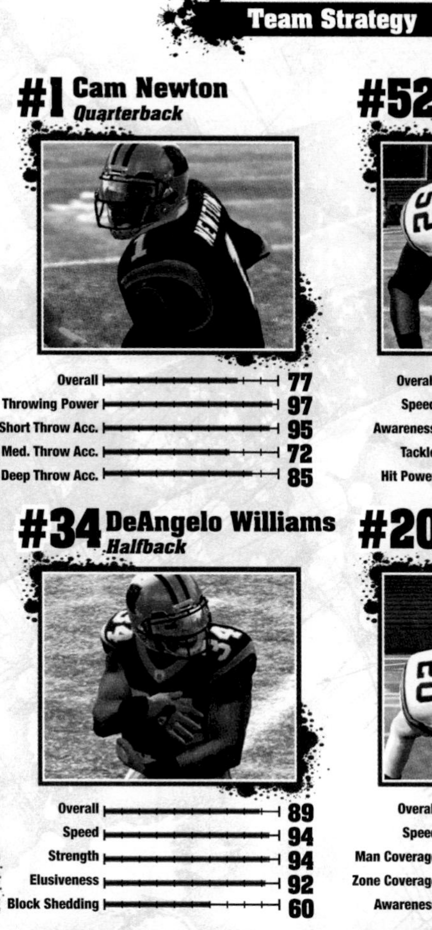

#1 Cam Newton
Quarterback

Overall	77
Throwing Power	97
Short Throw Acc.	95
Med. Throw Acc.	72
Deep Throw Acc.	85

#34 DeAngelo Williams
Halfback

Overall	89
Speed	94
Strength	94
Elusiveness	92
Block Shedding	60

#33 Mike Goodson
Halfback

Overall	74
Speed	93
Strength	95
Elusiveness	91
Block Shedding	81

#52 Jon Beason
Middle Linebacker

Overall	97
Speed	85
Awareness	96
Tackle	97
Hit Power	92

#20 Chris Gamble
Cornerback

Overall	86
Speed	92
Man Coverage	93
Zone Coverage	86
Awareness	76

#91 Everette Brown
Right Enf

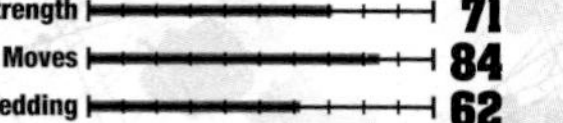

Overall	70
Speed	83
Strength	71
Finesse Moves	84
Block Shedding	62

DEFENSIVE STRENGTH CHART

5-2 Normal

FS #23
SS #30
CB #31
ROLB #50
MLB #52
CB #20
RE #96
DT #92
DT #99
DT #97
LE #95

Dime Normal

FS #23
SS #30
CB #31
CB #41
MLB #97
CB #22
CB #20
RE #96
DT #97
DT #99
LE #95

OVR 90 or Greater
OVR between 60-69
OVR between 80-89
OVR 59 or lower
OVR between 70-79

Key Player Substitution

Player: Jason Williams

Position: #1 ROLB

Key Stat: 86 Speed

What He Brings: This sub will free up your starting ROLB to move to RE to rush the passer. Williams has solid man coverage and can really excel while being user-controlled.

Playbook Tips

Offensive Style: Run Heavy

Offense

- Rookie QB Cam Newton will be under pressure to learn the offense quickly—thankfully he is a gifted athlete.
- Carolina's backfield will look different this season, but a two-back system still works best.
- Carolina has 64 shotgun passing plays, so Newton can take a dropback similar to what he ran in college.

Defense

- New coach Ron Rivera will employ the 4-3 defense but may look to sprinkle in elements of the 3-4.
- Use plenty of Nickel as the Panthers' two LBs are stronger than the secondary.
- Chris Gamble has been quietly playing solid on the edge for Carolina; keep him on the other team's number one WR.

OFFENSIVE FORMATIONS

FORMATION	# OF PLAYS
Gun Doubles	18
Gun Empty Base	9
Gun Spread Y-Slot	12
Gun Split Slot	15
Gun Snugs Flip	12
Gun Trips TE	15
Gun Y-Trips Open	18
I-Form Pro	18
I-Form Pro Twins	12
I-Form Tight Pair	15
Singleback Ace	18
Singleback Ace Pair	12
Singleback Ace Pair Flex	12
Singleback Bunch	12
Singleback Panther Doubles	18
Singleback Spread Flex	12
Singleback Tight Slots	12
Strong Pro	18
Strong Close	15
Weak Twins	12
Wildcat Panther	3

OFFENSIVE PLAYCOUNTS

PLAY TYPE	# OF PLAYS
Quick Pass	16
Standard Pass	56
Shotgun Pass	64
Play Action Pass	49
Inside Handoff	42
Outside Handoff	12
Pitch	11
Counter	6
Draw	11

Three-Headed Rushing Attack

I-Form Pro Twins - HB Blast

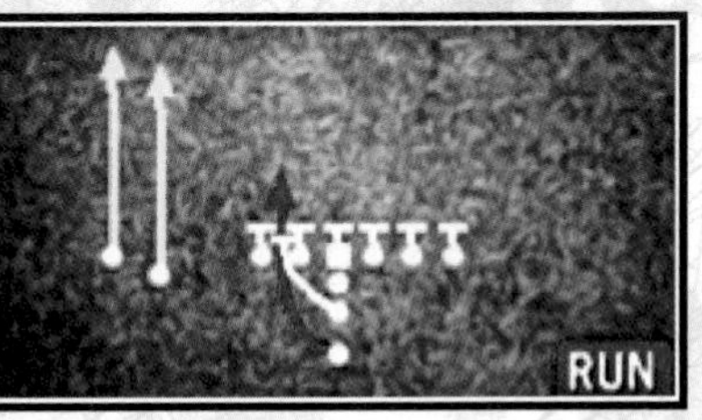

We love the deception of running multiple plays from one formation. Here we look to substitute our big HB Jonathan Stewart into the game. The design of the HB Blast is the opposite of the HB Toss. This will play to our advantage, as the defense will try to shade the right side of the field.

We look to bounce the run to the outside. The defensive linebacker has other plans. We have lost containment off the left edge, forcing us to redirect our run up the middle.

Stewart makes the cut upfield, and we pick up five tough yards. The defense did a great job at keeping containment on the outside edges. However, the defense cannot account for the middle of the field, and we take advantage of that.

PRO TIP Mixing up the style of run is very important. To have a full running attack, we need the ability to run to the left, middle, and right of the field.

I-Form Pro Twins—Iso

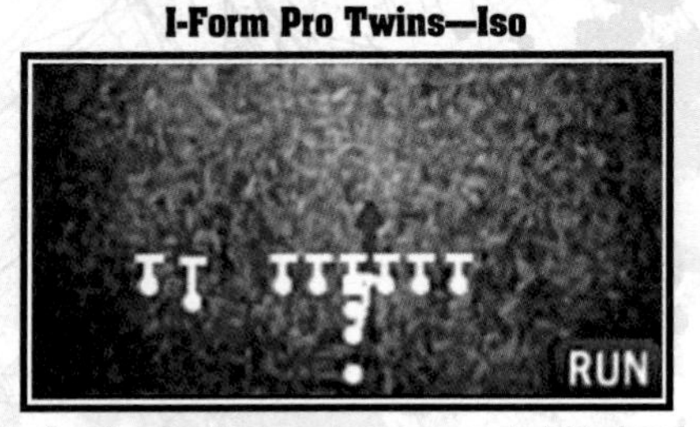

The Carolina Panthers are known as a straight-ahead rushing team that has always had solid FBs to get out in front. This attitude is true in *Madden NFL 12,* and the Iso is a great play to show it off.

At the snap, the QB gets the ball to the running back, who looks to get in behind the FB. The defense does a solid job holding the edge, but the Iso is a straight-ahead smashmouth run that can pick up solid chunks of yards consistently.

Since the defense was not expecting the run to the middle, it did not have linebackers ready to back up the linemen. This is a painful mistake because a talented back can really gain solid yards before the safety gets in to make a tackle. Use this play whenever the defense stops respecting the middle of the field. While it doesn't yield as many yards as the HB Toss, it can still move the chains.

PRO TIP Getting your top rushing threat 20 carries a game can really take the burden off a young QB.

I-Form Pro Twins - HB Toss

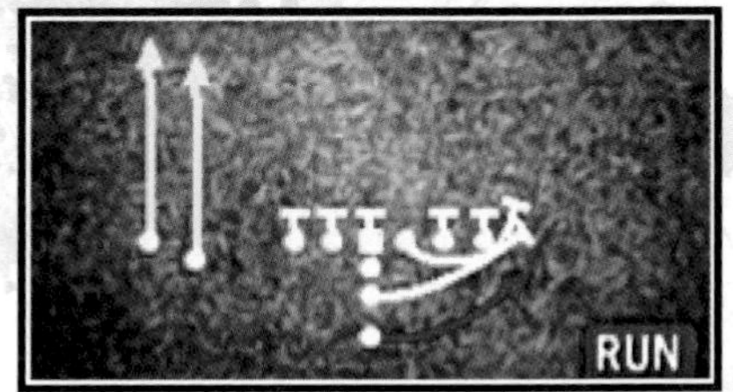

The HB Toss can be hit or miss if we are not patient in the run game. When used correctly, it can give us huge gains on the ground with our speedy HB. Do not rush to the outside. Make sure to follow your lead blockers, and do not outrun them as you move upfield.

The offensive line has made its push upfield. This is the critical point in the run due to the deep safety coming up to help with the run defense. Do not run outside the blocker. Be patient and let the FB engage his block with the safety.

We wait for the FB to deliver the crushing block, and we have open space to run into up the sideline. Patience is the difference between a four-yard gain and a touchdown.

PRO TIP If outside containment is lost with the HB Toss, cut your losses and move the ball back up the middle of the field to avoid losing yards.

Quick Pass

I-Form Pro Twins—PA TE Leak

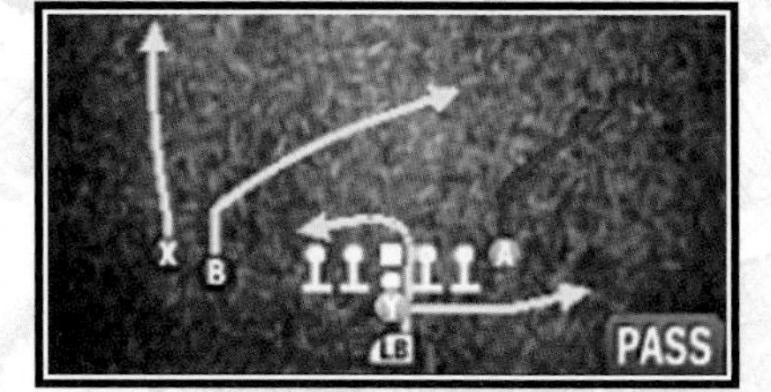

The PA TE Leak has been one of our favorite plays ever since the last generation of *Madden NFL*. By staying in our run formation, we can fool the defense and get an advantage at the snap.

The QB does a good job of selling the play fake, which will help our wideouts get an advantage and hopefully earn inside position. The two routes out of the backfield are solid for quick passes and are often forgotten about by the defense.

The defense lost inside position against the WR running across the middle of the field. The QB does a good job waiting to make the throw and leading it out in front. This play will instantly make your run game better, since the defense will have to be ready for this at all times.

PRO TIP You can cancel any play action by blocking the RB; this will get you the other passing routes without the wait.

Man Beater

Gun Snugs - Bench

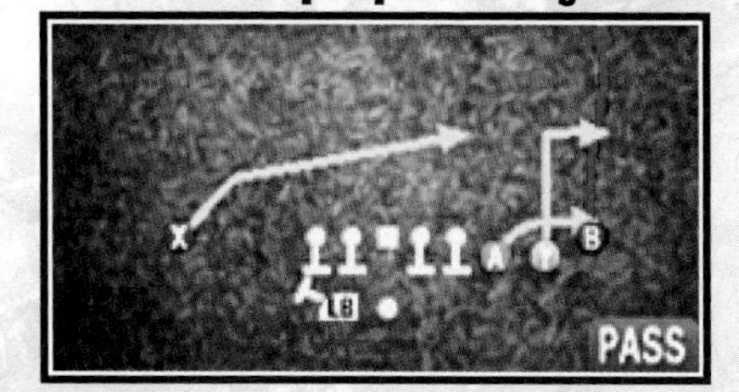

The Gun Snugs Bench has a high-low passing concept to the outside. We have two deep-corner routes and two short out routes. This play can be used to beat man and zone defensive coverage.

We read the defense is in a Cover 2 zone defense. We know that we called the perfect play. The "low" out routes will keep the short defender at bay while our "high" corner routes will be isolated against the deep safeties.

Our WR has the angle on the deep safety, and we deliver the pass for the big gain. Against a Cover 4 zone, look to the out routes on the sideline, as they should open up. Against man defensive coverage, we like the out routes as well.

PRO TIP Route running is a crucial rating for the success of the out routes. Use your best route runners here.

Zone Beater

Gun Y - Y - Trips Open - Strong Flood

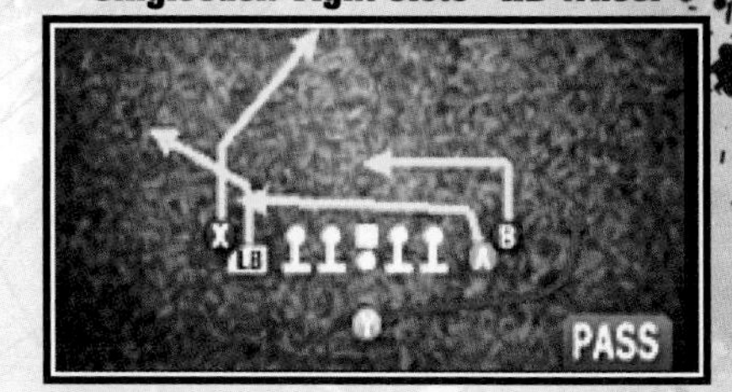

The Strong Flood is a great passing concept that looks to attack zone coverage to the right of the field and to beat man-to-man coverage to the left. We match up David Gettis to the left as we look to get him into the open field. Will it be man or zone coverage by the defense?

Gettis gets inside position on the defensive back. However, we still are not sure if the defense is in man or zone coverage. If it is man coverage, Gettis will be wide open as he approaches the middle of the field.

The defense is indeed in man defensive coverage, and we deliver the ball to Gettis. He uses his speed to get extra yards after the catch. Against zone coverage, look to the WR in the flat. The vertical route will pull the zone coverage deep and will target the WR running the deep out route!

PRO TIP WR David Gettis is a versatile threat in the passing game. He has the size and speed to play every down. Get him the ball often.

Base Play

Singleback Tight Slots - HB Wheel

If there is a perfect play in the game, the Singleback Tight Slots HB Wheel might just be it. It has quick passing options and man-to-man beaters, and it puts pressure on the defense deep and can beat the zone. This is our favorite play in the Carolina playbook because of its multiple threats.

At the snap of the ball, we see that our HB on the wheel route is wide open in the flat. We can check down to the HB for the easy gain, but we decide to check our other options downfield.

Our decision is the right one. We see our emerging star WR David Gettis open on the post. We deliver the pass and haul it in for the touchdown. Against man coverage, look to the flat and the crossing patterns over the middle of the field.

PRO TIP Mix the run in from this formation to help open up the deep post downfield.

NEW ENGLAND PATRIOTS

OFFENSIVE SCOUTING REPORT

The New England Patriots dominated the regular season with a 14-2 record during 2010. The Patriots were once again led by future Hall of Fame QB Tom Brady and his 36 TD passes. Despite trading one of the biggest *Madden NFL* threats in WR Randy Moss last season, the Patriots are poised to be a great team in *Madden NFL 12*. Tom Brady is one of the few QBs who has the accuracy to go along with his throw power. RB Danny Woodhead has solid speed and showed that he is a receiving threat out of the backfield. WR Wes Welker is capable of tearing up defenses underneath with his agility and acceleration. Focus on TE Aaron Hernandez in the open field, and switch to TE Rob Gronkowski in the red zone since he is a bigger target. Look to spread the field with New England and capitalize on their tremendous depth at skill positions. There is no doubt that the Patriots will be used heavily online this season.

DEFENSIVE SCOUTING REPORT

The New England Patriots' defense is predicated on Vince Wilfork's ability to control the middle of the field. Wilfork is one of the best defensive tackles in *Madden NFL 12*. He should be able to anchor the Patriots' defensive line and allow their linebackers to fill running lanes. The defensive secondary has a rising star in Devin McCourty, whom you can leave on an island in one-on-one situations. McCourty's covering skills allow for extreme flexibility with the Patriots' defensive schemes. The Patriots lack a true pass rush but do have a few athletic linebackers who can get after the quarterbacks.

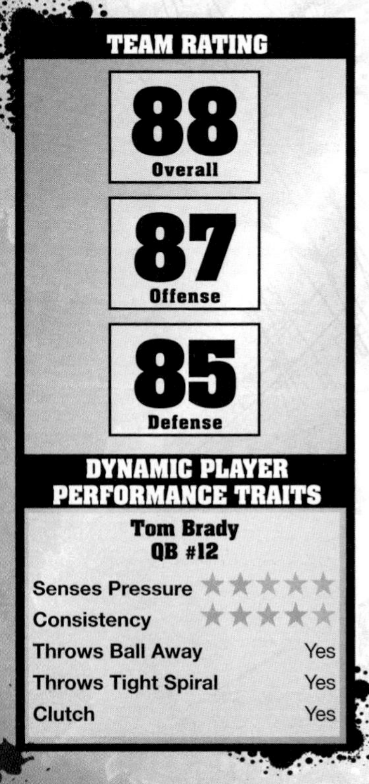

TEAM RATING

88	Overall
87	Offense
85	Defense

DYNAMIC PLAYER PERFORMANCE TRAITS

Tom Brady
QB #12

Senses Pressure	★★★★★
Consistency	★★★★★
Throws Ball Away	Yes
Throws Tight Spiral	Yes
Clutch	Yes

RATINGS BY POSITION

Quarterbacks	99	Defensive Tackles	96
Halfbacks	82	Outside Linebackers	76
Fullbacks	81	Middle Linebackers	92
Wide Receivers	81	Cornerbacks	85
Tight Ends	84	Free Safeties	83
Tackles	85	Strong Safeties	86
Guards	82	Kickers	87
Centers	89	Punters	77
Defensive Ends	84		

DEPTH CHART

POS	OVR	FIRST NAME	LAST NAME
3DRB	82	Danny	Woodhead
C	89	Dan	Koppen
C	57	Ryan	Wendell
CB	87	Devin	McCourty
CB	82	Leigh	Bodden
CB	72	Kyle	Arrington
CB	72	Jonathan	Wilhite
CB	68	Darius	Butler
DT	96	Vince	Wilfork
DT	69	Myron	Pryor
DT	70	Kyle	Love
FB	81	Sammy	Morris
FS	83	Brandon	Meriweather
FS	79	James	Sanders
HB	82	BenJarvus	Green-Ellis
HB	82	Danny	Woodhead
HB	69	Shane	Vereen
HB	67	Stevan	Ridley
K	87	Stephen	Gostkowski
KOS	87	Stephen	Gostkowski
KR	76	Brandon	Tate
KR	87	Devin	McCourty
LE	84	Ty	Warren
LE	73	Ron	Brace
LE	67	Brandon	Deaderick
LG	93	Logan	Mankins
LG	59	Thomas	Austin
LOLB	77	Rob	Ninkovich
LOLB	65	Eric	Moore
LOLB	73	Marques	Murrell
LS	63	Matt	Katula
LT	88	Matt	Light
LT	75	Nate	Solder
LT	74	Nick	Kaczur
MLB	92	Jerod	Mayo
MLB	79	Brandon	Spikes
MLB	73	Gary	Guyton
MLB	66	Dane	Fletcher
P	77	Zoltan	Mesko
PR	73	Julian	Edelman
QB	99	Tom	Brady
QB	66	Brian	Hoyer
QB	69	Ryan	Mallett
RE	84	Mike	Wright
RE	82	Marcus	Stroud
RE	61	Landon	Cohen
RG	71	Dan	Connolly
RG	67	Marcus	Cannon
RG	65	Rich	Ohrnberger
ROLB	75	Jermaine	Cunningham
ROLB	75	Tully	Banta-Cain
RT	81	Sebastian	Vollmer
RT	65	Quinn	Ojinnaka
SS	86	Pat	Chung
SS	79	Jarrad	Page
SS	63	Josh	Barrett
TE	84	Rob	Gronkowski
TE	82	Aaron	Hernandez
TE	73	Alge	Crumpler
WR	77	Deion	Branch
WR	90	Wes	Welker
WR	76	Brandon	Tate
WR	73	Julian	Edelman
WR	62	Taylor	Price
WR	63	Matthew	Slater

OFFENSIVE STRENGTH CHART

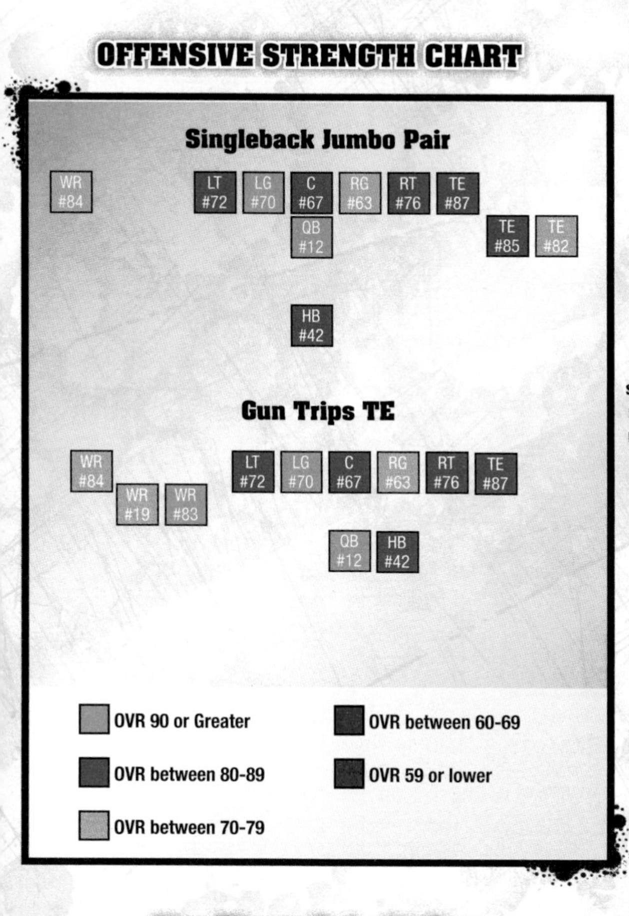

Key Player Substitution

Player: Brandon Tate

Position: #2 WR

Key Stat: 94 Speed

What He Brings: Look to get Brandon Tate into the game as the Patriots' best overall deep threat. He can help open up routes underneath for Wes Welker.

#12 Tom Brady *Quarterback*

Overall	99
Throwing Power	95
Short Throw Acc.	99
Med. Throw Acc.	96
Deep Throw Acc.	89

#83 Wes Welker *Wide Reciever*

Overall	90
Speed	85
Catch	96
Route Running	97
Acceleration	96

#19 Brandon Tate *Wide Reciever*

Overall	76
Speed	94
Catch	74
Route Running	64
Acceleration	95

#75 Vince Wilfork *Defensive Tackle*

Overall	96
Speed	55
Strength	97
Power Moves	91
Block Shedding	93

#51 Jerod Mayo *Middle Linebacker*

Overall	92
Speed	85
Awareness	77
Tackle	97
Hit Power	89

#24 Jonathan Wilhite *Cornerback*

Overall	72
Speed	92
Man Coverage	77
Zone Coverage	76
Awareness	68

DEFENSIVE STRENGTH CHART

3-4 Odd

FS #31, SS #25, CB #23, MLB #55, MLB #51, CB #32, ROLB #96, RE #99, DT #75, LE #94, LOLB #50

Sub 2-3-6 Even

FS #31, SS #25, CB #23, CB #27, MLB #51, SS #44, CB #32, ROLB #96, RE #99, LE #94, LOLB #50

OVR 90 or Greater
OVR between 60-69
OVR between 80-89
OVR 59 or lower
OVR between 70-79

Key Player Substitution

Player: Jonathan Wilhite

Position: #2 CB

Key Stat: 92 Speed

What He Brings: Jonathan Wilhite has the athleticism that it takes to be an every-down corner in *Madden NFL 12*.

Playbook Tips

Offensive Style: Pass Heavy

Offense

- While the Patriots have many short throws, Tom Brady is elite and can make any throw in the game.
- Using Wes Welker on slot screens is a great way to set up the defense to get beaten deep.
- Don't sleep on using the Patriots' bulk at TE to create a solid heavy package for rushing the ball.

Defense

- The Patriots have two safeties who can really force the ball loose on hit sticks, so keep them near the line of scrimmage.
- On passing downs, use Jermaine Cunningham to rush the QB with his elite athletic ability.
- On the other side, use LB Gary Guyton to create backside pressure off the edge.

OFFENSIVE FORMATIONS

FORMATION	# OF PLAYS
Gun 5WR Patriot	12
Gun Ace Pair Flex	12
Gun Bunch	12
Gun Empty Y-Flex	9
Gun Normal Flex WK	12
Gun Pats Wing TE	21
Gun Pats Wing Trips	24
Gun Snugs Flip	9
Gun Split Patriot	12
Gun Spread Flex	12
Gun Trips Open	9
Gun Trips TE	12
I-Form TE Flip	12
I-Form Tight	12
I-Form Tight Pair	12
Singleback Bunch	12
Singleback Ace Pair Twins	12
Singleback Deuce Wing	15
Singleback Doubles Pats	21
Singleback Jumbo Pair	9
Strong Pro	18
Strong Twins	15

OFFENSIVE PLAYCOUNTS

PLAY TYPE	# OF PLAYS
Quick Pass	18
Standard Pass	36
Shotgun Pass	110
Play Action Pass	45
Inside Handoff	33
Outside Handoff	15
Pitch	8
Counter	5
Draw	10

Three-Headed Rushing Attack

Singleback Jumbo Pair—HB Belly Weak

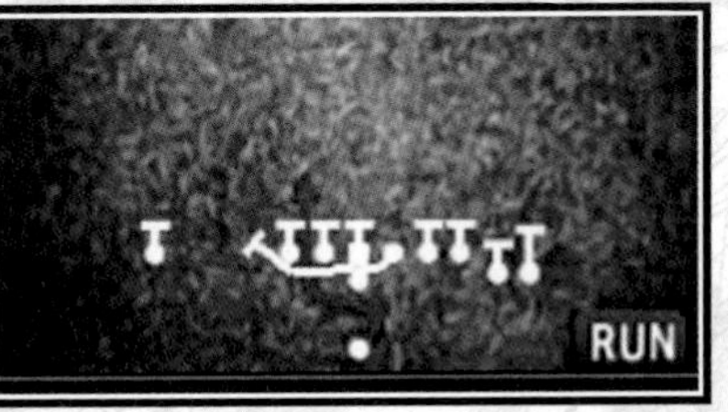

Having New England's two rising star TEs split out to the right will really draw attention over to that side of the formation. This makes it the perfect time to call the HB Belly Weak.

The offense will employ a pulling RG as the lead blocker on the play. The HB Belly Weak is similar to a counter play but is designed to just cut one gap over and remain inside. The fake step right is very similar and a good way to hold the defense.

The LB does look to shoot through the gap created by the pulling guard. However, our RB makes one cut and continues on the designed run play. While this doesn't have the threat to go the distance of the counter, it is a great way to make the defense respect the weak side of the formation.

PRO TIP If you're in true run mode, add Nate Solder at the TE position. His excellent blocking skills will dominate LBs.

Singleback Jumbo Pair—HB Dive

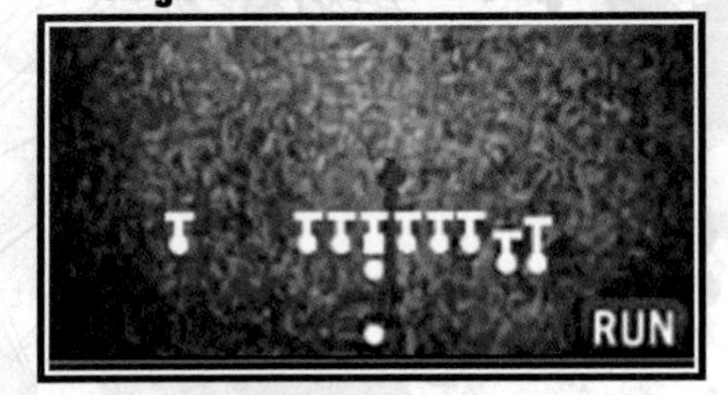

When you're using Singleback, the HB will have no lead blocker. This means he will have to choose the hole depending on what he sees from the linebackers. QB Tom Brady is great at reading the defense and will only call this play when his team has the advantage in the box.

The back takes the snap and has the option of the hole to the left or the right. A great way to make up for the lack of a lead blocker is to start at one hole and cut back at the last second. This will hopefully cause the defender to run into a wall of blockers at the line.

The Patriots have two different style backs for this run. BenJarvus Green-Ellis will look to lay down the law with a more punishing style and is not afraid to take on a linebacker. Danny Woodhead will hide behind his lineman before bursting through the seam and looking to make defenders miss.

PRO TIP For short yardage, don't dance at the line. Put the back's head down and run straight ahead.

Singleback Jumbo Pair - Power O

The New England Patriots have a trio of TEs who make it extremely difficult for defenses in the NFL to match up against. The Singleback Jumbo Pair is a formation that we like to use to take advantage of these TEs. What makes the Patriots difficult to defend is not being able to key in on the run or pass.

The Power O is a great play to run strong side with our three-TE package. Our HB has a wall of blockers leading the way. Outside containment has been lost as we see the defensive back closing in off the edge.

We cut the run back up inside, and our TEs go to work. We get the extra block we need to spring the big run. When running the Power O, be sure to follow your pulling offensive linemen. He will often deliver the crushing blow downfield.

PRO TIP Use the play action from this formation. The Patriots possess a trio of TEs who can dominant the run and pass game.

Quick Pass

Singleback Jumbo Pair - PA Power O

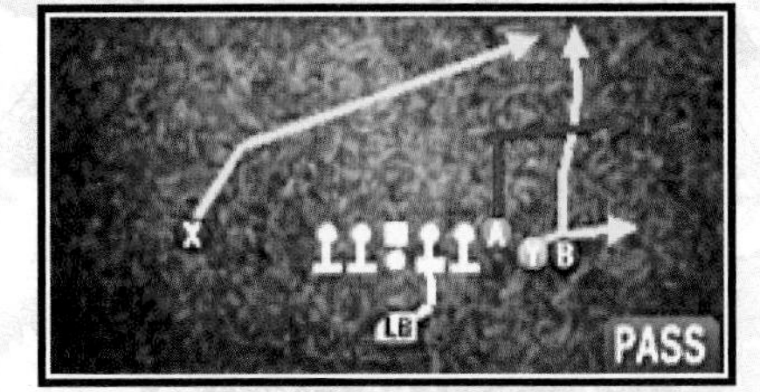

We line up in the same formation as the previous play, and we look to run the PA Power O. All-Pro Tom Brady runs an amazing play action, and with an effective run game, we can expect our TEs to do damage as receivers off the play action.

The play action has occurred, and we quickly scan the defense downfield. We read the defensive zone blitz and see that our TE in the flat is wide open. Make sure to get the pass to the TE before he reaches the sideline.

Brady delivers the perfect pass to the TE before he reaches the sideline. We have room to run up the sideline and gain extra yards. The play action caught the defense off guard as they anticipated the run. They also got caught in the zone blitz and didn't guard the flat.

PRO TIP The Patriots' TEs are versatile. Do not be afraid to use them in shotgun passing situations.

Man Beater

Gun 5 WR Patriot - WR Screen

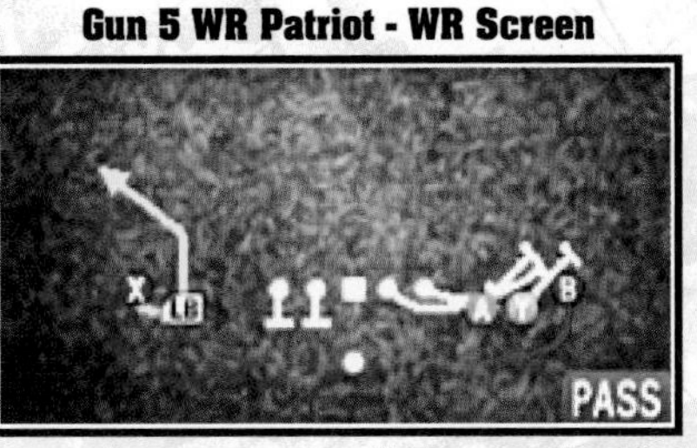

When we play an opponent with an aggressive blitz package, the 5WR Patriot formation is good for spreading out the defense. The Patriots have tools in the passing game that will make the WR Screen a big-time threat. WR Wes Welker is our main target because of his great agility and acceleration.

Welker gets into position after the snap. The defense is caught in the blitz and is exposed as our blockers get into position. Screens can hit for a touchdown every time you call upon them.

The pass is delivered, and we get upfield at full speed quickly. Make sure to follow your blockers to spring free. The WR Screen will make your opponent think twice about blitzing.

PRO TIP Be careful when running WR Screens, as your QB can take big-time hits. The offensive line pulls for the screen, which exposes your QB to injury.

Zone Beater

Gun Ace Pair Flex - TE Spot

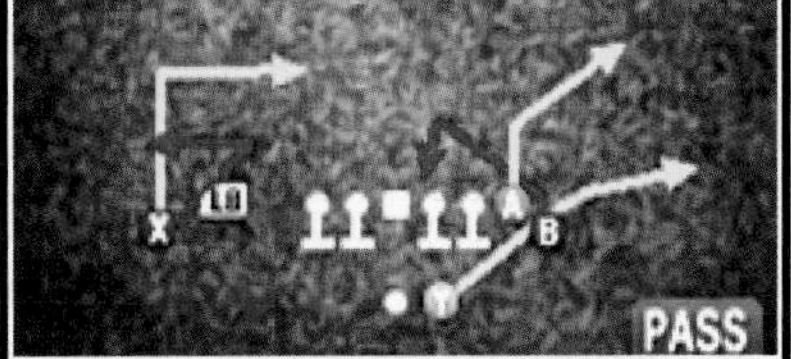

With the Gun Ace Pair formation, we substitute RB Danny Woodhead into the game, as he is a better passing threat out of the backfield. We are looking to isolate him to the flat. The defense has been using man blitz against us, and we want to get Woodhead matched up in the open field with a slower linebacker.

The pressure is coming off the edge, and we can see Woodhead is already open in the flat. The alignment of the formation forces the inside linebacker to cover Woodhead as he goes to the flat. The linebacker does not have the speed to cover Woodhead, and we should get a big gain.

The pass is delivered, and we streak up the sideline before we get pushed out of bounds. Woodhead creates major matchup problems for any defense. His electric speed and amazing hands make him a threat out of the backfield.

Base Play

Trips TE - Deep Fork

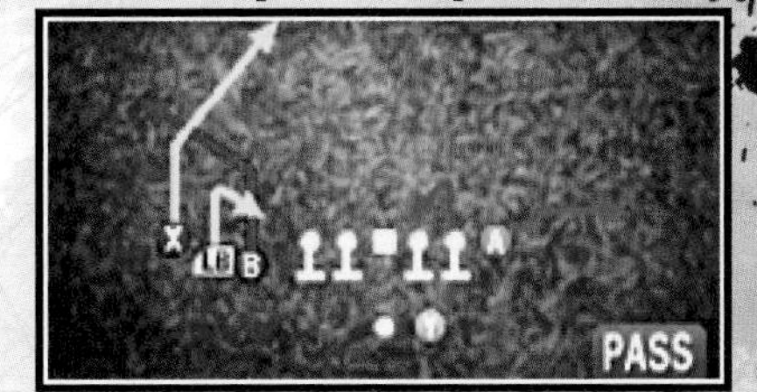

The Trips TE Deep Fork is one of the best plays in the game. We have a Trips formation to our left and delayed blue routes by our TE and HB. The blue routes will first look to block and then release. To our trips side we have amazing deep route options that will put pressure on both zone and man defensive coverages.

At the snap of the ball, we read the defense is in a Cover 3 zone. We are not worried about the blitz, as we have two blue routes helping in pass protection. We quickly look to our "scissor" concept downfield. The post and corner are targeting the deep safety. We look to see who will free up as the play develops.

The safety gives our post inside release, and we deliver the perfect ball for the touchdown. The Trips TE Deep Fork is a very difficult play to defend. Sending pressure will not work because of blue routes helping in pass protection. Zone defense also will find it hard to defend our deep routes!

OAKLAND RAIDERS

OFFENSIVE SCOUTING REPORT

Despite average ratings across the board, Oakland really excels with its depth and speed. RB Darren McFadden exploded last season, and his combination of strength and speed make him a tough tackle and a receiving threat out of the backfield. The WR core possesses great size and speed from WR Louis Murphy and Darrius Heyward-Bey. The Raiders' playbook allows for dynamic return man Jacoby Ford to play above his rating in the slot. Don't forget to sneak FB Marcel Reece into your game plan, as he is one of the most athletic players at his position. QB Jason Campbell has the arm strength; also use him if you want a vertical attack. QB Bruce Gradkowski allows for a "dink and dunk" scheme. The Oakland defense will force the opponent into hurrying its throws, which will lead to good field position and big points in *Madden NFL 12*.

DEFENSIVE SCOUTING REPORT

Speed, speed, and more speed. The Oakland Raiders have so much speed in *Madden NFL 12* that they are hands down the best defense in the game. Rookie defensive back DeMarcus Van Dyke has blistering speed, and while he may not be highly rated he is a playmaker and you should get him on the field. Defensive tackle Richard Seymour will anchor the defensive line for the Raiders and can single-handedly alter opponents' running schemes. Safety Tyvon Branch is a monster in the secondary who has the speed to hang with any receiver in the game as well as play in the box to help with run support. Make sure to utilize your LBs at DE with the LB pass rush package in passing situations.

RATINGS BY POSITION

Position	Rating
Quarterbacks	81
Halfbacks	87
Fullbacks	83
Wide Receivers	74
Tight Ends	89
Tackles	80
Guards	82
Centers	72
Defensive Ends	79
Defensive Tackles	93
Outside Linebackers	80
Middle Linebackers	82
Cornerbacks	92
Free Safeties	84
Strong Safeties	87
Kickers	86
Punters	98

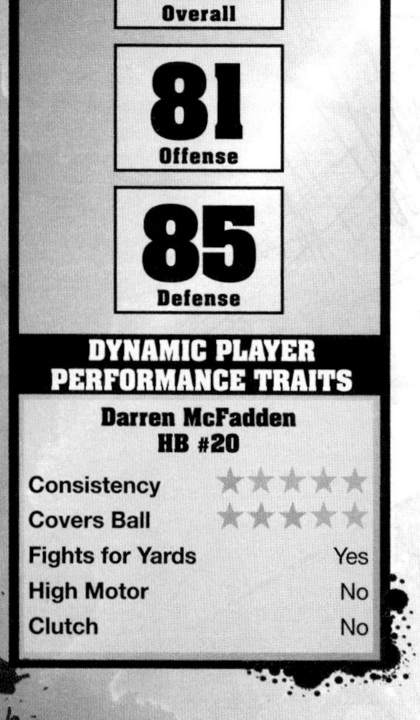

TEAM RATING

76 Overall

81 Offense

85 Defense

DYNAMIC PLAYER PERFORMANCE TRAITS

Darren McFadden
HB #20

Trait	
Consistency	★★★★★
Covers Ball	★★★★★
Fights for Yards	Yes
High Motor	No
Clutch	No

DEPTH CHART

POS	OVR	FIRST NAME	LAST NAME
3DRB	75	Michael	Bush
C	72	Stefen	Wisniewski
C	72	Samson	Satele
CB	98	Nnamdi	Asomugha
CB	85	Stanford	Routt
CB	76	Chris	Johnson
CB	64	Walter	McFadden
CB	65	Jeremy	Ware
DT	93	Richard	Seymour
DT	85	Tommy	Kelly
DT	79	John	Henderson
DT	70	Desmond	Bryant
FB	83	Marcel	Reece
FB	58	Manase	Tonga
FS	84	Michael	Huff
FS	73	Hiram	Eugene
FS	68	Stevie	Brown
HB	87	Darren	McFadden
HB	75	Michael	Bush
HB	63	Taiwan	Jones
HB	67	Rock	Cartwright
K	86	Sebastian	Janikowski
KOS	86	Sebastian	Janikowski
KR	74	Jacoby	Ford
KR	67	Rock	Cartwright
LE	78	Lamarr	Houston
LE	67	Jarvis	Moss
LG	87	Robert	Gallery
LG	71	Bruce	Campbell
LOLB	72	Quentin	Groves
LOLB	75	Thomas	Howard
LOLB	61	Bruce	Davis
LS	50	Jon	Condo
LT	81	Jared	Veldheer
LT	64	Daniel	Loper
MLB	82	Rolando	McClain
MLB	70	Ricky	Brown
P	98	Shane	Lechler
PR	68	Johnnie Lee	Higgins
QB	81	Jason	Campbell
QB	75	Bruce	Gradkowski
QB	66	Kyle	Boller
RE	80	Matt	Shaughnessy
RE	79	Trevor	Scott
RG	76	Cooper	Carlisle
RG	64	Roy	Schuening
ROLB	87	Kamerion	Wimbley
ROLB	65	Sam	Williams
ROLB	58	Travis	Goethel
RT	78	Mario	Henderson
RT	65	Joe	Barksdale
SS	87	Tyvon	Branch
SS	75	Michael	Mitchell
SS	65	Jerome	Boyd
TE	89	Zach	Miller
TE	65	Brandon	Myers
TE	61	Kevin	Brock
WR	75	Louis	Murphy
WR	72	Darrius	Heyward-Bey
WR	74	Jacoby	Ford
WR	68	Johnnie Lee	Higgins
WR	72	Chaz	Schilens
WR	60	Denarius	Moore

OFFENSIVE STRENGTH CHART

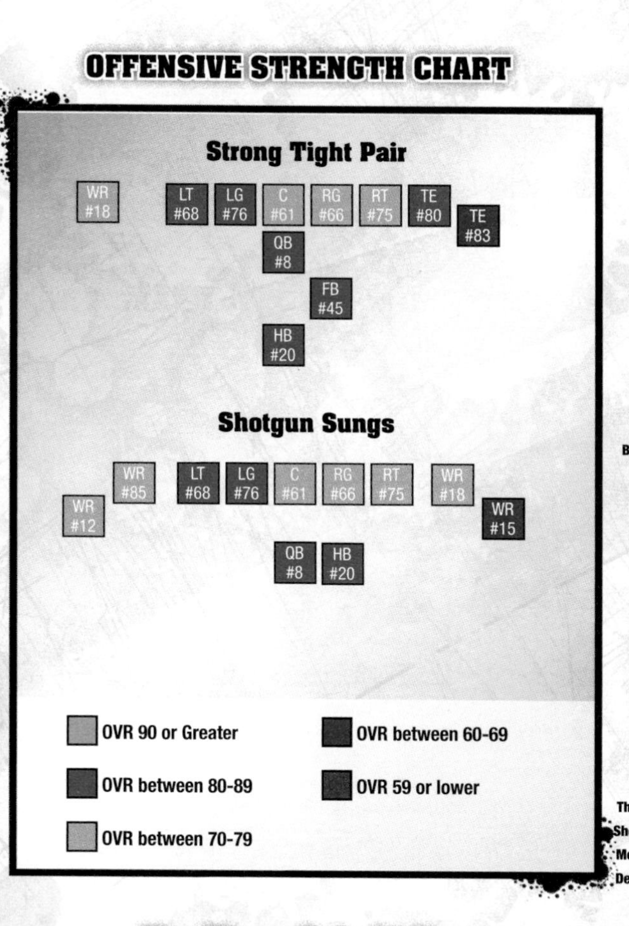

Key Player Substitution

Player: Darrius Heyward-Bey

Position: #1 WR Slot

Key Stat: 97 Speed

What He Brings: Heyward-Bey is the style of WR that makes a perfect number one in *Madden NFL*. He has good size and can outrun almost any defender in the game.

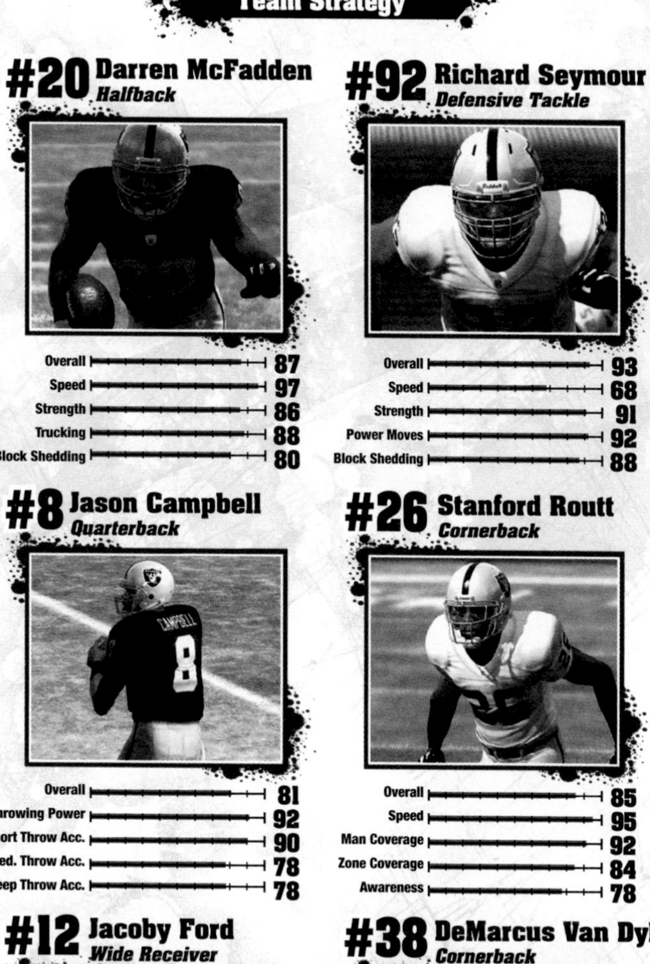

#20 Darren McFadden
Halfback

- Overall 87
- Speed 97
- Strength 86
- Trucking 88
- Block Shedding 80

#92 Richard Seymour
Defensive Tackle

- Overall 93
- Speed 68
- Strength 91
- Power Moves 92
- Block Shedding 88

#8 Jason Campbell
Quarterback

- Overall 81
- Throwing Power 92
- Short Throw Acc. 90
- Med. Throw Acc. 78
- Deep Throw Acc. 78

#26 Stanford Routt
Cornerback

- Overall 85
- Speed 95
- Man Coverage 92
- Zone Coverage 84
- Awareness 78

#12 Jacoby Ford
Wide Receiver

- Overall 74
- Speed 98
- Catch 79
- Route Running 68
- Acceleration 97

#38 DeMarcus Van Dyke
Cornerback

- Overall 66
- Speed 98
- Man Coverage 76
- Zone Coverage 72
- Awareness 45

DEFENSIVE STRENGTH CHART

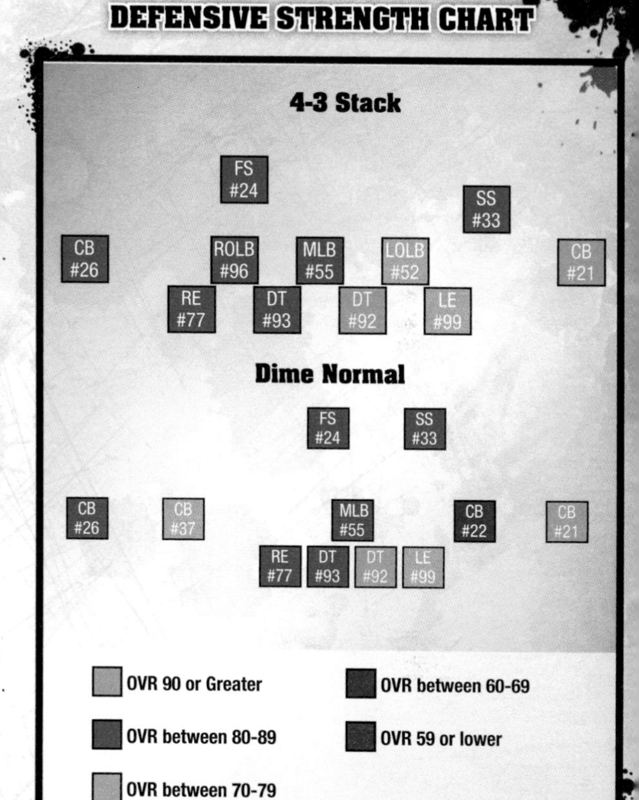

Key Player Substitution

Player: John Henderson

Position: #1 LE in Run Situations

Key Stat: 95 Strength

What He Brings: John Henderson can still stop the run but is buried deep at DT. Look to use his strength at LE against the run.

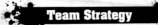

Playbook Tips

Offensive Style: Run Balanced

Offense

- Oakland has great off tackle runs in its playbook for people who want to bang it off the edge.
- Darren McFadden really exploded into the mainstream last season; his talents can carry Oakland's offense.
- Utilize QB Bruce Gradkowski when you need short consistent throws to move the chains.

Defense

- The Raiders D-line is strong enough to stop the run without too much support from the secondary.
- In passing situations, allow Oakland's OLBs to rush off the edge with their elite speed.
- Keep as many CBs on the field as possible; they have the speed to make plays on the ball.

OFFENSIVE FORMATIONS

FORMATION	# OF PLAYS
Gun Doubles On	21
Gun Normal Y-Flex	15
Gun Split Y-Flex	15
Gun Spread Flex	12
Gun Trey Open	18
Gun Y-Trips WK	18
Gun Snugs	9
I-Form Pro	15
I-Form Pro Twins	18
I-Form TE Flip	12
I-Form Tight	15
I-Form Tight Pair	15
Singleback Ace	21
Singleback Ace Twins	15
Singleback Ace Pair Slot	15
Singleback Bunch Base	12
Singleback Doubles	15
Singleback Wing Trio	15
Strong H Pro	15
Strong Tight Pair	12

OFFENSIVE PLAYCOUNTS

PLAY TYPE	# OF PLAYS
Quick Pass	18
Standard Pass	51
Shotgun Pass	70
Play Action Pass	67
Inside Handoff	43
Outside Handoff	20
Pitch	11
Counter	3
Draw	11

Three-Headed Rushing Attack

I-Form TE Flip—HB Iso

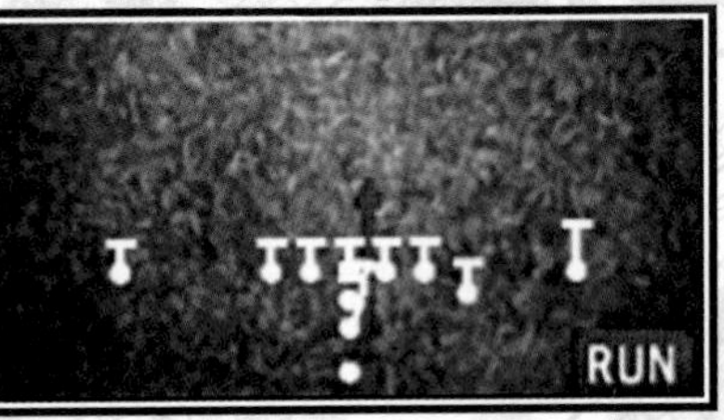

The I-Form TE Flip has the TE on the strong side playing back from the line of scrimmage. The HB Iso gives you a great way to pick up yards on third and short with the Raiders.

The left side of the line is more open at the snap, but we must have discipline and stay to our lane. The HB Iso is meant to hit one gap, and running it properly will pay off here.

The defense was not ready for a run to the middle, and our two linemen have headed into the second level and are looking to punish the safeties. The back looks to make a cut behind his blocker to engage the defender into his block and then head in for a TD.

PRO TIP Add your best blocking TE into the game on short yardage situations to really get a push forward.

I-Form TE Flip—HB Blast Wk

The HB Blast to the weak side is still a power run, but it allows our team to attack inside the tackles. When you have a strong guard like Robert Gallery inside, it is good to use his strength to run behind.

While the defender is able to get some penetration in the backfield, the FB stops him before he can do any real damage. Most players will take the run outside here, but the CBs are waiting, and the run is not designed to block there.

Instead, cut the run back inside the line and pick up as much as possible. This is the optimal way to run this play and will not allow the defense to stack the strong side of the box when they see this formation.

PRO TIP If the defense blows containment outside, cut hard and get to the edge.

I-Form TE Flip - Off Tackle

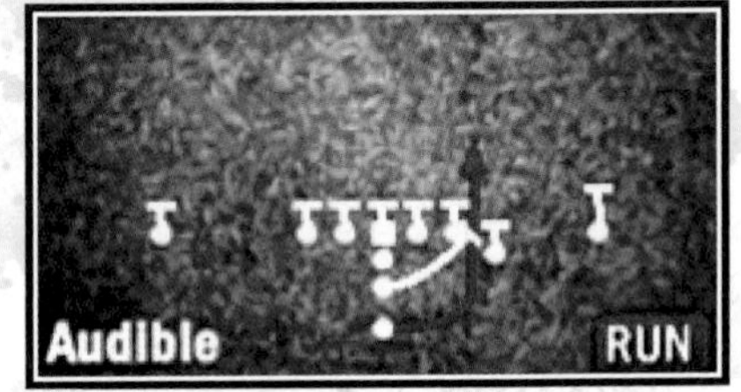

The Off Tackle from the I-Form TE Flip is a staple run of the Oakland Raiders. It can go outside and can cut up inside the tackle if needed. HB Darren McFadden makes this play a TD threat.

McFadden receives the handoff, and we can see that the TE has blown his block. The inside defender has gained position to blow the play up in the backfield. The Off Tackle's design allows us to use McFadden's explosive speed to bust it outside.

We follow our blocks and get outside. McFadden goes for the spin move to get a few extra yards. Cover up the ball when making spin or juke moves, as you are more prone to fumble.

PRO TIP Do not look to only run outside with the Off Tackle. If the defense has outside containment, cut it back inside.

Quick Pass

Strong H Pro - Oak Y - Post

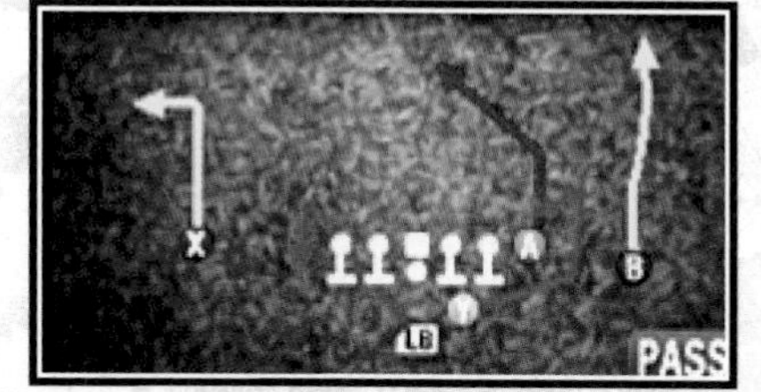

When the defense is blitzing you heavily, we love to call upon the Strong H Pro Oak Y-Post. We use it because of the blue routes in the backfield. Our blue routes will first look to block and then release into the open field. This gives us time in the pocket without worrying about the pressure.

Our FB steps up into the pocket and looks to aid in pass protection. We anticipated the blitz, but the defense dropped into man defensive coverage.

Our FB now releases into the flat, and we deliver the ball for the short gain. If the defense did send pressure, we would look to target the post route and our sideline routes.

PRO TIP FB Marcel Reese has amazing speed, and most teams in *Madden NFL 12* will not be able to account for him.

Man Beater

Gun Spread Flex - PA Deep Outs

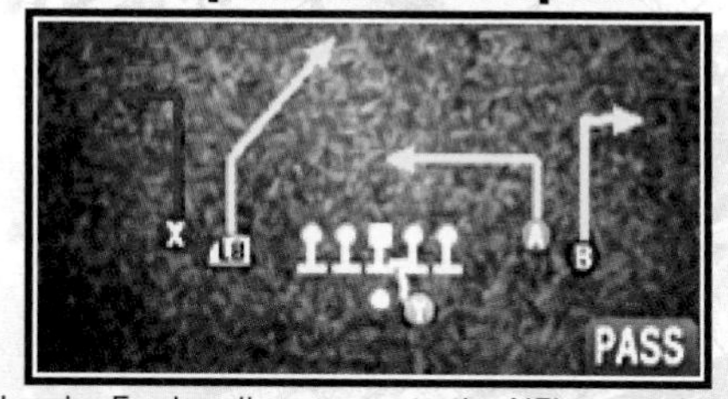

Jacoby Ford really came onto the NFL scene last season as a serious deep threat. With the PA Deep Outs, we are looking for the defense to bite on the play action and sneak the deep pass down the middle of the field to him.

Ford's defenders bite hard on the play action, and we should have him wide open in the middle of the field. We have to be wary of the safety stepping up and laying a crushing blow on the smaller Ford.

We get the pass delivered just in time. Ford makes the grab and the safety delivers the big hit. This play is high risk, high reward. Ford is a smaller WR and will often drop the ball when hit this hard by the safety. Also, play action from Shotgun can work against us if the defense is blitzing.

PRO TIP Have the HB block to cancel the play action. This will help us avoid the sack against the blitz.

Zone Beater

Gun Wing Trio - Curl Flat Corner

The Curl Flat Corner passing concept is one of the best ways to attack zone defensive coverage. We are looking to flood the defense by attacking specific spots on the field. Against a Cover 2 zone, the corner route will be open. Against a Cover 4 zone, look to the flat. Our curl option is a solid route for all defenses.

The defense is in a Cover 4 zone. The deep corner route is defended, but our flat route is wide open. Do not throw late to the flat. Before every play, decide if you will throw to the flat if it is open.

We act quickly and once again get the ball to our big TE Zach Miller. The defense covered all our deep options with the Cover 4 zone. They conceded the short flat route, and we take what they give us.

PRO TIP Often we are forced to settle for what the defense gives us. Do not force passes into coverage.

Base Play

Singleback Ace Pair Slot - PAY - Drag Wheel

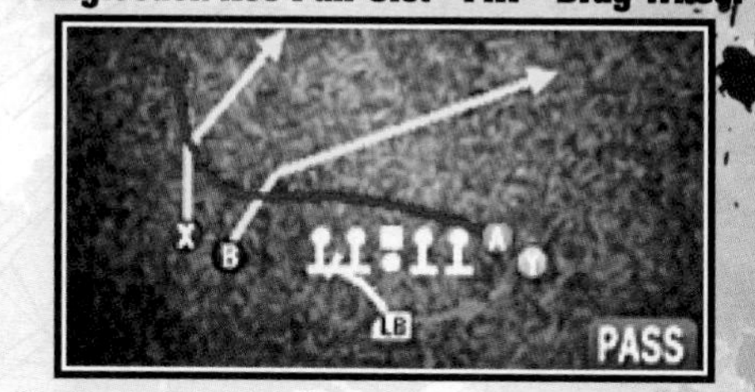

The Oakland Raiders have a threat at the TE position in Zach Miller. We like to use play action to get him the ball. Darren McFadden is such a big threat on the ground that play action will open many things up in the passing game.

Notice the inside linebacker bite on the play action. This will allow for Miller to get behind the zone and make the easy catch!

The play action fools defense, and Miller gets into the open field and picks up the big gain. The safety is the last line of defense and delivers a crushing blow, but not before we pick up the huge gain.

PRO TIP Consider using FB Marcel Reece at TE. He has amazing speed and athletic ability and can play both FB and TE.

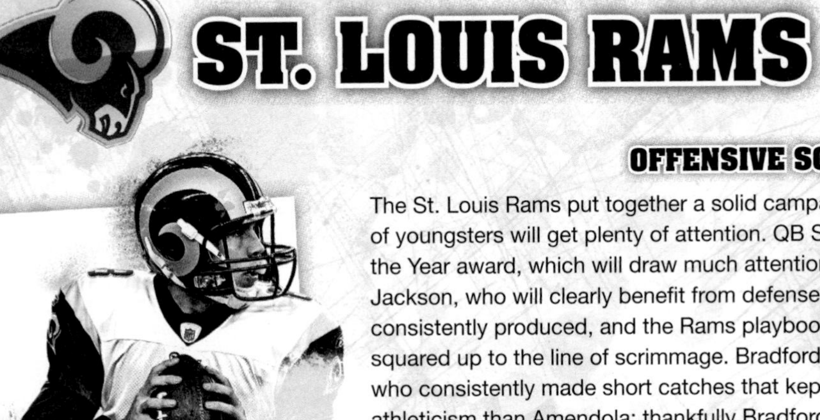

ST. LOUIS RAMS

OFFENSIVE SCOUTING REPORT

The St. Louis Rams put together a solid campaign in the 2010 NFL season. This talented group of youngsters will get plenty of attention. QB Sam Bradford is fresh off the Offensive Rookie of the Year award, which will draw much attention from defenses. This is good news for RB Steven Jackson, who will clearly benefit from defenses focusing their attention elsewhere. Jackson has consistently produced, and the Rams playbook has plenty of powerful runs that get his body squared up to the line of scrimmage. Bradford's accuracy was beneficial to WR Danny Amendola, who consistently made short catches that kept the chains moving. The Rams will need more athleticism than Amendola; thankfully Bradford found a nice speedy target in WR Mark Clayton. If WR Donnie Avery and Clayton can stay healthy, the Rams will have a great tandem in *Madden NFL 12*!

DEFENSIVE SCOUTING REPORT

Steve Spagnuolo is still working on building the defense of his dreams. He has one cornerstone piece with DE Chris Long. The biggest acquisition for the Rams during the off-season was the drafting of Robert Quinn. Quinn has potential to be one of the premier pass rushers in the game. Also watch out for linebacker James Laurinaitis, as he has the playmaking ability to disrupt offenses in the passing game. The Rams are an up-and-coming team in *Madden NFL 12*.

TEAM RATING

Overall	78
Offense	84
Defense	80

DYNAMIC PLAYER PERFORMANCE TRAITS

Sam Bradford
QB #8

Consistency	★★★★★
Senses Pressure	★★★★★
Throws Ball Away	Yes
Throws Tight Spiral	Yes
Clutch	No

RATINGS BY POSITION

Quarterbacks	85
Halfbacks	94
Fullbacks	71
Wide Receivers	76
Tight Ends	72
Tackles	85
Guards	84
Centers	86
Defensive Ends	84
Defensive Tackles	82
Outside Linebackers	75
Middle Linebackers	87
Cornerbacks	78
Free Safeties	77
Strong Safeties	79
Kickers	86
Punters	92

DEPTH CHART

POS	OVR	FIRST NAME	LAST NAME
3DRB	94	Steven	Jackson
C	86	Jason	Brown
C	63	Drew	Miller
CB	80	Ronald	Bartell
CB	76	Bradley	Fletcher
CB	68	Justin	King
CB	71	Kevin	Dockery
CB	69	Jerome	Murphy
DT	82	Fred	Robbins
DT	75	Gary	Gibson
DT	77	Clifton	Ryan
DT	63	Darell	Scott
FB	71	Brit	Miller
FS	77	James	Butler
FS	66	Darian	Stewart
FS	62	Jonathan	Nelson
HB	94	Steven	Jackson
HB	62	Kenneth	Darby
HB	59	Keith	Toston
HB	59	Chauncey	Washington
K	86	Josh	Brown
KOS	86	Josh	Brown
KR	75	Danny	Amendola
KR	64	Mardy	Gilyard
LE	89	Chris	Long
LE	62	George	Selvie
LE	57	Eugene	Sims
LG	87	Jacob	Bell
LG	76	Mark	Setterstrom
LOLB	72	Larry	Grant
LOLB	69	Chris	Chamberlain
LOLB	67	Bryan	Kehl
LS	66	Chris	Massey
LT	83	Rodger	Saffold
LT	63	Ryan	McKee
MLB	87	James	Laurinaitis
MLB	58	Josh	Hull
MLB	51	Maurice	Simpkins
P	92	Donnie	Jones
PR	75	Danny	Amendola
QB	85	Sam	Bradford
QB	68	A.J.	Feeley
QB	56	Thaddeus	Lewis
RE	78	Robert	Quinn
RE	82	James	Hall
RE	62	C.J.	Ah You
RG	80	Hank	Fraley
RG	72	John	Greco
ROLB	78	Na'il	Diggs
ROLB	69	David	Vobora
ROLB	61	David	Nixon
RT	87	Jason	Smith
RT	63	Renardo	Foster
SS	79	Craig	Dahl
SS	60	Jermale	Hines
TE	72	Billy	Bajema
TE	71	Daniel	Fells
TE	71	Lance	Kendricks
WR	78	Mark	Clayton
WR	74	Brandon	Gibson
WR	75	Danny	Amendola
WR	71	Laurent	Robinson
WR	69	Danario	Alexander
WR	64	Mardy	Gilyard

OFFENSIVE STRENGTH CHART

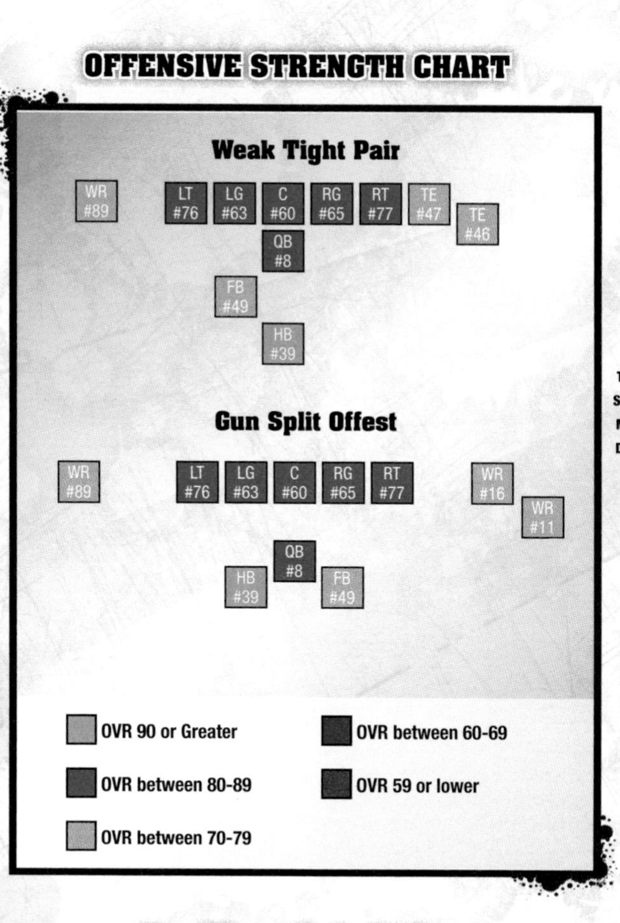

Key Player Substitution

Player: Donnie Avery

Position: #1 WR Slot

Key Stat: 96 Speed

What He Brings: Despite an injury last season, Donnie Avery remains a solid threat. If he can become a go-to WR for Sam Bradford, the rest of the WRs fit in perfectly behind him.

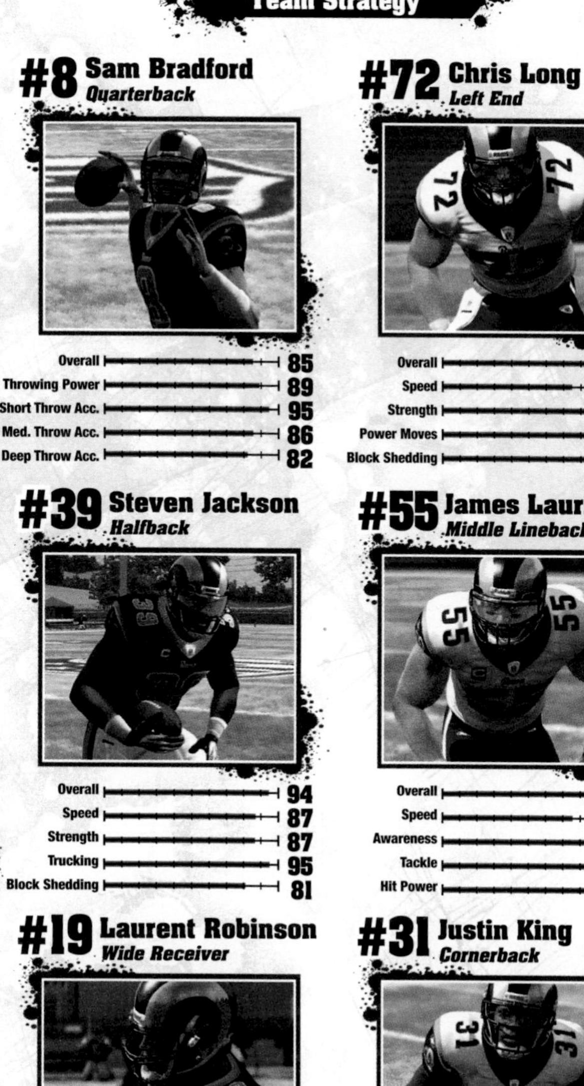

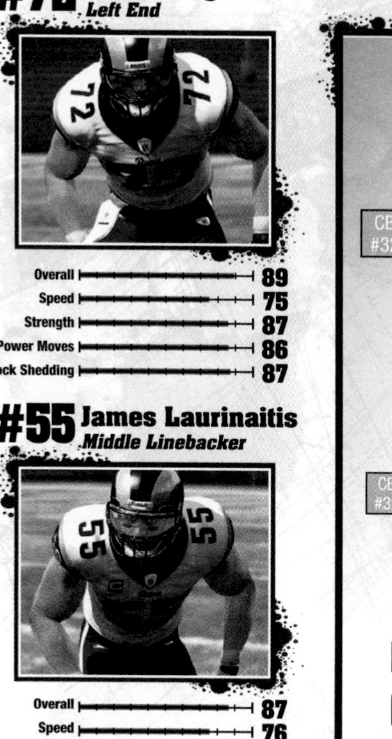

#31 Justin King

Cornerback

Overall	68
Speed	95
Man Coverage	76
Zone Coverage	64
Awareness	65

DEFENSIVE STRENGTH CHART

4-3 Stack

FS #37, SS #43, CB #32, ROLB #53, MLB #55, LOLB #59, CB #24, RE #94, DT #71, DT #98, LE #72

Dime Normal

FS #37, SS #47, CB #32, CB #31, MLB #55, CB #35, CB #24, RE #94, DT #71, DT #98, LE #72

OVR 90 or Greater

OVR between 60-69

OVR between 80-89

OVR 59 or lower

OVR between 70-79

Key Player Substitution

Player: Justin King

Position: #2 CB

Key Stat: 95 Speed

What He Brings: Justin King needs to be on the field every snap. He is a tremendous athlete and will improve the defense instantly.

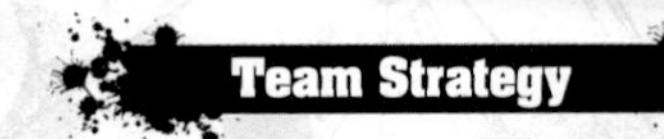

Playbook Tips

Offensive Style: Run Balanced

Offense

- Steven Jackson is a workhorse who can run without a fullback leading the charge.
- Sam Bradford showed great accuracy in his first season, look to work the ball over the middle of the field.
- The team has average talent at the WR core, so really focus on good route concepts over individual matchups.

Defense

- Steve Spagnuolo has done a good job dialing up blitzes at the right moment—work them in on third and long.
- The defensive line has improved and shouldn't need much help from the safeties in run support.
- Keep MLB James Laurinaitis on the field on the field for as many snaps as possible; he is a sure tackler.

OFFENSIVE FORMATIONS

FORMATION	# OF PLAYS
Gun Doubles On	15
Gun Empty Trey	12
Gun Snugs Flip	12
Gun Split Offset	21
Gun Spread Y-Slot	18
Gun Trey Open	15
Gun Trips TE	18
Gun Y-Trips WK	15
I-Form Pro	18
I-Form Slot Flex	15
I-Form Twin TE	15
Singleback Ace	12
Singleback Ace Pair Twins	12
Singleback Bunch	19
Singleback Doubles	18
Singleback Jumbo	12
Singleback Y-Trips	15
Strong Pro	18
Strong Twins Flex	12
Weak Tight Pair	12
Strong Twins Flex	12

OFFENSIVE PLAYCOUNTS

PLAY TYPE	# OF PLAYS
Quick Pass	17
Standard Pass	54
Shotgun Pass	89
Play Action Pass	51
Inside Handoff	36
Outside Handoff	17
Pitch	
Counter	5
Draw	12

Three-Headed Rushing Attack

Strong Twins Flex—Counter Weak

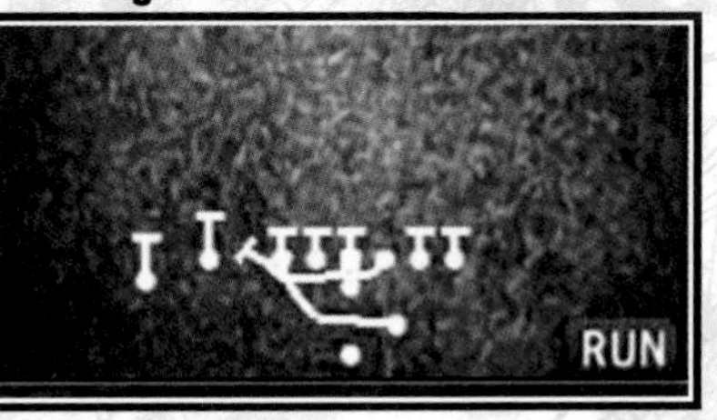

The Counter Weak is a great way to run back to the weak side. However, in this example the defense was overplaying the WRs. Since they are not strong blockers, we look to playmaker to the opposite side and still use the misdirection to pick up a huge gain.

By flipping the play back right when the defense overloads, we can have an outside run that will be open against man defense. The LG now pulls out to the right and looks to get outside. Jackson heads left but quickly cuts back to take the handoff right.

This extra delay gives the FB time to get outside and lead this run to the edge. You should have a good idea by the presnap defense if the counter will be taken inside or outside, but don't be afraid to make a cut if the situation changes.

PRO TIP Use the right thumbstick at the line of scrimmage to playmaker the run; it will frustrate defenses who think they are set up to stop you.

Strong Twins Flex—HB Iso

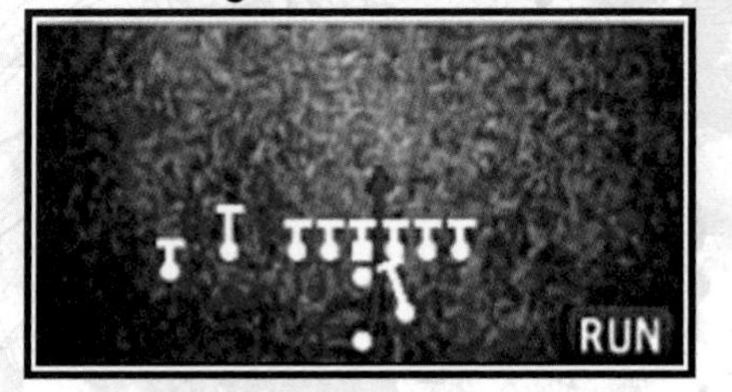

The Strong Twins Flex is a great formation, but it would be nothing without this solid quick run audible down. The importance of being able to pick up short yardage is very important. You must have the confidence to say "You cannot stop me from getting this 1 yard." The HB Iso is that type of run.

Most iso runs that we encounter have the FB lined up directly in front of the HB. However, the FB is offset due to the strong I look. This gives him a nice angle on the rush and allows us to head right at the snap.

Don't be tempted by the hole that appears to the left side of the formation. Our blocking is set up to the middle gap and will allow the back to break big runs when followed properly. Jackson is one of the best at slipping through tight holes on power runs.

PRO TIP A three-headed rushing attack is best when your main running threat can complete all three styles—Jackson is that good!

Strong I Twins Flex - Off Tackle

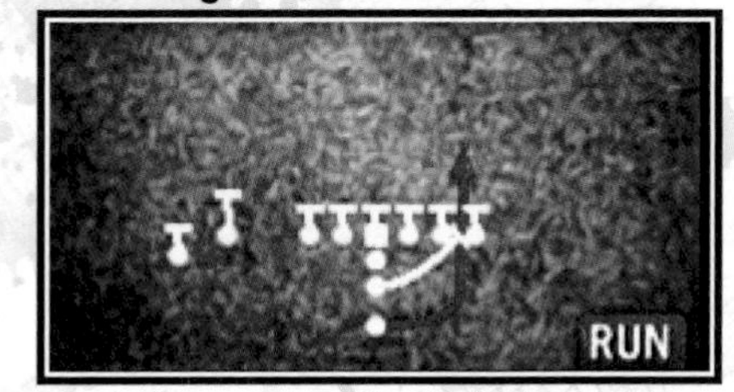

Steven Jackson has been the driving force behind the St. Louis Rams for many seasons. We want to get him the ball as often as we can. Steven Jackson can handle the load; make sure to keep his backups on the bench. The Off Tackle is a fantastic run, as it allows Jackson to use his great vision to decide which running lane to attack.

Jackson gets the handoff and looks to get upfield. A few running lanes have opened up, and we can go inside or outside. Because of Jackson's size, we are not worried about running between the tackles with him.

We choose to break the play up inside, as Jackson is a tough runner. We make contact with the linebacker and fight for a few extra yards. Over the course of the game, Jackson's tough running will pay off as the defense tires out.

Quick Pass

Gun Close Split - HB Wheel

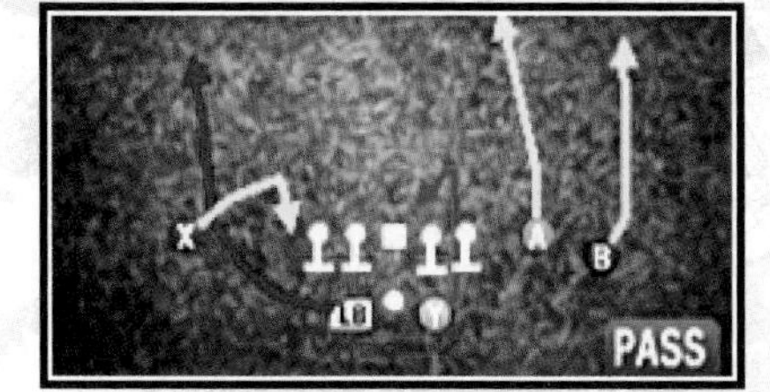

Not only is HB Steven Jackson dangerous as a runner, but he is a threat as a receiver as well. In this play, we have Jackson running out on a wheel route. The wheel route is effective for all styles of defense. Against the Cover 2 zone, wait for the route to clear past the flat defender and deliver the pass. Against the Cover 3 zone, deliver the pass just as Jackson breaks outside the line of scrimmage.

The defense is in a man blitz, and we drop back and read that Jackson is open in the flat. We do not wait for him to clear past the zone defense; the zone coverage is weak because of the blitz.

Jackson makes the catch toward the sideline before he is finally pushed out of bounds. Zone blitzing can be confusing, but it has a major weakness in defending the flat and sidelines. Jackson helps to expose the zone blitz for the short gain.

PRO TIP When facing the zone blitz, understand that most zone blitzes have three defenders deep and three defenders short.

Man Beater

Gun Doubles On - Slot Post

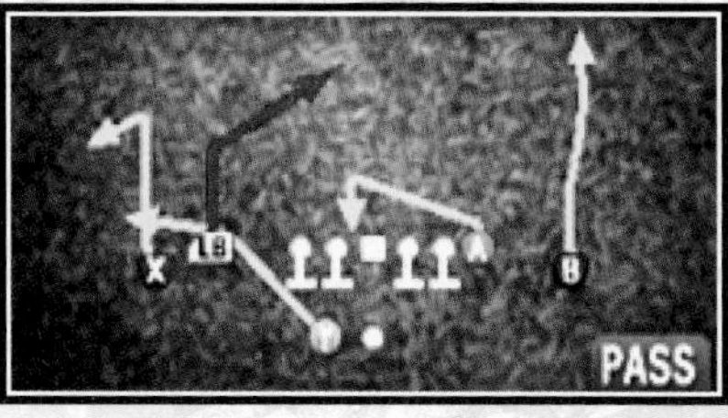

The Slot Post from Gun Doubles On has a high-low read over the middle of the field. The TE is running a short curl while the slot WR is going deep over the middle. This route combination is nice against the zone blitz and against man coverage.

The defense is not blitzing, and they are in a man-to-man coverage. The TE is already in his curl route while the slot WR is getting inside position against his defender. We can check down to the TE if need be, or we can wait to see if the slot WR opens up over the middle.

Our patience pays off, as our slot WR is able to get separation over the middle of the field. The safety is closing in for the big hit. As we brace for this, remember to cover up the ball!

PRO TIP Watch out for the defense playing a man-to-man robber defense.

Zone Beater

Singleback Y - Trips WK - 4 Verticals

The defense has tried to attack us with zone coverage blitzing and man coverage blitzing. They are now looking to play a standard Cover 2 zone, which can be difficult to beat if you are not attacking it properly. When we expect a Cover 2 zone, there is no better play to call than 4 Verticals.

Our WR makes his move at the defensive back. We have four vertical routes looking to attack the zone deep. The defense will have only two defenders deep and have five defenders short. They will not be able to account for all our deep options.

The defense simply does not have the number of players protecting the deep part of the field. The goal of the 4 Vertical is to flood the defense deep for the easy completion.

PRO TIP Key in on the safeties when reading zone coverage schemes. If no one drops over the deep middle of the field, then the defense is play a Cover 2 zone.

Base Play

Singleback Close Bunch - Mesh Post

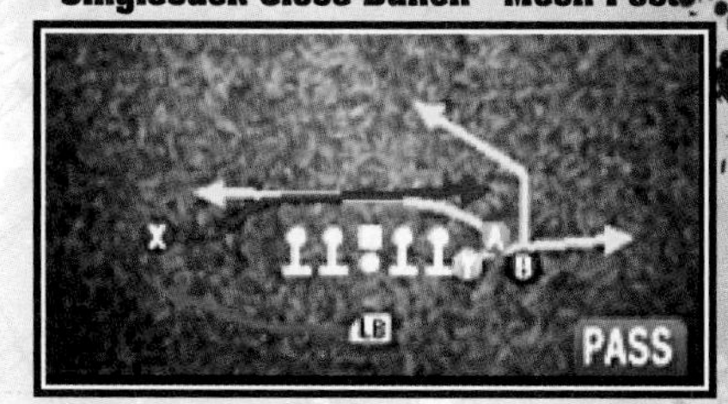

The Mesh Post from the Singleback Close Bunch might be the most balanced play in the Rams' playbook. We are able to attack man defensive coverage with our mesh over the middle of the field. The flat route is great for zone and man blitzes, and our post route is great for beating the Cover 2 zone.

We come to the line of scrimmage confident, no matter what defense is thrown at us. At the snap of the ball, we read man blitz and immediately check our TE running to the flat.

He is wide open against the aggressive defense. We get upfield and gain huge yardage, as the defense was out of position. The blitz means that there is no help in the secondary for the defense to take down our TE.

PRO TIP For a high-risk, high-reward play, hang in the pocket and look for the post down the middle of the field.

BALTIMORE RAVENS

OFFENSIVE SCOUTING REPORT

The Baltimore Ravens are set to be a top-tier team in *Madden NFL 12*. Joe Flacco has continued to improve his accuracy to go along with a cannon arm. The Ravens have strong pass catchers, including WR Anquan Boldin and TE Todd Heap. Work Rookie WR Torrey Smith into your game plan to test slower CBs deep. Let Flacco air it out. RB Ray Rice has elite agility and acceleration out of the backfield. While Rice is a threat on the ground, he also possesses great hands out of the backfield. The Ravens have always had the defense in *Madden NFL*; now the offense is waiting to be unleashed.

DEFENSIVE SCOUTING REPORT

The Baltimore Ravens' defensive squad rivals only the Raiders' as having the best overall defense in *Madden NFL 12*. The overall speed that the Ravens possess puts them as a top-tier team defensively. Anchoring the entire project is Ray Lewis. He has been controlling the middle of the field for over a decade and he shows no signs of slowing down. He is still one of the best linebackers in the game. Ed Reed is the ultimate ball hawk and patrols the secondary looking to make QBs pay for making mistakes. The defensive line of the Ravens is also stacked with some big boys. Terrence Cody and Haloti Ngata have amazing strength as well as block shedding. Overall, the Ravens defense will win you games down the stretch by forcing turnovers and stopping the offense in clutch situations.

TEAM RATING

86	Overall
88	Offense
88	Defense

DYNAMIC PLAYER PERFORMANCE TRAITS

Ray Rice
RB #27

Consistency	
Cover Ball	
Fights for Yards	Yes
High Motor	Yes
Clutch	No

RATINGS BY POSITION

Quarterbacks	88
Halfbacks	92
Fullbacks	90
Wide Receivers	81
Tight Ends	84
Tackles	83
Guards	90
Centers	91
Defensive Ends	90
Defensive Tackles	83
Outside Linebackers	88
Middle Linebackers	95
Cornerbacks	79
Free Safeties	98
Strong Safeties	86
Kickers	88
Punters	96

DEPTH CHART

POS	OVR	FIRST NAME	LAST NAME
3DRB	92	Ray	Rice
C	91	Matt	Birk
C	72	Chris	Chester
CB	82	Josh	Wilson
CB	75	Lardarius	Webb
CB	81	Domonique	Foxworth
CB	76	Jimmy	Smith
CB	63	Chykie	Brown
DT	83	Kelly	Gregg
DT	71	Terrence	Cody
DT	71	Brandon	McKinney
FB	90	Le'Ron	McClain
FB	76	Jason	McKie
FS	98	Ed	Reed
FS	77	Tom	Zbikowski
HB	92	Ray	Rice
HB	79	Willis	McGahee
HB	60	Jalen	Parmele
HB	60	Anthony	Allen
K	88	Billy	Cundiff
KOS	88	Billy	Cundiff
KR	58	David	Reed
KR	82	Josh	Wilson
LE	82	Cory	Redding
LE	78	Paul	Kruger
LE	63	Pernell	McPhee
LG	95	Ben	Grubbs
LG	65	Bryan	Mattison
LOLB	81	Jarret	Johnson
LOLB	58	Prescott	Burgess
LS	50	Morgan	Cox
LT	82	Michael	Oher
LT	63	Oniel	Cousins
MLB	95	Ray	Lewis
MLB	79	Jameel	McClain
MLB	72	Dannell	Ellerbe
MLB	69	Tavares	Gooden
P	96	Sam	Koch
PR	75	Lardarius	Webb
QB	88	Joe	Flacco
QB	79	Marc	Bulger
QB	67	Hunter	Cantwell
RE	97	Haloti	Ngata
RE	55	Arthur	Jones
RE	53	Lamar	Divens
RG	85	Marshal	Yanda
RG	63	Tony	Moll
ROLB	94	Terrell	Suggs
ROLB	63	Brendon	Ayanbadejo
RT	84	Jared	Gaither
RT	70	Jah	Reid
RT	62	Ramon	Harewood
SS	86	Dawan	Landry
SS	66	Haruki	Nakamura
TE	84	Todd	Heap
TE	72	Ed	Dickson
TE	65	Dennis	Pitta
WR	87	Anquan	Boldin
WR	86	Derrick	Mason
WR	69	Torrey	Smith
WR	61	Marcus	Smith
WR	67	Brandon	Jones
WR	65	Tandon	Doss

OFFENSIVE STRENGTH CHART

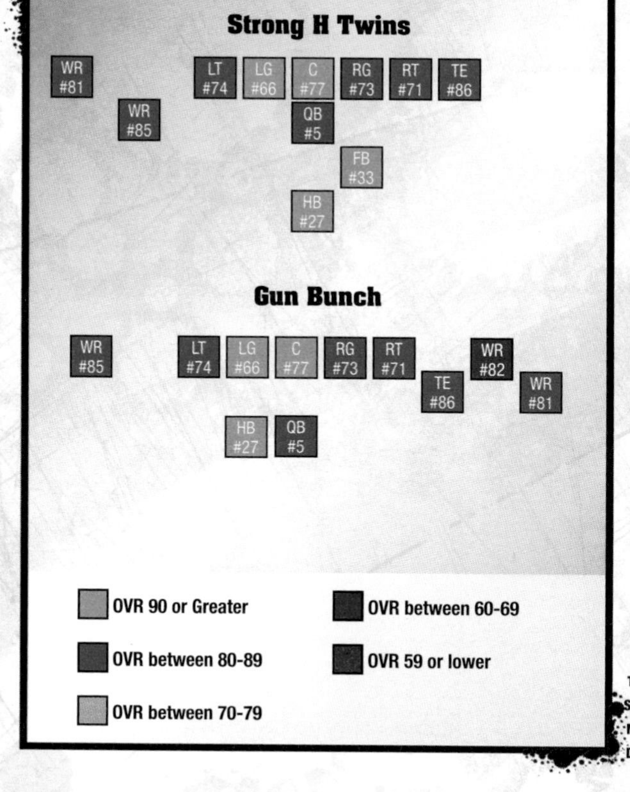

Key Player Substitution

Player: Tyrod Taylor

Position: #2 QB

Key Stat: 87 Speed

What He Brings: Tyrod Taylor can punish the defense if they forget to watch the outside. Bring him in once every half to try and catch them off guard.

#27 Ray Rice
Halfback

Overall	92
Speed	90
Strength	96
Elusiveness	92
Block Shedding	80

#5 Joe Flacco
Quarterback

Overall	88
Throwing Power	96
Short Throw Acc.	92
Med. Throw Acc.	86
Deep Throw Acc.	78

#6 Tyrod Taylor
Quarterback

Overall	62
Throwing Power	92
Short Throw Acc.	88
Med. Throw Acc.	75
Deep Throw Acc.	65

#20 Ed Reed
Free Safety

Overall	98
Speed	93
Tackle	59
Hit Power	75
Play Recognition	99

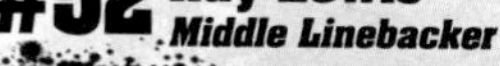

#52 Ray Lewis
Middle Linebacker

Overall	95
Speed	83
Awareness	95
Tackle	94
Hit Power	98

#22 Jimmy Smith
Cornerback

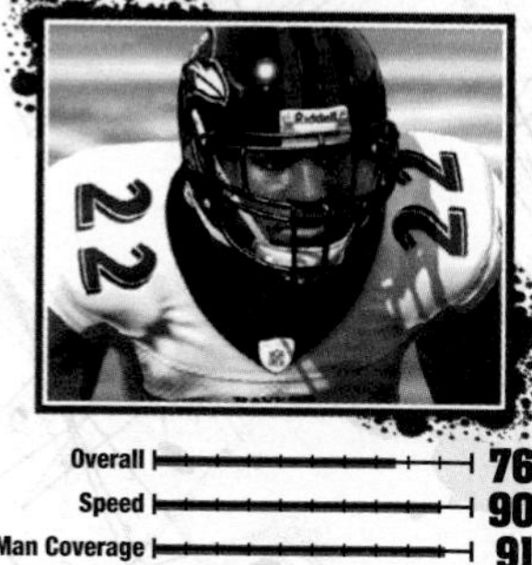

Overall	76
Speed	90
Man Coverage	91
Zone Coverage	84
Awareness	46

DEFENSIVE STRENGTH CHART

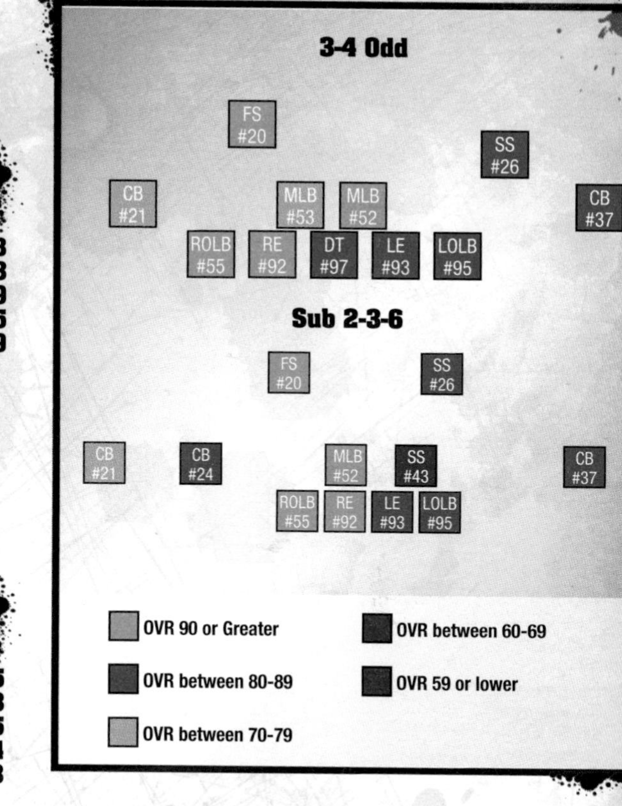

Key Player Substitution

Player: Tavares Gooden

Position: #1 LOLB

Key Stat: 86 Speed

What He Brings: With Gooden buried on the depth chart at MLB, look to use his speed off the edge in pass-rushing situations at LOLB. Pairing him with Terrell Suggs will be a nightmare for the opposing QB.

Playbook Tips

Offensive Style: Run Balanced

Offense

- Joe Flacco has a tremendous arm and can really throw outside the numbers to his big targets.
- Ray Rice has ascended to the top tier of RBs this season. Feature him exclusively as your workhorse back.
- Anquan Boldin gives Flacco a consistent target inside who can help build confidence.

Defense

- Haloti Ngata and Terrence Cody have an awesome one-two strength combination that will lock up the run game.
- Ray Lewis is still one of the best LBs in the league.
- Unleash Terrell Suggs off the edge in passing situations to make the offense keep extra blockers in the game.

OFFENSIVE FORMATIONS

FORMATION	# OF PLAYS
Gun Bunch	9
Gun Raven Empty	12
Gun Raven Trips	9
Gun Split Raven	18
Gun Spread Y-Flex	12
Gun Trey Open	12
Gun Wing Trips	15
I-Form Pro	18
I-Form Tight Pair	15
I-Form Twins Flex	12
Singleback Ace	12
Singleback Ace Pair	15
Singleback Bunch	12
Singleback Doubles Flex	21
Singleback F Pair Twins	18
Singleback Jumbo	12
Strong Close	12
Strong H Twins	15
Strong H Twin TE	9
Weak H Pro	15
Weak Close Flip	18

OFFENSIVE PLAYCOUNTS

PLAY TYPE	# OF PLAYS
Quick Pass	19
Standard Pass	40
Shotgun Pass	59
Play Action Pass	66
Inside Handoff	50
Outside Handoff	19
Pitch	13
Counter	7
Draw	8

Three-Headed Rushing Attack

Strong H Close Flip—Counter Weak

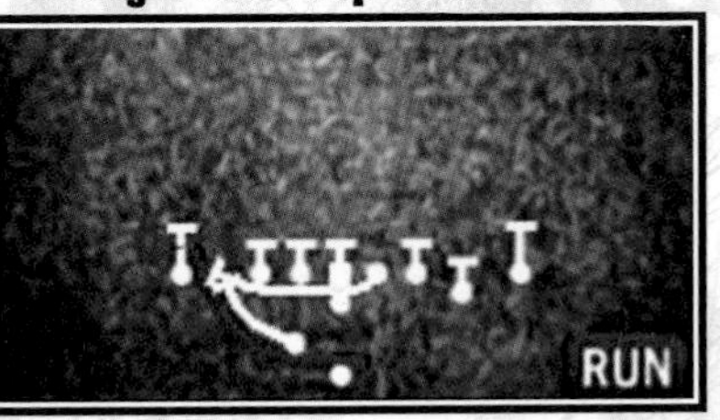

The Strong H Close Flip is a great formation that most online players have not gotten too many reps against. Most gamers employ the Strong Close, so using this formation can really catch the defense off guard. Let's take a look at the Counter Weak, which will allow our HB to get outside to the weak side.

Since the FB is lined up on the weak side, he can hit the outside before the right guard arrives. Look to key off him to determine whether to take the run inside or outside. Be patient; this run looks bad at the start, but the blocking will arrive by the time the ball carrier does.

The back starts making his way outside and can clearly see the safety is tracking him upfield. A great player here will cut the run back inside the tackle. This should propel the WR to latch on to the safety and can be the block we need to spring us into a huge gain.

PRO TIP Make sure to place your best run-blocking WR out to the right for this run. He can pick up blocks once he gets downfield.

Strong H Close Flip—HB Lead

The HB Lead is a different style of up-the-middle run than most in the game. The FB who is offset actually attacks a different gap than the RB. This can be successful because if the defense over-pursues the initial read from the FB, they will be out of position.

At the snap, our back focuses on hitting his assigned gap, but this plan is quickly derailed when the LB waits in the gap for him. The ability to cut back is what makes Ray Rice one of the top backs in the game. He can now follow his FB and look to pick up a block.

The hard cut seals off the defender who was just about to blow the play up. With a guard sneaking through to the second level, there is no telling how many yards we can pick up. There are not many power runs that allow us to hit two gaps consistently, but the HB Lead is one of them.

PRO TIP The HB Lead is a staple run of a power attack like Baltimore's; run it with military discipline.

Strong H Close Flip - HB Draw

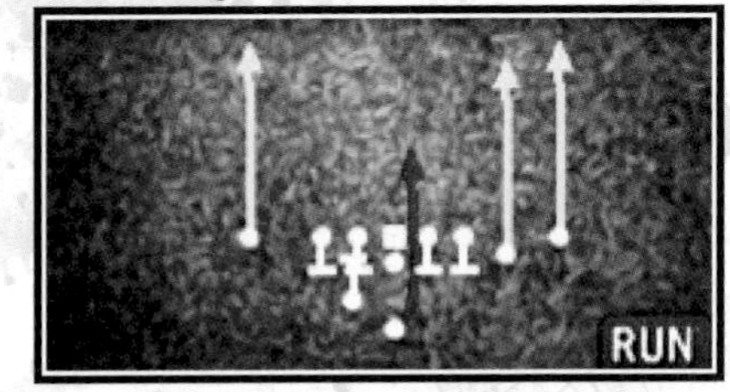

When running HB Draws, the best plan is to find the first hole you see after the snap of the ball. Any hesitation can affect the success of the play. Blocking the play with a fake pass will make the defense respect the pass. Once the coverage drops back to play the pass, you will burst ahead for positive yards.

After the snap of the ball, we see a few inside holes. Look to get upfield as quickly as possible. If the running lanes inside are clogged, look to bounce the run outside.

Once we get upfield, we will have our blockers at the second level helping to chip the linebackers. We will also have our WR helping in the run game.

PRO TIP Patience, patience, patience! The key to successful HB Draws is waiting for your blocks to develop and attacking the open running lanes once they have opened.

Quick Pass

Strong H Close - PA Boot Screen

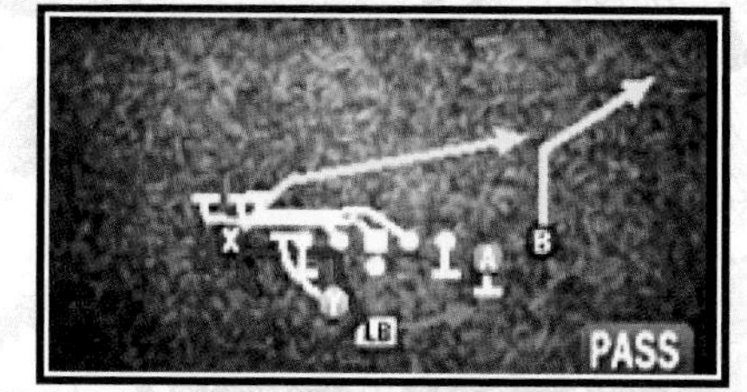

We love the PA Boot Screen. This play is so unique in that we have a play action and then a screen to our HB. Your opponent should be caught off guard, allowing you to take complete advantage. Look for the uncovered HB after the play action and get upfield as quick as possible.

Wait for the blockers to get into position before you make the throw to the HB. There is nothing worse you can do on a screen play than give the ball off prior to the blockers getting into position. If the screen is guarded, look to take off with the QB or simply throw the ball away.

HB Ray Rice may not have top-end speed, but his agility and acceleration are elite. Good things will happen once he gets the ball in the open field!

PRO TIP Reblock the FB to get him on a better blocking assignment; his original blocking assignment often lets the defense in untouched.

Man Beater

Gun Ravens Empty - Ravens Wheel

We decide to come out in an Empty set to put pressure on the defense, as they have been blitzing us all game. The Empty set is great for signaling out where pressure appears to be coming from. In this example, the defense is again zone blitzing us, and we are looking to attack the defense in the soft part of the zone. A general rule of thumb about blitzing zone defenses is that coverage deep will have a three-man shell. Coverage short will also have three defenders matched up against the offense.

This play calls for two of the WRs running wheel routes. They will initially break to the flat and then burst upfield. Wheel routes are great for beating man and zone coverages. We can see that the wheel route has opened up against the zone blitz. However, we are looking to pick up more yards on this play.

The WR on the post breaks to the middle of the field and finds the open spot in the zone defense. We see the deep safety over the top, the short middle linebacker underneath, and finally the trailing safety is out of position. The zone blitz is vulnerable to a player who knows and understands how to attack it properly.

Zone Beater

Gun Bunch - Ravens Bunch Out

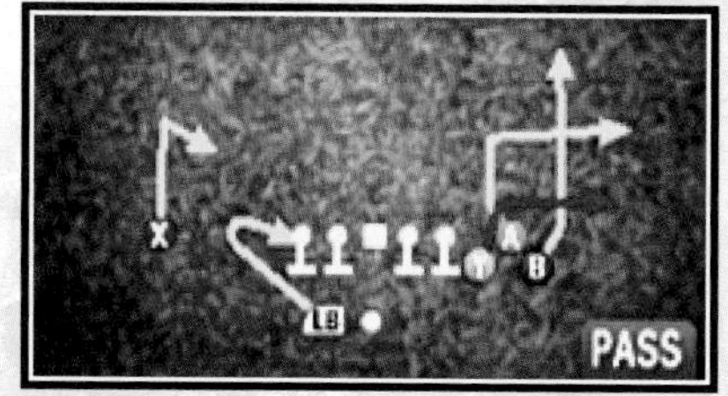

The defense is again playing zone coverage as we come out in one of our favorite zone-beating formations. Instead of bringing the zone blitz, this time the defense drops eight defenders into the secondary. The holes we had during the zone blitz have closed now that the defense has dropped more in coverage. HB Ray Rice is on a blue route to help in pass protection. We anticipated the defense to blitz again.

Rice steps up in the pocket and awaits the oncoming rush. However, there are no oncoming defenders for him to block. We wait just a bit longer and then Rice will release to the flat.

The defenses' three-man pass rush cannot apply enough pressure to force us into making a bad decision with the ball. We are able to hang in the pocket and wait for Rice to release. The ball is delivered while the defense drops back away from Rice. We are able to scamper upfield for the big gain.

Base Play

Gun Ravens Trips - Slants

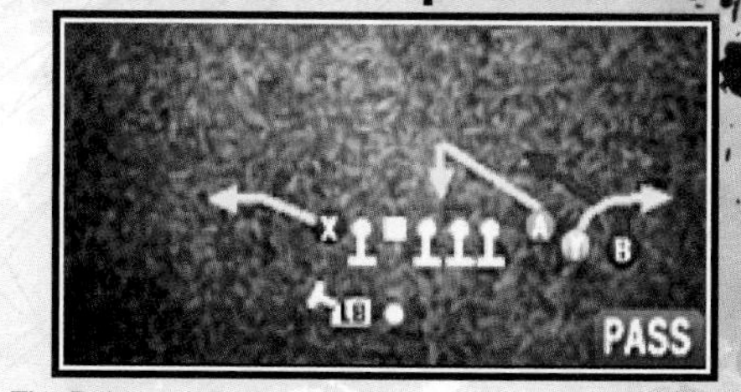

The Baltimore Ravens are the only team to possess the Gun Offset Trips formation. We love this formation because we have a Trips formation to the right of the field to attack zone coverage. We also have isolated our TE to the left of the field. The defense needs to account for the unbalanced line, which helps to give our TE on the line of scrimmage a free release at the snap of the ball.

The defense is in a zone blitz; we know this because we see the safeties drop back into a Cover 2 zone. The zone blitz leaves the middle of the field wide open. The WR begins to take his cut toward the vacant part of the field and quickly cuts back on a curl.

We deliver the high pass to our WR, who makes the grab just prior to the safety's big hit. The zone blitz brought quick pressure, but we were able to find the open whole and pick up the first down.

WASHINGTON REDSKINS

OFFENSIVE SCOUTING REPORT

The Redskins shook up their roster and come into the season with some solid young talent on offense. Their style will shift to focus more on short passes that allow WRs to make plays after the catch. Rookie WR Leonard Hankerson gives the team some much-needed size and athleticism at the wideout position. WR Anthony Armstrong must be an X-factor for your offense. He is capable of averaging big gains and will be forced to do so with even more attention on him this year. Rookie RB Roy Helu will fit perfectly with the zone-blocking scheme from the Redskins' playbook. WR Brandon Banks showed elite agility on special teams, and a good game plan will focus on getting him the ball in space. No matter who plays QB for Washington, look to elite TE Chris Cooley, who can consistently get free running routes against linebackers. Their defense will keep them competitive online, and if their draft works, look out for the Redskins in *Madden NFL 12*.

DEFENSIVE SCOUTING REPORT

The Washington Redskins have a dynamic duo in the defensive secondary. LaRon Landry and DeAngelo Hall are one of the best one-two punches in *Madden NFL 12*. Not only is Landry fast, but also he can lay big hit sticks with his amazing hit power. Hall has elite speed and can cover from sideline to sideline as well as end zone to end zone. Brian Orakpo is a solid rusher off the edge who looks to make sure the QB can't even get the ball off. The Redskins' defensive line has some potential but will need to prove its worth. The Redskins can make some serious noise with their defense this coming year. Make sure to check them out and see if you can harness the power of LaRon Landry!

TEAM RATING

74 Overall

79 Offense

83 Defense

DYNAMIC PLAYER PERFORMANCE TRAITS

LaRon Landry
SS #30

Consistency	★★★★★
Confidence	★★★★★
Big Hitter	Yes
High Motor	Yes
Clutch	No

RATINGS BY POSITION

Quarterbacks	76
Halfbacks	79
Fullbacks	82
Wide Receivers	75
Tight Ends	87
Tackles	78
Guards	76
Centers	63
Defensive Ends	76
Defensive Tackles	76
Outside Linebackers	81
Middle Linebackers	91
Cornerbacks	83
Free Safeties	90
Strong Safeties	90
Kickers	66
Punters	83

DEPTH CHART

POS	OVR	FIRST NAME	LAST NAME
3DRB	66	James	Davis
C	63	Will	Montgomery
C	58	Erik	Cook
CB	86	DeAngelo	Hall
CB	80	Carlos	Rogers
CB	69	Kevin	Barnes
CB	64	Reggie	Jones
CB	61	Byron	Westbrook
DT	76	Ma'ake	Kemoeatu
DT	83	Albert	Haynesworth
DT	71	Jarvis	Jenkins
DT	65	Anthony	Bryant
FB	82	Mike	Sellers
FB	49	Darrel	Young
FS	90	O.J.	Atogwe
FS	75	Kareem	Moore
FS	75	Reed	Doughty
HB	79	Ryan	Torain
HB	65	Keiland	Williams
HB	66	James	Davis
K	66	Graham	Gano
KOS	66	Graham	Gano
KR	61	Brandon	Banks
KR	61	Byron	Westbrook
LE	78	Adam	Carriker
LE	76	Phillip	Daniels
LE	60	Rob	Jackson
LG	75	Kory	Lichtensteiger
LG	62	Maurice	Hurt
LOLB	74	Ryan	Kerrigan
LOLB	75	Lorenzo	Alexander
LOLB	60	Edgar	Jones
LS	56	Nick	Sundberg
LT	80	Trent	Williams
LT	63	Selvish	Capers
MLB	91	London	Fletcher
MLB	81	Rocky	McIntosh
MLB	62	H.B.	Blades
MLB	59	Perry	Riley
P	83	Josh	Bidwell
PR	61	Brandon	Banks
QB	76	Rex	Grossman
QB	82	Donovan	McNabb
QB	66	John	Beck
RE	73	Kedric	Golston
RE	72	Vonnie	Holliday
RE	66	Jeremy	Jarmon
RG	77	Artis	Hicks
RG	75	Mike	Williams
ROLB	88	Brian	Orakpo
ROLB	63	Chris	Wilson
ROLB	52	Markus	White
RT	76	Stephon	Heyer
RT	64	Clint	Oldenburg
SS	90	LaRon	Landry
SS	73	Chris	Horton
SS	72	Macho	Harris
TE	87	Chris	Cooley
TE	79	Fred	Davis
TE	62	Logan	Paulsen
WR	85	Santana	Moss
WR	77	Anthony	Armstrong
WR	64	Roydell	Williams
WR	61	Brandon	Banks
WR	59	Terrence	Austin
WR	64	Malcolm	Kelly

OFFENSIVE STRENGTH CHART

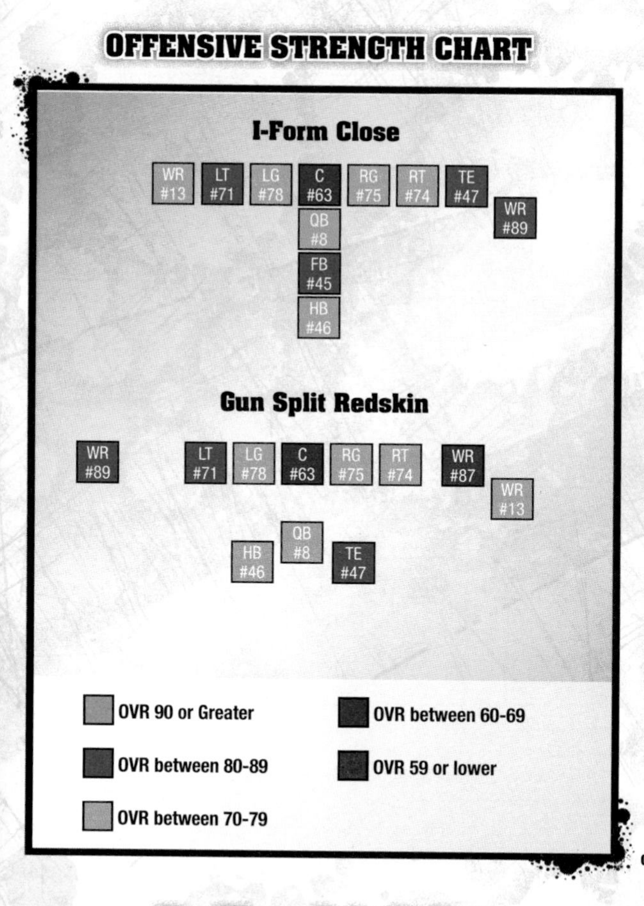

#13 Anthony Armstrong
Wide Receiver

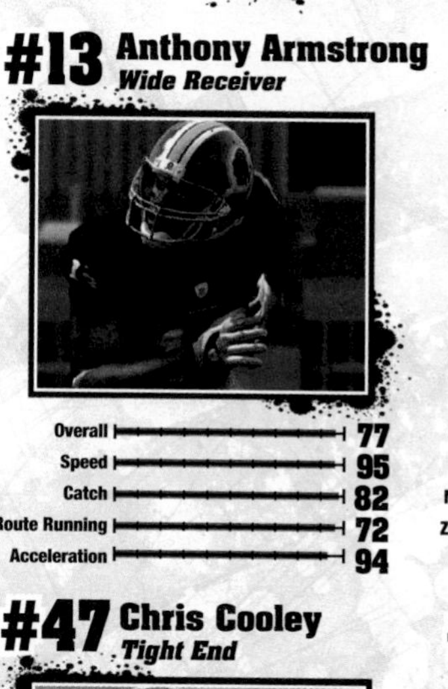

Overall	77
Speed	95
Catch	82
Route Running	72
Acceleration	94

#23 DeAngelo Hall
Cornerback

Overall	86
Speed	97
Man Coverage	86
Zone Coverage	94
Awareness	82

#47 Chris Cooley
Tight End

Overall	87
Speed	78
Catch	87
Jump	85
Catch in Traffic	85

#30 LaRon Landry
Strong Safety

Overall	90
Speed	92
Tackle	88
Hit Power	97
Play Recognition	70

#10 Roy Helu
Halfback

Overall	65
Speed	93
Strength	88
Elusiveness	76
Block Shedding	69

#56 Perry Riley
Middle Linebacker

Overall	59
Speed	83
Awareness	37
Tackle	85
Hit Power	90

DEFENSIVE STRENGTH CHART

3-4 Odd

FS #27
SS #30
CB #22
MLB #52
MLB #59
CB #23
ROLB #98
RE #64
DT #96
LE #94
LOLB #97

Sub 2-3-6

FS #27
SS #30
CB #22
CB #25
MLB #59
SS #48
CB #23
ROLB #98
RE #64
LE #94
MLB #52

OVR 90 or Greater
OVR between 60-69
OVR between 80-89
OVR 59 or lower
OVR between 70-79

Key Player Substitution

Player: Roy Helu

Position: #1 RB

Key Stat: 95 Acceleration

What He Brings: Roy Helu proved he could carry the load in college and now he deserves the chance at the NFL level. Allow him to use his 93 speed rating to attack the defense.

Key Player Substitution

Player: Phillip Daniels

Position: #1 LE in Run Situations

Key Stat: 94 Strength

What He Brings: Daniels can be brought in to stuff the run in short yardage situations.

Playbook Tips

Offensive Style: Balanced

Offense

- If young WRs Anthony Armstrong and Leonard Hankerson continue developing, this team will have threats very soon!
- The Redskins don't rely on any one player at RB—look to ride the hot streak.
- Help out your QB by looking for Chris Cooley in the middle of the field; he is not afraid to head into traffic.

Defense

- The Redskins have plenty of money tied up in their defense—hopefully this is the season they live up to the expectations.
- DeAngelo Hall had an on-the-field resurgence last season, but he has always been a warrior on the virtual gridiron.
- As Brian Orakpo develops, he will become a top talent at the OLB spot.

OFFENSIVE FORMATIONS

FORMATION	# OF PLAYS
Gun Doubles	18
Gun Empty Y-Flex	12
Gun Snugs Flip	9
Gun Split Redskin	18
Gun Spread Flex WK	12
Gun Wing Trio WK	12
I-Form Close	15
I-Form Pro	15
I-Form Twins Flex	12
Singleback Ace	21
Singleback Ace Pair	12
Singleback Ace Twins	12
Singleback Bunch	18
Singleback Jumbo	12
Singleback Normal Skins	21
Singleback Tight Doubles	15
Singleback Twin TE Slot	15
Singleback Y-Trips	18
Strong Close	15
Weak Pro	18

OFFENSIVE PLAYCOUNTS

PLAY TYPE	# OF PLAYS
Quick Pass	17
Standard Pass	75
Shotgun Pass	61
Play Action Pass	58
Inside Handoff	36
Outside Handoff	23
Pitch	12
Counter	4
Draw	8

Three-Headed Rushing Attack

Strong Close—Quick Toss

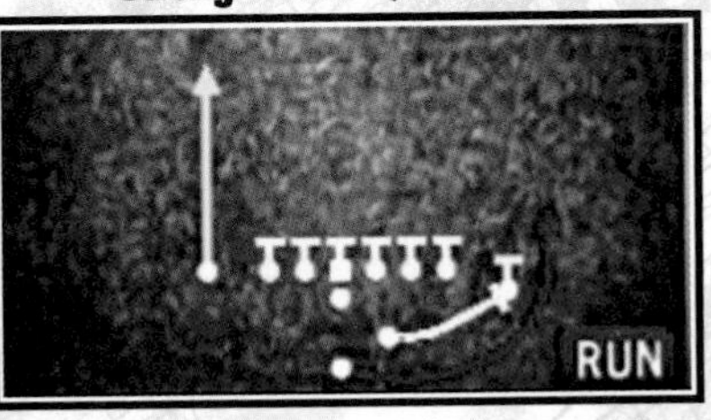

The Quick Toss is a great way to beat a man defense that lacks outside discipline. This is a play that we are consistently audibling to with our offense. Utilize it when the defense is loading up to stop the run to the middle and you will rarely get stopped in the backfield.

Here, the QB reads that the defense is in man coverage, so he motions the WR inside to clear out space to the edge. He will turn quickly at the snap and look to toss the ball out to the HB, who will already be on his way.

The FB does a great job getting outside the formation and providing a lead block for the HB. The HB has two defenders approaching from his left, but he can outrun them due to a poor angle of pursuit. Keep heading towards the sideline and pick up as much as possible.

PRO TIP Get your fastest HB into the game for this run—give rookie Roy Helu a shot.

Strong Close—HB Slip Screen

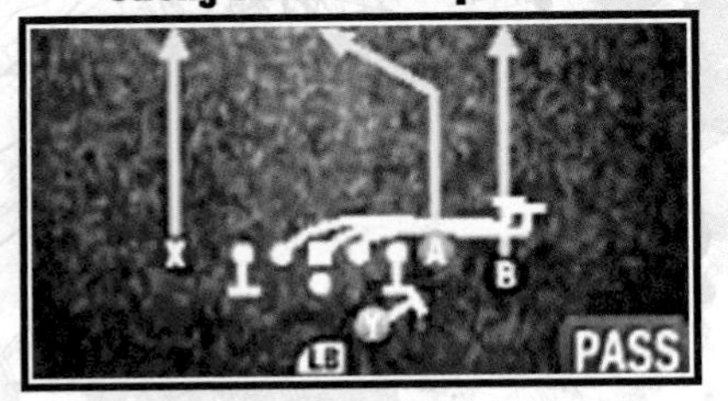

The HB Slip Screen is a great way to beat a defense that is trying to blitz to stop the run. Some teams simply don't have the size up front to slow down the consistent rushing attack, so they will look send defenders; this is where the screen becomes a clutch addition to the run game.

A great way to make the screen effective is to roll the QB to the opposite side of the screen. This adds some length to the throw but it really helps pull the defenders away from where the play will end up going. Be sure to be ready to get the ball out of your hands, as the offensive line pulls on the play.

As the HB catches the ball, he has a clear field to the outside and a wall of defenders protecting him to the inside. This is a perfect setup and the defense will have to think twice about blitzing the run. When playing online, a defender must now respect this formation and user-control a player since the screen could be coming at any moment.

Strong I Close - Off Tackle

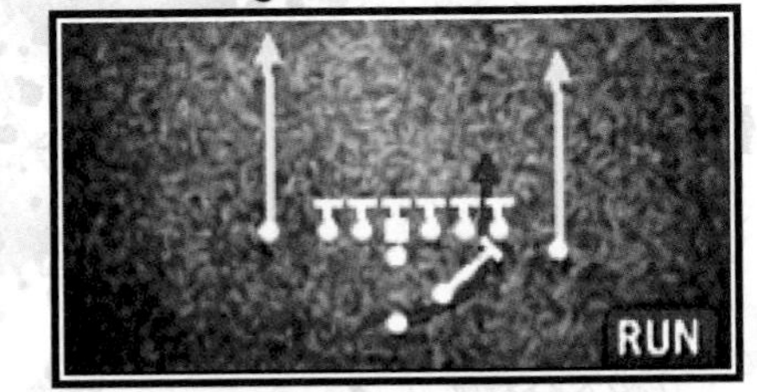

Every NFL team wants the running game to be a vital part of their offensive scheme. HB Ryan Torain emerged last season to carry the heavy lifting for the Redskins. Having a consistent runner in the backfield is crucial for success over the long run. The Strong Close HB Off Tackle is the perfect fit for Torain.

At the snap of the ball, we see an inside running lane and our WR downfield sealing off the outside edge. The beauty of the Off Tackle is its ability to run inside and out. The inside running lane is the more secure option while the outside hole has the big play potential.

We decide to hit the outside running lane in the hopes our WR can hold his block. As we approach, the defensive player breaks off his block and looks to make a play on Torain. We bulldoze over the defensive back and take on the safety. If we can break the safety's tackle, we will have open field ahead.

PRO TIP Use motion in the run game. Motion the flanker WR to the left and snap the ball as he approaches the offensive line.

Quick Pass

I-Close - Skins Drag

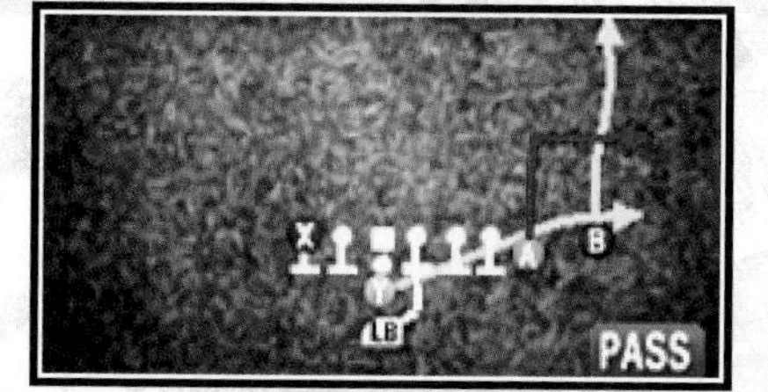

The Redskins have several great power-run formations. The I-Close formation is similar to the Strong Close formation in that the defense will focus entirely on the run. The Skins Drag has a great deep route to one of our best downfield WRs. We expect the defense to send extra defenders to aid in run support. At the snap of the ball, we will look deep to see if there is any safety coverage.

We immediately look deep and see if there is any safety help over the top. The blitz is coming, and our deep threat has a few steps on the defensive back. There is no safety coverage, so we can take the chance going deep.

The pressure was closing in, but the blitz left the defense exposed in the secondary. The defensive back could not keep up with our speedy WR. He makes an amazing catch in the end zone for a touchdown!

PRO TIP Use Block for both the HB and FB for extra protection for the deep ball.

Man Beater

Gun Split Redskins - Slot Seam

When facing the blitz, the Split Redskins Slot Seam has three routes that expose the defensive coverage. Both the routes out of the backfield are quick hitters while our slot WR runs an amazing deep route. Against zone coverage, the deep in and curl route are great options.

The defense is blitzing and is in man-to-man coverage. The pressure is coming off the edge, and the deep safety is responsible for covering our HB out of the backfield. We get ready to deliver the pass before the safety can make a play on the ball.

Our HB makes the catch, as the safety is a few yards back. We get upfield for a nice gain. Beating the blitz is all about being prepared and knowing your hot reads.

PRO TIP Use Block for both players in the backfield and target the slot WR downfield. This is high-risk, high-reward play.

Zone Beater

Gun Empty Y - Flex - Corners

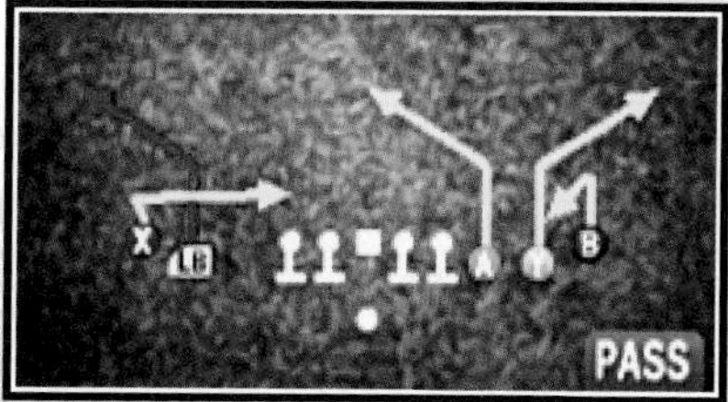

The Gun Empty Y-Flex Corners is our favorite play in the Redskins' playbook to beat defensive zone coverage. We love this play because of its ability to attack the zone downfield. Against the Cover 2 zone, we can read the coverage deep and find either of the corner routes or the post over the middle. Against the Cover 3 zone, we will have one-on-one matchups downfield. Our final way to beat zone coverage is when we face a Cover 4. The underneath in and curl routes will sit under the deep defenders for the easy gain.

Going into the play, we have TE Chris Cooley as our primary read. We recognize the zone blitz and see that the defense is in a Cover 3. The middle of the field is wide open. We wait for Cooley to make his cut on the post and then deliver the ball.

We deliver the ball to Cooley, and he hauls in the pass. The Empty Flex Corners play is one of our most reliable plays to use to beat just about every coverage in the game.

Base Play

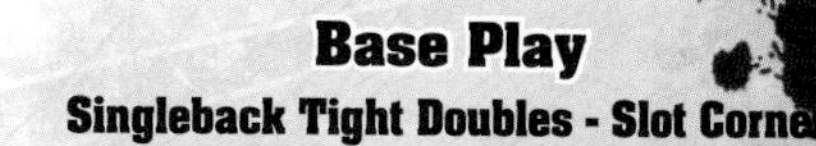

Singleback Tight Doubles - Slot Corner

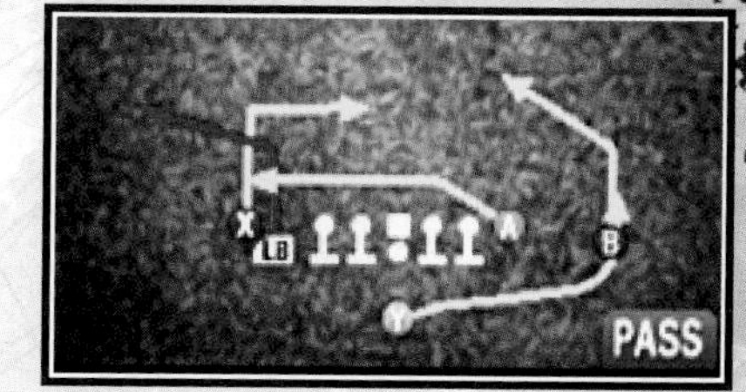

The Singleback Tight Doubles Slot Corner crushes zone defensive coverage. With this play, we want to spotlight our TE Chris Cooley. He runs a drag route through the middle of the field. Having a sure-handed TE gives our QB a safety valve in the passing game.

As the play develops, we see that the defense is completely drawn toward Cooley. He is such a threat in the passing game that he has drawn the attention of two underneath zone defenders. This allows our WR running the corner route to be wide open behind the defense!

Although Cooley was our first option, we must always be on our toes. We could have forced the pass into double coverage, but we adapted to what the defense was doing and hit the WR in the corner for the big gain.

PRO TIP Against the blitz, check down to either Cooley on the drag or the HB in the flat.

NEW ORLEANS SAINTS

OFFENSIVE SCOUTING REPORT

The New Orleans Saints were a popular team in *Madden NFL* last season after an incredible Super Bowl run. However, their *Madden NFL 12* squad will actually give gamers a better overall attack. With the zone coverage being revamped in *Madden NFL 12*, not only will the Saints' defense be improved, but their offense will now be able to attack the tough areas of the field. The Saints' meal ticket is QB Drew Brees, who shines with his accuracy. The Saints' playbook has zone-smashing formations that allow big targets like WR Marques Colston and TE Jimmy Graham to open windows for Brees. Use faster WRs like Devery Henderson against man coverage while sticking with higher-rated catching WRs against zone coverage. RB Mark Ingram finally gives the Saints a balance on offense that takes their focus off of speed. When you take a lead early with their aerial assault, look to slow your drives in the second half by relying on the Heisman Trophy winner Ingram. The Saints' playbook also has excellent routes for the HB to run out of the backfield. Use a faster back with a high catch rating in this situation.

DEFENSIVE SCOUTING REPORT

The Saints' defense wasn't as strong last season because of its overall lack of team speed. However, this will all change thanks to the new zone coverage play in *Madden NFL 12*. The Saints will now be able to blanket the field and use their physical players to change the game. The Saints have a very physical secondary that can make WRs work to get off the line of scrimmage. This will let the pass rush work upfield and put pressure on the QB. Jonathan Vilma will continue to be a staple in the middle of the field for this defense and someone who strikes fear into his opponents.

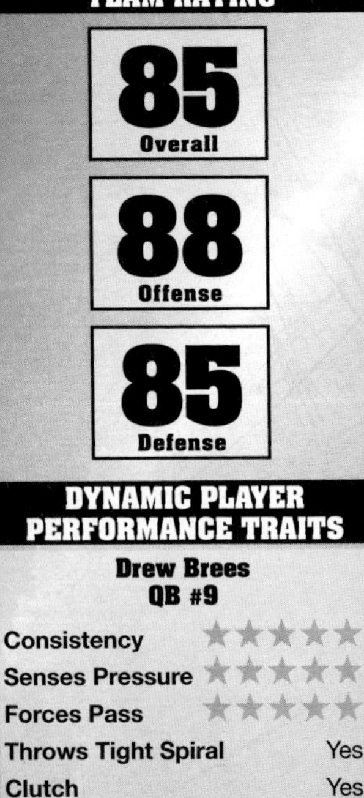

TEAM RATING

85	Overall
88	Offense
85	Defense

DYNAMIC PLAYER PERFORMANCE TRAITS

Drew Brees
QB #9

Consistency	★★★★★
Senses Pressure	★★★★★
Forces Pass	★★★★★
Throws Tight Spiral	Yes
Clutch	Yes

RATINGS BY POSITION

Quarterbacks	96
Halfbacks	78
Fullbacks	82
Wide Receivers	80
Tight Ends	77
Tackles	84
Guards	97
Centers	80
Defensive Ends	83
Defensive Tackles	86
Outside Linebackers	78
Middle Linebackers	91
Cornerbacks	88
Free Safeties	85
Strong Safeties	86
Kickers	78
Punters	

DEPTH CHART

POS	OVR	FIRST NAME	LAST NAME
3DRB	73	Reggie	Bush
C	80	Jonathan	Goodwin
C	65	Matt	Tennant
CB	90	Jabari	Greer
CB	86	Tracy	Porter
CB	73	Patrick	Robinson
CB	76	Randall	Gay
CB	68	Johnny	Patrick
DT	86	Sedrick	Ellis
DT	86	Shaun	Rogers
DT	77	Remi	Ayodele
DT	74	Tony	Hargrove
FB	82	Heath	Evans
FB	62	Jed	Collins
FS	85	Malcolm	Jenkins
FS	82	Darren	Sharper
FS	72	Usama	Young
HB	78	Pierre	Thomas
HB	79	Mark	Ingram
HB	73	Reggie	Bush
HB	74	Chris	Ivory
K	78	Garrett	Hartley
KOS	81	Thomas	Morstead
KR	62	Courtney	Roby
KR	77	Robert	Meachem
LE	77	Cameron	Jordan
LE	75	Alex	Brown
LE	74	Jimmy	Wilkerson
LG	96	Carl	Nicks
LG	63	Roger	Allen III
LOLB	78	Danny	Clark
LOLB	73	Jo-Lonn	Dunbar
LOLB	58	Stanley	Arnoux
LS	46	Jason	Kyle
LT	80	Jermon	Bushrod
LT	70	Charles	Brown
MLB	91	Jonathan	Vilma
MLB	68	Martez	Wilson
MLB	64	Marvin	Mitchell
MLB	55	Anthony	Waters
P	81	Thomas	Morstead
PR	78	Lance	Moore
QB	96	Drew	Brees
QB	67	Chase	Daniel
QB	65	Sean	Canfield
RE	88	Will	Smith
RE	59	Jeff	Charleston
RE	58	Greg	Romeus
RG	98	Jahri	Evans
RG	63	Brian	De La Puente
ROLB	78	Scott	Shanle
ROLB	80	Kawika	Mitchell
RT	88	Jon	Stinchcomb
RT	68	Zach	Strief
SS	86	Roman	Harper
SS	75	Pierson	Prioleau
SS	66	Chris	Reis
TE	77	Jimmy	Graham
TE	76	David	Thomas
TE	61	Tory	Humphrey
WR	88	Marques	Colston
WR	76	Devery	Henderson
WR	77	Robert	Meachem
WR	78	Lance	Moore
WR	62	Courtney	Roby
WR	61	Adrian	Arrington

OFFENSIVE STRENGTH CHART

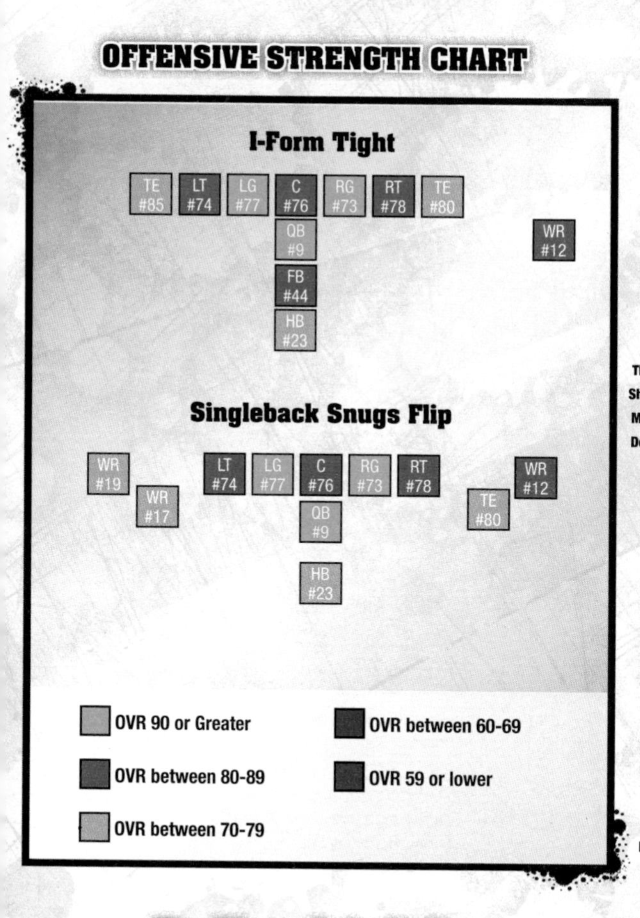

Key Player Substitution

Player: Devery Henderson

Position: #3 WR Slot

Key Stat: 98 Speed

What He Brings: Devery Henderson is one of the fastest players in *Madden NFL 12*. By placing him in the slot we can use his straight-ahead speed to our advantage.

#9 Drew Brees
Quarterback

Overall	96
Throwing Power	88
Short Throw Acc.	95
Med. Throw Acc.	92
Deep Throw Acc.	85

#12 Marques Colston
Wide Receiver

Overall	88
Speed	83
Catch	96
Route Running	92
Acceleration	85

#80 Jimmy Graham
Tight End

Overall	77
Speed	85
Catch	81
Jump	92
Catch in Traffic	77

#51 Jonathan Vilma
Middle Linebacker

Overall	91
Speed	84
Awareness	92
Tackle	93
Hit Power	84

#22 Tracy Porter
Cornerback

Overall	86
Speed	93
Man Coverage	93
Zone Coverage	86
Awareness	79

#28 Usama Young
Free Safety

Overall	72
Speed	90
Tackle	60
Hit Power	40
Play Recognition	58

DEFENSIVE STRENGTH CHART

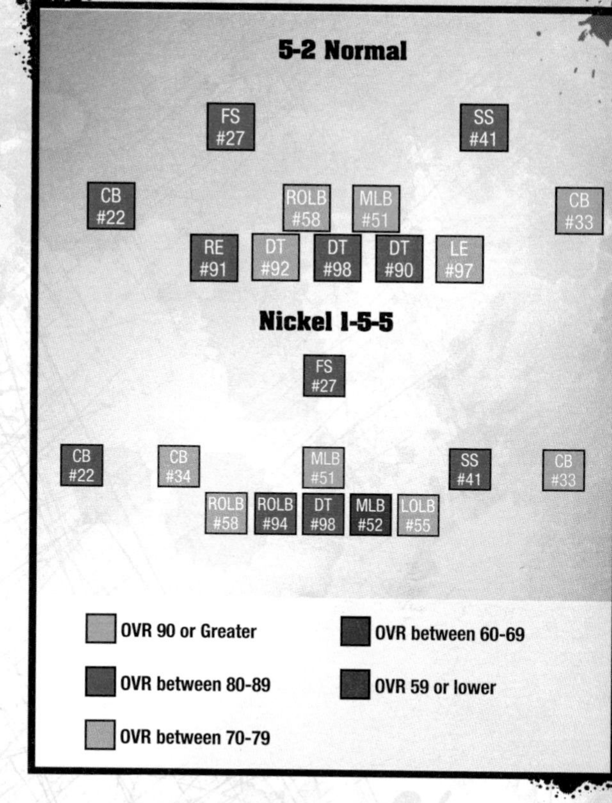

Key Player Substitution

Player: Darren Sharper

Position: #4 CB (46 Speed Package Only)

Key Stat: 91 Awareness

What He Brings: The 46 speed package will place the fourth CB in the LB spot in the box. By placing Sharper in here, we can get all of his pop.

Playbook Tips

Offensive Style: Pass Heavy

Offense

- Try using rookie RB Mark Ingram in the Strong Close formation, because he can break runs inside or outside.
- Drew Brees is pivotal for offenses who demand accuracy from their QB; he can hit any window.
- Marques Colston and Jimmy Graham are big targets who can get open on the sideline.

Defense

- Jonathan Vilma is an incredible talent who should be on the field for every defensive snap.
- The Saints have cornerbacks that do a great job getting up in the WRs' faces and forcing them to work off the line.
- Sending a blitz on third and long is a good idea since the defensive line lacks an elite pass rusher.

OFFENSIVE FORMATIONS

FORMATION	# OF PLAYS
Gun 4WR Saints Trey	15
Gun Doubles WK	15
Gun Empty Trey	12
Gun Empty Y-Saints	12
Gun Split Offset	12
Gun Spread Y-Slot	15
Gun Tight	12
Gun Wing Trio WK	18
I-Form Pro	15
I-Form Tight	15
I-Form Twins Flex	21
Singleback Ace	18
Singleback Bunch Base	12
Singleback Doubles	15
Singleback Jumbo	12
Singleback Snugs Flip	18
Singleback Twin TE Flex	15
Singleback Y-Trips	18
Strong Close	12
Weak H Twins	12

OFFENSIVE PLAYCOUNTS

PLAY TYPE	# OF PLAYS
Quick Pass	15
Standard Pass	58
Shotgun Pass	85
Play Action Pass	48
Inside Handoff	38
Outside Handoff	9
Pitch	12
Counter	5
Draw	11

Three-Headed Rushing Attack

I-Form Tight - HB Toss

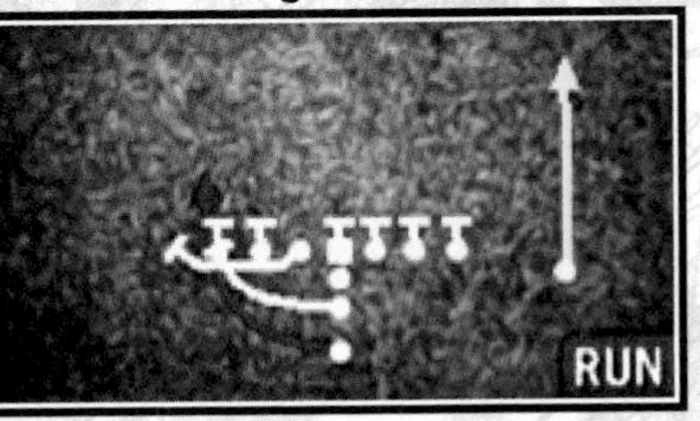

A perfect complementing play for the HB Blast is the I-Form Tight HB Toss. For this play, we substitute our faster HB into the game as we look to get the ball toward the outside of the field. We love this play because of its potential. If the defense can reach the edge and push the run back toward the middle of the field, be sure to cut the run back inside.

As our HB gets the toss, our FB lays a great block on the last outside defender. We can now use our HB's explosive speed to get to the outside.

We look to shake the safety who is closing in on the HB. Rather than trying to run through the defender, we quickly try to juke past him.

PRO TIP If the defense breaks in on the outside, move back up toward the middle of the field and cut your losses short.

I-Form Tight—HB Iso

The I-Form Tight—HB Iso is a great way to take the defense's focus away from the passing game. While New Orleans is known for their great QB and talent on the outside, they are also able to close out football games with this type of running attack.

The Saints have two of the best guards in the game—they can really clear holes up the middle. Look to follow the FB straight through the hole and into the second tier of the defense.

The HB Iso is used to move the chains and close out football games. Don't get too fancy trying to make cuts and moves. Cover up the football and keep the clock running. A turnover could really put your defense in a tough spot.

PRO TIP Mark Ingram is the perfect back for achieving success with this run.

I-Form Tight - HB Blast

The HB Blast from the I-Form Tight formation is designed to run behind the left tackle. The I-Tight is a true power run formation and complements the other runs from this formation. You can expect to move the chains drive after drive when running the HB Blast.

Pierre Thomas is our HB of choice for this play. Thomas follows the fullback up toward the blocks being made by the offensive line. We look to the outside edge to see if we can break the run outside. The defense has done a good job of keeping containment outside.

We continue moving between the tackles and follow our blockers upfield. Thomas is a tough runner and is able to get upfield quickly. We are almost in the secondary for the big gain.

PRO TIP At the snap of the ball, look to bounce the ball outside for the big gain. If the hole is closed, follow the design of the play inside.

Quick Pass

I-Form Tight—Saints Swing Screen

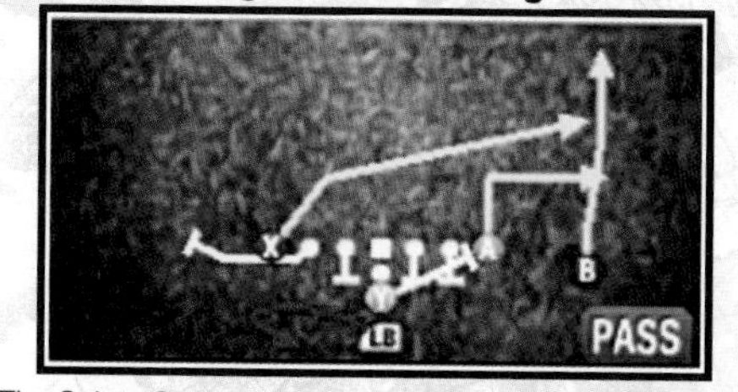

The Saints Swing Screen is a unique play in the Saints' playbook. Head coach Sean Payton is a fan of calling unique plays to catch the defense off guard. Look to use the Saints Swing Screen to catch aggressive defenses in bad spots.

The LG will be our only blocker on this screen out to the left. The action of the play is to roll the QB right, and the natural routes coming across the field will give the defense no clue that they are about to be beaten.

Roll the QB out to the right and look for crossing routes. Once the screen is set up, look to bullet a pass out to the HB, who will be ready. Once he hauls in the catch, the HB should try to get outside against man defense or cut off his block against zone.

PRO TIP If the screen is covered, simply stay calm and look to one of the routes on the right side of the field.

Man Beater

Gun Tight - Saints Spots Shake

The Saints have a nice Gun Tight formation for facing man-to-man defense. Against the blitz it is even better! The compression of the set helps to create natural rubs and picks, which allow our offensive players to get open in coverage. We like to highlight our HB in the Saints Spot Shake as he runs a route out of the backfield; this is very difficult for the defense to account for.

As the play develops, our HB will break out to the flat and will force his man defender to get into position quickly. The speed of our HB is what makes this play so difficult to defend. A quick pass from our QB can spring our HB for a big gain.

The blitz was on, and we were able to pick up a huge gain as we ran toward the sideline. The man defender was too slow in covering our HB and had no extra help in the defensive secondary.

PRO TIP When running this play, make sure that your fastest HB is in the backfield and that this is your first read against the blitz.

Zone Beater

Gun Empty Y - Saints - Quick Screens

A high-powered blitzing defense has been the staple of the *Madden NFL* community over the past few seasons. Being able to beat defensive pressure is vital to the success of any offensive scheme. Quick Screens is a great play to attack any blitz in the game. The design of the play allows us to attack the outside edge of the field. Blitzing defenses are most vulnerable in this area, and we are able to capitalize for big plays in the passing game.

The pressure on this play is coming from the slot defenders on both sides of the offensive line. We quickly scan the field and see both our screen routes getting into position.

Our blocking WR blocks the man defender just enough to spring us free into the secondary. The speed of our HB takes this play to the next level. Every time the defense blitzes, we look to be just as aggressive in the passing game.

Base Play

Gun 4 WR Saints Trey - Saints HB Angle

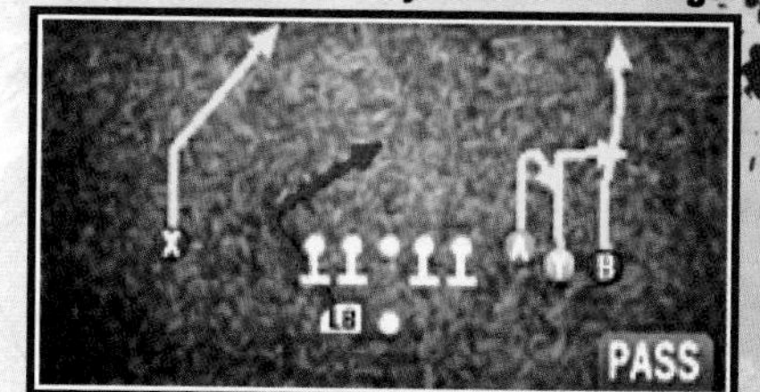

The flexibility of the Saints HB Angle makes it one of the best plays in the entire game. The HB's route out of the backfield is ideal for man defensive coverage and for any blitz packages. To the right of the field, we have a trips alignment with a curl route for beating man-to-man and an out and streak pattern to help beat zone coverage. Our isolated WR to the left is on a deep post, which is a nice route to stretch the defense down field.

We see the defense is playing man-to-man and has dropped a zone defender over the middle of the field to stop our HB's angle route. Our next read is to the curl route. The big-target WR is getting into his route and looks to be in good position against his defender.

The pass is delivered high to only where our WR can get it. He hauls in the pass and picks up the first down. The defense will find it difficult to stop this play no matter what defense they are in!

PRO TIP Position your best downfield WR on the deep post. This is a big time route that can shape how the defense will want to cover you.

SEATTLE SEAHAWKS

OFFENSIVE SCOUTING REPORT

The Seattle Seahawks shocked the world by defeating the defending Super Bowl Champion Saints in the first round of the play-offs. In *Madden NFL 12*, Seattle will shock you with their toughness, which leads to a very balanced attack. By starting the agile Leon Washington at RB, Seattle gets the speed boost that it desperately needs. Don't rely too heavily on Washington for short yardage; instead pass the duties to Marshawn Lynch. Lynch showed he is capable of making big runs in tough situations last season and is a beast in *Madden NFL 12*. On the outside, reenergized WR Mike Williams has the size and is a solid possession WR. On the other side, utilize WR Golden Tate and take advantage of his speed.

DEFENSIVE SCOUTING REPORT

The Seahawks' defense has the ability to be very solid with the right adjustments. The Hawks have solid linebackers who can control the run game. The defensive line is also very solid against the run and can often get penetration into the backfield. In the secondary, Earl Thomas looks to make a name for himself as a threat to force turnovers if you throw his way. Seattle does have solid CBs who can defend average talent, but work on a scheme that allows your OLBs to work towards the QB and rush his throws to help them out.

RATINGS BY POSITION

Quarterbacks	84	Defensive Tackles	85
Halfbacks	81	Outside Linebackers	83
Fullbacks	76	Middle Linebackers	88
Wide Receivers	75	Cornerbacks	82
Tight Ends	76	Free Safeties	82
Tackles	80	Strong Safeties	84
Guards	76	Kickers	88
Centers	74	Punters	81
Defensive Ends	83		

TEAM RATING

76	Overall
81	Offense
84	Defense

DYNAMIC PLAYER PERFORMANCE TRAITS

Marshawn Lynch
HB #24

Consistency	★★★★★
Covers Ball	★★★★★
Fights for Yards	Yes
High Motor	No
Clutch	Yes

DEPTH CHART

POS	OVR	FIRST NAME	LAST NAME
3DRB	77	Justin	Forsett
C	74	Chris	Spencer
C	62	Chris	White
CB	87	Marcus	Trufant
CB	76	Kelly	Jennings
CB	67	Walter	Thurmond III
CB	62	Roy	Lewis
CB	59	Kennard	Cox
DT	85	Brandon	Mebane
DT	77	Junior	Siavii
DT	78	Colin	Cole
DT	64	Craig	Terrill
FB	76	Michael	Robinson
FS	82	Earl	Thomas
FS	78	Jordan	Babineaux
FS	59	Mark	LeGree
HB	81	Marshawn	Lynch
HB	77	Justin	Forsett
HB	75	Leon	Washington
K	88	Olindo	Mare
KOS	88	Olindo	Mare
KR	75	Leon	Washington
KR	77	Justin	Forsett
LE	87	Chris	Clemons
LE	79	Raheem	Brock
LE	60	Dexter	Davis
LG	73	Tyler	Polumbus
LG	74	Stacy	Andrews
LG	81	Chester	Pitts
LOLB	82	Aaron	Curry
LOLB	62	Matt	McCoy
LOLB	62	K.J.	Wright
LS	47	Clint	Gresham
LT	83	Russell	Okung
LT	62	Paul	McQuistan
MLB	88	Lofa	Tatupu
MLB	63	Joe	Pawelek
P	83	Jon	Ryan
PR	75	Leon	Washington
QB	84	Matt	Hasselbeck
QB	73	Charlie	Whitehurst
QB	66	J.P.	Losman
RE	78	Red	Bryant
RE	73	Kentwan	Balmer
RE	70	Jay	Richardson
RG	79	Max	Unger
RG	74	John	Moffitt
RG	74	Mike	Gibson
ROLB	83	David	Hawthorne
ROLB	68	Will	Herring
ROLB	79	LeRoy	Hill
RT	76	James	Carpenter
RT	75	Sean	Locklear
RT	70	William	Robinson
SS	84	Lawyer	Milloy
SS	69	Kam	Chancellor
TE	76	John	Carlson
TE	67	Cameron	Morrah
TE	63	Anthony	McCoy
WR	83	Mike	Williams
WR	71	Ben	Obomanu
WR	72	Brandon	Stokley
WR	70	Deon	Butler
WR	71	Golden	Tate
WR	69	Ruvell	Martin

OFFENSIVE STRENGTH CHART

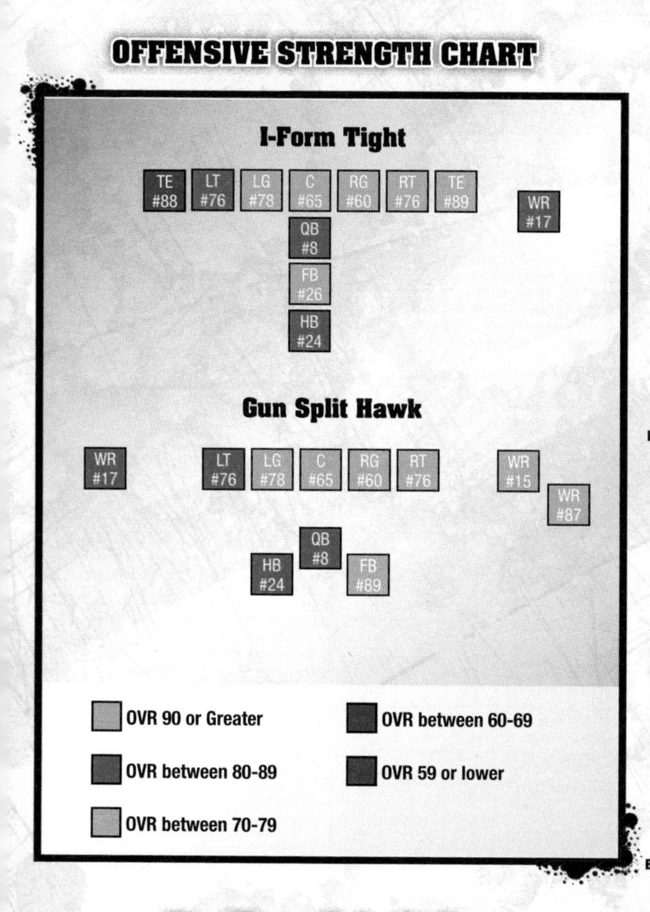

Key Player Substitution

Player: Cameron Morrah

Position: #1 TE

Key Stat: 84 Speed

What He Brings: While John Carlson is solid all around, bring Morrah in the game to really stretch the defense out.

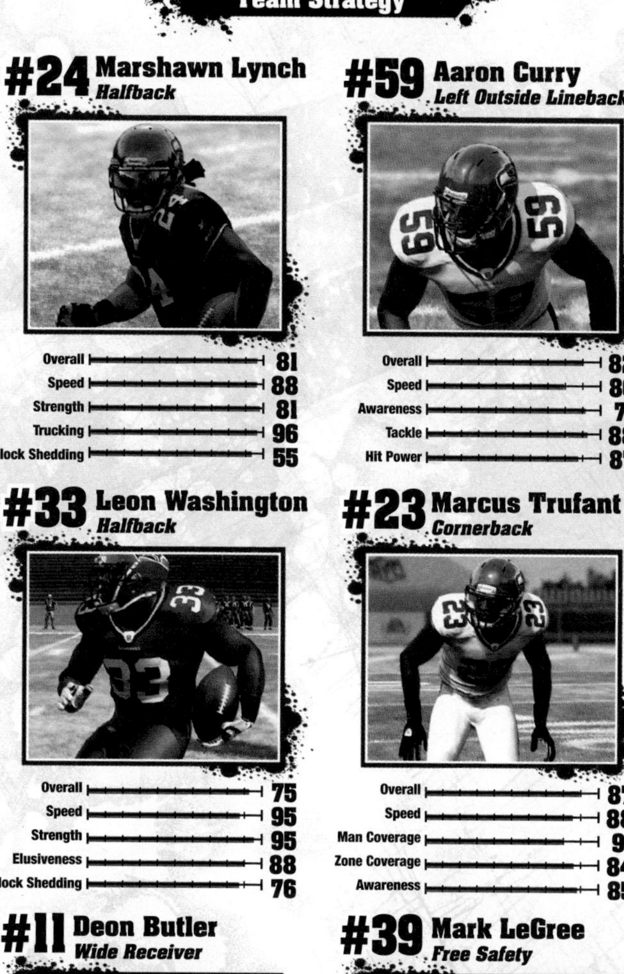

#24 Marshawn Lynch
Halfback

Overall	81
Speed	88
Strength	81
Trucking	96
Block Shedding	55

#33 Leon Washington
Halfback

Overall	75
Speed	95
Strength	95
Elusiveness	88
Block Shedding	76

#11 Deon Butler
Wide Receiver

Overall	70
Speed	95
Catch	81
Route Running	81
Acceleration	93

#59 Aaron Curry
Left Outside Linebacker

Overall	82
Speed	86
Awareness	71
Tackle	88
Hit Power	87

#23 Marcus Trufant
Cornerback

Overall	87
Speed	88
Man Coverage	91
Zone Coverage	84
Awareness	85

#39 Mark LeGree
Free Safety

Overall	59
Speed	90
Tackle	67
Hit Power	53
Play Recognition	42

DEFENSIVE STRENGTH CHART

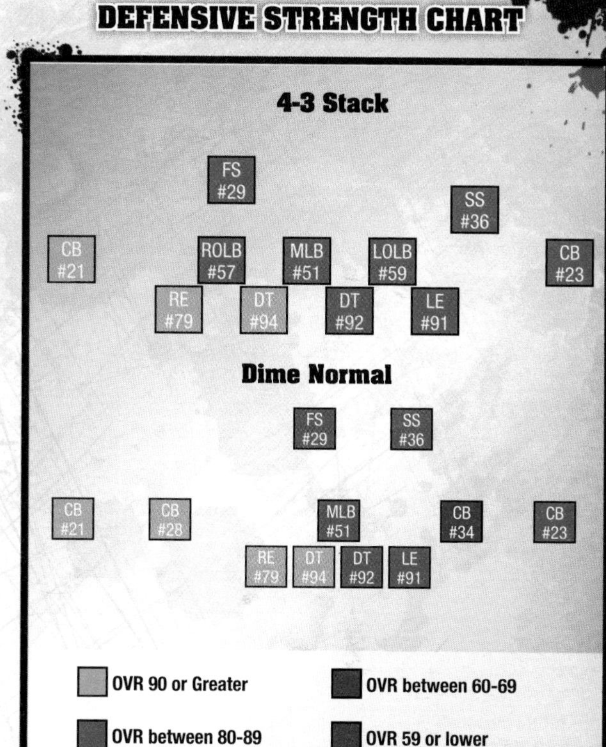

Key Player Substitution

Player: Aaron Curry

Position: #1 LE on Passing Downs

Key Stat: 88 Acceleration

What He Brings: If the offense brings in multiple WRs, forcing the defense to use Dime, bring Aaron Curry into the game to rush the passer off the edge. If the defense doesn't keep an RB in the game to block, he can run past most tackles.

Playbook Tips

Offensive Style: Pass Balanced

Offense

- Use Marshawn Lynch in short-yardage situations, even if the defense is expecting run.
- Leon Washington is a threat not only on special teams, but on routes out of the backfield too.
- Pete Carroll will continue to install his offense, which already won the Panthers a playoff game under his guidance.

Defense

- Aaron Curry is a strong rusher in passing situations, so don't be afraid to sub him at DE.
- Controlling safety Earl Thomas is a great way to fortify the middle of your defense.
- The Seahawks' defense tackles very well on the outside.

OFFENSIVE FORMATIONS

FORMATION	# OF PLAYS
Gun Doubles On	15
Gun Empty Trey	12
Gun Split Hawk	15
Gun Spread	18
Gun Trey Open	15
Gun Y-Trips WK	
I-Form Normal	21
I-Form Slot Flex	12
I-Form Tight	15
Singleback Ace	18
Singleback Ace Pair Twins	12
Singleback Bunch	15
Singleback Doubles	18
Singleback Double Flex	12
Singleback Jumbo Z	18
Singleback Snugs	9
Strong I Normal	15
Strong I Twin TE	12
Weak I Twins	15

OFFENSIVE PLAYCOUNTS

PLAY TYPE	# OF PLAYS
Quick Pass	18
Standard Pass	52
Shotgun Pass	63
Play Action Pass	58
Inside Handoff	37
Outside Handoff	16
Pitch	11
Counter	7
Draw	10

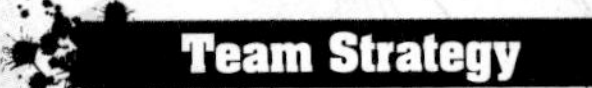

Three-Headed Rushing Attack

Strong Normal—Counter Weak

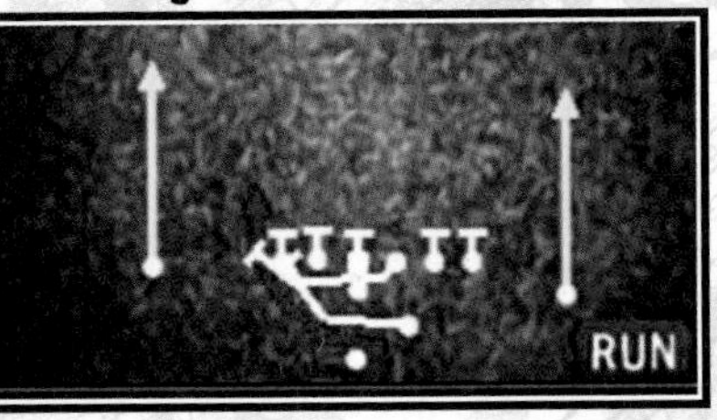

The Counter Weak is a very common run that we see from strong formations, thanks to the FB's alignment in the formation. Every time we find a set with this run, we use it to open up the weak-side rushing game and keep the defense honest.

The RG appears to attack the center at the snap of this play, this which be a problem since the counter takes an extra second to set up. Thankfully our pulling right guard will pick him up before any damage is done.

The guard's block allows the FB to stay out in front and be our lead blocker on the play. The RB does a good job keeping the run inside since this run lacks any chance to go the distance. His ability to break tackles serves him best inside because he is not a threat to outrun anyone on the edge.

PRO TIP The Counter Weak will be best used with HB Leon Washington, who has a great blend of speed and agility.

Strong Normal - Stretch

The Strong Normal is a great formation that has plenty of power to the outside. A stretch will be effective because of where the FB lines up to the right side. He will be able to get around the corner and create a seal.

At the snap, the WRs clear out of their area and look to take a defender with them. The FB starts to head out and looks to clear the gap between the tackle and the TE. The middle of the defense opens up, but our RB knows he has no support from his team there. He instead stays on track and tries to break the run outside.

The HB does a good job not outrunning his blocks until everything is set up. Once he determines his attack, he starts his boost and really puts on a hard cut to the edge. He should have a full head of steam when the safety approaches and he should try to run him over.

PRO TIP A great user will recognize the handoff motion of the stretch and look to contain the outside.

Strong I Pro - HB Dive

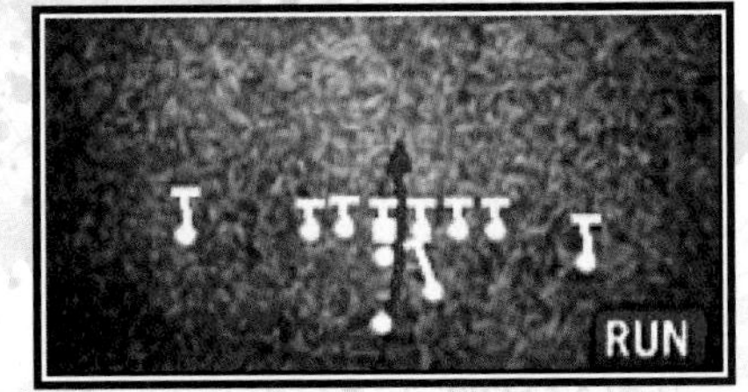

The Strong I Pro is a running set that allows you to play a smashmouth-style of offense. With a TE on the line of scrimmage and a FB offset in the backfield, we force the defense to respect the threat of the run. On the outside, we still have the ability to go downfield in the passing game with our split end and flanker.

The design of the Strong I Pro HB Dive is to attack the defense in the middle of the field. At the snap of the ball, always look outside to see if there is room to run. If there is no running room, look to get upfield.

We are able to cut through the defensive line and fight for a few hard yards. It's important to cover up the ball when running between the tackles. Our ball carrier is vulnerable to oncoming hits, which could result in fumbles.

PRO TIP The design of this run is for the A gap. Only look to run outside as a change of pace.

Quick Pass

Singleback Double Flex - Curl Flats

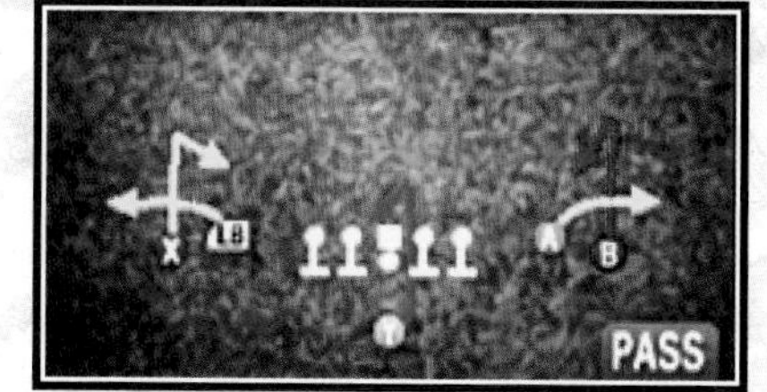

Under center spread formations are a nice way to attack the defense horizontally. What we like so much about the Curl Flats is its ability to quickly attack a vulnerable defense. Just before the snap of the ball, look at your slot WRs; if they aren't covered, you will want to deliver the pass as soon as you snap the ball.

As we line up under center, we see that our slot WR is uncovered. This is our signal that the defense is in some type of defensive blitz coverage. The only thing left to do here is quickly hit our WR in the flat!

We hit our WR in stride as he breaks upfield. The defense gave us a major tell when they didn't line up to cover our WR. Little things such as this make all the difference between a win and loss.

PRO TIP Substitute your fastest WRs into each slot. This will help to increase yards after a catch.

Man Beater

Singleback Double Flex - HB Draw

The HB Draw is a great play to complement our last breakdown. When the defense adjusts to defend against our quick pass to the flat, we will counter their adjustment. If the defense has their defender line defending the slot WR, they will be out of position to defend the run. The HB Draw looks like a pass initially and then results in a run.

Here we see the defense is now defending the slot WR. This is our key to run the HB Draw. The defense won't have enough defenders near the line of scrimmage to defend the run.

Our HB gets upfield and gashes the defense for a big gain. We are now playing the ultimate head game with the defense. They won't know who to cover!

PRO TIP With HB Draws, be patient and let your blocks develop. As soon as you see your running lane, move upfield.

Zone Beater

Gun Empty Trey - Strong Flood

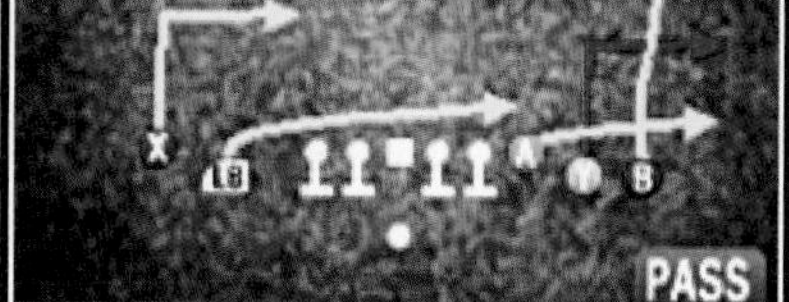

The Gun Empty Trey Strong Flood is a play that has a ton of options with which to attack the defense. We love this formation because of its trips alignment to the right and its isolated WR to the left. We can easily beat man-to-man and zone defensive coverage with this play.

At the snap of the ball, we roll right to create better passing angles for the natural flow of the play. We first look to our flat WR and then immediately look to our isolated WR on the left running his crossing pattern.

The defense is in a Cover 2 zone and has taken away our flat route. As we glance back to the middle of the field, we see a window to hit our WR on the crossing route. We were able to successfully attack the defense without having any presnap reads of what they were doing. Another great option against a Cover 2 zone would have been our deep streak route. If you plan on going downfield, we recommend you stay in the pocket.

Base Play

Gun Spread - Inside Cross

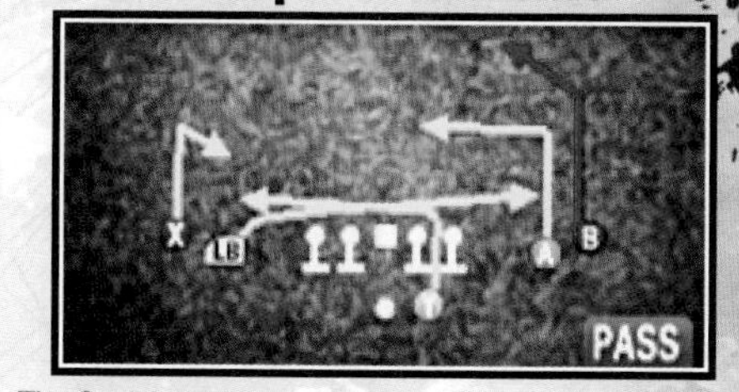

The Seahawks have numerous HBs who are dangerous threats in the game. The Inside Cross is a man-to-man beater that highlights our explosive HB. We sub in HB Leon Washington for this play, as we are looking to match up Washington against the slower linebacker.

As Washington makes his break, you can see that the linebacker isn't able to move with Washington's speed. As Washington makes his break toward the sideline, we deliver the ball.

Washington makes the grab in the open field and has room to gain yards after the catch. We keyed in on a mismatch on the field and took full advantage.

PRO TIP Use a speedy HB for this play. The slower the HB, the less effective he will be against the linebacker.

PITTSBURGH STEELERS

OFFENSIVE SCOUTING REPORT

The Steelers came up just one drive shy of winning a seventh Super Bowl title last season. For the right type of player, Pittsburgh will be a dominating force in *Madden NFL 12*. The playbook allows for QB Ben Roethlisberger, or "Big Ben," to hang tough in the pocket and wait for routes downfield to develop. Stud WR Mike Wallace has the speed to threaten defenses deep, and Big Ben is tough enough to make plays with his legs, allowing Wallace the time to slip behind the defense. Helping out is RB Rashard Mendenhall, who will pick up tough yards game after game. He is tough enough to carry the bulk of the rushes and features a solid Truck rating. WR Hines Ward and TE Heath Miller flat-out make tough catches and hang on to the ball. This will keep the chains moving for the Steelers in *Madden NFL 12*.

DEFENSIVE SCOUTING REPORT

The success of the Steelers' defense lies with safety Troy Polamalu. He can fly into the box against the run or drop back and latch on to any ball thrown in his direction. This seemingly gives the Steelers an extra defender on every play. While the QB must worry about Polamalu, Pittsburgh's four incredibly balanced and speedy linebackers could be rushing from anywhere on the field. The zone blitzing scheme they run is devastating with the right personnel, and they have it in *Madden NFL 12*. This includes hard-hitting safety Ryan Clark, who can punish opponents who try to throw into the middle of the defense.

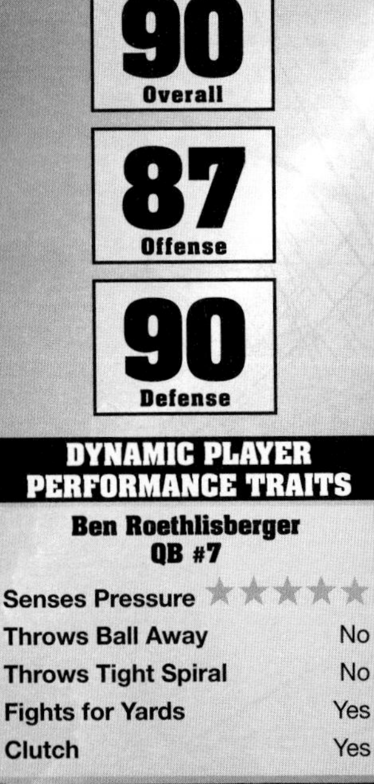

TEAM RATING

90	Overall
87	Offense
90	Defense

DYNAMIC PLAYER PERFORMANCE TRAITS

Ben Roethlisberger QB #7

Senses Pressure	★★★★★
Throws Ball Away	No
Throws Tight Spiral	No
Fights for Yards	Yes
Clutch	Yes

RATINGS BY POSITION

Quarterbacks	94
Halfbacks	88
Fullbacks	69
Wide Receivers	83
Tight Ends	85
Tackles	83
Guards	75
Centers	88
Defensive Ends	90
Defensive Tackles	92
Outside Linebackers	96
Middle Linebackers	90
Cornerbacks	81
Free Safeties	83
Strong Safeties	99
Kickers	73
Punters	79

DEPTH CHART

POS	OVR	FIRST NAME	LAST NAME
3DRB	88	Rashard	Mendenhall
C	88	Maurkice	Pouncey
C	70	Doug	Legursky
CB	85	Ike	Taylor
CB	77	Bryant	McFadden
CB	68	William	Gay
CB	70	Anthony	Madison
CB	68	Curtis	Brown
DT	92	Casey	Hampton
DT	77	Chris	Hoke
DT	65	Steve	McClendon
FB	69	David	Johnson
FB	53	Jamie	McCoy
FS	83	Ryan	Clark
FS	67	Ryan	Mundy
HB	88	Rashard	Mendenhall
HB	66	Isaac	Redman
HB	60	Jonathan	Dwyer
HB	62	Baron	Batch
K	73	Shaun	Suisham
KOS	73	Shaun	Suisham
KR	70	Emmanuel	Sanders
KR	69	Antonio	Brown
LE	91	Aaron	Smith
LE	79	Ziggy	Hood
LG	75	Chris	Kemoeatu
LG	65	Keith	Williams
LG	66	Dorian	Brooks
LOLB	93	LaMarr	Woodley
LOLB	66	Jason	Worilds
LS	69	Greg	Warren
LT	82	Max	Starks
LT	73	Jonathan	Scott
LT	64	Tony	Hills
MLB	90	Lawrence	Timmons
MLB	91	James	Farrior
MLB	81	Larry	Foote
MLB	57	Stevenson	Sylvester
P	79	Daniel	Sepulveda
PR	69	Antonio	Brown
QB	94	Ben	Roethlisberger
QB	71	Byron	Leftwich
QB	74	Charlie	Batch
RE	88	Brett	Keisel
RE	74	Cameron	Heyward
RE	57	Ra'Shon	Harris
RG	74	Ramon	Foster
RG	63	Chris	Scott
ROLB	98	James	Harrison
ROLB	61	Chris	Carter
ROLB	59	Baraka	Atkins
RT	84	Flozell	Adams
RT	71	Marcus	Gilbert
RT	82	Willie	Colon
SS	99	Troy	Polamalu
SS	69	Will	Allen
SS	60	Tuff	Harris
TE	85	Heath	Miller
TE	67	Matt	Spaeth
TE	59	Eugene	Bright
WR	86	Hines	Ward
WR	87	Mike	Wallace
WR	76	Antwaan	Randle El
WR	70	Emmanuel	Sanders
WR	69	Arnaz	Battle
WR	69	Antonio	Brown

OFFENSIVE STRENGTH CHART

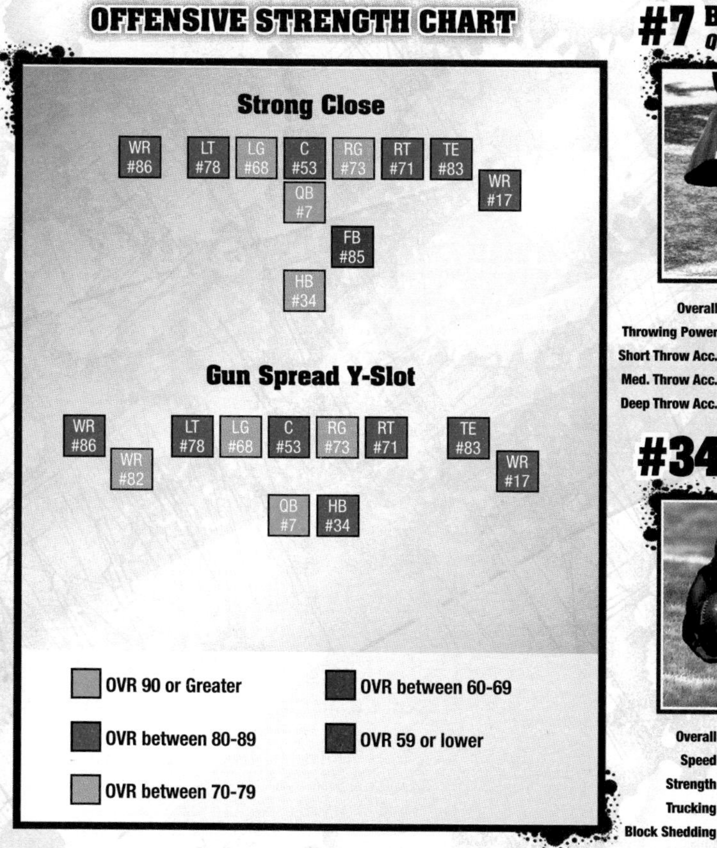

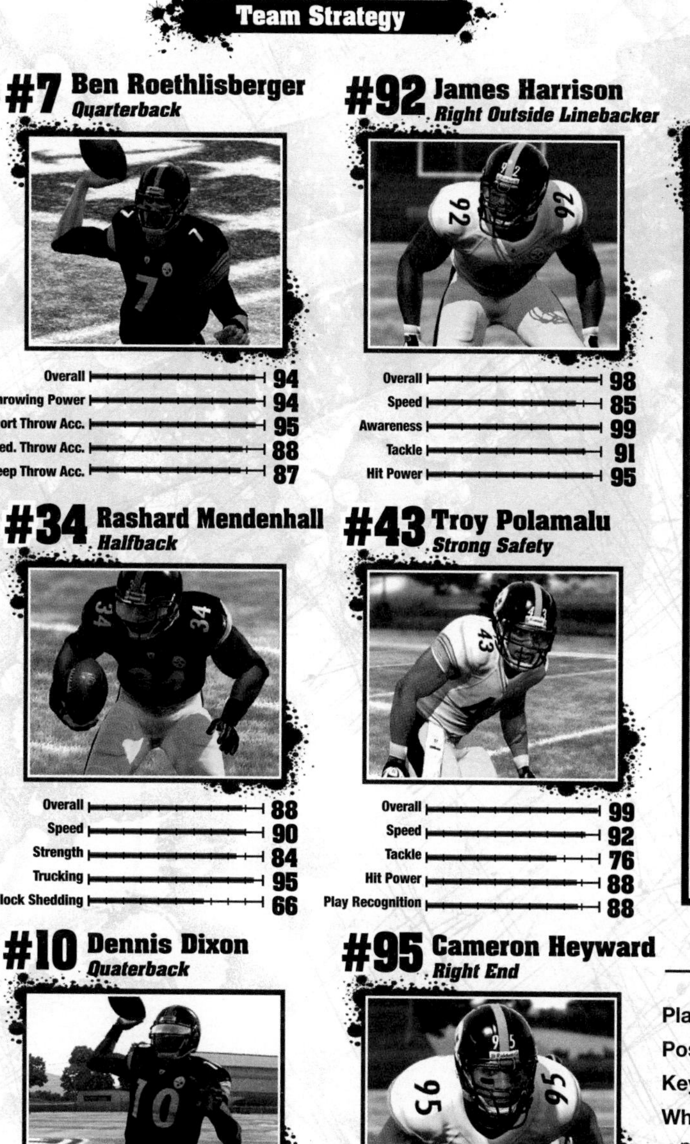

DEFENSIVE STRENGTH CHART

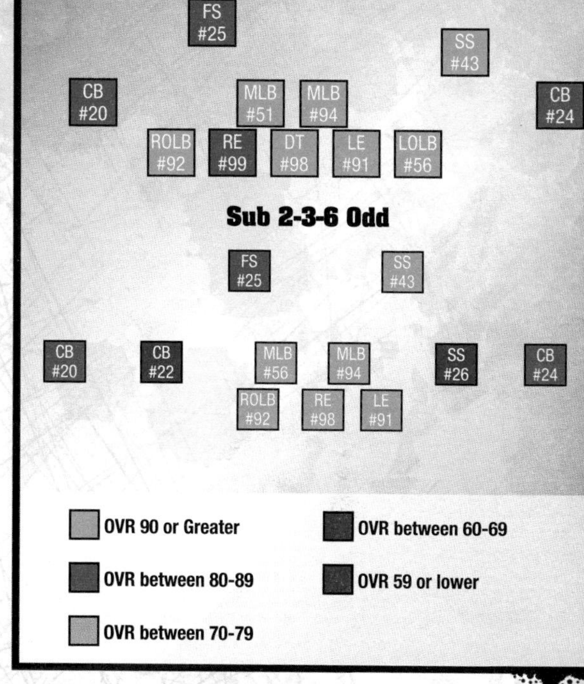

Key Player Substitution

Player: Emmanuel Sanders

Position: #2 WR

Key Stat: 94 Speed

What He Brings: Allow Sanders to get in the game by bumping him up the depth chart over Hines Ward. He has tremendous speed and can break the game open. Keep Ward in for run-block situations.

Key Player Substitution

Player: Cameron Heyward

Position: #2 DT

Key Stat: 91 Strength

What He Brings: Let this talented rookie onto the field during pass-rushing situations. He can still hold up against the run but should get more penetration against the pass.

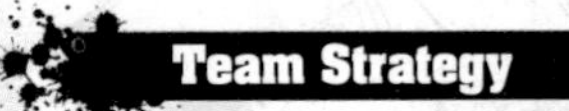

Playbook Tips

Offensive Style: Run Balanced

Offense

- Look to hit WR Mike Wallace on a deep post early in the game, this can catch the defense off guard.
- The Steelers have a great runner in between the tackles with Rashard Mendenhall, use him north and south.
- The Steelers line may need help from extra TEs to help give Big Ben time to look downfield.

Defense

- Pittsburgh loves to send their fast LBs off the edge in its 3-4 defensive scheme.
- Troy Polamalu will play the run even when you don't bring him into the box, he is that good.
- Simply allow the strong but slower Defensive Line to hold their own and let the Lb's run free.

OFFENSIVE FORMATIONS

FORMATION	# OF PLAYS
Gun 5WR Trips	
Gun Bunch WK	9
Gun Doubles On	12
Gun Empty Steeler	15
Gun Snugs	9
Gun Split Close	12
Gun Spread Y-Slot	15
Gun Trips HB WK	
Gun Trio	15
Gun Y-Trips WK	18
I-Form Tight	15
I-Form Tight Pair	15
Singleback Ace	15
Singleback Ace Pair Twins	15
Singleback Bunch	15
Singleback Jumbo	12
Singleback Pitt Doubles	21
Singleback Pitt Y-Trips	15
Strong Close	15
Weak Flex Twins	15

OFFENSIVE PLAYCOUNTS

PLAY TYPE	# OF PLAYS
Quick Pass	18
Standard Pass	45
Shotgun Pass	100
Play Action Pass	42
Inside Handoff	32
Outside Handoff	10
Pitch	11
Counter	10
Draw	10

Three-Headed Rushing Attack

Singleback Jumbo—Counter Wk

The Singleback Jumbo formation is a great way to get extra TEs into the game who can really help out in run blocking. The Counter Wk is a great way to use the weak side if the defense pays too much attention to the added TEs.

The initial step to the right freezes the linebacker and keeps him from shooting through the weak-side gap and locking up the run. This also allows the back time to let the pulling guard get out in front of the defense. Don't be scared—the play is designed to run left and it will work best if you follow your blocks.

The RB cuts back inside the defense as the cornerback does a good job holding down the edge. This will force the defense to not overload the strong side on future run plays.

PRO TIP Get Hines Ward into the game to run-block, he is one of the best in *Madden NFL 12*!

Singleback Jumbo—HB Toss Strong

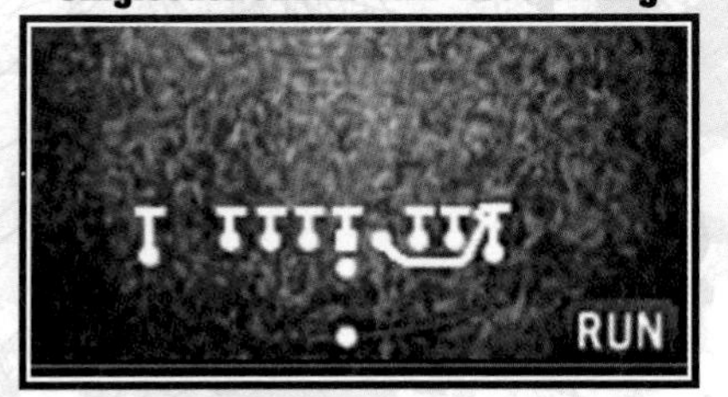

A toss to the strong side is a great way to beat the defense for big gains. With all of the extra strength that your dual TEs bring into the game, look to toss the ball out behind them.

The defense was completely overplaying the toss to the strong side, and rather than switch to the counter, we simply playmaker the run to the weak side. The defense is now totally out of position. This will allow our LG to pull to the right and become our blocker. Don't ever snap the ball if you're not confident that the play will work. Look to make an adjustment.

The HB catches the ball and will easily get to the edge of the defense. Only a safety is standing between him and a huge gain. Thankfully, Mendenhall is a solid back with a wide array of moves. During the next few strides, set up one move and execute it.

PRO TIP Because we allowed Dennis Dixon to hand off the ball, the defense will be worried that he might be in the game for a play fake.

Singleback Jumbo - Inside Zone

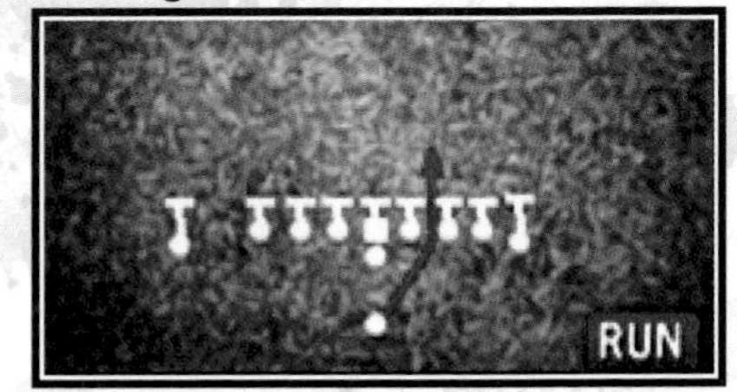

The Singleback Jumbo formation is solid when looking to run the ball as the staple of your offense. The formation calls for an extra TE to be lined up on the line of scrimmage. This extra TE gives us a serious threat in the running and passing games. The Inside Zone is designed to find the open running lane inside and out.

As we receive the handoff, we quickly look over the defense and find our open running lanes. Our HB Rashard Mendenhall has the ability to run between the tackles, and he has enough speed to run outside.

We find an opening running lane through the middle of the field for the big gain. Mendenhall powers through deep into the secondary. Going outside is temping because of the big play potential, but follow your blocks as they develop.

PRO TIP Motion your flanker WR in toward the offensive line for better run blocking.

Quick Pass

Strong Close - Slot Trail

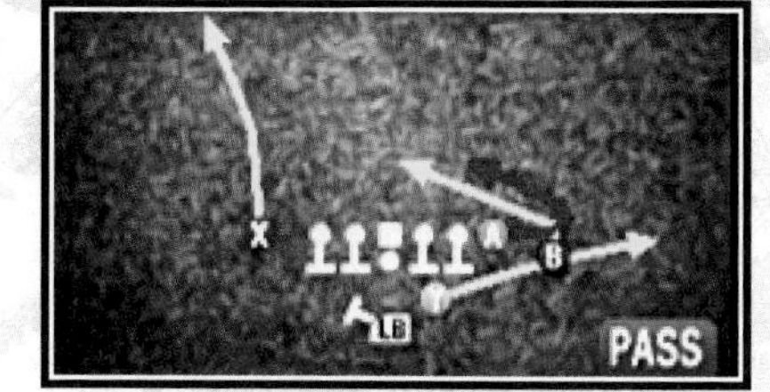

We love using deception in the passing game. The Strong Close formation should make your opponent first think run. We are trying to catch the defense off guard and hit them deep downfield. The Slot Trail also has a few short options that we can use to attack the defense underneath.

The defense is bringing a man-to-man blitz. We know that because they are in a blitz that they should be vulnerable against the deep ball. Notice the FB has picked up the defense blitz.

Our speedy WR gets behind his man-to-man defender deep in the secondary. We deliver the deep pass and haul in the grab with a amazing diving catch.

PRO TIP Substitute your fastest WR for your downfield threat.

Man Beater

Gun Tight - Mesh

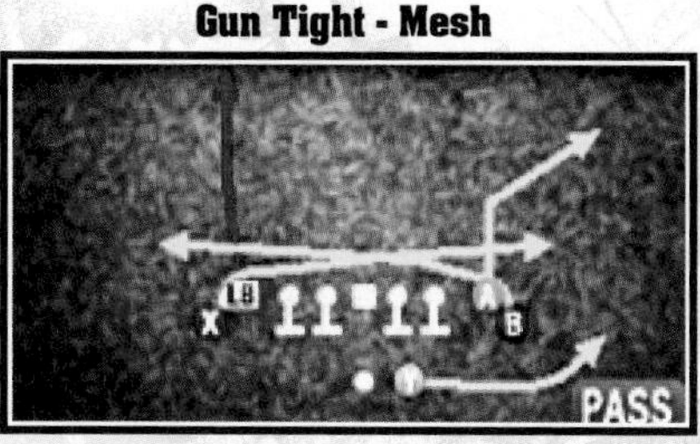

When facing man coverage, the Gun Tight Mesh is one of the better plays in this playbook. The compression of the set allows for picks and rubs while the WRs progress on their routes. This play has a few options for attacking man-to-man and zone. Against man-to-man, the dual drag routes will be our first option. We then look to the HB in the flat and finally to the deep streak. When facing zone coverage, look toward the WR running the deep corner.

Both of our drag WRs have become open at the snap of the ball. We will wait for them to clear into the open field before we deliver the pass. We know that the defense is not blitzing because of the two deep safeties in coverage.

We hang in the pocket and deliver the pass as our WR breaks toward the sideline. If pressure is coming, look to get the pass out to the WR as soon as they open up.

PRO TIP When facing pressure, block the HB for extra pass protection.

Zone Beater

Gun Trio - Pitt Smash

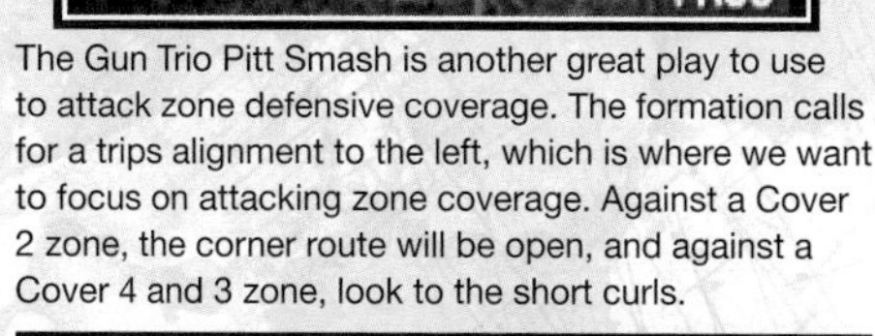

The Gun Trio Pitt Smash is another great play to use to attack zone defensive coverage. The formation calls for a trips alignment to the left, which is where we want to focus on attacking zone coverage. Against a Cover 2 zone, the corner route will be open, and against a Cover 4 and 3 zone, look to the short curls.

The defense drops into a Cover 2 zone; we notice this because the deep safeties split the secondary in halves at the snap of the ball. Our WR begins his cut for the corner route, and we can see the open space behind the zone defense.

We deliver the pass to the WR as he approaches the sideline. The WR makes the catch and gets past the deep safety in coverage.

PRO TIP Against a zone blitz, look for the short curls. The defense won't be able to cover both curls.

Base Play

Singleback Pitt Doubles - FL Middle

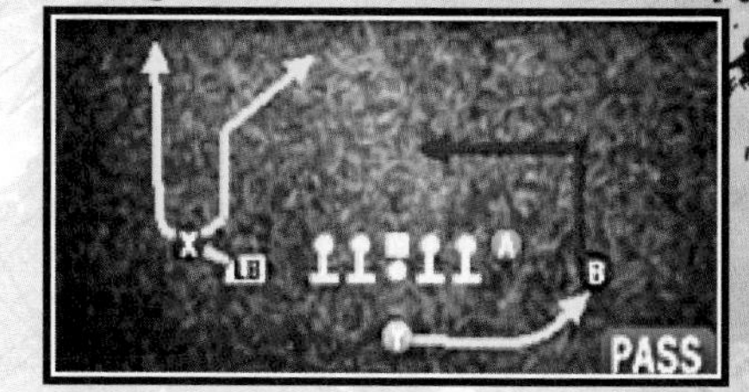

When attacking zone defensive coverage, the FL Middle from Singleback Pitt Doubles is one of our favorites from this playbook. The wheel route that our slot WR runs will attack the flat and then the deep sideline. This a nice option when facing a Cover 2 zone and a blitzing zone defense.

Here we see the defense is in a Cover 2 zone and our slot WR is being guarded in the flat. However, because he is running a wheel route, he will begin his move upfield shortly after he gets to the flat. Notice the zone defender is passing off the WR to the deep safety.

We squeeze the throw to the WR as he is between the flat defender and the deep safety. The WR makes the catch down the sideline in the soft spot of the zone.

PRO TIP The slot WR should have a high Catch rating. When delivering passes against zone defenses, expect big hits on the ball carrier.

HOUSTON TEXANS

OFFENSIVE SCOUTING REPORT

The Texans scored big last season by committing to relative unknown RB Arian Foster. Foster exploded onto the scene and led the NFL in rushing. In *Madden NFL 12*, look to use Foster early to open up the passing lanes for the Matt Schaub to Johnson combo. Andre Johnson is an elite talent with the size and speed to challenge any CB in the game. At TE, Owen Daniels gives you a big target in the tight spaces over the middle of the field. Houston has been stockpiling talent for the last few seasons, and this will be the *Madden NFL* season it is all unleashed.

DEFENSIVE SCOUTING REPORT

The Houston Texans will switch to a 3-4 look this season under new defensive coordinator Wade Phillips. This should allow newly converted LOLB Mario Williams to use his elite talent and athleticism to rush off the edge. On the other side, the Texans picked up J.J. Watt in the draft, and he will be a nice addition to the core. DeMeco Ryans and Brian Cushing are a great one-two combo; they keep the middle of the field clear against the run or the pass at LB. While the secondary doesn't have great speed, Houston will likely have some success with a zone scheme this year in *Madden NFL 12*.

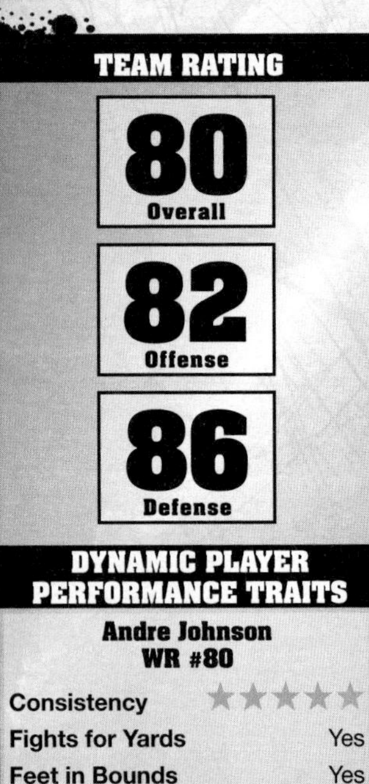

TEAM RATING

80 Overall

82 Offense

86 Defense

DYNAMIC PLAYER PERFORMANCE TRAITS

Andre Johnson
WR #80

Consistency	★★★★★
Fights for Yards	Yes
Feet in Bounds	Yes
High Motor	Yes
Clutch	Yes

RATINGS BY POSITION

Quarterbacks	88
Halfbacks	92
Fullbacks	91
Wide Receivers	83
Tight Ends	86
Tackles	85
Guards	81
Centers	79
Defensive Ends	83
Defensive Tackles	75
Outside Linebackers	81
Middle Linebackers	90
Cornerbacks	72
Free Safeties	80
Strong Safeties	80
Kickers	83
Punters	81

DEPTH CHART

POS	OVR	FIRST NAME	LAST NAME
3DRB	73	Derrick	Ward
C	79	Chris	Myers
C	65	Shelley	Smith
CB	75	Kareem	Jackson
CB	69	Brice	McCain
CB	75	Jason	Allen
CB	70	Brandon	Harris
CB	62	Sherrick	McManis
DT	75	Shaun	Cody
DT	68	Earl	Mitchell
DT	71	Damione	Lewis
FB	91	Vonta	Leach
FB	61	James	Casey
FS	80	Glover	Quin Jr.
FS	71	Troy	Nolan
FS	65	Torri	Williams
HB	92	Arian	Foster
HB	73	Derrick	Ward
HB	72	Steve	Slaton
HB	69	Ben	Tate
K	83	Neil	Rackers
KOS	83	Neil	Rackers
KR	74	Jacoby	Jones
KR	72	Steve	Slaton
LE	85	Antonio	Smith
LE	74	Amobi	Okoye
LG	86	Wade	Smith
LG	77	Kasey	Studdard
LOLB	88	Mario	Williams
LOLB	70	Tim	Jamison
LOLB	71	Xavier	Adibi
LS	55	Jonathan	Weeks
LT	80	Duane	Brown
LT	63	Rashad	Butler
LT	62	Derek	Newton
MLB	89	DeMeco	Ryans
MLB	86	Brian	Cushing
MLB	70	Zac	Diles
MLB	68	Darryl	Sharpton
P	81	Matt	Turk
PR	74	Jacoby	Jones
QB	88	Matt	Schaub
QB	70	Dan	Orlovsky
QB	72	Matt	Leinart
RE	80	J.J.	Watt
RE	65	Tim	Bulman
RG	75	Mike	Brisiel
RG	73	Antoine	Caldwell
ROLB	73	Connor	Barwin
ROLB	69	Brooks	Reed
ROLB	64	Mark	Anderson
RT	90	Eric	Winston
RT	65	Cole	Pemberton
SS	80	Bernard	Pollard
SS	69	Dominique	Barber
SS	69	Quintin	Demps
TE	86	Owen	Daniels
TE	70	Joel	Dreessen
TE	67	Garrett	Graham
WR	97	Andre	Johnson
WR	78	Kevin	Walter
WR	74	Jacoby	Jones
WR	61	Dorin	Dickerson
WR	61	David	Anderson
WR	52	Derrick	Townsel

OFFENSIVE STRENGTH CHART

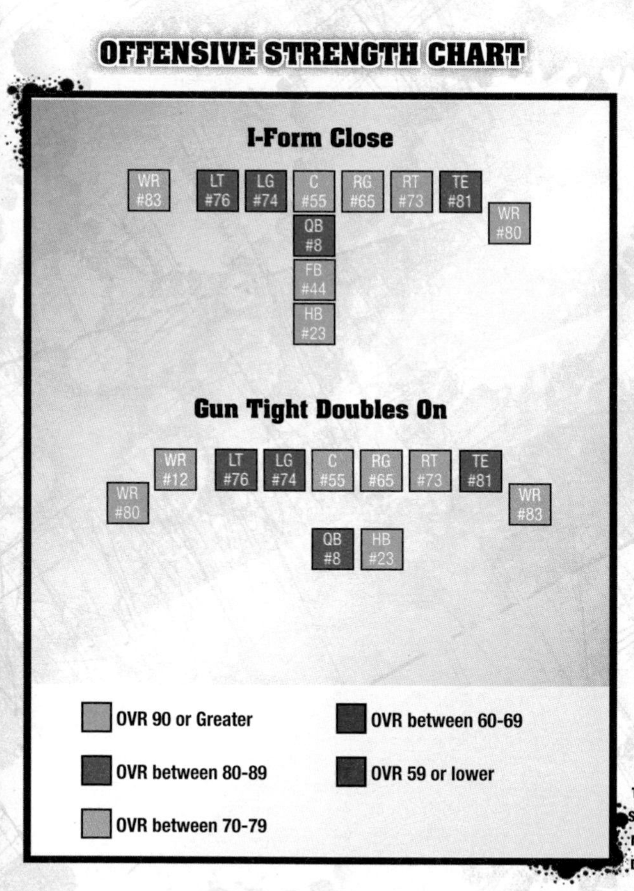

Key Player Substitution

Player: Steve Slaton

Position: #1 Third Down RB

Key Stat: 93 Speed

What He Brings: Arian Foster is a workhorse back who can handle the load, but to keep him fresh for the fourth quarter, look to get Steve Slaton some work as a receiving threat on third down.

#80 Andre Johnson
Wide Receiver

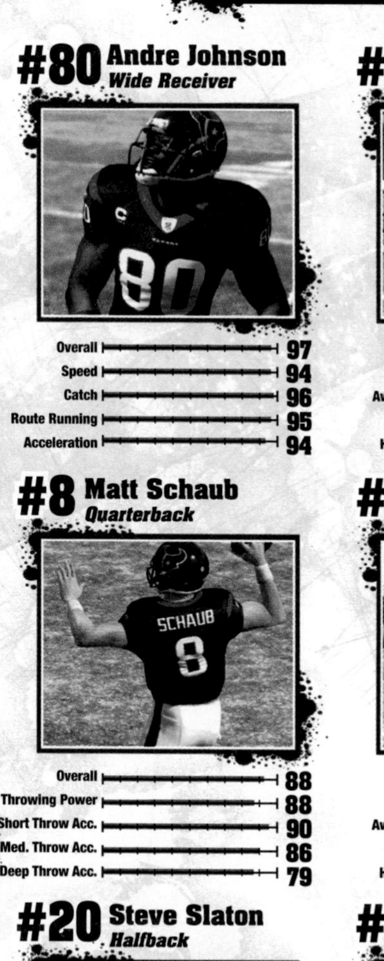

Overall	97
Speed	94
Catch	96
Route Running	95
Acceleration	94

#8 Matt Schaub
Quarterback

Overall	88
Throwing Power	88
Short Throw Acc.	90
Med. Throw Acc.	86
Deep Throw Acc.	79

#20 Steve Slaton
Halfback

Overall	72
Speed	93
Strength	94
Elusiveness	85
Block Shedding	74

#90 Mario Williams
Left Outside Linebacker

Overall	88
Speed	84
Awareness	86
Tackle	83
Hit Power	81

#56 Brian Cushing
Middle Linebacker

Overall	86
Speed	84
Awareness	79
Tackle	91
Hit Power	88

#21 Brice McCain
Cornerback

Overall	69
Speed	95
Man Coverage	78
Zone Coverage	74
Awareness	55

DEFENSIVE STRENGTH CHART

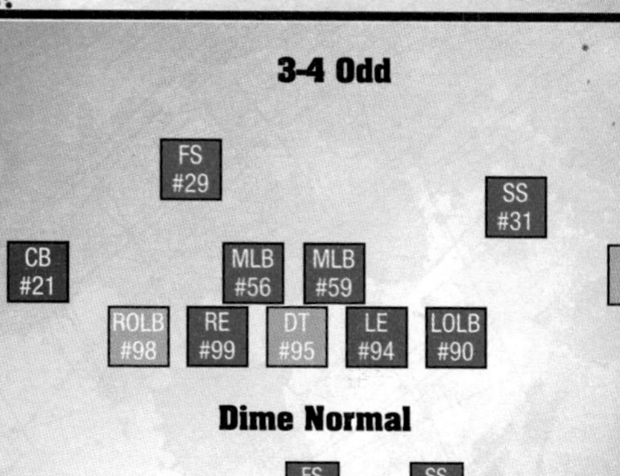

Dime Normal

FS #29 | SS #31

CB #21 | CB #30 | MLB #59 | CB #26 | CB #25

RE #99 | DT #92 | DT #95 | LE #94

OVR 90 or Greater

OVR between 60-69

OVR between 80-89

OVR 59 or lower

OVR between 70-79

Key Player Substitution

Player: Quintin Demps

Position: #1 SS Slot

Key Stat: 89 Speed

What He Brings: Bernard Pollard is solid against the run, but with the Texans having to play pass-happy teams in their division, including Indy, start Demps and leave him out there in passing situations.

Playbook Tips

Offensive Style: Balanced

Offense

- Andre Johnson is on the short list of best WRs in the game. This is due to his unique blend of size and speed.
- Arian Foster emerged onto the scene last year as a powerful running back who can have a big game against any defense.
- Utilizing Matt Schaub in a medium-passing game really works to his core stats.

Defense

- Houston will employ a 3-4 look this season with DE Mario Williams lining up off the edge.
- DeMeco Ryans and Brian Cushing are two players to leave on the field in Nickel passing situations.
- If Amobi Okoye can stay healthy, this can be the season he finally breaks out and anchors the line.

OFFENSIVE FORMATIONS

FORMATION	# OF PLAYS
Gun Bunch	18
Gun Doubles	18
Gun Empty Y-Flex	12
Gun Snugs Flip	9
Gun Split Texan	12
Gun Tight Doubles On	9
Gun Y-Trips HB WK	15
I-Form Close	12
I-Form Pro	24
I-Form Tight Pair	15
I-Form Twins Flex	9
Singleback Ace	12
Singleback Ace Close	12
Singleback Ace Twins	21
Singleback Doubles	21
Singleback Jumbo Z	9
Singleback Tight Doubles	15
Singleback Wing Trio	15
Strong Close	18
Weak Pro	12
Weak Twins	12

OFFENSIVE PLAYCOUNTS

PLAY TYPE	# OF PLAYS
Quick Pass	20
Standard Pass	62
Shotgun Pass	69
Play Action Pass	57
Inside Handoff	36
Outside Handoff	18
Pitch	13
Counter	2
Draw	13

Three-Headed Rushing Attack

Singleback Ace Close—HB Stretch

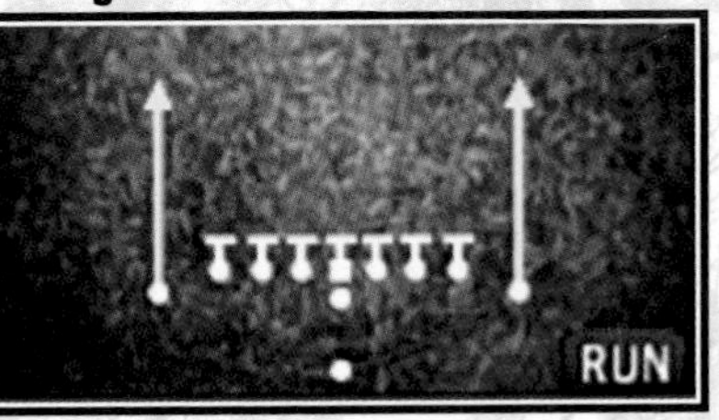

With a renewed identity behind star RB Arian Foster, the Texans will look to punish the defense this season. The HB Stretch is the perfect run to prove that last season was not a fluke. It is a powerful run behind this compressed look.

Foster receives the stretch handoff from the QB and immediately looks to head down the line of scrimmage. The TE is also working out in front of Foster to prevent any penetration from the outside of the formation.

The defender slips past the WR, who works his way downfield to pick up the safety. We can either allow the TE to pick him up or we can simply attempt to make him miss. He is already stumbling, and a strong back like Foster will easily be able to shake him off.

PRO TIP Arian Foster has the perfect combo of size and speed; he can cut it inside or attack the edge.

Singleback Ace Close—HB Sweep

The HB Sweep is a very important run for the Texans. It forces the defense to play zone to really attempt to stop it. Otherwise man coverage will get pulled inside and the defense will get beaten.

The staple of the sweep is a quick pitch and a pulling guard out in front. Since we don't have the luxury of a fullback in this formation, we will need the guard to lead the way for us.

The defense is pursuing on the back side of the play, but we can simply outrun them because they have a poor angle. We have our blocker out in front ready to take on a smaller defender and spring us for a chance to get to the end zone.

PRO TIP If you find yourself playing a defense with elite speed, try HB Steve Slaton.

Singleback Ace Close - Zone Weak

Last season, HB Arian Foster stormed onto the NFL scene and gave the Texans a huge boost in their run game. One of the main focal points of your offense will go through him. The Zone Weak is a great inside and outside style of run. Foster has just enough speed to make him a dangerous outside threat and is tough enough to run between the tackles.

We receive the handoff and look for the open running lane. Remember to look both inside and outside for running room. You can use the Zone Weak for both inside and outside running.

Foster finds running room and busts through to the defensive secondary. Once we get a back like Foster moving, it is difficult to take him down. We are able to get into the end zone for the touchdown.

PRO TIP Look to use the Truck stick to smash through your opponents with a big HB like Foster.

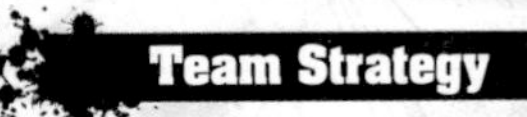

Quick Pass

Singleback Tight Doubles - PA Rollout

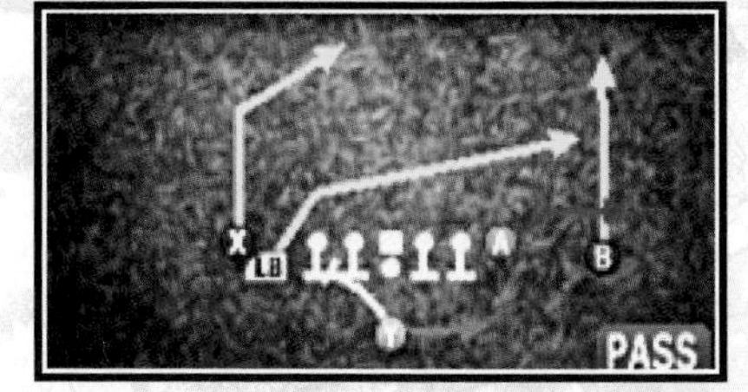

As an offense, one of our goals is to fool the defense so that they can't clue in on what we are trying to do offensively. The PA Rollout is a nice play that gives us a few homerun routes and great pass protection with short passing options underneath the defense.

Here we are highlighting our TE again as he looks to block at the snap of the ball. Soon after his initial block, he will release into the flat as a passing option. Not only are we running play action to fool the defense, but we are also trying to fool them with our TE on a delayed blue route.

Our TE releases into the flat, and the defense doesn't account for him. We are able to pick up a nice gain before the defense takes him down!

PRO TIP Slide protect to the side of the TE to help free him on his delayed release.

Man Beater

Gun Tight Doubles On - Texan Cross

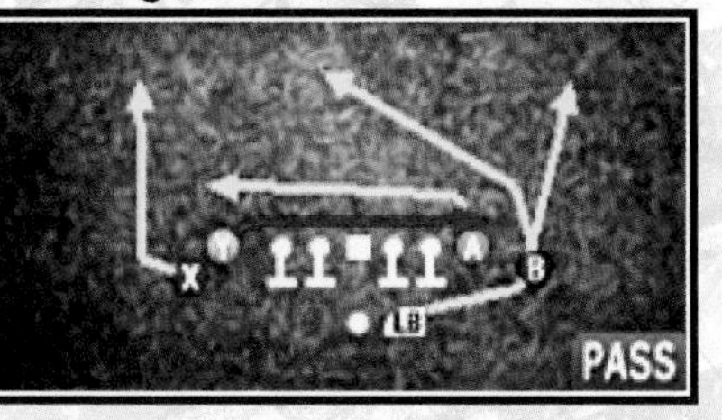

The Texan Cross is a great play where we look to highlight our all-pro WR Andre Johnson. The design of the play has him running a drag across the field. We wait for Johnson to open into space before we deliver the ball. What is also great about this play is all the options we have on the field. The HB runs a great route to beat any style of blitzing defense, and we look to use him as our safety valve.

Johnson is initially covered as the play develops. Wait for Johnson to open up over the middle of the field. As soon as you have a passing window, deliver the ball.

The pass is delivered on the money, and Johnson hauls the catch in over two defenders. Throwing to a WR like Johnson gives us a lot of room to avoid making mistakes.

PRO TIP Look to attack the defense with the deep post if they are in a Cover 2 zone or any type of blitzing defense!

Zone Beater

Gun Bunch - Corner Strike

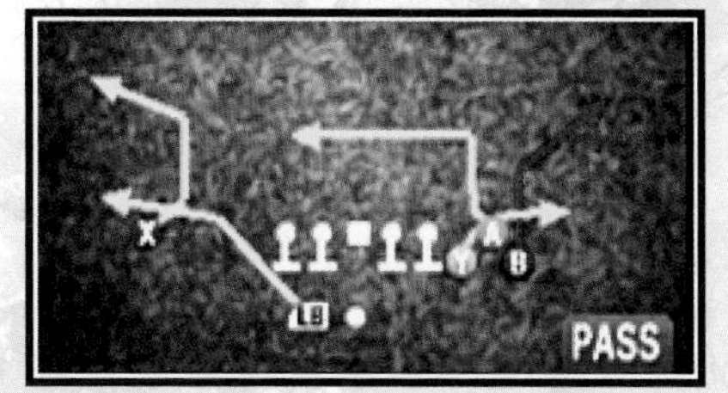

Attacking zone defense coverage is all about using overloads from trips and bunch formations. The Gun Bunch Corner Strike has a few options we can use to attack any zone defensive coverage. The flat route is great against a Cover 4 zone, and the corner route is solid for a Cover 2 zone. Sit back and read the defense and deliver the ball to the open WR.

The defense is in a Cover 2 zone, and we see that the flat defender is forced to choose who he will defend. As our WR running to the flat makes his break, our corner route should be open up top.

Our Corner route opens up as the play develops, and we deliver the ball to the WR down the sideline. At the snap of the ball, we had to read the defensive coverage and then find the open passing window.

PRO TIP Look to attack zone defensive coverage with bigger WRs and TEs.

Base Play

Singleback Ace Close - Texan Drag

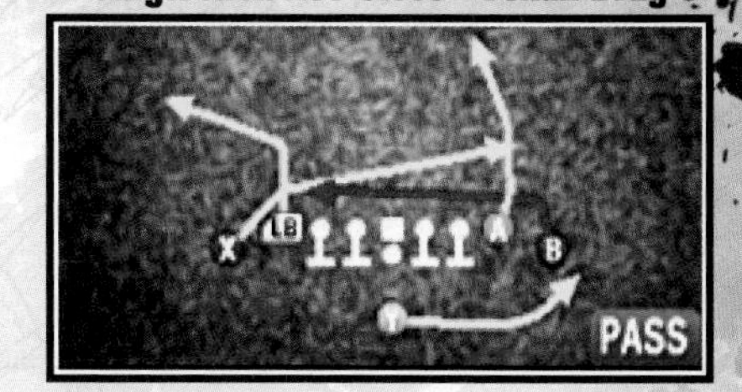

One of the most important aspects of any play is its ability to beat man-to-man and zone defensive coverages. The Singleback Ace Close Texan Drag gives us options to beat both styles of defense. The dual drags over the middle of the field are great for attacking man-to-man, and the corner routes are great against all zone defensive coverages.

The defense is in a man-to-man blitz, and the pressure is coming in quick. Our drag routes haven't opened up underneath, but we do see our TE breaking free with no help in the defensive secondary.

We deliver the throw in stride to our big TE for the touchdown. Finding holes in the defense is all about progression of your reads. We first looked to the drags and saw they were covered and then looked to our next option for the score.

PRO TIP Using the TE in the passing game can really open up your offense. TEs don't have the speed we think of for big play potential. However, their size helps to create mismatches for the defense.

TENNESSEE TITANS

OFFENSIVE SCOUTING REPORT

While the QB situation in Tennessee is unclear, one thing is for certain: Chris Johnson will be an explosive RB in *Madden NFL 12*! New head coach Mike Munchak is a former NFL lineman and will commit to an offense heavily featuring Johnson. Look to start rookie QB Jake Locker, who has plenty of athletic ability on the virtual gridiron. While scrambling won't be used as heavily as in previous years, Locker can still make plays with his feet. At WR, focus on getting the ball to Kenny Britt, whose toughness and catch in traffic ratings are amazing.

DEFENSIVE SCOUTING REPORT

The Titans will undergo changes this season to their defensive scheme, but one thing that will remain the same is their physical play. CB Cortland Finnegan is a hard-nosed football player who makes his opponents work for every yard. The Titans will have to work on generating a pass rush but did pick up Derrick Morgan in the draft to help out. Michael Griffin remains solid in the secondary and can play any style called upon him. If the Titans' offense can grind out drives, this defense will be able to shorten the game and get some wins.

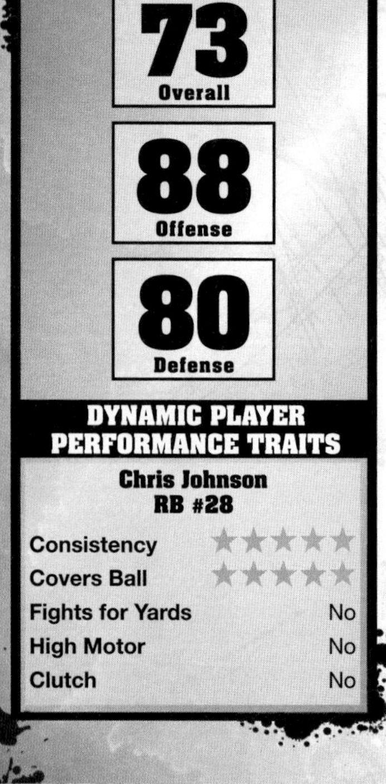

RATINGS BY POSITION

Quarterbacks	74	Defensive Tackles	84
Halfbacks	96	Outside Linebackers	79
Fullbacks	88	Middle Linebackers	88
Wide Receivers	83	Cornerbacks	84
Tight Ends	78	Free Safeties	91
Tackles	91	Strong Safeties	87
Guards	82	Kickers	95
Centers	73	Punters	63
Defensive Ends	86		

DEPTH CHART

POS	OVR	FIRST NAME	LAST NAME
3DRB	96	Chris	Johnson
C	73	Eugene	Amano
C	63	Kevin	Matthews
CB	90	Cortland	Finnegan
CB	78	Alterraun	Verner
CB	71	Jason	McCourty
CB	61	Ryan	Mouton
CB	61	Pete	Ittersagen
DT	84	Jason	Jones
DT	84	Tony	Brown
DT	75	Jovan	Haye
DT	68	Sen'Derrick	Marks
FB	88	Ahmard	Hall
FS	91	Michael	Griffin
FS	74	Vincent	Fuller
FS	66	Robert	Johnson
HB	96	Chris	Johnson
HB	72	Javon	Ringer
HB	63	Stafon	Johnson
HB	62	Jamie	Harper
K	95	Rob	Bironas
KOS	95	Rob	Bironas
KR	70	Marc	Mariani
KR	67	Damian	Williams
LE	90	Jason	Babin
LE	71	William	Hayes
LE	63	Hall	Davis
LG	80	Leroy	Harris
LG	69	Ryan	Durand
LOLB	74	Gerald	McRath
LOLB	64	Patrick	Bailey
LOLB	68	Jamie	Winborn
LS	51	Ken	Amato
LT	91	Michael	Roos
LT	66	Troy	Kropog
MLB	88	Stephen	Tulloch
MLB	67	Colin	McCarthy
MLB	65	Colin	Allred
P	63	Brett	Kern
PR	70	Marc	Mariani
QB	74	Jake	Locker
QB	77	Kerry	Collins
QB	60	Rusty	Smith
RE	81	Dave	Ball
RE	71	Jacob	Ford
RE	77	Derrick	Morgan
RG	83	Jake	Scott
RG	54	Fernando	Velasco
ROLB	84	Will	Witherspoon
ROLB	72	Akeem	Ayers
ROLB	66	Rennie	Curran
RT	91	David	Stewart
RT	70	Michael	Otto
SS	87	Chris	Hope
SS	65	Donnie	Nickey
SS	67	Nick	Schommer
TE	78	Bo	Scaife
TE	70	Craig	Stevens
TE	76	Jared	Cook Jr.
WR	86	Kenny	Britt
WR	78	Nate	Washington
WR	84	Randy	Moss
WR	75	Justin	Gage
WR	67	Damian	Williams
WR	68	Lavelle	Hawkins

OFFENSIVE STRENGTH CHART

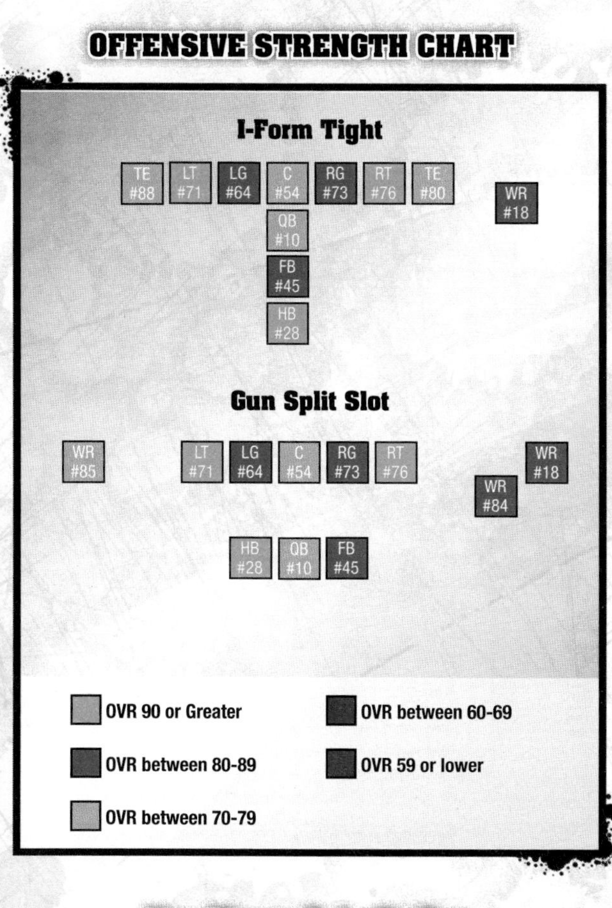

Key Player Substitution

Player: Jared Cook Jr.

Position: #1 TE

Key Stat: 85 Speed

What He Brings: Jared Cook Jr. is a beast on the virtual gridiron. He has a great frame that allows him to be a safety valve for his QB and the speed to go with it.

#28 Chris Johnson
Halfback

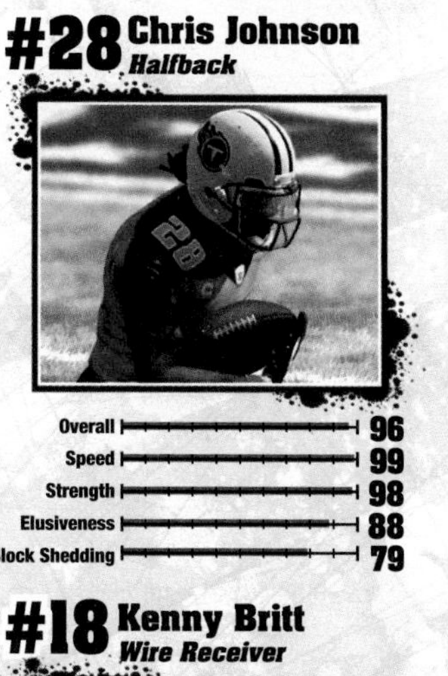

Overall	96
Speed	99
Strength	98
Elusiveness	88
Block Shedding	79

#18 Kenny Britt
Wire Receiver

Overall	86
Speed	88
Catch	86
Route Running	85
Acceleration	91

#89 Jared Cook Jr.
Tight End

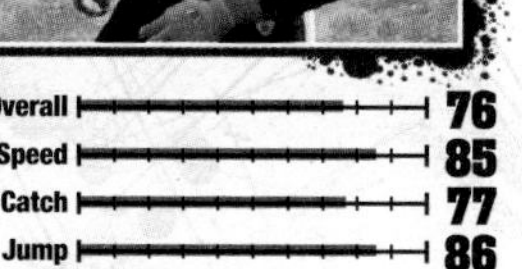

Overall	76
Speed	85
Catch	77
Jump	86
Catch in Traffic	78

#31 Cortland Finnegan
Cornerback

Overall	90
Speed	91
Man Coverage	88
Zone Coverage	91
Awareness	85

#33 Michael Griffin
Free Safety

Overall	91
Speed	88
Tackle	75
Hit Power	74
Play Recognition	84

#32 Robert Johnson
Free Safety

Overall	66
Speed	86
Tackle	64
Hit Power	63
Play Recognition	60

DEFENSIVE STRENGTH CHART

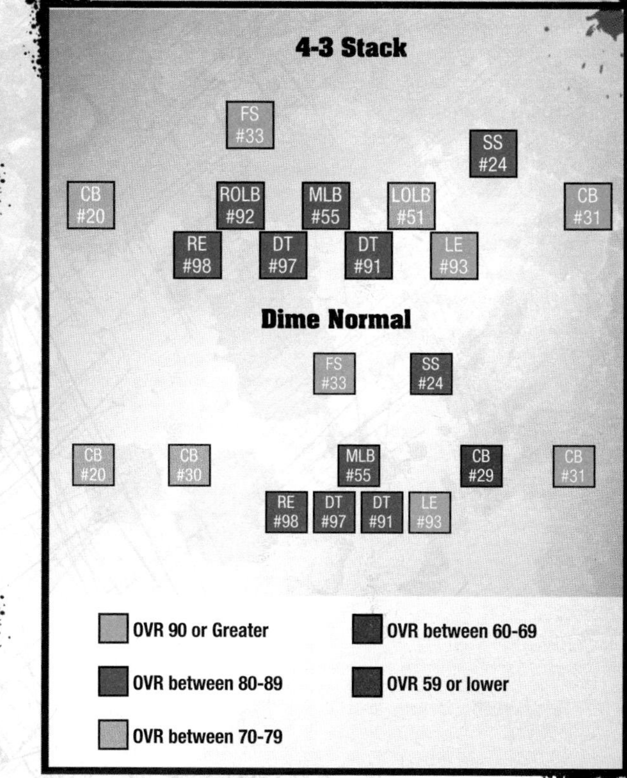

Key Player Substitution

Player: Derrick Morgan

Position: #1 RE

Key Stat: 87 Acceleration

What He Brings: Derrick Morgan is a great talent and should see the field immediately. He can hold his own against the run and the pass.

Playbook Tips

Offensive Style: Run Balanced

Offense

- Rookie QB Jake Locker will have to use his athletic ability while learning the offense on the fly.
- Chris Johnson should get the heavy majority of the carries as he can break the game wide open.
- The Titans should look to bring multiple TEs into the game to help in run and pass protection.

Defense

- Cortland Finnegan's toughness and heart make it tough to get off the line against him.
- New defensive coordinator Jerry Gray looks to add bulk to the line to help slow down the run game.
- Play extra-loose defense to extend drives because minimizing the number of possessions will benefit your offense's ground attack.

OFFENSIVE FORMATIONS

FORMATION	# OF PLAYS
Gun Double Flex	15
Gun Doubles	15
Gun Doubles WK	18
Gun Empty Spread	9
Gun Split Slot	15
Gun Y-Trips Open	12
Gun Y-Trips WK	18
I-Form H Pro	21
I-Form Tight	12
I-Form Tight Pair	12
Singleback Ace	21
Singleback Ace Pair	18
Singleback Bunch	12
Singleback Doubles	18
Singleback Y-Trips	18
Singleback Snugs Flip	12
Singleback Trey Open	12
Strong Pro	21
Strong Pro Twins	15
Weak Pro	18

OFFENSIVE PLAYCOUNTS

PLAY TYPE	# OF PLAYS
Quick Pass	19
Standard Pass	69
Shotgun Pass	63
Play Action Pass	55
Inside Handoff	41
Outside Handoff	19
Pitch	11
Counter	14
Draw	10

Three-Headed Rushing Attack

I-Form Tight—Iso

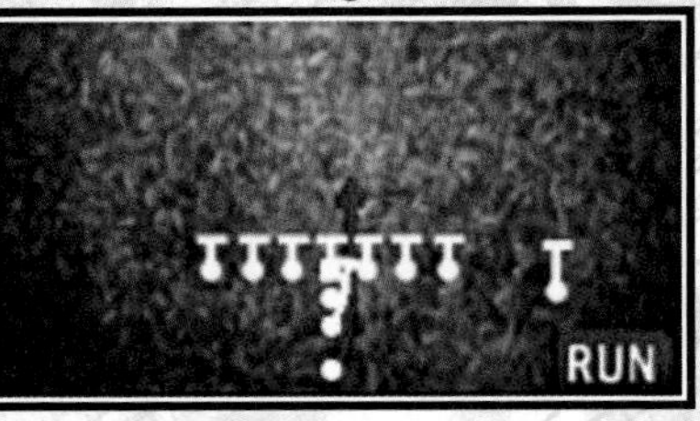

I-Form Tight is a great power run formation that most teams use to pick up short yardage. However, when you have a talent like Chris Johnson, there is no such thing as short yardage—every play is a threat to go the distance.

The initial double-team by our interior linemen does a great job of creating two holes. Since the LB is disciplined in his assignment, we stay with our FB and head up the middle.

Our linemen release the double-team and head into the second level. The defender misses the HB in the backfield and now we have a convoy. With the safety unblocked, we will simply head to the left and leave him in the dust. Johnson is that talented as a RB and will make defenses who over-pursue pay big time.

PRO TIP Former lineman and new head coach Mike Munchak will be sure to commit to Johnson and a power rushing attack.

I Form Tight - HB Lead Toss

Having a HB like Chris Johnson in the backfield strikes fear into any defense. His blazing speed is perfect for the HB Lead Toss. We look to attack the outside edge of the defense with this play and put pressure on the defense to match Johnson's speed. If the defense contains the outside edge, look to cut your losses and move the ball back upfield.

We catch the toss and are off to the races with Johnson. His speed will be tough for defenses to match on the outside. Look to reach the edge and cut upfield as soon as you have the running angle.

Johnson gets to the corner and turns on the jets. The defense is late in reaching him before he gets deep down the sideline. The HB Toss has big play potential written all over it and can open many other plays for the offense.

PRO TIP Speed is the most important aspect to the success of the HB Toss. If Johnson is tired, avoid calling the HB Lead Toss.

I Form Tight - HB Stretch

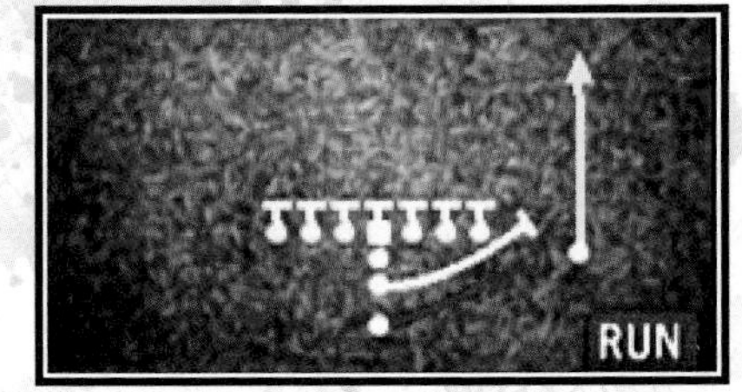

The HB Stretch is another run that we like to use to take advantage of Johnson's speed. The HB Lead Toss broke to the left of the field, and with the HB Stretch, we are looking to attack the defense to the right of the field. This run helps get the ball to the HB toward the outside of the field to where the HB can quickly get into the secondary.

Our wall of blockers has opened up a serious hole toward the outside of the field. Look to follow your FB to gain the extra push into the defensive secondary.

Johnson has only one man to beat, and that is the deep safety. We put the juke move on just before we are taken down for a huge gain on the run.

PRO TIP Follow your block by the FB. He will lead you to the open running lane.

Quick Pass

I-Form Tight—PA HB Wheel

By staying in the power run formation and adding a play action pass, we can look to slow down the LBs' pursuit of the RB. Use this play after a few successful runs to keep the defense guessing.

Our QB does a great job of selling the fake, and Johnson continues down the field on his route. Our QB will now roll to his strong side, where his receiving options should be coming open.

When you roll the pocket, you cut down half the field and make it very easy for the QB to rifle through his progressions. With the defense closing in, we simply dump the ball into the flat, which lost containment on the play fake.

PRO TIP If you get time, unleash the deep wheel route to the HB because no LB can match up with his speed.

Man Beater

Gun Split Slot - HB Screen

Another great way to attack any blitzing-style defense is with the HB Screen. The aggressive nature of the blitz forces the defenses into the backfield. We then look to sneak the screen in with blockers in front to take advantage of the aggressive defense. Chris Johnson's speed will be a huge factor in the success of this play.

Here comes the pressure! The defense has a clear path to the QB; meanwhile, Johnson is getting into position for the screen.

The blitz leaves no extra defenders in the secondary to help defend against the screen. With the extra blockers and Johnson's blazing speed, the HB Screen has big play potential.

PRO TIP At the snap of the ball, roll away from pressure with the QB. Then set up for the pass to the HB.

Zone Beater

Singleback Y - Trips Open - Levels

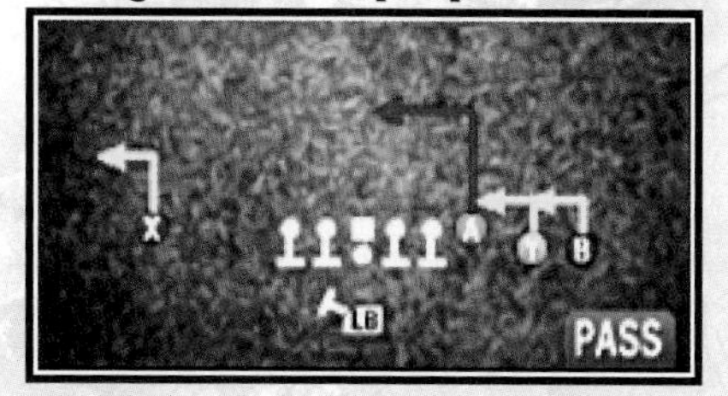

Without a doubt, one of the best ways to beat zone defense is with the Levels passing concept. This overloads the defense with the same route but at all different depths. This makes it extremely difficult for any zone to defend.

Here we see the zone defender is letting our WR through on the short in route. Over the top, we see another WR running the same route but deeper downfield. We wait for the routes to develop and find the open WR.

We get the ball to our underneath WR and look to move upfield. Running levels is a surefire way to beat a zone defense. Do not key in on any WR prior to the play happening. You have to react to which WR opens up and then deliver the ball.

PRO TIP Route running is very important when running Levels. Substitute in your best route runners for this play.

Base Play

Singleback Snugs - Stick

Singleback Snugs Stick is a very quick developing play that we like to use when facing a man-to-man blitz. Both our slot WRs will break to the flat while our split-end WRs will sit on short curl routes. This play is great for one-on-one matchups.

The defense is lined up to attack the offensive A gap. We see the overload in the middle by the linebackers and anticipate the blitz. At the snap of the ball, we want to look to our left slot WR in the flat.

The pressure came quickly, but we got the ball out to our WR just as quick. With no help in the defensive secondary, this play can result in big plays time after time.

PRO TIP Watch out for the defense playing a Cover 2 zone. If there is a flat defender, this play could get you a pick 6.

The Minnesota Vikings' attack is predicated on the success of star RB Adrian Peterson. He possesses 95+ ratings in crucial categories, including speed, agility, and acceleration. Pounding the rock will force the defense to commit to the run and will open up the passing lanes for talented WRs Percy Harvin and Sidney Rice. The Vikings have three options at QB coming into the season: Joe Webb, Tarvaris Jackson, Christian Ponder. All three have very good mobility and must use their athleticism to stress the defense. These plays focus on short passes to talented playmakers. The Vikings have committed to a run-first offense and will have success if they get into manageable third-down situations.

DEFENSIVE SCOUTING REPORT

The Vikings have one of the top-tier defensive lines in the game. When you can dominate the line of scrimmage, playing defense seems to come easier. Jared Allen leads the pass-rushing portion of the line while Kevin Williams holds down the run game. Antoine Winfield has shown his ability to make game-changing plays in the secondary. The Vikings are a solid team that will benefit from the improved zone coverage. This will help hide some of the team's speed deficiencies while leading to more sacks for the line.

TEAM RATING

74 Overall

83 Offense

85 Defense

DYNAMIC PLAYER PERFORMANCE TRAITS

Adrian Peterson
RB #28

Consistency	★★★★★
Covers Ball	★★★★★
Fights for Yards	Yes
High Motor	Yes
Clutch	No

RATINGS BY POSITION

Quarterbacks	73
Halfbacks	97
Fullbacks	77
Wide Receivers	81
Tight Ends	84
Tackles	80
Guards	82
Centers	73
Defensive Ends	91
Defensive Tackles	97
Outside Linebackers	86
Middle Linebackers	88
Cornerbacks	86
Free Safeties	71
Strong Safeties	78
Kickers	96
Punters	77

DEPTH CHART

POS	OVR	FIRST NAME	LAST NAME
3DRB	72	Toby	Gerhart
C	73	John	Sullivan
C	64	Jon	Cooper
CB	90	Antoine	Winfield
CB	81	Cedric	Griffin
CB	70	Asher	Allen
CB	66	Chris	Cook
CB	65	Brandon	Burton
DT	97	Kevin	Williams
DT	86	Pat	Williams
DT	74	Jimmy	Kennedy
DT	66	Christian	Ballard
DT	65	Fred	Evans
FB	77	Naufahu	Tahi
FB	41	Ryan	D'Imperio
FS	71	Madieu	Williams
FS	63	Eric	Frampton
HB	97	Adrian	Peterson
HB	72	Toby	Gerhart
HB	66	Lorenzo	Booker
HB	65	Albert	Young
K	96	Ryan	Longwell
KOS	96	Ryan	Longwell
KR	85	Percy	Harvin
KR	72	Toby	Gerhart
LE	88	Ray	Edwards
LE	67	Everson	Griffen
LG	92	Steve	Hutchinson
LG	73	Chris	DeGeare
LG	65	Seth	Olsen
LOLB	82	Ben	Leber
LOLB	62	Erin	Henderson
LOLB	54	Kenny	Onatolu
LS	63	Cullen	Loeffler
LT	85	Bryant	McKinnie
LT	61	Patrick	Brown
MLB	88	E.J.	Henderson
MLB	69	Jasper	Brinkley
MLB	63	Ross	Homan
P	77	Chris	Kluwe
PR	70	Greg	Camarillo
QB	73	Christian	Ponder
QB	66	Joe	Webb
QB	72	Tarvaris	Jackson
RE	94	Jared	Allen
RE	69	Brian	Robison
RE	50	D'Aundre	Reed
RG	71	Anthony	Herrera
RG	69	Ryan	Cook
ROLB	90	Chad	Greenway
ROLB	71	Heath	Farwell
RT	75	Phil	Loadholt
RT	64	DeMarcus	Love
RT	67	Thomas	Welch
SS	78	Husain	Abdullah
SS	76	Jamarca	Sanford
SS	72	Tyrell	Johnson
TE	84	Visanthe	Shiancoe
TE	73	Kyle	Rudolph
TE	66	Jim	Kleinsasser
WR	85	Percy	Harvin
WR	85	Sidney	Rice
WR	74	Bernard	Berrian
WR	70	Greg	Camarillo
WR	63	Greg	Lewis

OFFENSIVE STRENGTH CHART

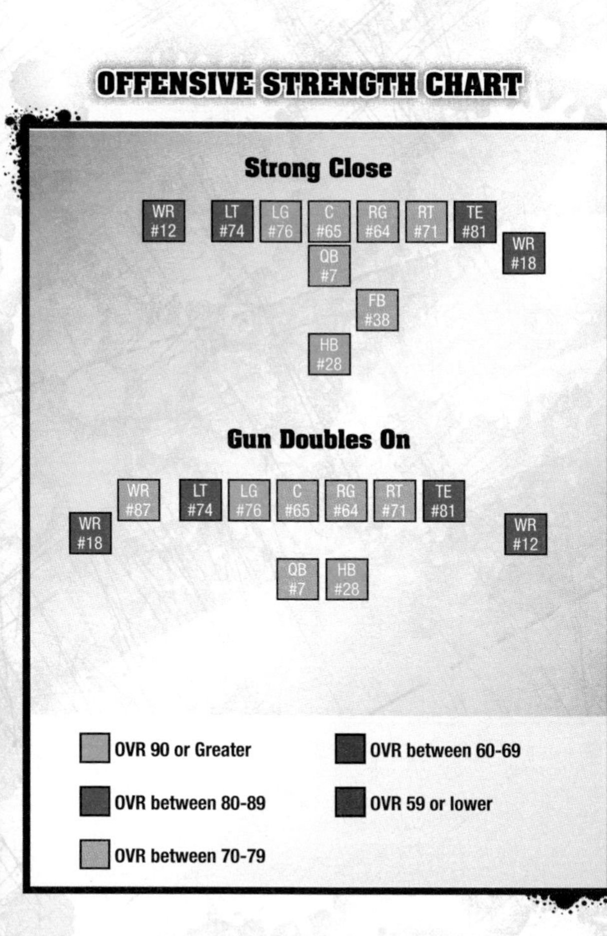

Key Player Substitution

Player: Joe Webb

Position: #2 QB Slot

Key Stat: 86 Speed

What He Brings: Joe Webb has the extra speed to turn the corner and really stress the defense. If you prefer a mobile QB, start him over Christian Ponder.

#28 Adrian Peterson *Halfback*

Overall	97
Speed	97
Strength	98
Elusiveness	97
Block Shedding	60

#12 Percy Harvin *Wide Receiver*

Overall	85
Speed	96
Catch	84
Route Running	77
Acceleration	98

#14 Joe Webb *Quarterback*

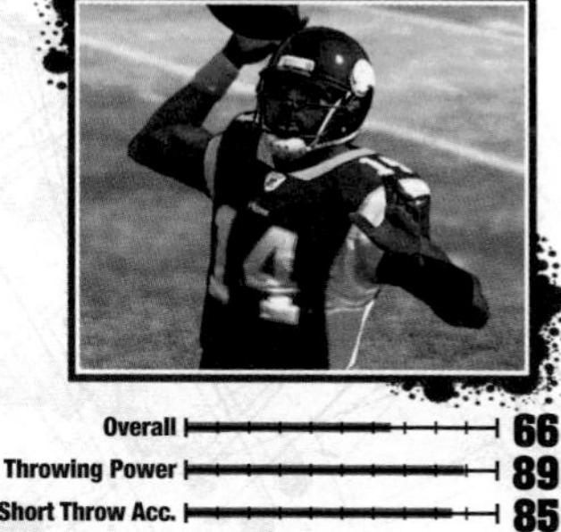

Overall	66
Throwing Power	89
Short Throw Acc.	85
Med. Throw Acc.	66
Deep Throw Acc.	67

#69 Jared Allen *Right End*

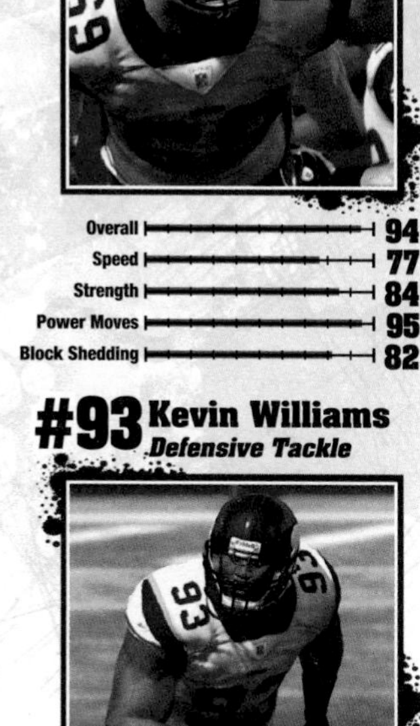

Overall	94
Speed	77
Strength	84
Power Moves	95
Block Shedding	82

#93 Kevin Williams *Defensive Tackle*

Overall	97
Speed	70
Strength	92
Power Moves	87
Block Shedding	92

#25 Tyrell Johnson *Strong Safety*

Overall	72
Speed	89
Tackle	70
Hit Power	74
Play Recognition	55

DEFENSIVE STRENGTH CHART

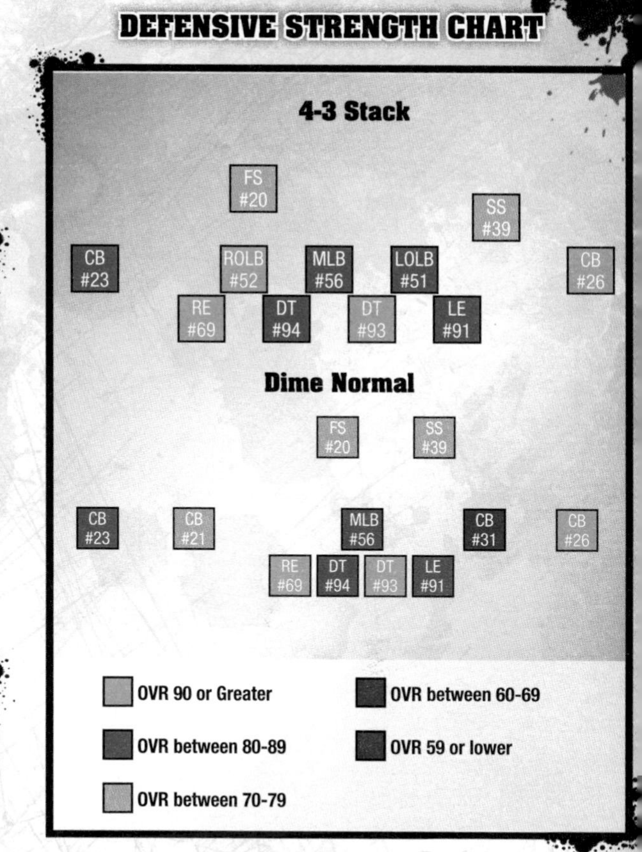

Key Player Substitution

Player: Tyrell Johnson

Position: #1 SS

Key Stat: 92 Jump

What He Brings: Tyrell Johnson has been a gem for the last few seasons. While user-controlling Johnson, you can challenge bigger WRs who look to make possession catches on the sidelines.

Playbook Tips

Offensive Style: Run Balanced

Offense

- Without a great QB, look to work Adrian Peterson heavily into your offense.
- The Vikings have QBs who can stretch the defense with their legs and help cut down the field on throws.
- Percy Harvin has the ability to break the game open from multiple positions; get him the ball in space.

Defense

- Jared Allen is a one-man wrecking crew, so blitz sparingly and allow him to harass the QB all game.
- The Vikings' defensive line is strong up the middle; leave the safeties out of the box at the start of the game.
- Minnesota's overall defensive speed is fairly slow, but the new zone coverage should help them keep up.

OFFENSIVE FORMATIONS

FORMATION	# OF PLAYS
Full House Normal House	12
Gun Double Flex	15
Gun Doubles On	19
Gun Empty Trey	12
Gun Snugs Flip	12
Gun Split Viking	12
Gun Trey Open	15
Gun Y-Trips WK	18
I-Form Pro	18
I-Form Slot Flex	15
I-Form Tight Pair	12
Singleback Ace	15
Singleback Ace Pair Twins	12
Singleback Ace Twins	15
Singleback Bunch	18
Singleback Doubles	18
Singleback Jumbo Z	9
Singleback Y-Trips	18
Strong Close	12
Strong Pro	12
Weak Pro	12

OFFENSIVE PLAYCOUNTS

PLAY TYPE	# OF PLAYS
Quick Pass	19
Standard Pass	62
Shotgun Pass	72
Play Action Pass	50
Inside Handoff	43
Outside Handoff	15
Pitch	11
Counter	7
Draw	13

Three-Headed Rushing Attack

Singleback Ace - Outside Zone

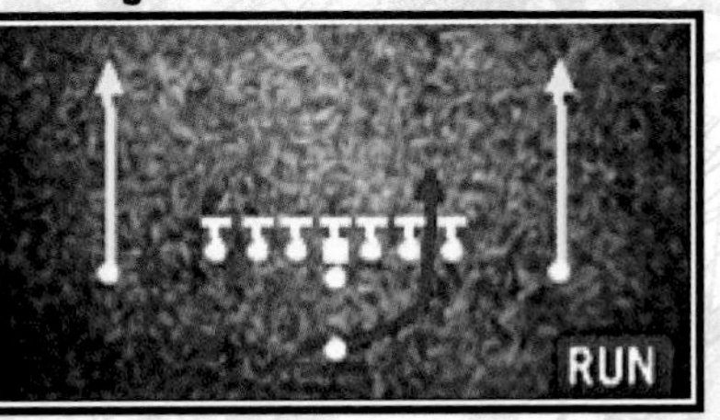

Having a dynamic HB like Adrian Peterson in the backfield means a few things for the offense. It means getting the ball to Peterson toward the outside, where his speed can take advantage of slower defenses, and it means finding as many ways as possible to get him the ball. The Outside Zone is a great run that capitalizes on Peterson's strengths as an HB.

We get the handoff and see that we can either run through the defender or try to run around him. Peterson has the speed to get outside, but he also has the power to run over the defender.

This time around, we choose to break the run outside and use Peterson's speed to get the extra yards. We then plow through the defense as they take us down on the sideline.

PRO TIP Be quick with your decisions. Before the snap of the ball, know where you want to go with the ball and stick with that plan.

Singleback Ace— HB Dive

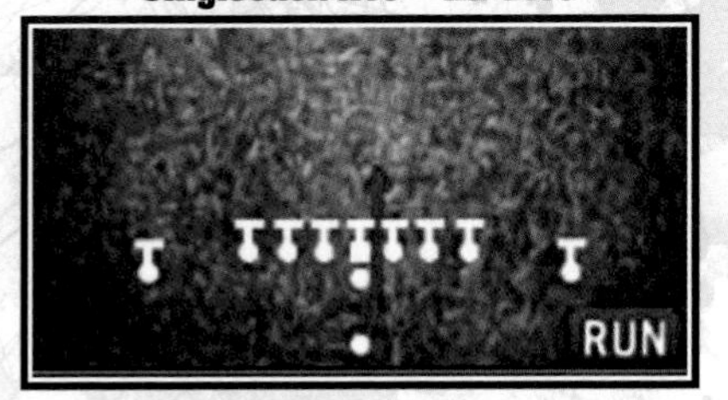

The HB Dive from the Ace formation is an incredibly balanced run. It allows Peterson to hit the run to either side of the center. The defense must remain balanced but also is very spread out due to the lineup of this Singleback set.

Without a fullback to block, a QB must be ready to audible out of this play if the defense stacks LBs in the middle of the field. Here, the box is open so Peterson gets the handoff and our interior line blows open a hole to the right side.

Adrian Peterson wastes no time getting back to the line of scrimmage on this run. Once he breaks into the second level, he can unleash the wide array of moves that make him the top running back in *Madden NFL 12*.

PRO TIP Cover up the ball if the defense swarms into the middle to prevent game-changing fumbles.

Singleback Ace - Pump Draw

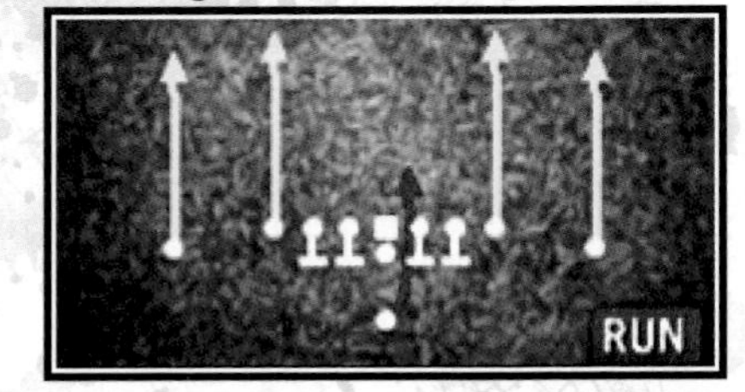

The Pump Draw is a very unique play and is another option to get the ball into Adrian Peterson's hands. At the snap of the ball, our QB will pump fake and try to freeze the defense. We then get the handoff and look to move upfield with Peterson.

Notice the pump fake and the defender dropping back into coverage. This is exactly what we were hoping for with this play. As soon as we get the ball, look to move upfield through an open running lane.

The defense is out of position, and there is only one man left to beat! It shouldn't be too hard to shake one defender in the defensive secondary.

PRO TIP With any draws, be sure to wait for your offensive line to push upfield.
If you outrun your blocks, you can count on losing yards with this play.

Quick Pass

Fullhouse - WRDBL Shake

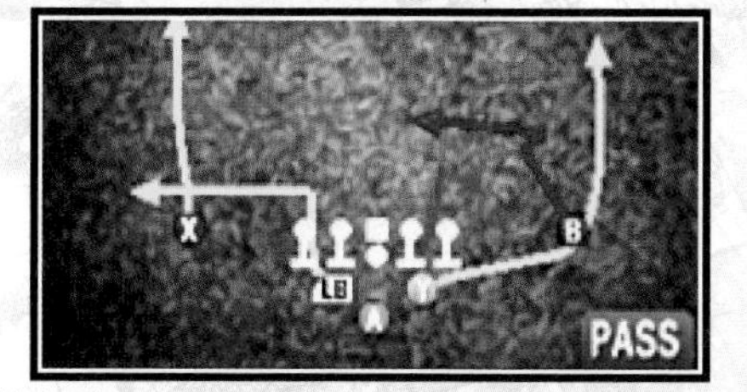

This has been our favorite play for the past few seasons. The WR DBL Shake has so many options for beating blitzing defenses that it will make your opponent's head spin! Our main option is the TE in the backfield. He runs an amazing out and up route that we like to throw quickly to. Next look to your HB running into the flat, and finally look for the HB on the delay blue route.

The defense is in a man-to-man blitz, and the pressure is coming in quickly. We see our TE getting into position, and we just have to hang in the pocket a split second longer before we deliver the ball.

We deliver the ball before the pressure can get to the QB, and we are into the secondary with no defenders around us. Beating the blitz can be frustrating for your opponent. They expect to get the QB and fluster you in the process. However, with the right play and the right reads, we are able to attack the blitz with success!

PRO TIP Make sure you have your best receiving TE in for this play. There is nothing worse than calling the right play but having your receiver drop the ball.

Man Beater

Gun Trey Open - WR Screen

The Vikings have another threat that is not Adrian Peterson. In the passing game, WR Percy Harvin is that explosive threat. The WR Screen from the Gun Trey Open is a play that targets Harvin's speed in a major way. At the snap of the ball, get the ball out to him quickly and follow your blockers upfield.

Here we see that Harvin is in position as the QB gets ready to make the pass. Our offensive line is getting in position to deliver the blocks downfield. This play is great when facing any type of blitzing defense.

We make the grab and bolt down the sideline for the easy score. Harvin has the speed to outrun the defenders, especially with blockers helping to lead the way.

PRO TIP Roll away from any oncoming pressure with the QB and then deliver the pass to the WR once he gets into position.

Zone Beater

Gun Split Viking - Vike's Go

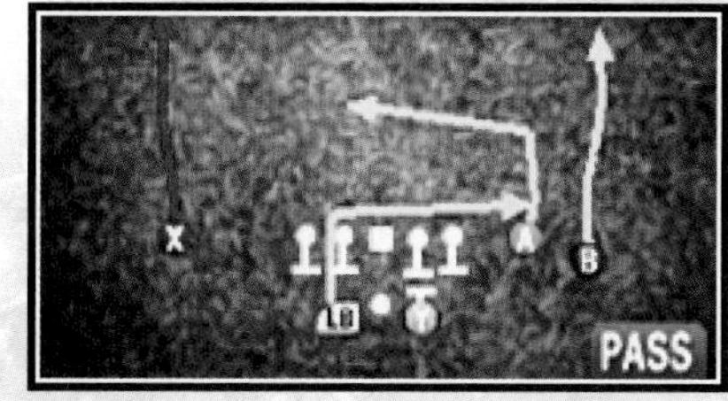

The Vike's Go is a play in which we like to highlight one of our bigger WRs down the sideline. When facing the zone, the sideline can be an area to expose the defense. We use our big WR to post up smaller defenders down the field.

The defense is in a Cover 3 zone, and we know this by seeing the three-deep defenders dropping back into coverage. We know that we should have a one-on-one matchup down the sideline against the zone defender.

As our WR breaks down the sideline, we throw the deep pass, looking to get into a jump ball battle with the deep defender. Our WR hauls in the pass and gets into the end zone for the score.

PRO TIP When going for jump balls, make sure you have the height advantage with your WR.

Base Play

Singleback Ace—PA All Go

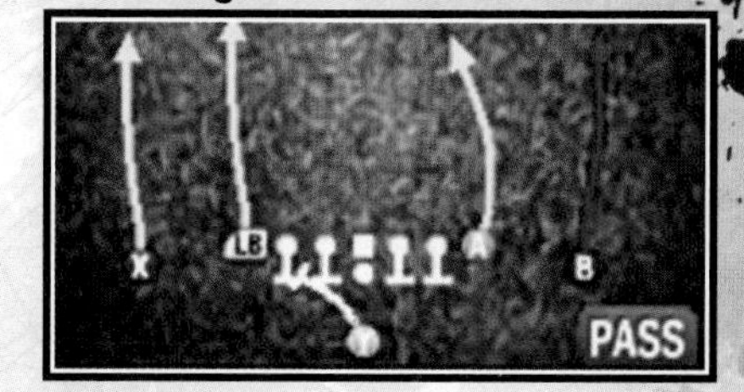

The PA All Go is a great play out of a balanced formation. The fake works because it is the same formation as our three-headed rushing attack. Depending on how we read the defense, we can easily make changes to the play. Drags and curls are great for beating man defense, while zone coverage can be exploited by leaving the WRs on their go routes.

The QB sells the fake to Adrian Peterson, who must be respected because he is a top-notch running back. If this freezes the defense for a second, our WRs will be able to get behind them in hopes of hauling in a deep pass.

Ponder sees that his best WR, Percy Harvin, has earned a step against his defender. He simply takes a strong step into the pocket and lobs the pass downfield. Harvin can run onto any ball thrown out in front but is also strong enough to go up and fight for the football in the air.

PRO TIP To make this a true base play, cancel the play action and look to hot route WRs depending on the coverage you read presnap.

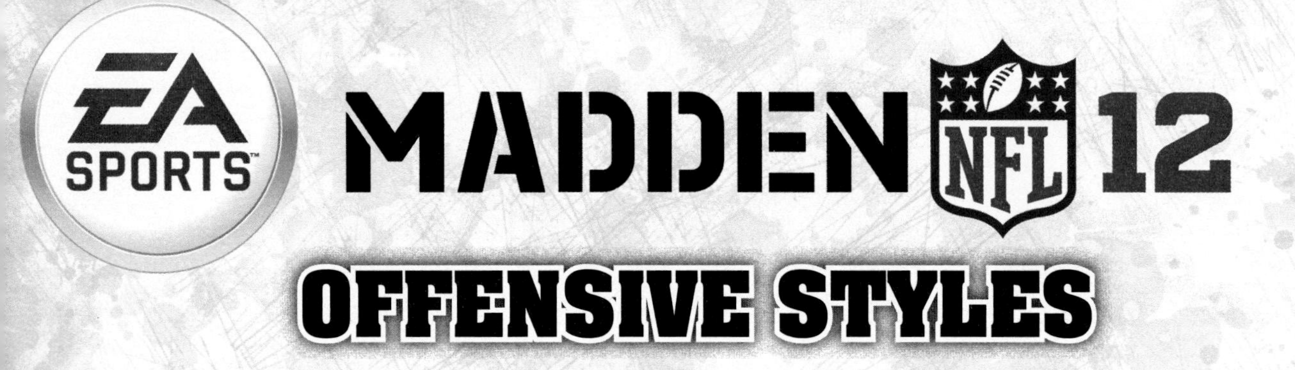

Contents

GAME PLANS

Every time you enter a game in *Madden NFL 12*, you have the option of selecting a playbook. You can choose one of the 32 teams' playbooks, or you can run a specific style of offense. Here are breakdowns of the six styles to choose from in the game: Balanced, Balanced Pass, Balanced Run, Power Run, West Coast, and Run N Gun. Select a book based on what personnel you have and what type of offense you are looking to run. If you want to air out the ball look at Balanced Pass, but if you have an elite running back, try out the Power Run. These offensive books are also a great place to start when making your own custom playbook!

Each attack consists of seven plays to start with; you should install the audibles and work on your scheme in practice mode. Here are the play types we use for each system:

Three-Headed Rushing Attack: This gives us a good formation to come out and pound the ball in. Set two of the three runs as your audibles, and the third will be your quick-run audible down. Now you can attack the defense left, middle, or right at the press of a button.

Quick Pass: Set this play as your third audible and use it on short yardage or if you expect the blitz to be coming.

Man Beater (Compressed Set): Set this as the fourth audible and use it if you pick up a man-to-man defensive look before the snap; this can help you create space against your defender.

Zone Beater (Compressed or Trips Set): Your fifth audible should be the play you go to if you get a zone read; use this play to flood the zone and free up a receiver down the field.

Base Play (Balanced or Hybrid Set): We come out in this play in most situations; it allows us to get a read on the defense and has routes that can beat both man and zone coverage. Look to get comfortable in this play and with audibling in and out of it quickly.

PRO TIP Learn where your players go when audibling to different formations; how can you maximize your playmakers?

BALANCED PLAYBOOK BREAKDOWN

The balanced offensive attack was absolutely dominant in *Madden NFL 10* and just may be making a resurgence this season. For players who don't like to tip the defense off to their game plan, the Balanced playbook has plenty of formations that allow you to run or pass all over the defense. This playbook has the very popular Full House formation along with great I-Form runs to gash your opponent with runs and quick passes. If the defense starts to crowd the box, look to run some of the solid shotgun plays in this book. Our favorite sets include Gun Snugs Flip, Singleback Trips Open, and Gun Y-Trips HB Wk. All of these sets working together will give you *balance*!

Three-Headed Rushing Attack

I-Form Tight—HB Lead Toss

Toss it out to the weak side

If the defense starts to lock on to the interior run, we can quickly toss the ball outside to our speedy RB. Most weak-side runs are counters; very rarely do you see a toss. With the LG pulling, wait patiently for the run to be set up before cutting outside. This is a great run to catch an overly aggressive defense with.

The blockers get around the edge

At the snap of the ball, our FB and LG start to pull and create a nice blocking convoy for our RB. Rather than holding down turbo right away, make sure the blocks get set up before deciding whether to take the ball out around the edge.

The defense lost containment on the edge

The RB's eyes light up as he receives the ball and sees that his team has won the battle to block the edge of the field. He can now use his speed to get into space, and if he can make one man miss, this could be a huge gain. This run works best when the defense is sloppy and loses assignments, and it should be used accordingly. Running to the weak side can be risky if you don't set it up properly, but it gives the defense something to worry about at all times.

I-Form Tight—Iso

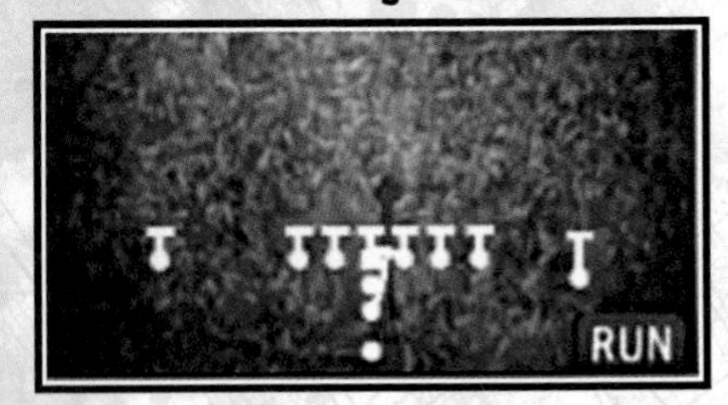

Force the D to stop you

An Iso run is nothing flashy, but when you come out in a tight formation, the defense knows you mean business. By adding extra bulk into the game, the defense will be forced to counter and bring in slower players to combat your look. Here we want the fullback to do most of the work and just let the halfback follow him to pick up as many yards as possible.

Full speed ahead

With most running plays, gamers are cautioned not to use turbo until the blocks set up. However, when running an Iso, you want to get the ball to the HB as quickly as possible and get him running forward immediately. Some runs allow you the luxury of choosing a lane or cutting back, but here we simply want to follow our powerful FB into the line of scrimmage.

The battle is won at the line

Our team pancakes the defenders and our RB can now run freely. Notice how he is keeping his eyes on the second level and watching the safety despite the distance. This is giving him the ability to set up for a move once the defender approaches him. The Iso won't often be broken for long touchdowns, but it is the perfect run to keep the chains moving and the defense watching the middle of the field.

I-Form Tight—Power O

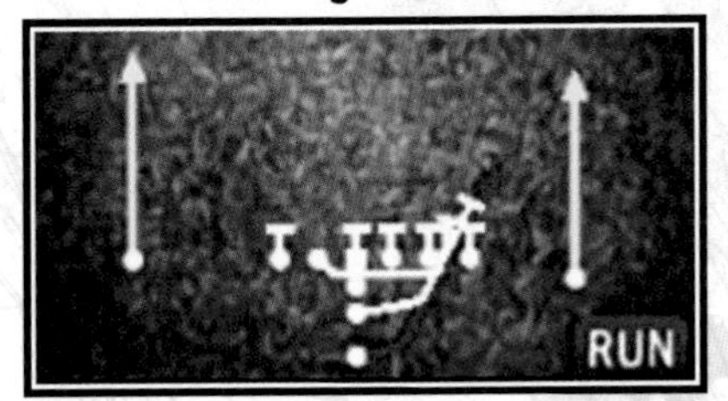

Inside or outside here

The Power O is a great run for the three-headed rushing attack because it can be taken between the tackles or broken outside. At the snap, the guard pulls around to the edge, and we can read his block and determine what hole to hit.

Lots of beef out in front

With two huge blockers out in front of the RB, now is the time to find out what hole to attack. The inside might be open for a decent gain, but the LB appears to be filling it in. If we can set up our block, it's possible to hit the edge with our RB's great agility.

Gotta go inside to get outside

The guard does a great job of picking up the edge rusher, who has slipped off his block. Our back appears to be bottled inside, but this cut draws in the defense and allows the edge to be open. With the TE getting into the second level, one good cut means big yards for the offense. Make sure to know what situation you are in on offense; if you need short yards, look to bang the Power O up the middle—otherwise be patient and find the right hole. When used with other runs, this I-Form Tight attack can be deadly.

Quick Pass

Full House Normal Wide—WR Dbl Shake

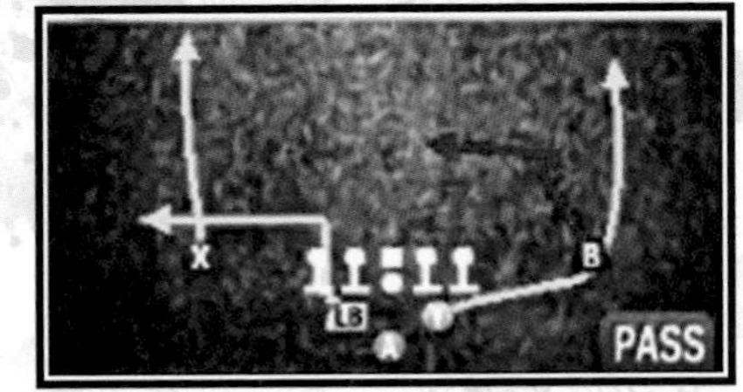

Money in the red zone

The Full House has been one of our favorite formations over the last few seasons. Because we have three options in the backfield, the defense is almost always on its heels. By switching up our targets, we can force the defense to play back and allow the offense to be the aggressor.

Bullet the pass in

This route out of the backfield is great for beating the blitz, picking up short yardage, and converting in the red zone. Make sure to throw a bullet pass and really work on the timing. Learn to trust the throw—it is very hard to intercept since the player uses his body to shield off the defender.

Put your head down and rumble

If the defense starts to key in and user-control the play, flip the play and utilize the route to the right side! We also have the blue route releasing out of the backfield—this is a great route to wait on and roll out since the defense will forget about it. If in the red zone, put both WRs on fades and simply lob it up and let the computer make the catch. So many options on this play!

Man Beater

Gun Snugs Flip—Mesh

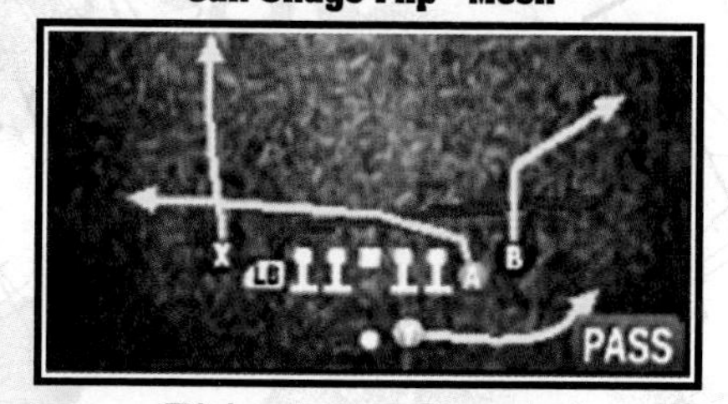

This is a classic compressed set

The Mesh play is great for beating man coverage since defenders will be forced to run through tight spaces over the middle of the field. The throw takes place right in front of the QB, which means it will be accurate and he can get a great read on the defense.

Waiting for separation

The compressed set is a great way to cause a lot of congestion in the middle of the field. The defenders will either be forced to switch off or run the risk of bumping into each other and losing a step on their men. On this play, put the right-side slot receiver on a drag route. He is already on something similar, but the hot routed drag will get him more space to operate.

Lead the pass out in front

If you have a mismatch like WR against LB, you will gain separation if you are patient. If you can lead the pass out in front of the WR, he can turn upfield when he catches the ball and pick up some extra yards. This is a great way to get the defense out of man and focused onto the middle of the field.

Zone Beater

Singleback Trips Open—Slot Drive

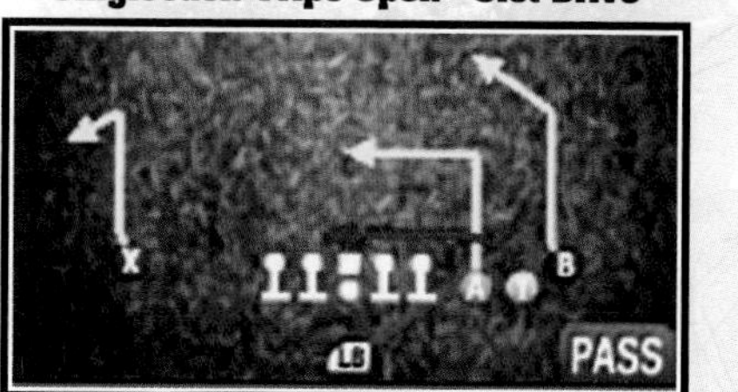

Three receivers on the right will flood the zone

By using a trips formation, the defense will be vulnerable when in zone coverage, due to the offense's ability to have multiple players in one area of the field. Here, we are using a levels-style concept to put pressure on the defense.

Drawing plenty of attention

The key to this play is the ability of the middle WR to draw the attention of the LB. If he can draw him across the middle of the field, the deep ball can be thrown in the soft spot underneath the deep zones. If the LB sags back, simply look to hit the area he vacates across the middle of the field.

Fit it in the window

If you have success deep, the defense may sit back in Cover 4; one reason this play is excellent is the HB releasing to the trips side of the formation. All three WRs clear out and the HB fills into open space in the flat. This will force the defense to keep a defender short or abandon their zone defense all together.

Base Play

Gun Y-Trips HB Wk—Double Drags

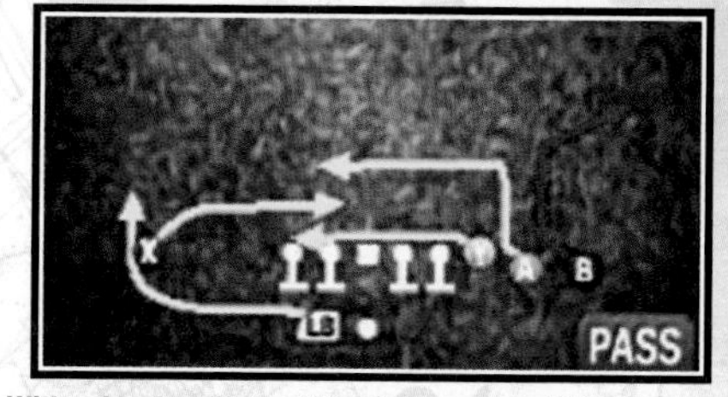

With a few hot routes, this play has everything you need

On the right-hand side of this formation, we like to curl the outside WR, which will let us beat man coverage during our second progression. The TE should be placed onto a slant out, as this will help beat zone coverage.

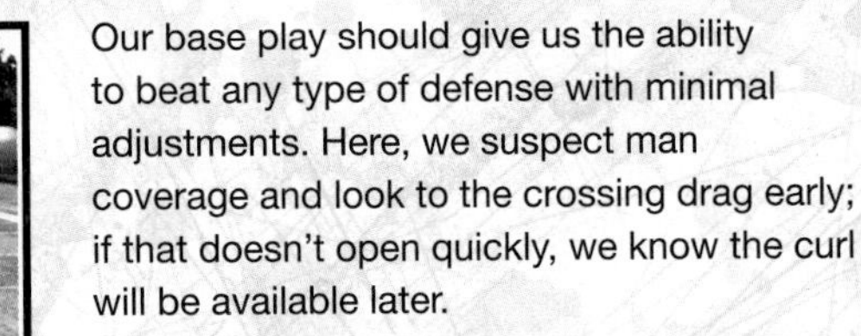

The inside route does a great job holding the defender

Our base play should give us the ability to beat any type of defense with minimal adjustments. Here, we suspect man coverage and look to the crossing drag early; if that doesn't open quickly, we know the curl will be available later.

He shields his defender away from the ball

If we get zone coverage, we can hit the slot WR on his initial burst, but he usually does a great job of attracting the defense. By slanting the TE, we get a great route to the sideline that can be caught for a possession catch. If we get a zone read before the snap, look to streak the outside right WR to clear out space instead of the curl. This also has a great flat route by the HB as a safety valve, or he can block for extra protection.

BALANCED PASS PLAYBOOK BREAKDOWN

The Balanced Pass playbook sounds like it would be a pass-first attack, but it contains some of the best running formations in the game! If you can establish a ground attack with the popular Strong Close formation, you will quickly open up the passing game and be able to use this book's true strength. For top *Madden NFL* players, the Gun Snugs Flip formation has been one of the best in recent years. This book has these sets in both shotgun (Gun Snugs Flip) and under center (Singleback Tight Flex), which can really frustrate defenses. With plenty of shotgun plays, the Balanced Pass playbook is perfect for the team that has solid depth at WR but appreciates the art of running the ball. Even if this attack is not for you, know its formations, because you will likely see many of its plays used online by your opponents!

Three-Headed Rushing Attack

Strong Close—HB Dive

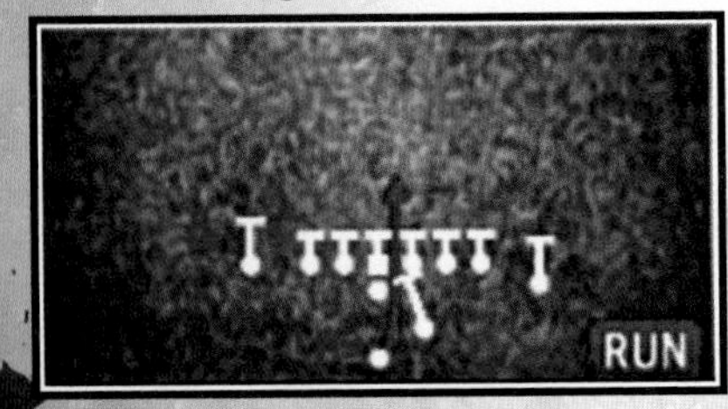

Hit them straight ahead

While most three-headed rushing attacks consist of left, middle, and right runs, the balanced pass attack is unique since we look to attack the middle, the B gap, and then outside the tackle with our runs. The HB Dive is a good straight-ahead run that can be used to attack the A gap. It has more flexibility than the Iso, which is our usual middle run.

Follow your blockers

The blockers do a great job of opening up holes into the second level. The HB Dive gives us the ability to go left, unlike the Iso run, but our best chance of success on this play is to stick behind our blockers.

Hit the second level

The back does a good job exploding through the line. Look to cover up the ball if you get into traffic with defenders swarming in. If the defense is playing a three-down line and leaving the middle open, you must pound them up the middle. Motion the WR from the right and block him when he gets to the center. Make the opponent respect this run.

Strong Close—HB Off Tackle

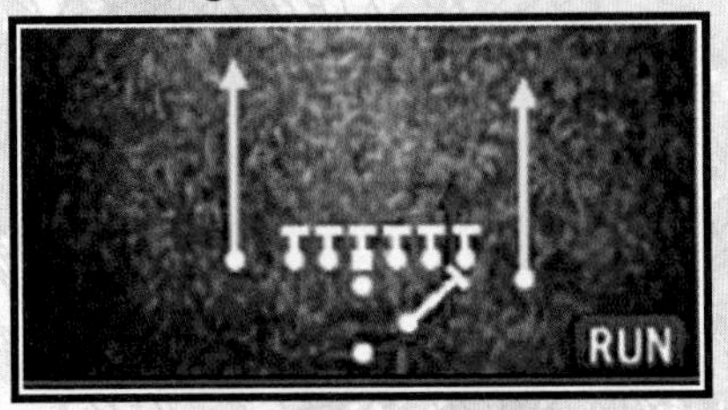

The best run in the book

The HB Off Tackle is a run that tells the defense, "Here is what I am doing, now go ahead and stop it." While the run is designed to be banged off the edge, you can either hit it up the middle or take it wide depending on how the defense plays. The WRs do a great job clearing out, and you are left to read the fullback's block.

Note the handoff angle

The fullback takes an inside release here and looks to seal the inside of the formation. Reading where he goes is a key to the success of this run. Our optimal lane here is running off the RT, who should be able to seal his defender and hold the edge.

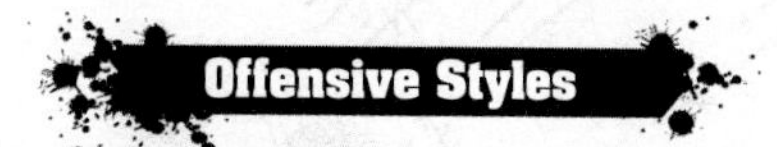

The fullback seals inside

Once we get off tackle, we can see that the TE is powering his defender back and the WR who is downfield is working his man. Now that we are back to the line of scrimmage, pick up as many yards as possible and work on setting up downfield blocks. If you can suck a defender inside before cutting back out, the HB Off Tackle can reap huge rewards.

Strong Close—Quick Toss

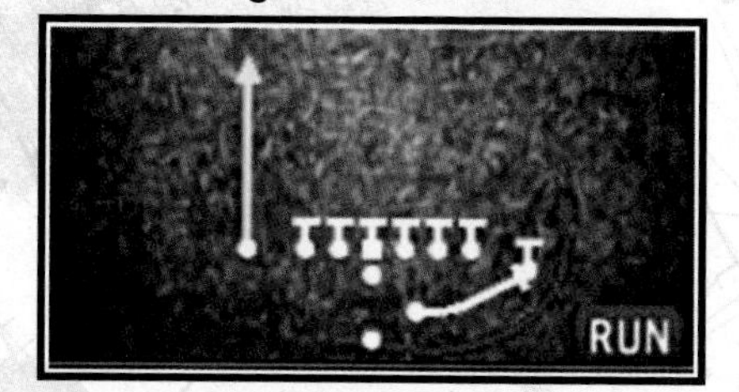

Quickly beat the D outside

The difference between the HB Off Tackle and the Quick Toss is the style of run. While both go to the right side of the field, one uses blocking and power, while the Quick Toss looks to catch the defense off guard or not playing disciplined football. If the defense is worried about the HB Dive and HB Off Tackle, they will be putting more defenders in between the tackles to stop the run—now is the perfect time to quickly toss it outside and work to get the edge.

He grabs the toss and heads outside

While this run can be blown up in the backfield, we should have a pretty good idea of when it is going to work. This is a run that we call when we see the defense is suspect—you shouldn't call this run otherwise. If the CB stays wide, cut inside on the FB; otherwise, get as far away from the line as possible with a speedy RB.

The running back loves seeing the FB out in front

Against man defense, motion the WR on the right across the formation. While you lose him as a blocker, his defender should follow him and clear up space to the edge. He is a weak blocker, and using motion makes it look like this is the HB Dive since we use the same motion! Follow the FB and look to break contain on the defense.

Quick Pass

Strong Close—Y Trail

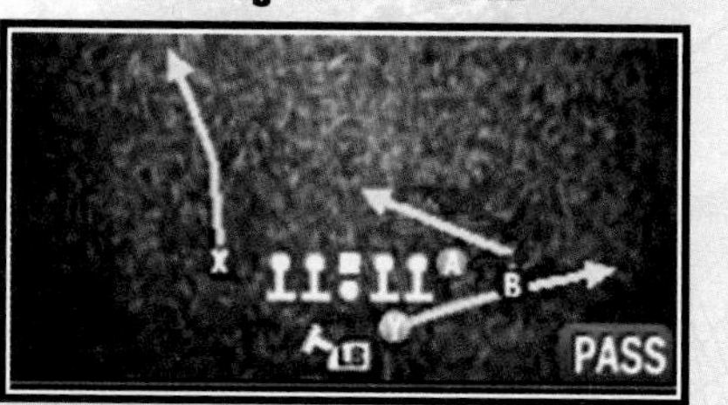

The D will be thinking run

When we stay in the Strong Close formation, the defense will be forced to respect the run and likely will be vulnerable to the quick pass. The sharp cut by the TE is simply one of the hardest routes for man coverage to defend.

The TE sets up his man

The FB and TE appear to be running the same route at the snap. If the defense runs blitzes and forgets to man the FB, simply leak the ball to the him in the flat and break down the sideline. Otherwise, wait for the TE to head back over the middle of the field. If you roll the QB, you can create a two-on-one vs. the defender in the flat; Playmaker the FB and force the defender to choose the QB or the FB.

The TE explodes onto the led pass

A stud TE like Jermichael Finley will burn his man consistently over the middle of the field. Lead the pass out in front and let him pick up yards after the catch. You also have the ability to get him the ball before his cut if the LB doesn't line up directly over the TE.

Man Beater

Gun Split TE—TE Out

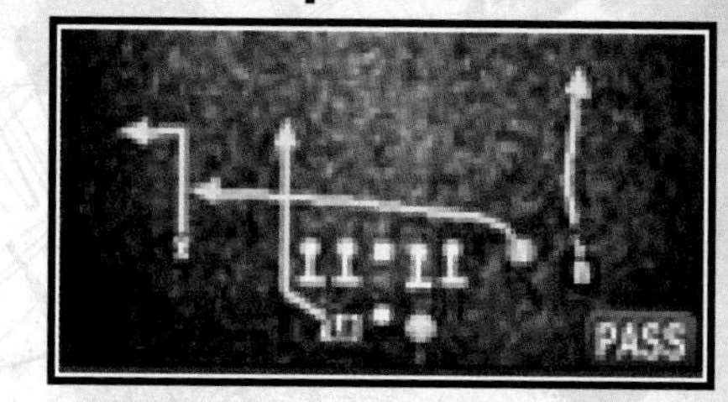

There are great progressions on this play

Hot route the WR on the left to a curl. This gives the TE Out play three different routes that can roast man coverage.

Check this area of the field first

Start by looking to throw the HB a bullet pass if the defender does not get good positioning. Next, look for the TE, who is crossing over the middle and can get separation from slower linebackers. If these routes don't open up, the curl on the left side of the field will be reaching its window and you can throw a bullet pass to shield the defender.

Find the mismatch

The RB does a good job earning inside position against the defender, and the QB rockets a pass inside underneath the safety. If we suspect a blitz, look to block the back to the right of our QB—the extra time can allow us to get through all of our reads or bomb one deep to the outside right WR if he is left one-on-one.

Zone Beater

Gun Snugs Flip—Bench Switch

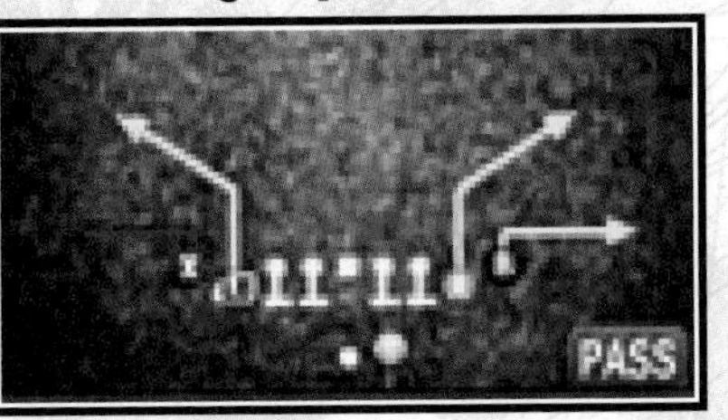

Demolish Cover 2 or Cover 3

By utilizing a four verticals attack, we can really stress zone coverages that don't keep that many defenders deep. Simply wait to see which WR the zone lets run free and deliver a strike downfield.

The safety chooses the streak

Our four routes all start out on streaks, but as the two outside players cut, the defense is forced to make a choice. Our routes do a great job of getting behind flat zones and simply flood deep zones.

The corner route is wide open

The QB has time to lay out a nice throw to the wide side of the field. The defense tries to recover, but the defender was pulled too far away by the streak. If the defense plays Cover 4, simply hit the releasing blue route underneath out of the backfield. You can also use slant outs to create this play if you see the coverage you want to attack.

Base Play

Singleback Tight Flex—Shallow Cross

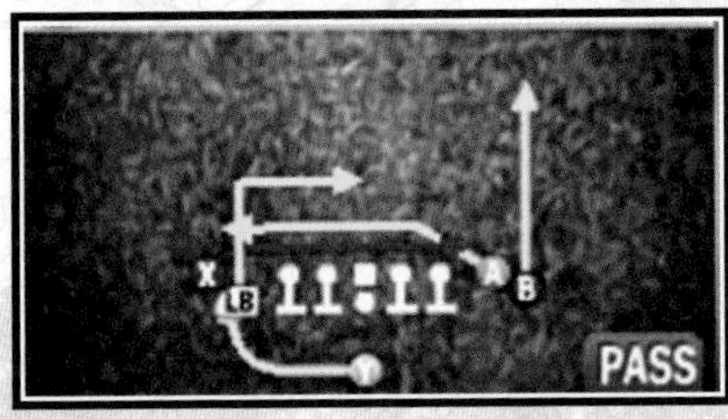

A tremendous base formation

The most common tight looks are out of shotgun, but the Balanced Pass playbook has a unique under-center tight formation. It forces the defense to respect the run and can easily beat man and zone coverage.

The defender follows the crossing route

The crossing routes will free up against man coverage, while the in route will sneak behind zone coverage. Here the LB makes a mistake by following the crossing WR too far over the middle and leaves a big space behind him.

Great catch over the middle

The WR starts his cut inside at a very good depth and hauls in the pass. If the defender does not follow the crossing route in zone coverage, simply wait for a window to open up and hit the short WR. This is a very safe throw in front of the QB, and it will come open against either type of coverage.

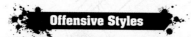

BALANCED RUN PLAYBOOK BREAKDOWN

Three-Headed Rushing Attack

Strong Pro—Counter Weak

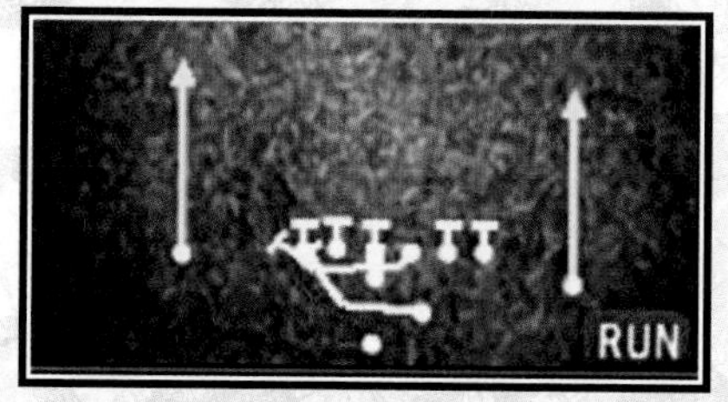

Use the misdirection to get outside

The Counter Weak is our favorite run to counter an aggressive defense. If we can get the defenders to take one step the wrong way, we will really have the advantage on this run. The WRs do a great job clearing out in this formation.

The back takes a fake step while his guard pulls

The back lets the guard get set up to the left before taking the snap. Once he pulls in the ball, it's his job to read whether to cut the run inside or bounce it outside. The ideal route is between the guard and FB before heading outside.

Set the FB up to block wide

The defender on the edge does a good job of staying outside and not getting sucked in. This forces the RB to stay inside of his FB. By not using turbo, we can wait until the FB gets outside and demolishes the CB, who is simply no match for the stronger blocker. Most players will just run outside and run into the defender; be patient and set up your blockers.

Strong Pro—HB Dive

Straight through the A gap

The HB Dive will help set up all your other runs and passing plays. Run this play until the defense shows it can consistently stop it. Once the defense crams the middle, utilize your other running plays.

Green is the perfect style back here

The QB will hand the rock off to the HB while the FB powers forward and terminates defenders. The dive is great because we can quickly shift to the weak side if the defense overcommits to the primary gap. Most of the time, though, the play will follow its main assignment and pick up 5 yards.

Into the second level

The back puts his head down after he breaks through the line of scrimmage and can likely bowl over a weaker tackling safety. While the dive doesn't often go the distance, it helps keep the defense worried about long drives. Motion the WR on the right against zone coverage and snap him when he gets behind the center.

Strong Pro—HB Stretch

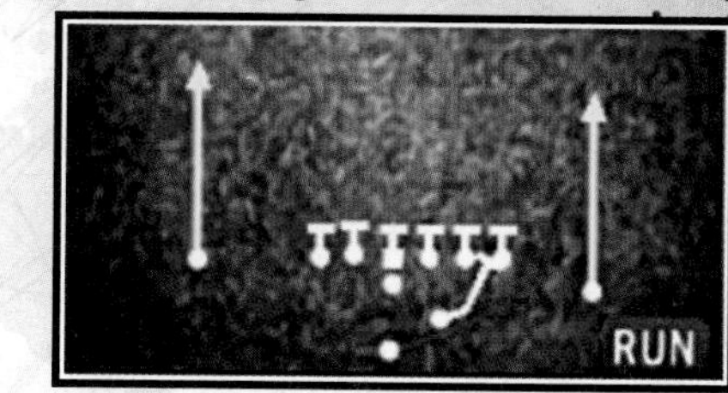

Use the stretch to go off tackle

The HB Stretch is a run seen only in a few offenses. It is a great way to quickly get outside without giving up the potential penetration that often hits Quick Toss–style runs. The QB runs the ball over instead of pitching it, but the goal is still to get outside.

Give the HB the ball

The RB shouldn't worry about the handoff; his main focus should be reading his blocks. If a lineman misses a block on the weak side don't worry—simply run away from the defender. We can cut this run inside the tackle if the outside is bottled up.

The FB pins the block inside

The HB starts his step much like when he's running the counter, but instead he continues on his way. Here, the FB seals the edge and the HB starts his cut outside. This can be frustrating for a defense that finally stops the middle run but just loses contain and gives up a big gain.

Quick Pass

Strong Pro—F Angle

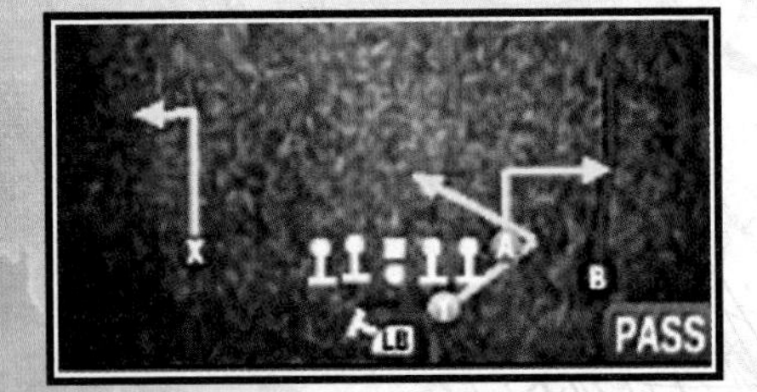

The defense will be looking to blitz

Because we're staying in the Strong Pro formation, the defense should not be expecting pass. Once you pick up a few first downs with the ground game, you should feel the defense tighten to the line. If you feel they lose contain or are frustrated, look to beat them with a quick pass.

The FB starts to the flat

The FB will start out to the flat, and when the LB finally catches up to him, he will cut inside and smoke the defender. Hit him with a quick bullet pass upfield.

A sharp cut earns him inside position

If the defense sits back, we have the out route by the TE as our second read. Make sure to change the outside route to a curl instead of a dig route. The concept is the same, but it is a little better for beating the defense and will be a great third read.

Man Beater

Gun Doubles On—Drag Unders

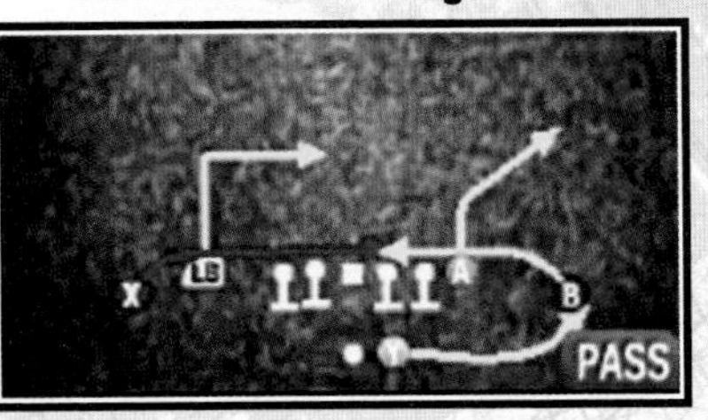

Four ways to smoke the defense

While Drag Unders appears to be a man beater due to the crossing route, it is actually the two other routes that work best. Depending on where the defense lines up in man, the in or corner route can seal position and lead to a possession catch.

Great route running is key

On this play, our TE holds the defender on his back and makes a sharp cut to the outside. Our QB leads the pass out in front and gives the TE space to make the catch away from traffic.

The big target works the outside

The drag routes will develop later because they cross from a wider depth than normal, but the in route that works the middle of the field can be used to beat an overly aggressive user-player.

Zone Beater

Singleback Wing Trio—Four Verticals

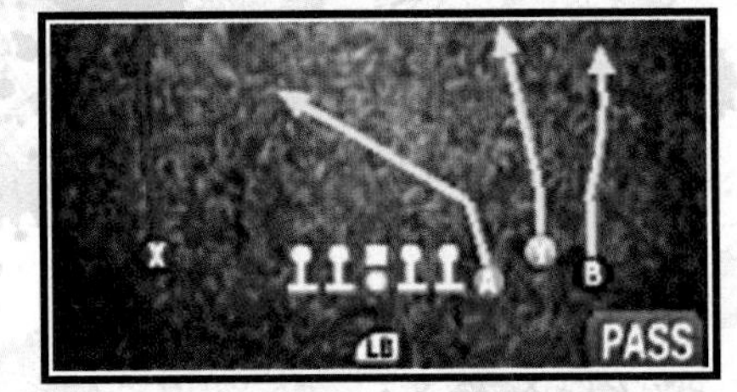

Get a zone read and call this play

By utilizing Four Verticals, we can really stress zone coverages in the deep middle of the field. Wait until the WRs cross into the second tier of the defense and zip it into the open window.

The safety chooses the streak

Our four routes all start out on streaks, but the route over the middle starts to cut over the middle at an angle. As the defender passes off the WR, he has no idea that his teammate must guard two offensive players at once.

The corner route is wide open

The sooner you make the throw, the easier it will be for the QB. If you can put some air underneath it, you will give the WR time to get underneath it. This is easier against Cover 2 and Cover 3. Look to hit the blue route releasing underneath against Cover 4.

Base Play

Wildcat—Power

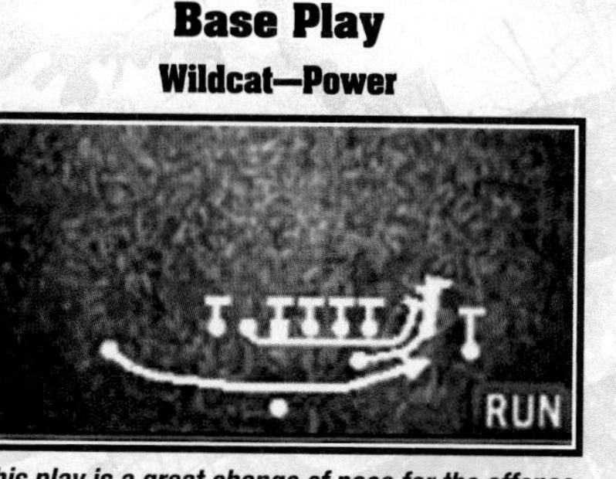

This play is a great change of pace for the offense

This is more of a specialty play than a true base play, but when used at the right time it can catch the defense off guard.

TIP

For a base formation with your five sets, use the Gun Split Offset, since you can't audible from Wildcat.

Keep the ball at the snap

The primary running back will line up at QB and take the snap. The secondary RB motions across the formation and gives the player the option of handing him the ball or keeping it himself. Hold down turbo and keep the ball—this will give you a nice boost toward the line of the scrimmage.

Pitch it outside

The defense should try to contain this run from breaking outside. If they overcommit outside, keep the ball and burst toward the line of scrimmage. If the defense loses containment, pitch the ball out to the HB who just faked the handoff. This is a nice little trick that can fool the defense, but make sure to pitch it only when that option is available because it can be risky.

POWER RUN PLAYBOOK BREAKDOWN

Three-Headed Rushing Attack

Strong I Twin TE—Counter Weak

This is a great run to break contain

The counter is a perfect way to break a run to the edge. The more patient you are when waiting for blocks to materialize, the more yards you are likely to gain.

Defense gets penetration

Here is an example where the counter gets penetrated from the edge. Thankfully, our FB immediately heads out and heads off the pressure. Now, we simply have to navigate around the defender.

The pulling guard now leads

In most cases, the pulling guard picks up the first player to get in. However, since the DE wasn't fooled by our misdirection, the FB picks up the job. Now, the HB should work his run to the guard and allow him to get in front. By waiting for him to set up, we will have help in picking up yards.

Strong I Twin TE—HB Dive Weak

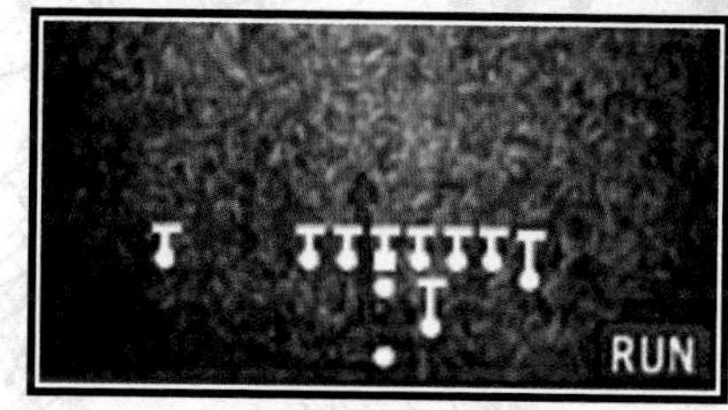

Our quick audible down

Having the ability to audible down to a run means the defense can't sit back and play pass coverage. While the HB Dive Weak is not a true power run, it is perfect when we need to remind the defense to respect our run game.

To the left side of the line

The HB Dive Weak sends the FB to a spot similar to the one for the HB Dive, but the back is set to hit the weak side of the line. The linemen open up a huge hole on the weak side of the line. The back can now choose to follow the FB for a shot at big yards, or just take the huge hole for the sure gain.

The defender runs past the back

The defender on the right guard breaks his block, but the halfback is already moving his way to the line of scrimmage. If it's short yardage, call Playmaker and shift the run to the right. This will make it more of a powerful dive and allow it to pick up the yards to move the chains. The FB locks in on the LB, and our back's focus is to get in behind him.

Strong I Twin TE—Toss Strong

The Twin TE formation comes in handy

The addition of an extra TE on the strong side of the line makes tossing it out wide devastating against non-base defensive packages like Nickel.

The TEs let the FB run free

The TEs are great blockers compared to WRs. They seal off the edge and let the FB go find someone to block. The HB shouldn't lay on the gas yet, since no defender has penetrated through the line.

Now there's just the safety to avoid

The FB heads back towards the middle, leaving the safety eyeing us. Thankfully, our lineman has broken into the second level, and we look to cut back to give him time to make the block. A lineman should be able to pancake the safety and leave us heading for the end zone.

Quick Pass

Full House Wide—Angle Swing

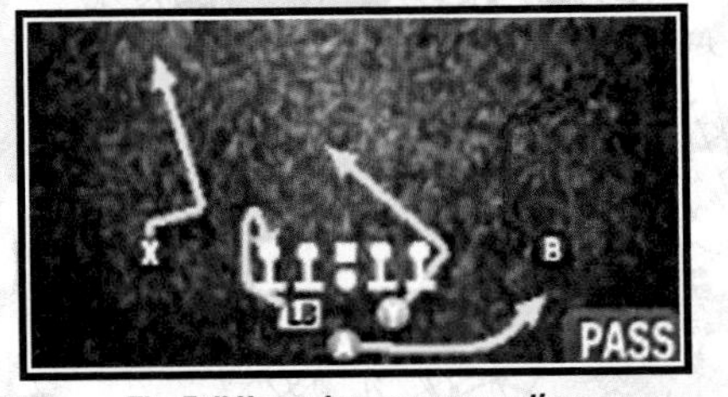

The Full House has so many options

With the Power Run playbook, you always want to make the defense fear the run. The Full House adds three great options that can go any which way, leaving the defense guessing. We will use this as an extension of the run game and look to hit a quick pass.

This is the best quick-pass route in the game

This play can be flipped so either player can run this route. This play will beat man or zone depending on when the QB throws the ball. Look to deliver the ball quickly if the blitz is on, or wait for the route to smoke the coverage.

Deliver the ball in stride

Try to streak the opposite route; you should get a very quickly passable route from the backfield. If you curl the outside routes, you will have two good options out wide to beat man coverage.

Man Beater

Weak I Twin WR—WR Cross

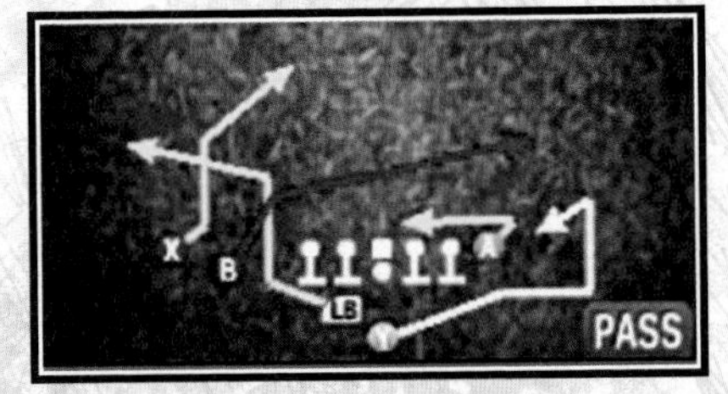

Keep everything in tight

With a true power run attack, we like to keep heavier personnel on the field. Usually our man beaters are created by speedier players getting mismatched. Since we have slower players, we will have to use possession-style catches to beat the defense.

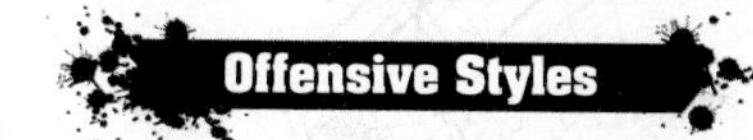

The TE appears to be going outside

The TE is our first read; he starts to head outside but cuts back in. This is a unique route in the game, and it really shakes the defender. Work on the timing because it is a very uncommon route.

The target uses his hips to seal the defender outside

The crossing patterns will work across the middle if the defense covers the TE short. Make sure to cancel the auto-motion to the RB; otherwise this play will be sniffed out by the defense. You can either block the RB for more time or drag him.

Zone Beater

Shotgun Wing Trips—Slot Option

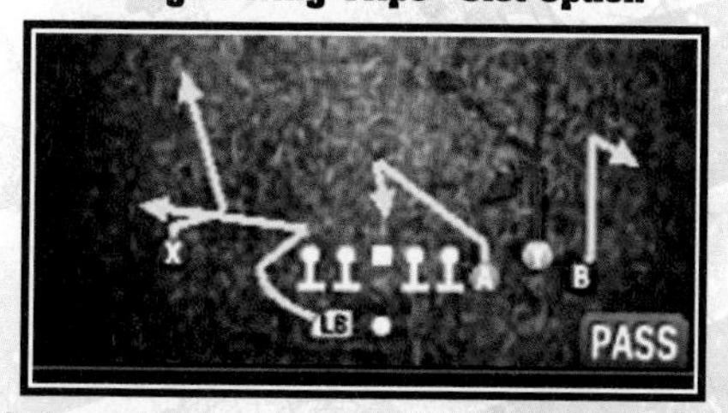

Option routes are common in NCAA Football*, but less so in* Madden NFL

The option route on this play makes this one of the most dynamic plays in the game. An aware WR should know what the coverage is and determine his route based on the defense.

The option route doesn't let the safety pass off his route

The safety drops down into the box and our WR quickly reads Cover 3. The slot WR on the option route correctly chooses to continue on his route up the seam. This draws away the defender and takes the top off the D.

The comeback sits nicely in the zone

The outside WR was passed off to the safety, but he was taken out of the play. Our player sits right in a soft spot of the zone for a huge gain. If the safety did listen and pick up the outside WR, our slot option would react differently and likely be open!

Base Play

Singleback Bunch—Flanker Drive

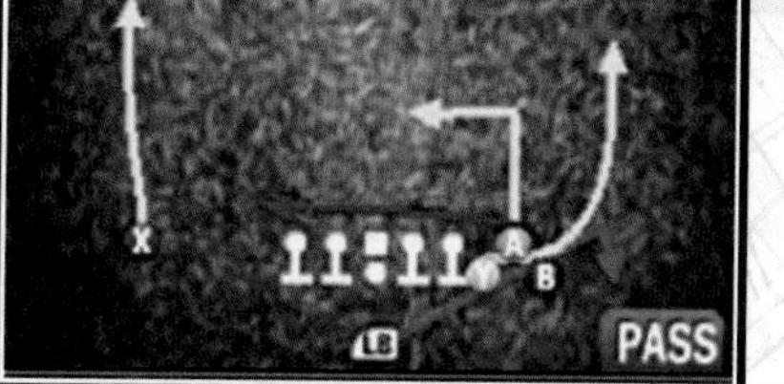

A bunch look that can beat man as well

Flanker Drive has been a very popular play in recent years. The wheel route to the outside has the ability to motion out and beat zone coverage. The blue route in the backfield is also a plus.

Good route running over the middle

Over the middle, we have two routes running at different depths. Both drags and in routes this season have the capability to beat man. So, look to hit whichever route gets open first or creates more separation.

Both routes smoke their man

By sending the lone WR left on a curl, we can beat zone coverage and have a final safety valve out wide. If the defense sits back in zone, we can hit the blue route receiver out of the backfield, who will release after picking up a block.

WEST COAST PLAYBOOK BREAKDOWN

Three-Headed Rushing Attack

Far Tight Twins—Quick Toss

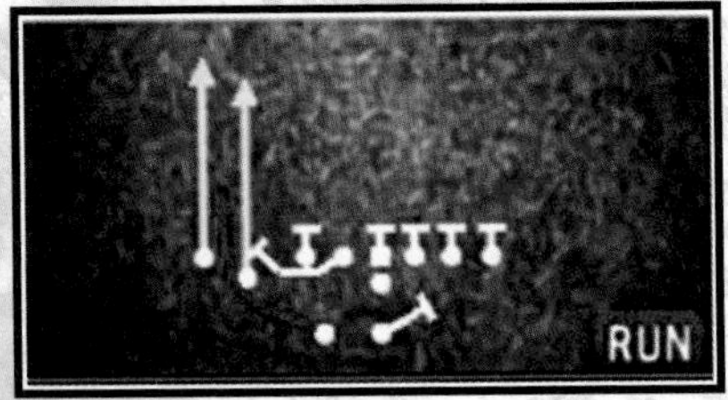

A devastating quick run

The Quick Toss usually is our run to the right, but with this formation it's the perfect way to quickly run left. The WRs will clear out at the snap, leaving the guard to block out in front.

Everyone clears out

Even if a defender breaks inside, the run will completely leave him in the dust. Our only concern should be a CB in Cover 2 who stays out wide. If this happens, swing back inside the pulling guard.

Shifty running backs rule

This is the perfect run for a fast back; don't toss it to your FB unless you know it's *wide open*. Agile backs will get one-on-one with defenders in space and can quickly leave them behind.

Far Tight Twins—FB Dive

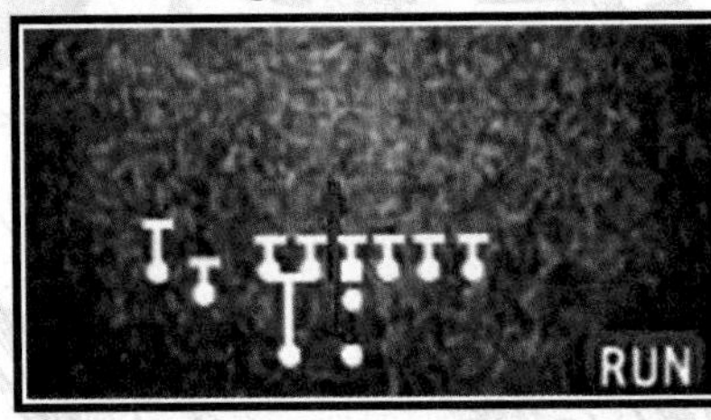

Quickly hit the gap

While handing off to the RB is most common and lets the FB block, simply giving it to the FB can catch the defense off guard. If you see a soft spot in the middle of the line, call this play to capitalize.

The ball is out in a hurry

If you don't have the luxury of a fast FB, sub in a backup running back who has some trucking ability. If you motion the RB towards the line, he can give you a block for a change!

The FB breaks into the second level

When a fullback gets into the second level, don't get cute. Make sure to cover up the football and lean forward to get extra yards when tackled. This is a unique running formation, and FB Dive is one of the few quickly developing runs it has to offer.

Far Tight Twins—HB Sweep

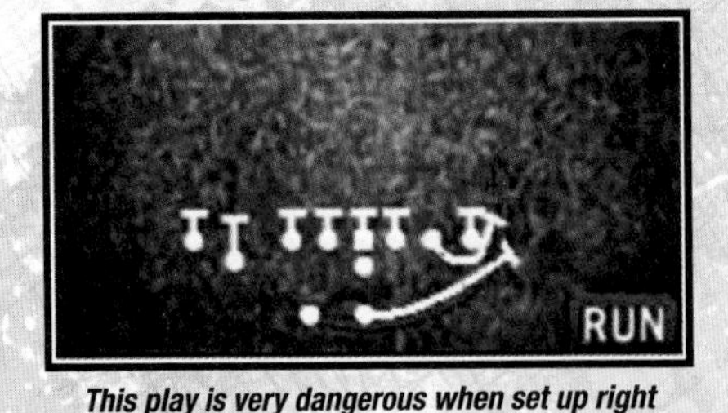

This play is very dangerous when set up right

The sweep from Far Tight Twins is a run that takes a few strides to get going, but it can literally set up a wall of blockers.

Blockers are getting set up nicely

At the snap, the runner heads out to the right side of the formation and collects the ball from the QB. Most sweeps involve pitches, but this formation hands it off due to the setup. Our WRs are on the side we are running away from, which keeps defenders away.

Tons of room around the corner

Look to turbo immediately upon receiving the ball. Since it takes a few extra seconds to get the handoff, the risk of penetration into the backfield is too great to wait around for. Look to kick it out to the edge and pick up as much as possible.

QUICK PASS

Far Pro—HB Seam

Five quick options make this deadly

The Far Pro allows us to keep a similar split backfield. The initial cut on the HB Seam is a unique route and should give us the ability to shoot a pass in.

Read the LB

The LB appears to be blitzing at the snap instead of manning up the HB. We will simply wait for him to get into the line and then toss it over his head.

Zip it in and pick up more

If the LB sits back, we still can get the ball to the HB, but the yards after catch won't be as great. Instead, the TE out route should get open depending on the pre-snap lineup. Put the outside WRs on curl routes to give you a late window.

Man Beater

Singleback Tight Doubles—Curl Drag

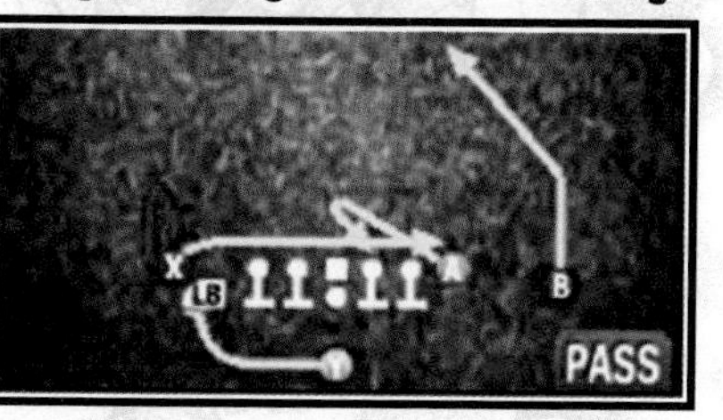

Compressed sets smash man

Singleback Tight Doubles is a very popular formation used by the online player. The tight look to the left causes confusion for the defense and allows a free release in most situations.

The defenders switch

The little curl route starts from the inside and forces the defenders to switch off. Look to hit the curl before he turns, and get him going outside. Otherwise, wait until you get a good window on the crossing pattern and throw a strike.

Our WR earns separation

After you run this play a few times, a smart user will bring a defender into the middle of the field to help out. If you have a dynamic talent on the outside, leave the post route and let it fly out in front.

Zone Beater

Singleback Bunch Swap—Seattle

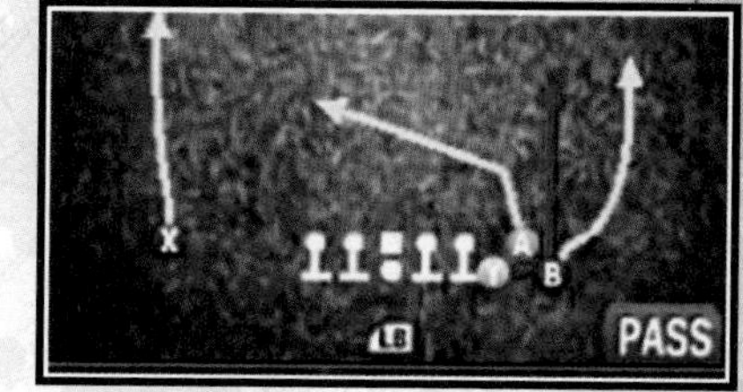

Seattle is a great concept

The inside wheel route is very commonly motioned to the outside to beat man coverage. Here we will use that route as a decoy.

The defender passes off the outside man

The short defender passes his man outside, but he is already beaten to the inside of the field and he won't be able to recover.

The seam is ripped open

f the zone defender over the inside of the ield tries to guard the seam, our route hat cuts to the middle of the field will get open. This is the easiest throw for the QB o complete, so take it when it becomes available.

Base Play

Gun Snugs Flip—PA WR Seam

Double blue routes

Utilizing double blue routes can really frustrate a defense that thinks they have a play locked up, only to get beaten to the flat. Cancel the play action to give your QB more time to stress the defense with his legs.

Cancel the play action and roll the pocket

At the snap, the defense tries to bring some pressure, but the newly blocked HB picks it up. The delayed routes will pick up any pressure from the outside before releasing to the flat. We can also put the HB on a route if we catch the defense asleep.

Free release to the flat

This play really needs to be user-controlled to be stopped—since it has mirror routes to both sides it is very hard. If the defense brings too many people up to the line of scrimmage, simply bomb a deep pass over the middle to the post.

RUN N GUN PLAYBOOK BREAKDOWN

Three-Headed Rushing Attack

Strong Pro—Counter Weak

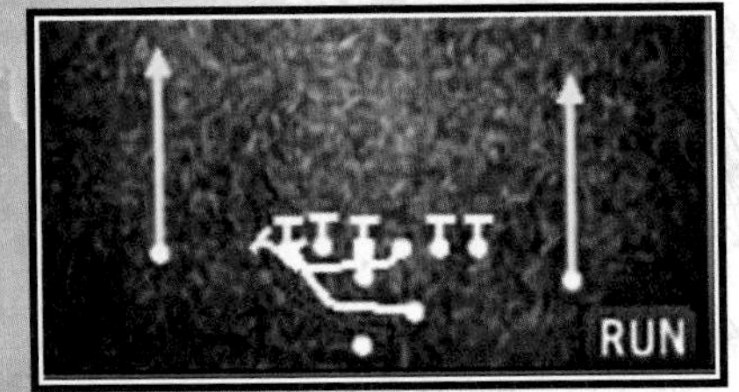

A great way to keep the defense from stacking the strong side

The Counter Weak from Strong Pro is a devastating run. Make sure to motion the far right WR over against zone coverage to pick up an extra blocker.

The HB attempts to freeze the linebackers

As the guard and FB pull to the left, our HB appears to be going right. However, this is simply a fake and the runner cuts back right to receive the handoff.

Two hogs out in front

The run works as planned as no defenders break through the line. We now have two enormous blockers out in front and looking to take on smaller secondary players. This will keep the defense from over-playing the strong side.

Strong Pro—HB Blast

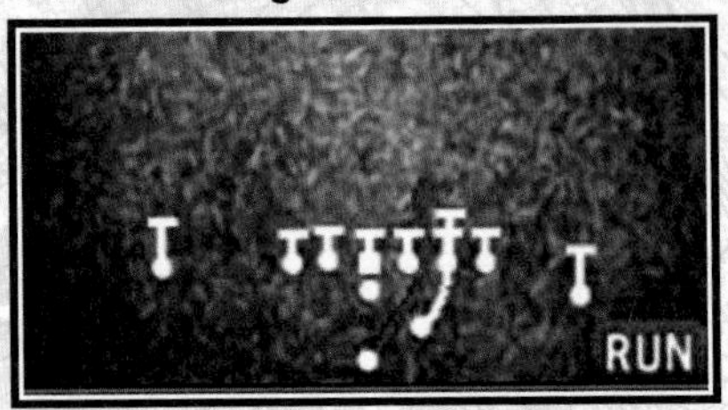

The FB blocks a different gap than he does on the dive

The HB Blast is a no-nonsense run that will pick up chunks of yards against a defense on its heels. The FB blocks the B gap as the HB takes it up the middle. This is different than a dive, but it can be just as effective.

Pretend to follow the FB

The FB gets to the line and seals off his blocker. When the HB gets to the line he will have to choose to sneak behind the FB or go to the middle of the line. By faking right, he sucks in the linebacker before cutting back—this is elite running.

Then hit your assigned hole hard

The running back breaks into the second level of the defense, and only the safeties can prevent him from getting a touchdown. Cover up the ball and barrel ahead for a few more yards. This will cause a headache for the defense, especially if you have a lead.

Strong Pro—HB Toss

Put a speedy RB in the game

The HB Toss is a great way to catch a scrambling defense off guard. If you successfully run up the middle and then call a hurry-up run, the defense should suspect a similar attack. While they are scrambling to get set up, patiently call the HB Toss and get ready to burn them!

The HB waits for his blocks to set up

The WR clears out on this run, but if his defender is playing man, simply motion him across the formation to get rid of both of them completely. This will leave more space on the edge for us to rush to.

Make one move and go

The HB takes control of the ball and his eyes are focused ahead of him. Nobody is catching him from the weak side. With the safety backed up, he will have plenty of space to set up a move and continue on his way.

Quick Pass

Full House Normal Wide—WR Dbl Shake

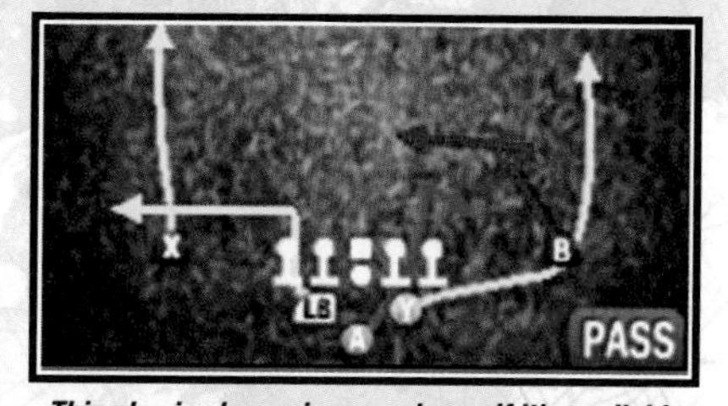

This play is always in our scheme if it's available

We have already covered the WR Dbl Shake, but it's so deadly that we include it any time we hit the red zone or need clutch yards on third and short.

Put a huge target in the game

By placing a big target with a high catch in traffic rating into the game, we can really own the middle of the field. Look to work the timing down with the receiver and throw a bullet pass.

He owns the middle of the field with his size

Make sure to flip the play every now and then so the user can't pick a side to defend. Fade both outside WRs in the red zone and throw a lob; the computer should get a nice catch for you. If all else fails roll out and hit the delayed blue route.

Man Beater

Gun Tight Flex—WR Cross

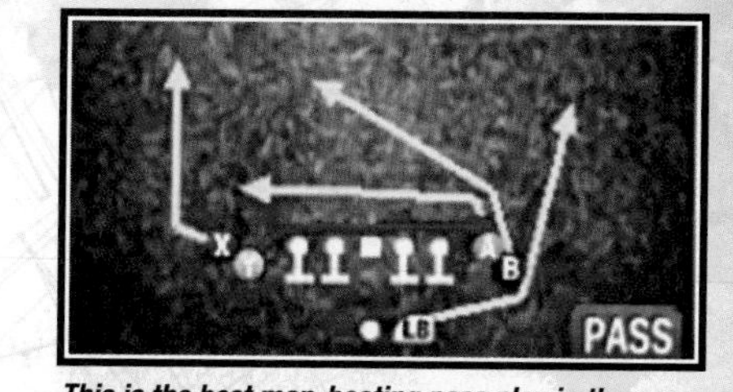

This is the best man-beating pass play in the game

Gun Tight Flex is an amazingly popular formation online and for good reason. It has the ability to pick up blitzes, and all the compression really puts pressure on man defense.

There's too much going on for the defense

On this play, look to the HB, and if the defense lines up poorly, hit him quickly in the flat. Drag the inside left WR; he will get placed on a better angle over the middle. The outside left route will consistently beat man coverage when it cuts back upfield. You must learn to trust this throw; it will force the defense to double cover or completely stop calling man.

Our deep route gets separation

The outside right WR is running a deep crossing route and does a great job of beating man or zone coverage. This throw takes longer to develop, so waiting can be risky. Look to lead the pass out in front and fit it under the safety. If you motion the inside left WR, it can help free him up on his drag.

Zone Beater

Gun Trey Open—Corner Strike

Three receivers to the right and a stock flat route

This is a great formation that gives us three WRs to the right side of the formation. The flat route will do a great job holding Cover 2 and Cover 3 defenders short and allowing routes to get behind him. Since we can't call a flat route as a hot route, it's nice to have a play where it's available.

The flat route holds the short defender

The WR who runs an in route gets deep enough up the seam to draw attention. This is the key to the play—if he runs a normal in route, he won't get far enough upfield for anyone to care about him.

The corner route fits underneath the safety

The corner route is perfect if we can get enough time to protect the QB. The DB starts to get into his backpedal because he thinks the WR is going deep. However, as soon as his hips turn, our player cuts to the sideline and sits inside the zone with a great catch.

Base Play

Singleback Ace Twins—Slot Under

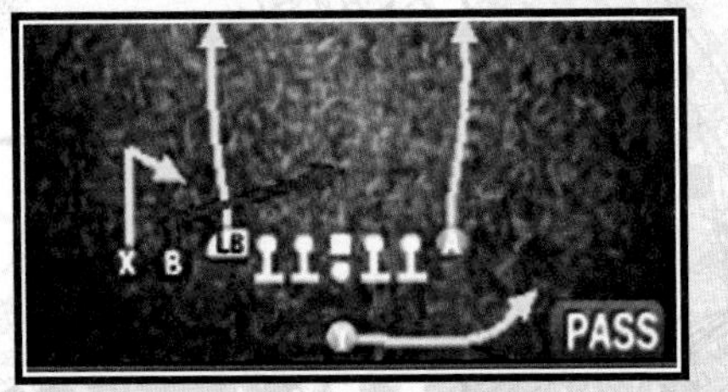

This is a great personnel package to audible from

Singleback Ace Twins is a great formation that has tremendous balance. You can feel confident in audibling to other plays with this formation. On Slot Under, the seam will get open in zone as the unique slant will flood the middle.

Waiting for routes to develop

By placing the outside left WR on a curl route, we have a good second progression if the inside slant can't shake loose. That is a solid stock slant route, though, and gets some help from the streak in the middle.

The WR breaks one and is gone

The QB does a great job releasing the ball as his WR is turning. The defender can't bring down the ball carrier, who had one-on-one coverage on the outside due to the pressure in the seams. Our speedy WR turns upfield and goes in for a touchdown!

MADDEN NFL 12

DEFENSIVE SCHEMES

Contents

In this chapter we break down the four most basic formations in the game. These will be the most used formations throughout the *Madden NFL 12* season. We will break down the 3-4, 4-3, Nickel, and Dime formations, giving you the "Five Sets for Success," which will help to catapult you up the leaderboard. Whether you play online or offline these plays will help to generate pressure and confuse your opponent!

3-4 DEFENSIVE SCHEME

Run Defense

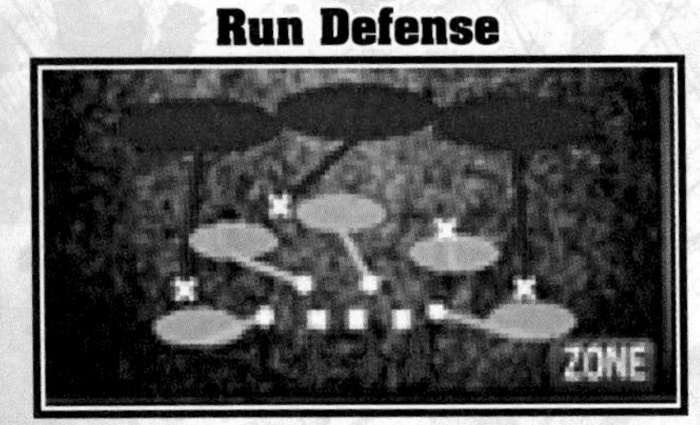

3-4 Over—Cover 3 (Inverted Cover 2)

We use the 3-4 Over—Cover 3 zone as our run defense, and with a few adjustments we turn it into an inverted Cover 2. User-control the FS in the box and look to make a play on the ball carrier at the snap of the ball.

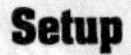

Setup

- Pinch the defensive line.
- Crash the defensive line out.
- Hot route the DT to a QB spy.
- Shade the coverage in.
- User-control the FS in the box.

Nowhere to go

The HB has nowhere to go as our inverted Cover 2 holds down the line of scrimmage. If the offense had fooled us we would have been ready with tons of coverage on the field. Remember to drop back into coverage with the FS if it is a pass.

Base Play

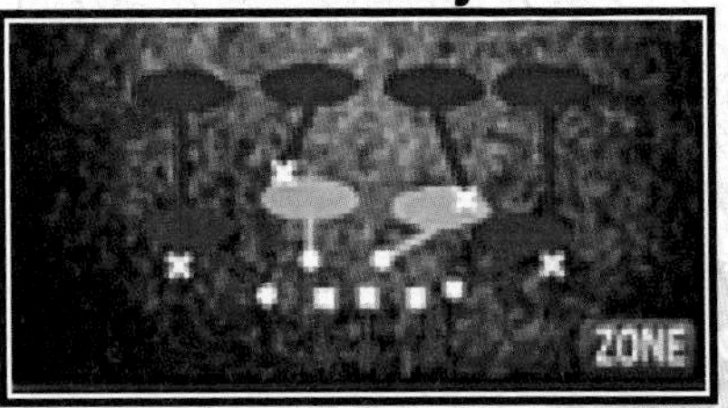

3-4 Over—Drop Zone

Using the 3-4 Over—Drop Zone allows us to play every basic defense in the game. The Drop Zone is unique because it has buzz routes designed into the play. This is ideal for max coverage defenses.

Setup

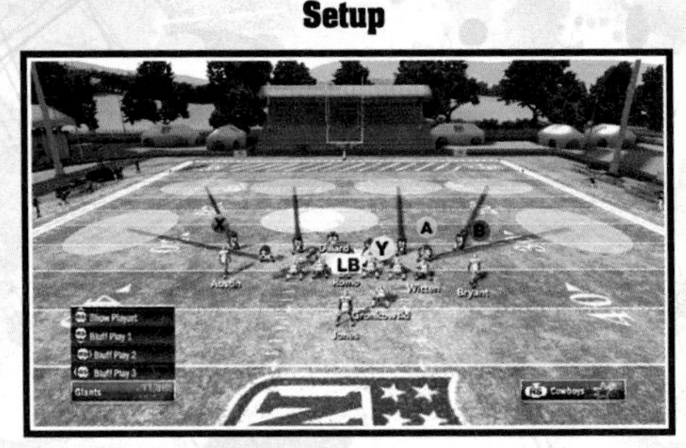

- Pinch the defensive line.
- Hot route the DT to a QB spy.
- User-control the left-of-screen MLB in coverage.

Coverage sack

We got the coverage sack. The QB couldn't find anyone open downfield and was forced to hold onto the ball. Expect lots of coverage sacks when using this defense.

Man/Zone Blitz

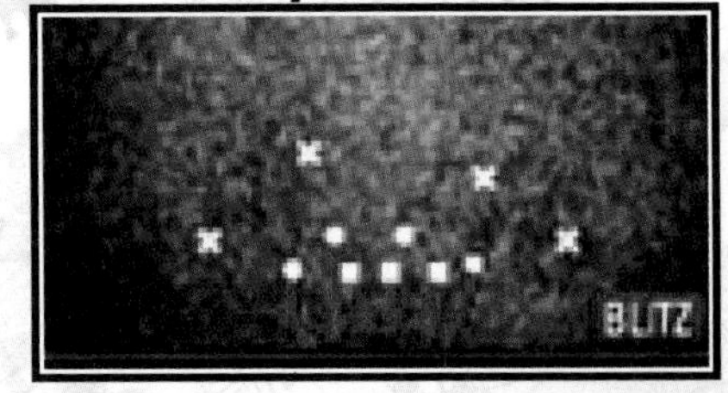

3-4 Over—Sting Pinch (Man)

In combination with the Cover 3 zone the Pinch is our man-to-man blitz. Pressure will come off either edge depending on where the offensive line slide protects. The heat will be quick, so look to make a big play and watch out for quick passes.

Setup

- Pinch the defensive line.
- Globally blitz both outside linebackers.
- Reblitz the left-of-screen MLB and stack him in the left A gap.
- User-control the defender covering the HB.

The receiver in the flat is tackled for a short gain

We didn't get a sack or turnover, but the offense was forced to pass to the short flat. Our linebacker makes the tackle and the offense gets a short gain.

3-4 Over—Cover 3 (Zone)

Setup

- Pinch the defensive line.
- Globally blitz both outside linebackers.
- Reblitz the left-of-screen MLB and stack in the left A gap.
- Shade the safeties in.
- User-control the FS in the short flat.

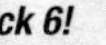

Pick 6!

We get a nice user pick because the pressure was getting to the QB. The last play the QB read we were in man-to-man, and he thought that he could squeeze a pass over the middle to one-on-one coverage. However, our zone defender was waiting for the mistake and capitalized with a pick 6!

Red Zone

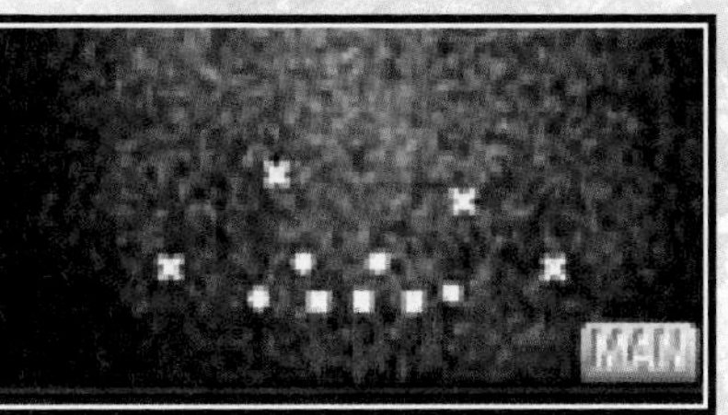

3-4 Under—Double Man

In the red zone we need to be careful of the fade lob, so we call on the 3-4 Over—Double Man. Both outside receivers will be double covered, and we can expect to lock down the fade lob to the outside.

Setup

- Pinch the defensive line.
- Hot route both DEs into hook zones.
- User-control the blitzing MLB in coverage.

Our double-team works perfectly

Double coverage will work the majority of the time against the fade lob in the red zone. Make sure to watch for quick passes near the line of scrimmage.

X-Factor

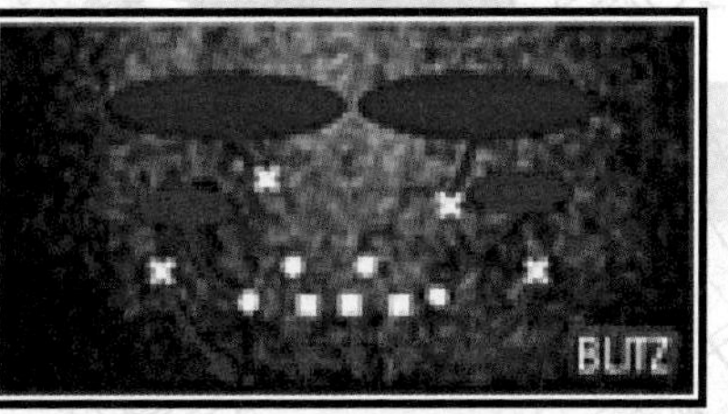

3-4 Under—CB Dogs Blitz

Blitzes from the cornerback spot haven't been a hot trend over the past few years, but in *Madden NFL 12* and with the resurgence of zone coverage we think there is value in them. The 3-4 Over—CB Dogs Blitz has buzz zones already assigned to the play, which helps the setup of this play to be extremely quick.

Setup

- Pinch the defensive line.
- Hot route both DEs into hook zones.
- Hot route the left-of-screen MLB into a deep zone and user-control him deep.

Sack!

The QB looks to roll out because this defense looks very similar to our max coverage defense. Instead of rolling into green grass he ran right into our pressure!

Keep expanding your 3-4 Over scheme and work one extra play into it each week. The more plays you add the better your defense can be in the long run. For the short term focus on these five plays for the specific situations and work on the setups until you know them like the back of your hand!

4-3 DEFENSIVE SCHEME

Run Defense

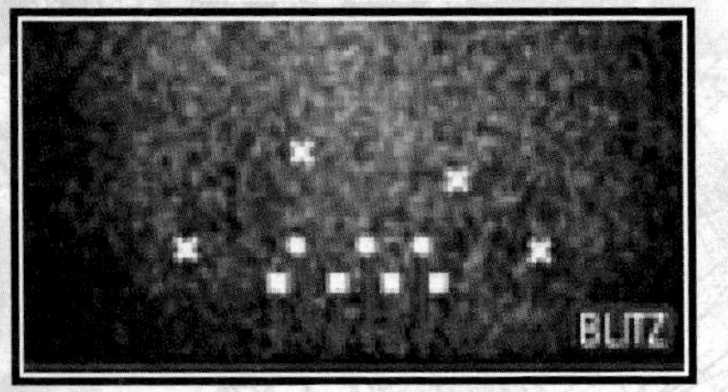

4-3 Normal—Thunder Smoke

We chose the Thunder Smoke as our run defense because of its all-out commitment to stopping the run. One offensive player will be left uncovered, so be careful of any play action passes—the offense will be able to exploit our pass coverage.

Setup

- Show blitz.
- Globally blitz all linebackers.
- User-control the defender covering the HB.

The HB has nowhere to go and is taken down for a loss

This run defense has all gaps on the offensive line filled, so be sure to step up into the box with your user defender and make a play on the ball carrier.

Base Play

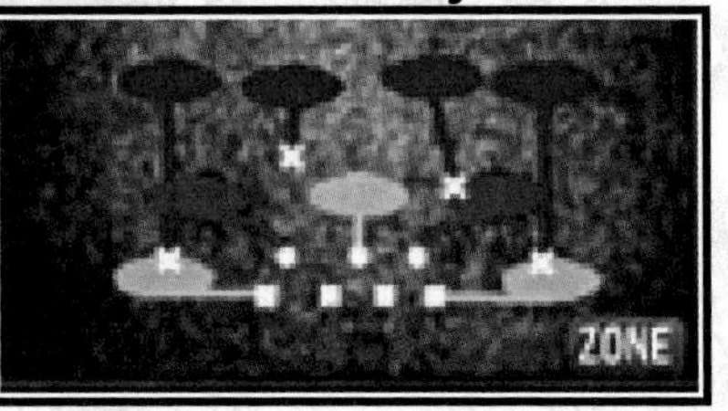

4-3 Normal—Cover 4 Flats

The Cover 4 Flats is a unique play in that the DEs drop into flat zones rather than pass rush the QB. This means that our base play is already set up for the ultimate coverage defense. We don't need to make any adjustments for it to be effective.

Setup

- Show blitz.

Interception

Our linebacker drops back and makes a play on the ball. This play calls for nine defenders dropping into coverage. Keep in mind that you can call every basic coverage by using your quick audibles.

Man/Zone Blitz

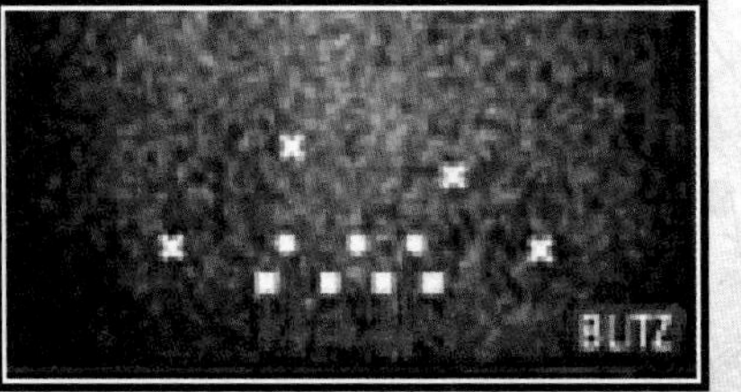

4-3 Normal—OLB Fire Man (Man)

The OLB Fire Man is a Cover 0 blitz that we use to bring pressure off the edge of the offensive line. We make a few adjustments to better the coverage of the play, but the pressure remains intact.

Setup

- Show blitz.
- Hot route the right-of-screen DT to a QB contain.
- Hot route the right-of-screen DE to a QB spy.
- User-control the defender covering the HB.

The pressure comes off the left edge untouched

The QB contain looks to draw the attention of the offensive line to the right of the field. The QB spy will slow down any type of crossing pattern. Combine this with pressure off the left edge and we can expect to get a lot of stops with the OLB Fire Man.

Setup

4-3 Normal—Cover 3 (Zone)

- Show blitz.
- Hot route the right-of-screen DT to a QB contain.
- Hot route the right-of-screen DE to a QB spy.
- User-control the FS in the short left flat.

Our DE gets to the QB before he can get off the pass

This time the QB dropped back expecting to see man-to-man defense. The QB read the blitz and expected the defense to be running the same play, so his initial read of the defense was wrong.

Red Zone

4-3 Normal—QB Contain

In the red zone we look to either slow down the fade lob to the outside or control any quick pass out of the backfield. The QB Contain has the outside linebackers on contain routes, which will help stop any quick pass out of the backfield as well as defend the fade lob.

Setup

- Pinch the defensive line.
- User-control the defender covering the HB.

The WR makes the catch but is out of bounds

The QB contain defenders will drop wide at the snap of the ball and be in position to close in on a pass to the HB out of the backfield. They will also defend any pass to the flats. With the lob pass the contain defenders can recover to aid in bringing down the WR.

X-Factor

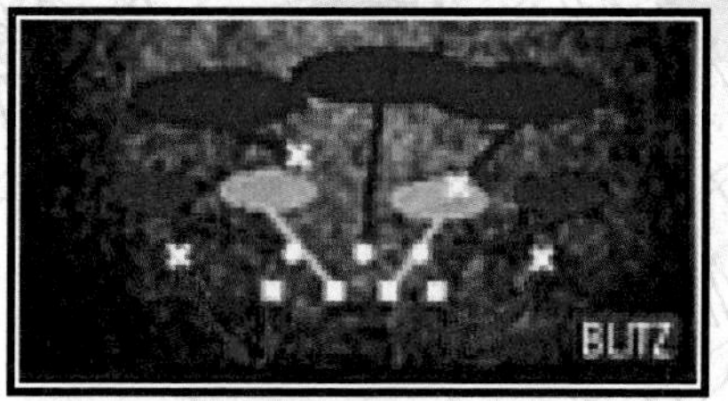

4-3 Normal—CB Dogs Zone

Pressure out wide will help to catch your opponent off guard. Not to mention, this play has one of the best pre-play setups in the game. The coverage on the field is excellent and we can still sneak pressure off the edge as the play develops.

Setup

- Pinch the defensive line.
- Hot route both DTs to QB spy.

Another sack!

The QB has nowhere to go with the ball. All his deep options have zone defenders defending them, and the underneath routes are covered by our QB spy defenders and buzz zones. We get the sack on the play and change the landscape of the game!

NICKEL DEFENSIVE SCHEME

Run Defense

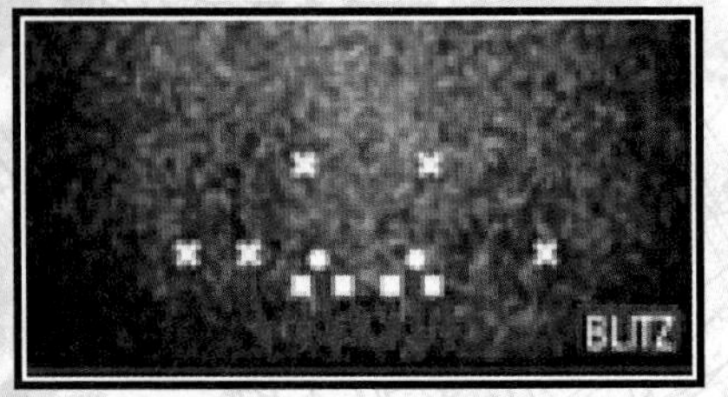

Nickel Normal—Under Smoke

The Nickel Normal—Under Smoke is a Cover 0 defense that has an attack-first, ask-questions-later mentality. This defense is perfect for stopping the run, and we use it in late-game situations to get a stop on defense.

Setup

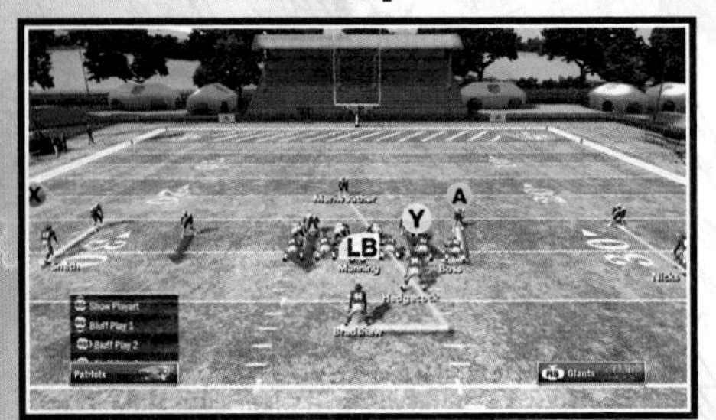

- Pinch the defensive line.
- Globally blitz both LBs.
- User-control the deep safety covering the HB.

Nothing happening here!

We make the play with our user defender. All the running lanes were closed off by our defenders. We stayed on the HB with our user defender and made a play to take down the ball carrier.

Base Play

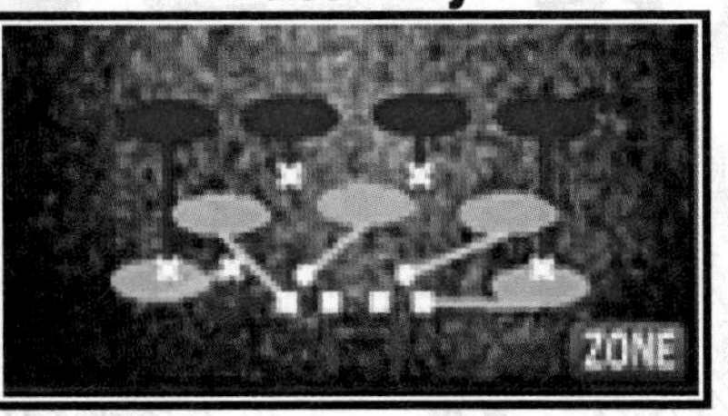

Nickel Normal—9 Velcro

The 9 Velcro is another play that calls for nine defenders dropping back into coverage. This is a max coverage defense that can be used to play a bend-but-don't-break defense.

Setup

- Pinch the defensive line.
- Hot route the left-of-screen DT into a QB spy.

The WR makes the catch but for a short gain

Mix in your other basic coverages, such as Cover 3 and Cover 2 zone and 2 Man Under. You can play max coverage defenses with them as well. Drop extra defensive linemen to fill holes in the defense.

Man/Zone Blitz

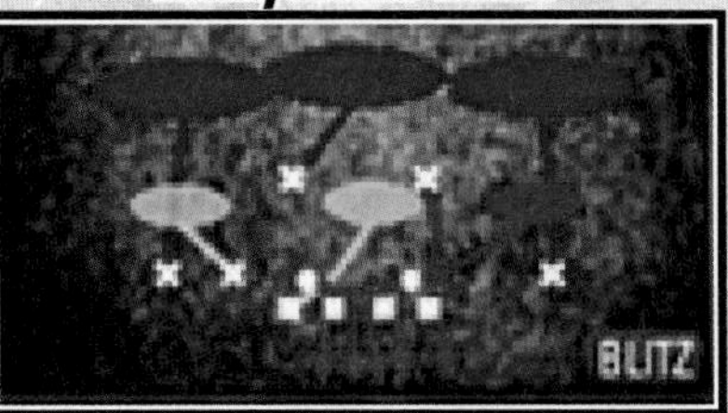

Nickel Normal—Mid Zone Blitz (Zone)

The Nickel formation creates interesting pressure that can't be duplicated by any other formation in the game. We stack our blitzing plays in the right-of-screen A gap. We are sending four pass rushers after the QB, and in most cases the offensive line will slide to pick the pressure up. However, with the Nickel formation the alignment of the defensive line allows the DE to come after the QB untouched.

Setup

- Globally blitz the linebackers.
- Hot route the left-of-screen DT to a QB contain.
- Hot route the nickelback to a buzz zone.
- User-control the deep FS in the deep zone.

Instant pressure

The Nickel formation will bring some of the best pressure in *Madden NFL 12*. The pressure we can generate from this formation is unique and can only be done from this formation.

Setup

Nickel Normal—DB Blitz (Man)

- Globally blitz the linebackers.
- Hot route the left-of-screen DT to a QB contain.
- User-control the deep FS covering the HB.

We quick-audible to our man-to-man blitz in the Nickel formation

The quick audible down from the Nickel formation allows us to bring the same pressure as the Mid Zone Blitz but has man-to-man coverage behind it. We confuse the offense and get the sack for a huge loss!

Red Zone

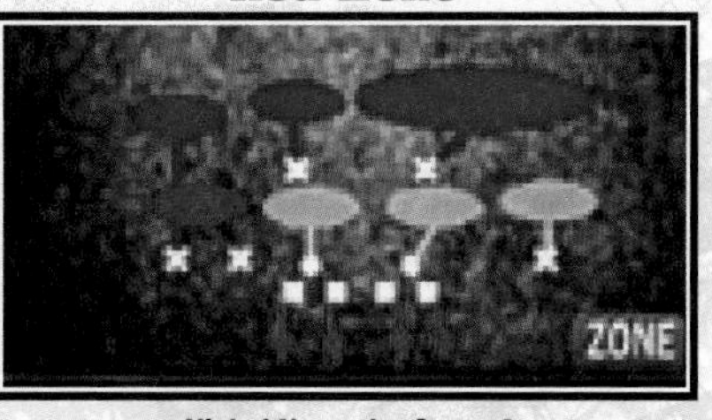

Nickel Normal—Cover 6

The Cover 6 is a great play to use when we are in the extended red zone. The defense calls for one side of the field to have Cover 2 coverage and the other to have Cover 4 coverage. This can be great in the red zone because the field will shrink, helping to make the zones in the Cover 6 that much better.

Setup

- Crash the defensive line out.
- Hot route the right-of-screen DE into a buzz zone.

The QB throws an interception

The QB threw into triple coverage as he read the Cover 2 on one side of the field and thought he had a chance to go deep on the defense. Our defense capitalizes on the mistake and makes the interception.

X-Factor

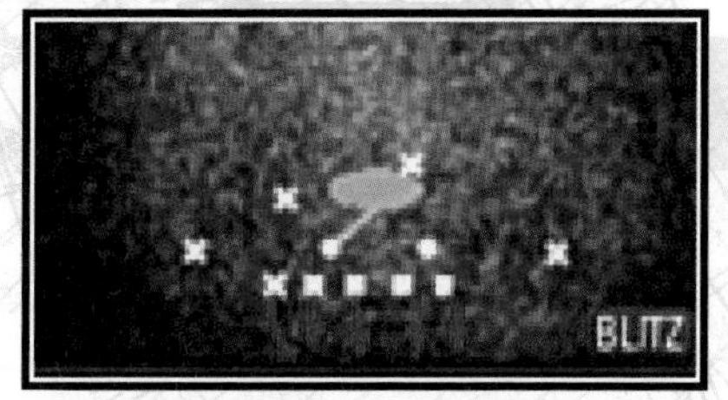

Nickel Strong—NB Blitz

We change up the variation of the formation to the Nickel Strong. This places the nickelback closer to the offensive line, which puts him in better position to blitz the offense.

Setup

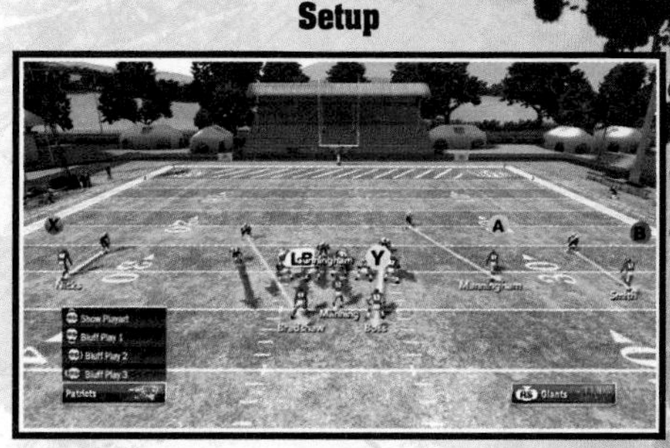

- Shift the defensive line left.
- Hot route the left-of-screen LB to blitz and stack him in the left A gap.

This play is unblockable

No matter the slide protection, pressure will get in with this play. The pressure is quick and it will cause opponents headaches all season long. We create a massive overload on the left of the field. We send five defenders at three offensive linemen. This forces the offense to slide protect to pick the pressure up. We have a weak-side pass rusher who will get after the QB if the offense does slide protect.

DIME DEFENSIVE SCHEME

Run Defense

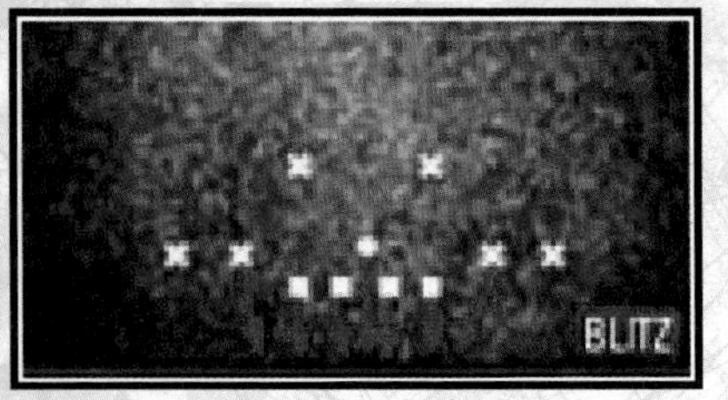

Dime Normal—All Out Blitz

This defense is great if you have an aggressive mind-set. We stack the box with defenders and tell the offense to run on us if they dare.

Setup

- Pinch the defensive line.
- User-control the FS who is covering the HB.

Bottled up!

The HB is swarmed by defenders and has nowhere to go. We make a commitment that we will stop the run with all our effort. This play can lock down any rushing attack, but be careful—it is prone to giving up big runs.

Base Play

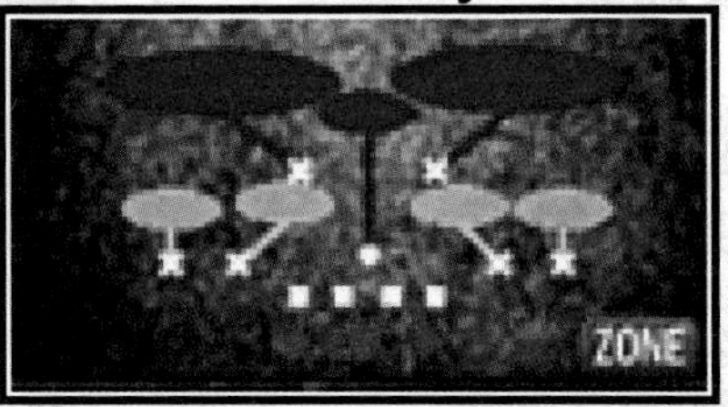

Dime Normal—Cover 2 Buc

The Cover 2 Buc isn't the typical Cover 4 that we like to use as our base defense, but it is unique because the pass rush angles are very different. With a dominant defensive line this play can cause major issues for offensive lines.

Setup

- Pinch the defensive line.
- Hot route both outside CBs to buzz zones.

The defense gets to the QB before he can make the pass

The pass rush from this play can often result in an instant sack. The stunting defensive linemen will crash hard on the offensive line, freeing a defender to come untouched through the A gap. This play is unique, so make sure you implement it into your defensive scheme.

Man/Zone Blitz

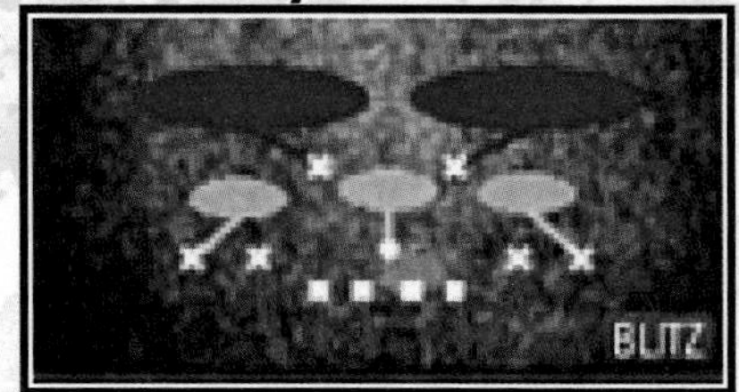

Dime Normal—Strike 2 Deep (Zone)

The Strike 2 Deep has been a *Madden NFL* favorite for many years now. It is extremely effective, and if you plan on using a Dime scheme this is a must-have play to integrate into your defensive game plan. The pressure comes off the edge quickly, and when you combine it correctly with the man-to-man version this play can be devastating.

Setup

- Reblitz the right-of-screen DT.
- Position the blitzing cornerbacks closer to the DEs.

Pressure flies off the edge!

Our pressure gets to the QB in no time. We force a fumble on the play. The beauty of sending outside pressure is that if the offense slide protects the pressure will sneak in off the back edge.

Setup

Dime Normal—DB Blitz (Man)

- Reblitz the right-of-screen DT.
- Position the blitzing cornerbacks closer to the DEs.
- User-control the defender covering the HB.

Different play, same pressure

The pressure once again gets to the QB, and he is left scratching his head after this play. This combination of man/zone blitzing is one of our favorites. The setups are quick and easy, and the play really delivers some intense pressure!

The Ultimate X-Factor

For this X-Factor we are going to use the Dime formation but bring pressure off both edges. We are hoping we really confuse our opponent into making bad decisions with the ball. Use it in the red zone as well!

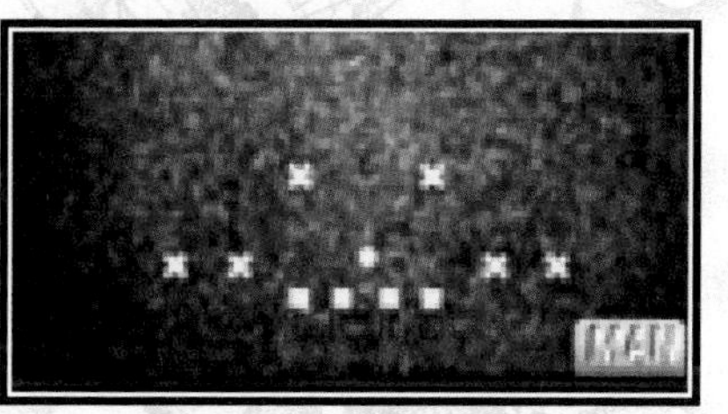

Dime Normal—Wk Overload 3

The Wk Overload will bring pressure off the left edge. In combination with the Fire Fox Zone it is one of the best duos in the game.

Setup

- None.

The pressure comes in quickly, so offenses need to be ready. Our goal is to get them to think that pressure is coming from one angle, and then we can squeeze pressure in off the opposite edge.

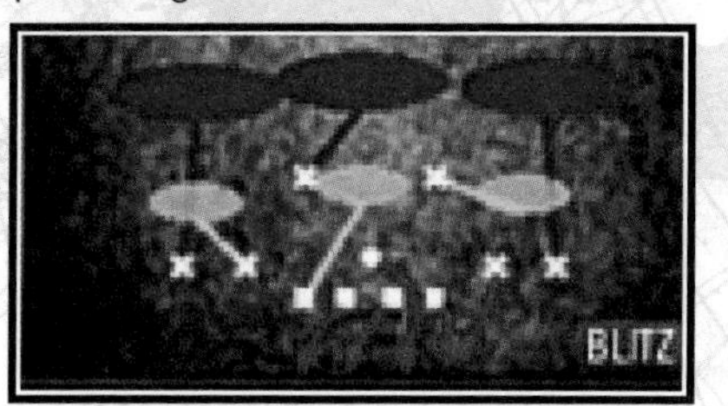

Dime Normal—Fox Fire Zone

On the opposite edge of the Wk Overload 3 we are looking to bring in pressure from our blitzing cornerback. We want the defense to feel uncomfortable in the pocket, and we believe that with the mix of our other defenses that can absolutely be the case.

Setup

- Move both cornerbacks closer to the defensive end.
- Hot route the nickelback to a buzz zone.

We take down the QB for a huge loss

Our defense steps up and makes a play by sacking the QB.

FRANCHISE FANTASY DRAFT

In this chapter we break down a fantasy draft that had seven users picking their teams to best fit their schemes and game plans. Fantasy drafting is one of our favorite all-time features in the *Madden NFL* series. It allows you to pick your ultimate team for how you play the game. Add in a few friends and you can really extend the life of the mode. We showcase the top 10 for each team and break down each owner's mind-set during the draft. Zfarls drafted for the New York Giants and Sgibs drafted for the New England Patriots.

Draft Order

- Oakland Raiders—6th pick
- St. Louis Rams—16th pick
- New York Giants—20th pick
- Kansas City Chiefs—22nd pick
- New England Patriots—25th pick
- San Diego Chargers—30th pick
- Denver Broncos—31st pick

Oakland Raiders Draft Results (6th overall pick)

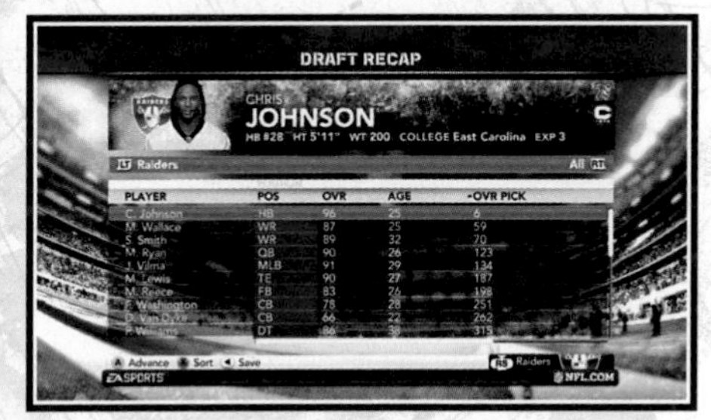

The Raiders' owner put a major emphasis on being able to run the ball, and with the 6th pick in the first round the team took speedster HB Chris Johnson. The focal point of the offense will be Johnson and his speed, creating mismatch problems for defenses. The speed picks didn't stop there—the next two picks for the Raiders were speed WRs. Mike Wallace and veteran Steve Smith were taken with the 2nd- and 3rd-round picks. The Raiders grabbed a great value pick with Matt Ryan, who fell all the way to the 4th round. The first four picks were all about offense, and with the 5th-round choice the Raiders looked to Jonathan Vilma. Vilma will control the middle of the field for both running and passing situations. With the 6th-round pick the Raiders continued to finish out their offense as they selected TE Marcedes Lewis. A big moment in the draft was when the Raiders selected FB Marcel Reece with their 7th-round pick; many believed that this was far too early for Reece to be selected in the draft. Picks 8–10 were all defensive selections, where the Raiders continued to draft more speed for their cover corners with Fabian Washington and rookie DeMarcus Van Dyke. Veteran Pat Williams was selected to anchor the middle of the defensive line.

Overall Draft Score: B-

- Great selections were made in rounds 1–4.
- Matt Ryan was a steal in the 4th round.
- TE Marcedes Lewis was drafted a few rounds early.
- FB Marcel Reece was drafted many rounds early.
- Emphasis on speed in the secondary was important for the Raiders, and they selected two of the fastest CBs in the game.

St. Louis Rams Draft Results (16th overall pick)

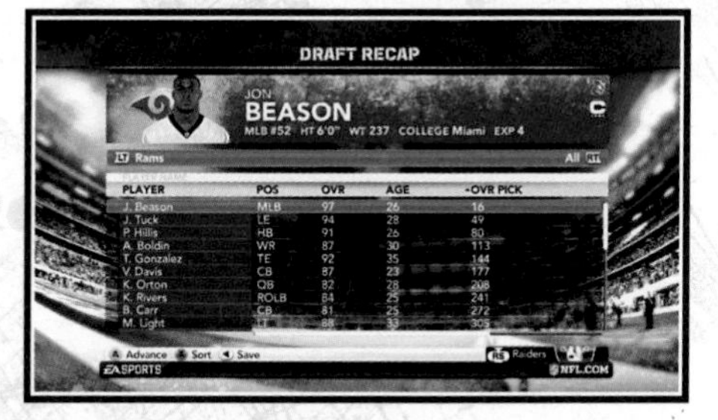

Going into the draft the Rams owner made it clear that defense was his number one priority. He believes that defense wins championships and wanted to stick to this agenda in the draft. With the 16th pick in the 1st round the Rams selected MLB Jon Beason. Beason has the speed and the coverage ability to be a monster in defensive coverage as well as run support. With their 2nd-round pick the Rams selected DE Justin Tuck. Tuck is one of the best DEs in the game and can play both inside and outside on the defensive line. The next three picks for the Rams were all offensive as they selected HB Peyton Hillis, WR Anquan Boldin, and TE Tony Gonzalez. With their 6th-round pick the Rams selected cover CB Vontae Davis with hopes that he can shut down the opponents' number one WR. The Rams needed a QB in the 7th round and selected veteran Kyle Orton. With their 8th- and 9th-round selections the Rams went back to the defensive side of the ball and selected OLB Keith Rivers and CB Brandon Carr. The Rams shocked the entire draft when they selected LT Matt Light with their 10th-round selection.

Overall Draft Score: C+

- The Rams' 1st- and 2nd-round selections were great.
- They got away from their initial game plan. Defense was a priority but three of the first five selections were offensive players.
- LT Matt Light was drafted many rounds early.
- CB Brandon Carr was drafted many rounds early.

New York Giants Draft Results (20th overall pick)

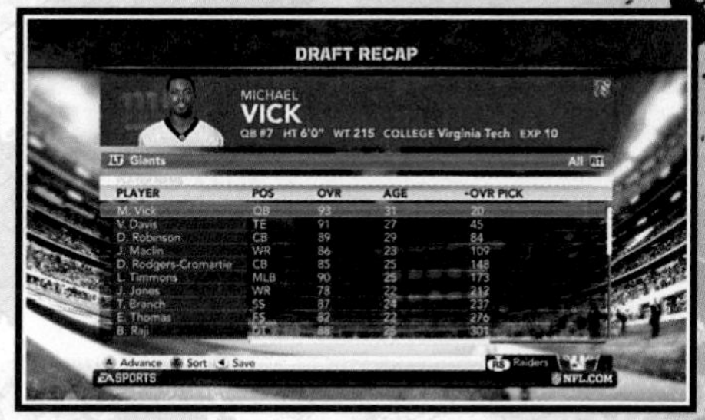

At the start of the draft the Giants' owner, Zfarls, stated he was going to select QB Mike Vick with his first selection if he was there. Vick is arguably the most dominant player in *Madden NFL 12,* and with the 20th selection in the first round Zfarls and the Giants selected Vick. This has to be the pick of the draft as Vick is the ultimate game changer and falling to the 20th selection is unbelievable. Zfarls continued to surround Vick with offensive weapons to maximize his potential. With their 2nd-round pick the Giants selected TE Vernon Davis, who is a great run blocker as well as downfield receiving threat. The 3rd-round selection was CB Dunta Robinson. Speedster WR Jeremy Maclin was taken with the Giants' 4th-round pick to give Vick another threat outside. Zfarls looked to get more speed in his defensive secondary as he grabbed one of the best CBs in *Madden NFL 12* in Dominique Rodgers-Cromartie. To hold down the middle of the field the Giants selected MLB Lawrence Timmons. Potentially the ultimate sleeper pick of the draft was when Zfarls drafted WR Julio Jones with the 6th-round pick. Jones can stretch the field with his speed and creates major mismatches with his height. To square off his defensive secondary Zfarls drafted safeties Tyvon Branch and Earl Thomas in the 8th and 9th rounds. DT B.J. Raji was selected with the Giants' 10th overall selection.

Overall Draft Score: A-

- Vick was the best pick of the draft.
- There were great picks up and down for offense and defense.
- The picks focused on surrounding Vick with offensive playmakers.
- The defense is big and fast.

Kansas City Chiefs Draft Results (22nd Overall Pick)

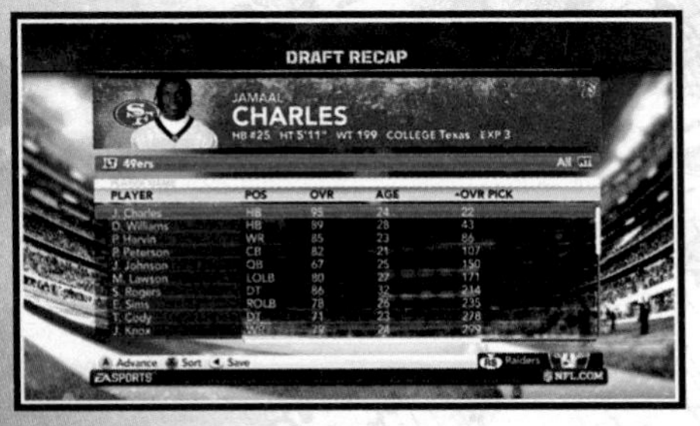

The Kansas City Chiefs focused on overall team balance. They drafted HBs Jamaal Charles and DeAngelo Williams with their 1st- and 2nd-round picks. They wanted to make sure that their backfield was solid up and down the depth chart. The Chiefs continued to draft speed as they selected WR Percy Harvin in the 3rd round and rookie CB Patrick Peterson in the 4th round. A wild card selection for the Chiefs' 5th-round pick was *Madden NFL* gem Josh Johnson. The focus of the Chiefs' offense will revolve around the HBs and Johnson's ability to scramble and make short throws. With the Chiefs' 6th- and 8th-round picks they selected value picks with LBs Manny Lawson and Ernie Sims. Sims and Lawson are lower-rated LBs but they are playmakers with their speed. The Chiefs rounded out their top 10 picks with two more value selections in DT Terrence Cody and WR Johnny Knox.

Overall Draft Score: A-

- Drafting two elite HBs is a bit of a waste of talent early on. Wait until later in the draft to find a value pick at HB who can be just as effective if needed.
- The selection of Josh Johnson is interesting. It could work out in their favor, but any type of passing game could be difficult to run.
- Picks 5–10 are absolutely amazing. Each player drafted is elite at specific ratings.

New England Patriots Draft Results (25th Overall Pick)

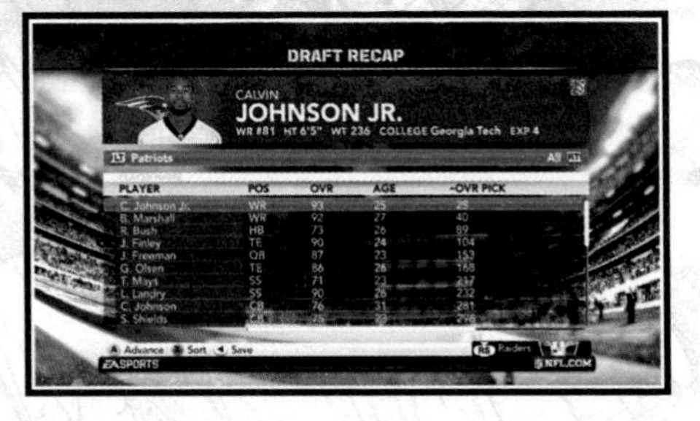

Just as owner Zfarls explained he would be drafting Michael Vick with his first pick if available so did owner Sgibs of the Patriots. He also explained that he was going to be drafting the best overall *Madden NFL* player with each pick. He would fill out his team according to his needs and would select that player even if it meant taking him early. There is no doubt that with Sgibs's first pick he snagged the best available player in Calvin Johnson. AT 6'5" and 95 speed Johnson is easily the best WR in *Madden NFL*. With a pass-first mentality Sgibs drafted Brandon Marshall to round out his outside receiving threats. A bit of a shock to most was when the Patriots selected HB Reggie Bush in the 3rd round. TE Jermichael Finley was selected with the 4th-round pick and QB Josh Freeman was taken in the 5th round. Sgibs once again reached in the 6th round as he selected TE Greg Olsen. With his first six selections Sgibs had selected his starting offensive lineup and with his next four picks moved to his defensive secondary. He selected CBs Taylor Mays, LaRon Landry, Chris Johnson, and Sam Shields.

Overall Draft Score: B+

- Sgibs stuck with his game plan but did take a few reach picks to get what he wanted.
- HB Reggie Bush was selected a few rounds early.
- HB Greg Olsen was selected a few rounds early.
- Selections 7–10 were excellent.

San Diego Chargers Draft Results (30th Overall Pick)

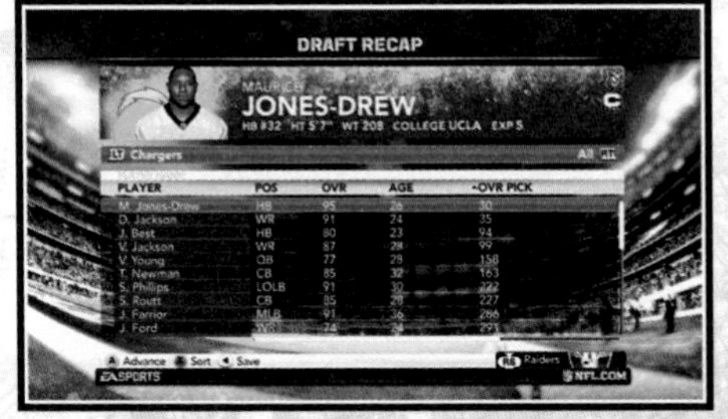

The San Diego Chargers had another owner who was looking for overall balance with his team. With his first selection he snagged HB Maurice Jones-Drew with the 30th pick in the first round. WR DeSean Jackson was selected in the 2nd round and many owners were moaning and groaning with this selection! HB Jahvid Best was selected in the 3rd round, where many thought this was a bit early for Best. With the 4th and 5th picks the Chargers selected WR Vincent Jackson and QB Vince Young. The Chargers then moved to defense as they selected four of their next five picks on the defensive side of the ball. CB Terence Newman was selected in the 6th round while LB Shaun Phillips was selected in the 7th. Picks 8 and 10 were great steals for the Chargers as they selected CB Stanford Routt and WR Jacoby Ford.

Overall Draft Score: B+

- HB Jahvid Best was selected a few rounds early.
- Many great overall players were selected.
- There were no wow picks but many solid players.
- Jacoby Ford was a great pick in the 10th round.

Denver Broncos Draft Results (31st Overall Pick)

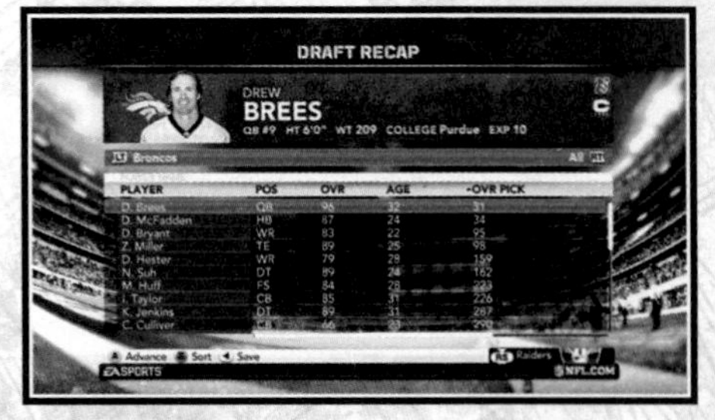

The Broncos' focus was geared towards picking a dominant offense and then worrying about defense later on. With their 1st-round selection they grabbed Drew Brees. To give Brees a weapon to hand the ball off to the Broncos selected HB Darren McFadden. We love this pick for McFadden as he is a threat both in the run game and as a receiving option. With their 3rd- and 4th-round picks the Broncos selected WR Dez Bryant and TE Zach Miller. Both are great picks and are major threats in the passing game. To give their offense more speed the Broncos selected Devin Hester with their 5th-round pick. Once the starters on offense were selected the Broncos owner moved towards the defensive side of the ball, and the remaining five picks were all defense. DT Ndamukong Suh was the

Broncos' first defensive selection, and with the 9th pick the Broncos selected another big DT with Kris Jenkins. Michael Huff and Ike Taylor were selected for the defensive secondary, and a major wow moment took place when the Broncos selected CB Chris Culliver in the 10th round.

Overall Draft Score: B+

- The offense for the Chiefs is explosive.
- They surrounded Drew Brees with great offensive targets.
- CB Chris Culliver as a 10th-round pick was a major surprise; he should have been selected many rounds later.

Who was the winner of the draft? Who do you think was the best overall team? How would you select your team? To see a matchup between the Giants (Zfarls) and the Patriots (Sgibs) head on over to (madden 12 prima football website to check out who won this matchup!

Team Selection

Franchise mode received major attention in the off season. There is a tremendous number of new options and responsibilities you must take on when taking your team from worst to first. One of the most important things is choosing who to start your franchise with; it is always one of the best moments when you open *Madden NFL* up every season. The obvious choice for most gamers is to pick their favorite team and try to carry them to Super Bowl greatness. However, some players like to choose a random squad and try to learn their system. What makes a team a good franchise pick? It depends on the type of player, and since you will be spending tons of time in this mode, think of these questions first:

- Does this team have the type of players for the system I want to run as head coach?
- How is this team's cap situation—will I be able to add any pieces via free agency?
- Is this a young team ready to rise to the top with the right coach?
- Should I be worried about the age of my team—are any of my stars on the decline?
- Is my QB a true franchise cornerstone, or will I need to find another player to lead my team?

Solid Teams Ready to Win Now

Green Bay Packers

Green Bay is ready to pursue a second straight Super Bowl. QB Aaron Rodgers has tremendous weapons at the receiving position, and the secondary is tops in the league. The defense has plenty of good years ahead of them. Focus on finding depth and youth on the offensive line. Green Bay is a great team overall, and trading for an explosive HB would make them impossible to defend.

Make sure to keep your star QB protected, because it will be very hard to win without him.

Atlanta Falcons

The Falcons proved they were an elite team last season by posting the top record in the NFC. By adding WR Julio Jones, Atlanta is packed with talent on the outside. QB Matt Ryan also has great talent at the HB position if you prefer a ground-and-pound style. The secondary has a few rising stars at CB as well. Look to add a game-breaker at the LB position to really shore up the defense.

Look to rebuild your stock of draft picks by finding a desperate franchise to swap with.

Baltimore Ravens

Baltimore has been one of the most consistent teams in the last decade thanks to their defense. While some of their players are getting older, Baltimore still has a great chance to win in the next few seasons. If you choose them for your franchise, QB Joe Flacco has a solid RB in Ray Rice to help close out games. Anquan Boldin is a true threat on the outside, while TE Todd Heap can be a safety blanket over the middle. Baltimore has the pieces to win it all right now!

Focus on free agents who can help your team now!

Teams to Build With

Carolina Panthers

CAM
NEWTON
QB 1
HT 6'6"
WT 250
COLLEGE AUBURN

Carolina had the first overall selection in the draft and went with Heisman winner Cam Newton. By using his unique blend of speed and power, you can really keep the defense on their toes. Look to add a playmaker at WR for the young QB to develop a relationship with. On defense, Carolina is strong but should look to get faster through the draft. They are implementing a new system but should be able to build a winner in a few seasons!

Bring in an older QB and assign him a role as mentor!

Arizona Cardinals

The Cardinals have one of the best secondaries in *Madden NFL 12*. If you are the type of player who loves to play pass defense and user-control the safety, consider choosing Arizona. The first priority is finding a QB who can get the ball to star WR Larry Fitzgerald. Find a QB who has the attributes for the type of offense you want to run. The Cardinals were a few minutes from winning the big one just a few seasons ago, and with the right trade they could be right back there!

Look for players who have one special skill and utilize them for specific roles

Cleveland Browns

OFFENSE 82

The Browns had a solid season and found two new stars in QB Colt McCoy and *Madden NFL 12* cover man Peyton Hillis. These two will be solid for years to come. If you can find a way to add a few playmakers on the outside to pair with Joshua Cribbs, the Browns will be in the playoffs sooner rather than later. On defense, Joe Haden has half the field on lock. Look to find a player who can speed up the pass rush and the Browns will be considered a threat in no time.

There will be many hard decisions about who to keep and who to cut in Franchise mode. Winning in the NFL on a consistent basis is one of the hardest things to do in sports. Stay focused and learn to make the tough decisions. If you can keep building your team and focus on the long term, there is no doubt you will one day be called a champion!

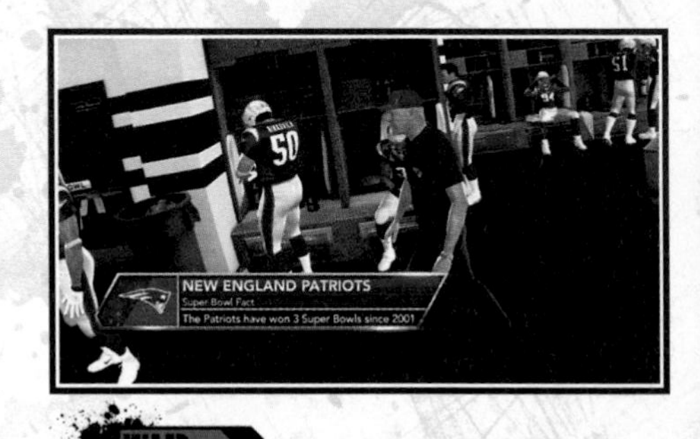

The Patriots have won 3 Super Bowls since 2001

TIP

Focus on re-signing players before their deal is up—this can help save money!

NOTE

Players who are more into simming the franchise than playing games should make sure to set their coaching scheme to maximize the team's ability to win.

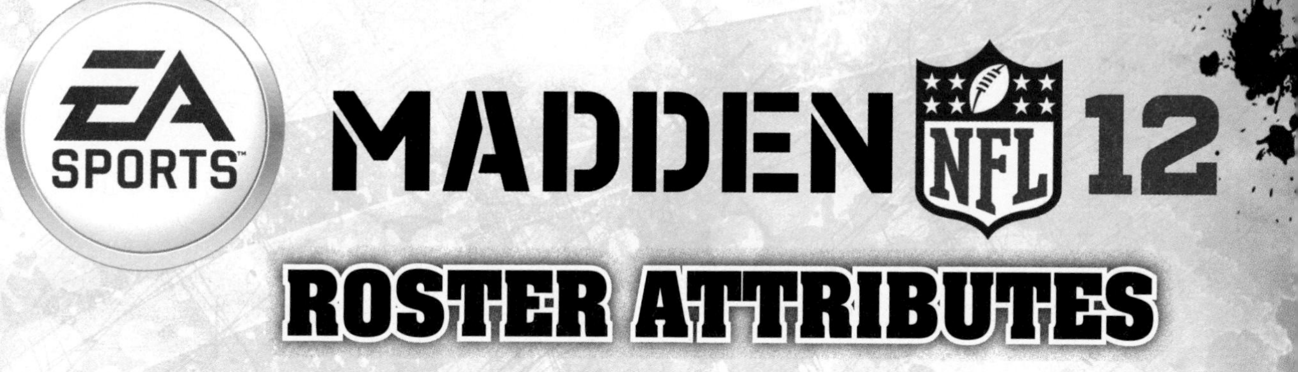

ROSTER ATTRIBUTES

Contents

QUARTERBACKS

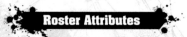

Name		OVR	SPD	AWR	PWR	ACU
Tom	Brady	99	58	98	95	97
Aaron	Rodgers	98	79	88	95	92
Peyton	Manning	98	60	99	94	96
Drew	Brees	96	64	95	88	96
Philip	Rivers	96	63	94	90	96
Ben	Roethlisberger	94	70	87	94	89
Michael	Vick	93	91	80	96	85
Matt	Ryan	90	65	87	89	89
Tony	Romo	88	73	85	91	86
Joe	Flacco	88	73	83	96	84
Matt	Schaub	88	62	87	88	90
Josh	Freeman	87	74	77	97	83
Eli	Manning	87	65	87	90	86
Matt	Cassel	86	69	85	85	84
Sam	Bradford	85	73	72	89	89
Jay	Cutler	85	71	75	98	84
Kevin	Kolb	84	72	77	88	80
Matt	Hasselbeck	84	67	87	86	83
David	Garrard	83	77	83	90	80
Mark	Sanchez	83	69	77	88	83
Carson	Palmer	83	54	85	89	85
Donovan	McNabb	82	74	82	94	76
Kyle	Orton	82	64	83	84	85
Ryan	Fitzpatrick	81	75	82	80	84
Jason	Campbell	81	70	72	92	78
Matthew	Stafford	80	70	71	97	81
Marc	Bulger	79	55	85	84	86
Vince	Young	77	85	65	90	76
Cam	Newton	77	83	49	97	81
Tim	Tebow	77	80	69	88	76
Colt	McCoy	77	74	73	80	86
Chad	Henne	77	66	70	94	75
Kerry	Collins	77	52	83	89	76
Shaun	Hill	76	69	79	79	86
Rex	Grossman	76	60	76	90	79
Jon	Kitna	76	56	84	84	79
Alex	Smith	75	76	72	85	78
Blaine	Gabbert	75	75	50	90	83
Matt	Flynn	75	75	75	79	80
Bruce	Gradkowski	75	70	73	78	84
Chad	Pennington	75	65	80	69	89
Jake	Locker	74	83	44	95	74
Charlie	Batch	74	53	83	82	79

QUARTERBACKS

Name		OVR	SPD	AWR	PWR	ACU
Seneca	Wallace	73	84	71	78	74
Christian	Ponder	73	73	50	84	84
Matt	Moore	73	67	70	86	75
Charlie	Whitehurst	73	65	68	88	77
Jake	Delhomme	73	64	76	84	75
Trent	Edwards	73	63	74	82	84
Mark	Brunell	73	60	85	79	77
Troy	Smith	72	83	67	87	71
Tarvaris	Jackson	72	83	65	94	70
Luke	McCown	72	74	72	85	74
Brady	Quinn	72	71	66	86	75
Caleb	Hanie	72	69	72	83	73
Chris	Redman	72	56	82	77	82
Matt	Leinart	72	54	69	85	77
Andy	Dalton	71	66	58	85	82
Byron	Leftwich	71	54	68	93	77
Colin	Kaepernick	70	85	46	92	75
Dennis	Dixon	70	84	65	84	70
Josh	McCown	70	77	71	78	79
Kellen	Clemens	70	66	69	88	74
Dan	Orlovsky	70	65	70	78	76
Sage	Rosenfels	70	62	62	85	84
Jimmy	Clausen	70	57	54	90	78
Derek	Anderson	70	56	68	95	75
Tyler	Thigpen	69	75	62	82	75
John	Skelton	69	72	58	96	71
Cam	Weber	69	70	45	92	79
Chris	Simms	69	63	68	87	78
Billy	Volek	69	55	74	81	79
Ryan	Mallett	69	51	41	98	79
Drew	Stanton	68	70	65	85	74
Max	Hall	68	66	63	79	81
Ricky	Stanzi	68	62	52	86	81
Jim	Sorgi	68	62	77	74	78
Chris	Greisen	68	55	67	81	80
A.J.	Feeley	68	54	69	85	76
Josh	Johnson	67	88	60	89	68
Stephen	McGee	67	75	57	83	69
Charlie	Frye	67	68	65	77	79
Chase	Daniel	67	66	58	83	75
Mike	Kafka	67	63	59	79	82
Brodie	Croyle	67	55	68	88	77
Patrick	Ramsey	67	54	68	89	72

QUARTERBACKS

Name		OVR	SPD	AWR	PWR	ACU
Hunter	Cantwell	67	52	57	94	72
Joe	Webb	66	86	60	89	67
Kyle	Boller	66	70	68	90	67
J.P.	Losman	66	68	65	93	67
Brian	Hoyer	66	65	62	87	73
John	Beck	66	64	70	78	80
Graham	Harrell	66	56	68	78	85
T.J.	Yates	66	55	51	80	80
Brian	St.Pierre	66	52	75	77	79
Terrelle	Pryor	65	90	40	90	68
Wayne	Campbell	65	77	40	87	77
Kevin	O'Connell	65	74	60	85	68
Hope	Bromley	65	74	40	90	75
David	Hansen	65	73	40	92	74
Andre	Thomas	65	70	45	87	81
David	Carr	65	67	65	87	72

FULLBACKS

Name		OVR	SPD	STR	RUN BLK	PASS BLK
Ovie	Mughelli	94	72	86	78	48
Vonta	Leach	91	69	84	82	52
Le'Ron	McClain	90	79	81	68	50
Lousaka	Polite	90	75	84	83	60
Lawrence	Vickers	90	73	82	73	50
Ahmard	Hall	88	76	81	72	60
Tony	Richardson	88	74	74	65	55
Leonard	Weaver	87	79	81	62	55
Mike	Karney	86	74	82	67	51
Montell	Owens	84	82	77	58	55
Greg	Jones	84	78	79	62	50
Marcel	Reece	83	89	76	72	54
Madison	Hedgecock	83	67	84	74	60
Heath	Evans	82	77	76	59	60
Mike	Sellers	82	70	78	67	62
Sammy	Morris	81	82	76	51	53
John	Kuhn	79	79	77	60	52
Earnest	Graham	78	80	76	60	55
John	Conner	78	72	75	68	59
Naufahu	Tahi	77	78	86	70	59
Moran	Norris	77	65	85	74	48
Michael	Robinson	76	78	79	65	52
Owen	Schmitt	76	73	85	62	44

FULLBACKS

Name		OVR	SPD	STR	RUN BLK	PASS BLK
Jerome	Felton	76	73	80	71	55
Jason	McKie	76	67	78	65	55
Jacob	Hester	73	83	70	60	50
Tim	Castille	73	76	76	64	54
Korey	Hall	73	74	76	70	48
Deon	Anderson	72	73	80	66	47
Jeremi	Johnson	72	66	82	68	52
Bear	Pascoe	72	65	78	72	62
Brit	Miller	71	76	75	63	54
Corey	McIntyre	71	75	85	72	52

HALFBACKS

Name		OVR	SPD	ACC	AGI	CAR
Adrian	Peterson	97	97	97	98	81
Chris	Johnson	96	99	99	98	91
Jamaal	Charles	95	98	98	98	87
Maurice	Jones-Drew	95	94	95	96	87
Steven	Jackson	94	87	90	87	95
Michael	Turner	93	87	89	83	98
Arian	Foster	92	91	93	91	92
Ray	Rice	92	90	98	96	91
Frank	Gore	91	92	94	92	84
Peyton	Hillis	91	87	91	86	85
DeAngelo	Williams	89	94	93	94	92
Matt	Forte	89	91	89	88	89
LeSean	McCoy	88	93	96	96	86
Rashard	Mendenhall	88	90	88	84	89
Darren	McFadden	87	97	97	86	82
Ahmad	Bradshaw	85	93	96	94	72
Knowshon	Moreno	85	88	96	97	78
Ronnie	Brown	84	91	90	89	90
LaDainian	Tomlinson	84	90	89	87	86
Thomas	Jones	84	86	85	85	93
Tiki	Barber	83	88	92	88	83
Danny	Woodhead	82	94	96	96	81
Joseph	Addai	82	90	93	94	85
Brian	Westbrook	82	88	90	90	84
Ryan	Grant	82	87	82	81	91
BenJarvus	Green-Ellis	82	84	87	79	98
Felix	Jones	81	96	96	92	75
Jonathan	Stewart	81	90	86	82	90
Marshawn	Lynch	81	88	86	81	93

HALFBACKS

Name		OVR	SPD	ACC	AGI	CAR
Cedric	Benson	81	87	86	82	80
LeGarrette	Blount	81	86	88	83	80
Jahvid	Best	80	96	97	97	80
Fred	Jackson	80	88	87	85	85
Shonn	Greene	80	87	92	84	77
Clinton	Portis	80	87	85	87	83
Ricky	Williams	80	85	86	84	75
Brandon	Jacobs	80	85	83	77	93
Darren	Sproles	79	94	97	97	72
Ryan	Torain	79	86	88	82	92
Willis	McGahee	79	85	81	80	87
Mark	Ingram	79	85	95	90	94
Pierre	Thomas	78	86	85	84	84
Kevin	Faulk	78	85	87	87	78
Jerome	Harrison	77	92	93	95	73
Ryan	Mathews	77	91	88	88	84
James	Starks	77	91	89	86	85
Justin	Forsett	77	91	94	93	76
Maurice	Morris	77	88	89	87	78
Fred	Taylor	77	88	84	85	74
Chester	Taylor	77	86	88	88	72
Mike	Tolbert	77	83	88	75	91
Correll	Buckhalter	76	87	89	82	83
Carnell	Williams	76	87	86	86	77
C.J.	Spiller	75	95	97	95	79
Leon	Washington	75	95	95	95	68
Bernard	Scott	75	93	92	90	75
Tim	Hightower	75	84	87	76	76
Michael	Bush	75	84	85	80	86
Marion	Barber	75	80	82	79	87
Mike	Goodson	74	93	95	95	62
Chris	Ivory	74	88	85	79	79
Tashard	Choice	74	87	91	86	86
Julius	Jones	74	87	84	84	81
Kevin	Smith	74	85	81	78	87
Rashad	Jennings	74	84	87	83	85
Jason	Snelling	74	81	86	79	88
Reggie	Bush	73	96	97	97	64
Beanie	Wells	73	88	82	82	83
Ryan	Williams	73	87	94	92	73
Derrick	Ward	73	86	87	79	81
LenDale	White	73	79	82	75	93

HALFBACKS

Name		OVR	SPD	ACC	AGI	CAR
LaRod	Stephens-Howling	72	93	95	94	73
Steve	Slaton	72	93	93	94	57
Donald	Brown	72	89	86	82	80
Brandon	Jackson	72	89	92	92	74
Javon	Ringer	72	88	95	88	81
Mikel	Leshoure	72	85	93	83	97
Toby	Gerhart	72	85	82	86	77
Laurence	Maroney	71	89	76	77	85
Kendall	Hunter	71	88	93	91	77
Mike	Bell	71	85	86	76	86
Montario	Hardesty	71	85	88	87	84
Mewelde	Moore	71	85	88	88	69
Mike	Hart	71	79	88	85	88
Dominic	Rhodes	70	84	88	86	75
Daniel	Thomas	70	83	89	87	74
DeMarco	Murray	69	93	91	82	74
Shane	Vereen	69	90	85	89	70
Ben	Tate	69	89	92	87	77
Jacquizz	Rodgers	69	84	97	94	83
Ladell	Betts	69	83	79	78	83
Ryan	Moats	68	88	92	89	69
Delone	Carter	68	85	88	85	84
Anthony	Dixon	68	83	87	78	86
Dion	Lewis	67	85	87	93	75
Jason	Wright	67	82	85	80	76
Rock	Cartwright	67	82	88	75	84
Stevan	Ridley	67	81	88	78	92
Lorenzo	Booker	66	92	93	93	64
James	Davis	66	91	92	83	87
Deji	Karim	66	90	92	90	74

WIDE RECEIVERS

Name		OVR	SPD	ACC	CAT	JUM
Andre	Johnson	97	94	94	96	93
Roddy	White	96	92	94	95	93
Larry	Fitzgerald	96	87	89	98	99
Reggie	Wayne	95	87	93	98	87
Calvin	Johnson Jr.	93	95	94	91	99
Greg	Jennings	93	94	95	94	91
Brandon	Marshall	92	88	87	96	92
DeSean	Jackson	91	99	98	91	87
Dwayne	Bowe	91	88	88	86	97

WIDE RECEIVERS

Name		OVR	SPD	ACC	CAT	JUM
Wes	Welker	90	85	96	96	71
Steve	Smith	89	95	92	88	89
Miles	Austin	89	94	91	88	89
Hakeem	Nicks	89	90	93	90	94
Brandon	Lloyd	88	92	93	95	92
Marques	Colston	88	83	85	96	90
Mike	Wallace	87	98	98	88	88
Santonio	Holmes	87	95	94	87	88
Vincent	Jackson	87	91	84	89	97
Anquan	Boldin	87	86	85	88	86
Jeremy	Maclin	86	95	93	89	87
Steve	Johnson	86	88	92	84	91
Kenny	Britt	86	88	91	86	90
Derrick	Mason	86	86	90	91	85
Hines	Ward	86	85	83	89	80
Santana	Moss	85	96	95	88	87
Percy	Harvin	85	96	98	84	90
Braylon	Edwards	85	92	88	75	98
Chad	Ochocinco	85	91	93	88	90
Sidney	Rice	85	89	87	87	96
Terrell	Owens	85	88	81	81	87
Randy	Moss	84	95	84	87	95
Mike	Williams	84	88	92	89	94
Steve	Smith	84	87	88	91	86
Dez	Bryant	83	94	96	88	98
Mike	Williams	83	84	88	91	94
Pierre	Garcon	82	95	95	78	90
Donald	Driver	82	85	83	87	83
Lee	Evans	81	96	92	86	85
Michael	Crabtree	81	88	90	88	92
Mario	Manningham	80	92	96	80	95
Mike	Sims-Walker	80	90	86	84	91
A.J.	Green	80	89	90	89	92
Malcom	Floyd	80	89	82	87	97
Devin	Hester	79	98	98	76	90
Johnny	Knox	79	97	97	86	89
Mike	Thomas	79	93	95	87	92
Josh	Cribbs	79	92	96	69	90
Roy	Williams	79	90	86	84	92
Jordy	Nelson	79	88	90	85	84
Austin	Collie	79	87	89	92	80
Jerricho	Cotchery	79	83	85	85	86
Julio	Jones	78	94	90	83	96

WIDE RECEIVERS

Name		OVR	SPD	ACC	CAT	JUM
Nate	Burleson	78	93	91	82	92
Nate	Washington	78	93	92	80	93
Steve	Breaston	78	91	94	81	91
Lance	Moore	78	88	94	87	80
Josh	Morgan	78	87	91	82	90
Mark	Clayton	78	86	92	83	87
Davone	Bess	78	85	96	95	77
Kevin	Walter	78	83	84	87	84
T.J.	Houshman-dzadeh	78	83	82	85	78
Anthony	Armstrong	77	95	94	82	93
Robert	Meachem	77	94	89	77	88
Deion	Branch	77	88	92	85	81
Jason	Avant	77	82	83	85	82
Devery	Henderson	76	98	96	79	83
Donnie	Avery	76	96	95	78	85
Eddie	Royal	76	95	97	80	87
Brandon	Tate	76	94	95	74	91
Brad	Smith	76	92	91	76	87
Arrelious	Benn	76	89	82	79	89
Michael	Jenkins	76	87	77	82	92
Antwaan	Randle El	76	87	90	76	86
Mohamed	Massaquoi	76	86	91	82	90
James	Jones	76	86	89	84	85
Earl	Bennett	76	85	87	85	80
Louis	Murphy	75	93	91	78	92
Danny	Amendola	75	85	94	88	76
Justin	Gage	75	80	79	85	94
Jacoby	Ford	74	98	97	79	88
Bernard	Berrian	74	96	88	77	88
David	Gettis	74	94	95	79	88
Dexter	McCluster	74	93	96	81	80
Jacoby	Jones	74	93	88	78	88
Jerome	Simpson	74	91	93	82	91
Jordan	Shipley	74	88	92	83	77
Patrick	Crayton	74	87	86	85	83
Brian	Hartline	74	87	92	85	79
Brandon	Gibson	74	87	88	76	86
Andre	Caldwell	74	86	88	78	90
Early	Doucet	74	86	89	77	82
Chris	Chambers	74	86	83	80	92
Demaryius	Thomas	73	96	92	81	95
Julian	Edelman	73	86	87	82	84

WIDE RECEIVERS

Name		OVR	SPD	ACC	CAT	JUM
Legedu	Naanee	73	84	86	83	80
Jabar	Gaffney	73	83	87	88	80
Ted	Ginn	72	97	95	65	88
Darrius	Heyward-Bey	72	97	96	68	92
Chaz	Schilens	72	92	94	79	94
Devin	Aromashodu	72	89	92	77	91
Brandon	Stokley	72	84	87	83	77
Roscoe	Parrish	71	95	97	76	84
Golden	Tate	71	93	89	83	90
Laurent	Robinson	71	92	94	74	89
Jonathan	Baldwin	71	91	85	82	97
Harry	Douglas	71	91	94	77	89
Jason	Hill	71	87	89	76	88
Buster	Davis	71	86	88	77	83
Brandon	LaFell	71	86	85	78	87
Ben	Obomanu	71	86	88	81	86
Kelley	Washington	71	84	87	76	88
Deon	Butler	70	95	93	81	88
Emmanuel	Sanders	70	94	95	82	92
Marc	Mariani	70	92	92	76	82
Joey	Galloway	70	91	90	80	77
Eric	Weems	70	90	94	77	82
Brian	Robiskie	70	89	86	85	85
Randall	Cobb	70	89	93	81	86
Anthony	Gonzalez	70	88	92	82	79
Greg	Little	70	87	84	84	95
Greg	Camarillo	70	82	84	83	82
Troy	Williamson	69	94	93	74	74
Torrey	Smith	69	92	97	79	92
Antonio	Brown	69	92	94	74	84
Danario	Alexander	69	87	83	78	97
Sammie	Stroughter	69	86	93	81	82
Eric	Decker	69	85	88	86	82
David	Nelson	69	84	87	78	88
Arnaz	Battle	69	80	83	76	77
Ruvell	Martin	69	79	84	78	87
Johnnie Lee	Higgins	68	94	96	72	89
Donte'	Stallworth	68	94	89	72	78
Devin	Thomas	68	91	92	70	88
Lavelle	Hawkins	68	91	93	74	90
Chansi	Stuckey	68	87	91	77	81
Bryant	Johnson	68	87	86	76	87

WIDE RECEIVERS

Name		OVR	SPD	ACC	CAT	JUM
Vincent	Brown	68	81	87	84	89
Maurice	Stovall	68	80	79	77	88
Leonard	Hankerson	67	92	86	81	90
Brandon	Jones	67	91	88	74	84
Kevin	Curtis	67	90	87	80	75
Micheal	Spurlock	67	88	93	74	84
Titus	Young	67	88	96	84	81
Damian	Williams	67	88	82	84	84
Blair	White	67	84	86	84	74
Jerheme	Urban	67	83	86	76	79
Michael	Clayton	67	81	82	73	86
Andre	Roberts	66	91	90	75	84
Rashied	Davis	66	88	90	71	85
Seyi	Ajirotutu	66	88	82	75	85
Greg	Salas	66	85	85	83	88
Brian	Finneran	66	73	75	80	77
Demetrius	Williams	65	89	85	75	90
Sam	Giguere	65	85	90	74	83
Dane	Sanzen-bacher	65	85	79	81	75
Sam	Hurd	65	83	85	79	84
Austin	Pettis	65	83	86	82	88
Tandon	Doss	65	83	86	88	87
David	Clowney	64	92	93	73	89
Marcus	Easley	64	91	85	75	88
Jerrel	Jernigan	64	90	95	80	83
Mardy	Gilyard	64	88	94	73	85
Kris	Durham	64	87	80	82	84
Matthew	Willis	64	86	88	73	85
Brooks	Foster	64	86	86	70	88
Riley	Cooper	64	86	77	75	87

TIGHT ENDS

Name		OVR	SPD	AWR	CAT	JUM
Antonio	Gates	99	84	95	94	92
Dallas	Clark	96	87	93	96	82
Jason	Witten	96	75	94	95	80
Tony	Gonzalez	92	78	95	90	88
Vernon	Davis	91	90	77	82	94
Jermichael	Finley	90	86	75	87	95
Marcedes	Lewis	90	73	88	90	78
Kellen	Winslow	89	83	83	85	92
Zach	Miller	89	82	85	87	85
Chris	Cooley	87	78	87	87	85
Greg	Olsen	86	87	78	86	89
Owen	Daniels	86	83	85	88	82
Dustin	Keller	85	86	74	83	88
Heath	Miller	85	72	85	87	75
Todd	Heap	84	82	87	89	88
Visanthe	Shiancoe	84	80	81	84	86
Rob	Gronkowski	84	79	70	87	84
Benjamin	Watson	83	85	80	80	86
Jacob	Tamme	83	83	80	90	73
Brent	Celek	83	77	88	83	75
Aaron	Hernandez	82	84	67	88	87
Jeremy	Shockey	81	77	84	83	84
Brandon	Pettigrew	81	73	85	76	76
Jermaine	Gresham	80	83	65	84	87
Fred	Davis	79	79	72	82	87
Bo	Scaife	78	78	80	82	83
Jimmy	Graham	77	85	67	81	92
Randy	McMichael	77	73	74	77	88
Kevin	Boss	77	73	73	80	88
Jared	Cook Jr.	76	85	67	77	86
Tony	Moeaki	76	81	68	85	74
David	Thomas	76	74	73	76	84
John	Carlson	76	73	77	79	80
Tony	Scheffler	75	82	74	85	86
Evan	Moore	75	78	69	85	88
Leonard	Pope	75	75	75	74	86
Anthony	Fasano	75	69	84	82	68
Donald	Lee	74	74	74	73	79
Desmond	Clark	74	69	80	76	83
Shawn	Nelson	73	83	58	77	87
Zach	Miller	73	83	62	74	84
Kyle	Rudolph	73	80	54	84	84
Martellus	Bennett	73	78	54	76	94
Alge	Crumpler	73	68	75	74	75
Ed	Dickson	72	83	62	79	82
Alex	Smith	72	74	74	74	82
Kris	Wilson	72	72	67	76	85
Daniel	Graham	72	70	73	63	70
Billy	Bajema	72	68	75	73	76
Travis	Beckum	71	84	65	85	85
Lance	Kendricks	71	76	56	81	86

LEFT TACKLES

Name		OVR	STR	AWR	RUN BLK	PASS BLK
Jake	Long	97	97	88	97	95
Joe	Thomas	95	92	88	96	94
D'Brickashaw	Ferguson	94	90	88	95	92
Ryan	Clady	92	91	87	89	96
Jordan	Gross	92	90	96	94	93
Michael	Roos	91	95	87	95	91
Marcus	McNeill	89	92	85	85	94
Jason	Peters	89	96	86	95	88
Joe	Staley	88	86	88	85	89
Matt	Light	88	88	93	87	92
Chad	Clifton	88	93	95	81	93
Sam	Baker	87	91	81	86	92
Donald	Penn	87	93	86	92	87
Branden	Albert	86	89	79	90	88
Bryant	McKinnie	85	96	89	96	86
Andrew	Whitworth	85	95	88	94	86
Doug	Free	84	84	81	84	92
Rodger	Saffold	83	86	73	79	91
Russell	Okung	83	86	70	82	90
Jeff	Backus	83	92	91	82	90
Michael	Oher	82	98	69	95	84
Max	Starks	82	96	87	94	87
Jared	Veldheer	81	91	68	89	85
Eugene	Monroe	81	88	73	86	89
Trent	Williams	80	90	69	88	86
Duane	Brown	80	90	76	87	82
Charlie	Johnson	80	90	81	82	86
Jermon	Bushrod	80	90	75	84	88
David	Diehl	77	88	90	87	80
Anthony	Castonzo	76	86	62	83	88
Anthony	Collins	76	91	70	88	85
Nate	Solder	75	84	60	87	85
Garry	Williams	75	91	72	86	82
Frank	Omiyale	75	91	76	82	83
Gabe	Carimi	74	92	62	94	78
Levi	Jones	74	87	73	86	78
Nick	Kaczur	74	93	75	81	80
Barry	Sims	74	87	82	88	86
Derek	Sherrod	73	84	58	84	85
Demetrius	Bell	73	83	72	83	78
William	Beatty	73	80	60	83	87
Kevin	Shaffer	73	88	80	81	84

LEFT TACKLES

Name		OVR	STR	AWR	RUN BLK	PASS BLK
Shawn	Andrews	73	97	68	95	80
Jonathan	Scott	73	87	71	82	84
Levi	Brown	70	91	69	86	77
Charles	Brown	70	80	49	87	78
Tony	Ugoh	69	86	70	79	82
Alex	Barron	69	88	69	84	79
Brandon	Frye	67	87	58	74	78
T.J.	Lang	67	88	58	86	74
Troy	Kropog	66	78	64	83	84

LEFT GUARDS

Name		OVR	STR	AWR	RUN BLK	PASS BLK
Carl	Nicks	96	96	86	92	90
Ben	Grubbs	95	94	84	94	87
Kris	Dielman	94	93	90	92	89
Logan	Mankins	93	91	90	94	84
Steve	Hutchinson	92	93	97	92	82
Brian	Waters	91	95	98	95	85
Todd	Herremans	90	91	87	88	93
Mike	Iupati	88	94	67	95	81
Robert	Gallery	87	92	80	94	75
Jacob	Bell	87	86	84	82	89
Eric	Steinbach	86	88	88	81	87
Wade	Smith	86	89	82	90	82
Travelle	Wharton	85	85	73	86	88
Chris	Williams	84	88	75	79	87
Rob	Sims	84	93	83	84	89
Justin	Blalock	83	92	76	88	79
Daryn	Colledge	82	82	77	78	85
Andy	Levitre	82	86	73	85	87
Kyle	Kosier	82	85	83	85	82
Vince	Manuwai	82	93	82	92	76
Ben	Hamilton	81	81	80	85	75
Chester	Pitts	81	89	77	85	81
Reggie	Wells	81	87	80	83	83
Rich	Seubert	81	86	87	86	79
Leroy	Harris	80	89	75	85	78
Richie	Incognito	79	90	70	88	77
Zane	Beadles	78	85	66	84	85
Keydrick	Vincent	78	93	78	89	77
Evan	Mathis	77	82	68	82	84

LEFT GUARDS

Name		OVR	STR	AWR	RUN BLK	PASS BLK
Kasey	Studdard	77	92	72	87	78
Nate	Livings	77	90	75	86	75
Mark	Setterstrom	76	84	66	84	84
Kyle	DeVan	76	89	65	84	80
Jon	Asamoah	75	86	52	87	81
Kory	Lichten-steiger	75	84	64	84	76
Billy	Yates	75	86	74	86	82
Matthew	Slauson	75	88	69	84	78
Chris	Kemoeatu	75	94	78	87	76
Nate	Garner	74	91	69	85	78
Clint	Boling	74	83	63	78	83
Chad	Rinehart	74	87	60	84	77
Mackenzy	Bernadeau	74	98	54	85	75
Stacy	Andrews	74	93	77	85	76
Tyler	Polumbus	73	87	64	73	80
Ted	Larsen	73	78	61	78	83
Ikechuku	Ndukwe	73	87	72	83	76
Chris	DeGeare	73	91	68	79	75
Rex	Hadnot	72	87	68	84	78
Derrick	Dockery	72	92	76	86	73
Bruce	Campbell	71	90	35	79	86
Cory	Procter	71	85	74	84	80

CENTERS

Name		OVR	STR	AWR	RUN BLK	PASS BLK
Nick	Mangold	97	94	93	92	93
Jeff	Saturday	95	87	98	87	95
Shaun	O'Hara	92	89	92	92	94
Matt	Birk	91	86	99	92	88
Todd	McClure	90	83	98	90	85
Dan	Koppen	89	85	95	85	93
Alex	Mack	88	93	77	93	87
Maurkice	Pouncey	88	92	75	92	88
Andre	Gurode	87	94	91	93	85
Ryan	Kalil	86	86	80	90	84
Nick	Hardwick	86	86	89	86	90
Jason	Brown	86	92	84	91	82
Jeff	Faine	85	85	88	85	89
Brad	Meester	85	87	95	89	80
Scott	Wells	84	86	88	82	88

CENTERS

Name		OVR	STR	AWR	RUN BLK	PASS BLK
Eric	Heitmann	84	91	85	92	86
Casey	Wiegmann	83	79	90	85	85
Olin	Kreutz	82	90	92	83	85
Dominic	Raiola	80	85	86	81	79
Jonathan	Goodwin	80	84	78	81	90
Mike	Pouncey	79	89	61	88	86
Chris	Myers	79	87	79	86	84
Jamaal	Jackson	78	88	84	87	80
Kyle	Cook	78	89	73	87	83
Justin	Hartwig	77	85	78	86	88
Geoff	Hangartner	77	86	79	86	83
Jake	Grove	77	86	81	88	82
Jason	Spitz	77	87	78	85	80
Casey	Rabach	75	83	83	78	86
Russ	Hochstein	75	85	82	84	82
Chris	Spencer	74	86	66	84	88
Joe	Berger	74	85	75	84	75
Brett	Romberg	74	82	77	83	81
Jeremy	Zuttah	73	86	71	84	75
Eugene	Amano	73	85	75	82	81
John	Sullivan	73	84	76	82	75
Scott	Mruczkowski	73	83	74	83	84
Rudy	Niswanger	73	84	75	87	76
Chris	Chester	72	82	64	84	79
Samson	Satele	72	82	71	82	78
Stefen	Wisniewski	72	83	61	84	79
Rodney	Hudson	71	82	62	80	84
J.D.	Walton	71	82	65	85	80
Steve	Vallos	71	87	68	83	80
Lyle	Sendlein	71	80	73	81	85
David	Baas	71	86	66	87	77
Doug	Legursky	70	87	68	85	78
Greg	Warren	69	78	82	74	80
Josh	Beekman	69	86	65	83	78
Andy	Alleman	68	79	65	72	79

RIGHT GUARDS

Name		OVR	STR	AWR	RUN BLK	PASS BLK
Jahri	Evans	98	96	92	93	94
Chris	Snee	96	93	91	94	92
Josh	Sitton	92	92	84	92	88
Brandon	Moore	90	91	80	94	86

RIGHT GUARDS

Name		OVR	STR	AWR	RUN BLK	PASS BLK
Bobbie	Williams	89	95	94	94	81
Davin	Joseph	88	91	77	90	85
Harvey	Dahl	87	91	76	94	85
Ryan	Lilja	86	88	87	85	89
Marshal	Yanda	85	86	75	86	85
Chris	Kuper	84	84	81	82	86
Uche	Nwaneri	84	94	79	91	84
Leonard	Davis	84	98	90	95	84
Justin	Smiley	83	86	78	82	84
Jake	Scott	83	86	87	86	85
Eric	Wood	82	88	74	87	77
Deuce	Lutui	82	96	77	88	82
Hank	Fraley	80	88	88	87	77
Louis	Vasquez	80	96	74	90	79
Chilo	Rachal	79	91	68	84	73
Max	Unger	79	84	74	85	81
Adam	Snyder	79	92	73	88	78
Artis	Hicks	77	89	74	88	84
Mike	Pollak	76	82	65	80	85
John	Jerry	76	93	64	88	72
Danny	Watkins	76	89	45	84	88
Cooper	Carlisle	76	87	78	84	77
Geoff	Schwartz	76	92	68	86	78
Adam	Goldberg	76	87	78	83	85
Mike	Brisiel	75	87	70	82	78
Roberto	Garza	75	90	74	82	82
Stephen	Peterman	75	92	81	85	79
Mike	Williams	75	95	79	87	74
Donald	Thomas	74	88	68	83	73
Ramon	Foster	74	87	65	86	75
Mike	Gibson	74	86	65	82	77
John	Moffitt	74	87	58	88	76
Antoine	Caldwell	73	82	58	84	72
John	Greco	72	83	64	82	76
Lance	Louis	72	87	63	79	71
Shawn	Lauvao	72	89	65	84	78
Max	Jean-Gilles	72	95	71	91	78
Floyd	Womack	72	95	78	87	75
Dan	Connolly	71	87	68	79	79
Shawn	Murphy	71	87	70	83	69
Anthony	Herrera	71	89	73	86	74
Adrian	Jones	70	84	64	81	83

RIGHT GUARDS

Name		OVR	STR	AWR	RUN BLK	PASS BLK
Trai	Essex	70	86	72	76	86
Phil	Costa	70	93	64	74	78
Pat	McQuistan	70	91	65	85	83
Johan	Asiata	69	84	62	73	84
David	Binn	69	75	86	70	65

RIGHT TACKLES

Name		OVR	STR	AWR	RUN BLK	PASS BLK
Tyson	Clabo	93	90	88	94	87
David	Stewart	91	93	88	89	90
Kareem	McKenzie	91	96	93	95	86
Eric	Winston	90	85	82	86	91
Vernon	Carey	90	93	87	91	87
Jon	Stinchcomb	88	91	92	85	92
Jason	Smith	87	91	72	91	86
Damien	Woody	86	91	90	87	80
Mark	Tauscher	86	91	92	89	80
Ryan	Harris	85	87	80	85	87
Eben	Britton	85	90	76	89	85
Jeff	Otah	85	96	76	96	80
Jammal	Brown	84	90	82	87	82
Jared	Gaither	84	92	73	85	89
Flozell	Adams	84	97	90	92	78
Ryan	Diem	83	90	89	81	88
Bryan	Bulaga	82	82	65	86	85
Willie	Colon	82	89	78	86	84
Sebastian	Vollmer	81	91	71	83	85
Gosder	Cherilus	80	92	73	86	84
Langston	Walker	79	93	83	89	78
Mario	Henderson	78	87	75	79	86
Winston	Justice	78	89	68	82	84
Barry	Richardson	78	92	69	86	78
Marc	Colombo	78	93	85	90	76
Tyron	Smith	77	85	50	84	86
Brandon	Keith	77	87	66	83	80
Anthony	Davis	77	93	58	89	73
Dennis	Roland	77	87	74	88	79
Tony	Pashos	77	90	76	86	74
James	Carpenter	76	91	53	88	77
Jeromey	Clary	76	86	78	86	78
Stephon	Heyer	76	93	76	87	79

RIGHT TACKLES

Name		OVR	STR	AWR	RUN BLK	PASS BLK
Andre	Smith	76	93	56	93	78
James	Lee	75	87	66	84	78
Sean	Locklear	75	86	75	84	82
J'Marcus	Webb	75	88	65	83	78
Phil	Loadholt	75	93	69	92	75
Khalif	Barnes	74	90	69	88	74
Adam	Terry	74	88	68	86	87
Jeremy	Bridges	74	89	73	84	75
John	St. Clair	74	93	84	83	73
Ryan	O'Callaghan	74	94	74	87	74
Wayne	Hunter	72	92	70	86	76
Herb	Taylor	71	85	65	78	80
Marcus	Gilbert	71	92	45	80	84
Vladimir	Ducasse	71	93	45	85	84
Corey	Hilliard	71	90	64	82	79
Jeremy	Trueblood	71	91	73	87	74
Kirk	Chambers	71	87	72	85	74
Erik	Pears	70	83	67	83	71

DEFENSIVE TACKLES

Name		OVR	ACC	STR	AWR	TAC
Kevin	Williams	97	88	92	88	91
Vince	Wilfork	96	84	97	92	88
Richard	Seymour	93	79	91	92	87
Kyle	Williams	93	85	88	92	95
Jay	Ratliff	92	85	89	85	88
Casey	Hampton	92	74	98	95	93
Ndamukong	Suh	89	88	95	75	94
Kris	Jenkins	89	76	97	85	86
B.J.	Raji	88	81	95	74	86
Aubrayo	Franklin	88	77	95	87	91
Jonathan	Babineaux	87	86	87	83	83
Terrance	Knighton	87	77	94	78	91
Sedrick	Ellis	86	87	90	78	83
Corey	Williams	86	88	90	79	82
Mike	Patterson	86	87	88	88	90
Paul	Soliai	86	74	96	84	89
Shaun	Rogers	86	69	98	77	87
Pat	Williams	86	67	97	96	90
Tommy	Kelly	85	74	92	79	85
Brandon	Mebane	85	87	91	73	80
Jason	Jones	84	82	86	75	82

DEFENSIVE TACKLES

Name		OVR	ACC	STR	AWR	TAC
Tommie	Harris	84	90	83	82	75
Tyson	Alualu	84	86	90	73	86
Barry	Cofield	84	80	92	77	92
Domata	Peko	84	79	90	80	85
Tony	Brown	84	84	87	77	84
Albert	Haynesworth	83	83	96	75	83
Kelly	Gregg	83	67	90	96	85
Jamal	Williams	83	64	97	90	87
Fred	Robbins	82	77	92	85	85
Gerald	McCoy	81	95	89	60	80
Chris	Canty	81	77	86	78	86
Sione	Pouha	81	81	94	82	87
Anthony	Adams	81	74	88	87	86
Antonio	Garay	81	75	89	78	85
Ahtyba	Rubin	81	75	95	79	88
Ron	Edwards	81	76	93	85	84
Brodrick	Bunkley	79	77	93	73	80
John	Henderson	79	69	95	84	85
Colin	Cole	78	75	88	77	82
Nick	Fairley	77	94	86	48	85
Tank	Johnson	77	82	82	75	72
Corey	Peters	77	88	80	66	77
Pat	Sims	77	84	91	72	84
Marques	Douglas	77	78	83	83	80
Chris	Hovan	77	83	84	85	75
Remi	Ayodele	77	78	87	70	78
Matt	Toeaina	77	74	93	74	80
Clifton	Ryan	77	82	86	75	73
Fili	Moala	77	79	81	75	84
Chris	Hoke	77	74	88	83	84
Junior	Siavii	77	60	94	79	88
Ronald	Fields	77	66	88	79	85
Ed	Johnson	76	74	86	76	74
Ma'ake	Kemoeatu	76	55	96	82	83
Jovan	Haye	75	73	87	72	79
Ryan	McBean	75	76	85	73	79
Gary	Gibson	75	80	84	69	76
Antonio	Dixon	75	80	87	65	79
Daniel	Muir	75	72	87	74	79
Jay	Alford	75	84	85	70	83
Shaun	Cody	75	82	84	75	86
Tony	Hargrove	74	81	78	72	73
Peria	Jerry	74	84	83	55	74

DEFENSIVE TACKLES

Name		OVR	ACC	STR	AWR	TAC
Sammie	Hill	74	81	90	66	75
Marcus	Thomas	74	84	87	62	74
Phil	Taylor	74	70	94	55	89
Dan	Williams	74	70	95	66	88
Jimmy	Kennedy	74	77	90	75	77
Bryan	Robinson	74	69	82	74	68
Rocky	Bernard	73	82	87	73	76
Geno	Atkins	72	94	85	57	67
Antonio	Johnson	72	78	82	70	74
Kevin	Vickerson	72	70	88	71	78
Derreck	Robinson	72	68	84	72	65
Jarvis	Jenkins	71	82	90	50	87
Brian	Schaefering	71	70	82	75	77
Brian	Price	71	87	85	45	75
Derek	Landri	71	79	82	70	80
Damione	Lewis	71	76	85	73	75
Atiyyah	Ellison	71	70	86	67	79
Roy	Miller	71	76	88	68	78
C.J.	Mosley	71	72	88	70	81
Ryan	Sims	71	76	88	70	75
Brandon	McKinney	71	74	89	70	82
Terrence	Cody	71	70	97	56	92
Drake	Nevis	70	86	77	58	80
Jurrell	Casey	70	88	84	46	88
Desmond	Bryant	70	78	79	60	79
Kyle	Love	70	75	85	55	77
Tank	Tyler	70	78	90	65	72
Howard	Green	70	76	84	67	74
Thomas	Johnson	70	68	86	71	77
Louis	Leonard	70	69	94	74	80
Marvin	Austin	69	92	83	39	77
Terrell	McClain	69	81	96	47	79
Linval	Joseph	69	84	94	55	74

LEFT DEFENSIVE END

Name		OVR	SPD	ACC	STR	AGI
Justin	Tuck	94	84	92	87	75
Robert	Mathis	93	86	96	76	85
Aaron	Smith	91	66	76	91	65
Jason	Babin	90	74	84	79	75
Shaun	Ellis	90	66	78	92	65
Chris	Long	89	75	83	87	77
Charles	Johnson	88	78	90	81	76

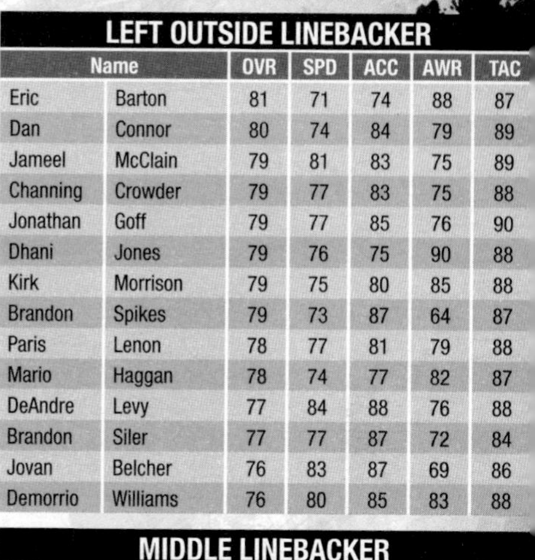

LEFT DEFENSIVE END

Name		OVR	SPD	ACC	STR	AGI
Ray	Edwards	88	76	87	83	76
Kendall	Langford	88	69	77	88	67
Chris	Clemons	87	79	88	75	82
Cliff	Avril	85	81	88	74	83
Antonio	Smith	85	73	82	83	69
Ty	Warren	84	64	73	90	64
Ryan	Pickett	83	63	78	94	62
Marcell	Dareus	82	73	78	92	72
Israel	Idonije	82	72	85	85	70
Cory	Redding	82	69	85	87	69
Calais	Campbell	80	75	84	82	73
Raheem	Brock	79	77	87	75	71
Ziggy	Hood	79	66	78	85	67
Jason	Pierre-Paul	78	84	97	72	86
Adrian	Clayborn	78	76	78	85	73
Juqua	Parker	78	74	86	80	76
Paul	Kruger	78	74	79	79	72
Adam	Carriker	78	74	79	86	69
Lamarr	Houston	78	72	82	88	70
Jarvis	Green	78	63	78	83	70
Cameron	Jordan	77	78	84	88	77
Jason	Hunter	77	77	84	69	79
Lawrence	Jackson	77	77	83	79	71
Kroy	Biermann	77	73	84	82	75
Kenyon	Coleman	77	67	74	83	67
Brandon	Graham	76	80	82	77	75
Robert	Geathers	76	78	86	75	74
Corey	Wootton	76	74	82	84	73
Jacques	Cesaire	76	73	78	80	72
Tyson	Jackson	76	69	74	87	66
Charles	Grant	76	69	75	78	69
Jeremy	Mincey	76	68	85	82	75
Phillip	Daniels	76	63	72	93	64
Isaac	Sopoaga	76	52	75	93	57
Alex	Brown	75	78	87	75	75
Jonathan	Fanene	75	73	85	78	71
Jamaal	Anderson	75	71	76	83	75
Corey	Liuget	75	68	84	91	72
Shaun	Smith	75	60	72	94	60
Greg	Hardy	74	75	87	77	78
Jimmy	Wilkerson	74	72	77	84	71
Amobi	Okoye	74	66	83	86	65
Robert	Ayers	73	78	85	81	76
Victor	Abiamiri	73	69	80	80	77

RIGHT DEFENSIVE END

Name		OVR	SPD	ACC	STR	AGI
Haloti	Ngata	97	68	81	99	70
Julius	Peppers	95	85	96	85	88
Jared	Allen	94	77	86	84	74
Dwight	Freeney	93	87	96	80	85
Trent	Cole	93	84	93	78	78
John	Abraham	93	81	88	85	74
Justin	Smith	92	73	81	88	68
Elvis	Dumervil	91	84	95	78	82
Osi	Umenyiora	89	84	95	74	80
Darnell	Dockett	89	73	88	89	70
Cullen	Jenkins	89	68	86	90	67
Will	Smith	88	76	84	87	74
Brett	Keisel	88	73	79	88	73
Aaron	Kampman	86	75	82	85	67
Randy	Starks	86	66	77	95	62
Carlos	Dunlap	85	84	88	82	82
Antwan	Odom	84	74	86	87	76
Luis	Castillo	84	65	80	97	64
Mike	Wright	84	60	78	90	63
Dwan	Edwards	83	64	78	91	65
Trevor	Pryce	83	64	72	93	65
James	Hall	82	75	84	79	72
Marcus	Stroud	82	54	77	94	61
Glenn	Dorsey	81	69	87	88	67
Dave	Ball	81	68	76	87	66
Mike	Devito	81	63	77	89	64
J.J.	Watt	80	76	82	90	72
Matt	Shaughnessy	80	73	84	85	69
Kyle	Vanden Bosch	80	69	74	85	67
Trevor	Scott	79	79	85	74	73
Mathias	Kiwanuka	79	73	84	80	72
Robert	Quinn	78	83	94	78	85
Jared	Odrick	78	68	84	88	64
Red	Bryant	78	68	82	94	64
Justin	Bannan	78	63	69	92	62
Igor	Olshansky	78	60	76	91	64
Derrick	Morgan	77	74	87	82	73
Gerard	Warren	76	61	78	90	60
Robaire	Smith	76	59	75	86	63
Marcus	Benard	75	80	87	72	76
Tyler	Brayton	75	70	80	83	69
Da'Quan	Bowers	74	78	82	83	82
Cameron	Heyward	74	73	81	91	69
Marcus	Spears	74	64	78	88	67
David	Veikune	73	75	84	74	76
Phillip	Merling	73	72	84	82	77
Kedric	Golston	73	63	80	85	66
Kentwan	Balmer	73	55	78	92	62
Jabaal	Sheard	72	82	87	68	74
Darryl	Tapp	72	78	84	74	73
Michael	Bennett	72	71	77	81	68
Vonnie	Holliday	72	59	66	87	60

LEFT OUTSIDE LINEBACKER

Name		OVR	SPD	ACC	AWR	TAC
Patrick	Willis	98	90	96	90	98
Jon	Beason	97	85	93	96	97
Ray	Lewis	95	83	86	95	94
Brian	Urlacher	94	84	89	95	96
Jerod	Mayo	92	85	91	77	97
David	Harris	92	79	87	90	96
Jonathan	Vilma	91	84	90	92	93
London	Fletcher	91	79	83	98	98
James	Farrior	91	75	77	97	96
Lawrence	Timmons	90	85	93	82	93
Karlos	Dansby	90	79	87	91	92
Curtis	Lofton	90	79	84	86	96
Daryl	Smith	90	78	86	88	93
Bart	Scott	90	77	84	93	92
DeMeco	Ryans	89	76	86	90	96
Lofa	Tatupu	88	79	92	90	95
Stephen	Tulloch	88	79	85	85	97
Nick	Barnett	88	78	87	86	91
E.J.	Henderson	88	74	78	87	95
Paul	Posluszny	87	76	86	85	93
James	Laurinaitis	87	76	86	82	95
Takeo	Spikes	87	75	80	97	90
Derrick	Johnson	86	84	88	88	89
Brian	Cushing	86	84	88	79	91
Barrett	Ruud	86	79	84	88	91
Gary	Brackett	86	77	84	96	90
A.J.	Hawk	85	82	86	85	89
Rey	Maualuga	83	80	89	77	90
Stephen	Cooper	83	76	83	83	90
Bradie	James	83	76	81	86	92
D'Qwell	Jackson	83	75	83	84	93
Rolando	McClain	82	81	87	73	90
Desmond	Bishop	82	77	81	79	85
Keith	Brooking	82	74	77	94	88
Rocky	McIntosh	81	82	88	74	88
Larry	Foote	81	73	79	81	88
Gerald	Hayes	81	72	82	82	86
Eric	Barton	81	71	74	88	87
Dan	Connor	80	74	84	79	89
Jameel	McClain	79	81	83	75	89
Channing	Crowder	79	77	83	75	88
Jonathan	Goff	79	77	85	76	90
Dhani	Jones	79	76	75	90	88
Kirk	Morrison	79	75	80	85	88
Brandon	Spikes	79	73	87	64	87
Paris	Lenon	78	77	81	79	88
Mario	Haggan	78	74	77	82	87
DeAndre	Levy	77	84	88	76	88
Brandon	Siler	77	77	87	72	84
Jovan	Belcher	76	83	87	69	86
Demorrio	Williams	76	80	85	83	88

MIDDLE LINEBACKER

Name		OVR	SPD	ACC	AWR	TAC
Patrick	Willis	98	90	96	90	98
Jon	Beason	97	85	93	96	97
Ray	Lewis	95	83	86	95	94
Brian	Urlacher	94	84	89	95	96
Jerod	Mayo	92	85	91	77	97
David	Harris	92	79	87	90	96
Jonathan	Vilma	91	84	90	92	93
London	Fletcher	91	79	83	98	98
James	Farrior	91	75	77	97	96
Lawrence	Timmons	90	85	93	82	93
Karlos	Dansby	90	79	87	91	92
Curtis	Lofton	90	79	84	86	96
Daryl	Smith	90	78	86	88	93
Bart	Scott	90	77	84	93	92
DeMeco	Ryans	89	76	86	90	96
Lofa	Tatupu	88	79	92	90	95
Stephen	Tulloch	88	79	85	85	97
Nick	Barnett	88	78	87	86	91
E.J.	Henderson	88	74	78	87	95
Paul	Posluszny	87	76	86	85	93
James	Laurinaitis	87	76	86	82	95
Takeo	Spikes	87	75	80	97	90
Derrick	Johnson	86	84	88	88	89
Brian	Cushing	86	84	88	79	91
Barrett	Ruud	86	79	84	88	91
Gary	Brackett	86	77	84	96	90
A.J.	Hawk	85	82	86	85	89
Rey	Maualuga	83	80	89	77	90
Stephen	Cooper	83	76	83	83	90

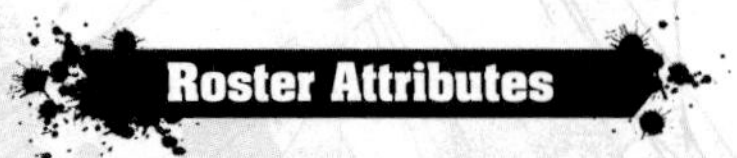

MIDDLE LINEBACKER

Name		OVR	SPD	ACC	AWR	TAC
Bradie	James	83	76	81	86	92
D'Qwell	Jackson	83	75	83	84	93
Rolando	McClain	82	81	87	73	90
Desmond	Bishop	82	77	81	79	85
Keith	Brooking	82	74	77	94	88
Rocky	McIntosh	81	82	88	74	88
Larry	Foote	81	73	79	81	88
Gerald	Hayes	81	72	82	82	86
Eric	Barton	81	71	74	88	87
Dan	Connor	80	74	84	79	89
Jameel	McClain	79	81	83	75	89
Channing	Crowder	79	77	83	75	88
Jonathan	Goff	79	77	85	76	90
Dhani	Jones	79	76	75	90	88
Kirk	Morrison	79	75	80	85	88
Brandon	Spikes	79	73	87	64	87
Paris	Lenon	78	77	81	79	88
Mario	Haggan	78	74	77	82	87
DeAndre	Levy	77	84	88	76	88
Brandon	Siler	77	77	87	72	84
Jovan	Belcher	76	83	87	69	86
Demorrio	Williams	76	80	85	83	88

RIGHT OUTSIDE LINEBACKER

Name		OVR	SPD	ACC	AWR	TAC
DeMarcus	Ware	98	86	97	91	88
James	Harrison	98	85	88	99	91
Terrell	Suggs	94	85	95	88	87
Lance	Briggs	93	78	84	91	95
Tamba	Hali	91	78	90	86	92
Chad	Greenway	90	79	86	86	94
Cameron	Wake	89	84	94	79	85
Brian	Orakpo	88	84	92	76	88
James	Anderson	87	85	92	83	90
Kamerion	Wimbley	87	79	93	80	87
Keith	Rivers	84	87	91	76	87
Will	Witherspoon	84	84	85	87	86
Keith	Bulluck	84	84	82	89	85
Calvin	Pace	84	79	87	80	84
Justin	Durant	83	85	87	79	88
Jason	Taylor	83	82	84	92	74
David	Hawthorne	83	79	83	84	93
David	Bowens	83	76	81	88	84
Geno	Hayes	82	84	89	78	88
Scott	Fujita	82	77	83	88	85
Mike	Peterson	82	77	81	88	85

RIGHT OUTSIDE LINEBACKER

Name		OVR	SPD	ACC	AWR	TAC
David	Thornton	82	73	81	90	89
Clint	Session	81	84	86	75	85
Joey	Porter	81	76	82	88	82
Stewart	Bradley	81	75	83	79	87
Shawne	Merriman	80	83	86	76	77
Kawika	Mitchell	80	78	86	75	81
Von	Miller	79	87	94	60	84
LeRoy	Hill	79	76	84	85	85
Ernie	Sims	78	88	90	66	85
Parys	Haralson	78	80	90	77	76
Scott	Shanle	78	78	85	85	85
Na'il	Diggs	78	73	80	89	82
Antwan	Applewhite	77	82	87	74	80
Aldon	Smith	76	82	96	56	81
Sean	Weatherspoon	75	83	86	66	90
Brandon	Johnson	75	82	88	68	77
Jermaine	Cunningham	75	82	89	68	77
Larry	English	75	79	85	68	76
Tully	Banta-Cain	75	76	85	76	73
Akeem	Jordan	74	84	87	71	75
Brad	Jones	74	82	86	70	84
Connor	Barwin	73	84	87	72	79
Jyles	Tucker	72	77	83	67	76
Charlie	Anderson	72	75	84	74	80
Akeem	Ayers	72	74	87	58	80
Clint	Sintim	71	83	81	62	81
Erik	Walden	71	77	86	68	79
Heath	Farwell	71	76	80	74	80
Zak	DeOssie	71	75	82	64	76
Zack	Follett	71	74	84	68	83

CORNERBACKS

Name		OVR	SPD	ACC	AGI	AWR
Darrelle	Revis	99	93	96	96	92
Nnamdi	Asomugha	98	93	93	94	93
Champ	Bailey	97	95	94	97	98
Asante	Samuel	94	90	95	99	95
Charles	Woodson	93	88	90	91	98
Tramon	Williams	92	93	95	95	84
Brandon	Flowers	91	89	94	93	84
Cortland	Finnegan	90	91	93	92	85
Leon	Hall	90	88	89	89	89
Jabari	Greer	90	88	93	92	88
Corey	Webster	90	87	92	91	89
Antoine	Winfield	90	85	87	88	96
Johnathan	Joseph	89	95	95	93	86

CORNERBACKS

Name		OVR	SPD	ACC	AGI	AWR
Dunta	Robinson	89	93	95	95	86
Rashean	Mathis	89	91	92	94	87
Quentin	Jammer	89	89	88	89	84
Vontae	Davis	87	93	97	95	76
Devin	McCourty	87	93	94	93	74
Marcus	Trufant	87	88	94	98	85
DeAngelo	Hall	86	97	96	95	82
Antonio	Cromartie	86	96	97	97	85
Tracy	Porter	86	93	95	94	79
Andre'	Goodman	86	92	94	89	83
Chris	Gamble	86	92	93	95	76
Joe	Haden	86	90	97	97	72
Aqib	Talib	86	89	94	96	76
Brent	Grimes	86	88	94	92	82
Charles	Tillman	86	86	90	87	84
Dominique	Rodgers-Cromartie	85	98	98	98	71
Terence	Newman	85	97	94	95	85
Stanford	Routt	85	95	94	90	78
Ike	Taylor	85	95	92	92	79
Kelvin	Hayden	85	87	88	92	86
Terrell	Thomas	85	86	91	89	79
Ronde	Barber	85	83	89	89	97
Sheldon	Brown	84	87	91	90	86
Nate	Clements	84	86	90	92	84
Al	Harris	84	84	83	87	92
Terrence	McGee	83	92	95	95	82
Antoine	Cason	83	89	94	93	79
Patrick	Peterson	82	97	93	96	60
Josh	Wilson	82	95	94	88	76
Leigh	Bodden	82	86	88	88	84
Prince	Amukamara	81	93	94	90	58
Richard	Marshall	81	93	91	92	74
Domonique	Foxworth	81	92	93	94	80
Will	Allen	81	91	88	91	82
Eric	Wright	81	89	91	91	78
Jerraud	Powers	81	88	92	91	77
Shawntae	Spencer	81	88	93	91	78
Brandon	Carr	81	87	88	89	78
Cedric	Griffin	81	85	87	90	78
Tim	Jennings	80	94	95	91	77
Leodis	McKelvin	80	93	94	95	71
Carlos	Rogers	80	88	92	88	76
Ronald	Bartell	80	87	88	88	79
Chris	Carr	79	91	94	88	75
Dimitri	Patterson	79	88	91	89	73

CORNERBACKS

Name		OVR	SPD	ACC	AGI	AWR
Aaron	Ross	79	88	93	93	76
Fabian	Washington	78	98	96	91	75
Chris	Houston	78	93	95	89	75
Alterraun	Verner	78	87	90	92	72
Mike	Jenkins	77	93	94	91	67
Ellis	Hobbs	77	90	91	94	77
Drayton	Florence	77	86	88	88	78
Bryant	McFadden	77	85	86	89	80
Chris	Johnson	76	97	96	91	72
Phillip	Buchanon	76	96	97	92	75
Kelly	Jennings	76	91	93	93	75
Jimmy	Smith	76	90	89	92	46
Sean	Smith	76	89	88	92	66
Bradley	Fletcher	76	86	92	87	68
Randall	Gay	76	83	87	89	83
Brian	Williams	76	80	86	85	80
Sam	Shields	75	97	97	88	67
Gregory	Toler	75	93	89	90	69
Bruce	Johnson	75	93	93	91	67
Lardarius	Webb	75	93	95	95	60
Justin	Tryon	75	92	93	90	66
Derek	Cox	75	92	90	92	69
Alphonso	Smith	75	90	92	90	74
Kareem	Jackson	75	90	85	86	69
Jason	Allen	75	90	91	91	70
Zackary	Bowman	74	91	92	93	69
Ras-I	Dowling	74	90	85	85	51
Kyle	Wilson	74	89	93	95	48
Lito	Sheppard	74	88	92	93	76
Joselio	Hanson	74	86	88	88	74
Patrick	Robinson	73	92	94	92	42
Captain	Munnerlyn	73	89	94	88	58
Javier	Arenas	73	88	93	94	55
Mike	Adams	73	87	83	84	77
Pacman	Jones	72	93	94	94	64
Jonathan	Wilhite	72	92	93	87	68
Kyle	Arrington	72	89	90	89	68
Tarell	Brown	72	87	93	90	61
William	James	72	86	88	87	75
Tye	Hill	71	97	93	92	66
Jason	McCourty	71	89	92	91	64
D.J.	Moore	71	88	91	95	65
Aaron	Williams	71	87	93	90	52

FREE SAFETY

Name		OVR	SPD	ACC	AGI	AWR
Ed	Reed	98	93	91	94	97
Nick	Collins	95	92	95	92	86
Antoine	Bethea	93	89	91	89	85
Michael	Griffin	91	88	92	92	83
O.J.	Atogwe	90	89	92	85	85
Kerry	Rhodes	88	84	87	85	87
Chris	Harris	88	79	87	83	88
Brian	Dawkins	87	84	85	83	92
Eric	Weddle	87	84	88	87	85
Malcolm	Jenkins	85	87	93	89	73
Antrel	Rolle	85	86	93	94	78
Michael	Huff	84	93	94	93	85
Jairus	Byrd	84	87	93	94	72
Louis	Delmas	84	87	93	91	67
Brandon	Meriweather	83	91	92	93	73
Tanard	Jackson	83	86	88	87	69
Ryan	Clark	83	81	85	81	81
Earl	Thomas	82	93	91	93	64
Darren	Sharper	82	84	80	82	91
Eugene	Wilson	81	85	88	86	74
Chris	Crocker	81	83	90	81	80
Thomas	DeCoud	80	87	90	86	72
Glover	Quin Jr.	80	86	88	87	68
Abram	Elam	80	83	89	84	75
Dashon	Goldson	79	86	89	88	67
James	Sanders	79	78	84	79	82
Jordan	Babineaux	78	85	87	83	76
Eric	Smith	78	79	86	87	74
Nate	Allen	77	88	92	87	66
Tom	Zbikowski	77	88	85	87	70
James	Butler	77	80	85	86	74
Chris	Clemons	76	92	95	87	65
Sherrod	Martin	76	88	91	89	67
Alan	Ball	76	87	91	85	65
Brodney	Pool	76	87	89	88	71
Gibril	Wilson	76	82	84	84	74
Kareem	Moore	75	88	90	88	66
Darcel	McBath	75	85	91	91	60
Marlin	Jackson	75	82	83	84	72
Reed	Doughty	75	79	85	77	74
Darrell	Stuckey	74	89	85	88	62
Gerald	Alexander	74	86	90	87	63
Vincent	Fuller	74	86	91	82	69
Jon	McGraw	74	75	79	76	77
Rahim	Moore	73	83	82	89	58
Hiram	Eugene	73	83	86	81	67
Kendrick	Lewis	73	82	86	85	57
Usama	Young	72	90	87	95	69
Al	Afalava	72	80	86	83	68
Chris	Conte	71	88	84	77	57
Don	Carey	71	87	91	88	55

STRONG SAFETY

Name		OVR	SPD	ACC	AGI	TAC
Troy	Polamalu	99	92	94	95	76
Adrian	Wilson	92	85	87	86	85
LaRon	Landry	90	92	93	88	88
Eric	Berry	88	92	95	90	82
Quintin	Mikell	88	88	86	82	76
Tyvon	Branch	87	95	91	85	83
Yeremiah	Bell	87	85	86	84	88
Chris	Hope	87	79	85	81	84
Pat	Chung	86	86	89	90	82
Dawan	Landry	86	82	84	81	81
Roman	Harper	86	82	85	77	87
Donte	Whitner	85	88	88	91	87
T.J.	Ward	85	86	84	84	84
Jim	Leonhard	85	84	88	86	72
Charles	Godfrey	84	91	94	90	72
Bob	Sanders	84	85	86	84	65
Lawyer	Milloy	84	77	80	77	76
Deon	Grant	83	84	86	89	69
William	Moore	82	85	84	85	76
Kenny	Phillips	81	90	93	92	74
Sean	Jones	81	86	84	87	74
Renaldo	Hill	80	83	88	86	67
Erik	Coleman	80	81	82	81	80
Bernard	Pollard	80	79	86	83	81
Melvin	Bullitt	79	87	90	86	75
Craig	Dahl	79	86	88	87	76
Bryan	Scott	79	79	83	77	79
Jarrad	Page	79	79	84	80	67
Husain	Abdullah	78	87	91	85	75
Reggie	Smith	78	85	90	88	69
Ken	Hamlin	78	84	82	83	71
Michael	Lewis	78	75	82	77	86
Morgan	Burnett	77	87	82	86	77
Courtney	Greene	77	86	89	83	74
Chinedum	Ndukwe	77	85	85	81	75
Steve	Gregory	77	85	88	85	72
Gerald	Sensabaugh	77	85	84	84	70
Charlie	Peprah	77	82	85	79	76
Roy	Williams	77	75	80	70	85
Jamarca	Sanford	76	84	86	79	74
Atari	Bigby	76	82	83	81	74
Aaron	Francisco	76	78	83	77	67
Reggie	Nelson	75	93	89	94	55
Michael	Mitchell	75	87	88	87	76
Michael	Johnson	75	85	90	85	72
George	Wilson	75	82	90	86	72
Brandon	McGowan	75	82	85	81	72
Pierson	Prioleau	75	80	76	78	64
Danieal	Manning	74	96	96	93	65
Josh	Bullocks	74	85	88	85	55
C.C.	Brown	74	80	83	81	73
Sabby	Piscitelli	73	87	88	78	74

KICKERS

Name		OVR	KPW	KAC
Ryan	Longwell	96	91	93
Rob	Bironas	95	96	93
Nate	Kaeding	93	91	96
Robbie	Gould	93	92	95
John	Carney	91	85	90
David	Akers	90	87	90
Adam	Vinatieri	90	88	91
Jay	Feely	89	91	92
John	Kasay	89	87	91
Billy	Cundiff	88	98	88
Olindo	Mare	88	93	88
Jason	Hanson	88	86	88
Shayne	Graham	87	87	92
Stephen	Gostkowski	87	90	94
Phil	Dawson	87	92	89
Sebastian	Janikowski	86	98	87
Josh	Brown	86	97	87
Joe	Nedney	85	90	88
Matt	Bryant	84	88	92
Neil	Rackers	83	94	87
Rian	Lindell	83	89	87
Josh	Scobee	81	96	86
Matt	Prater	80	97	87
Dan	Carpenter	79	93	91
Garrett	Hartley	78	93	89
Ryan	Succop	77	92	90
Jeff	Reed	75	89	84
Kris	Brown	75	90	84
Lawrence	Tynes	74	88	86
Shaun	Suisham	73	89	88
Mike	Nugent	73	91	84
Mason	Crosby	72	98	81
Connor	Barth	71	89	88
Nick	Folk	71	88	84
David	Buehler	67	96	81
Alex	Henery	66	94	84
Graham	Gano	66	91	83
Dave	Rayner	66	92	82
Rhys	Lloyd	66	97	76

PUNTERS

Name		OVR	KPW	KAC
Shane	Lechler	98	96	94
Sam	Koch	96	91	99
Donnie	Jones	92	98	95
Andy	Lee	90	96	94
Mat	McBriar	90	97	92
Brian	Moorman	89	89	93
Dustin	Colquitt	88	90	97
Brad	Maynard	84	82	89
Mike	Scifres	83	96	92
Jon	Ryan	83	95	92
Brandon	Fields	83	93	94
Josh	Bidwell	83	82	88
Thomas	Morstead	81	96	89
Matt	Turk	81	79	87
Daniel	Sepulveda	79	90	95
Jason	Baker	79	86	89
Hunter	Smith	79	85	88
Michael	Koenen	79	93	86
Chris	Kluwe	77	93	88
Zoltan	Mesko	77	94	89
Tim	Masthay	76	94	88
Dave	Zastudil	76	90	87
Kevin	Huber	74	88	90
Ben	Graham	74	91	88
Pat	McAfee	73	95	86
Nick	Harris	73	87	88
Britton	Colquitt	72	91	89
Sav	Rocca	69	93	86
Kyle	Larson	69	84	88
Steve	Weatherford	66	85	83
Jeremy	Kapinos	65	89	84
Adam	Podlesh	63	92	81
Brett	Kern	63	93	85
Reggie	Hodges	62	89	82
Matt	Dodge	62	95	83
Robert	Malone	58	89	87

MADDEN NFL 12

The Official Player's Guide

Written by:

Gamer Media, Inc.
(Zach Farley & Steve Gibbons)

Senior Product Marketing Manager: Donato Tica
Product Marketing Manager: Paul Giacomotto
Copyeditor: Deana Shields
Design & Layout: Jody Seltzer & Bryan Neff
Manufacturing: Stephanie Sanchez
Production Support: Alexander Musa

Prima Games would like to thank: Moya Nickodem, Anthony Stevenson, Jennica Pearson, Brent Coyle, Annie Gottshalk, Justin Dewiel, Mike Scantlebury, Larry Richart, Anthony White, Donny Moore, A.J. Dembroski, John Coleman, Lorraine Honrada, Daniel Davis, Randy Hembrador, Michelle Manahan and Jim Stadelman.

From the authors - Thank you for purchasing this guide. Both Zfarls and SGibs would not be here without the support we have gotten from you all. A very special thanks to both our families and friends! We would not have been able to accomplish this guide without their help throughout the years. And finally, an extra special thanks to everyone at EA SPORTS and Justin Dewiel. Long live pao de queijo. Good luck and happy gaming!

ISBN: 978-0-307-89054-2
Printed in the United States of America

11 12 13 14 DD 10 9 8 7 6 5 4 3 2 1

Prima Games
An Imprint of Random House, Inc.
3000 Lava Ridge Court, Suite 100
Roseville, CA 95661
www.primagames.com